# Visit the Web site for

# Understanding Western Society

## bedfordstmartins.com/mckaywestunderstanding

## FREE Online Study Guide

### Get instant feedback on your progress with

- Chapter self-tests
- Key terms review
- Map quizzes
- Timeline activities
- Note-taking outlines
- Chapter study guide steps

## FREE History Research and Writing Help

### Refine your research skills and find plenty of good sources with

- A database of useful images, maps, documents, and more at *Make History*
- A guide to online sources for history
- Help with writing history papers
- A tool for building a bibliography
- Tips on avoiding plagiarism

# Understanding Western Society

## A BRIEF HISTORY

**VOLUME 2** **From the Age of Exploration to the Present**

**John P. McKay**
University of Illinois at Urbana-Champaign

**Bennett D. Hill**
Late of Georgetown University

**John Buckler**
Late of the University of Illinois at Urbana-Champaign

**Clare Haru Crowston**
University of Illinois at Urbana-Champaign

**Merry E. Wiesner-Hanks**
University of Wisconsin–Milwaukee

**Joe Perry**
Georgia State University

**BEDFORD/ST. MARTIN'S**
Boston • New York

**In Memoriam**
**John Buckler**
**1945–2011**

FOR BEDFORD/ST. MARTIN'S
*Publisher for History:* Mary Dougherty
*Executive Editor for History:* Traci M. Crowell
*Director of Development for History:* Jane Knetzger
*Developmental Editor:* Kathryn Abbott
*Senior Production Editor:* Lori Chong Roncka
*Senior Production Supervisor:* Nancy Myers
*Executive Marketing Manager:* Jenna Bookin Barry
*Editorial Assistant:* Robin Soule
*Production Assistants:* Laura Winstead and Elise Keller
*Copyeditor:* Susan Moore
*Indexer:* Leoni Z. McVey
*Cartography:* Mapping Specialists, Ltd.
*Photo Researchers:* Carole Frohlich and Elisa Gallagher, The Visual Connection Image Research, Inc.
*Permissions Manager:* Kalina K. Ingham
*Senior Art Director:* Anna Palchik
*Text Designer:* Brian Salisbury
*Cover Designer:* Donna Lee Dennison
*Cover Art:* Jean Béraud, *At the Café*, ca. 1900. The Bridgeman Art Library.
*Composition:* NK Graphics
*Printing and Binding:* RR Donnelley and Sons

*President:* Joan E. Feinberg
*Editorial Director:* Denise B. Wydra
*Director of Marketing:* Karen R. Soeltz
*Director of Production:* Susan W. Brown
*Associate Director, Editorial Production:* Elise S. Kaiser
*Managing Editor:* Elizabeth M. Schaaf

Library of Congress Control Number: 2011931600

Manufactured in the United States of America.

6  5  4  3  2  1
f  e  d  c  b  a

*For information, write:* Bedford/St. Martin's, 75 Arlington Street, Boston, MA 02116    (617-399-4000)

ISBN-13: 978–0–312–66887–7 (Combined edition)
ISBN-13: 978–0–312–66888–4 (Volume 1)
ISBN-13: 978–0–312–66889–1 (Volume 2)

# Preface

**U**nderstanding Western Society grew out of many conversations about the teaching, study, and learning of history in the last decade. We knew that many instructors wanted a Western Civilization text that introduced students to the broad sweep of history but that also re-created the lives of ordinary men and women in appealing human terms. We knew that instructors wanted a text that presented cutting-edge scholarship in new fields of historical inquiry. We also came to realize that a growing number of instructors thought that their students needed a brief text, either because instructors were assigning more supplemental reading or because they thought their students would be better able to grasp key concepts given less detail. Finally, many instructors wanted a text that would help students focus as they read, that would keep their interest in the material, and that would encourage students to learn historical-thinking skills. We are extremely proud to introduce a textbook designed to address all of these concerns—*Understanding Western Society: A Brief History.*

## Narrative

*Understanding Western Society* presents the broad sweep of the history of Western civilization through the lens of social history. History as a discipline never stands still, and over the last several decades cultural history has joined social history as a source of dynamism. The focus on cultural history highlights the interplay between men's and women's lived experiences. Historical scholarship also has increasingly emphasized the global context of European history, and *Understanding Western Society* reflects that trend. Among the global topics of *Understanding Western Society* are examinations of the steppe peoples of Central Asia, of Muslim views of the Crusades, of the Atlantic world, and of the processes of decolonization and globalization. In addition, scholarship on gender is woven throughout the narrative and in sections on Frankish queens, medieval prostitutes, and female humanists. The politics of gender and gender roles during the French and industrial revolutions are explored as well.

In response to the calls for a less comprehensive text, in developing *Understanding Western Society*, we shortened the narrative of the parent text, *A History of Western Society*, by 30 percent. We condensed and combined thematically related sections and aimed throughout the text to tighten our exposition while working hard to retain topical balance, up-to-date scholarship, and lively, accessible writing. The result is a brief edition that preserves the narrative flow, balance, and power of the full-length work, and that allows students to better discern overarching trends and connect these with the individuals who animate the past.

## Pedagogy and Features

In trying to create a text that would help students grasp key concepts, maintain their interest in reading, and help them develop historical thinking skills, we then joined this brief narrative with an innovative design and unique pedagogy. *Understanding Western Society*'s chapter architecture supports students' reading and helps them to grasp key themes and ideas. All chapters open with a succinct statement about the main themes and events of the chapter, designed to establish clear learning outcomes. Chapters are organized into three to six main sections, with **section headings crafted as questions** to facilitate active reading. **Chapter-opening chronologies** underscore the sequence of events, and definitions in the margins explain **key terms**, providing on-the-page reinforcement and a handy tool for review. **Chapter locators** across the bottom of each two-page spread keep students focused on where they are in the chapter and help them see how the material they are reading connects to what they have already reviewed and to what is coming next.

We also reconsidered the traditional review that comes at the end of the chapter. Each chapter includes a "**Looking Back, Looking Ahead**" conclusion that provide an insightful synthesis of the chapter's main developments, while connecting them to events that students will encounter in the chapters to come. Each chapter ends with a step-by-step "**Chapter Study Guide**" that not only helps students with the basic material but also encourages them to move beyond a basic knowledge of what happened in the past to a more nuanced grasp of how events relate to each other, and a better understanding of why the past matters. In essence, the chapter-review sections provide the tools to help students develop the skills of historical analysis and interpretation while also helping them to read and think critically. We hope that this combination of design and pedagogy will help students grasp meaning as they read and also model how historians think, how they pose questions, and how they answer those questions with evidence and interpretation.

Other features of the book further reinforce historical thinking, expand upon the narrative, and offer opportunities for classroom discussion and assignments. In our years of teaching Western Civilization, we have often noted that students really come alive when they encounter stories about real people in the past. Thus, each chapter includes an "**Individuals in Society**" biographical essay that offers a brief study of an individual or group, informing students about the societies in which these people lived. The spotlighting of individuals, both famous and obscure, underscores the book's attention to cultural and intellectual developments, highlights human agency, and reflects changing interests within the historical profession as well as the development of "microhistory." Biographical essays in *Understanding Western Society* include features on Cyrus the Great who in the sixth century B.C.E. founded the Persian Empire; Glückel of Hameln, a German-Jewish widow who lived in the seventeenth century; and Josiah Wedgwood, the eighteenth-century English potter.

Each chapter also includes a primary source feature, "**Listening to the Past**," chosen to extend and illuminate a major historical issue considered in each chapter through the presentation of a single original source or several voices on the subject. Each opens with an introduction and closes with "Questions for Analysis" that invite students to evaluate the evidence as historians would. Selected for their interest and importance, and carefully fitted into their historical context, these sources allow students to observe how history has been shaped by individuals. Documents include Eirik the Red's tenth-century saga of his voyages to North America; Denis Diderot's fictional account of a voyage to Tahiti from the eighteenth century; and the 1959 "kitchen debate" between the U.S. vice president Richard Nixon and the Soviet premier Nikita Khrushchev.

We are particularly proud of the illustrative component of our work—the art and map program. Although this is a brief book, over 400 illustrations, all contemporaneous with the subject matter, reveal to today's visually attuned students how the past speaks in pictures as well as in words. Recognizing students' difficulties with geography, we also offer 87 full-size, full-color maps and 61 spot maps. Each chapter includes a "**Mapping the Past**" activity that helps improve students' geographical literacy and a "**Picturing the Past**" visual activity that gives students valuable skills in reading and interpreting images.

The new directions in format and pedagogy that are the hallmark of *Understanding Western Society* have not changed the central mission of the book since it first appeared in its original format, which is to introduce students to the broad sweep of Western Civilization in a fresh yet balanced manner. As we have made changes, large and small, we have always sought to give students and teachers an integrated perspective so that they could pursue—on their own or in the classroom—those historical questions that they find particularly exciting and significant. We hope students will then take the habits of thinking developed in the history classroom with them, for understanding the changes of the past might help them to handle the ever-faster pace of change in today's world.

## Acknowledgments

It is a pleasure to thank the many instructors who read and critiqued the manuscript through its development:

James H. Adams, Pennsylvania State University, Abington
Gemma Albanese, Dawson College
Robert Anxiaux, Eastfield College
Deborah C. Bjelajac, Florida State College at Jacksonville
Eugene Boia, Cleveland State University

Elizabeth Collins, Triton College
Ian Drummond, Gordon College
Bobbie Harris, Hillsborough Community College
John S. Kemp, Truckee Meadows Community College
Peter J. Klem, Great Basin College
James A. Lenaghan, The Ohio State University
Carol Levin, University of Nebraska–Lincoln
Heidi J. Manzone, University of North Florida
David B. Mock, Tallahassee Community College
Wesley Moody, Florida State College at Jacksonville
Ellen Howell Myers, San Antonio College
Laura M. Nelson, West Virginia University
Rosemary Fox Thurston, New Jersey City University

It is also a pleasure to thank the many editors who have assisted us over the years, first at Houghton Mifflin and now at Bedford/St. Martin's. At Bedford/St. Martin's, these include developmental editor Kathryn Abbott; associate editors Lynn Sternberger and Jack Cashman; editorial assistant Robin Soule; executive editor Traci M. Crowell; director of development Jane Knetzger; publisher for history Mary Dougherty; photo researchers Carole Frohlich and Elisa Gallagher; text permissions editor Elaine Kosta; and Lori Chong Roncka, senior production editor, with the assistance of Laura Winstead and the guidance of managing editor Elizabeth Schaaf and assistant managing editor John Amburg. Other key contributors were text designer Brian Salisbury, senior art director Anna Palchik, copyeditor Susan Moore, proofreaders Janet Cocker and Angela Morrison, indexer Leoni Z. McVey, and senior art director–cover designer Donna Dennison. We would also like to thank editorial director Denise Wydra and president Joan E. Feinberg.

Many of our colleagues at the University of Illinois, the University of Wisconsin–Milwaukee, and Georgia State University continue to provide information and stimulation, often without even knowing it. We thank them for it. The authors also thank the many students they have taught over the years. Their reactions and opinions helped shape this book. Merry Wiesner-Hanks would, as always, like to thank her husband Neil, without whom work on this project would not be possible. Clare Haru Crowston thanks her husband Ali, and her children Lili, Reza, and Kian, who are a joyous reminder of the vitality of life that we try to showcase in this book. John McKay expresses his deep appreciation to JoAnn McKay for her keen insights and unfailing encouragement. Joe Perry thanks Andrzej S. Kaminski and the expert team assembled at Lazarski University for their insightful comments and is most grateful to Joyce de Vries for her unstinting support and encouragement.

Each of us has benefited from the criticism of his or her coauthors, although each of us assumes responsibility for what he or she has written. John Buckler has written the first six chapters; building on text originally written by Bennett Hill, Merry Wiesner-Hanks has assumed primary responsibility for Chapters 7 through 14; building on text originally written by Bennett Hill and John McKay, Clare Crowston has assumed primary responsibility for Chapters 15 through 20; John McKay has written and revised Chapters 21 through 25; and Joe Perry has written and revised Chapters 26 through 31, building on text originally written by John McKay.

# Brief Contents

# Contents

## 15 European Exploration and Conquest

### 1450–1650  416

# 16 Absolutism and Constitutionalism in Europe

## ca. 1589–1725   450

# 17 Toward a New Worldview

## 1540–1789   488

## 18 The Expansion of Europe
### 1650–1800   520

## 19 The Changing Life of the People
### 1700–1800   552

## 20 The Revolution in Politics

### 1775–1815   582

## 21 The Revolution in Energy and Industry

### ca. 1780–1850   614

# 22 Ideologies and Upheavals

**1815–1850   642**

# 23 Life in the Emerging Urban Society

**1840–1900   672**

## 24 The Age of Nationalism
1850–1914   702

## 25 The West and the World
1815–1914   734

## 26 War and Revolution

1914–1919   766

## 27 The Age of Anxiety

ca. 1900–1940   802

# 28 Dictatorships and the Second World War

### 1919–1945    832

# 29 Cold War Conflict and Consensus

### 1945–1965    868

## 30 Challenging the Postwar Order
### 1960–1991   902

## 31 Europe in an Age of Globalization
### 1990 to the Present   936

# Maps, Figures, and Tables

## Maps

# Figures and Tables

# Special Features

## Listening to the Past

## Individuals in Society

Adopters of *Understanding Western Society: A Brief History* and their students have access to abundant extra resources, including documents, presentation and testing materials, the acclaimed Bedford Series in History and Culture volumes, and much much more. See below for more information, visit the book's catalog site at **bedfordstmartins.com/mckaywestunderstanding/catalog**, or contact your local Bedford/St. Martin's sales representative.

## Get the Right Version for Your Class

To accommodate different course lengths and course budgets, *Understanding Western Society: A Brief History* is available in several different versions and e-book formats, which are available at a substantial discount.

- Combined edition (Chapters 1–31) — available in paperback and e-book formats
- Volume 1: From Antiquity to the Enlightenment (Chapters 1–17) — available in paperback and e-book formats
- Volume 2: From the Age of Exploration to the Present (Chapters 15–31) — available in paperback and e-book formats

The online, interactive **Bedford e-Book** can be examined or purchased at a discount at **bedfordstmartins.com/mckaywestunderstanding**; if packaged with the print text, it is available at no extra cost. Your students can also purchase *Understanding Western Society: A Brief History* in other popular e-book formats for computers, tablets, and e-readers.

## Online Extras for Students

The book's companion site at **bedfordstmartins.com/mckaywestunderstanding** gives students a way to read, write, and study, and it helps them find and access quizzes and activities, study aids, and history research and writing help.

free *Online Study Guide.* Available at the companion site, this popular resource provides students with quizzes and activities for each chapter, including multiple-choice self-tests that focus on important concepts; a flash card activity that tests students' knowledge of key terms; timeline activities that emphasize causal relationships; and map activities intended to strengthen students' geography skills. Instructors can monitor students' progress through an online Quiz Gradebook or receive e-mail updates.

free *Research, Writing, and Anti-plagiarism Advice.* Available at the companion site, Bedford's **History Research and Writing Help** includes the textbook authors' **Suggested Reading** organized by chapter; **History Research and Reference Sources**, with links to history-related databases, indexes, and journals; **More Sources and How to Format a History Paper**, with clear advice on how to integrate primary and secondary sources into research papers and how to cite and format sources correctly; **Build a Bibliography**, a simple Web-based tool known as The Bedford Bibliographer that generates bibliographies in four commonly used documentation styles; and **Tips on Avoiding Plagiarism**, an online tutorial that reviews the consequences of plagiarism and features exercises to help students practice integrating sources and recognize acceptable summaries.

## Resources for Instructors

Bedford/St. Martin's has developed a wide range of teaching resources for this book and for this course. They range from lecture and presentation materials to assessment tools and course-management options. Most can be downloaded or ordered at **bedfordstmartins.com/ mckaywest understanding/catalog**.

***HistoryClass for Understanding Western Society.*** HistoryClass, a Bedford/St. Martin's Online Course Space, puts the online resources available with this textbook in one convenient and completely customizable course space. There you and your students can access an interactive e-book and primary-sources reader; maps, images, documents, and links; chapter review quizzes; interactive multimedia exercises; and research and writing help. In HistoryClass you can get all our premium content and tools and assign, rearrange, and mix them with your own resources. For more information, visit **yourhistoryclass.com**.

***Bedford Coursepack for Blackboard, WebCT, Desire2Learn, Angel, Sakai, or Moodle.*** We have free content to help you integrate our rich content into your course-management system. Registered instructors can download coursepacks with no hassle and no strings attached. Content includes our most popular free resources and book-specific content for *Understanding Western Society: A Brief History*. Visit **bedfordstmartins.com/cms** to see a demo, find your version, or download your coursepack.

***Instructor's Resource Manual.*** The instructor's manual offers both experienced and first-time instructors tools for preparing for lecture and running discussions. It includes chapter-review material, teaching strategies, and a guide to chapter-specific supplements available for the text.

***Computerized Test Bank.*** Each chapter of the test bank includes a mix of fresh, carefully crafted multiple-choice, matching, short-answer, and essay questions. It also contains the Review, Visual Activity, Map Activity, Individuals in Society, and Listening to the Past questions from the textbook and model answers for each. The questions appear in Microsoft Word format and in easy-to-use test-bank software that allows instructors to easily add, edit, re-sequence, and print questions and answers. Instructors can also export questions into a variety of formats, including WebCT and Blackboard.

***PowerPoint Maps, Images, Lecture Outlines, and i>clicker Content.*** Look good and save time with *The Bedford Lecture Kit*. These presentation materials are downloadable individually from the Instructor Resources tab at **bedfordstmartins.com/mckaywestunderstanding/catalog** and are available on *The Bedford Lecture Kit* **Instructor's Resource CD-ROM**. They include ready-made and fully customizable PowerPoint multimedia presentations built around lecture outlines with embedded maps, figures, and selected images from the textbook and with detailed instructor notes on key points. Also available are maps and selected images in JPEG and PowerPoint formats; content for i>clicker, a classroom response system, in Microsoft Word and PowerPoint formats; the Instructor's Resource Manual in Microsoft Word format; and outline maps in PDF format for quizzing or handing out. All files are suitable for copying onto transparency acetates.

***Overhead Map Transparencies.*** This set of full-color acetate transparencies includes 130 maps for the Western Civilization course.

***Make History — Free Documents, Maps, Images, and Web Sites.*** *Make History* combines the best Web resources with hundreds of maps and images, to make it simple to find the source material you need. Browse the collection of thousands of resources by course or by topic, date, and type. Each item has been carefully chosen and helpfully annotated to make it easy to find exactly what you need. Available at **bedfordstmartins.com/makehistory**.

***Videos and Multimedia.*** A wide assortment of videos and multimedia CD-ROMs on various topics in Western civilization is available to qualified adopters through your Bedford/St. Martin's sales representative.

## Package and Save Your Students Money

For information on free packages and discounts up to 50 percent, visit **bedfordstmartins.com/ mckaywestunderstanding/catalog**, or contact your local Bedford/St. Martin's sales representative.

***Bedford e-Book.*** The e-book for this title, described above, can be packaged with the print text at no additional cost.

**Sources of Western Society, Second Edition.** This two-volume primary-source collection provides a rich selection of sources to accompany *Understanding Western Society: A Brief History*. Each chapter features five to six written and visual sources that present history from well-known figures and ordinary individuals alike. A "Viewpoints" feature highlights two or three sources that address the same topic from different perspectives. Document headnotes as well as reading and discussion questions promote student understanding. Available free when packaged with the print text.

**Sources of Western Society e-Book.** The reader is also available as an e-book. When packaged with the print or electronic version of the textbook, it is available for free.

**The Bedford Series in History and Culture.** More than one hundred titles in this highly praised series combine first-rate scholarship, historical narrative, and important primary documents for undergraduate courses. Each book is brief, inexpensive, and focused on a specific topic or period. For a complete list of titles, visit **bedfordstmartins.com/history/series**. Package discounts are available.

**Rand McNally Atlas of Western Civilization.** This collection of over fifty full-color maps highlights social, political, and cross-cultural change and interaction from classical Greece and Rome to the post-industrial Western world. Each map is thoroughly indexed for fast reference. Available for $3.00 when packaged with the print text.

**The Bedford Glossary for European History.** This handy supplement for the survey course gives students historically contextualized definitions for hundreds of terms—from *Abbasids* to *Zionism*—that they will encounter in lectures, reading, and exams. Available free when packaged with the print text.

**Trade Books.** Titles published by sister companies Hill & Wang; Farrar, Straus and Giroux; Henry Holt and Company; St. Martin's Press; Picador; and Palgrave Macmillan are available at a 50 percent discount when packaged with Bedford/St. Martin's textbooks. For more information, visit **bedfordstmartins.com/tradeup**.

**A Pocket Guide to Writing in History.** This portable and affordable reference tool by Mary Lynn Rampolla provides reading, writing, and research advice useful to students in all history courses. Concise yet comprehensive advice on approaching typical history assignments, developing critical reading skills, writing effective history papers, conducting research, using and documenting sources, and avoiding plagiarism—enhanced with practical tips and examples throughout—have made this slim reference a bestseller. Package discounts are available.

**A Student's Guide to History.** This complete guide to success in any history course provides the practical help students need to be effective. In addition to introducing students to the nature of the discipline, author Jules Benjamin teaches a wide range of skills from preparing for exams to approaching common writing assignments, and explains the research and documentation process with plentiful examples. Package discounts are available.

**The Social Dimension of Western Civilization.** Combining current scholarship with classic pieces, this reader's forty-eight secondary sources, compiled by Richard M. Golden, hook students with the fascinating and often surprising details of how everyday Western people worked, ate, played, celebrated, worshiped, married, procreated, fought, persecuted, and died. Package discounts are available.

**The West in the Wider World: Sources and Perspectives.** Edited by Richard Lim and David Kammerling Smith, this first college reader to focus on the central historical question "How did the West become the West?" offers a wealth of written and visual source materials to reveal the influence of non-European regions on the origins and development of Western Civilization. Package discounts are available.

# How to use this book to figure out what's really important

The **chapter title** tells you the subject of the chapter and identifies the time span that will be covered.

# 15

# European Exploration and Conquest

## 1450–1650

The **chapter introduction** identifies the most important themes, events, and people that will be explored in the chapter.

Before 1450 Europeans were relatively marginal players in a centuries-old trading system that linked Africa, Asia, and Europe. Elites everywhere prized Chinese porcelains and silks, while wealthy members of the Celestial Kingdom, as China called itself, wanted ivory and black slaves from Africa, and exotic goods and peacocks from India. African people wanted textiles from India and cowrie shells from the Maldives in the Indian Ocean. Europeans craved Asian silks and spices but they had few desirable goods to offer their trading partners.

The European search for better access to Asian trade led to a new overseas empire in the Indian Ocean and the accidental discovery of the Western Hemisphere. Within a few decades European colonies in South and North America would join this worldwide web. Europeans came to dominate trading networks and political empires of truly global proportions. The era of globalization had begun.

Global contacts created new forms of cultural exchange, assimilation, conversion, and resistance. Europeans struggled to comprehend the peoples and societies they found and sought to impose European cultural values on them. New forms of racial prejudice emerged, but so did new openness and curiosity about different ways of life. Together with the developments of the Renaissance and the Reformation, the Age of Discovery—as the period of European exploration and conquest from 1450 to 1650 is known—laid the foundations for the modern world. ■

416

Memorizing facts and dates for a history class won't get you very far. That's because history isn't just about "facts." It's also about understanding cause and effect and the significance of people, places, and events from the past that still have relevance to your world today. This textbook is designed to help you focus on what's truly significant in the history of Western societies and to give you practice thinking like a historian.

**Life in the Age of Discovery.** A detail from an early-seventeenth-century Flemish painting depicting maps, illustrated travel books, a globe, a compass, and an astrolabe. The voyages of discovery revolutionized Europeans' sense of space and inspired a passion among the wealthy for collecting objects related to navigation and travel. (National Gallery, London/Art Resource, NY)

## Chapter Preview

▶ What were the limits of world contacts before Columbus?

▶ How and why did Europeans undertake voyages of expansion?

▶ What was the impact of conquest?

▶ How did Europe and the world change after Columbus?

▶ How did expansion change European attitudes and beliefs?

The **Chapter Preview** lists the questions that open each new section of the chapter and will be addressed in turn on the following pages. You should think about answers to these as you read.

# Each section has tools that help you focus on what's important.

The **question in red** asks about the specific topics being discussed in this section. Pause to answer each one after you read the section.

## ▼ What were the limits of world contacts before Columbus?

Historians now recognize that a type of world economy, known as the Afro-Eurasian trade world, linked the products and people of Europe, Asia, and Africa in the fifteenth century. The West was not the dominant player before Columbus, and the European voyages derived from a desire to share in and control the wealth coming from the Indian Ocean.

### The Trade World of the Indian Ocean

The Indian Ocean was the center of the Afro-Eurasian trade world. It was a crossroads for commercial and cultural exchange between China, India, the Middle East, Africa, and Europe (Map 15.1). From the seventh through the fourteenth centuries, the volume of this trade steadily increased, declining only during the years of the Black Death.

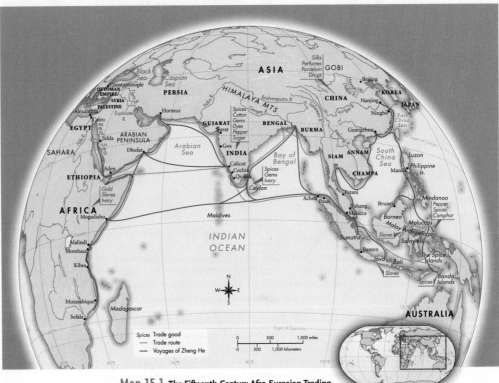

**Map 15.1 The Fifteenth-Century Afro-Eurasian Trading World** After a period of decline following the Black Death and the Mongol invasions, trade revived in the fifteenth century. Muslim merchants dominated trade, linking ports in East Africa and the Red Sea with those in India and the Malay Archipelago. Chinese Admiral Zheng He's voyages (1405–1433) followed the most important Indian Ocean trade routes, in the hope of imposing Ming dominance of trade and tribute.

Chapter 15
**European Exploration and Conquest • 1450–1650**
418

CHAPTER LOCATOR    What were the limits of world contacts before Columbus?

The **chapter locator** at the bottom of the page puts this section in the context of the chapter as a whole, so you can see how this section relates to what's coming next.

Merchants congregated in a series of multicultural, cosmopolitan port cities strung around the Indian Ocean. The most developed area of this commercial web was in the South China Sea. In the fifteenth century the port of Malacca became a great commercial entrepôt (AHN-truh-poh), a trading post to which goods were shipped for storage while awaiting redistribution to other places.

The Mongol emperors opened the doors of China to the West, encouraging Europeans like the Venetian trader and explorer Marco Polo to do business there. Marco Polo's tales of his travels from 1271 to 1295 and his encounter with the Great Khan fueled Western fantasies about the Orient. After the Mongols fell to the Ming Dynasty in 1368, China entered a period of agricultural and commercial expansion, population growth, and urbanization. Historians agree that China had the most advanced economy in the world until at least the start of the eighteenth century.

China also took the lead in exploration, sending Admiral Zheng He's fleet along the trade web as far west as Egypt. From 1405 to 1433, each of his seven expeditions involved hundreds of ships and tens of thousands of men. Court conflicts and the need to defend against renewed Mongol encroachment led to the abandonment of the expeditions after the deaths of Zheng He and the emperor. China's turning away from external trade opened new opportunities for European states to claim a decisive role in world trade.

Another center of trade in the Indian Ocean was India, the crucial link between the Persian Gulf and the Southeast Asian and East Asian trade networks. The subcontinent had ancient links with its neighbors to the northwest: trade between South Asia and Mesopotamia dates back to the origins of human civilization. Arab merchants who circumnavigated India on their way to trade in the South China Sea established trading posts along the southern coast of India, where the cities of Calicut and Quilon became thriving commercial centers. India was an important contributor of goods to the world trading system; much of the world's pepper was grown there, and Indian cotton textiles were highly prized.

## The Columbian Exchange

The migration of peoples to the New World led to an exchange of animals, plants, and disease, a complex process known as the Columbian exchange. Columbus brought sugar plants on his second voyage; Spaniards also introduced rice and bananas from the Canary Islands, and the Portuguese carried these items to Brazil. Everywhere they settled, the Spanish and Portuguese brought and raised wheat with labor provided by the encomienda system. Grapes and olives brought over from Spain did well in parts of Peru and Chile.

Apart from wild turkeys and game, Native Americans had no animals for food. Moreover, they did not domesticate animals for travel or to use as beasts of burden, except for alpacas and llamas in the Inca Empire. On his second voyage in 1493 Columbus introduced horses, cattle, sheep, dogs, pigs, chickens, and goats. The multiplication of these animals proved spectacular. In turn, Europeans returned home with many food crops that become central elements of their diet.

Disease was perhaps the most important form of exchange. The wave of catastrophic epidemic disease that swept the Western Hemisphere after 1492 can be seen as an extension of the swath of devastation wreaked by the Black Death in the 1300s, first on Asia and then on Europe. The world after Columbus was thus unified by disease as well as by

**Columbian exchange** The exchange of animals, plants, and diseases between the Old and the New Worlds.

## Chapter Chronology

| | |
|---|---|
| 1443 | Portuguese establish first African trading post at Arguin |
| 1492 | Columbus lands in the Americas |
| 1511 | Portuguese capture Malacca from Muslims |
| 1518 | Spanish king authorizes slave trade to New World colonies |
| 1519–1522 | Magellan's expedition circumnavigates the world |
| 1521 | Cortés conquers the Mexica Empire |
| 1533 | Pizarro conquers Inca Empire |
| 1602 | Dutch East India Company established |

**Chapter chronologies** show the sequence of events and underlying developments in the chapter.

**Key terms** in the margins give you background on important people, ideas, and events. Use these for reference while you read, but also think about which terms are emphasized and why they matter.

How and why did Europeans undertake voyages of expansion?

What was the impact of conquest?

How did Europe and the world change after Columbus?

How did expansion change European attitudes and beliefs?

# The Chapter Study Guide provides a process that will build your understanding and your historical skills.

## ▪ Chapter 15 Study Guide

Online Study Guide
bedfordstmartins.com/mckaywestunderstanding

**STEP 1**
**Identify** the key terms and explain their significance.

> **Step 1**
>
> **GETTING STARTED** Below are basic terms about this period in the history of Western civilization. Can you identify each term below and explain why it matters? To do this exercise online, go to bedfordstmartins.com/mckaywestunderstanding.

| TERMS | WHO (OR WHAT) AND WHEN | WHY IT MATTERS |
|---|---|---|
| conquistador, p. 422 | | |
| caravel, p. 423 | | |
| Ptolemy's *Geography*, p. 423 | | |
| Treaty of Tordesillas, p. 430 | | |
| Mexica Empire, p. 431 | | |
| Inca Empire, p. 433 | | |
| viceroyalties, p. 435 | | |
| encomienda system, p. 435 | | |
| Columbian exchange, p. 437 | | |

**STEP 2**
**Analyze** differences and similarities among ideas, events, people, or societies discussed in the chapter.

> **Step 2**
>
> **MOVING BEYOND THE BASICS** The exercise below requires a more advanced understanding of the chapter material. Examine the nature and impact of European exploration and conquest by filling in the chart below. What were the motives behind expansion? Why did monarchs support overseas expeditions? Why did men like Columbus undertake such dangerous journeys? Identify key conquests and discoveries for each nation. Then, describe the impact of exploration and colonization in the Americas in both the New World, Europe, and Africa. When you are finished, consider the following question: What intended and unintended consequences resulted from European expansion? To do this exercise online, go to bedfordstmartins.com/mckaywestunderstanding.

| EXPLORATION 1492–1600 | MOTIVES FOR EXPLORATION AND SETTLEMENT | CONQUESTS AND DISCOVERIES | IMPACT IN NEW WORLD | IMPACT IN EUROPE | IMPACT IN AFRICA |
|---|---|---|---|---|---|
| Portugal | | | | | |
| Spain | | | | | |
| France | | | | | |
| England | | | | | |

**Visit** the FREE Online Study Guide at **bedfordstmartins.com/mckaywestunderstanding** to do these steps online and to check how much you've learned.

**Step 3**

**PUTTING IT ALL TOGETHER** Now that you've reviewed key elements of the chapter, take a step back and try to see the big picture. Remember to use specific examples from the chapter in your answers. To do this exercise online, go to bedfordstmartins.com/mckaywestunderstanding.

**STEP 3**
**Answer** the big-picture questions using specific examples or evidence from the chapter.

### WORLD CONTACTS BEFORE COLUMBUS

- How did trade connect the civilizations of Africa, Asia, and Europe prior to 1492? Which states were at the center of global trade? Which were at the periphery? Why?

- Why were Europeans at a trading disadvantage prior to 1492? How did geography limit European participation in world trade? What role did Europe's economy and material culture play in this context?

### THE EUROPEAN VOYAGES OF DISCOVERY

- Why were Europeans so eager to gain better access to Asia and Asian trade? How did fifteenth-century economic and political developments help stimulate European expansion?

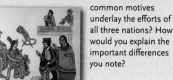

- Compare and contrast Spanish, French, and English exploration and colonization of the New World. What common motives underlay the efforts of all three nations? How would you explain the important differences you note?

### THE IMPACT OF CONQUEST

- What kinds of societies and governments did Europeans seek to establish in the Americas? What light does the nature of colonial society shed on the motives behind European expansion and European views of the indigenous peoples of the Americas?

- What was the Columbian exchange? How did it transform both Europe and the Americas?

- How did European expansion give rise to new ideas about race?

### EUROPE AND THE WORLD AFTER COLUMBUS

- What role did increasing demand for sugar play in shaping the economy and society of the New World? Why were sugar and slavery so tightly linked?

- If Europe was at the periphery of the global trading system prior to 1492, where was it situated by the middle of the sixteenth century? What had changed? What had not?

- How did expansion complicate Europeans' understanding of themselves and their place in the world?

■ **In Your Own Words** Imagine that you must explain Chapter 15 to someone who hasn't read it. What would be the most important points to include and why?

**ACTIVE RECITATION**
**Explain** the important points in your own words to make sure you have a firm grasp of the chapter material.

449

The notion of "the West" has ancient origins. Ideas about the West and the distinction between West and East derived originally from the ancient Greeks. Greek civilization grew up in the shadow of earlier civilizations to the south and east of Greece, especially Egypt and Mesopotamia. Greeks defined themselves in relation to these more advanced cultures, which they saw as "Eastern." Greeks were also the first to use the word *Europe* for a geographic area, taking the word from the name of a minor goddess. They set Europe in opposition to "Asia" (who was also a minor goddess), by which they meant both what we now call Asia and what we call Africa. Later Europeans divided certain regions of the world into the "Near East" of the eastern Mediterranean, Arabian Peninsula and northeastern Africa, and the "Far East" of Asia.

The Greeks passed this conceptualization on to the Romans, who saw themselves clearly as "the West." For some Romans, Greece remained part of the West, while other Romans came to view Greek traditions as vaguely "Eastern." To Romans, the East was more sophisticated and more advanced, but also decadent and somewhat immoral. Roman value judgments shape preconceptions, stereotypes, and views of differences to this day between the West and the East—what were also called the "Occident" and the "Orient." We can see these reflected in comments about the "mysterious East" or "oriental ways of thinking."

Greco-Roman ideas about the West were passed on to people who lived in western and northern Europe, who saw themselves as the inheritors of this classical tradition and thus as the West. When these Europeans established colonies outside of Europe beginning in the late fifteenth century, they regarded what they were doing as taking Western culture with them, even though many aspects of Western culture, such as Christianity, had actually originated in what Europeans by that point regarded as the East. With colonization, *Western* came to mean those cultures that included significant numbers of people of European ancestry, no matter where on the globe they were located.

In the early twentieth century, educators and other leaders in the United States became worried that many people, especially young people, were becoming cut off from European intellectual and cultural traditions. They encouraged the establishment of college and university courses focusing on "Western civilization," the first of which was taught at Columbia University in 1919. This was intended to broaden students' knowledge about the Western world as the United States emerged from its isolation to become a world leader after World War I. In designing the course, faculty included cultures that as far back as the ancient Greeks had been considered Eastern, such as Egypt and Mesopotamia, describing these as the "cradles of Western civilization." This conceptualization and this course spread to other colleges and universities, evolving into what became known as the introductory Western civilization course, the staple of historical instruction for generations of college students in North America.

After World War II, divisions between the West and the East changed again. Now there was a new division between East and West within Europe, with *Western* coming to imply a capitalist economy and *Eastern* the communist Eastern bloc. Thus, Japan became Western, and some Greek-speaking areas of Europe, Eastern. The collapse of communism in the Soviet Union and eastern Europe in the 1980s brought yet another refiguring, with much of eastern Europe joining the European Union, originally a Western organization.

At the beginning of the twenty-first century, "Western" still suggests a capitalist economy, but it also has certain cultural connotations, such as individualism and competition, which some see as negative and others see as positive. Thus throughout its long history, the meaning of "the West" has shifted, but in every era it has meant more than a geographical location.

## Cities and States in Southwest Asia and the Nile Valley

Ten thousand years ago, humans were living in most parts of the planet. They had designed technologies to meet the challenges presented by deep forests and jungles, steep mountains, and blistering deserts. As the climate changed, they adapted, building boats to cross channels created by

| HIEROGLYPHIC | REPRESENTS | UGARITIC | PHOENICIAN | GREEK | ROMAN |
|---|---|---|---|---|---|
|  | Throw stick |  |  | Γ | G |
|  | Man with raised arms |  |  | E | E |
|  | Basket with handle |  |  | K | K |
|  | Water |  |  | M | M |
|  | Snake |  |  | N | N |
|  | Eye |  |  | O | O |
|  | Mouth |  |  | Π | P |
|  | Head |  |  | P | R |
|  | Pool with lotus flowers |  | W | Σ | S |
|  | House |  |  | B | B |
|  | Ox-head |  | K | A | A |

**Origins of the Alphabet** This figure shows the origin of many of the letters of our alphabet. As peoples encountered a form of writing, each altered the sign without changing its value. (**Source:** A. B. Knapp, *The History and Culture of Ancient Western Asia and Egypt*, 1/e. Copyright © 1988 Wadsworth, a part of Cengage Learning, Inc. Reproduced by permission. www.cengage.com/permissions.)

melting glaciers, and finding new sources of food when old sources were no longer plentiful. In some places the new sources included domesticated plants and animals, which allowed people to live in much closer proximity to one another than they had as foragers.

That close proximity created opportunities, as larger groups of people pooled their knowledge to deal with life's challenges, but it also created problems. Human history from that point on can be seen as a response to these opportunities, challenges, and conflicts. As small villages grew into cities, people continued to develop technologies and systems to handle new issues. They created structures of governance based on something beyond the kin group to control their more complex societies, along with military forces and taxation systems to support the structures of governance. In some places they invented writing to record taxes, inventories, and payments, and they later put writing to other uses, including the preservation of stories, traditions, and history. The first places where these new technologies and systems were introduced were the Tigris and Euphrates River Valleys of southwest Asia and the Nile Valley of northeast Africa, areas whose history became linked through trade connections, military conquests, and migrations.

Writing was perhaps the most important of these new technologies. Written sources provide a wider range of information about past societies than is available from physical evidence alone, which means that we know much more about the societies that left written records than about those that did not. Writing was developed to meet the needs of the more complex urban societies that are often referred to as civilizations, and particularly to meet the needs of the state, a new structure of governance distinct from tribes and kinship groups. In states, a small share of the population is able to coerce resources out of everyone else, and leaders gain and maintain power through organized violence, bureaucracies, systems of taxation, and written laws. These laws generally created more elaborate social and gender hierarchies.

States first developed in Mesopotamia, the land between the Euphrates and Tigris Rivers. Starting in the southern part of Mesopotamia known as Sumeria, sustained agriculture reliant on irrigation resulted in larger populations, a division of labor, and the growth of cities. Priests and rulers invented ways to control and organize these complex societies, including armies, taxation systems, and cuneiform writing. Conquerors from the north unified Mesopotamian city-states into larger empires and spread Mesopotamian culture over a large area. The most significant of these was the Babylonian Empire, which under King Hammurabi in 1790 B.C.E. developed a written code of law and expanded trade connections.

During the third millennium B.C.E., a period known as the Old Kingdom, Egypt grew into a cohesive state under a single ruler in the valley of the Nile, which provided rich farmland and an avenue of communication. The Egyptians developed powerful beliefs in life after death, and the focal point of religious and political life was the pharaoh, a god-king who commanded the wealth, resources, and people of Egypt. For long stretches of history Egypt was prosperous and secure in the fertile Nile Valley, although at times various groups migrated in seeking better lives or invaded and conquered. Very often these newcomers adopted aspects of Egyptian religion, art, and politics, and the Egyptians adopted aspects of the newcomers' cultures, such as techniques used by the Hyksos in making and casting bronze. During the period known as the New Kingdom (ca. 1550–1070 B.C.E.), warrior-pharaohs expanded their power beyond the Nile Valley and created the first Egyptian empire, during which they first fought and then allied with the iron-using Hittites. After the collapse of the New Kingdom, the Nubian rulers of Kush conquered Egypt, and another group,

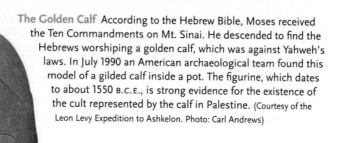

**The Golden Calf** According to the Hebrew Bible, Moses received the Ten Commandments on Mt. Sinai. He descended to find the Hebrews worshiping a golden calf, which was against Yahweh's laws. In July 1990 an American archaeological team found this model of a gilded calf inside a pot. The figurine, which dates to about 1550 B.C.E., is strong evidence for the existence of the cult represented by the calf in Palestine. (Courtesy of the Leon Levy Expedition to Ashkelon. Photo: Carl Andrews)

the Phoenicians, came to dominate trade in the Mediterranean, spreading a letter alphabet.

For several centuries after the collapse of New Kingdom Egypt, a Semitic people known as the Hebrews or the Israelites controlled a small state on the western end of the Fertile Crescent. Their most important legacy was not political, but rather a new form of religious belief, Judaism, based on the worship of a single all-powerful god, Yahweh. The Hebrews wrote down their religious ideas, traditions, laws, advice literature, prayers, hymns, history, and prophecies in a series of books, which came to define the Hebrews as a people. This group of books, the Hebrew Bible, describes the Covenant between Yahweh and the Hebrew people and sets out laws and traditions that structured Hebrew society and family life. Reverence for these written texts was passed from Judaism to the other Western monotheistic religions that grew from it, Christianity and Islam.

In the ninth century B.C.E. the Assyrians began a rise to power from northern Mesopotamia, creating an empire by means of often brutal military conquest. Assyria's success was also due to sophisticated, farsighted, and effective military tactics, technical skills, and organization.

From a base in what is now southern Iran, the Persians established an even larger empire, developing effective institutions of government and building roads. Though conquerors, the Persians, unlike the Assyrians, usually respected their subjects and allowed them to practice their native customs, traditions, and religions. Around 600 B.C.E. a new religion based on the teachings of the prophet Zoroaster grew in Persia. This religion emphasized the individual's responsibility to choose between good and evil.

The cultures of ancient Mesopotamia, Egypt, and Persia were the originators of many things that later became part of the West, including agriculture, cities, states, writing, bureaucracies, systems of taxation, and religious ideas. Of these, writing may have been the most significant, because it created records and therefore was the origin of what many people understand as history.

## The Greeks

The people of ancient Greece developed a culture that fundamentally shaped the civilization of the western part of Eurasia. The Greeks were the first in the Mediterranean and neighboring areas to explore most of the philosophical questions that still concern thinkers today. Going beyond mythmaking, the Greeks strove to understand the world in logical, rational terms. The result was the birth of philosophy and science, subjects as important to many Greeks as religion. Drawing on their day-by-day experiences, the Greeks also developed the concept of politics, and their contributions to literature still fertilize intellectual life today.

The history of the Greeks is divided into two broad periods: the Hellenic, roughly the time between the founding of the first complex societies in the area that is now the Greek islands and mainland, about 3500 B.C.E., and the rise of the kingdom of Macedonia in the north of Greece in 338 B.C.E.; and the Hellenistic, the years from the reign of Alexander the Great (336–323 B.C.E.) through the spread of Greek culture from Spain to India (ca. 100 B.C.E.). During the Hellenic period, Greeks developed a distinctive form of city-state known as the *polis* and made lasting cultural and intellectual achievements. In the Hellenistic period Macedonian and Greek armies defeated the Persian Empire and built new cities and kingdoms. During their conquests they blended their ideas and traditions with those of the societies they encountered, creating a vibrant culture.

In its earliest history, Greece's mountainous terrain and lack of navigable rivers led to the development of small, independent communities and political fragmentation. Some groups of people joined together in kingdoms, notably those of the Minoans on Crete and the Mycenaeans on the mainland, but the rugged terrain prohibited the growth of a great empire like those of Mesopotamia and Egypt. The fall of these kingdoms led to a period known as the Greek Dark Age (ca. 1100–ca. 800 B.C.E.). However, Greek culture survived, and Greeks developed the independent city-state, known as the polis, in which individuals governed themselves without elaborate political machinery. The physical, religious, and political form of the polis varied from place to place, but everywhere it was relatively small, reflecting the fragmented geography of Greece.

The maturation of the polis coincided with an era, later termed the Archaic Age (ca. 800–ca. 500 B.C.E.), that gave rise to two developments of lasting importance. The first was the spread of the Greek people, who now ventured as far east as the Black Sea and as far west as the Atlantic Ocean. The second development was the rise of Sparta and Athens, which formed new social and political structures. Sparta created a military state in which men remained in the army most of their lives and women concentrated on raising healthy soldiers. After much social conflict, Athens created a democracy in which male citizens both voted for their leaders and had a direct voice in an assembly. As was the case in all democracies in ancient Greece, women, slaves, and outsiders could not be citizens.

In the classical period, between 500 and 336 B.C.E., Greek civilization reached its highest peak in politics, thought, and art, even as it engaged in violent conflicts. The Greeks successfully defended themselves from Persian invasions but nearly destroyed themselves in the Peloponnesian War, which pitted Sparta and its allies against Athens and its allies. In the last half of the fifth century B.C.E. the brilliant Athenian leader Pericles turned Athens into the showplace of Greece by sponsoring the building of temples and other buildings. He also oversaw the creation of statues and carvings that showed the gods in human form and highlighted Athenian victories. In other artistic developments, wealthy Athenians paid for theater performances in which dramatists used their art in attempts to portray, understand, and resolve life's basic conflicts. During the classical period the Greeks honored a variety of gods and goddesses with rituals and festivals, but they did not look to religion for moral guidance. This period also saw the rise of philosophy; and Socrates, Plato, and Aristotle began a broad examination of the universe and the place of humans in it.

In the middle of the fourth century B.C.E. the Greek city-states were conquered by King Philip II and his son Alexander, rulers of Macedonia to the north of Greece. A brilliant military leader, Alexander then conquered the entire Persian Empire, along with many territories to the east of Persia. He also founded new cities in which Greek and local populations mixed. His successors continued to build cities and colonies, which became powerful instruments in the spread of Greek culture and in the blending of Greek traditions and ideas with those of other peoples. Greek became the common language of learning and business, which made trade easier and contributed to the prosperity of this era.

The mixing of peoples in the Hellenistic era influenced religion, philosophy, and science. The Hellenistic kings built temples to the old Olympian gods and established cults like those in earlier Greek cities. But because many people found these spiritually unsatisfying, they turned instead to mystery religions.

**The Acropolis of Athens** These buildings embody the noblest spirit of Greek architecture. From the entrance visitors walk through the Propylaea and its pillars (lower center). Ahead opens the grand view of the Parthenon, still noble in ruins (center). To the left stands the Erechtheum, the whole a monument to Athens itself. (Courtesy, Sotiris Toumbis Editions)

In these religions, which blended Greek and non-Greek elements, followers gained secret knowledge in initiation rituals and were promised eternal life. Others turned to practical philosophies instead of religion; these provided advice on how to live a good life. In the scholarly realm, advances were made in mathematics, astronomy, and mechanical design. The greatest thinker of the Hellenistic period was Archimedes, who devised new artillery for military purposes and created a screw to draw water from a lower to a higher level, among other inventions. Also during this period, physicians used observation and dissection to better understand the way the human body works and to develop treatments for disease.

Throughout both the Hellenic and Hellenistic periods, the ancient Greeks built on the achievements of earlier societies in the eastern Mediterranean, but they also added new elements. These included history, drama, philosophy, science, and realistic art. The Greek world was largely conquered by the Romans, and the various Hellenistic monarchies became part of the Roman Empire. In cultural terms the lines of conquest were reversed: the Romans derived their alphabet from the Greek alphabet, though they changed the letters somewhat. Roman statuary was modeled on Greek and was often, in fact, made by Greek sculptors, who found ready customers among wealthy Romans. Furthermore, the major Roman gods and goddesses were largely the same as Greek ones, though they had different names. Although the Romans did not seem to have been particularly interested in the speculative philosophy of Socrates and Plato, they were drawn to the more practical philosophies of the Epicureans and Stoics. And like the Hellenistic Greeks, many Romans became dissatisfied with traditional religions, turning instead to mystery religions that offered secret knowledge and promised eternal life.

The influence of the ancient Greeks was not limited to the Romans. Art and thought in northern India was shaped by the blending of Greek and Buddhist traditions. European thinkers and writers made conscious attempts to return to classical ideals in art, literature, and philosophy during the Renaissance. In America political leaders from the Revolutionary era on decided that important government buildings should be modeled on the Parthenon or other temples, complete with marble statuary of their own heroes. In some ways, capitol buildings in the United States are good symbols of the legacy of Greece — gleaming ideals of harmony, freedom, democracy, and beauty that (as with all ideals) do not always correspond with realities.

# The Romans

Like the Persians under Cyrus and the Macedonians under Alexander, the Romans conquered vast territories. Their singular achievement lay in their ability to incorporate conquered peoples into the Roman system. Unlike the Greeks, who mostly refused to share citizenship, the Romans extended citizenship first to other peoples in Italy and later to inhabitants of Roman provinces. After a grim period of civil war that ended in 31 B.C.E., the emperor Augustus restored peace and expanded Roman power and law as far east as the Euphrates River, creating the institution that the modern world calls the "Roman Empire."

Roman history is usually divided into two periods. The first is the republic (509–27 B.C.E.), the age in which Rome grew from a small group of cities in the middle of the Italian peninsula to a state that ruled much of the Mediterranean. Its republican government aimed to share power rather than concentrate it in a monarchy. The second period is the empire (27 B.C.E.–476 C.E.), when the republican constitution gave way to rule by a single individual, and when Rome's large territory eventually was split into eastern and western halves.

In its earliest development, Roman culture was influenced by the Etruscans, people who established permanent

Julius Caesar In this bust, the sculptor portrays Caesar as a man of power and intensity. The bust is a study of determination and an excellent example of Roman portraiture. (Museo Archeologico Nazionale Naples/Scala/Art Resource, NY)

settlements in northern and central Italy that evolved into cities resembling the Greek city-states. The Etruscans introduced Romans to urbanism, industry, trade, and the alphabet. Under Etruscan rule, the Romans prospered, making contact with the larger Mediterranean world, while the city of Rome continued to grow. In 509 B.C.E. the Romans won independence from Etruscan rule and continued to expand their territories. They also established a republic that functioned through a shared government of the people, directed by the senate, and summarized by the expression SPQR — *senatus populusque Romanus*, meaning "the Roman senate and people." In the resolution to a social conflict known as the Struggle of the Orders, nobles and ordinary people created a state administered by magistrates elected from the entire population and established a uniform law code.

In a series of wars, the Romans conquered the Mediterranean, creating an overseas empire that brought them unheard of power and wealth. Yet social unrest came in the wake of the war, opening unprecedented opportunities for ambitious generals who wanted to rule Rome like an empire. Civil war ensued, and it appeared as if the great politician and general Julius Caesar would emerge victorious, but he was assassinated by a group of senators. After his assassination and another period of civil war, his grandnephew Augustus finally restored peace and order to Rome. Augustus did not create a new office for himself but instead assumed control over many of the offices that traditionally had been held by separate people. His tenure clearly marked the end of the republic, and without specifically saying so, Augustus created the office of emperor. One of the most momentous aspects of his reign was the further expansion of Roman territories.

Augustus's success in creating solid political institutions was tested by the ineptness of some leaders who followed him, but later in the first century C.E. Rome entered a period of political stability, prosperity, and relative peace that lasted until the end of the second century C.E. During this period, later dubbed the *pax Romana*, the city of Rome became the magnificent capital of the empire, increasingly adorned with beautiful buildings and improved urban housing, and harboring a well-fed populace. To entertain the public, Roman rulers presented gladiatorial games and chariot races. The Roman provinces and frontiers also saw extensive prosperity in the second century through the growth of agriculture, trade, and industry, among other factors. As the Roman Empire expanded eastward from Europe, it met opposition, yet even during the fighting, commerce among the Romans and peoples who lived in central and southern Asia thrived along a series of trade routes.

One of the most significant developments during the time of Augustus was the beginning of Christianity. Christianity was a religion created by the followers of Jesus of Nazareth, a Jewish man who taught that belief in his divinity led to eternal life. His followers spread their belief across the Roman Empire, transforming Christianity from a Jewish sect into a new religion. Christian groups were informal at first, but by the second century they began to develop hierarchical institutions modeled on those of Rome. At first many pagans in the Roman Empire misunderstood Christian practices and rites, and they feared that the gods would withdraw their favor from the Roman Empire because of the Christian insistence that the pagan gods either did not exist or were evil spirits. As a result, Christians suffered sporadic persecution under certain Roman emperors. Gradually, however, tensions between pagans and Christians lessened, particularly as Christianity modified its teachings to make them more acceptable to wealthy and educated Romans.

In terms of politics and economics, the prosperity of the Roman Empire in the second century C.E. gave way in the third century to a period of civil war, barbarian invasions, and conflict with foreign armies. These disrupted agriculture, trade, and production; they also damaged the flow of taxes and troops. At the close of the third century the emperor Diocletian ended the period of chaos, in part because he recognized that the empire had become too great for one man to handle. He therefore divided it into a western and an eastern half, assuming direct control of the eastern part and giving a colleague the rule of the western part. Diocletian and his successor, Constantine, also took rigid control of the struggling economy, but their efforts were not successful. Free tenant farmers lost control of their lands, exchanging them for security that landlords offered against barbarians and other threats. Meanwhile, tolerance of Christianity grew, and Constantine legalized the practice of this religion throughout the empire. The symbol of all the changes in the empire became the establishment of its new capital, Constantinople, the new Rome.

From the third century onward the Western Roman Empire slowly disintegrated. The last Roman emperor in the West, Romulus Augustus, was deposed by the Ostrogothic chieftain Odoacer in 476, but much of the empire had already come under the rule of various barbarian tribes well before this. Thus despite the efforts of emperors and other leaders, by the fifth century the Western Roman Empire no longer existed.

Scholars have long seen the fall of the Western Roman Empire era as one of the great turning points in Western history — the end of the classical era. In the fourteenth century they began the practice of dividing Western history into different periods — eventually, the ancient, medieval, and modern eras. Those categories still shape the way that Western history is taught and learned.

No large-scale story of rise and fall captures the experience of everyone, of course. For many people in the Roman world, neither the change from republic to empire nor the end of the empire altered their lives very much. They farmed or worked in cities, and hoped for the best for their families. They took in new ideas but blended them with old traditions. Thus there was continuity along with change.

## The Early Middle Ages

The transition from ancient to medieval was a slow process, not a single event. The primary agents in this process of change were the barbarian tribes whose migrations broke the Roman Empire apart. The barbarians brought different social, political, and economic structures with them. Although Greco-Roman art and architecture still adorned the land and people continued to travel on Roman roads, the roads were rarely maintained, and travel itself was much less secure than during the empire. Merchants no longer traded over long distances, so people's access to goods produced outside their local area plummeted. Barbarian kings relied on officials trained in Roman law, and Latin remained the language of scholarly communication and the Christian Church, but knowledge about technological processes such as the making of glass and roof tiles declined or disappeared. There was intermarriage and cultural assimilation among Romans and barbarians, but there was also violence and great physical destruction.

The Eastern Roman Empire, called the Byzantine Empire, did not fall to barbarian invasions, however. During the sixth and seventh centuries the Byzantine Empire survived waves of attacks, owing to effective military leadership and to fortifications around Constantinople. From this strong position Byzantine emperors organized and preserved Roman institutions, and the Byzantine Empire lasted until 1453, nearly a millennium longer than the Roman Empire in the West. In particular, the emperor Justinian oversaw creation of the *Code*, which distilled the legal genius of the Romans into a coherent whole, eliminated outmoded laws and contradictions, and clarified the law itself. Just as they valued the law, the Byzantines prized education, and because of them many masterpieces of ancient Greek literature survived to influence the intellectual life of the modern world. In mathematics and science, the Byzantines passed Greco-Roman learning on to the Arabs, and they discovered an explosive compound, "Greek fire," that saved Constantinople from Arab assault. The Byzantines also devoted a great deal of attention to medicine, and their general level of medical competence was far higher than that of western Europeans.

Along with Byzantium, the Christian Church was an important agent of continuity in the transition from ancient to medieval. Christianity gained the support of the fourth-century emperors and gradually adopted the Roman system of hierarchical organization. The church possessed able administrators and leaders whose skills were tested in the chaotic environment of the end of the Roman Empire in the West.

**Homage and Fealty** In this manuscript illumination, a vassal kneels before the lord, places his clasped hands between those of the lord, and declares, "I become your man." Although the rites of entering a feudal relationship varied widely across Europe and sometimes were entirely verbal, we have a few illustrations of them. Sometimes the lord handed over a clump of earth, representing the fief, and the ceremony concluded with a kiss, symbolizing the peace between them. (ONB/Vienna, Picture Archive, Cod. 2262, fol. 174 v.)

Bishops expanded their activities, and in the fifth century the bishops of Rome, taking the title "pope," began to stress their supremacy over other Christian communities. Monasteries offered opportunities for individuals to develop deeper spiritual devotion and also provided a model of Christian living, methods that advanced agricultural development, and places for education and learning. Missionaries and church officials spread Christianity within and far beyond the borders of what had been the Roman Empire, transforming a small sect into the most important and wealthiest institution in Europe.

Christian thinkers reinterpreted the classics in a Christian sense, incorporating elements of Greek and Roman philosophy and of various pagan religious groups into Christian teachings. Of these early thinkers, Augustine of Hippo was the most influential. His ideas about sin, free will, and sexuality shaped western European thought from the fifth century on. Missionaries and priests got pagan and illiterate peoples to understand and become more accepting of Christianity by preaching the basic teachings of the religion, stressing similarities between pagan customs and beliefs and those of Christianity, and introducing the ritual of penance and the veneration of saints.

Classical and Christian traditions modified those of barbarian society, although barbarian political systems were very different from those of Rome. Barbarians generally had no notion of the state as we use the term today; they thought in social, not political, terms. The basic social unit was the tribe, made up of kin groups formed by families. Family groups lived in small agriculture-based villages, where there were great differences in wealth and status. Most barbarian kingdoms were weak and short-lived, though the kingdom of the Franks was relatively more unified and powerful. Rulers first in the Merovingian Dynasty of the fifth century, and then in the Carolingian of the eighth century, used military victories, strategic marriage alliances, and the help of the church to enhance their authority. Carolingian government reached the peak of its power under Charlemagne (ruled 768–814), who continued the expansionist policies of his ancestors, extending the Frankish kingdom to include all of continental Europe except Spain, Scandinavia, southern Italy, and the Slavic areas of the East, and allying himself with the papacy.

In the seventh century, a new force emerged that had a dramatic impact on much of Europe and western Asia — Islam. The diverse Arab tribes were transformed into a powerful political and social force by the teachings of the Prophet Muhammad. The Muslims adopted and adapted Greek, Byzantine, and Persian political and cultural institutions. Superb horsemen and fighters, the Arabs conquered much of the Middle East and North Africa in the name of Islam, and in the eighth century they crossed into Europe, eventually defeating the weak barbarian kingdom in Spain and gaining control of most of the Iberian Peninsula. Muslim-controlled Spain, known as al-Andalus, was the most advanced society in Europe in terms of agriculture, science, and medicine. Some Christian residents assimilated to Muslim practices, but hostility between the two groups was also evident.

Charlemagne's empire broke down in the late ninth century, and continental Europe was fractured politically. No European political power was strong enough to put up effective resistance to external attack, which came from many directions. Vikings from Scandinavia carried out raids for plunder along the coasts and rivers of Europe. They traveled as far as Iceland, Greenland, North America, and Russia. In many places they set up permanent states, as did the Magyars, who came into central Europe from the east. From the south came Muslims, who conquered Sicily and drove northward into Italy. All these invasions as well as civil wars weakened the power of kings, and local nobles became the strongest powers against external threats. They established a new form of decentralized government, later known as feudalism. Common people turned to nobles for protection, paying with their land, labor, and freedom.

## The High and Late Middle Ages

Beginning in the last half of the tenth century, the invasions that had contributed to European fragmentation gradually ended, and domestic disorder slowly subsided. Feudal rulers began to develop new institutions of law and government that enabled them to assert their power over lesser lords and the general population. Centralized states slowly crystallized, first in western Europe in the eleventh century, and then in eastern and northern Europe as well. An era of relative stability and prosperity followed, generally known as the "High Middle Ages," which lasted until climate change and disease brought calamity in the fourteenth century.

**Ox Team Plowing** From an eleventh-century calendar showing manorial occupations, this illustration for January—the time for sowing winter wheat—shows two pair of oxen pulling a wheeled plow. Wheeled plows allowed for faster work and deeper tillage, but they still required large inputs of human labor. Here one man prods the animals, a second directs the plow blade, and a third drops seed in the ground. (© British Library Board, Cott. Tib. B.V.3, Min. Pt 1)

At the same time that rulers expanded their authority, energetic popes built their power within the Western Christian church. They asserted their superiority over kings and emperors, though these moves were sometimes challenged by those secular rulers. Monasteries continued to be important places for learning and devotion, and new religious orders were founded. Meanwhile, Christianity expanded into Europe's northern and eastern regions, and Christian rulers expanded their holdings in Muslim Spain. On a more personal scale, religion structured people's daily lives and the yearly calendar.

A papal call to retake the holy city of Jerusalem from the Muslims led to nearly two centuries of warfare between Christians and Muslims. Christian warriors, clergy, and settlers moved out in all directions from western and central Europe, so that through conquest and colonization border regions were gradually incorporated into a more uniform European culture. The enormous popular response to the pope's call reveals the influence of the papacy and a new sense that war against the church's enemies was a duty of nobles. The Crusades were initially successful, and small Christian states were established in the Middle East. They did not last very long, however, and other effects of the Crusades were disastrous: Jewish communities in Europe were regularly attacked; relations between the Western and Eastern Christian churches were poisoned by the Crusaders' attack on Constantinople; and Christian-Muslim relations became more uniformly hostile than they had been earlier.

For most people, the High Middle Ages did not bring dramatic change. The vast majority of medieval Europeans were rural peasants who lived in small villages and worked their own and their lords' land. Peasants led hard lives, and most were bound to the land, although there were some opportunities for social mobility. Nobles were a tiny fraction of the total population, but they exerted great power over all aspects of life. Aristocratic values and attitudes, often called chivalry, shaded all aspects of medieval culture. Medieval towns and cities grew initially as trading centers and recruited people from the countryside with the promise of greater freedom and new possibilities. They also became centers of production, and merchants and artisans formed guilds to protect their livelihoods. Not everyone in medieval towns and cities shared in the prosperity, however; many residents lived hand-to-mouth on low wages.

The towns that became centers of trade and production in the High Middle Ages also developed into cultural and intellectual centers. Trade brought in new ideas as well as merchandise, and in many cities a new type of educational institution—the university—emerged from cathedral and municipal schools. Universities developed theological, legal, and medical courses of study based on classical models and provided trained officials for the new government and church bureaucracies. People also wanted permanent visible representations of their piety, and church and city leaders supported the building of churches and cathedrals as symbols of their Christian faith and their civic pride. Cathedrals grew larger and more sumptuous, with high towers, soaring arches, and exquisite stained-glass windows in a style known as Gothic. New types of vernacular literature arose in which poems, songs, and stories were written down in local dialects.

In the fourteenth century the prosperity of the High Middle Ages ended. Bad weather brought poor harvests, which contributed to an international economic depression and fostered disease. The Black Death caused enormous population losses and had social, psychological, and economic consequences. Additional difficulties included the Hundred Years' War between England and France, which devastated much of the French countryside and bankrupted England; a schism among rival popes that weakened the Western Christian Church; and peasant and worker frustrations that exploded in uprisings. These revolts were usually crushed, though noble landlords were not always successful in reasserting their rights to labor services instead of cash rents.

Despite the calamities of the fourteenth century, medieval Europe continues to fascinate us today. We go to medieval banquets, fairs, and even weddings; visit castle-themed hotels and amusement parks; watch movies about knights and their conquests; play video games in which we become warriors, trolls, or sorcerers; and read stories with themes of great quests, some set in the Middle Ages and some set in places that just seem medieval, with humble but brave villagers, beautiful ladies, powerful wizards, and gorgeous warriors on horseback. From all these amusements the Middle Ages emerges as a strange and wonderful time, when people's emotions were more powerful, challenges more dangerous, and friendships more lasting than in the safe, shallow, fast-paced modern world.

In reality few of us would want to live in the real Middle Ages, when most people worked in the fields all day, a banquet meant a piece of tough old rooster instead of the usual meal of pea soup and black bread, and even wealthy lords lived in damp and drafty castles. We do not really want to return to a time when one-third to one-half of all children died before age five and alcohol was the only real pain reliever.

## The Renaissance and the Reformation

The contemporary appeal of the Middle Ages is an interesting phenomenon, particularly because it stands in such sharp contrast to the attitude of educated Europeans who lived in the centuries immediately afterward. They were the ones who dubbed the period "middle" and viewed the soaring cathedrals as "Gothic," because they thought that only the uncouth Goths could have invented such a disunified style. They saw their own era as the one to be celebrated and the Middle Ages as best forgotten. First in Italy and then elsewhere, these scholars, writers and artists thought that they were living in a new golden age, later termed the Renaissance, French for *rebirth*. The word *renaissance* was used initially to describe art that seemed to recapture, or perhaps even surpass, the glories of the classical past, and then came to be used for many aspects of life of the period. The new attitude diffused slowly out of Italy, with the result that the Renaissance "happened" at different times in different parts of Europe.

The Renaissance was characterized by self-conscious awareness among fourteenth- and fifteenth-century Italians—particularly scholars and writers known as humanists—that they were living in a new era. Key to this attitude was a serious interest in the Latin classics, a belief in individual potential, and a more secular attitude toward life. Humanists opened schools for boys and young men to train them for active lives of public service, but they had doubts about whether humanist education was appropriate for women. As humanism spread to northern Europe, religious concerns became more pronounced, and Christian humanists set out plans for the reform of church and society. Their ideas were spread to a much wider audience than those of early humanists as a result of the development of the printing press with movable metal type, which revolutionized communication. Interest in the classical past and in the individual shaped Renaissance art in terms of style and subject matter. Also important to Renaissance art were the wealthy patrons who helped fund it.

Social hierarchies in the Renaissance developed new features that contributed to the modern social hierarchies of race, class, and gender. The distinction between free people and slaves was one such hierarchy. Although in the Renaissance slavery in Europe was not limited to Africans, increasing numbers of black Africans entered Europe as slaves to supplement the labor force, and black skin color was increasingly viewed as a mark of inferiority. In terms of class, the medieval hierarchy of orders based on function in society intermingled with a new hierarchy that created a new social elite whose status was based on wealth. In regard to gender, the Renaissance debate about women led many to discuss women's nature and proper role in society, a discussion sharp-

Botticelli, *Primavera* (Spring), ca. 1482  Framed by a grove of orange trees, Venus, goddess of love, is flanked on her right by Flora, goddess of flowers and fertility, and on her left by the Three Graces, goddesses of banquets, dance, and social occasions. Above, Venus's son Cupid, the god of love, shoots darts of desire, while at the far right the wind god Zephyrus chases the nymph Chloris. The entire scene rests on classical mythology, though some art historians claim that Venus is an allegory for the Virgin Mary. Botticelli captured the ideal for female beauty in the Renaissance: slender, with pale skin, a high forehead, red-blond hair, and sloping shoulders. (Digital image © The Museum of Modern Art/Licensed by Scala/Art Resource, NY)

ened by the presence of a number of ruling queens in this era. Nevertheless, women continued to lag behind men in social status and earnings.

During the Renaissance, the feudal monarchies of medieval Europe gradually evolved into nation-states. Beginning in the fifteenth century rulers in western Europe used aggressive methods to build up their governments, reducing violence, curbing unruly nobles, and establishing domestic order. They emphasized royal majesty and royal sovereignty and insisted on the respect and loyalty of all subjects. War and diplomacy were important ways that states increased their power, but so was marriage. Because almost all of Europe was ruled by hereditary dynasties, claiming and holding resources involved shrewd marital alliances.

Religious reformers carried out even more dramatic changes than did humanists, artists, or rulers. Calls for reform of the Christian Church began very early in its history and continued throughout the Middle Ages, but in the sixteenth century these calls gained wide acceptance. The Western Christian Church, generally known as the Roman Catholic Church, had serious problems that stretched from local parishes and monasteries to the pope in Rome. Many individuals and groups were discontented with the power and wealth of the church, and even with some basic church teachings. This discontent helps explain why the ideas of one reformer, Martin Luther, found such a ready audience. Luther and other Protestants developed a new understanding of Christian doctrine that emphasized faith, the power of God's grace, and the centrality of the Bible. Protestant ideas were attractive to the literate middle classes, and they spread rapidly through preaching, hymns, and the printing press. Some reformers developed more radical ideas about baptism, the ownership of property, and the separation between church and state. Both Protestants and Catholics regarded these ideas as dangerous, and radicals were banished or executed. The progress of the Reformation was shaped by the political situation in the Holy Roman Empire, the decentralization of which allowed the Reformation to spread. In England the king's need for a church-approved divorce triggered the break with Rome, and a Protestant church was established. Protestant ideas also spread into France and eastern Europe. In all these areas, a second generation of reformers, most prominently John Calvin, developed their own theology and plans for institutional change.

The Roman Catholic Church responded slowly to the Protestant challenge, but by the middle of the sixteenth century the papacy was leading a movement for reform within the church that became known as the Catholic Reformation. Popes supported improvements in education for clergy, banned the selling of church offices, established a special court to deal with suspected heretics, and required bishops to live in their territories rather than in palaces in Rome. Every diocese, the territory governed by a bishop, was supposed to establish a seminary for training clergy. In terms of doctrine, popes and the general council of the church that met at Trent (1545–1563) reaffirmed existing Catholic teachings on the importance of tradition as well as Scripture and the importance of good works as well as faith. New religious orders such as the Jesuits and the Ursulines spread Catholic ideas through teaching, and in the case of the Jesuits through missionary work.

Religious differences led to riots, civil wars, and international conflicts in the later sixteenth century. In France and the Netherlands, Calvinist Protestants and Catholics attacked each other, and religious differences mixed with political and economic grievances. Long civil wars resulted, with the civil war in the Netherlands becoming an international conflict. War ended in France with the Edict of Nantes, in which Protestants were given some civil rights, and in the Netherlands with the division of the country into a Protestant north and a Catholic south. The era of religious wars was also marked by the most extensive witch persecutions in European history, as both Protestants and Catholics tried to rid their cities and states of people they regarded as linked to the Devil.

The Renaissance and the Reformation are often seen as key to the creation of the modern world. The radical changes of these times contained many elements of continuity, however. Artists, humanists, and religious reformers looked back to the classical era and early Christianity for inspiration, viewing those times as better and purer than their own. Political leaders played important roles in cultural and religious developments, just as they had for centuries in Europe and other parts of the world.

The events of the Renaissance and Reformation thus were linked with earlier developments, and they were also closely connected with another important element in the modern world: European exploration and colonization, which you will study in depth in Chapter 15 of this book. Renaissance monarchs paid for expeditions' ships, crews, and supplies, expecting a large share of any profits gained and increasingly viewing overseas territory as essential to a strong state. Only a week after Martin Luther stood in front of Emperor Charles V at a meeting of German rulers in the city of Worms declaring his independence in matters of religion, Ferdinand Magellan, a Portuguese sea captain using Spanish ships, was killed by indigenous people in a group of islands off the coast of southeast Asia. Charles V had provided the backing for Magellan's voyage, the first to circumnavigate the globe. Magellan viewed one of the purposes of his trip as the spread of Christianity, and later in the sixteenth century institutions created as part of the Catholic Reformation, including the Jesuit order, would operate in European colonies overseas as well as in Europe itself. The islands where Magellan was killed were later named the Philippines, in honor of Charles's son Philip. The desire for fame, wealth, and power that was central to the Renaissance, and the religious zeal central to the Reformation, were thus key to the European voyages and to colonial ventures as well.

# 15

# European Exploration and Conquest

## 1450–1650

Before 1450 Europeans were relatively marginal players in a centuries-old trading system that linked Africa, Asia, and Europe. Elites everywhere prized Chinese porcelains and silks, while wealthy members of the Celestial Kingdom, as China called itself, wanted ivory and black slaves from Africa, and exotic goods and peacocks from India. African people wanted textiles from India and cowrie shells from the Maldives in the Indian Ocean. Europeans craved Asian silks and spices but they had few desirable goods to offer their trading partners.

The European search for better access to Asian trade led to a new overseas empire in the Indian Ocean and the accidental discovery of the Western Hemisphere. Within a few decades European colonies in South and North America would join this worldwide web. Europeans came to dominate trading networks and political empires of truly global proportions. The era of globalization had begun.

Global contacts created new forms of cultural exchange, assimilation, conversion, and resistance. Europeans struggled to comprehend the peoples and societies they found and sought to impose European cultural values on them. New forms of racial prejudice emerged, but so did new openness and curiosity about different ways of life. Together with the developments of the Renaissance and the Reformation, the Age of Discovery—as the period of European exploration and conquest from 1450 to 1650 is known—laid the foundations for the modern world. ■

**Life in the Age of Discovery.** A detail from an early-seventeenth-century Flemish painting depicting maps, illustrated travel books, a globe, a compass, and an astrolabe. The voyages of discovery revolutionized Europeans' sense of space and inspired a passion among the wealthy for collecting objects related to navigation and travel. (National Gallery, London/Art Resource, NY)

# Chapter Preview

- ▶ What were the limits of world contacts before Columbus?

- ▶ How and why did Europeans undertake voyages of expansion?

- ▶ What was the impact of conquest?

- ▶ How did Europe and the world change after Columbus?

- ▶ How did expansion change European attitudes and beliefs?

# ▼ What were the limits of world contacts before Columbus?

Historians now recognize that a type of world economy, known as the Afro-Eurasian trade world, linked the products and people of Europe, Asia, and Africa in the fifteenth century. The West was not the dominant player before Columbus, and the European voyages derived from a desire to share in and control the wealth coming from the Indian Ocean.

## The Trade World of the Indian Ocean

*gold & slaves*

The Indian Ocean was the center of the Afro-Eurasian trade world. It was a crossroads for commercial and cultural exchange between China, India, the Middle East, Africa, and Europe (Map 15.1). From the seventh through the fourteenth centuries, the volume of this trade steadily increased, declining only during the years of the Black Death.

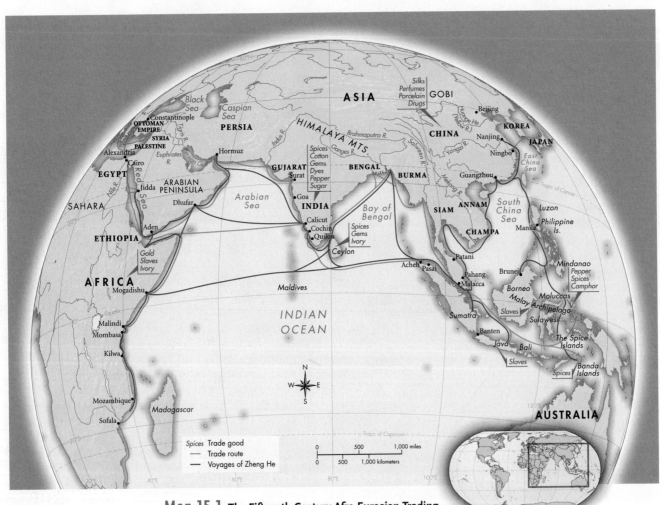

**Map 15.1 The Fifteenth-Century Afro-Eurasian Trading World** After a period of decline following the Black Death and the Mongol invasions, trade revived in the fifteenth century. Muslim merchants dominated trade, linking ports in East Africa and the Red Sea with those in India and the Malay Archipelago. Chinese Admiral Zheng He's voyages (1405–1433) followed the most important Indian Ocean trade routes, in the hope of imposing Ming dominance of trade and tribute.

Chapter 15
European Exploration and
Conquest • 1450–1650

418

CHAPTER LOCATOR

What were the limits of world contacts before Columbus?

Merchants congregated in a series of multicultural, cosmopolitan port cities strung around the Indian Ocean. The most developed area of this commercial web was in the South China Sea. In the fifteenth century the port of Malacca became a great commercial entrepôt (AHN-truh-poh), a trading post to which goods were shipped for storage while awaiting redistribution to other places.

The Mongol emperors opened the doors of China to the West, encouraging Europeans like the Venetian trader and explorer Marco Polo to do business there. Marco Polo's tales of his travels from 1271 to 1295 and his encounter with the Great Khan fueled Western fantasies about the Orient. After the Mongols fell to the Ming Dynasty in 1368, China entered a period of agricultural and commercial expansion, population growth, and urbanization. Historians agree that China had the most advanced economy in the world until at least the start of the eighteenth century.

China also took the lead in exploration, sending Admiral Zheng He's fleet along the trade web as far west as Egypt. From 1405 to 1433, each of his seven expeditions involved

**The Port of Banten in Western Java** Influenced by Muslim traders and emerging in the early sixteenth century as a Muslim kingdom, Banten evolved into a thriving entrepôt. The city stood on the trade route to China and, as this Dutch engraving suggests, in the seventeenth century the Dutch East India Company used Banten as an important collection point for spices purchased for sale in Europe. (Archives Charmet/The Bridgeman Art Library)

How and why did Europeans undertake voyages of expansion?

What was the impact of conquest?

How did Europe and the world change after Columbus?

How did expansion change European attitudes and beliefs?

hundreds of ships and tens of thousands of men. Court conflicts and the need to defend against renewed Mongol encroachment led to the abandonment of the expeditions after the deaths of Zheng He and the emperor. China's turning away from external trade opened new opportunities for European states to claim a decisive role in world trade.

Another center of trade in the Indian Ocean was India, the crucial link between the Persian Gulf and the Southeast Asian and East Asian trade networks. The subcontinent had ancient links with its neighbors to the northwest: trade between South Asia and Mesopotamia dates back to the origins of human civilization. Arab merchants who circumnavigated India on their way to trade in the South China Sea established trading posts along the southern coast of India, where the cities of Calicut and Quilon became thriving commercial centers. India was an important contributor of goods to the world trading system; much of the world's pepper was grown there, and Indian cotton textiles were highly prized.

## The Trading States of Africa

Africa also played an important role in the world trade system before Columbus. By 1450 Africa had a few large and developed empires along with hundreds of smaller states. From 1250 until its defeat by the Ottomans in 1517, the Mamluk Egyptian empire was one of the most powerful on the continent. Its capital, Cairo, was a center of Islamic learning and religious authority as well as a hub for Indian Ocean trade goods. Sharing in Cairo's prosperity was the African highland state of Ethiopia, a Christian kingdom with scattered contacts with European rulers. On the east coast of Africa, Swahili-speaking city-states engaged in the Indian Ocean trade. Cities like Mogadishu and Mombasa were known for their prosperity and culture.

In the fifteenth century most of the gold that reached Europe came from Sudan in West Africa and from the Akan (AH-kahn) peoples living near present-day Ghana (GAH-nuh). Transported across the Sahara by Arab and African traders on camels, the gold was sold in the ports of North Africa. Other trading routes led to the Egyptian cities of Alexandria and Cairo, where the Venetians held commercial privileges.

Nations inland that sat astride the north-south caravan routes grew wealthy from this trade. In the mid-thirteenth century the kingdom of Mali emerged as an important player on the overland trade route. In later centuries the diversion of gold away from the trans-Sahara routes would weaken the inland states of Africa politically and economically.

Gold was one important object of trade; slaves were another. Slavery was practiced in Africa, as virtually everywhere else in the world, before the arrival of Europeans. Arabic and African merchants took West African slaves to the Mediterranean to be sold in European, Egyptian, and Middle Eastern markets and also brought eastern Europeans to West Africa as slaves. In addition, Indian and Arabic merchants traded slaves in the coastal regions of East Africa.

## The Ottoman and Persian Empires

The Middle East served as an intermediary for trade between Europe, Africa, and Asia and was also an important supplier of goods for foreign exchange, especially silk and cotton. Two great rival empires, the Persian Safavids (sah-FAH-vidz) and the Turkish Ottomans, dominated the region.

The Persians' Shi'ite Muslim faith clashed with the Ottomans' adherence to Sunnism. Economically, the two competed for control over western trade routes to the East. Under Sultan Mohammed II (r. 1451–1481), the Ottomans captured Europe's largest city, Constantinople, in May 1453. Renamed Istanbul, the city became the capital of the Ottoman Empire. By the mid-sixteenth century the Ottomans controlled the sea trade

Chapter 15
**European Exploration and**
**420**     **Conquest • 1450–1650**

CHAPTER LOCATOR   |    What were the limits of world contacts before Columbus?

on the eastern Mediterranean, Syria, Palestine, Egypt, and the rest of North Africa, and their power extended into Europe as far west as Vienna.

Ottoman expansion frightened Europeans. In France in the sixteenth century, twice as many books were printed about the Turkish threat as about the American discoveries. The strength of the Ottomans helps explain some of the missionary fervor Christians brought to new territories. It also raised economic concerns. With trade routes to the east in the hands of the Ottomans, Europeans needed to find new trade routes.

## Genoese and Venetian Middlemen

Compared to the East, Europe constituted a minor outpost in the world trading system. European craftsmen produced few products to rival those of Asia. In the late Middle Ages, the Italian city-states of Venice and Genoa controlled the European luxury trade with the East.

In 1304 Venice established formal relations with the sultan of Mamluk Egypt, opening operations in Cairo, the gateway to Asian trade. Venetian merchants specialized in expensive luxury goods like spices, silks, and carpets, which they obtained from middlemen in the eastern Mediterranean and Asia Minor.

The Venetians exchanged Eastern luxury goods for European products they could trade abroad, including Spanish and English wool, German metal goods, Flemish textiles, and silk cloth made by their own craftsmen using imported raw materials. Eastern demand for such goods was low. To make up the difference, the Venetians earned currency in the shipping industry and through trade in firearms and slaves.

Venice's ancient rival was Genoa. In the wake of the Crusades, Genoa dominated the northern route to Asia through the Black Sea. Expansion in the thirteenth and fourteenth centuries took the Genoese as far as Persia and the Far East. In 1291 they sponsored a failed expedition into the Atlantic in search of India. This voyage reveals the long roots of Genoese interest in Atlantic exploration.

In the fifteenth century, with Venice claiming victory in the spice trade, the Genoese shifted focus from trade to finance and from the Black Sea to the western Mediterranean. Located on the northwestern coast of Italy, Genoa had always been active in the western Mediterranean, trading with North African ports, southern France, Spain, and even England and Flanders through the Strait of Gibraltar. When Spanish and Portuguese voyages began to explore the western Atlantic (see pages 424–425), Genoese merchants, navigators, and financiers provided their skills to the Iberian monarchs.

A major element of both Venetian and Genoese trade was slavery. Merchants purchased slaves, many of whom were fellow Christians, in the Balkans. After the loss of the Black Sea—and thus the source of slaves—to the Ottomans, the Genoese sought new supplies of slaves in the West, taking the Guanches (indigenous peoples from the Canary Islands), Muslim prisoners and Jewish refugees from Spain, and by the early 1500s both black and Berber Africans. With the growth of Spanish colonies in the New World,

**The Taking of Constantinople by the Turks, April 22, 1453** The Ottoman conquest of the capital of the Byzantine Empire in 1453 sent shock and despair through Europe. Capitalizing on the city's strategic and commercial importance, the Ottomans made it the center of their empire. (Bibliothèque nationale de France)

Genoese and Venetian merchants would become important players in the Atlantic slave trade.

Italian experience in colonial administration, slaving, and international trade and finance served as a model for the Iberian states as they pushed European expansion to new heights. Mariners, merchants, and financiers from Venice and Genoa—most notably Christopher Columbus—played a crucial role in bringing the fruits of this experience to the Iberian Peninsula and to the New World.

## ▼ How and why did Europeans undertake voyages of expansion?

As we have seen, Europe was by no means isolated before the voyages of exploration and its "discovery" of the New World. But because they did not produce many products desired by Eastern elites, Europeans were modest players in the Indian Ocean trading world. As Europe recovered after the Black Death, new European players entered the scene with new technology, eager to spread Christianity and to undo Italian and Ottoman domination of trade with the East.

### Causes of European Expansion

European expansion had multiple causes. By the middle of the fifteenth century, Europe was experiencing a revival of population and economic activity after the lows of the Black Death. This revival created demands for luxury goods, especially spices, from the East. The fall of Constantinople and subsequent Ottoman control of trade routes created obstacles to fulfilling these demands. Europeans needed to find new sources of precious metal to trade with the Ottomans, or trade routes that bypassed the Ottomans.

Religious fervor was another important catalyst for expansion. The passion and energy ignited by the Christian *reconquista* (reconquest) of the Iberian Peninsula encouraged the Portuguese and Spanish to continue the Christian crusade. Just seven months separated the Spanish conquest of Granada, the last remaining Muslim state on the Iberian Peninsula, and Columbus's departure across the Atlantic. Since the remaining Muslim states, such as the mighty Ottoman Empire, were too strong to defeat, Iberians turned their attention elsewhere.

Combined with eagerness for profits and to spread Christianity was the desire for glory and the urge to chart new waters. Scholars have frequently described the European discoveries as a manifestation of Renaissance curiosity about the physical universe. The detailed journals kept by European voyagers attest to their wonder and fascination with the new peoples and places they visited.

Individual explorers combined these motivations in unique ways. Christopher Columbus was a devout Christian who was increasingly haunted by messianic obsessions in the last years of his life. As Portuguese explorer Bartholomew Diaz put it, his own motives were "to serve God and His Majesty, to give light to those who were in darkness and to grow rich as all men desire to do." When the Portuguese explorer Vasco da Gama reached the port of Calicut, India, in 1498 and a native asked what he wanted, he replied, "Christians and spices."[1] The bluntest of the Spanish conquistadors, Hernando Cortés, announced as he prepared to conquer Mexico, "I have come to win gold, not to plow the fields like a peasant."[2]

Eagerness for exploration was heightened by a lack of opportunity at home. After the reconquista, young men of the Spanish upper classes found their economic and political opportunities greatly limited. The ambitious turned to the sea to seek their fortunes.

**conquistador** Spanish for "conqueror"; Spanish soldier-explorers, such as Hernando Cortés and Francisco Pizarro, who sought to conquer the New World for the Spanish crown.

**Chapter 15**
**European Exploration and Conquest** • 1450–1650

422

CHAPTER LOCATOR | What were the limits of world contacts before Columbus?

Whatever the reasons, the voyages were made possible by the growth of government power. The Spanish monarchy was stronger than before and in a position to support foreign ventures. In Portugal explorers also looked to the monarchy, to Prince Henry the Navigator in particular (pages 424–425), for financial support and encouragement. Like voyagers, monarchs shared a mix of motivations, from the desire to please God to the desire to win glory and profit from trade. Competition among European monarchs was an important factor in encouraging the steady stream of expeditions that began in the late fifteenth century.

Ordinary sailors were ill paid, and life at sea meant danger, overcrowding, unbearable stench, and hunger. For months at a time, 100 to 120 people lived and worked in a space of 1,600 to 2,000 square feet. Men chose to join these miserable crews to escape poverty at home, to continue a family trade, to win a few crumbs of the great riches of empire, or to find better lives as illegal immigrants in the colonies.

The people who stayed at home had a powerful impact on the process. Royal ministers and factions at court influenced monarchs to provide or deny support for exploration. The small number of people who could read served as an audience for tales of fantastic places and unknown peoples. Cosmography, natural history, and geography aroused enormous interest among educated people in the fifteenth and sixteenth centuries.

*The Travels of Sir John Mandeville* The author of this tale claimed to be an English knight who traveled extensively in the Middle East and Asia from the 1320s to the 1350s. Although historians now consider the work a skillful fiction, it had a great influence on how Europeans understood the world at the time. This illustration, from an edition published around 1410, depicts Mandeville approaching a walled city on the first stage of his voyage to Constantinople (© British Library Board)

## Technology and the Rise of Exploration

Technological developments in shipbuilding, weaponry, and navigation provided another impetus for European expansion. Since ancient times, most seagoing vessels had been narrow, open boats called galleys, propelled largely by slaves or convicts manning the oars. Though well suited to the placid waters of the Mediterranean, galleys could not withstand the rougher conditions in the Atlantic. The need for sturdier craft, as well as population losses caused by the Black Death, forced the development of a new style of ship that would not require much manpower to sail. In the course of the fifteenth century, the Portuguese developed the caravel, a small, light, three-mast sailing ship. The caravel held more cargo and was much more maneuverable than the galley. When fitted with cannon, it could dominate larger vessels.

Great strides in cartography and navigational aids were also made during this period. In 1406 Arab scholars reintroduced Europeans to Ptolemy's *Geography*. Written in the second century C.E., the work synthesized the geographical knowledge of the classical world. Ptolemy's work provided significant improvements over medieval cartography, showing the world as round and introducing the idea of latitude and longitude to plot position accurately. It also contained crucial errors. Unaware of the Americas, Ptolemy showed the world as much smaller than it is, so that Asia appeared not very distant from

**caravel** A small, maneuverable, three-mast sailing ship developed by the Portuguese in the fifteenth century that gave the Portuguese a distinct advantage in exploration and trade.

**Ptolemy's *Geography*** A second century C.E. work that synthesized the classical knowledge of geography and introduced the concepts of longitude and latitude. Reintroduced to Europeans in 1406 by Arab scholars, its ideas allowed cartographers to create more accurate maps.

How and why did Europeans undertake voyages of expansion?  What was the impact of conquest?  How did Europe and the world change after Columbus?  How did expansion change European attitudes and beliefs?

423

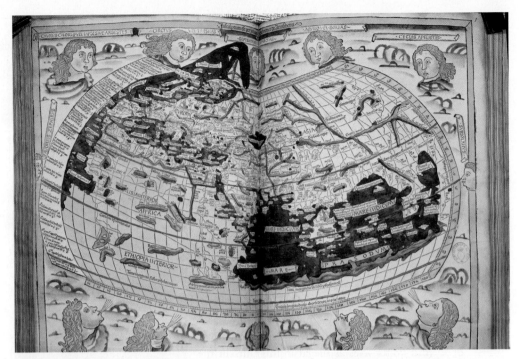

**Ptolemy's *Geography*** The recovery of Ptolemy's *Geography* in the early fifteenth century gave Europeans new access to ancient geographical knowledge. This 1486 world map, based on Ptolemy, is a great advance over medieval maps but contains errors with significant consequences for future exploration. It shows a single continent watered by a single ocean, with land covering three-quarters of the world's surface. Africa and Asia are joined with Europe, making the Indian Ocean a land-locked sea and rendering the circumnavigation of Africa impossible. The continent of Asia is stretched far to the east, greatly shortening the distance from Europe to Asia via the Atlantic. (Giraudon/Art Resource, NY)

Europe to the west. Based on this work, cartographers fashioned new maps that combined classical knowledge with the latest information from mariners.

The magnetic compass enabled sailors to determine their direction and position at sea. The astrolabe, an instrument invented by the ancient Greeks and perfected by Muslim navigators, was used to determine the altitude of the sun and other celestial bodies. It permitted mariners to plot their latitude, that is, their precise position north or south of the equator.

Like the astrolabe, much of the new technology that Europeans used on their voyages was borrowed from the East. Gunpowder, the compass, and the sternpost rudder were Chinese inventions. The lateen sail, which allowed European ships to tack against the wind, was a product of the Indian Ocean trade world and was brought to the Mediterranean on Arab ships. Advances in cartography also drew on the rich tradition of Judeo-Arabic mathematical and astronomical learning in Iberia. In exploring new territories, European sailors thus called on techniques and knowledge developed over centuries in China, the Muslim world, and the Indian Ocean.

## The Portuguese Overseas Empire

Portugal had a long history of seafaring and navigation. Blocked from access to western Europe by Spain, the Portuguese turned to the Atlantic and North Africa, whose waters they knew better than did other Europeans.

In the early phases of Portuguese exploration, Prince Henry (1394–1460), a younger son of the king, played a leading role. A nineteenth-century scholar dubbed Henry "the

Chapter 15
European Exploration and
Conquest • 1450–1650

424

CHAPTER LOCATOR

What were the limits of world contacts before Columbus?

Navigator" because of his support for the study of geography and navigation and for the annual expeditions he sponsored down the western coast of Africa.

The objectives of Portuguese exploration policy included desires for military glory; crusades to Christianize Muslims and to locate a mythical Christian king of Africa, Prester John; and the quest to find gold, slaves, and an overseas route to the spice markets of India. Portugal's conquest of Ceuta, an Arab city in northern Morocco, in 1415 marked the beginning of European overseas expansion. In the 1420s, under Henry's direction, the Portuguese began to settle the Atlantic islands of Madeira (ca. 1420) and the Azores (1427). In 1443 they founded their first African commercial settlement at Arguin in North Africa. By the time of Henry's death in 1460, his support for exploration was vindicated by thriving sugar plantations on the Atlantic islands, the first arrival of enslaved Africans in Portugal (see page 439), and new access to African gold.

The Portuguese next established trading posts and forts on the gold-rich Guinea coast and penetrated into the African continent all the way to Timbuktu (Map 15.2). By 1500 Portugal controlled the flow of African gold to Europe.

The Portuguese then pushed farther south down the west coast of Africa. In 1487 Bartholomew Diaz rounded the Cape of Good Hope at the southern tip, but storms and a threatened mutiny forced him to turn back. A decade later Vasco da Gama succeeded in rounding the Cape while commanding a fleet in search of a sea route to India. With the help of an Indian guide, da Gama reached the port of Calicut in India. He returned to Lisbon loaded with spices and samples of Indian cloth, having proved the possibility of lucrative trade with the East via the Cape route. Thereafter, a Portuguese convoy set out for passage around the Cape every March.

Lisbon became the entrance port for Asian goods into Europe, but this was not accomplished without a fight. Muslim-controlled port city-states had long controlled the rich spice trade of the Indian Ocean, and they did not surrender it willingly. Portuguese cannon blasted open the port of Malacca in 1511, followed by Calicut, Ormuz, and Goa. The bombardment of these cities laid the foundation for Portuguese imperialism in the sixteenth and seventeenth centuries.

In March 1493, between the voyages of Diaz and da Gama, Spanish ships under a Genoese mariner named Christopher Columbus (1451–1506), in the service of the Spanish crown, entered Lisbon harbor. Spain also had begun the quest for an empire.

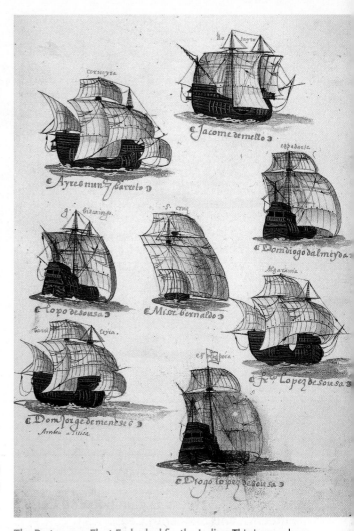

**The Portuguese Fleet Embarked for the Indies** This image shows a Portuguese trading fleet in the late fifteenth century bound for the riches of the Indies. Between 1500 and 1635 over nine hundred ships sailed from Portugal to ports on the Indian Ocean, in annual fleets composed of five to ten ships. (British Museum/HarperCollins Publishers/The Art Archive)

## The Problem of Christopher Columbus

In order to understand Christopher Columbus in the context of his own time, we need to ask several questions. First, what kind of man was Columbus, and what forces or influences shaped him? Second, in sailing westward from Europe, what were his goals? Third, did he achieve his goals, and what did he make of his discoveries?

How and why did Europeans undertake voyages of expansion? | What was the impact of conquest? | How did Europe and the world change after Columbus? | How did expansion change European attitudes and beliefs?

425

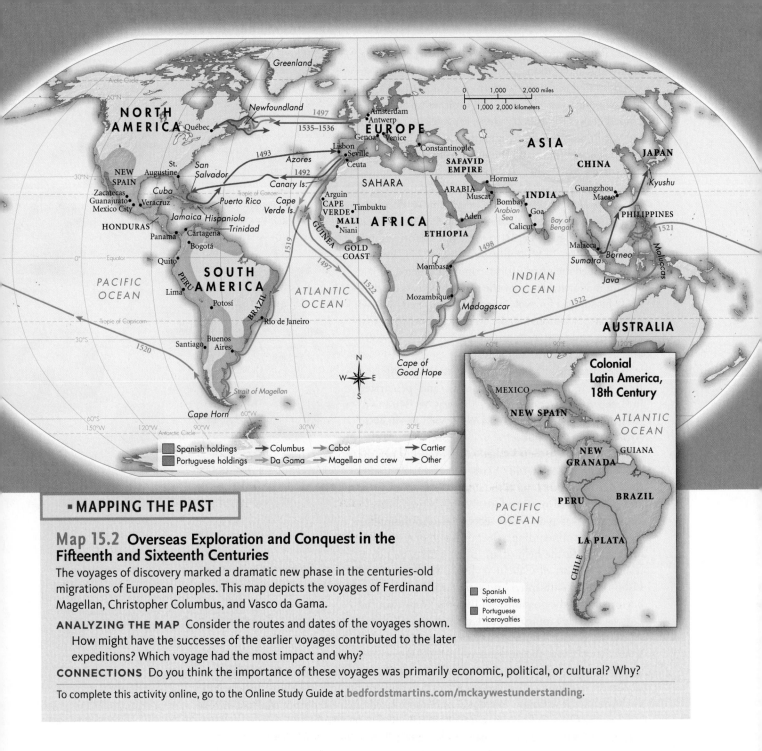

The voyages of Ferdinand Magellan, Christopher Columbus, and Vasco da Gama depicted on map.

Map labels include: Greenland, NORTH AMERICA, Newfoundland, Québec, EUROPE, Amsterdam, Antwerp, Genoa, Venice, ASIA, Constantinople, CHINA, JAPAN, Lisbon, Seville, Ceuta, SAFAVID EMPIRE, Hormuz, Guangzhou, Kyushu, Macao, NEW SPAIN, St. Augustine, San Salvador, Azores, Canary Is., SAHARA, ARABIA, Muscat, INDIA, Bombay, Goa, PHILIPPINES, Zacatecas, Cuba, Puerto Rico, Cape Verde Is., Arguin, CAPE VERDE, Timbuktu, Aden, Calicut, Bay of Bengal, Guanajuato, Veracruz, Mexico City, MALI, AFRICA, ETHIOPIA, Niani, GUINEA, Arabian Sea, Malacca, Borneo, Moluccas, HONDURAS, Jamaica, Hispaniola, Trinidad, Panama, Cartagena, GOLD COAST, Mombasa, Sumatra, Java, Bogotá, Quito, PERU, SOUTH AMERICA, BRAZIL, ATLANTIC OCEAN, INDIAN OCEAN, Mozambique, PACIFIC OCEAN, Lima, Potosí, Rio de Janeiro, Madagascar, AUSTRALIA, Santiago, Buenos Aires, Strait of Magellan, Cape of Good Hope, Cape Horn

Dates on routes: 1497, 1535–1536, 1493, 1492, 1519, 1497, 1522, 1498, 1521, 1522, 1520

Legend:
- Spanish holdings — Columbus — Cabot — Cartier
- Portuguese holdings — Da Gama — Magellan and crew — Other

Colonial Latin America, 18th Century: MEXICO, NEW SPAIN, ATLANTIC OCEAN, NEW GRANADA, GUIANA, PACIFIC OCEAN, PERU, BRAZIL, LA PLATA, CHILE

Legend:
- Spanish viceroyalties
- Portuguese viceroyalties

## ▪ MAPPING THE PAST

## Map 15.2 Overseas Exploration and Conquest in the Fifteenth and Sixteenth Centuries

The voyages of discovery marked a dramatic new phase in the centuries-old migrations of European peoples. This map depicts the voyages of Ferdinand Magellan, Christopher Columbus, and Vasco da Gama.

**ANALYZING THE MAP** Consider the routes and dates of the voyages shown. How might have the successes of the earlier voyages contributed to the later expeditions? Which voyage had the most impact and why?

**CONNECTIONS** Do you think the importance of these voyages was primarily economic, political, or cultural? Why?

To complete this activity online, go to the Online Study Guide at bedfordstmartins.com/mckaywestunderstanding.

Columbus's westward voyages embodied a long-standing Genoese ambition to circumvent Venetian domination of eastward trade, which was now being claimed by the Portuguese. Columbus was very knowledgeable about the sea. He had worked as a mapmaker, and he was familiar with such fifteenth-century Portuguese navigational developments as *portolans* — written descriptions of the courses along which ships sailed — and the use of the compass as a nautical instrument. His successful thirty-three-day voyage to the Caribbean owed a great deal to his seamanship.

Columbus was also a deeply religious man. He began the *Journal* of his voyage to the Americas in the form of a letter to Ferdinand and Isabella of Spain:

*On 2 January in the year 1492, when your Highnesses had concluded their war with the Moors who reigned in Europe, I saw your Highnesses' banners victoriously raised on the towers of the Alhambra, the citadel of the city, and the Moorish king come out of the city gates and kiss the hands of your Highnesses and the prince, My Lord. And later in that same month, on the grounds of information I had given your Highnesses concerning the lands of India . . . your Highnesses decided to send me, Christopher Columbus, to see these parts of India and the princes and peoples of those lands and consider the best means for their conversion.*[3]

Columbus had witnessed the Spanish conquest of Granada and shared fully in the religious and nationalistic fervor surrounding that event. Like the Spanish rulers and most Europeans of his age, he understood Christianity as a missionary religion that should be carried to places where it did not exist.

What was the object of this first voyage? Columbus gave the answer in the very title of the expedition, "The Enterprise of the Indies." He wanted to find a direct ocean trading route to Asia. Rejected for funding by the Portuguese in 1483 and by Ferdinand and Isabella in 1486, the project finally won the backing of the Spanish monarchy in 1492. The Spanish crown named Columbus viceroy over any territory he might discover and gave him one-tenth of the material rewards of the journey. Based on Ptolemy's *Geography* and other texts, he expected to pass the islands of Japan and then land on the east coast of China.

How did Columbus interpret what he had found, and in his mind did he achieve what he had set out to do? Columbus's small fleet left Spain on August 3, 1492. He landed on an island in the Bahamas, which he christened San Salvador, on October 12, 1492. Columbus believed he had found some small islands off the east coast of Japan. In a letter he wrote to Ferdinand and Isabella on his return to Spain, Columbus described the natives as handsome, peaceful, and primitive people. Believing he was in the Indies, he called them "Indians," a name that was later applied to all inhabitants of the Americas. Columbus concluded that they would make good slaves and could quickly be converted to Christianity. (See "Listening to the Past: Columbus Describes His First Voyage," page 428.)

Scholars have identified the inhabitants of the islands as the Taino people, speakers of the Arawak language, who inhabited Hispaniola (modern-day Haiti and Dominican Republic) and other islands in the Caribbean. Columbus received reassuring reports from Taino villagers of the presence of gold and of a great king in the vicinity. From San Salvador, Columbus sailed southwest, believing that this course would take him to Japan or the coast of China. He landed instead on Cuba on October 28. Deciding that he must be on the mainland near the coastal city of Quinsay (now Hangzhou), he sent a small embassy inland with letters from Ferdinand and Isabella and instructions to locate the grand city.

**Columbus's First Voyage to the New World, 1492–1493**

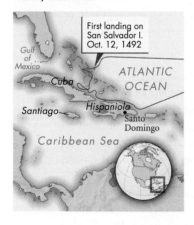

First landing on San Salvador I. Oct. 12, 1492

Gulf of Mexico

ATLANTIC OCEAN

Cuba

Santiago — Hispaniola
Santo Domingo

Caribbean Sea

The landing party found only small villages. Confronted with this disappointment, Columbus focused on trying to find gold or other valuables among the peoples he had discovered. The sight of Taino people wearing gold ornaments on Hispaniola seemed to prove that gold was available in the region. In January, confident that its source would soon be found, he headed back to Spain to report on his discovery.

Over the next decades, the Spanish would follow a policy of conquest and colonization in the New World. On his second voyage, Columbus forcibly subjugated the island of Hispaniola and enslaved its indigenous peoples. On this

# LISTENING TO THE PAST

## Columbus Describes His First Voyage

*On his return voyage to Spain in January 1493, Christopher Columbus composed a letter intended for wide circulation and had copies of it sent ahead to Isabella and Ferdinand. Because the letter sums up Columbus's understanding of his achievements, it is considered the most important document of his first voyage. Remember that his knowledge of Asia rested heavily on Marco Polo's* Travels, *published around 1298.*

Since I know that you will be pleased at the great success with which the Lord has crowned my voyage, I write to inform you how in thirty-three days I crossed from the Canary Islands to the Indies, with the fleet which our most illustrious sovereigns gave me. I found very many islands with large populations and took possession of them all for their Highnesses; this I did by proclamation and unfurled the royal standard. No opposition was offered.

I named the first island that I found "San Salvador," in honour of our Lord and Saviour who has granted me this miracle. . . . When I reached Cuba, I followed its north coast westwards, and found it so extensive that I thought this must be the mainland, the province of Cathay.* . . . From there I saw another island eighteen leagues eastwards which I then named "Hispaniola.". . .†

Hispaniola is a wonder. The mountains and hills, the plains and meadow lands are both fertile and beautiful. They are most suitable for planting crops and for raising cattle of all kinds, and there are good sites for building towns and villages. The harbours are incredibly fine and there are many great rivers with broad channels and the majority contain gold.‡ The trees, fruits and plants are very different from those of Cuba. In Hispaniola there are many spices and large mines of gold and other metals.§ . . .

The inhabitants of this island, and all the rest that I discovered or heard of, go naked, as their mothers bore them, men and women alike. A few of the women, however, cover a single place with a leaf of a plant or piece of cotton which they weave for the purpose. They have no iron or steel or arms and are not capable of using them, not because they are not strong and well built but because they are amazingly timid. All the weapons they have are canes cut at seeding time, at the end of which they fix a sharpened stick, but they have not the courage to make use of these, for very often when I have sent two or three men to a village to have conversation with them a great number of them have come out. But as soon as they saw my men all fled immediately, a father not even waiting for his son. And this is not because we have harmed any of them; on the contrary, wherever I have gone and been able to have conversation with them, I have given them some of the various things I had, a cloth and other articles, and received nothing in exchange. But they have still remained incurably timid.

True, when they have been reassured and lost their fear, they are so ingenuous and so liberal with all their possessions that no one who has not seen them would believe it. If one asks for anything they have they never say no. On the contrary, they offer a share to anyone with demonstrations of heartfelt affection, and they are immediately content with any small thing, valuable or valueless, that is given them. I forbade the men to give them bits of broken crockery, fragments of glass or tags of laces, though if they could get them they fancied them the finest jewels in the world. . . .

I hoped to win them to the love and service of their Highnesses and of the whole Spanish nation and to persuade them to collect and give us of the things which they possessed in abundance and which we needed. They have no religion and are not idolaters; but all believe that power and goodness dwell in the sky and they are firmly convinced that I have come from the sky with these ships and people. In this belief they gave me a good reception everywhere, once they had overcome their fear; and this is not because they are stupid — far from it, they are men of great intelligence, for they navigate all those seas, and give a marvellously good account of every thing — but because they have never before seen men clothed or ships like these. . . .

In all these islands the men are seemingly content with one woman, but their chief or king is allowed more than twenty. The women appear to work more

and subsequent voyages, Columbus brought with him settlers for the new Spanish territories, along with agricultural seed and livestock. Columbus himself, however, had little interest in or capacity for governing. Revolt soon broke out against him and his brother on Hispaniola. A royal expedition sent to investigate returned the brothers to Spain in chains. Columbus was quickly cleared of wrongdoing, but he did not recover his authority over the territories.

Columbus was very much a man of his times. To the end of his life in 1506, he believed that he had found small islands off the coast of Asia. He never realized the scope of his achievement: he found a vast continent unknown to Europeans, except for a fleeting

Chapter 15
**European Exploration and**
**428**  **Conquest • 1450–1650**

CHAPTER LOCATOR | What were the limits of world contacts before Columbus?

will give them as much gold as they require, if they will render me some very slight assistance; also I will give them all the spices and cotton they want. . . . I will also bring them as much aloes as they ask and as many slaves, who will be taken from the idolaters. I believe also that I have found rhubarb and cinnamon and there will be countless other things in addition. . . .

So all Christendom will be delighted that our Redeemer has given victory to our most illustrious King and Queen and their renowned kingdoms, in this great matter. They should hold great celebrations and render solemn thanks to the Holy Trinity with many solemn prayers, for the great triumph which they will have, by the conversion of so many peoples to our holy faith and for the temporal benefits which will follow, for not only Spain, but all Christendom will receive encouragement and profit.

This is a brief account of the facts. Written in the caravel off the Canary Islands.**

15 February 1493

At your orders   THE ADMIRAL ❯❯

**Source:** From *The Four Voyages of Christopher Columbus*, edited and translated by J. M. Cohen (Penguin Classics, 1969). Copyright © J. M. Cohen, 1969. Reproduced by permission of Penguin Books, Ltd.

Christopher Columbus, by Ridolfo Ghirlandaio. Friend of Raphael and teacher of Michelangelo, Ghirlandaio (1483–1561) enjoyed distinction as a portrait painter, and so we can assume that this is a good likeness of the older Columbus. (Scala/ Art Resource, NY)

## QUESTIONS FOR ANALYSIS

1. How did Columbus explain the success of his voyage?
2. What was Columbus's view of the Native Americans he met?
3. Evaluate his statements that the Caribbean islands possessed gold, cotton, and spices.

than the men and I have not been able to find out if they have private property. As far as I could see whatever a man had was shared among all the rest and this particularly applies to food. . . . In another island, which I am told is larger than Hispaniola, the people have no hair. Here there is a vast quantity of gold, and from here and the other islands I bring Indians as evidence.

In conclusion, to speak only of the results of this very hasty voyage, their Highnesses can see that I

*Cathay is the old name for China. In the logbook and later in this letter, Columbus accepts the native story that Cuba is an island that can be circumnavigated in something more than twenty-one days, yet he insists here and during the second voyage that it is part of the Asiatic mainland.

†Hispaniola is the second largest island of the West Indies. Haiti occupies the western third of the island, the Dominican Republic the rest.

‡This did not prove to be true.

§These statements are also inaccurate.

**Actually, Columbus was off Santa Maria in the Azores.

Viking presence centuries earlier. He could not know that the scale of his discoveries would revolutionize world power, raising issues of trade, settlement, government bureaucracy, and the rights of native and African peoples.

## Later Explorers

The Florentine navigator Amerigo Vespucci (veh-SPOO-chee) (1454–1512) realized what Columbus had not. Writing about his discoveries on the coast of modern-day Venezuela, Vespucci stated: "Those new regions which we found and explored with the

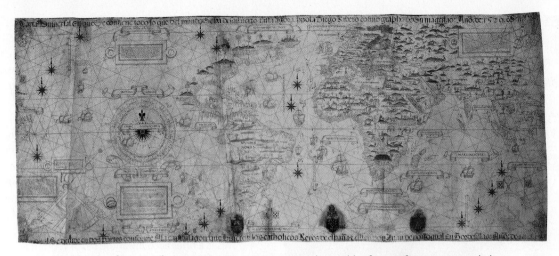

**World Map of Diogo Ribeiro, 1529** This map integrates the wealth of new information provided by European explorers in the decades after Columbus's 1492 voyage. Working on commission for the Spanish king Charles V, mapmaker Diogo Ribeiro incorporated new details on Africa, South America, India, the Malay Archipelago, and China. Note the inaccuracy in his placement of the Moluccas, or Spice Islands, which are much too far east. This "mistake" was intended to serve Spain's interests in trade negotiations with the Portuguese. (Biblioteca Apostolica Vaticana)

fleet . . . we may rightly call a New World." In recognition of Amerigo's bold claim, the continent was named for him.

To settle competing claims to the Atlantic discoveries, Spain and Portugal turned to Pope Alexander VI. The resulting Treaty of Tordesillas (tor-duh-SEE-yuhs) in 1494 gave Spain everything to the west of an imaginary north-south line drawn down the Atlantic and Portugal everything to the east. This arbitrary division worked in Portugal's favor when in 1500 an expedition led by Pedro Alvares Cabral, en route to India, landed on the coast of Brazil, which Cabral claimed as Portuguese territory.

The search for profits determined the direction of Spanish exploration and expansion into South America. With insignificant profits from the Caribbean compared to the enormous riches that the Portuguese were reaping in Asia, Spain renewed the search for a western passage to Asia. In 1519 Charles V of Spain commissioned Ferdinand Magellan (1480–1521) to find a direct sea route to the spices of the Moluccas off the southeast coast of Asia. Magellan sailed southwest across the Atlantic to Brazil, and after a long search along the coast he located the treacherous straits that now bear his name (see Map 15.1). After passing through the straits, his fleet sailed north up the west coast of South America and then headed west into the Pacific toward the Malay Archipelago. Some of these islands were conquered in the 1560s and named the "Philippines" for Philip II of Spain.

Terrible storms, disease, starvation, and violence haunted the expedition. Sailors on two of Magellan's five ships attempted mutiny on the South American coast; one ship was lost, and another ship deserted and returned to Spain before even traversing the straits. Magellan himself was killed in a skirmish in the Philippines. The expedition had enough survivors to man only two ships, and one of them was captured by the Portuguese. One ship with only eighteen men returned to Spain from the east by way of the Indian Ocean, the Cape of Good Hope, and the Atlantic in 1522. The voyage—the first to circumnavigate the globe—had taken close to three years.

Despite the losses, this voyage revolutionized Europeans' understanding of the world by demonstrating the vastness of the Pacific. Although the voyage made a small profit in spices, the westward passage to the Indies was too long and dangerous for commercial purposes. Spain soon abandoned the attempt to oust Portugal from the Eastern spice trade and concentrated on exploiting her New World territories.

**Treaty of Tordesillas** The 1494 agreement giving Spain everything to the west of an imaginary line drawn down the Atlantic and giving Portugal everything to the east.

Chapter 15
European Exploration and
**430**   Conquest • 1450–1650

CHAPTER LOCATOR     What were the limits of world contacts before Columbus?

The English and French also set sail across the Atlantic during the early days of exploration in search of a northwest passage to the Indies. In 1497 John Cabot, a Genoese merchant living in London, discovered Newfoundland. The next year he returned and explored the New England coast. These forays proved futile, and the English established no permanent colonies in the territories they explored. Between 1576 and 1578, Martin Frobisher made three voyages in and around the Canadian bay that now bears his name. Frobisher hopefully brought a quantity of ore back to England with him, but it proved to be worthless.

Early French exploration of the Atlantic was equally frustrating. Between 1534 and 1541 Frenchman Jacques Cartier made several voyages and explored the St. Lawrence region of Canada, searching for a passage to the wealth of Asia. When this hope proved vain, the French turned to a new source of profit within Canada itself: trade in beaver pelts and other furs. French fisherman also competed with Spanish and English for the teeming schools of cod they found in the Atlantic waters around Newfoundland.

## Spanish Conquest in the New World

In 1519 the Spanish sent an exploratory expedition from their post in Cuba to the mainland under the command of the conquistador Hernando Cortés (1485–1547). Accompanied by six hundred men, sixteen horses, and ten cannon, Cortés was to launch the conquest of the Mexica Empire. Its people were later called the Aztecs, but now most scholars prefer to use the term *Mexica* (meh-SHEE-kuh) to refer to them and their empire.

The Mexica Empire was ruled by Montezuma II (r. 1502–1520) from his capital at Tenochtitlán (tay-noch-teet-LAHN), now Mexico City. Larger than any European city of the time, it was the heart of a sophisticated civilization with advanced mathematics,

**Mexica Empire** Also known as the Aztec Empire, a large and complex Native American civilization in modern Mexico and Central America that possessed advanced mathematical, astronomical, and engineering technology.

**The Aztec Capital of Tenochtitlán** Occupying a large island, Tenochtitlán was laid out in concentric circles. The administrative and religious buildings were at the heart of the city, which was surrounded by residential quarters. Cortés himself marveled at the city in his letters: "The city is as large as Seville or Córdoba. . . . There are bridges, very large, strong, and well constructed, so that, over many, ten horsemen can ride abreast. . . . The city has many squares where markets are held. . . . There is one square . . . where there are daily more than sixty thousand souls, buying and selling. In the service and manners of its people, their fashion of living was almost the same as in Spain, with just as much harmony and order." (The Newberry Library)

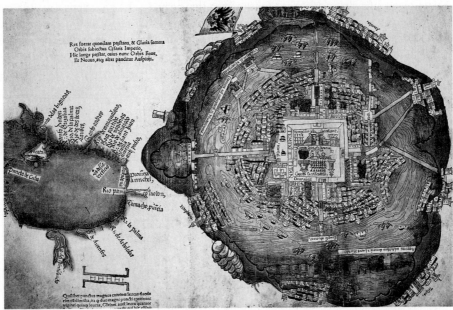

## ▪ PICTURING THE PAST

### Doña Marina Translating for Hernando Cortés During His Meeting with Montezuma

In April 1519 Doña Marina (or La Malinche as she is known in Mexico) was among twenty women given to the Spanish as slaves. Fluent in Nahuatl (NAH-wah-tuhl) and Yucatec (YOO-kuh-tehk) Mayan (spoken by a Spanish priest accompanying Cortés), she acted as an interpreter and diplomatic guide for the Spanish. She had a close relationship with Cortés and bore his son, Don Martín Cortés, in 1522. This image was created by Tlaxcalan artists shortly after the conquest of Mexico and represents one indigenous perspective on the events. (The Granger Collection, NY)

**ANALYZING THE IMAGE** What role does Doña Marina (far right) appear to be playing in this image? Does she appear to be subservient or equal to Cortés (right, seated)? How did the painter indicate her identity as non-Spanish?

**CONNECTIONS** How do you think the native rulers negotiating with Cortés might have viewed her? What about a Spanish viewer of this image? What does the absence of other women here suggest about the role of women in these societies?

To complete this activity online, go to the Online Study Guide at bedfordstmartins.com/mckaywestunderstanding.

astronomy, and engineering, with a complex social system, and with oral poetry and historical traditions.

Cortés landed on the coast of the Gulf of Mexico on April 21, 1519. The Spanish camp was soon visited by delegations of unarmed Mexica leaders bearing gifts and news of

Chapter 15
**European Exploration and Conquest • 1450–1650**

**432**

CHAPTER LOCATOR | What were the limits of world contacts before Columbus?

their great emperor. Cortés quickly realized that he could exploit internal dissension within the empire to his own advantage. The Mexica state religion necessitated constant warfare against neighboring peoples to secure captives for religious sacrifices and laborers for agricultural and building projects. Conquered peoples were required to pay tribute to the Mexica state through their local chiefs.

Cortés forged an alliance with the Tlaxcalas and other subject kingdoms, which chafed under the tribute demanded by the Mexicas. In October a combined Spanish-Tlaxcalan force occupied the city of Chollolan and massacred many thousand inhabitants. Strengthened by this display of power, Cortés made alliances with other native kingdoms. In November 1519, with a few hundred Spanish men and some six thousand indigenous warriors, Cortés marched on Tenochtitlán.

Montezuma refrained from attacking the Spaniards as they advanced toward his capital and welcomed Cortés and his men into Tenochtitlán. Other native leaders attacked the Spanish, but Montezuma relied on the advice of his state council, itself divided, and on the dubious loyalty of tributary communities. Montezuma's long hesitation proved disastrous. When Cortés—with incredible boldness—took Montezuma hostage, the emperor's influence over his people crumbled.

During the ensuing attacks and counter-attacks, Montezuma was killed. The Spaniards and their allies escaped from the city and began gathering forces and making new alliances against the Mexica. In May 1520 Cortés led a second assault on Tenochtitlán. Spanish victory in late summer 1521 was hard-won and greatly aided by the effects of smallpox, which had weakened and reduced the Mexica population. After the defeat of Tenochtitlán, Cortés and other conquistadors began the systematic conquest of Mexico. Over time, a series of indigenous kingdoms fell under Spanish domination, although not without decades of resistance.

More surprising than the defeat of the Mexicas was the fall of the remote Inca Empire. Perched more than 9,800 feet above sea level, the Incas were isolated from other indigenous cultures. Like the Mexicas, the Incas had created a civilization that rivaled the Europeans in population and complexity.

At the time of the Spanish invasion the Inca Empire had been weakened by disease and warfare. An epidemic of disease, possibly smallpox, had begun spreading among the people. Even worse, the empire had been embroiled in a civil war over succession. The Spanish conquistador Francisco Pizarro (ca. 1475–1541) landed on the northern coast of Peru on May 13, 1532, the very day Atahualpa (ah-tuh-WAHL-puh) won control of the empire after five years of fighting. As Pizarro advanced across the Andes toward Cuzco, Atahualpa was proceeding to the capital for his coronation.

**Inca Empire** The vast and sophisticated Peruvian empire centered at the capital city of Cuzco that was at its peak from 1438 until 1532.

Like Montezuma in Mexico, Atahualpa was aware of the Spaniards' movements. He sent envoys to greet the Spanish and invite them to meet him in the provincial town of Cajamarca. His plan was to lure the Spaniards into a trap, seize their horses and ablest men for his army, and execute the rest. Instead, the Spaniards ambushed and captured him, collected an enormous ransom in gold, and then executed him in 1533. The Spanish now marched on the capital of the empire itself, profiting once again from internal conflicts to form alliances with local peoples. When Cuzco fell in 1533, the Spanish plundered immense riches in gold and silver.

As with the Mexica, decades of violence and resistance followed the defeat of the Incan capital. Nevertheless, Spanish conquest opened a new chapter in European relations with the New World. It was not long before rival European nations attempted to forge their own overseas empires.

**Invasion of Tenochtitlán, 1519–1521**

Texcoco
Otumba   Zautla   Jalapa
Gulf of Mexico
Veracruz
Tlaxcala
Tenochtitlán   Cholula

→ Cortés's original route, 1519
→ Cortés's retreat, 1520
→ Cortés's return route, 1520–1521

## Early French and English Settlement in the New World

For over a hundred years, the Spanish and the Portuguese dominated settlement in the New World. The first English colony was founded at Roanoke (in what is now North Carolina) in 1585. After a three-year loss of contact with England, the settlers were found to have disappeared; their fate remains a mystery. The colony of Virginia, founded at Jamestown in 1607, had better luck and gained a steady hold producing tobacco for a growing European market. While these colonies originated as bases for harassing Spanish shipping, settlement on the coast of New England was undertaken for different reasons. There, radical Protestants sought to escape Anglican repression in England and begin new lives. The small and struggling outpost of Plymouth (1620) was followed by Massachusetts (1630), which grew into a prosperous settlement. Religious disputes in Massachusetts itself led to the dispersion of settlers into the new communities of Providence, Connecticut, Rhode Island, and New Haven. Catholics acquired their own settlement in Maryland (1632) and Quakers in Pennsylvania (1681).

Where the Spanish established whole-scale dominance over Mexico and Peru, English settlements hugged the Atlantic coastline. This did not prevent conflict with the indigenous inhabitants over land and resources. The haphazard nature of English colonization also led to conflicts of authority within the colonies. As the English crown grew more interested in colonial expansion, efforts were made to acquire the territory between New England in the north and Virginia in the south. This would allow the English to unify their holdings and overcome French and Dutch competition on the North American mainland.

French navigator and explorer Samuel de Champlain founded the first permanent French settlement, at Quebec, in 1608. Ville-Marie, latter-day Montreal, was founded in 1642. The French were energetic and industrious traders and explorers. Following the waterways of the St. Lawrence, the Great Lakes, and the Mississippi, they ventured into much of North America. In 1682 French explorer LaSalle descended the Mississippi to the Gulf of Mexico, opening the way for French occupation of Louisiana.

While establishing their foothold in the north, the French slowly acquired new territories in the West Indies. These included Cayenne (1604), St. Christophe (1625), Martinique, Guadeloupe, and Saint-Domingue (1697) on the western half of the island of Hispaniola. These islands became centers of tobacco and then sugar production. French ambitions on the mainland and in the Caribbean sparked a century-long competition with the English that culminated in the Seven Years' War from 1756 to 1763. France lost Canada and Louisiana, but retained profitable colonies in the West Indies. France regained part of Louisiana by treaty in 1800 and sold it to the United States in 1803.

European involvement in the Americas led to profound transformation of pre-existing indigenous societies and the rise of a transatlantic slave trade. It also led to an acceleration of global trade and cultural exchange. Over time, the combination of indigenous, European, and African cultures gave birth to new societies in the New World. In turn, the profits of trade and the impact of cultural exchange greatly influenced European society.

## ▼ What was the impact of conquest?

The growing European presence in the New World transformed its land and its peoples forever. Violence and disease wrought devastating losses, while surviving peoples encountered new political, social, and economic organizations imposed by Europeans. The Columbian exchange brought infectious diseases to the Americas, but it also gave new crops to the Old World that altered consumption patterns in Europe and across the globe (see page 437).

Chapter 15
**European Exploration and**
**434    Conquest • 1450–1650**

CHAPTER LOCATOR    What were the limits of world contacts before Columbus?

## Colonial Administration

In the sixteenth century the Spanish crown divided its New World territories into four **viceroyalties** or administrative divisions: New Spain, with the capital at Mexico City; Peru, with the capital at Lima; New Granada, with Bogotá as its administrative center; and La Plata, with Buenos Aires as the capital (see Map 15.2).

Within each territory, the viceroy, or imperial governor, exercised broad military and civil authority as the direct representative of Spain. The viceroy presided over the *audiencia* (ow-dee-EHN-see-ah), a board of twelve to fifteen judges that served as his advisory council and the highest judicial body. Later, King Charles III (r. 1759–1788) introduced the system of intendants to Spain's New World territories. These royal officials possessed broad military, administrative, and financial authority within their intendancies and were responsible not to the viceroy but to the monarchy in Madrid. The Portuguese governed their colony of Brazil in a similar manner. After the union of the crowns of Portugal and Spain in 1580, Spanish administrative forms were introduced.

## Impact of European Settlement on the Lives of Indigenous Peoples

Before Columbus's arrival, the Americas were inhabited by thousands of groups of indigenous peoples with different languages and cultures. Their patterns of life varied widely, from hunter-gatherer tribes organized into tribal confederations to large-scale agriculture-based empires connecting bustling cities and towns. The best estimate is that the peoples of the Americas numbered around 50 million in 1492.

Their lives were radically transformed by the arrival of Europeans. In the sixteenth century perhaps two hundred thousand Spaniards immigrated to the New World. Conquistadors carved out vast estates called haciendas in temperate grazing areas and imported Spanish livestock for the kinds of ranching with which they were familiar. In coastal tropical areas, the Spanish erected huge plantations to supply sugar to the European market. Around 1550 silver was discovered in present-day Bolivia and Mexico. To work the cattle ranches, sugar plantations, and silver mines, the conquistadors first turned to the indigenous peoples.

The Spanish quickly established the **encomienda system**, in which the Crown granted the conquerors the right to employ groups of Native Americans as laborers or to demand tribute from them in exchange for providing food and shelter. In practice, the encomienda system was a legalized form of slavery.

The new conditions and hardships imposed by conquest and colonization resulted in enormous native population losses. The major cause of death was disease. Having little or no resistance to diseases brought from the Old World, the inhabitants of the New World fell victim to smallpox, typhus, influenza, and other illnesses. Another factor was overwork. Unaccustomed to forced labor, native workers died in staggering numbers. Moreover, forced labor diverted local people from agricultural work, leading to malnutrition, reduced fertility rates, and starvation. Women forced to work were separated from their infants, leading to high infant mortality rates in a population with no livestock to supply alternatives to breast milk. Malnutrition and hunger in turn lowered resistance to disease. Finally, many indigenous peoples also died through outright violence in warfare.[4]

The Franciscan Bartolomé de Las Casas (1474–1566) documented the brutal treatment of indigenous peoples at the hands of the Spanish:

> To these quiet Lambs . . . came the Spaniards like most c(r)uel Tygres, Wolves and Lions, enrag'd with a sharp and tedious hunger; for these forty years past, minding nothing else

**viceroyalties** The name for the four administrative units of Spanish possessions in the Americas: New Spain, Peru, New Granada, and La Plata.

**encomienda system** A system whereby the Spanish crown granted the conquerors the right to forcibly employ groups of Indians; it was a disguised form of slavery.

How and why did Europeans undertake voyages of expansion?    What was the impact of conquest?    How did Europe and the world change after Columbus?    How did expansion change European attitudes and beliefs?

435

Español con India,
Mestizo.

Mestizo con Española
Castizo.

Mulato con Española,
Morisco.

Morisco con Española
Chino.

Lobo con China
Gibaro.

Gibaro con Mulata
Albarazado.

Sanbaigo con Loba
Calpamulato.

Calpamulato con Canbuja
Tenteen el Aire.

*but the slaughter of these unfortunate wretches, whom with divers kinds of torments neither seen nor heard of before, they have so cruelly and inhumanely butchered, that of three millions of people which Hispaniola itself did contain, there are left remaining alive scarce three hundred persons.*[5]

Las Casas and other missionaries asserted that the Indians had human rights, and through their persistent pressure the Spanish emperor Charles V abolished the worst abuses of the encomienda system in 1531.

The pattern of devastating disease and population loss established in the Spanish colonies was repeated everywhere Europeans settled. The best estimate is that the native population declined from roughly 50 million in 1492 to around 9 million by 1700. It is important to note, however, that native populations and cultures did survive the conquest period, sometimes by blending with European incomers and sometimes by maintaining cultural autonomy.

For colonial administrators the main problem posed by the astronomically high death rate was the loss of a subjugated labor force to work the mines and sugar plantations. The search for fresh sources of labor gave birth to the new tragedy of the Atlantic slave trade (see page 440).

## Life in the Colonies

Many factors helped to shape life in European colonies, including geographic location, religion, indigenous cultures and practices, patterns of European settlement, and the cultural attitudes and official policies of the European nations that claimed them as empire. Throughout the New World, Europeanized settlements were hedged by immense borderlands of European and non-European contact.

Women played a crucial role in the creation of new identities and the continuation of old ones. The first explorers formed unions with native women, through coercion or choice, and relied on them as translators and guides and to form alliances with indigenous powers. As settlement developed, the character of each colony was influenced by the presence or absence of European women. Where women and children accompanied men, as in the British colonies and the Spanish mainland

**Mixed Races** The unprecedented mixing of peoples in the Spanish New World colonies inspired great fascination. An elaborate terminology emerged to describe the many possible combinations of indigenous, African, and European blood, which were known collectively as *castas*. This painting belongs to a popular genre of the eighteenth century depicting couples composed of individuals of different ethnic origin and the children produced of their unions. (Schalkwijk/Art Resource, NY)

CHAPTER LOCATOR    What were the limits of world contacts before Columbus?

colonies, new settlements took on European languages, religion, and ways of life that have endured, with input from local cultures, to this day. Where European women did not, as on the west coast of Africa and most European outposts in Asia, local populations largely retained their own cultures, to which male Europeans acclimatized themselves.

Most women who crossed the Atlantic were Africans, constituting four-fifths of the female newcomers before 1800.[6] Wherever slavery existed, masters profited from their power to engage in sexual relations with enslaved women. One important difference among European colonies was in the status of children born from such unions. In some colonies, mostly those dominated by the Portuguese, Spanish, or French, substantial populations of free blacks descended from the freed children of such unions. In English colonies, masters were less likely to free children they fathered with female slaves.

The mixing of indigenous people with Europeans and Africans created whole new populations and ethnicities as well as complex self-identities. In Spanish America the word mestizo—*métis* in French—described people of mixed Native American and European descent. The blanket terms "mulatto" and "people of color" were used for those of mixed African and European origin. With its immense slave-based plantation agriculture system, large indigenous population, and relatively low Portuguese immigration, Brazil developed a particularly complex racial and ethnic mosaic.

## The Columbian Exchange

The migration of peoples to the New World led to an exchange of animals, plants, and disease, a complex process known as the Columbian exchange. Columbus brought sugar plants on his second voyage; Spaniards also introduced rice and bananas from the Canary Islands, and the Portuguese carried these items to Brazil. Everywhere they settled, the Spanish and Portuguese brought and raised wheat with labor provided by the encomienda system. Grapes and olives brought over from Spain did well in parts of Peru and Chile.

Apart from wild turkeys and game, Native Americans had no animals for food. Moreover, they did not domesticate animals for travel or to use as beasts of burden, except for alpacas and llamas in the Inca Empire. On his second voyage in 1493 Columbus introduced horses, cattle, sheep, dogs, pigs, chickens, and goats. The multiplication of these animals proved spectacular. In turn, Europeans returned home with many food crops that become central elements of their diet.

Disease was perhaps the most important form of exchange. The wave of catastrophic epidemic disease that swept the Western Hemisphere after 1492 can be seen as an extension of the swath of devastation wreaked by the Black Death in the 1300s, first on Asia and then on Europe. The world after Columbus was thus unified by disease as well as by trade and colonization.

**Columbian exchange** The exchange of animals, plants, and diseases between the Old and the New Worlds.

## ▼ How did Europe and the world change after Columbus?

The centuries-old Afro-Eurasian trade world was forever changed by the European voyages of discovery and their aftermath. For the first time, a truly global economy emerged in the sixteenth and seventeenth centuries, and it forged new links among far-flung peoples, cultures, and societies. The ancient civilizations of Europe, Africa, the Americas, and Asia confronted each other in new and rapidly evolving ways. Those confrontations often led to conquest and exploitation, but they also contributed to cultural exchange and renewal.

# INDIVIDUALS IN SOCIETY

## Juan de Pareja

**DURING THE LONG WARS OF THE RECONQUISTA,** Muslims and Christians captured each other in battle and used the defeated as slaves. As the Muslims were gradually eliminated from Iberia in the fifteenth and sixteenth centuries, the Spanish and Portuguese turned to the west coast of Africa for a new supply of slaves. Most slaves worked as domestic servants, rather than in the fields. Some received specialized training as artisans.

Not all people of African descent were slaves, and some experienced both freedom and slavery in a single lifetime. The life and career of Juan de Pareja (pah-REH-huh) illustrates the complexities of the Iberian slave system and the heights of achievement possible for those who achieved freedom.

Pareja was born in Antequera, an agricultural region and the old center of Muslim culture near Seville in southern Spain. Of his parents

**Velázquez, *Juan de Pareja* (1650).** (The Metropolitan Museum of Art, Fletcher Fund, Rogers Fund, and Bequest of Miss Adelaide Milton de Groot [1876–1967], by exchange, supplemented by gifts from friends of the Museum, 1971. [1971.86]. Image © 1986 The Metropolitan Museum of Art)

we know nothing. Because a rare surviving document calls him a "mulatto," one of his parents must have been white and the other must have had some African blood. In 1630 Pareja applied to the mayor of Seville for permission to travel to Madrid to visit his brother and "to perfect his art." The document lists his occupation as "a painter in Seville." Since it mentions no other name, it is reasonable to assume that Pareja arrived in Madrid a free man. Sometime between 1630 and 1648, however, he came into the possession of the artist Diego Velázquez (1599–1660); Pareja became a slave.

How did Velázquez acquire Pareja? By purchase? As a gift? Had Pareja fallen into debt or committed some crime and thereby lost his freedom? We do not know. Velázquez, the greatest Spanish painter of the seventeenth century, had a large studio with many assistants. Pareja was set to grinding powders to make colors and to preparing canvases. He must have demonstrated ability because when Velázquez went to Rome in 1648, he chose Pareja to accompany him.

In 1650, as practice for a portrait of Pope Innocent X, Velázquez painted Pareja. The portrait shows Pareja dressed in fine clothing and gazing self-confidently at the viewer. Displayed in Rome in a public exhibition of Velázquez's work, the painting won acclaim from his contemporaries. That same year, Velázquez signed the document that gave Pareja his freedom, to become effective in 1654. Pareja lived out the rest of his life as an independent painter.

What does the public career of Pareja tell us about the man and his world? Pareja's career suggests that a person of African descent might fall into slavery and yet still acquire professional training and work alongside his master in a position of confidence. Moreover, if lucky enough to be freed, a former slave could exercise a profession and live his own life in Madrid. Pareja's experience was far from typical for a slave in the 1600s, but it reminds us of the myriad forms that slavery took in this period.

**Sources:** Jonathan Brown, *Velázquez: Painter and Courtier* (New Haven, Conn.: Yale University Press, 1986); *Grove Dictionary of Art* (New York: Macmillan, 2000); Sister Wendy Beckett, *Sister Wendy's American Collection* (New York: HarperCollins Publishers, 2000), p. 15.

### QUESTIONS FOR ANALYSIS

1. Since slavery was an established institution in Spain, speculate on Velázquez's possible reasons for giving Pareja his freedom.
2. To what extent was Pareja a marginal person in Spanish society? Was he an insider or an outsider to Spanish society?

What were the limits of world contacts before Columbus?

# Sugar and Slavery

Throughout the Middle Ages slavery was deeply entrenched in the Mediterranean, but it was not based on race; many slaves were white. How, then, did black African slavery enter the European picture and take root in South and then North America? In 1453 the Ottoman capture of Constantinople halted the flow of white slaves from the eastern Mediterranean. The successes of the Iberian reconquista also meant that the supply of Muslim captives had drastically diminished. Cut off from its traditional sources of slaves, Mediterranean Europe then turned to sub-Saharan Africa, which had a long history of slave trading. (See "Individuals in Society: Juan de Pareja," left.) As Portuguese explorers began their voyages along the western coast of Africa, one of the first commodities they sought was slaves.

In the 1440s and 1450s, the first slaves were simply seized by small raiding parties. Portuguese merchants soon found that it was easier to trade with local leaders, who were accustomed to dealing in slaves captured through warfare with neighboring powers. From 1490 to 1530 Portuguese traders brought between three hundred and two thousand black slaves to Lisbon each year (Map 15.3).

**Map 15.3** **Seaborne Trading Empires in the Sixteenth and Seventeenth Centuries** By the mid-seventeenth century, trade linked all parts of the world except for Australia. Notice that trade in slaves was not confined to the Atlantic but involved almost all parts of the world.

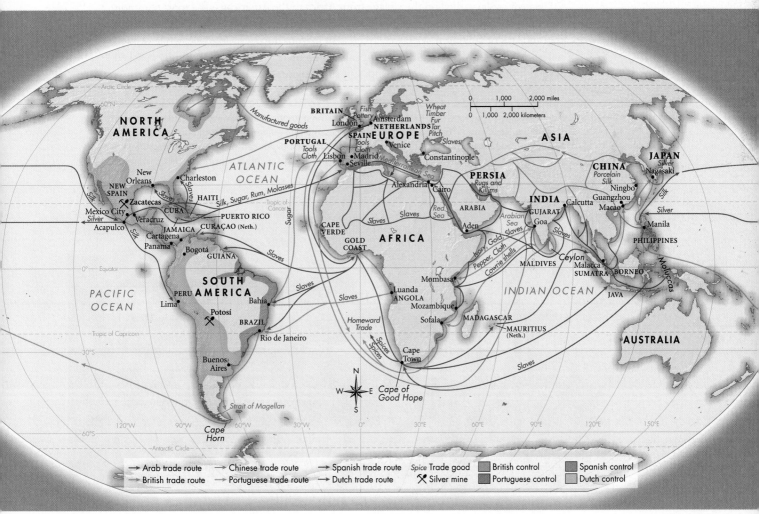

In this stage of European expansion, the history of slavery became intertwined with the history of sugar. Originally sugar was an expensive luxury that only the very affluent could afford, but population increases and monetary expansion in the fifteenth century led to increasing demand. The establishment of sugar plantations on the Canary and Madeira Islands in the fifteenth century testifies to this demand.

Sugar was a particularly difficult and demanding crop to produce for profit. Seed-stems were planted by hand, thousands to the acre. When mature, the cane had to be harvested and processed rapidly to avoid spoiling, forcing days and nights of work with little rest. Moreover, its growing season was virtually constant, meaning that there was no fallow period when workers could recuperate. The demands of sugar production were only increased with the invention of roller mills to crush the cane more efficiently. Yields could be augmented, but only if a sufficient labor force was found to supply the mills. Europeans solved the labor problem by forcing first native islanders and then enslaved Africans to provide the backbreaking work.

Sugar gave New World slavery its distinctive shape. The trans-Atlantic slave trade began in 1518 when the Spanish king Charles I authorized traders to bring African slaves to New World colonies. The Portuguese brought the first slaves to Brazil around 1550; by 1600 four thousand were being imported annually. After its founding in 1621, the Dutch West India Company transported thousands of Africans to Brazil and the Caribbean, mostly to work on sugar plantations. In the late seventeenth century, with the chartering of the Royal African Company, the English got involved.

Before 1700, when slavers decided it was better business to improve conditions, some 20 percent of slaves died on the voyage from Africa to the Americas.[7] The most common cause of death was from dysentery induced by poor quality food and water, intense crowding, and lack of sanitation. Men were often kept in irons during the passage, while women and girls were considered fair game for sailors. To increase profits, slave traders packed several hundred captives on each ship. On sugar plantations, death rates among slaves

**A New World Sugar Refinery, Brazil** Sugar was the most important and most profitable plantation crop in the New World. This image shows the processing and refinement of sugar on a Brazilian plantation. Sugar cane was grown, harvested, and processed by African slaves who labored under brutal and ruthless conditions to generate enormous profits for plantation owners. (The Bridgeman Art Library/Getty Images)

from illness and exhaustion were extremely high, leading to a constant stream of new shipments of slaves from Africa.

In total, scholars estimate that European traders embarked over 10 million African slaves across the Atlantic from 1518 to 1800 (of whom roughly 8.5 million disembarked), with the peak of the trade occurring in the eighteenth century.[8] By comparison, only 2 to 2.5 million Europeans migrated to the New World during the same period. Enslaved Africans worked in an infinite variety of occupations: as miners, soldiers, sailors, servants, and artisans and in the production of cotton, rum, indigo, tobacco, wheat, corn, and, most predominantly, sugar.

## Spanish Silver and Its Economic Effects

The sixteenth century has often been called Spain's golden century, but silver mined in the Americas was the true source of Spain's incredible wealth. In 1545 the Spanish dis-covered an extraordinary source of silver at Potosí (poh-toh-SEE) (in present-day Bolivia) in territory conquered from the Inca Empire. By 1550 Potosí yielded perhaps 60 percent of all the silver mined in the world. From Potosí and the mines at Zacatecas (za-kuh-TAY-kuhs) and Guanajuato (gwah-nah-HWAH-toh) in Mexico, huge quantities of precious metals poured forth. Between 1503 and 1650, 35 million pounds of silver and over 600,000 pounds of gold entered Seville's port. Spanish predominance, however, proved temporary.

In the sixteenth century Spain experienced a steady population increase, creating a sharp rise in the demand for food and goods. Spanish colonies in the Americas also demanded consumer goods that were not pro-duced in the colonies, such as cloth and luxury goods. Since Spain had expelled some of its best farmers and businessmen — the Muslims and Jews — in the fifteenth century, the Spanish economy was suffering and could not meet the new demands. The excess of demand over supply led to widespread inflation. The result was a rise in production costs and a further decline in Spain's pro-ductive capacity.

Silver did not cause the initial inflation. It did, how-ever, exacerbate the situation, and, along with the ensu-ing rise in population, the influx of silver significantly contributed to the upward spiral of prices. Inflation se-verely strained government budgets. Several times be-tween 1557 and 1647, Spain's King Philip II and his successors wrote off the state debt, thereby undermining confidence in the government and leaving the economy in shambles. After 1600, when the population declined, prices gradually stabilized.

As Philip II paid his armies and foreign debts with silver bullion, Spanish inflation was transmitted to the rest of Europe. Between 1560 and 1600 much of Eu-rope experienced large price increases. Because money bought less, people who lived on fixed incomes, such as nobles, were badly hurt. Those who owed fixed sums of money, such as the middle class, prospered because in

**Philip II, ca. 1533** This portrait of Philip II as a young man and crown prince of Spain is by the celebrated artist Titian, who was court painter to Philip's father, Charles V. After taking the throne, Philip became another great patron of the artist. (Prado, Madrid/Index/The Bridgeman Art Library.)

a time of rising prices, debts lessened in value each year. Food costs rose most sharply, and the poor fared worst of all.

In many ways, though, it was not Spain but China that controlled the world trade in silver. The Chinese demanded silver for their products and for the payment of imperial taxes. China was thus the main buyer of world silver, absorbing half the world's production. The silver market drove world trade, with New Spain and Japan being mainstays on the supply side and China dominating the demand side. The world trade in silver is one of the best examples of the new global economy that emerged in this period.

## The Birth of the Global Economy

With the Europeans' discovery of the Americas and their exploration of the Pacific, the entire world was linked for the first time in history by seaborne trade. The opening of that trade brought into being three successive commercial empires: the Portuguese, the Spanish, and the Dutch.

The Portuguese were the first worldwide traders. In the sixteenth century they controlled the sea route to India (see Map 15.3). From their fortified bases at Goa on the Arabian Sea and at Malacca on the Malay Peninsula, ships carried goods to the Portuguese settlement at Macao in the South China Sea. From Macao Portuguese ships loaded with Chinese silks and porcelains sailed to the Japanese port of Nagasaki and to the Philippine port of Manila, where Chinese goods were exchanged for Spanish silver from New Spain. Throughout Asia the Portuguese traded in slaves. The Portuguese exported horses from Mesopotamia and copper from Arabia to India; from India they exported hawks and peacocks for the Chinese and Japanese markets. Back to Portugal they brought Asian spices that had been purchased with textiles produced in India and with gold and ivory from East Africa. They also shipped back sugar from their colony in Brazil, produced by African slaves whom they had transported across the Atlantic.

Coming to empire a few decades later than the Portuguese, the Spanish were determined to claim their place in world trade. The Spanish Empire in the New World was basically a land empire, but across the Pacific the Spaniards built a seaborne empire centered at Manila in the Philippines. The city of Manila served as the transpacific bridge between Spanish America and China. In Manila, Spanish traders used silver from American mines to purchase Chinese silk for European markets. After 1640, however, the Spanish silk trade declined in the face of stiff competition from Dutch imports.

In the seventeenth century the Dutch challenged the Spanish and Portuguese empires. Drawing on their commercial wealth and long experience in European trade, the Dutch emerged by the end of the century as the most powerful worldwide seaborne trading power. The Dutch Empire was built on spices. The Dutch East India Company was founded in 1602 with the stated intention of capturing the spice trade from the Portuguese.

The Dutch set their sights on gaining direct access to and control of the Indonesian sources of spices. The Dutch fleet, sailing from the Cape of Good Hope in Africa and avoiding the Portuguese forts in India, steered directly for Indonesia (see Map 15.3). In return for assisting Indonesian princes in local squabbles and disputes with the Portuguese, the Dutch won broad commercial concessions. Through agreements, seizures, and outright war, they gained control of the western access to the Indonesian archipelago in the first half of the seventeenth century. Gradually, they acquired political domination over the archipelago itself. By the 1660s the Dutch had managed to expel the Portuguese from Ceylon and other East Indian islands, thereby establishing control of the lucrative spice trade.

Not content with challenging the Portuguese in the Indian Ocean, the Dutch also aspired to a role in the Americas. Founded in 1621 in a period of war with Spain, the Dutch West India Company aggressively sought to open trade with North and South

Chapter 15
European Exploration and
Conquest • 1450–1650

442

CHAPTER LOCATOR | What were the limits of world contacts before Columbus?

**Goods from the Global Economy** After the discovery of the Americas, a wave of new items entered European markets. Spices from Southeast Asia were a driving force behind the new global economy and among the most treasured European luxury goods. They were used not only for cooking but also as medicines and health tonics. This fresco shows a fifteenth-century Italian pharmacist measuring out spices for a customer. (Alfredo Dagli Orti/The Art Archive)

America and capture Spanish territories there. The company captured or destroyed hundreds of Spanish ships, seized the Spanish silver fleet in 1628, and captured portions of Brazil and the Caribbean. The Dutch also successfully interceded in the transatlantic slave trade, bringing much of the west coast of Africa under Dutch control.

Dutch efforts to colonize North America were less successful. The colony of New Netherland, governed from New Amsterdam (modern-day New York City), was hampered by lack of settlement and weak governance and was easily captured by the British in 1664.

## ▼ How did expansion change European attitudes and beliefs?

The age of overseas expansion heightened Europeans' contacts with the rest of the world. These contacts gave birth to new ideas about the inherent superiority or inferiority of different races, in part to justify European participation in the slave trade.

Cultural encounter also inspired more positive views. The essays of Michel de Montaigne epitomized a new spirit of skepticism and cultural relativism, while the plays of William Shakespeare reflected his efforts to come to terms with the cultural complexity of his day.

## New Ideas About Race

At the beginning of the transatlantic slave trade, most Europeans would have thought of Africans, if they thought of them at all, as savages—because of their eating habits, morals, clothing, and social customs—and as barbarians because of their language and methods of war. They grouped Africans into the despised categories of pagan heathens or Muslim infidels. Africans were certainly not the only peoples subject to such dehumanizing attitudes. Jews were also viewed as an alien group that was, like Africans, naturally given to sin and depravity. More generally, elite people across Europe were accustomed to viewing the peasant masses as a lower form of humanity.

As Europeans turned to Africa for new sources of slaves, they drew on and developed ideas about Africans' primitiveness and barbarity to defend slavery and even argue that enslavement benefited Africans by bringing the light of Christianity to heathen peoples. Over time, the institution of slavery fostered a new level of racial inequality. Africans gradually became seen as utterly distinct from and wholly inferior to Europeans. From rather vague assumptions about non-Christian religious beliefs and a general lack of civilization, Europeans developed increasingly rigid ideas of racial superiority and inferiority to safeguard the growing profits gained from plantation slavery. Black skin became equated with slavery itself as Europeans at home and in the colonies convinced themselves that blacks were destined by God to serve them as slaves in perpetuity.

Support for this belief went back to the Greek philosopher Aristotle's argument that some people are naturally destined for slavery and to biblical associations between darkness and sin. After 1700 the emergence of new methods of observing and describing nature led to the use of science to define race. From referring to a nation or an ethnic group, henceforth "race" would mean biologically distinct groups of people, whose physical differences produced differences in culture, character, and intelligence.

## Michel de Montaigne and Cultural Curiosity

Racism was not the only possible reaction to the new worlds emerging in the sixteenth century. Decades of religious fanaticism, bringing civil anarchy and war, led both Catholics and Protestants to doubt that any one faith contained absolute truth. Added to these doubts was the discovery of peoples in the New World who had radically different ways of life. These shocks helped produce ideas of skepticism and cultural relativism in the sixteenth and seventeenth centuries. Skepticism is a school of thought founded on doubt that total certainty or definitive knowledge is ever attainable. Cultural relativism suggests that one culture is not necessarily superior to another, just different. Both notions found expression in the work of Frenchman Michel de Montaigne (duh mahn-TAYN) (1533–1592).

Montaigne developed a new literary genre, the essay—from the French *essayer*, meaning "to test or try"—to express his thoughts and ideas. Published in 1580, Montaigne's *Essays* consisted of short personal reflections. Intended to be accessible to ordinary people, Montaigne wrote in French rather than Latin and in an engaging conversational style.

Montaigne's essay "On Cannibals" reveals the impact of overseas discoveries on his consciousness. In contrast to the prevailing views of the time, he rejected the notion that one culture is superior to another. Speaking of native Brazilians, he wrote:

Chapter 15
**European Exploration and**
**444** **Conquest • 1450–1650**

CHAPTER LOCATOR | What were the limits of world contacts before Columbus?

> *I find that there is nothing barbarous and savage in this nation [Brazil], . . . except, that everyone gives the title of barbarism to everything that is not according to his usage; as, indeed, we have no other criterion of truth and reason, than the example and pattern of the opinions and customs of the place wherein we live. . . . They are savages in the same way that we say fruits are wild, which nature produces of herself and by her ordinary course; whereas, in truth, we ought rather to call those wild whose natures we have changed by our artifice and diverted from the common order.*[9]

In his own time and throughout the seventeenth century, few would have agreed with Montaigne's challenge to ideas of European superiority. The publication of his ideas, however, contributed to a basic shift in attitudes. Montaigne inaugurated an era of doubt.

## William Shakespeare and His Influence

In addition to the essay as a literary genre, the period fostered remarkable creativity in other branches of literature. England — especially in the latter part of Queen Elizabeth I's reign and in the first years of her successor, James I (r. 1603–1625) — witnessed remarkable literary expression.

The undisputed master of the period was the dramatist William Shakespeare, whose genius lay in the originality of his characterizations, the diversity of his plots, his understanding of human psychology, and his unexcelled gift for language. Born in 1564, Shakespeare was a Renaissance man with a deep appreciation of classical culture, individualism, and humanism.

**Titus Andronicus** With classical allusions, fifteen murders and executions, a Gothic queen who takes a black lover, and incredible violence, this early Shakespearean tragedy (1594) was a melodramatic thriller that enjoyed enormous popularity with the London audience. The shock value of a dark-skinned character on the English stage is clearly shown in this illustration. (Reproduced by permission of the Marquess of Bath, Longleat House, Warminster, Wilts)

Like Montaigne, Shakespeare's work reveals the impact of the new discoveries and contacts of his day. The title character of *Othello* is described as a "Moor of Venice." In Shakespeare's day, the term *moor* referred to Muslims of Moroccan or North African origin, including those who had migrated to the Iberian Peninsula. It could also be applied, though, to natives of the Iberian Peninsula who converted to Islam or to non-Muslim Berbers in North Africa. To complicate things even more, references in the play to Othello as "black" in skin color have led many to believe that Shakespeare intended him to be a sub-Saharan African, and he is usually depicted as such in modern performances. This confusion in the play reflects the uncertainty in Shakespeare's own day about racial and religious classifications.

The character of Othello is both vilified in racist terms by his enemies and depicted as a brave warrior, a key member of the city's military leadership, and a man capable of winning the heart of an aristocratic white woman. In contrast to the prevailing view of Moors as inferior, Shakespeare presents Othello as a complex human figure. Shakespeare's play thus demonstrates both the intolerance of contemporary society and the possibility for some individuals to look beyond racial stereotypes.

Shakespeare's last play, *The Tempest*, displays a similar interest in race and race relations. The plot involves the stranding on an island of sorcerer Prospero and his daughter Miranda. There Prospero finds and raises Caliban, a native of the island, whom he instructs in his own language and religion. After Caliban's attempted rape of Miranda, Prospero enslaves him, earning the rage and resentment of his erstwhile pupil. Modern scholars often note the echoes between this play and the realities of imperial conquest and settlement in Shakespeare's day. It is no accident, they argue, that the poet portrayed Caliban as a monstrous dark-skinned island native who was best-suited for slavery. Shakespeare himself borrows words from Montaigne's essay "On Cannibals," suggesting that he may have intended to criticize, rather than endorse, racial intolerance. Shakespeare's work shows us one of the finest minds of the age grasping to come to terms with the racial and religious complexities around him.

# ←LOOKING BACK LOOKING AHEAD→

JUST THREE YEARS SEPARATED the posting of Martin Luther's "Ninety-five Theses" in 1517 from Ferdinand Magellan's discovery of the Pacific Ocean in 1520. Within a few short years, the religious unity of Western Europe and its notions of terrestrial geography were shattered. Old medieval certainties about Heaven and earth collapsed. In the ensuing decades, Europeans struggled to come to terms with religious difference at home and the multitudes of new peoples and places they encountered abroad. These processes were intertwined, as Puritans and Quakers fled religious persecution at home to colonize the New World and the new Jesuit order proved its devotion to the pope by seeking Catholic converts across the globe. While some Europeans were fascinated and inspired by this new diversity, too often the result was violence. Europeans endured decades of civil war between Protestants and Catholics, and indigenous peoples suffered massive population losses as a result of European warfare, disease, and exploitation. Tragically, both Catholic and Protestant religious leaders condoned the African slave trade that was to bring suffering and death to millions of Africans.

Even as the voyages of discovery contributed to the fragmentation of European culture, they also belonged to longer-term processes of state centralization and consolidation. The new monarchies of the Renaissance produced stronger and wealthier governments capable of financing the huge expenses of exploration and colonization. Competition to gain overseas colonies became an integral part of European politics. Spain's investment in conquest proved spectacularly profitable and yet, as we will see in Chapter 16, the ultimate result was a weakening of its power. Other European nations took longer to realize financial gain, yet over time the Netherlands, England, and France reaped tremendous profits from colonial trade, which helped them build modernized, centralized states. The path from medieval Christendom to modern nation-states led through religious warfare and global encounter. ■

- **For a list of suggested readings for this chapter, visit** *bedfordstmartins.com/mckaywestunderstanding*.

- **For primary sources from this period, see** *Sources of Western Society*, Second Edition.

- **For Web sites, images, and documents related to topics in this chapter, see Make History at** *bedfordstmartins.com/mckaywestunderstanding*.

## Step 1

**GETTING STARTED** Below are basic terms about this period in the history of Western civilization. Can you identify each term below and explain why it matters? To do this exercise online, go to bedfordstmartins.com/mckaywestunderstanding.

| TERMS | WHO (OR WHAT) AND WHEN | WHY IT MATTERS |
|---|---|---|
| conquistador, p. 422 | | |
| caravel, p. 423 | | |
| Ptolemy's *Geography*, p. 423 | | |
| Treaty of Tordesillas, p. 430 | | |
| Mexica Empire, p. 431 | | |
| Inca Empire, p. 433 | | |
| viceroyalties, p. 435 | | |
| encomienda system, p. 435 | | |
| Columbian exchange, p. 437 | | |

## Step 2

**MOVING BEYOND THE BASICS** The exercise below requires a more advanced understanding of the chapter material. Examine the nature and impact of European exploration and conquest by filling in the chart below. What were the motives behind expansion? Why did monarchs support overseas expeditions? Why did men like Columbus undertake such dangerous journeys? Identify key conquests and discoveries for each nation. Then, describe the impact of exploration and colonization in the Americas in both the New World, Europe, and Africa. When you are finished, consider the following question: What intended and unintended consequences resulted from European expansion? To do this exercise online, go to bedfordstmartins.com/mckaywestunderstanding.

| EXPLORATION 1492–1600 | MOTIVES FOR EXPLORATION AND SETTLEMENT | CONQUESTS AND DISCOVERIES | IMPACT IN NEW WORLD | IMPACT IN EUROPE | IMPACT IN AFRICA |
|---|---|---|---|---|---|
| Portugal | | | | | |
| Spain | | | | | |
| France | | | | | |
| England | | | | | |

# PUTTING IT ALL TOGETHER
Now that you've reviewed key elements of the chapter, take a step back and try to see the big picture. Remember to use specific examples from the chapter in your answers. To do this exercise online, go to bedfordstmartins.com/mckaywestunderstanding.

## WORLD CONTACTS BEFORE COLUMBUS

- How did trade connect the civilizations of Africa, Asia, and Europe prior to 1492? Which states were at the center of global trade? Which were at the periphery? Why?

- Why were Europeans at a trading disadvantage prior to 1492? How did geography limit European participation in world trade? What role did Europe's economy and material culture play in this context?

## THE EUROPEAN VOYAGES OF DISCOVERY

- Why were Europeans so eager to gain better access to Asia and Asian trade? How did fifteenth-century economic and political developments help stimulate European expansion?

- Compare and contrast Spanish, French, and English exploration and colonization of the New World. What common motives underlay the efforts of all three nations? How would you explain the important differences you note?

## THE IMPACT OF CONQUEST

- What kinds of societies and governments did Europeans seek to establish in the Americas? What light does the nature of colonial society shed on the motives behind European expansion and European views of the indigenous peoples of the Americas?

- What was the Columbian exchange? How did it transform both Europe and the Americas?

- How did European expansion give rise to new ideas about race?

## EUROPE AND THE WORLD AFTER COLUMBUS

- What role did increasing demand for sugar play in shaping the economy and society of the New World? Why were sugar and slavery so tightly linked?

- If Europe was at the periphery of the global trading system prior to 1492, where was it situated by the middle of the sixteenth century? What had changed? What had not?

- How did expansion complicate Europeans' understanding of themselves and their place in the world?

## ■ In Your Own Words
Imagine that you must explain Chapter 15 to someone who hasn't read it. What would be the most important points to include and why?

# 16

# Absolutism and Constitutionalism in Europe

## ca. 1589–1725

The seventeenth century was a period of transformation in Europe. Agricultural and manufacturing slumps meant that many people struggled to feed themselves and their families, and population rates stagnated or even fell. Religious and dynastic conflicts led to almost constant war and dramatic growth in the size of armies. To pay for these armies, governments created bureaucracies to collect greatly increased taxes. Despite these obstacles, European states succeeded in gathering more power. By 1680 much of the unrest that originated with the Reformation was resolved.

The crises of the seventeenth century were not limited to western Europe. Central and eastern Europe experienced even more catastrophic dislocation, with German lands serving as the battleground of the Thirty Years' War and borders constantly vulnerable to attack from the east. In Prussia and in Habsburg Austria absolutist states emerged in the aftermath of this conflict. Russia and the Ottoman Turks also developed absolutist governments. These empires seemed foreign and exotic to western Europeans, who saw them as the antithesis of their political, religious, and cultural values. Beneath the surface, however, these eastern governments shared many similarities with western ones.

While absolutism emerged as the solution to crisis in many European states, a small minority adopted a different path, placing sovereignty in the hands of privileged groups rather than the Crown. Historians refer to states where power was limited by law as "constitutional." The two most important seventeenth-century constitutionalist states were England and the Dutch Republic. Constitutionalism should not be confused with democracy. The elite rulers of England and the Dutch Republic pursued familiar policies of increased taxation, government authority, and social control. Nonetheless, they served as influential models to onlookers across Europe as a form of government that checked the power of a single ruler. ■

**Life in Absolutist France.** King Louis XIV receives foreign ambassadors to celebrate a peace treaty. The king grandly occupied the center of his court, which in turn served as the pinnacle for the French people and, at the height of his glory, for all of Europe. (Erich Lessing/Art Resource, NY)

# Chapter Preview

▶ What made the seventeenth century an "age of crisis"?

▶ Why did France rise and Spain fall in this period?

▶ What explains the rise of absolutism in Austria and Prussia?

▶ What was distinctive about Russia and the Ottoman Empire?

▶ Where and why did constitutionalism triumph?

▶ What developments do baroque art and music reflect?

# ▼ What made the seventeenth century an "age of crisis"?

Historians often refer to the seventeenth century as an "age of crisis." After the economic and demographic growth of the sixteenth century, Europe faltered into stagnation and retrenchment. This was partially due to climate changes, but it also resulted from religious divides, increased governmental pressures, and war. Overburdened peasants and city-dwellers took action to defend themselves, sometimes profiting from conflicts to obtain relief. In the long run, however, governments proved increasingly able to impose their will on the populace.

*wars*
*famines*
*uprisings*

## Peasant Life in the Midst of Economic Crisis

In the seventeenth century most Europeans lived in the countryside. The hub of the rural world was the small peasant village centered on a church and a manor. In western Europe, a small number of peasants in each village owned enough land to feed themselves and had the livestock and plows necessary to work their land. These independent farmers were leaders of the peasant village. They employed the landless poor, rented out livestock and tools, and served as agents for the noble lord. Below them were small landowners and tenant farmers who did not have enough land to be self-sufficient. These

**An English Food Riot** Nothing infuriated ordinary women and men more than the idea that merchants and landowners were withholding grain from the market in order to push high prices even higher. In this cartoon an angry crowd hands out rough justice to a rich farmer accused of hoarding. (Courtesy of the Trustees of the British Museum)

Chapter 16
**Absolutism and Constitutionalism
in Europe • ca. 1589–1725**

452

CHAPTER LOCATOR | What made the seventeenth century an "age of crisis"?

families sold their best produce on the market to earn cash for taxes, rent, and food. At the bottom were the rural workers who worked as dependent laborers and servants. In eastern Europe, the vast majority of peasants toiled as serfs for noble landowners and did not own land in their own right (see the next section).

Rich or poor, east or west, bread was the primary element of the diet. Peasants paid stiff fees to the local miller for grinding grain into flour and sometimes to the lord for the right to bake bread in his oven. Bread was most often accompanied by a soup made of roots, herbs, beans, and perhaps a small piece of salt pork. An important annual festival in many villages was the killing of the family pig. The whole family gathered to help, sharing a rare abundance of meat with neighbors and carefully salting the extra and putting down the lard.

European rural society lived on the edge of subsistence. Because of the crude technology and low crop yield, peasants were constantly threatened by scarcity and famine. In the seventeenth century a period of colder and wetter climate throughout Europe, dubbed the "little ice age" by historians, meant a shorter farming season with lower yields. The result was recurrent famines that significantly reduced the population of early modern Europe. Most people did not die of outright starvation, but rather of diseases brought on by malnutrition and exhaustion.

Given the harsh conditions of life, industry also suffered. The output of woolen textiles, one of the most important European manufactures, declined sharply in the first half of the seventeenth century. Food prices were high, wages stagnated, and unemployment soared. This economic crisis was not universal: it struck various regions at different times and to different degrees. In the middle decades of the century, Spain, France, Germany, and England all experienced great economic difficulties; but these years were the golden age of the Netherlands.

The urban poor and peasants were the hardest hit. When the price of bread rose beyond their capacity to pay, they frequently expressed their anger by rioting. In towns they invaded bakers' shops to seize bread and resell it at a "just price." In rural areas they attacked convoys taking grain to the cities. Women often led these actions, since their role as mothers gave them some impunity in authorities' eyes. Historians have labeled this vision of a world in which community needs predominate over competition and profit a moral economy.

## The Return of Serfdom in the East

While economic and social hardship was common across Europe, important differences existed between east and west. In the west the demographic losses of the Black Death allowed peasants to escape from serfdom as they acquired enough land to feed themselves as well as the livestock and ploughs necessary to work their land. In eastern Europe seventeenth-century peasants had largely lost their ability to own land independently. Eastern lords dealt with the labor shortages caused by the Black Death by restricting the

## Chapter Chronology

| | |
|---|---|
| ca. 1500–1650 | Consolidation of serfdom in eastern Europe |
| 1533–1584 | Reign of Ivan the Terrible in Russia |
| 1589–1610 | Reign of Henry IV in France |
| 1598–1613 | Time of Troubles in Russia |
| 1620–1740 | Growth of absolutism in Austria and Prussia |
| 1642–1649 | English civil war, which ends with execution of Charles I |
| 1643–1715 | Reign of Louis XIV in France |
| 1653–1658 | Military rule in England under Oliver Cromwell (the Protectorate) |
| 1660 | Restoration of English monarchy under Charles II |
| 1665–1683 | Jean-Baptiste Colbert applies mercantilism to France |
| 1670 | Charles II agrees to re-Catholicize England in secret agreement with Louis XIV |
| 1670–1671 | Cossack revolt led by Stenka Razin |
| ca. 1680–1750 | Construction of baroque palaces |
| 1682 | Louis XIV moves court to Versailles |
| 1682–1725 | Reign of Peter the Great in Russia |
| 1683–1718 | Habsburgs push the Ottoman Turks from Hungary |
| 1685 | Edict of Nantes revoked |
| 1688–1689 | Glorious Revolution in England |
| 1701–1713 | War of the Spanish Succession |

Why did France rise and Spain fall in this period?

What explains the rise of absolutism in Austria and Prussia?

What was distinctive about Russia and the Ottoman Empire?

Where and why did constitutionalism triumph?

What developments do baroque art and music reflect?

453

**Estonian Serfs in the 1660s** The Estonians were conquered by German military nobility in the Middle Ages and reduced to serfdom. The German-speaking nobles ruled the Estonian peasants with an iron hand, and Peter the Great reaffirmed their domination when Russia annexed Estonia. (Mansell Collection/Time Life Pictures/Getty Images)

right of their peasants to move to take advantage of better opportunities elsewhere. Moreover, lords steadily took more and more of their peasants' land and arbitrarily imposed heavier and heavier labor obligations. By the early 1500s lords in many eastern territories could command their peasants to work for them without pay for as many as six days a week.

The power of the lord reached far into serfs' everyday lives. Not only was their freedom of movement restricted, but they required permission to marry or could be forced to marry. Lords could reallocate the lands worked by their serfs at will or sell serfs apart from their families.

Between 1500 and 1650 the consolidation of serfdom in eastern Europe was accompanied by the growth of commercial agriculture, particularly in Poland and eastern Germany. As economic expansion and population growth resumed after 1500, eastern lords increased the production of their estates by squeezing sizable surpluses out of the impoverished peasants. They then sold these surpluses to foreign merchants, who exported them to the growing cities of wealthier western Europe.

It was not only the peasants who suffered in eastern Europe. With the approval of kings, landlords systematically undermined the medieval privileges of the towns and the power of the urban classes. The population of the towns and the urban middle classes declined greatly. This development both reflected and promoted the supremacy of noble landlords in most of eastern Europe in the sixteenth century.

## The Thirty Years' War

In the first half of the seventeenth century, the fragile balance of life was violently upturned by the ravages of the Thirty Years' War (1618–1648). The Holy Roman Empire was a confederation of hundreds of principalities, independent cities, duchies, and other polities loosely united under an elected emperor. The uneasy truce between Catholics and Protestants created by the Peace of Augsburg in 1555 deteriorated as the faiths of various areas shifted. Lutheran princes felt compelled to form the Protestant Union (1608), and Catholics retaliated with the Catholic League (1609). Each alliance was determined that the other should make no religious or territorial advance. Dynastic interests were also involved; the Spanish Habsburgs strongly supported the goals of their Austrian relatives: the unity of the empire and the preservation of Catholicism within it.

The war is traditionally divided into four phases. The first, or Bohemian, phase (1618–1625) was characterized by civil war in Bohemia between the Catholic League and the Protestant Union. In 1620 Catholic forces defeated Protestants at the Battle of the White Mountain. The second, or Danish, phase of the war (1625–1629) — so called because of the leadership of the Protestant king Christian IV of Denmark (r. 1588–1648) — witnessed additional Catholic victories.

Chapter 16
**Absolutism and Constitutionalism in Europe • ca. 1589–1725**

454

CHAPTER LOCATOR | What made the seventeenth century an "age of crisis"?

The third, or Swedish, phase of the war (1630–1635) began with the arrival in Germany of the Swedish king Gustavus Adolphus (r. 1594–1632) and his army. Gustavus Adolphus intervened to support the empire's Protestants. The French chief minister, Cardinal Richelieu (ree-shuh-LYOO), subsidized the Swedes, hoping to weaken Habsburg power in Europe. Gustavus Adolphus won two important battles but was fatally wounded in combat. The final, or French, phase of the war (1635–1648) was prompted by Richelieu's concern that the Habsburgs would rebound after the death of Gustavus Adolphus. Richelieu declared war on Spain and sent military as well as financial assistance. Finally, in October 1648 peace was achieved.

The 1648 **Peace of Westphalia** that ended the Thirty Years' War marked a turning point in European history. Conflicts fought over religious faith ended. The treaties recognized the independent authority of more than three hundred German princes (Map 16.1), reconfirming the emperor's severely limited authority. The Augsburg agreement of 1555 became permanent, adding Calvinism to Catholicism and Lutheranism as legally permissible creeds.

**Peace of Westphalia** The name of a series of treaties that concluded the Thirty Years' War in 1648 and marked the end of large-scale religious violence in Europe.

**Map 16.1 Europe After the Thirty Years' War** This map shows the political division of Europe after the Treaty of Westphalia (1648) ended the war. Which country emerged from the Thirty Years' War as the strongest European power? What dynastic house was that country's major rival in the early modern period?

Why did France rise and Spain fall in this period?

What explains the rise of absolutism in Austria and Prussia?

What was distinctive about Russia and the Ottoman Empire?

Where and why did constitutionalism triumph?

What developments do baroque art and music reflect?

The Thirty Years' War was probably the most destructive event for the central European economy and society prior to the world wars of the twentieth century. Perhaps one-third of urban residents and two-fifths of the rural population died, leaving entire areas depopulated. Trade in southern German cities was virtually destroyed. Agricultural areas suffered catastrophically. Many small farmers lost their land, allowing nobles to enlarge their estates and consolidate their control.[1]

## Achievements in State-Building

In this context of economic and demographic depression, monarchs began to make new demands on their people. Traditionally, historians have distinguished between the "absolutist" governments of France, Spain, Central Europe, and Russia and the constitutionalist governments of England and the Dutch Republic. Whereas absolutist monarchs gathered all power under their personal control, English and Dutch rulers were obliged to respect laws passed by representative institutions. More recently, historians have emphasized commonalities among these powers. Despite their political differences, all these states shared common projects of protecting and expanding their frontiers, raising new taxes, consolidating central control, and competing for the new colonies opening up in the New and Old Worlds.

Rulers who wished to increase their authority encountered formidable obstacles. Without paved roads, telephones, or other modern technology, it took weeks to convey orders from the central government to the provinces. Rulers also suffered from lack of information about their realms, making it impossible to police and tax the population effectively. Local power structures presented another serious obstacle. Nobles, the church, provincial and national assemblies, town councils, guilds, and other bodies held legal privileges, which could not easily be rescinded. In some kingdoms many people spoke a language different from the Crown's, further diminishing their willingness to obey its commands. Nonetheless, over the course of the seventeenth century both absolutist and constitutional governments achieved new levels of central control. This increased authority focused in four areas in particular: greater taxation, growth in armed forces, larger and more efficient bureaucracies, and the increased ability to compel obedience from their subjects.

**The Professionalization of the Swedish Army** Swedish king Gustavus Adolphus, surrounded by his generals, gives thanks to God for the safe arrival of his troops in Germany during the Thirty Years' War. A renowned military leader, the king imposed constant training drills and rigorous discipline on his troops, which contributed to their remarkable success in the war. (Courtesy of The Army Museum, Stockholm)

## Warfare and the Growth of Army Size

The driving force of seventeenth-century state-building was warfare, characterized by dramatic changes in the size and style of armies. Medieval armies had been raised by feudal lords for particular wars or campaigns, after which the troops were disbanded. In the seventeenth century monarchs took command of recruiting and maintaining armies—in peacetime as well as wartime. New techniques for training and deploying soldiers

Chapter 16
**Absolutism and Constitutionalism in Europe • ca. 1589–1725**

456

CHAPTER LOCATOR | What made the seventeenth century an "age of crisis"?

meant a rise in the professional standards of the army. Along with professionalization came an explosive growth in army size. The French took the lead, with the army growing from roughly 125,000 men in the Thirty Years' War to 340,000 at the end of the seventeenth century.[2] In response, France's neighbors greatly increased the size of their own armies and formed defensive coalitions for protection from French aggression.

Other European powers were quick to follow the French example. The rise of absolutism in central and eastern Europe led to a vast expansion in the size of armies. Great Britain followed a similar, albeit distinctive pattern. Instead of building a land army, the British focused on naval forces and eventually built the largest navy in the world.

## Popular Political Action

In the seventeenth century increased pressures of taxation and warfare led to an increase in popular uprisings. Popular revolts were extremely common in England, France, Spain, Portugal, and Italy in the mid-seventeenth century. In 1640 Philip IV of Spain faced revolt in Catalonia, the economic center of his realm. At the same time he struggled to put down uprisings in Portugal and in the northern provinces of the Netherlands. In 1647 the city of Palermo, in Spanish-occupied Sicily, exploded in protest over food shortages caused by a series of bad harvests. Fearing public unrest, the city government subsidized the price of bread, attracting even more starving peasants from the countryside. When Madrid ordered an end to subsidies, municipal leaders decided to lighten the loaf rather than raise prices. Not fooled by this change, local women led a bread riot, shouting "Long live the king and down with the taxes and the bad government!" As riot transformed to armed revolt, the insurgency spread to the rest of the island and eventually to Naples on the mainland. Apart from affordable food, rebels demanded the suppression of extraordinary taxes and participation in municipal government. Some dreamed of a republic in which noble tax exemptions would be abolished. Despite initial successes, the revolt lacked unity and strong leadership and could not withstand the forces of the state.

In France urban uprisings became a frequent aspect of the social and political landscape. Beginning in 1630 and continuing on and off through the early 1700s, major insurrections occurred at Dijon, Bordeaux (bor-DOH), Montpellier, Lyons, and Amiens. All were characterized by deep popular anger and violence directed at outside officials sent to collect taxes. These officials were sometimes seized, beaten, and hacked to death.

Municipal and royal authorities often struggled to overcome popular revolt. They feared that stern repressive measures, such as sending in troops to fire on crowds, would create martyrs and further inflame the situation, while forcible full-scale military occupation of a city would be very expensive. The limitations of royal authority gave some leverage to rebels, allowing them to gain concessions.

By the beginning of the eighteenth century, this leverage had largely disappeared. Municipal governments were better integrated into the national structure, and local authorities had prompt military support from the central government. People who publicly opposed royal policies and taxes received swift and severe punishment.

## ▼ Why did France rise and Spain fall in this period?

Kings in absolutist states asserted that, as they were chosen by God, they were responsible to God alone. They claimed exclusive power to make and enforce laws, denying any other institution or group the authority to check their power. Louis XIV of France

Why did France rise and Spain fall in this period?　　What explains the rise of absolutism in Austria and Prussia?　　What was distinctive about Russia and the Ottoman Empire?　　Where and why did constitutionalism triumph?　　What developments do baroque art and music reflect?

457

is often seen as the epitome of an "absolute" monarch. In truth, his success relied on collaboration with nobles, and thus his example illustrates both the achievements and the compromises of absolutist rule.

As French power rose in the seventeenth century, the glory of Spain faded. Once the fabulous revenue from American silver declined, Spain's economic stagnation could no longer be disguised, and the country faltered under weak leadership.

## The Foundations of Absolutism

Louis XIV's absolutism had long roots. In 1589 his grandfather Henry IV (r. 1589–1610), the founder of the Bourbon dynasty, acquired a devastated country. Civil wars between Protestants and Catholics had wracked France since 1561. Poor harvests had reduced peasants to starvation, and commercial activity had declined drastically.

Henry IV inaugurated a remarkable recovery by keeping France at peace during most of his reign. Although he had converted to Catholicism, he issued the Edict of Nantes, allowing Protestants the right to worship in 150 traditionally Protestant towns throughout France. He sharply lowered taxes and improved the infrastructure of the country, building new roads and canals and repairing the ravages of years of civil war. Despite his efforts at peace, Henry was murdered in 1610 by a Catholic zealot.

After the death of Henry IV his wife, the queen-regent Marie de' Medici, headed the government for the nine-year-old Louis XIII (r. 1610–1643). In 1628 Armand Jean du Plessis—Cardinal Richelieu (1585–1642)—became first minister of the French crown. Richelieu's maneuvers allowed the monarchy to maintain power within Europe and within its own borders despite the turmoil of the Thirty Years' War.

Cardinal Richelieu's domestic policies were designed to strengthen royal control. He extended the use of intendants, commissioners for each of France's thirty-two districts who were appointed directly by the monarch, to whom they were solely responsible. They recruited men for the army, supervised the collection of taxes, presided over the administration of local law, checked up on the local nobility, and regulated economic activities in their districts. As the intendants' power increased under Richelieu, so did the power of the centralized French state.

Under Richelieu, the French monarchy also acted to repress Protestantism. Louis personally supervised the siege of La Rochelle, an important port city and a major commercial center with strong ties to Protestant Holland and England. The fall of La Rochelle in October 1628 was one step in the removal of Protestantism as a strong force in French life.

Richelieu did not aim to wipe out Protestantism in the rest of Europe, however. His main foreign policy goal was to destroy the Catholic Habsburgs' grip on territories that surrounded France. Consequently, Richelieu supported Habsburg enemies, including Protestants. For the French cardinal, interests of state outweighed religious considerations.

Richelieu's successor as chief minister for the next child-king, the four-year-old Louis XIV, was Cardinal Jules Mazarin (1602–1661). Along with the regent, Queen Mother Anne of Austria, Mazarin continued Richelieu's centralizing policies. His struggle to increase royal revenues to meet the costs of war led to the uprisings of 1648–1653 known as the Fronde. In Paris, magistrates of the Parlement of Paris, the nation's most important court, were outraged by the crown's autocratic measures. These so-called robe nobles (named for the robes they wore in court) encouraged violent protest by the common people. As rebellion spread outside Paris and to the sword nobles (the traditional warrior nobility), civil order broke down completely. In 1651, when Anne's regency ended, much of the rebellion died away, and its leaders came to terms with the government.

the Fronde A series of violent uprisings during the early reign of Louis XIV triggered by growing royal control and oppressive taxation.

The violence of the Fronde had significant results for the future. The twin evils of noble rebellion and popular riots left the French wishing for peace and for a strong monarch to reimpose order. This was the legacy that Louis XIV inherited when he assumed personal control of the government in 1661 after the death of Mazarin.

Chapter 16
**Absolutism and Constitutionalism**
**in Europe • ca. 1589–1725**

458

CHAPTER LOCATOR | What made the seventeenth century an "age of crisis"?

**Hyacinthe Rigaud, *Louis XIV, King of France and Navarre*, 1701**
This was one of Louis XIV's favorite portraits of himself. He liked it so much that he had many copies of the portrait made, in full and half-size format. (Scala/Art Resource, NY)

**ANALYZING THE IMAGE**  Why do you think the king liked the portrait so much? What image of the king does it present to the viewer? What details does the painter include, and what impression do they convey?

**CONNECTIONS**  How does this representation of royal power compare with the images of Peter the Great (page 471) and Charles I (page 477)? Which do you find the most impressive, and why?

To complete this activity online, go to the Online Study Guide at bedfordstmartins.com/mckaywestunderstanding.

## Louis XIV and Absolutism

In the reign of Louis XIV (r. 1643–1715) the French monarchy reached the peak of absolutist development. Louis was a believer in the doctrine of the divine right of kings: God had established kings as his rulers on earth, and they were answerable ultimately to him alone. Kings were divinely anointed and shared in the sacred nature of divinity, but they could not simply do as they pleased. They had to obey God's laws and rule for the good of the people. To symbolize his central role in the divine order, when he was fifteen years old, Louis danced at a court ballet dressed as the sun, thereby acquiring the title of the "Sun King."

Louis worked very hard at the business of governing. He ruled his realm through several councils of state and insisted on taking a personal role in many of the councils' decisions. Despite increasing financial problems, Louis never called a meeting of the Estates General. The nobility, therefore, had no means of united expression or action. Nor did Louis have a first minister. In this way he kept himself free from worry about the inordinate power of a Richelieu.

Why did France rise and Spain fall in this period? | What explains the rise of absolutism in Austria and Prussia? | What was distinctive about Russia and the Ottoman Empire? | Where and why did constitutionalism triumph? | What developments do baroque art and music reflect?

Although personally tolerant, Louis hated division within the realm and insisted that religious unity was essential to his royal dignity and to the security of the state. He thus pursued the policy of Protestant repression launched by Richelieu. In 1685 Louis revoked the Edict of Nantes and took steps to suppress the Huguenots.

Despite his claims to absolute authority, there were multiple constraints on Louis's power. As a representative of divine power, he was obliged to rule in a way that seemed consistent with virtue and benevolent authority. He had to uphold the laws issued by his royal predecessors. Moreover, he also relied on the collaboration of nobles, who maintained social prestige and authority. Without their cooperation, it would have been impossible to extend his power throughout France or wage his many foreign wars. Louis's need to elicit noble cooperation led him to revolutionize court life at his palace at Versailles.

## Life at Versailles

Through most of the seventeenth century, the French court had no fixed home, following the monarch to his numerous palaces and country residences. In 1682 Louis moved his court and government to the newly renovated palace at Versailles. The palace quickly

**Pierre-Denis Martin, *View of the Chateau de Versailles, 1722*** Versailles began as a modest hunting lodge built by Louis XIII in 1623. His son, Louis XIV, spent decades enlarging and decorating the original chateau. In 1682 the new palace became the official residence of the Sun King and his court. (Châteaux de Versailles et de Trianon, Versailles/Réunion des Musées Nationaux/Art Resource, NY)

Chapter 16
**Absolutism and Constitutionalism**
460    in Europe • ca. 1589–1725

CHAPTER LOCATOR    What made the seventeenth century an "age of crisis"?

became the center of political, social, and cultural life. The king required all great nobles to spend at least part of the year in attendance on him there. Since he controlled the distribution of state power and wealth, nobles had no choice but to obey and compete with each other for his favor at Versailles.

Louis further revolutionized court life by establishing an elaborate set of etiquette rituals to mark every moment of his day, from waking up and dressing in the morning to removing his clothing and retiring at night. He required nobles to serve him in these rituals, and they vied for the honor of doing so. Endless squabbles broke out over what type of chair one could sit on at court and the order in which great nobles entered and were seated in the chapel for Mass.

These rituals may seem absurd, but they were far from meaningless or trivial. The king controlled immense resources and privileges; access to him meant favored treatment for government offices, military and religious posts, state pensions, honorary titles, and a host of other benefits. Courtiers sought these rewards for themselves and their family members and followers. A system of patronage—in which a higher-ranked individual protected a lower-ranked one in return for loyalty and services—flowed from the court to the provinces. Through this mechanism Louis gained cooperation from powerful nobles.

Although they were denied public offices and posts, women played a central role in the patronage system. At court the king's wife, mistresses, and other female relatives recommended individuals for honors, advocated policy decisions, and brokered alliances between noble factions. Noblewomen played a similar role among courtiers, bringing their family connections to marriage to form powerful social networks.

Louis XIV was an enthusiastic patron of the arts. He commissioned many sculptures and paintings for Versailles as well as performances of dance and music. Louis XIV also loved the stage, and in the plays of Molière and Racine his court witnessed the finest achievements in the history of the French theater.

With Versailles as the center of European politics, French culture grew in international prestige. French became the language of polite society and international diplomacy, gradually replacing Latin as the language of scholarship and learning. The royal courts of Sweden, Russia, Poland, and Germany all spoke French. France inspired a cosmopolitan European culture in the late seventeenth century that looked to Versailles as its center.

## French Financial Management Under Colbert

France's ability to build armies and fight wars depended on a strong economy. Fortunately for Louis, his controller general, Jean-Baptiste Colbert (1619–1683), proved to be a financial genius. Colbert's central principle was that the wealth and the economy of France should serve the state. To this end, from 1665 to his death in 1683, Colbert rigorously applied mercantilist policies to France.

Mercantilism is a collection of governmental policies for the regulation of economic activities by and for the state. It derives from the idea that a nation's international power is based on its wealth, specifically its supply of gold and silver. To accumulate wealth, a country always had to sell more goods abroad than it bought. To decrease the purchase of goods outside France, Colbert insisted that French industry should produce everything needed by the French people.

**mercantilism** A system of economic regulations aimed at increasing the power of the state based on the belief that a nation's international power was based on its wealth, specifically its supply of gold and silver.

To increase exports, Colbert supported old industries and created new ones. Colbert enacted new production regulations, created guilds to boost quality standards, and encouraged foreign craftsmen to immigrate to France. To encourage the purchase of French goods, he abolished many domestic tariffs and raised tariffs on foreign products. In 1664 Colbert founded the Company of the East Indies with (unfulfilled) hopes of competing with the Dutch for Asian trade.

Colbert also hoped to make Canada part of a vast French empire. He sent four thousand colonists to Quebec. Subsequently, the Jesuit Jacques Marquette and the merchant Louis Joliet sailed down the Mississippi River. Marquette and Joliet claimed possession of the land on both sides of the river as far south as present-day Arkansas. In 1684 French explorers continued down the Mississippi to its mouth and claimed vast territories for Louis XIV, naming the region "Louisiana."

During Colbert's tenure as controller general, Louis was able to pursue his goals without massive tax increases and without creating a stream of new offices. The constant pressure of warfare after Colbert's death, however, undid many of his economic achievements.

## Louis XIV's Wars

Louis XIV kept France at war for thirty-three of the fifty-four years of his personal rule. François le Tellier, Marquis de Louvois — Louis's secretary of state for war — equaled Colbert's achievements in the economic realm. Louvois created a professional army in the employ of the French state. Uniforms and weapons were standardized, and a rational system of training and promotion was devised. As in so many other matters, Louis's model was followed across Europe.

Louis's goal was to expand France to what he considered its natural borders. His armies managed to extend French borders to include important commercial centers in the Spanish Netherlands and Flanders as well as the entire province of Franche-Comté between 1667 and 1678. In 1681 Louis seized the city of Strasbourg, and three years later he sent his armies into the province of Lorraine. At that moment the king seemed invincible. In fact, Louis had reached the limit of his expansion. The wars of the 1680s and 1690s brought no additional territories but placed unbearable strains on French resources. Colbert's successors resorted to desperate measures to finance these wars, including devaluation of the currency and new taxes.

Louis's last war was endured by a French people suffering high taxes, crop failure, and widespread malnutrition and death. In 1700 the childless Spanish king Charles II (r. 1665–1700) died. His will bequeathed the Spanish crown and its empire to Philip of Anjou, Louis XIV's grandson. The will violated a prior treaty by which the European powers had agreed to divide the Spanish possessions between the king of France and the Holy Roman emperor, both brothers-in-law of Charles II. Claiming that he was following both Spanish and French interests, Louis broke with the treaty and accepted the will, thereby triggering the War of the Spanish Succession (1701–1713).

In 1701 the English, Dutch, Austrians, and Prussians formed the Grand Alliance against Louis XIV. War dragged on until 1713. The Peace of Utrecht, which ended the war, allowed Louis's grandson Philip to remain king of Spain on the understanding that the French and Spanish crowns would never be united. France surrendered Newfoundland, Nova Scotia, and the Hudson Bay territory to England, which also acquired Gibraltar, Minorca, and control of the African slave trade from Spain (Map 16.2).

The Peace of Utrecht marked the end of French expansion. Thirty-five years of war had given France the rights to all of Alsace and some commercial centers in the north. But at what price? In 1714 an exhausted France hovered on the brink of bankruptcy. It is no wonder that when Louis XIV died on September 1, 1715, many subjects felt as much relief as they did sorrow.

**Peace of Utrecht** A series of treaties, from 1713 to 1715, that ended the War of the Spanish Succession, ended French expansion in Europe, and marked the rise of the British Empire.

The Acquisitions of Louis XIV, 1668–1713

Paris

FRANCE

FRANCHE-COMTÉ

Territory gained
1668
1678
1713

**462**

Chapter 16
**Absolutism and Constitutionalism**
in Europe • ca. 1589–1725

CHAPTER LOCATOR | What made the seventeenth century an "age of crisis"?

Map 16.2 Europe After the Peace of Utrecht, 1714
(inset) North America, 1714

Legend:
- French Bourbon lands
- Spanish Bourbon lands
- Austrian Habsburg lands
- Prussian lands
- Great Britain
- Russian Empire
- —— Boundary of the Holy Roman Empire

Claims:
- British
- French
- Spanish

### ▪ MAPPING THE PAST

## Map 16.2 Europe After the Peace of Utrecht, 1715

The series of treaties commonly called the Peace of Utrecht ended the War of the Spanish Succession and redrew the map of Europe. A French Bourbon king succeeded to the Spanish throne. France surrendered the Spanish Netherlands (later Belgium) to Austria and recognized the Hohenzollern (hoh-uhn-ZAH-luhrn) rulers of Prussia. Spain ceded Gibraltar to Great Britain, for which it has been a strategic naval station ever since. Spain also granted Britain the *asiento*, the contract for supplying African slaves to America.

**ANALYZING THE MAP** Identify the areas on the map that changed hands as a result of the Peace of Utrecht. How did these changes affect the balance of power in Europe?

**CONNECTIONS** How and why did so many European countries possess scattered or discontiguous territories? What does this suggest about European politics in this period? Does this map suggest potential for future conflict?

To complete this activity online, go to the Online Study Guide at **bedfordstmartins.com/mckaywestunderstanding**.

## The Decline of Absolutist Spain in the Seventeenth Century

At the beginning of the seventeenth century, France's position appeared extremely weak. Struggling to recover from decades of religious civil war, France could not compete with Spain's European and overseas empire or its mighty military. Yet by the end of the century their positions were reversed.

| Why did France rise and Spain fall in this period? | What explains the rise of absolutism in Austria and Prussia? | What was distinctive about Russia and the Ottoman Empire? | Where and why did constitutionalism triumph? | What developments do baroque art and music reflect? |

**Spanish Troops** The long wars that Spain fought over Dutch independence, in support of Habsburg interests in Germany, and against France left the country militarily exhausted and financially drained by the mid-1600s. In this detail from a painting by Peeter Snayers, Spanish troops—thin, emaciated, and probably unpaid—straggle away from battle. (Prado, Madrid/Index/The Bridgeman Art Library)

By the early seventeenth century the seeds of Spanish disaster were sprouting. Between 1610 and 1650 Spanish trade with the colonies in the New World fell 60 percent due to competition from local industries in the colonies and from Dutch and English traders. At the same time, the mines that filled the empire's treasury started to run dry, and the quantity of metal produced steadily declined after 1620.

In Madrid, however, royal expenditures constantly exceeded income. To meet mountainous state debt, the Crown repeatedly devalued the coinage and declared bankruptcy, which resulted in the collapse of national credit. Meanwhile, manufacturing and commerce shrank. In contrast to the other countries of western Europe, Spain had a tiny middle class. The elite condemned moneymaking as vulgar and undignified. To make matters worse, the Crown expelled some three hundred thousand *Moriscos*, or former Muslims, in 1609, significantly reducing the pool of skilled workers and merchants. Those working in the textile industry were forced out of business by steep inflation that pushed their production costs to the point where they could not compete in colonial and international markets.[3]

Spanish aristocrats, attempting to maintain an extravagant lifestyle they could no longer afford, increased the rents on their estates. High rents and heavy taxes in turn drove the peasants from the land, leading to a decline in agricultural productivity. In cities wages and production stagnated.

The Spanish crown had no solutions to these dire problems. Philip III handed the running of the government over to the duke of Lerma, who used it to advance his personal and familial wealth. Philip IV left the management of his several kingdoms to Gaspar de Guzmán, Count-Duke of Olivares. Olivares did not lack energy and ideas, and he succeeded in devising new sources of revenue. But he clung to the belief that the solution to Spain's difficulties rested in a return to the imperial tradition of the sixteenth century. Unfortunately, the imperial tradition demanded the revival of war with the Dutch at the expiration of a twelve-year truce in 1622 and a long war with France over Mantua (1628–1659). These conflicts, on top of an empty treasury, brought disaster.

Chapter 16
**Absolutism and Constitutionalism
in Europe • ca. 1589–1725**

464

CHAPTER LOCATOR

What made the
seventeenth century an
"age of crisis"?

Spain's situation worsened with internal conflicts and fresh military defeats through the remainder of the seventeenth century. In 1640 Spain faced serious revolts in Catalonia and Portugal. In 1643 the French inflicted a crushing defeat on a Spanish army at Rocroi in what is now Belgium. By the Treaty of the Pyrenees of 1659, which ended the French-Spanish conflict, Spain was compelled to surrender extensive territories to France. In 1688 the Spanish crown reluctantly recognized the independence of Portugal. The era of Spanish dominance in Europe had ended.

# ▼ What explains the rise of absolutism in Austria and Prussia?

The rulers of eastern Europe also labored to build strong absolutist states in the seventeenth century. But they built on social and economic foundations far different from those in western Europe, namely serfdom and the strong nobility who benefited from it. The endless wars of the seventeenth century allowed monarchs to increase their power by building large armies, increasing taxation, and suppressing representative institutions. In exchange for their growing political authority, monarchs allowed nobles to remain as unchallenged masters of their peasants, a deal that appeased both king and nobility, but left serfs at the mercy of the lords.

## The Austrian Habsburgs

Like all of central Europe, the Habsburgs emerged from the Thirty Years' War impoverished and exhausted. Their efforts to destroy Protestantism in the German lands and to turn the weak Holy Roman Empire into a real state had failed. Defeat in central Europe encouraged the Habsburgs to turn away from a quest for imperial dominance and to focus inward and eastward in an attempt to unify their diverse holdings.

Habsburg victory over Bohemia during the Thirty Years' War was an important step in this direction. Ferdinand II (r. 1619–1637) drastically reduced the power of the Bohemian Estates, the largely Protestant representative assembly. He also confiscated the landholdings of Protestant nobles and gave them to loyal Catholic nobles and to the foreign aristocratic mercenaries who led his armies. After 1650 a large portion of the Bohemian nobility was of recent origin and owed its success to the Habsburgs.

With the support of this new nobility, the Habsburgs established direct rule over Bohemia. Under their rule the condition of the enserfed peasantry worsened substantially and Protestantism was stamped out. These changes were important steps in creating absolutist rule in Bohemia.

Ferdinand III (r. 1637–1657) continued to build state power. He centralized the government in the empire's German-speaking provinces, which formed the core Habsburg holdings. For the first time, a permanent standing army was ready to put down any internal opposition.

The Habsburg monarchy then turned east toward Hungary, which had been divided between the Ottomans and the Habsburgs in the early sixteenth century. Between 1683 and 1699 the Habsburgs pushed the Ottomans from most of Hungary and Transylvania. The recovery of all the former kingdom of Hungary was completed in 1718.

The Hungarian nobility, despite its reduced strength, effectively thwarted the full development of Habsburg absolutism. Throughout the seventeenth century Hungarian nobles rose in revolt against the Habsburgs. They never triumphed decisively, but neither were they crushed. In 1703, with the Habsburgs bogged down in the War of the

Why did France rise and Spain fall in this period?

**What explains the rise of absolutism in Austria and Prussia?**

What was distinctive about Russia and the Ottoman Empire?

Where and why did constitutionalism triumph?

What developments do baroque art and music reflect?

465

Spanish Succession, the Hungarians rose in one last patriotic rebellion under Prince Francis Rákóczy.

Rákóczy and his forces were eventually defeated, but the Habsburgs agreed to restore many of the traditional privileges of the aristocracy in return for Hungarian acceptance of hereditary Habsburg rule. Thus Hungary was never fully integrated into a centralized, absolute Habsburg state.

Despite checks on their ambitions in Hungary, the Habsburgs made significant achievements in state-building elsewhere by forging consensus with the church and the nobility. A sense of common identity and loyalty to the monarchy grew among elites in Habsburg lands. German became the language of the state, and Catholicism helped fuse a collective identity. Vienna became the political and cultural center of the empire.

## Prussia in the Seventeenth Century

In the fifteenth and sixteenth centuries, the Hohenzollern family had ruled parts of eastern Germany as the imperial electors of Brandenburg and the dukes of Prussia. When he came to power in 1640, the twenty-year-old Frederick William, later known as the "Great Elector," was determined to unify his three provinces and enlarge them by diplomacy and war. These provinces were Brandenburg; Prussia, inherited in 1618; and scattered holdings along the Rhine inherited in 1614 (Map 16.3). Each had its own estates, and

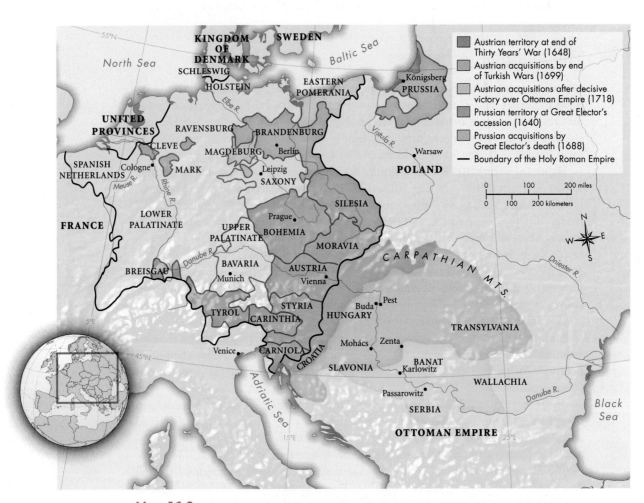

**Map 16.3 The Growth of Austria and Brandenburg-Prussia to 1748** Austria expanded to the southwest into Hungary and Transylvania at the expense of the Ottoman Empire. It was unable to hold the rich German province of Silesia, however, which was conquered by Brandenburg-Prussia.

Chapter 16
**Absolutism and Constitutionalism**
**in Europe • ca. 1589–1725**

466

CHAPTER LOCATOR   What made the seventeenth century an "age of crisis"?

taxes could not be levied without their consent. The estates of Brandenburg and Prussia were dominated by the nobility and the landowning classes, known as the Junkers.

In 1660 Frederick William persuaded Junkers in the estates to accept taxation without consent in order to fund a permanent army. They agreed to do so in exchange for reconfirmation of their own privileges, including authority over the serfs. Having won over the Junkers, the king crushed potential opposition to his power from the towns. One by one, Prussian cities were eliminated from the estates and subjected to new taxes on goods and services.

Thereafter, the estates' power declined rapidly, for the Great Elector had both financial independence and superior force. State revenue tripled during his reign, and the army expanded drastically. In 1701 the elector's son, Frederick I, received the elevated title of king of Prussia (instead of elector) as a reward for aiding the Holy Roman emperor in the War of the Spanish Succession.

**Junkers** The nobility of Brandenburg and Prussia, they were reluctant allies of Frederick William in his consolidation of the Prussian state.

## The Consolidation of Prussian Absolutism

Frederick William I, "the Soldiers' King" (r. 1713–1740), completed his grandfather's work, eliminating the last traces of parliamentary estates and local self-government. It was he who truly established Prussian absolutism and transformed Prussia into a military state. Frederick William summed up his life's philosophy in his instructions to his son: "A formidable army and a war chest large enough to make this army mobile in times of need can create great respect for you in the world, so that you can speak a word like the other powers."[4]

Frederick William and his ministers built an exceptionally honest and conscientious bureaucracy to administer the country and foster economic development. Twelfth in Europe in population, Prussia had the fourth largest army by 1740 and the best trained one.

Nevertheless, Prussians paid a heavy and lasting price for this achievement. Army expansion was achieved in part through forced conscription, which was declared lifelong in 1713. Desperate draftees fled the country or injured themselves to avoid service. Finally, in 1733 Frederick William I ordered that all Prussian men would undergo military training and serve as reservists in the army, allowing him to preserve both agricultural production and army size. To appease the Junkers, the king enlisted them to lead his growing army.

With all men harnessed to the war machine, Prussian civil society became rigid and highly disciplined. As a Prussian minister later summed up, "To keep quiet is the first civic duty."[5] Thus the policies of Frederick William I, combined with harsh peasant bondage and Junker tyranny, laid the foundations for a highly militaristic country.

**A Prussian Giant Grenadier** Frederick William I wanted tall, handsome soldiers. He dressed them in tight bright uniforms to distinguish them from the peasant population from which most soldiers came. He also ordered several portraits of his favorites, such as this one, from his court painter, J. C. Merk. Grenadiers wore the miter cap instead of an ordinary hat so that they could hurl their heavy grenades unimpeded by a broad brim. (The Royal Collection © 2010, Her Majesty Queen Elizabeth II)

Why did France rise and Spain fall in this period?

What explains the rise of absolutism in Austria and Prussia?

What was distinctive about Russia and the Ottoman Empire?

Where and why did constitutionalism triumph?

What developments do baroque art and music reflect?

**467**

# ▼ What was distinctive about Russia and the Ottoman Empire?

A favorite parlor game of nineteenth-century intellectuals was debating whether Russia was a Western (European) or non-Western (Asian) society. To this day, Russia differs from the West in some fundamental ways, though its history has paralleled that of the West in other aspects.

There was no question in the mind of Europeans, however, that the Ottomans were outsiders. Even absolutist rulers disdained Ottoman sultans as cruel and tyrannical despots. Despite stereotypes, the Ottoman Empire was in many ways more tolerant than its western counterparts, providing protection and security to other religions while maintaining the Muslim faith. The Ottoman state combined the Byzantine heritage of the territory it had conquered with Persian and Arab traditions. Flexibility and openness to other ideas and practices were sources of strength for the empire.

## The Mongol Yoke and the Rise of Moscow

The two-hundred-year period of rule by the Mongol khan (king) set the stage for the rise of absolutist Russia. The Mongols, a group of nomadic tribes from present-day Mongolia, established an empire that, at its height, stretched from Korea to eastern Europe. In the thirteenth century, the Mongols forced the Slavic princes to submit to their rule. The princes of Moscow became particularly adept at serving the Mongols. Ivan III (r. 1462–1505), known as Ivan the Great, successfully expanded the principality of Moscow toward the Baltic Sea.

By 1480 Ivan III felt strong enough to stop acknowledging the khan as his supreme ruler and to cease paying tribute to the Mongols. To legitimize their new autonomy, the princes of Moscow modeled themselves on the Mongol khans. Like the khans, they declared themselves to be autocrats, meaning that they were the sole source of power. The Muscovite state also forced weaker Slavic principalities to render tribute and borrowed Mongol institutions such as the tax system, postal routes, and census. Loyalty from the highest-ranking nobles, or boyars, helped the Muscovite princes consolidate their power.

Moscow, ca. 1300
Gains by 1505
Gains by 1584
Gains by 1725
Major battle

**The Expansion of Russia to 1725**

boyars The highest-ranking members of the Russian nobility.

Another source of legitimacy lay in Moscow's claim to the political and religious inheritance of the Byzantine Empire. After the fall of Constantinople to the Turks in 1453, the princes of Moscow saw themselves as the heirs of both the caesars (or emperors) and of Orthodox Christianity. The title tsar, first taken by Ivan IV in 1547, is in fact a contraction of *caesar*. The tsars considered themselves rightful and holy rulers, an idea promoted by Orthodox churchmen. The marriage of Ivan III to the daughter of the last Byzantine emperor further enhanced Moscow's claim to inherit imperial authority.

## The Tsar and His People

Developments in Russia took a chaotic turn with the reign of Ivan IV (r. 1533–1584), the famous "Ivan the Terrible," who ascended to the throne at age three. His mother died, possibly poisoned, when he was eight, leaving Ivan to suffer insults and neglect

**Russian Peasant** An eighteenth-century French artist visiting Russia recorded his impressions of the daily life of the Russian people in this etching of a fish merchant pulling his wares through a snowy village on a sleigh. Two caviar vendors behind him make a sale to a young mother standing at her doorstep with her baby in her arms. (From Jean-Baptiste Le Prince's second set of Russian etchings, 1765. Private Collection/www.amis-paris-petersbourg.org)

from the boyars at court. At age sixteen he suddenly pushed aside his hated advisers and crowned himself tsar.

Ivan's reign was successful in defeating the remnants of Mongol power, adding vast new territories to the realm, and laying the foundations for the huge, multiethnic Russian empire. After the sudden death of his beloved wife Anastasia Romanov, however, Ivan began a campaign of persecution against those he suspected of opposing him. Many were intimates of the court from leading boyar families, whom he had killed along with their families, friends, servants, and peasants. To further crush the power of the boyars, Ivan created a new service nobility, whose loyalty was guaranteed by their dependence on the state for noble titles and estates.

Ivan also moved toward making all commoners servants of the tsar. As landlords demanded more from the serfs who survived the wars and persecutions, growing numbers of peasants fled toward wild, recently conquered territories to the east and south. There they joined free groups and warrior bands known as **Cossacks** (KAH-sakz). The solution to the problem of peasant flight was to tie peasants ever more firmly to the land and to the noble landholders, who in turn served the tsar.

Simultaneously, Ivan bound urban traders and artisans to their towns and jobs so that he could tax them more heavily. The urban classes had no security in their work or property. These restrictions stood in sharp contrast to developments in western Europe. From nobles down to merchants and peasants, all of the Russian people were thus brought into the tsar's service. Ivan even made use of Cossack armies in forays to the southeast, forging a new alliance between Moscow and the Cossacks.

After the death of Ivan and his successor, Russia entered a chaotic period known as the "Time of Troubles" (1598–1613). While Ivan's relatives struggled for power, ordinary

**Cossacks** Free groups and outlaw armies originally comprising runaway peasants living on the borders of Russian territory from the fourteenth century onward. By the end of the sixteenth century they had formed an alliance with the Russian state.

Why did France rise and Spain fall in this period?    What explains the rise of absolutism in Austria and Prussia?    **What was distinctive about Russia and the Ottoman Empire?**    Where and why did constitutionalism triumph?    What developments do baroque art and music reflect?

469

**Saint Basil's Cathedral, Moscow** With its sloping roofs and colorful onion-shaped domes, Saint Basil's is a striking example of powerful Byzantine influences on Russian culture. According to tradition, an enchanted Ivan the Terrible blinded the cathedral's architects to ensure that they would never duplicate their fantastic achievement, which still dazzles the beholder in today's Red Square. (George Holton/Photo Researchers)

people suffered drought, crop failure, and plague. The Cossacks and peasants rebelled against nobles and officials, demanding fairer treatment. This social explosion from below brought the nobles together. They crushed the Cossack rebellion and elected Ivan's grandnephew, Michael Romanov, the new hereditary tsar (r. 1613–1645). (See "Listening to the Past: A German Account of Russian Life," page 472.)

Although the new tsar successfully reconsolidated central authority, he and his successors did not improve the lot of the common people. In 1649 a law extended serfdom to all peasants in the realm, giving lords unrestricted rights over their serfs and establishing penalties for harboring runaways. Social and religious uprisings among the poor and oppressed continued through the seventeenth century.

Despite the turbulence of the period, the Romanov tsars, like their Western counterparts, made several important achievements during the second half of the seventeenth century. After a long war, Russia gained land in Ukraine from Poland in 1667 and completed the conquest of Siberia by the end of the century. Territorial expansion was accompanied by growth of the bureaucracy and the army. Foreign experts were employed to help build and reform the Russian army, and Cossack warriors were enlisted to fight Siberian campaigns. The great profits from Siberia's natural resources funded the Romanovs' bid for Great Power status. Thus, Russian imperialist expansion to the east paralleled the western powers' exploration and conquest of the Atlantic world in the same period.

Chapter 16
**Absolutism and Constitutionalism
in Europe • ca. 1589–1725**

**470**

CHAPTER LOCATOR

What made the
seventeenth century an
"age of crisis"?

## The Reforms of Peter the Great

Heir to Romanov efforts at state-building, Peter the Great (r. 1682–1725) embarked on a tremendous campaign to accelerate and complete these processes. Possessing enormous energy and willpower, Peter was determined to build and improve the army and to continue the tsarist tradition of territorial expansion.

Fascinated by weapons and foreign technology, the tsar led a group of 250 Russian officials and young nobles on an eighteen-month tour of western European capitals. Traveling unofficially to avoid lengthy diplomatic ceremonies, Peter met with foreign kings and experts. He was particularly impressed with the growing power of the Dutch and the English, and he considered how Russia could profit from their example.

Returning to Russia, Peter entered into a secret alliance with Denmark and Poland to wage a sudden war of aggression against Sweden with the goal of securing access to the Baltic Sea and opportunities for westward expansion. Peter and his allies believed that their combined forces could win easy victories because Sweden was in the hands of a new and inexperienced king.

Eighteen-year-old Charles XII of Sweden (r. 1697–1718) surprised Peter. He defeated Denmark quickly in 1700, then turned on Russia. His well-trained professional army attacked and routed unsuspecting Russians besieging the Swedish fortress of Narva on the Baltic coast. Peter and the survivors fled in panic to Moscow. The attack marked the beginning of the long and brutal Great Northern War, which lasted from 1700 to 1721.

Peter responded to this defeat with measures designed to increase state power, strengthen his armies, and gain victory. He required all nobles to serve in the army or

**Peter the Great** This compelling portrait by Grigory Musikiysky captures the strength and determination of the warrior-tsar in 1723, after more than three decades of personal rule. In his hand Peter holds the scepter, symbol of royal sovereignty, and across his breastplate is draped an ermine fur, a mark of honor. In the background are the battleships of Russia's new Baltic fleet and the famous St. Peter and St. Paul Fortress that Peter built in St. Petersburg. Peter the Great commissioned this magnificent new crown (left) for himself for his joint coronation in 1682 with his half-brother Ivan. (portrait: Kremlin Museums, Moscow/ The Bridgeman Art Library; crown: Bildarchiv Preussischer Kulturbesitz/Art Resource, NY)

Why did France rise and Spain fall in this period?

What explains the rise of absolutism in Austria and Prussia?

**What was distinctive about Russia and the Ottoman Empire?**

Where and why did constitutionalism triumph?

What developments do baroque art and music reflect?

471

# LISTENING TO THE PAST

## A German Account of Russian Life

*Seventeenth-century Russia remained a remote and mysterious land for western and even central Europeans, who had few direct contacts with the tsar's dominion. Westerners portrayed eastern Europe as more "barbaric" and less "civilized" than their homelands. Thus they drew on eastern Europe's undeniably harsher social and economic conditions to posit a very debatable cultural and moral inferiority.*

*Knowledge of Russia came mainly from occasional travelers who had visited Muscovy and sometimes wrote accounts of what they saw. The most famous of these accounts was by the German Adam Olearius (ca. 1599–1671), who was sent to Moscow on three diplomatic missions in the 1630s. These missions ultimately proved unsuccessful, but they provided Olearius with a rich store of information for his* Travels in Muscovy, *from which the following excerpts are taken. Published in German in 1647 and soon translated into several languages (but not Russian), Olearius's unflattering but well-informed study played a major role in shaping European ideas about Russia.*

The government of the Russians is what political theorists call a "dominating and despotic monarchy," where the sovereign, that is, the tsar or the grand prince who has obtained the crown by right of succession, rules the entire land alone, and all the people are his subjects, and where the nobles and princes no less than the common folk—townspeople and peasants—are his serfs and slaves, whom he rules and treats as a master treats his servants. . . .

If the Russians be considered in respect to their character, customs, and way of life, they are justly to be counted among the barbarians. . . . The vice of drunkenness is so common in this nation, among people of every station, clergy and laity, high and low, men and women, old and young, that when they are seen now and then lying about in the streets, wallowing in the mud, no attention is paid to it, as something habitual. If a cart driver comes upon such a drunken pig whom he happens to know, he shoves him onto his cart and drives him home, where he is paid his fare. No one ever refuses an opportunity to drink and to get drunk, at any time and in any place, and usually it is done with vodka. . . .

The Russians being naturally tough and born, as it were, for slavery, they must be kept under a harsh and strict yoke and must be driven to do their work with clubs and whips, which they suffer without impatience, because such is their station, and they are accustomed to it. Young and half-grown fellows sometimes come together on certain days and train themselves in fisticuffs, to accustom themselves to receiving blows, and, since habit is second nature, this makes blows given as punishment easier to bear. Each and all, they are slaves and serfs. . . .

Because of slavery and their rough and hard life, the Russians accept war readily and are well suited to it. On certain occasions, if need be, they reveal themselves as courageous and daring soldiers. . . .

Although the Russians, especially the common populace, living as slaves under a harsh yoke, can bear and endure a great deal out of love for their masters, yet if the pressure is beyond measure, then it can be said of them: "Patience, often wounded, finally turned into fury." A dangerous indignation results, turned not so much against their sovereign as against the lower authorities, especially if the people have been much oppressed by them and by their supporters and have not been protected by the higher authorities. And once they are aroused and enraged, it is not easy to appease them. Then, disregarding all dangers that may ensue, they resort to every kind of violence and behave like madmen. . . . They own little; most of them have no feather beds; they lie on cushions, straw, mats, or their clothes; they sleep on benches and, in winter, like the non-Germans [natives] in Livonia, upon the oven, which serves them for cooking and is flat on the top; here husband, wife, children, servants, and maids huddle together. In some houses in the countryside we saw chickens and pigs under the benches and the ovens. . . . Russians are not used to delicate food and dainties; their daily food consists of porridge, turnips, cabbage, and cucumbers, fresh and pickled, and in Moscow mostly of big salt fish which stink badly, because of the thrifty use of salt, yet are eaten with relish. . . .

The Russians can endure extreme heat. In the bathhouse they stretch out on benches and let themselves be beaten and rubbed with bunches of birch twigs and wisps of bast (which I could not stand); and when they are hot and red all over and so exhausted that they can bear it no longer in the bathhouse, men and women rush outdoors naked and pour cold water over their bodies; in winter they even wallow in the snow and rub their skin with it as if it were soap; then they go back into the hot bathhouse. And since bathhouses are usually near rivers and brooks, they can throw themselves straight from the hot into the cold bath. . . .

in the civil administration—for life. Peter created schools and universities to produce skilled technicians and experts. One of his most hated reforms was requiring a five-year education away from home for every young nobleman. Peter established an interlocking military-civilian bureaucracy with fourteen ranks, and he decreed that all had to start at the bottom and work toward the top. Drawing on his experience abroad, Peter sought

Chapter 16
**Absolutism and Constitutionalism**
in Europe • ca. 1589–1725

472

CHAPTER LOCATOR | What made the seventeenth century an "age of crisis"?

**The brutality of serfdom is shown in this illustration from Olearius's *Travels in Muscovy*.** (University of Illinois Library, Champaign)

Generally noble families, even the small nobility, rear their daughters in secluded chambers, keeping them hidden from outsiders; and a bridegroom is not allowed to have a look at his bride until he receives her in the bridal chamber. Therefore some happen to be deceived, being given a misshapen and sickly one instead of a fair one, and sometimes a kinswoman or even a maidservant instead of a daughter; of which there have been examples even among the highborn. No wonder therefore that often they live together like cats and dogs and that wife-beating is so common among Russians. . . .

In the Kremlin and in the city there are a great many churches, chapels, and monasteries, both within and without the city walls, over two thousand in all. This is so because every nobleman who has some fortune has a chapel built for himself, and most of them are of stone. The stone churches are round and vaulted inside. . . . They allow neither organs nor any other musical instruments in their churches, saying: Instruments that have neither souls nor life cannot praise God. . . .

In their churches there hang many bells, sometimes five or six, the largest not over two hundredweights. They ring these bells to summon people to church, and also when the priest during mass raises the chalice. In Moscow, because of the multitude of churches and chapels, there are several thousand bells, which during the divine service create such a clang and din that one unaccustomed to it listens in amazement. **"**

**Source:** "A Foreign Traveler in Russia" excerpt from pp. 249–251 in *A Source Book for Russian History from Early Times to 1917*, volume 1, *Early Times to the Late Seventeenth Century*, edited by George Vernadsky, Ralph T. Fisher, Jr., Alan D. Ferguson, Andrew Lossky, and Sergel Pushkarev, compiler. Copyright © 1972 by Yale University Press. Used with permission of the publisher.

### QUESTIONS FOR ANALYSIS

1. How did Olearius characterize the Russians in general? What supporting evidence did he offer for his judgment?
2. How might Olearius's account help explain the social and religious uprisings of the seventeenth century (page 470)?
3. On the basis of these representative passages, why do you think Olearius's book was so popular and influential in central and western Europe?

talented foreigners and placed them in his service. These measures gradually combined to make the army and government more powerful and efficient.

Peter also greatly increased the service requirements of commoners. He established a regular standing army of more than two hundred thousand peasant-soldiers commanded by officers from the nobility. In addition, one hundred thousand men were brought

Why did France rise and Spain fall in this period?

What explains the rise of absolutism in Austria and Prussia?

**What was distinctive about Russia and the Ottoman Empire?**

Where and why did constitutionalism triumph?

What developments do baroque art and music reflect?

473

into the Russian army in special regiments of Cossacks and foreign mercenaries. To fund the army, taxes on peasants increased threefold during Peter's reign. Serfs were also arbitrarily assigned to work in the growing number of factories and mines that supplied the military.

Peter's new war machine was able to crush the army of Sweden in the Ukraine at Poltava in 1709, one of the most significant battles in Russian history. Russia's victory against Sweden was conclusive in 1721, and Estonia and present-day Latvia came under Russian rule for the first time. Russia became the dominant power in the Baltic and very much a European Great Power.

After his victory at Poltava, Peter channeled enormous resources into building a new Western-style capital on the Baltic to rival the great cities of Europe. The magnificent city of St. Petersburg was designed to reflect modern urban planning, with wide, straight avenues, buildings set in a uniform line, and large parks.

Peter the Great drafted twenty-five thousand to forty thousand men each summer to labor in St. Petersburg without pay. Many peasant construction workers died from hunger, sickness, and accidents. Nobles were ordered to build costly stone houses and palaces in St. Petersburg and to live in them most of the year. Merchants and artisans were also commanded to settle and build in the new capital. These nobles and merchants were then required to pay for the city's infrastructure. The building of St. Petersburg was, in truth, an enormous direct tax levied on the wealthy, with the peasantry forced to do the manual labor.

There were other important consequences of Peter's reign. For Peter, modernization meant westernization, and both Westerners and Western ideas flowed into Russia for the first time. He required nobles to shave their heavy beards and wear Western clothing. He obliged them to attend parties where young men and women would mix together and freely choose their own spouses. He forced a warrior elite to accept administrative service as an honorable occupation. From these efforts a new elite class of Western-oriented Russians began to emerge.

Peter's reforms were unpopular with many Russians. For nobles, one of Peter's most detested reforms was the imposition of unigeniture—inheritance of land by one son alone—cutting daughters and other sons from family property. For peasants, the reign of the tsar saw a significant increase in the bonds of serfdom, and the gulf between the enserfed peasantry and the educated nobility increased.

Peter's reforms were in some ways a continuation of Russia's distinctive history. He built on the service obligations of Ivan the Terrible and his successors, and his monarchical absolutism can be seen as the culmination of the long development of a unique Russian civilization. Yet the creation of a more modern army and state introduced much that was new and Western to Russia. This development paved the way for Russia to move somewhat closer to the European mainstream in its thought and institutions during the Enlightenment, especially under Catherine the Great.

## The Growth of the Ottoman Empire

Most Christian Europeans perceived the Ottomans as the antithesis of their own values and traditions and viewed the empire as driven by lust for warfare and conquest. In their view the fall of Constantinople was a catastrophe and the taking of the Balkans a form of despotic imprisonment. To Ottoman eyes, the world looked very different. The siege of Constantinople liberated the city from its long decline under the Byzantines. Rather than being a despoiled captive, the Balkans became a haven for refugees fleeing the growing religious intolerance of Western Christian powers.

The Ottomans came out of Central Asia as conquering warriors, settled in Anatolia (present-day Turkey), and, at their peak in the mid-sixteenth century, ruled one of the

Chapter 16
**Absolutism and Constitutionalism
in Europe • ca. 1589–1725**

474

CHAPTER LOCATOR | What made the seventeenth century an "age of crisis"?

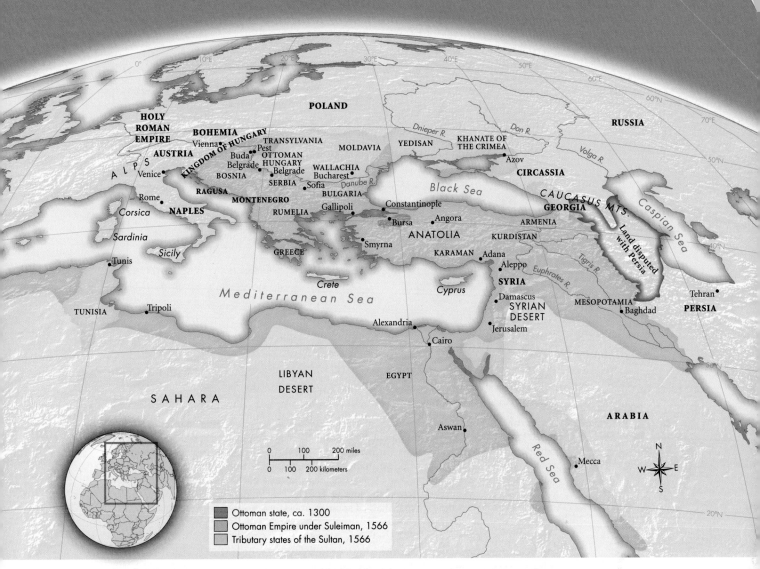

**Map 16.4  The Ottoman Empire at Its Height, 1566**  The Ottomans, like their great rivals the Habsburgs, rose to rule a vast dynastic empire encompassing many different peoples and ethnic groups. The army and the bureaucracy served to unite the disparate territories into a single state under an absolutist ruler.

most powerful empires in the world (see Chapter 15). Their possessions stretched from western Persia across North Africa and into the heart of central Europe (Map 16.4).

The Ottoman Empire was originally built on a unique model of state and society. There was an almost complete absence of private landed property. Agricultural land was the personal property of the **sultan**, and peasants paid taxes to use the land. There was therefore no security of landholding and no hereditary nobility.

The Ottomans also employed a distinctive form of government administration. The top ranks of the bureaucracy were staffed by the sultan's slave corps. Because Muslim law prohibited enslaving other Muslims, the sultan's agents purchased slaves along the borders of the empire. Within the realm, the sultan levied a "tax" of one thousand to three thousand male children on the conquered Christian populations in the Balkans every year. These young slaves were raised in Turkey as Muslims and were trained to fight and to administer. The most talented Ottoman slaves rose to the top of the bureaucracy, where they might acquire wealth and power. The less fortunate formed the core of the sultan's army, the **janissary corps**. By 1683 service in the janissary (JAN-uh-sehr-ee) corps

**sultan**  The ruler of the Ottoman Empire; he owned all the agricultural land of the empire and was served by an army and bureaucracy composed of highly trained slaves.

**janissary corps**  The core of the sultan's army, composed of slave conscripts from non-Muslim parts of the empire; after 1683 it became a volunteer force.

Why did France rise and Spain fall in this period?  What explains the rise of absolutism in Austria and Prussia?  What was distinctive about Russia and the Ottoman Empire?  Where and why did constitutionalism triumph?  What developments do baroque art and music reflect?

475

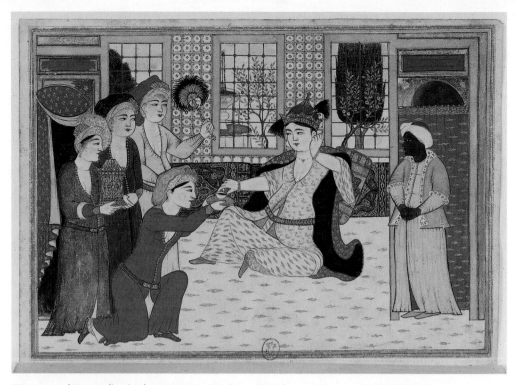

**Hürrem and Her Ladies in the Harem** In Muslim culture *harem* means a sacred place or a sanctuary. The term was applied to the part of the household occupied by women and children and forbidden to men outside the family. The most famous member of the Ottoman sultan's harem was Hürrem (1505–1585), wife of Suleiman the Magnificent. Captured, according to tradition, in modern-day Ukraine in a Tartar raid and brought to the harem as a slave-concubine, she quickly won the sultan's trust and affection. Suleiman's love for Hürrem led him to break all precedents and marry his concubine, a decision that shocked some courtiers. (Bibliothèque nationale de France)

had become so prestigious that the sultan ceased recruitment by force, and it became a volunteer army open to Christians and Muslims.

The Ottomans divided their subjects into religious communities, and each *millet,* or "nation," enjoyed autonomous self-government under its religious leaders. The Ottoman Empire recognized Orthodox Christians, Jews, Armenian Christians, and Muslims as distinct millets. The millet system created a powerful bond between the Ottoman ruling class and religious leaders, who supported the sultan's rule in return for extensive authority over their own communities. Each millet (MIH-luht) collected taxes for the state, regulated group behavior, and maintained law courts, schools, houses of worship, and hospitals for its people.

Sultans married women of the highest social standing, while keeping many concubines of low rank. To prevent the elite families into which they married from acquiring influence over government, sultans procreated only with their concubines and not with official wives. They also adopted a policy of allowing each concubine to produce only one male heir. At a young age, each son went to govern a province of the empire accompanied by his mother. These practices were intended to stabilize power and prevent a recurrence of the civil wars of the late fourteenth and early fifteenth centuries.

Sultan Suleiman undid these policies when he boldly married his concubine, a former slave of Polish origin named Hürrem, and had several children with her. Starting with Suleiman, imperial wives began to take on more power. Marriages were arranged between sultans' daughters and high-ranking servants, creating powerful new members of the imperial household. Over time, the sultan's exclusive authority waned in favor of a more bureaucratic administration.

**millet system** A system used by the Ottomans whereby subjects were divided into religious communities with each millet (nation) enjoying autonomous self-government under its religious leaders.

Chapter 16
**Absolutism and Constitutionalism
in Europe • ca. 1589–1725**

476

CHAPTER LOCATOR

What made the seventeenth century an "age of crisis"?

# ▼ Where and why did constitutionalism triumph?

While France, Prussia, Russia, and Austria developed the absolutist state, England and Holland evolved toward constitutionalism, which is the limitation of government by law. Constitutionalism also implies a balance between the authority and power of the government, on the one hand, and the rights and liberties of the subjects, on the other. By definition, all constitutionalist governments have a constitution. A nation's constitution may be embodied in one basic document, like the Constitution of the United States. Or it may be only partly formalized and include parliamentary statutes, judicial decisions, and a body of traditional procedures and practices, like the English and Dutch constitutions.

Despite their common commitment to constitutional government, England and the Dutch Republic represented significantly different alternatives to absolute rule. After decades of civil war and an experiment with republicanism, the English opted for a constitutional monarchy in 1688. England retained a monarch as the titular head of government but vested sovereignty in an elected parliament. Upon gaining independence from Spain in 1648, the Dutch rejected monarchical rule, adopting a republican form of government in which elected estates held supreme power.

**constitutionalism** A form of government in which power is limited by law and balanced between the authority and power of the government on the one hand, and the rights and liberties of the subject or citizen on the other hand; could include constitutional monarchies or republics.

**republicanism** A form of government in which there is no monarch and power rests in the hands of the people as exercised through elected representatives.

## Absolutist Claims in England

In 1603 Queen Elizabeth I (r. 1558–1603) of England's Scottish cousin James Stuart succeeded her as James I (r. 1603–1625). King James was well educated and had thirty-five years' experience as king of Scotland. But he was not as interested in displaying the majesty of monarchy as Elizabeth had been. Urged to wave at the crowds who waited to greet their new ruler, James complained that he was tired and threatened to drop his breeches "so they can cheer at my arse."[6]

James's greatest problem, however, stemmed from his absolutist belief that a monarch has a divine right to his authority and is responsible only to God. James went so far as to lecture the House of Commons: "There are no privileges and immunities which can stand against a divinely appointed King." Such a view ran directly counter to the long-standing English idea that a person's property could not be taken away without due process of law. James I and his son Charles I considered such constraints a threat to their divine-right prerogative. Consequently, at every Parliament between 1603 and 1640, bitter squabbles erupted

Van Dyck, *Charles I at the Hunt*, ca. 1635 Anthony Van Dyck was the greatest of Rubens's many students. In 1633 he became court painter to Charles I. This portrait of Charles just dismounted from a horse emphasizes the aristocratic bearing, elegance, and innate authority of the king. Van Dyck's success led to innumerable commissions by members of the court and aristocratic society. He had a profound influence on portraiture in England and beyond; some scholars believe that this portrait influenced Rigaud's 1701 portrayal of Louis XIV (see page 459). (Scala/Art Resource, NY)

Why did France rise and Spain fall in this period?

What explains the rise of absolutism in Austria and Prussia?

What was distinctive about Russia and the Ottoman Empire?

**Where and why did constitutionalism triumph?**

What developments do baroque art and music reflect?

477

between the Crown and the Commons. Charles I's attempt to govern without Parliament (1629–1640) and to finance his government by emergency taxes brought the country to a crisis.

## Religious Divides and the English Civil War

Religious issues also embittered relations between the king and the House of Commons. In the early seventeenth century increasing numbers of English people felt dissatisfied with the Church of England established by Henry VIII and reformed by Elizabeth. Many **Puritans** believed that the Reformation had not gone far enough. They wanted to "purify" the Anglican Church of Roman Catholic elements—elaborate vestments and ceremonials, bishops, and even the giving and wearing of wedding rings.

James I responded to such ideas by declaring, "No bishop, no king." For James, bishops were among the chief supporters of the throne. His son and successor, Charles I, further antagonized religious sentiments. Not only did he marry a Catholic princess, but he also supported the policies of the Archbishop of Canterbury William Laud (1573–1645). In 1637 Laud attempted to impose two new elements on church organization in Scotland: a new prayer book, modeled on the Anglican *Book of Common Prayer*, and bishoprics. The Presbyterian Scots rejected these elements and revolted. To finance an

**Puritans** Members of a sixteenth- and seventeenth-century reform movement within the Church of England that advocated purifying it of Roman Catholic elements, such as bishops, elaborate ceremonials, and wedding rings.

**Puritan Occupations** These twelve engravings depict typical Puritan occupations and show that the Puritans came primarily from the artisan and lower middle classes. The governing classes and peasants made up a much smaller percentage of the Puritans and generally adhered to the traditions of the Church of England. (Visual Connection Archive)

Chapter 16
**Absolutism and Constitutionalism**
in Europe • ca. 1589–1725

478

CHAPTER LOCATOR | What made the seventeenth century an "age of crisis"?

army to put down the Scots, King Charles was compelled to summon Parliament in November 1640.

Charles had ruled from 1629 to 1640 without Parliament, financing his government through extraordinary stopgap levies considered illegal by most English people. Most members of Parliament believed that such taxation without consent amounted to despotism. Consequently, they were not willing to trust the king with an army. Moreover, many supported the Scots' resistance to Charles's religious innovations. Accordingly, this Parliament, called the "Long Parliament" because it sat from 1640 to 1660, enacted legislation that limited the power of the monarch and made government without Parliament impossible.

In 1641 the Commons passed the Triennial Act, which compelled the king to summon Parliament every three years. The Commons impeached Archbishop Laud and then threatened to abolish bishops. King Charles, fearful of a Scottish invasion—the original reason for summoning Parliament—reluctantly accepted these measures.

The next act in the conflict was precipitated by the outbreak of rebellion in Ireland, where English governors and landlords had long exploited the people. In 1641 the Catholic gentry of Ireland led an uprising in response to a feared invasion by anti-Catholic forces of the British Long Parliament.

Without an army, Charles I could neither come to terms with the Scots nor respond to the Irish rebellion. After a failed attempt to arrest parliamentary leaders, Charles left London for the north of England where he recruited an army. In response, Parliament formed its own army, the New Model Army. During the spring of 1642 both sides prepared for war.

The English Civil War, 1642–1649

The English civil war (1642–1649) pitted the power of the king against that of the Parliament. After three years of fighting, Parliament's New Model Army defeated the king's armies at the battles of Naseby and Langport in the summer of 1645. Charles, though, refused to concede defeat. Both sides jockeyed for position, waiting for a decisive event. This arrived in the form of the army under the leadership of Oliver Cromwell, a member of the House of Commons and a devout Puritan. In 1647 Cromwell's forces captured the king and dismissed members of the Parliament who opposed his actions. In 1649 the remaining representatives, known as the "Rump Parliament," put Charles on trial for high treason. Charles was found guilty and beheaded on January 30, 1649.

## Cromwell and Puritanical Absolutism in England

With the execution of Charles, kingship was abolished and a commonwealth, or republican government, was proclaimed. Theoretically, legislative power rested in the surviving members of Parliament, and executive power was lodged in a council of state. In fact, the army that had defeated the king controlled the government, and Oliver Cromwell controlled the army. Though called the Protectorate, the rule of Cromwell (1653–1658) constituted military dictatorship.

The army prepared a constitution, the Instrument of Government (1653), that invested executive power in a lord protector (Cromwell) and a council of state. It provided for triennial parliaments and gave Parliament the sole power to raise taxes. But after repeated disputes, Cromwell dismissed Parliament in 1655, and the instrument was never formally endorsed. Cromwell continued the standing army and proclaimed quasi-martial law. He divided England into twelve military districts, each governed by a major general.

**Protectorate** The English military dictatorship (1653–1658) established by Oliver Cromwell following the execution of Charles I.

| Why did France rise and Spain fall in this period? | What explains the rise of absolutism in Austria and Prussia? | What was distinctive about Russia and the Ottoman Empire? | Where and why did constitutionalism triumph? | What developments do baroque art and music reflect? |

479

"The Royall Oake of Brittayne"  The chopping down of this tree, as shown in this cartoon from 1649, signifies the end of royal authority, stability, and the rule of law. As pigs graze (representing the unconcerned common people), being fattened for slaughter, Oliver Cromwell, with his feet in Hell, quotes Scripture. This is a royalist view of the collapse of Charles I's government and the rule of Cromwell. (Courtesy of the Trustees of the British Museum)

Reflecting Puritan ideas of morality, Cromwell's state forbade sports, kept the theaters closed, and rigorously censored the press.

On the issue of religion, Cromwell favored some degree of toleration, and the Instrument of Government gave all Christians except Roman Catholics the right to practice their faith. Cromwell had long associated Catholicism in Ireland with sedition and heresy, and he led an army there to reconquer the country in August 1649. Following Cromwell's reconquest, the English banned Catholicism in Ireland, executed priests, and confiscated land from Catholics for English and Scottish settlers. These brutal acts left a legacy of Irish hatred for England.

Cromwell adopted mercantilist policies similar to those of absolutist France. He enforced a Navigation Act (1651) requiring that English goods be transported on English ships. The act was a great boost to the development of an English merchant marine and brought about a short but successful war with the Dutch. Cromwell also welcomed the immigration of Jews because of their skills, and they began to return to England after four centuries of absence.

The Protectorate collapsed when Cromwell died in 1658 and his son succeeded him. Fed up with military rule, the English longed for a return to civilian government and, with it, common law and social stability. By 1660 they were ready to restore the monarchy.

## The Restoration of the English Monarchy

The Restoration of 1660 brought to the throne Charles II (r. 1660–1685), eldest son of Charles I. Both houses of Parliament were also restored, together with the established

Chapter 16
**Absolutism and Constitutionalism
in Europe • ca. 1589–1725**

**480**

CHAPTER LOCATOR    What made the
seventeenth century an
"age of crisis"?

Anglican Church. The Restoration failed to resolve two serious problems, however. What was to be the attitude of the state toward Puritans, Catholics, and dissenters from the established church? And what was to be the relationship between the king and Parliament?

To answer the first question, Parliament enacted the **Test Act** of 1673 against those outside the Church of England, denying them the right to vote, hold public office, preach, teach, attend the universities, or even assemble for meetings. In politics Charles II was determined to work well with Parliament. This intention did not last, however. Finding that Parliament did not grant him an adequate income, in 1670 Charles entered into a secret agreement with his cousin Louis XIV. The French king would give Charles two hundred thousand pounds annually, and in return Charles would relax the laws against Catholics, gradually re-Catholicize England, and convert to Catholicism himself. When the details of this treaty leaked out, a great wave of anti-Catholic sentiment swept England.

When James II (r. 1685–1688) succeeded his brother, the worst English anti-Catholic fears were realized. In violation of the Test Act, James appointed Roman Catholics to positions in the army, the universities, and local government. And he went further. Attempting to broaden his base of support with Protestant dissenters and nonconformists, James granted religious freedom to all.

Seeking to prevent the return of Catholic absolutism, a group of eminent persons in Parliament and the Church of England offered the English throne to James's Protestant daughter Mary and her Dutch husband, Prince William of Orange. In December 1688 James II, his queen, and their infant son fled to France. Early in 1689 William and Mary were crowned king and queen of England.

**Test Act** Legislation passed by the English parliament in 1673 to secure the position of the Anglican Church by stripping Puritans, Catholics, and other dissenters of the right to vote, preach, assemble, hold public office, and attend or teach at the universities.

## Constitutional Monarchy

The English call the events of 1688 and 1689 the "Glorious Revolution" because it replaced one king with another with a minimum of bloodshed. It also represented the destruction, once and for all, of the idea of divine-right monarchy. The revolution of 1688 established the principle that sovereignty, the ultimate power in the state, was divided between king and Parliament and that the king ruled with the consent of the governed.

The men who brought about the revolution framed their intentions in the Bill of Rights, which was formulated in direct response to Stuart absolutism. Law was to be made in Parliament; once made, it could not be suspended by the Crown. Parliament had to be called at least once every three years. The independence of the judiciary was established, and there was to be no standing army in peacetime. Protestants could possess arms, but the Catholic minority could not. No Catholic could ever inherit the throne. Additional legislation granted freedom of worship to Protestant dissenters, but not to Catholics.

The Glorious Revolution and the concept of representative government found its best defense in political philosopher John Locke's *Second Treatise of Civil Government* (1690). Locke (1632–1704) maintained that a government that oversteps its proper function—protecting the natural rights of life, liberty, and property—becomes a tyranny. By "natural" rights Locke meant rights basic to all men because all have the ability to reason. Under a tyrannical government, the people have the natural right to rebellion.

The events of 1688 and 1689 did not constitute a democratic revolution. The revolution placed sovereignty in Parliament, and Parliament represented the upper classes. The age of aristocratic government lasted at least until 1832 and in many ways until 1928, when women received full voting rights.

England's brief and chaotic experiment with republicanism under Oliver Cromwell convinced its people of the advantages of a monarchy, albeit with strong checks on royal authority. The eighteenth-century philosopher David Hume went so far as to declare that he would prefer England to be peaceful under an absolute monarch than in constant civil war as a republic. These sentiments would have found little sympathy among the proud burgers of the Dutch Republic.

Why did France rise and Spain fall in this period?    What explains the rise of absolutism in Austria and Prussia?    What was distinctive about Russia and the Ottoman Empire?    **Where and why did constitutionalism triumph?**    What developments do baroque art and music reflect?

481

# INDIVIDUALS IN SOCIETY

## Glückel of Hameln

**IN 1690 A JEWISH WIDOW IN THE SMALL GERMAN** town of Hameln in Lower Saxony sat down to write her autobiography. She wanted to distract her mind from the terrible grief she felt over the death of her husband and to provide her twelve children with a record "so you will know from what sort of people you have sprung, lest today or tomorrow your beloved children or grandchildren came and know naught of their family." Out of her pain and heightened consciousness, Glückel (1646–1724) produced an invaluable source for scholars.

She was born in Hamburg two years before the end of the Thirty Years' War. In 1649 the merchants of Hamburg expelled the Jews, who moved to nearby Altona, then under Danish rule. When the Swedes overran Altona in 1657–1658, the Jews returned to Hamburg "purely at the mercy of the Town Council." Glückel's narrative proceeds against a background of the constant harassment to which Jews were subjected — special papers, permits, bribes — and in Hameln she wrote, "And so it has been to this day and, I fear, will continue in like fashion."

When Glückel was "barely twelve," her father betrothed her to Chayim Hameln. She married at age fourteen. She describes him as "the perfect pattern of the pious Jew," a man who stopped his work every day for study and prayer, fasted, and was scrupulously honest in his business dealings. Only a few years older than Glückel, Chayim earned his living dealing in precious metals and in making small loans on pledges (pawned goods). This work required his constant travel to larger cities, markets, and fairs, often in bad weather, always over dangerous roads. Chayim consulted his wife about all his business dealings. As he lay dying, a friend asked if he had any last wishes. "None," he replied. "My wife knows everything. She shall do as she has always done." For thirty years Glückel had been his friend, full business partner, and wife. They had thirteen children, twelve of whom survived their father, eight then unmarried. As Chayim had foretold, Glückel succeeded in launching the boys in careers and in providing dowries for the girls.

Glückel's world was her family, the Jewish community of Hameln, and the Jewish communities into which her children married. Her social and business activities took her across Europe — from Amsterdam to Berlin, from Danzig to Vienna — so her world was neither narrow nor provincial. She took great pride that Prince Frederick of Cleves, later king of Prussia, danced at the wedding of her eldest daughter. The rising prosperity of Chayim's businesses allowed the couple to maintain up to six servants.

Glückel was deeply religious, and her culture was steeped in Jewish literature, legends, and mystical and secular works. Above all, she relied on the Bible. Her language, heavily sprinkled with scriptural references, testifies to a rare familiarity with the Scriptures.

Students who would learn about seventeenth-century business practices, the importance of the dowry in marriage, childbirth, Jewish life, birthrates, family celebrations, and even the meaning of life can gain a good deal from the memoirs of this extraordinary woman who was, in the words of one of her descendants, the poet Heinrich Heine, "the gift of a world to me."

## QUESTIONS FOR ANALYSIS

1. Consider the ways in which Glückel of Hameln was both an ordinary and an extraordinary woman of her times. Would you call her a marginal or a central person in her society?
2. How might Glückel's successes be attributed to the stabilizing force of absolutism in the seventeenth century?

**Source:** *The Memoirs of Glückel of Hameln* (New York: Schocken Books, 1977).

Although no images of Glückel exist, Rembrandt's *The Jewish Bride* suggests the mutual devotion that Glückel and her husband felt for one another. (Rijksmuseum-Stichting Amsterdam)

Chapter 16
**Absolutism and Constitutionalism**
in Europe • ca. 1589–1725

482

CHAPTER LOCATOR | What made the seventeenth century an "age of crisis"?

## The Dutch Republic in the Seventeenth Century

In the late sixteenth century the seven northern provinces of the Netherlands fought for and won their independence from Spain. The independence of the Republic of the United Provinces of the Netherlands was recognized in 1648 in the treaty that ended the Thirty Years' War. In this period, often called the "golden age of the Netherlands," Dutch ideas and attitudes played a profound role in shaping a new and modern worldview. At the same time, the United Provinces developed its own distinctive model of a constitutional state.

Rejecting the rule of a monarch, the Dutch established a republic, a state in which power rested in the hands of the people and was exercised through elected representatives. An oligarchy of wealthy businessmen called "regents" handled domestic affairs in each province's Estates (assemblies). The provincial Estates held virtually all the power. A federal assembly, or States General, handled foreign affairs and war, but it did not possess sovereign authority. All issues had to be referred back to the local Estates for approval, and each of the seven provinces could veto any proposed legislation.

In each province, the Estates appointed an executive officer, known as the **stadholder**, who carried out ceremonial functions and was responsible for military defense. Although in theory freely chosen by the Estates, in practice the reigning prince of Orange usually held the office of stadholder in several of the seven provinces of the Republic. This meant that tensions always lingered between supporters of the House of Orange and those of the staunchly republican Estates, who suspected the princes of harboring monarchical ambitions. When one of them, William III, took the English throne in 1688 with his wife, Mary, the republic simply continued without stadholders for several decades.

**stadholder** The executive officer in each of the United Provinces of the Netherlands, a position often held by the princes of Orange.

The political success of the Dutch rested on their commercial prosperity (see Chapter 15). The moral and ethical bases of that commercial wealth were thrift, frugality, and religious toleration. Jews enjoyed a level of acceptance and assimilation in Dutch business and general culture unique in early modern Europe. (See "Individuals in Society: Glückel of Hameln," left.) In the Dutch Republic, toleration paid off: it attracted a great deal of foreign capital and investment.

The Dutch came to dominate the shipping business by putting profits from their original industry—herring fishing—into shipbuilding. They boasted the lowest shipping rates and largest merchant marine in Europe, allowing them to undersell foreign competitors. Trade and commerce brought the Dutch the highest standard of living in Europe, perhaps in the world.

# ▼ What developments do baroque art and music reflect?

Rome and the revitalized Catholic Church of the later sixteenth century played an important role in the early development of the baroque style. The papacy and the Jesuits encouraged the growth of an intensely emotional, exuberant art. They wanted artists to appeal to the senses and thereby touch the souls and kindle the faith of ordinary church-goers while proclaiming the power and confidence of the reformed Catholic Church. In addition to this underlying religious emotionalism, the baroque drew its sense of drama, motion, and ceaseless striving from the Catholic Reformation.

Taking definite shape in Italy after 1600, the baroque style in the visual arts developed with exceptional vigor in Catholic countries. Yet baroque art was more than just "Catholic art" in the seventeenth century and the first half of the eighteenth. Protestants

Why did France rise and Spain fall in this period?

What explains the rise of absolutism in Austria and Prussia?

What was distinctive about Russia and the Ottoman Empire?

Where and why did constitutionalism triumph?

What developments do baroque art and music reflect?

483

Rubens, *Garden of Love*, 1633–1634 This painting is an outstanding example of the lavishness and richness of baroque art. Born and raised in northern Europe, Peter Paul Rubens trained as a painter in Italy. Upon his return to the Spanish Netherlands, he became a renowned and amazingly prolific artist, patronized by rulers across Europe. Rubens was a devout Catholic, and his work conveys the emotional fervor of the Catholic Reformation. (Scala/Art Resource, NY)

accounted for some of the finest examples of baroque style, especially in music. The baroque style spread partly because its tension and bombast spoke to an agitated age that was experiencing great violence and controversy in politics and religion.

In painting, the baroque reached maturity early with Peter Paul Rubens (1577–1640), the most outstanding and most representative of baroque painters. Studying in his native Flanders and in Italy, Rubens developed his own rich, sensuous, colorful style, which was characterized by animated figures, melodramatic contrasts, and monumental size. Rubens excelled in glorifying monarchs such as Queen Mother Marie de' Medici of France. He was also a devout Catholic; nearly half of his pictures treat Christian subjects. Yet one of Rubens's trademarks was fleshy, sensual nudes who populate his canvases as Roman goddesses, water nymphs, and remarkably voluptuous saints and angels.

In music, the baroque style reached its culmination almost a century later in the dynamic, soaring lines of the endlessly inventive Johann Sebastian Bach (1685–1750). Organist and choirmaster of several Lutheran churches across Germany, Bach was equally at home writing secular concertos and religious cantatas. Bach's organ music combined the baroque spirit of invention, tension, and emotion in an unforgettable striving toward the infinite.

Chapter 16
**Absolutism and Constitutionalism
in Europe • ca. 1589–1725**

**484**

CHAPTER LOCATOR

What made the seventeenth century an "age of crisis"?

# ← LOOKING BACK **LOOKING AHEAD** →

THE SEVENTEENTH CENTURY represented a difficult passage between two centuries of dynamism and growth. On one side lay the sixteenth century of religious enthusiasm and strife, overseas expansion, rising population, and vigorous commerce. On the other side stretched the eighteenth-century era of renewed population growth, economic development, and cultural flourishing. The first half of the seventeenth century was marked by the spread of religious and dynastic warfare across Europe, resulting in the death and dislocation of many millions. This catastrophe was compounded by recurrent episodes of crop failure, famine, and epidemic disease, all of which contributed to a stagnant economy and population loss. In the middle decades of the seventeenth century, the very survival of the European monarchies established in the Renaissance appeared in doubt.

With the re-establishment of order in the second half of the century, maintaining political and social stability appeared of paramount importance to European rulers and elites. In western and eastern Europe, a host of monarchs proclaimed their God-given and "absolute" authority to rule in the name of peace, unity, and good order. Rulers' ability to impose such claims in reality depended a great deal on compromise with local elites, who acquiesced to state power in exchange for privileges and payoffs. In this way, absolutism and constitutionalism did not always differ as much as they claimed. Both systems relied on political compromises forged from decades of strife.

The eighteenth century was to see this status quo thrown into question by new Enlightenment aspirations for human society, which themselves derived from the inquisitive and self-confident spirit of the scientific revolution. By the end of the century, demands for real popular sovereignty challenged the very bases of political order so painfully achieved in the seventeenth century. ■

- **For a list of suggested readings for this chapter, visit** *bedfordstmartins.com/mckaywestunderstanding*.

- **For primary sources from this period, see** *Sources of Western Society*, Second Edition.

- **For Web sites, images, and documents related to topics in this chapter, see Make History at** *bedfordstmartins.com/mckaywestunderstanding*.

| Why did France rise and Spain fall in this period? | What explains the rise of absolutism in Austria and Prussia? | What was distinctive about Russia and the Ottoman Empire? | Where and why did constitutionalism triumph? | **What developments do baroque art and music reflect?** |

# Chapter 16 Study Guide

Online Study Guide
bedfordstmartins.com/mckaywestunderstanding

## Step 1

**GETTING STARTED** Below are basic terms about this period in the history of Western civilization. Can you identify each term below and explain why it matters? To do this exercise online, go to bedfordstmartins.com/mckaywestunderstanding.

| TERMS | WHO (OR WHAT) AND WHEN | WHY IT MATTERS |
|---|---|---|
| Peace of Westphalia, p. 455 | | |
| the Fronde, p. 458 | | |
| mercantilism, p. 461 | | |
| Peace of Utrecht, p. 462 | | |
| Junkers, p. 467 | | |
| boyars, p. 468 | | |
| Cossacks, p. 469 | | |
| sultan, p. 475 | | |
| janissary corps, p. 475 | | |
| millet system, p. 476 | | |
| constitutionalism, p. 477 | | |
| republicanism, p. 477 | | |
| Puritans, p. 478 | | |
| Protectorate, p. 479 | | |
| Test Act, p. 481 | | |
| stadholder, p. 483 | | |

## Step 2

**MOVING BEYOND THE BASICS** The exercise below requires a more advanced understanding of the chapter material. Examine the growth of state power in France, Prussia, Austria, and England by filling in the chart below with descriptions of developments in four areas where these seventeenth-century governments achieved new levels of control: taxation, the armed forces, bureaucracies, and the ability to compel obedience from subjects. When you are finished, consider the following questions: Why did seventeenth-century governments place so much emphasis on increasing their military power? How did the need to maintain large armies shape other aspects of government? How did the growth of the state in England differ from the growth of the state in absolutist France, Prussia, and Austria? To do this exercise online, go to bedfordstmartins.com/mckaywestunderstanding.

| STATE | TAXATION | ARMED FORCES | BUREAUCRACIES | CONTROL OVER SUBJECTS |
|---|---|---|---|---|
| France | | | | |
| Prussia | | | | |
| Austria | | | | |
| England | | | | |

**PUTTING IT ALL TOGETHER** Now that you've reviewed key elements of the chapter, take a step back and try to see the big picture. Remember to use specific examples from the chapter in your answers. To do this exercise online, go to bedfordstmartins.com/mckaywestunderstanding.

### THE AGE OF CRISIS

- How did life for Europe's peasants change during the seventeenth century? Why was peasant life harder in eastern Europe than in western Europe?

- What conflicts and tensions underlay the warfare of the seventeenth century?

### ABSOLUTISM

- How and why did Louis XIV try to co-opt and control the French aristocracy? In practice, how "absolute" was his rule?

- Compare and contrast absolutism in Austria, Prussia, and Russia. What common problems and challenges did would-be absolutist rulers face in each of these three states?

- How did the Ottoman absolutist state differ from its European counterparts? To what do you attribute these differences?

### CONSTITUTIONAL STATES

- Why did the efforts of English monarchs to build an absolutist state fail? What groups and institutions in English society were most responsible for the triumph of constitutionalism?

- Compare and contrast the constitutional governments of England and the Netherlands. What role did merchant elites and commercial interests play in each state?

### BAROQUE ART AND MUSIC

- What role did religion play in the cultural developments of the seventeenth century? What do cultural developments tell us about the religious life of seventeenth-century Europeans?

- Why was baroque art and music so appealing to seventeenth-century Europeans? To what groups did it appeal the most? Why?

■ **In Your Own Words** Imagine that you must explain Chapter 16 to someone who hasn't read it. What would be the most important points to include and why?

# 17

# Toward a New Worldview

## 1540–1789

The intellectual developments of the seventeenth and eighteenth centuries created the modern worldview that the West continues to hold—and debate—to this day. In the seventeenth century fundamentally new ways of understanding the natural world emerged. Those leading the changes saw themselves as philosophers and referred to their field of study as "natural philosophy." In the nineteenth century scholars hailed these achievements as a "scientific revolution" that produced modern science as we know it. The new science created in the seventeenth century entailed the search for precise knowledge of the physical world based on the union of experimental observations with sophisticated mathematics. Whereas medieval scholars looked to authoritative texts like the Bible or the classics, seventeenth-century natural philosophers performed experiments and relied on increasingly complex mathematical calculations. The resulting conception of the universe and its laws remained in force until Einstein's discoveries in the first half of the twentieth century.

In the eighteenth century philosophers extended the use of reason from the study of nature to the study of human society. They sought to bring the light of reason to bear on the darkness of prejudice, outmoded traditions, and ignorance. Self-proclaimed members of an "Enlightenment" movement, they wished to bring the same progress to human affairs as their predecessors had brought to the understanding of the natural world. While the scientific revolution ushered in modern science, the Enlightenment created concepts of human rights, equality, progress, universalism, and tolerance that still guide Western societies today. At the same time, some people used their new understanding of reason to explain their own superiority, thus rationalizing such attitudes as racism and male chauvinism. ■

**Life During the Scientific Revolution.** This 1768 painting by Joseph Wright captures the popularization of science and experimentation during the Enlightenment. Here, a scientist demonstrates the creation of a vacuum by withdrawing air from a flask, with the air-deprived cockatoo serving as shocking proof of the experiment. (National Gallery, London/The Bridgeman Art Library)

# Chapter Preview

▶  How did European views of nature change in this period?

▶  What were the core principles of the Enlightenment?

▶  What did enlightened absolutism mean?

# ▼ How did European views of nature change in this period?

The emergence of modern science was a development of tremendous long-term significance. With the scientific revolution, which lasted roughly from 1540 to 1690, Western society began to acquire its most distinctive traits.

## Scientific Thought in 1500

The term *science* as we use it today only came into use in the nineteenth century. Prior to the scientific revolution, many different scholars and practitioners were involved in aspects of what came together to form science. One of the most important disciplines was **natural philosophy**, which focused on fundamental questions about the nature of the universe, its purpose, and how it functioned. In the early 1500s natural philosophy was still based primarily on the ideas of Aristotle. Medieval theologians such as Thomas Aquinas brought Aristotelian philosophy into harmony with Christian doctrines. According to the revised Aristotelian view, a motionless earth was fixed at the center of the universe, and it was encompassed by ten separate concentric crystal spheres in which were embedded the moon, sun, planets, and stars. Beyond the spheres was Heaven, with the throne of God and the souls of the saved. Angels kept the spheres moving in perfect circles.

Aristotle's cosmology made intellectual sense, but it could not account for the observed motions of the stars and planets. The great second-century Greek scholar Ptolemy (see Chapter 15) offered a solution to this dilemma. According to Ptolemy, the planets moved in small circles, called epicycles, each of which moved in turn along a larger circle or deferent. Ptolemaic astronomy was less elegant than Aristotle's neat nested circles and required complex calculations, but it provided a surprisingly accurate model for predicting planetary motion.

Aristotle's views, revised by medieval philosophers, also dominated thinking about physics and motion on earth. Aristotle had distinguished sharply between the world of the celestial spheres and that of the earth—the sublunar world. The spheres consisted of a perfect, incorruptible "quintessence," or fifth essence. The sublunar world, however, was made up of four imperfect, changeable elements: air, fire, water, and earth. Aristotle and his followers also believed that a uniform force moved an object at a constant speed and that the object would stop as soon as that force was removed.

Aristotle's ideas about astronomy and physics were accepted for two thousand years because they offered a commonsense

**The Aristotelian Universe as Imagined in the Sixteenth Century** A round earth is at the center, surrounded by spheres of water, air, and fire. Beyond this small nucleus, the moon, the sun, and the five planets were embedded in their own rotating crystal spheres, with the stars sharing the surface of one enormous sphere. Beyond, the heavens were composed of unchanging ether. (Image Select/Art Resource, NY)

**natural philosophy** An early modern term for the study of the nature of the universe, its purpose, and how it functioned; it encompassed what we would call "science" today.

explanation for the natural world and fit neatly with Christian doctrines placing humans on earth at the center of creation, with God and the angels in the eternal heavens above.

## Origins of the Scientific Revolution

Why did Aristotelian teachings give way to new views about the universe? The scientific revolution drew on long-term developments in European culture, as well as borrowings from Arabic scholars. The first important development was the university. By the thirteenth century permanent universities with professors and large student bodies had been established in western Europe. In the universities, medieval philosophers developed a limited but real independence from theologians and a sense of free inquiry.

In the fourteenth and fifteenth centuries leading universities established new professorships of mathematics, astronomy, and physics (natural philosophy) within their faculties of philosophy. Although the prestige of the new fields was low, critical thinking was now applied to scientific problems by a permanent community of scholars.

The Renaissance also stimulated scientific progress. Many ancient works were recovered, often through Arabic translations of the original Greek and Latin. In fields such as mathematics, the translations were accompanied by learned Arabic commentaries that went beyond ancient learning. Renaissance patrons played a role in funding scientific investigations, as they did for art and literature. In addition, Renaissance artists' turn toward realism and their use of geometry to convey three-dimensional perspective encouraged scholars to practice close observation and to use mathematics to describe the natural world. The rise of printing provided a faster and less expensive way to circulate knowledge across Europe.

The navigational problems of long sea voyages in the age of overseas expansion were another factor in the scientific revolution. Navigational problems were critical in the development of many new scientific instruments, such as the telescope, barometer, thermometer, pendulum clock, microscope, and air pump. Better instruments, which permitted more accurate observations, often led to important new knowledge.

Recent historical research has also focused on the contribution to the scientific revolution of practices now relegated far beyond the realm of science. For most of human history, interest in astronomy was inspired by belief that the changing relationships between planets and stars influenced events on earth. Many of the most celebrated astronomers were also astrologers. Used as a diagnostic tool in medicine, astrology formed a regular part of the curriculum of medical schools. Centuries-old practices of magic and alchemy also remained important traditions for participants in the scientific revolution. The idea that objects possessed hidden or "occult" qualities that allowed them to affect other objects was a particularly important legacy of the magical tradition.

## The Copernican Hypothesis

The first great departure from the medieval system was the work of the Polish cleric Nicolaus Copernicus (koh-PUHR-nih-kuhs) (1473–1543). After studies at the university of Kraków, Copernicus departed for Italy, where he studied astronomy, medicine,

## Chapter Chronology

| | |
|---|---|
| ca. 1540–1690 | Scientific revolution |
| ca. 1690–1789 | Enlightenment |
| ca. 1700–1789 | Growth of book publishing |
| 1720–1780 | Rococo style in art and decoration |
| 1740–1748 | War of Austrian Succession |
| 1740–1780 | Reign of the empress Maria Theresa |
| 1740–1786 | Reign of Frederick the Great of Prussia |
| ca. 1740–1789 | French salons led by elite women |
| 1756–1763 | Seven Years' War |
| 1762–1796 | Reign of Catherine the Great of Russia |
| 1765 | Philosophes publish *Encyclopedia: The Rational Dictionary of the Sciences, the Arts, and the Crafts* |
| 1780–1790 | Reign of Joseph II of Austria |
| 1791 | Establishment of the Pale of Settlement |

CHAPTER LOCATOR | How did European views of nature change in this period? | What were the core principles of the Enlightenment? | What did enlightened absolutism mean?

491

and church law at the famed universities of Bologna, Padua, and Ferrara. In his studies of astronomy, Copernicus came to believe that Ptolemy's cumbersome and occasionally inaccurate rules detracted from the majesty of a perfect creator. He preferred an ancient Greek idea: that the sun, rather than the earth, was at the center of the universe.

Finishing his university studies and returning to a church position in East Prussia, Copernicus worked on his hypothesis from 1506 to 1530. Without questioning the Aristotelian belief in crystal spheres or the idea that circular motion was divine, Copernicus theorized that the stars and planets, including the earth, revolved around a fixed sun. Fearing the ridicule of other astronomers, Copernicus did not publish his *On the Revolutions of the Heavenly Spheres* until 1543, the year of his death.

The Copernican hypothesis presented a revolutionary view of the universe and brought sharp attacks from religious leaders, especially Protestants, who objected to the idea that the earth moved but the sun did not. Protestant leaders John Calvin and Martin Luther condemned Copernicus. Luther noted that the theory was counter to the Bible: "as the Holy Scripture tells us, so did Joshua bid the sun stand still and not the earth."[1] Catholic reaction was milder at first. The Catholic Church had never held to literal interpretations of the Bible, and not until 1616 did it officially declare the Copernican hypothesis false.

Other events were almost as influential in creating doubts about traditional astronomical ideas. In 1572 a new star appeared and shone very brightly for almost two years. The new star, which was actually a distant exploding star, seemed to contradict the idea that the heavenly spheres were unchanging and therefore perfect. In 1577 a new comet suddenly moved through the sky, cutting a straight path across the supposedly impenetrable crystal spheres. It was time, as a sixteenth-century scientific writer put it, for "the radical renovation of astronomy."[2]

**Copernican hypothesis**
The idea that the sun, not the earth, is the center of the universe.

**Hevelius and His Wife** Portable sextants were used to chart a ship's position at sea by measuring the altitude of celestial bodies above the horizon. Astronomers used much larger sextants to measure the angular distances between two bodies. Here, Johannes Hevelius makes use of the great brass sextant at the Danzig observatory, with the help of his wife Elisabetha. Six feet in radius, this instrument was closely modeled on the one used by Tycho Brahe. (Houghton Library, Harvard College Library)

## Brahe, Kepler, and Galileo: Proving Copernicus Right

One astronomer who agreed with Copernicus was the Danish astronomer Tycho Brahe (TEE-koh BRAH-hee) (1546–1601). Brahe established himself as Europe's leading astronomer with his detailed observations of the new star of 1572. Aided by grants from the king of Denmark, Brahe built the most sophisticated observatory of his day.

Upon the king's death, Brahe acquired a new patron in the Holy Roman emperor Rudolph II and built a new observatory in Prague. In return for the emperor's support, he pledged to create new and improved tables of planetary motions, dubbed the *Rudolfine Tables*. For twenty years Brahe observed the stars and planets with the naked eye, compiling much more complete and accurate data than ever before. His limited understanding of mathematics and his sudden death in 1601, however, prevented him from making much sense out of his mass of data.

It was left to Brahe's young assistant, Johannes Kepler (YO-hah-nihs KEH-pluhr) (1571–1630), to rework Brahe's mountain of observations. A brilliant mathematician, Kepler was inspired by belief that the universe was built on mystical mathematical relationships and a musical harmony of the heavenly bodies.

Kepler's examination of his predecessor's findings convinced him that they could not be explained by Ptolemy's astronomy. Abandoning the notion of epicycles and deferents, Kepler developed three new and revolutionary laws of planetary motion. First, he demonstrated that the orbits of the planets around the sun are elliptical rather than circular. Second, he demonstrated that the planets do not move at a uniform speed in their orbits. When a planet is close to the sun it moves more rapidly, and it slows as it moves farther away from the sun. Finally, Kepler's third law stated that the time a planet takes to make its complete orbit is precisely related to its distance from the sun.

Kepler's contribution was monumental. Whereas Copernicus had speculated, Kepler proved mathematically the precise relations of a sun-centered (solar) system. His work demolished the old system of Aristotle and Ptolemy, and in his third law he came close to formulating the idea of universal gravitation (see page 495). In 1627 he also fulfilled Brahe's pledge by completing the Rudolfine Tables begun so many years earlier. These tables were used by astronomers for many years.

Kepler was not, however, the consummate modern scientist that his achievements suggest. His duties as court mathematician included casting horoscopes, and his own diary was based on astrological principles. He also wrote at length on cosmic harmonies and explained, for example, elliptical motion through ideas about the beautiful music created by the combined motion of the planets. His career exemplifies the complex interweaving of ideas and beliefs in the emerging science of his day.

While Kepler was unraveling planetary motion, a young Florentine named Galileo Galilei (ga-luh-LEE-oh ga-luh-LAY) (1564–1642) was challenging all

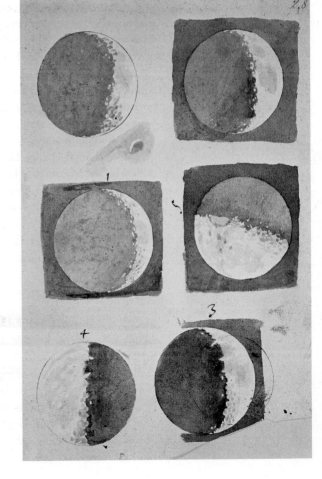

**Galileo's Telescopic Observations of the Moon**
Among the many mechanical devices Galileo invented was a telescope that could magnify objects twenty times (other contemporary telescopes could magnify objects only three times). Using this telescope, he obtained the empirical evidence that proved the Copernican system. He sketched many illustrations of his observations, including the six phases of the moon shown here. (moons: Scala/Art Resource, NY; telescope: Museum of Science, Florence/Art Resource, NY)

CHAPTER LOCATOR | How did European views of nature change in this period?    What were the core principles of the Enlightenment?    What did enlightened absolutism mean?

493

**experimental method** The approach, pioneered by Galileo, that the proper way to explore the workings of the universe was through repeatable experiments rather than speculation.

**law of inertia** A law formulated by Galileo that states that motion, not rest, is the natural state of an object, that an object continues in motion forever unless stopped by some external force.

the old ideas about motion. Galileo's great achievement was the elaboration and consolidation of the experimental method. That is, rather than speculate about what might or should happen, Galileo conducted controlled experiments to find out what actually did happen.

In some of his experiments Galileo measured the movement of a rolling ball across a surface, repeating the action again and again to verify his results. In his famous acceleration experiment, he showed that a uniform force—in this case, gravity—produced a uniform acceleration. Through another experiment, he formulated the law of inertia (ih-NUR-shuh). Rest was not the natural state of objects. Rather, an object continues in motion forever unless stopped by some external force. His discoveries proved Aristotelian physics wrong.

Galileo also applied the experimental method to astronomy. On hearing details about the invention of the telescope in Holland, Galileo made one for himself. He quickly discovered the first four moons of Jupiter, which clearly suggested that Jupiter could not possibly be embedded in any impenetrable crystal sphere as Aristotle and Ptolemy maintained. This discovery provided new evidence for the Copernican theory, in which Galileo already believed. Galileo then pointed his telescope at the moon. He wrote in 1610 in *Siderus Nuncius:*

> By the aid of a telescope anyone may behold [the Milky Way] in a manner which so distinctly appeals to the senses that all the disputes which have tormented philosophers through so many ages are exploded by the irrefutable evidence of our eyes, and we are freed from wordy disputes upon the subject.[3]

Reading these famous lines, one feels a crucial corner in Western civilization being turned. No longer should one rely on established authority. A new method of learning and investigating was being developed, one that proved useful in any field of inquiry. A historian investigating documents of the past, for example, is not so different from a Galileo studying stars and rolling balls.

As early as 1597, when Johannes Kepler sent Galileo an early publication defending Copernicus, Galileo wrote back agreeing with his position and confessing he lacked the courage to follow Kepler's example. Within the Catholic world, expressing public support for Copernicus was increasingly dangerous. In 1616 the Holy Office placed the works of Copernicus and his supporters, including Kepler, on a list of books Catholics were forbidden to read.

Out of caution Galileo silenced his beliefs for several years, until in 1623 he saw new hope with the ascension of Pope Urban VIII, a man sympathetic to developments in the new science. However, Galileo's 1632 *Dialogue on the Two Chief Systems of the World* went too far. Published in Italian and widely read, this work openly lampooned the traditional views of Aristotle and Ptolemy and defended those of Copernicus. Galileo was tried for heresy by the papal Inquisition. Imprisoned and threatened with torture, the aging Galileo recanted, "renouncing and cursing" his Copernican errors.

## Newton's Synthesis

Despite the efforts of the church, by about 1640 the work of Brahe, Kepler, and Galileo had been largely accepted by the scientific community. But the new findings failed to explain what forces controlled the movement of the planets and objects on earth. That challenge was taken up by English scientist Isaac Newton (1642–1727).

Newton was born into the lower English gentry in 1642 and he enrolled at Cambridge University in 1661. A genius who united the experimental and theoretical-mathematical sides of modern science, Newton was fascinated by alchemy and was also intensely religious. Like Kepler and other practitioners of the scientific revolution, he was far from being the perfect rationalist so glorified by writers in the eighteenth and nineteenth centuries.

Newton arrived at some of his most basic ideas about physics between 1664 and 1666. During this period, he later claimed to have discovered his law of universal gravitation as well as the concepts of centripetal force and acceleration. Not realizing the significance of his findings, the young Newton did not publish them, and upon his return to Cambridge he took up the study of optics. It was in reference to his experiments in optics that Newton outlined his method of scientific inquiry most clearly, explaining the need for scientists "first to enquire diligently into the properties of things, and to establish these properties by experiment, and then to proceed more slowly to hypotheses for the explanation of them."[4]

In 1684 Newton returned to physics and the preparation of his ideas for publication. The result appeared three years later in *Philosophicae Naturalis Principia Mathematica* (Mathematical Principles of Natural Philosophy). Newton's work presented a single explanatory system that could integrate the astronomy of Copernicus, as corrected by Kepler's laws, with the physics of Galileo and his predecessors. *Principia Mathematica* laid down Newton's three laws of motion, using a set of mathematical laws that explain motion and mechanics.

The key feature of the Newtonian synthesis was the law of universal gravitation. According to this law, every body in the universe attracts every other body in the universe in a precise mathematical relationship, whereby the force of attraction is proportional to the quantity of matter of the objects and inversely proportional to the square of the distance between them. The whole universe was unified in one coherent system. Newton's synthesis of mathematics with physics and astronomy prevailed until the twentieth century and established him as one of the most important figures in the history of science.

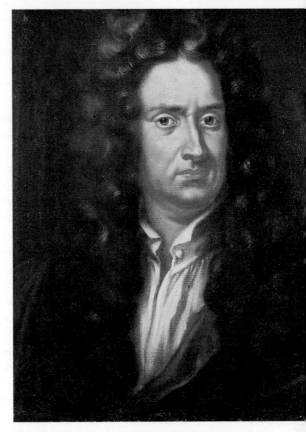

**Isaac Newton** This portrait suggests the depth and complexity of Isaac Newton. Is the powerful mind behind those piercing eyes thinking of science or of religion, or perhaps of both? (Scala/Art Resource, NY)

**law of universal gravitation**
Newton's law that all objects are attracted to one another and that the force of attraction is proportional to the object's quantity of matter and inversely proportional to the square of the distance between them.

## Bacon, Descartes, and the Scientific Method

The creation of a new science was not accomplished by a handful of brilliant astronomers working alone. Scholars in many fields sought answers to long-standing problems, sharing their results in a community that spanned Europe. One of the keys to the achievement of a new worldview in the seventeenth century was the development of better ways of obtaining knowledge about the world. Two important thinkers, Francis Bacon (1561–1626) and René Descartes (day-KAHRT) (1596–1650), were influential in describing and advocating for improved scientific methods based, respectively, on experimentation and mathematical reasoning.

The English politician and writer Francis Bacon was the greatest early propagandist for the new experimental method. Rejecting the Aristotelian and medieval method of using speculative reasoning to build general theories, Bacon argued that new knowledge had to be pursued through empirical research. The researcher who wants to learn more about leaves or rocks, for example, should not speculate about the subject but should rather collect a multitude of specimens and then compare and analyze them to derive general principles. Bacon's contribution was to formalize the empirical method, which had already been used by Brahe and Galileo, into the general theory of inductive reasoning known as empiricism.

**empiricism** A theory of inductive reasoning that calls for acquiring evidence through observation and experimentation rather than reason and speculation.

CHAPTER LOCATOR | **How did European views of nature change in this period?** | What were the core principles of the Enlightenment? | What did enlightened absolutism mean?

495

On the continent, more speculative methods retained support. As a twenty-three-year-old soldier serving in the Thirty Years' War, the French philosopher René Descartes experienced a life-changing intellectual vision one night in 1619. Descartes saw that there was a perfect correspondence between geometry and algebra and that geometrical spatial figures could be expressed as algebraic equations and vice versa. A major step forward in the history of mathematics, Descartes's discovery of analytic geometry provided scientists with an important new tool.

Descartes used mathematics to elaborate a highly influential vision of the workings of the cosmos. Drawing on ancient Greek atomist philosophies, Descartes developed the idea that matter was made up of identical "corpuscules" that collided together in an endless series of motions. All occurrences in nature could be analyzed as matter in motion and, according to Descartes, the total "quantity of motion" in the universe was constant. Descartes's mechanistic view of the universe depended on the idea that a vacuum was impossible, so that every action had an equal reaction, continuing in an eternal chain reaction. Although Descartes's hypothesis about the vacuum was proved wrong, his notion of a mechanistic universe intelligible through the physics of motion proved highly influential.

Descartes's greatest achievement was to develop his initial vision into a whole philosophy of knowledge and science. The Aristotelian cosmos was appealing in part because it corresponded with the evidence of the human senses. When the senses were proven to be wrong, Descartes decided it was necessary to doubt them and everything that could reasonably be doubted, and then, as in geometry, to use deductive reasoning from self-evident principles to ascertain scientific laws. Descartes's reasoning ultimately reduced all substances to "matter" and "mind" — that is, to the physical and the spiritual. Descartes believed that God had endowed man with reason for a purpose and that rational speculation could provide a path to the truths of creation. His view of the world as consisting of two fundamental entities is known as Cartesian dualism. Descartes's thought was highly

**Cartesian dualism**
Descartes's view that all of reality could ultimately be reduced to mind and matter.

## ▪ Major Contributors to the Scientific Revolution

| | |
|---|---|
| **Nicolaus Copernicus (1473–1543)** | *On the Revolutions of the Heavenly Spheres* (1543); theorized that the sun, rather than the earth, was the center of the galaxy |
| **Andreas Vesalius (1514–1564)** | *On the Structure of the Human Body* (1543) |
| **Tycho Brahe (1546–1601)** | Built observatory and compiled data for the Rudolfine Tables, a new table of planetary data |
| **Francis Bacon (1561–1626)** | Advocated experimental method, formalizing theory of inductive reasoning known as empiricism |
| **Galileo Galilei (1564–1642)** | Used telescopic observation to provide evidence for Copernican hypothesis; experimented to formulate laws of physics, such as inertia |
| **Johannes Kepler (1571–1630)** | Used Brahe's data to mathematically prove the Copernican hypothesis; his new laws of planetary motion united for the first time natural philosophy and mathematics; completed the Rudolfine Tables in 1627 |
| **William Harvey (1578–1657)** | Discovery of circulation of blood (1628) |
| **René Descartes (1596–1650)** | Used deductive reasoning to formulate the theory of Cartesian dualism |
| **Robert Boyle (1627–1691)** | Boyle's law (1662) governing the pressure of gases |
| **Isaac Newton (1642–1727)** | *Principia Mathematica* (1687); set forth the law of universal gravitation, synthesizing previous findings of motion and matter |

influential in France and the Netherlands, but less so in England, where experimental philosophy won the day.

Both Bacon's inductive experimentalism and Descartes's deductive mathematical reasoning had their faults. Bacon's inability to appreciate the importance of mathematics and his obsession with practical results clearly showed the limitations of antitheoretical empiricism. Likewise, some of Descartes's positions—he believed, for example, that it was possible to deduce the whole science of medicine from first principles—demonstrated the inadequacy of rigid, dogmatic rationalism. Although insufficient on their own, Bacon's and Descartes's extreme approaches are combined in the modern scientific method, which began to crystallize in the late seventeenth century.

## Science and Society

The rise of modern science had many consequences. First, it went hand in hand with the rise of a new and expanding social group—the international scientific community. Members of this community were linked together by common interests and shared values as well as by journals and learned scientific societies. Second, as governments intervened to support and sometimes direct research, the new scientific community became closely tied to the state and its agendas. National academies of science were created under state sponsorship in London in 1662, Paris in 1666, Berlin in 1700, and later across Europe. At the same time, scientists developed a critical attitude toward established authority that would inspire thinkers to question traditions in other domains as well.

Some things did not change in the scientific revolution. New "rational" methods for approaching nature did not question traditional inequalities between the sexes—and may have worsened them in some ways. When Renaissance courts served as centers of learning, talented noblewomen could find niches in study and research. The rise of a professional scientific community raised barriers for women because the new academies that furnished professional credentials did not accept female members.

There were, however, a number of noteworthy exceptions. In Italy, universities and academies did offer posts to women. Women across Europe were allowed to work as makers of wax anatomical models and as botanical and zoological illustrators. Women were also very much involved in informal scientific communities, attending salons, participating in scientific experiments, and writing learned treatises. Some female intellectuals were recognized as full-fledged members of the philosophical dialogue. In England, Margaret Cavendish, Anne Conway, and Mary Astell all contributed to debates about Descartes's mind-body dualism, among other issues.

The scientific revolution had few consequences for economic life and the living standards of the masses until the late eighteenth century. Thus the scientific revolution of the seventeenth century was first and foremost an intellectual revolution. For more than a hundred years its greatest impact was on how people thought and believed.

Finally, there is the question of the role of religion in the development of science. Just as some historians have argued that Protestantism led to the rise of capitalism, others have concluded

**Metamorphoses of the Caterpillar and Moth** Maria Sibylla Merian (1647–1717), the stepdaughter of a Dutch painter, became a celebrated scientific illustrator in her own right. Her finely observed pictures of insects in the South American colony of Surinam introduced many new species. For Merian, science was intimately tied with art: she not only painted but also bred caterpillars and performed experiments on them. Her two-year stay in Surinam, accompanied by a teenage daughter, was a daring feat for a seventeenth-century woman. (Bildarchiv Preussischer Kulturbesitz/Art Resource, NY)

CHAPTER LOCATOR | How did European views of nature change in this period? | What were the core principles of the Enlightenment? | What did enlightened absolutism mean?

497

that Protestantism was a fundamental factor in the rise of modern science. According to this view, Protestantism, particularly in its Calvinist varieties, made scientific inquiry a question of individual conscience, not of religious doctrine. The Catholic Church, in contrast, supposedly suppressed scientific theories that conflicted with its teachings and thus discouraged scientific progress. The truth is more complicated. All Western religious authorities — Catholic, Protestant, and Jewish — opposed the Copernican system to a greater or lesser extent until about 1630, by which time the scientific revolution was definitely in progress. The Catholic Church was initially less hostile than Protestant and Jewish religious leaders, and Italian scientists played a crucial role in scientific progress right up to the trial of Galileo in 1633. Thereafter, the Counter-Reformation church became more hostile to science, a change that helped account for the decline of science in Italy (but not in Catholic France) after 1640. At the same time, Protestant countries such as the Netherlands, Denmark, and England became quite "pro-science," especially countries that lacked a strong religious authority capable of imposing religious orthodoxy on scientific questions.

## Medicine, the Body, and Chemistry

The scientific revolution, which began with the study of the cosmos, soon inspired renewed study of the microcosm of the human body. For many centuries the ancient Greek physician Galen's explanation of the body carried the same authority as Aristotle's account of the universe. According to Galen, the body contained four humors: blood, phlegm, black bile, and yellow bile. Illness was believed to result from an imbalance of humors.

Swiss physician and alchemist Paracelsus (1493–1541) was an early proponent of the experimental method in medicine and pioneered the use of chemicals and drugs to address what he saw as chemical, rather than humoral, imbalances. Another experimentalist, Flemish physician Andreas Vesalius (1516–1564) studied anatomy by dissecting human bodies. In 1543, the same year Copernicus published *On the Heavenly Revolutions*, Vesalius issued *On the Structure of the Human Body*. Its two hundred precise drawings revolutionized the understanding of human anatomy. The experimental approach also led English royal physician William Harvey (1578–1657) to discover the circulation of blood through the veins and arteries in 1628. Harvey was the first to explain that the heart worked like a pump and to explain the function of its muscles and valves.

Irishman Robert Boyle (1627–1691) founded the modern science of chemistry. Following Paracelsus's lead, he undertook experiments to discover the basic elements of nature, which he believed was composed of infinitely small atoms. Boyle was the first to create a vacuum, thus disproving Descartes's belief that a vacuum could not exist in nature, and he discovered Boyle's law (1662), which states that the pressure of a gas varies inversely with volume.

## ▼ What were the core principles of the Enlightenment?

The scientific revolution was the single most important factor in the creation of the new worldview of the eighteenth-century Enlightenment. This worldview grew out of a rich mix of diverse and often conflicting ideas. For the writers who espoused them, these ideas competed vigorously for the attention of a growing public of well-educated readers, who remained a minority of the population.

Despite the diversity, three central concepts stand at the core of Enlightenment thinking. The most important and original idea was that the methods of natural science could

**Enlightenment** The influential intellectual and cultural movement of the late seventeenth and eighteenth centuries that introduced a new worldview based on the use of reason, the scientific method, and progress.

and should be used to examine and understand all aspects of life. This was what intellectuals meant by *reason*, a favorite word of Enlightenment thinkers. Nothing was to be accepted on faith; everything was to be submitted to rationalism, a secular, critical way of thinking. A second important Enlightenment concept was that the scientific method was capable of discovering the laws of human society as well as those of nature. This second concept led to the third key idea, that of progress. Armed with the proper method of discovering the laws of human existence, Enlightenment thinkers believed, it was at least possible for human beings to create better societies and better people.

**rationalism** A secular, critical way of thinking in which nothing was to be accepted on faith, and everything was to be submitted to reason.

## The Emergence of the Enlightenment

Loosely united by certain key ideas, the European Enlightenment (ca. 1690–1789) gained strength gradually and did not reach its maturity until about 1750. Yet it was the generation that came of age between the publication of Newton's *Principia* in 1687 and the death of Louis XIV in 1715 that tied the crucial knot between the scientific revolution and a new outlook on life. Talented writers of that generation popularized hard-to-understand scientific achievements for the educated elite.

A new generation came to believe that the human mind itself is capable of making great progress. Medieval and Reformation thinkers had been concerned primarily with the abstract concepts of sin and salvation. The humanists of the Renaissance had emphasized worldly matters (especially art and literature), but their inspiration came from the classical past. Enlightenment thinkers came to believe that their era had gone far beyond antiquity and that intellectual progress was very possible.

The excitement of the scientific revolution also generated doubt and uncertainty, contributing to a widespread crisis in late-seventeenth-century European thought. In the wake of the devastation wrought by the Thirty Years' War, some people asked whether ideological conformity in religious matters was really necessary. Others skeptically asked if religious truth could ever be known with absolute certainty and concluded that it could not.

The most famous of these skeptics was the French Huguenot Pierre Bayle (1647–1706). Bayle critically examined the religious beliefs and persecutions of the past in his *Historical and Critical Dictionary* (1697). Demonstrating that human beliefs had been extremely varied and very often mistaken, he concluded that nothing can ever be known beyond all doubt, a view known as skepticism.

Some Jewish scholars participated in the early Enlightenment movement. The philosopher Baruch Spinoza (1632–1677) was excommunicated by the relatively large Jewish community of Amsterdam for his controversial religious ideas. Spinoza believed that mind and body are united in one substance and that God and nature were

**Popularizing Science** The frontispiece illustration of Fontenelle's *Conversations on the Plurality of Worlds* (1686) invites the reader to share the pleasures of astronomy with an elegant lady and an entertaining teacher. The drawing shows the planets revolving around the sun. (© Roger-Viollet/The Image Works)

CHAPTER LOCATOR | How did European views of nature change in this period? | What were the core principles of the Enlightenment? | What did enlightened absolutism mean?

499

two names for the same thing. He envisioned a deterministic universe in which good and evil were merely relative values. Few of Spinoza's radical writings were published during his lifetime, but he is now recognized as among the most original thinkers of the early Enlightenment.

The rapidly growing travel literature on non-European lands and cultures was another cause of questioning among thinkers. In the wake of the great discoveries, Europeans were learning that the peoples of China, India, Africa, and the Americas all had their own very different beliefs and customs. Travel accounts helped change the perspective of educated Europeans. They began to look at truth and morality in relative, rather than absolute, terms. If anything was possible, who could say what was right or wrong?

Out of this period of intellectual turmoil came John Locke's *Essay Concerning Human Understanding* (1690), often viewed as the first major text of the Enlightenment. In this work Locke (1632–1704) set forth a new theory about how human beings learn and form their ideas. Whereas Descartes based his deductive logic on the conviction that certain first premises, or innate ideas, are imbued in all humans by God, Locke insisted that all ideas are derived from experience. The human mind at birth is like a blank tablet, or tabula rasa (tah-byuh-luh RAH-zuh) on which the environment writes the individual's understanding and beliefs. Human development is therefore determined by education and social institutions, for good or for evil. Locke's essay contributed to the theory of sensationalism, the idea that all human ideas and thoughts are produced as a result of sensory impressions. The *Essay Concerning Human Understanding* passed through many editions and translations and, along with Newton's *Principia*, was one of the dominant intellectual inspirations of the Enlightenment.

## The Influence of the Philosophes

By the time Louis XIV died in 1715, many of the ideas that would soon coalesce into the new worldview had been assembled. Yet Christian Europe was still strongly attached to its established political and social structures and its traditional spiritual beliefs. By 1775, however, a large portion of western Europe's educated elite had embraced many of the new ideas. This acceptance was the work of the philosophes, a group of influential intellectuals who proudly proclaimed that they were bringing the light of knowledge to their ignorant fellow creatures.

*Philosophe* is the French word for "philosopher," and it was in France that the Enlightenment reached its highest development. There were at least three reasons for this. First, French was the international language of the educated classes in the eighteenth century, and France was still the wealthiest and most populous country in Europe. Second, although French intellectuals were not free to openly criticize either church or state, they were not as strongly restrained as intellectuals in eastern and east-central Europe. Third, the French philosophes made it their goal to reach a larger audience of elites, many of whom were joined together in the eighteenth-century concept of the "republic of letters"—an imaginary transnational realm of the well-educated.

To appeal to the public and get around the censors, the philosophes wrote novels and plays, histories and philosophies, dictionaries and encyclopedias, all filled with satire and double meanings to spread their message. One of the greatest philosophes, the baron de Montesquieu (1689–1755), pioneered this approach in *The Persian Letters*, an extremely influential social satire published in 1721. This work consisted of letters supposedly written by two Persian travelers, Usbek and Rica, who as outsiders see European customs in unique ways and thereby allow Montesquieu a vantage point for criticizing existing practices and beliefs.

Like many Enlightenment philosophes, Montesquieu saw relations between men and women as representative of the overall social and political system. He used the oppression of women in the Persian harem, described in letters from Usbek's wives, to symbolize

philosophes A group of French intellectuals who proclaimed that they were bringing the light of knowledge to their fellow creatures in the Age of Enlightenment.

**Voltaire and Philosophes** This painting belongs to a series commissioned by Catherine the Great to depict daily life at the philosopher's retreat at Ferney in Switzerland. It shows Voltaire seated at the dinner table surrounded by his followers, including *Encyclopedia* editors Diderot and d'Alembert. The scene is imaginary, for Diderot never visited Ferney. (Photo by permission of the Voltaire Foundation, University of Oxford)

Eastern political tyranny. At the end of the book, the rebellion of Usbek's harem against the cruel eunuchs he left in charge demonstrates that despotism must ultimately fail.

Having gained fame by using wit as a weapon against cruelty and superstition, Montesquieu settled down on his family estate to study history and politics. His interest was partly personal. He was disturbed by the growth in royal absolutism under Louis XIV. But Montesquieu was also inspired by the example of the physical sciences, and he set out to apply the critical method to the problem of government in *The Spirit of Laws* (1748). The result was a comparative study of republics, monarchies, and despotisms.

Showing that forms of government were shaped by history, geography, and customs, Montesquieu focused on the conditions that would promote liberty and prevent tyranny. Admiring greatly the English balance of power among the king, the houses of Parliament, and the independent courts, he argued for a separation of powers, with political power divided and shared by a variety of classes and legal estates holding unequal rights and privileges. Apprehensive about the uneducated poor, Montesquieu was no democrat, but his theory of separation of powers had a great impact on the constitutions of the young United States in 1789 and of France in 1791.

The most famous and in many ways most representative philosophe was François Marie Arouet, who was known by the pen name Voltaire (1694–1778). In his long career, Voltaire wrote more than seventy witty volumes, hobnobbed with kings and queens, and died a millionaire because of shrewd business speculations. His early career, however, was turbulent, and he was arrested on two occasions for insulting noblemen. Voltaire moved to England for three years in order to avoid a longer prison term in France, and there he came to share Montesquieu's enthusiasm for English liberties and institutions.

CHAPTER LOCATOR | How did European views of nature change in this period? | **What were the core principles of the Enlightenment?** | What did enlightened absolutism mean?

501

**Madame du Châtelet** The marquise du Châtelet was fascinated by the new world system of Isaac Newton. She helped spread Newton's ideas in France by translating his *Principia* and by influencing Voltaire, her companion for fifteen years until her death. (Giraudon/Art Resource, NY)

Returning to France and soon threatened again with prison in Paris, Voltaire met Gabrielle-Emilie Le Tonnelier de Breteuil, marquise du Châtelet (SHAH-tuh-lay) (1706–1749), a gifted woman from the high aristocracy with a passion for science. Inviting Voltaire to live in her country house at Cirey in Lorraine and becoming his long-time companion, Madame du Châtelet studied physics and mathematics and published scientific articles and translations, including the first — and only — translation of Newton's *Principia* into French.

While living at Cirey, Voltaire wrote various works praising England and popularizing English scientific progress. Newton, he wrote, was history's greatest man, for he had used his genius for the benefit of humanity. "It is," wrote Voltaire, "the man who sways our minds by the prevalence of reason and the native force of truth, not they who reduce mankind to a state of slavery by force and downright violence . . . that claims our reverence and admiration."[5] In the true style of the Enlightenment, Voltaire mixed the glorification of science and reason with an appeal for better individuals and institutions.

Yet, like almost all of the philosophes, Voltaire was a reformer, not a revolutionary, in social and political matters. He pessimistically concluded that the best one could hope for in the way of government was a good monarch, since human beings "are very rarely worthy to govern themselves." Nor did Voltaire believe in social and economic equality in human affairs. The only realizable equality, Voltaire thought, was that "by which the citizen only depends on the laws which protect the freedom of the feeble against the ambitions of the strong."[6]

Voltaire's philosophical and religious positions were much more radical than his social and political beliefs. Voltaire believed in God, but his was a distant, deistic God. Drawing on Newton, he envisioned a mechanistic universe in which God acted like a great clockmaker who built an orderly system and then stepped aside and let it run. Above all, Voltaire and most of the philosophes hated all forms of religious intolerance, which they believed often led to fanaticism and savage, inhuman action.

The ultimate strength of the philosophes lay in their number, dedication, and organization. The philosophes felt keenly that they were engaged in a common undertaking that transcended individuals. Their greatest and most representative intellectual achievement was a group effort — the seventeen-volume *Encyclopedia: The Rational Dictionary of the Sciences, the Arts, and the Crafts*, edited by Denis Diderot (deh-nee DEE-duh-roh) (1713–1784) and Jean le Rond d'Alembert (dah-lum-BEHR) (1717–1783). The two men set out in 1751 to find coauthors who would examine the rapidly expanding whole of human knowledge. Even more fundamentally, they set out to teach people how to think critically and objectively about all matters.

The *Encyclopedia* survived initial resistance from the French government and the Catholic Church. Completed in 1765, it contained hundreds of thousands of articles by leading scientists, writers, skilled workers, and progressive priests, and it treated every aspect of life and knowledge. Science and the industrial arts were exalted, religion and immortality questioned. Intolerance, legal injustice, and out-of-date social institutions were openly criticized. The encyclopedists were convinced that greater knowledge would result in greater human happiness, for knowledge was useful and made possible economic, social, and political progress. Summing up the new worldview of the Enlightenment, the *Encyclopedia* was widely read, especially in less-expensive reprint editions, and it was extremely influential.

## The Enlightenment Outside of France

Historians now recognize the existence of important strands of Enlightenment thought outside of France. They have identified distinctive Enlightenment movements in eighteenth-century Italy, Spain, Greece, the Balkans, Poland, Hungary, and Russia. Different areas developed different forms of Enlightenment thinking. In England and Germany, scholars have described a more conservative Enlightenment that tried to integrate the findings of the scientific revolution with religious faith. After the Act of Union with England and Ireland in 1707, Scotland was freed from political crisis to experience a vigorous period of intellectual growth. The Scottish Enlightenment, centered in Edinburgh, was marked by an emphasis on pragmatic and scientific reasoning. Intellectual revival there was stimulated by the creation of the first public educational system in Europe.

The most important figure in Edinburgh was David Hume (1711–1776), whose carefully argued religious skepticism had a powerful impact at home and abroad. Building on Locke's teachings on learning, Hume argued that the human mind is really nothing but a bundle of impressions. These impressions originate only in sense experiences and our habits of joining these experiences together. Since our ideas ultimately reflect only our sense experiences, our reason cannot tell us anything about questions that cannot be verified by sense experience, such as the origin of the universe or the existence of God. Paradoxically, Hume's rationalistic inquiry ended up undermining the Enlightenment's faith in the power of reason.

## Urban Culture and Life in the Public Sphere

A series of new institutions and practices encouraged the spread of Enlightenment ideas in the late seventeenth and the eighteenth centuries. First, the European production and consumption of books grew significantly between 1700 and 1789. Moreover, the types

## ▪ Major Figures of the Enlightenment

| | |
|---|---|
| **Baruch Spinoza (1632–1677)** | Early Enlightenment thinker excommunicated from the Jewish religion for his concept of a deterministic universe |
| **John Locke (1632–1704)** | *Essay Concerning Human Understanding* (1690) |
| **Pierre Bayle (1647–1706)** | *Historical and Critical Dictionary* (1697) |
| **Montesquieu (1689–1755)** | *The Persian Letters* (1721); *The Spirit of Laws* (1748) |
| **Voltaire (1694–1778)** | Renowned French philosophe and author of more than seventy works |
| **David Hume (1711–1776)** | Central figure of the Scottish Enlightenment; *Of Natural Characters* (1748) |
| **Jean-Jacques Rousseau (1712–1778)** | *The Social Contract* (1762) |
| **Denis Diderot (1713–1784) and Jean le Rond d'Alembert (1717–1783)** | Editors of *Encyclopedia: The Rational Dictionary of the Sciences, the Arts, and the Crafts* (1765) |
| **Immanuel Kant (1724–1804)** | *What Is Enlightenment?* (1784); *On the Different Races of Man* (1775) |

CHAPTER LOCATOR | How did European views of nature change in this period? | What were the core principles of the Enlightenment? | What did enlightened absolutism mean?

503

of books people read changed dramatically. The proportion of religious and devotional books published in Paris declined after 1750; history and law held constant; the arts and sciences surged.

**reading revolution** The transition in Europe from a society where literacy consisted of patriarchal and communal reading of religious texts to a society where literacy was commonplace and reading material was broad and diverse.

Reading more books on many more subjects, the educated public in France and throughout Europe increasingly approached reading in a new way. The result was what some scholars have called a reading revolution. The old style of reading in Europe had been centered on a core of sacred texts. Reading had been patriarchal and communal, with the father of the family slowly reading the text aloud. Now reading involved a broader field of books that constantly changed. Reading became individual and silent, and texts

## ▪ PICTURING THE PAST

### Enlightenment Culture

An actor performs the first reading of a new play by Voltaire at the salon of Madame Geoffrin in this painting from 1755. Voltaire, then in exile, is represented by a bust statue. (Réunion des Musées Nationaux/Art Resource, NY)

**ANALYZING THE IMAGE** Which of these people do you think is the hostess, Madame Geoffrin, and why? Using details from the painting to support your answer, how would you describe the status of the people shown?

**CONNECTIONS** What does this image suggest about the reach of Enlightenment ideas to common people? To women? Does the painting of the coffeehouse on page 506 suggest a broader reach? Why?

To complete this activity online, go to the Online Study Guide at bedfordstmartins.com/ mckaywestunderstanding.

could be questioned. Subtle but profound, the reading revolution ushered in new ways of relating to the written word.

Conversation, discussion, and debate also played a critical role in the Enlightenment. Paris set the example, and other French and European cities followed. In Paris from about 1740 to 1789, a number of talented, wealthy women presided over regular social gatherings named after their elegant private drawing rooms, or **salons**. There they encouraged the exchange of observations on literature, science, and philosophy with great aristocrats, wealthy middle-class financiers, high-ranking officials, and noteworthy foreigners. Talented hostesses, or *salonnières* (sah-lahn-ee-EHRZ), mediated the public's examination of Enlightenment thought. As one philosophe described his Enlightenment hostess and her salon:

**salons** Regular social gatherings held by talented and rich Parisian women in their homes, where philosophes and their followers met to discuss literature, science, and philosophy.

> *She could unite the different types, even the most antagonistic, sustaining the conversation by a well-aimed phrase, animating and guiding it at will. . . . Politics, religion, philosophy, news: nothing was excluded. Her circle met daily from five to nine. There one found men of all ranks in the State, the Church, and the Court, soldiers and foreigners, and the leading writers of the day.*[7]

As this passage suggests, the salons created a cultural realm free from religious dogma and political censorship. There a diverse but educated public could debate issues and form its own ideas. Through their invitation lists, salon hostesses brought together members of the intellectual, economic, and social elites. In such an atmosphere, the philosophes, the French nobility, and the prosperous middle classes intermingled and influenced one another.

Elite women also exercised great influence on artistic taste. Soft pastels, ornate interiors, sentimental portraits, and starry-eyed lovers protected by hovering cupids were all hallmarks of the style they favored. This style, known as **rococo** (ruh-KOH-koh), was popular throughout Europe in the period from 1720 to 1780. It has been argued that feminine influence in the drawing room went hand in hand with the emergence of polite society and the general attempt to civilize a rough military nobility. Similarly, some philosophes championed greater rights and expanded education for women, claiming that the position and treatment of women were the best indicators of a society's level of civilization and decency.[8]

**rococo** A popular style in Europe in the eighteenth century, known for its soft pastels, ornate interiors, sentimental portraits, and starry-eyed lovers protected by hovering cupids.

While membership at the salons was restricted to the well-born, the well-connected, and the exceptionally talented, a number of institutions emerged for the rest of society. Lending libraries served an important function for people who could not afford their own books. The coffeehouses that first appeared in the late seventeenth century became meccas of philosophical discussion. In addition to these institutions, book clubs, Masonic lodges (groups of Freemasons, a secret egalitarian society that existed across Europe), and journals all played roles in the creation of a new **public sphere** that celebrated open debate informed by critical reason. The public sphere was an idealized space where members of society came together as individuals to discuss issues relevant to the society, economics, and politics of the day.

**public sphere** An idealized intellectual space that emerged in Europe during the Enlightenment, where the public came together to discuss important issues relating to society, economics, and politics.

What of the common people? Did they participate in the Enlightenment? Enlightenment philosophes did not direct their message to peasants or urban laborers. They believed that the masses had no time or talent for philosophical speculation and that elevating them would be a long, slow, potentially dangerous process.

There is some evidence, however, that the people were not immune to the words of the philosophes. At a time of rising literacy, book prices were dropping in cities and towns, and many philosophical ideas were popularized in cheap pamphlets. Moreover, even illiterate people had access to written material through the practice of public reading. Although they were barred from salons and academies, ordinary people were nonetheless exposed to the new ideas in circulation.

CHAPTER LOCATOR | How did European views of nature change in this period? | **What were the core principles of the Enlightenment?** | What did enlightened absolutism mean?

505

**Seventeenth-Century English Coffeehouse** By the seventeenth century, coffeehouses were popular throughout Europe and helped spread the ideas and values of the scientific revolution and the Enlightenment. (The Granger Collection, NY)

## Race and the Enlightenment

If philosophers did not believe the lower classes qualified for enlightenment, how did they regard individuals of different races? In recent years, historians have found in the scientific revolution and the Enlightenment a crucial turning point in European ideas about race. A primary catalyst for new ideas about race was the urge to classify nature unleashed by the scientific revolution's insistence on careful empirical observation. As scientists developed more elaborate taxonomies of plant and animal species, they also began to classify humans into hierarchically ordered "races" and to investigate the origins of race. The Comte de Buffon (komt duh buh-FOHN) argued that humans originated with one species that then developed into distinct races due largely to climatic conditions.

Enlightenment thinkers such as David Hume and Immanuel Kant (see page 510) helped popularize these ideas. In *Of Natural Characters* (1748), Hume wrote:

> *I am apt to suspect the negroes and in general all other species of men (for there are four or five different kinds) to be naturally inferior to the whites. There never was a civilized nation of any other complexion than white, nor even any individual eminent amongst them, no arts, no sciences. . . . Such a uniform and constant difference could not happen, in so many countries and ages if nature had not made an original distinction between these breeds of men.*[9]

Kant shared and elaborated Hume's views about race in *On the Different Races of Man* (1775), claiming that there were four human races, each of which had derived from a supposedly original race of "white brunette" people. According to Kant, the closest descendants of the original race were the white inhabitants of northern Germany. In deriving new physical characteristics, the other races had degenerated both physically and culturally from this origin.

Using the word *race* to designate biologically distinct groups of humans was new. Previously, Europeans grouped other peoples into "nations" based on their historical, political, and cultural affiliations, rather than on supposedly innate physical differences. Unsurprisingly, when European thinkers drew up a hierarchical classification of human species, their own "race" was placed at the top. Europeans had long believed they were culturally superior. Now emerging ideas about racial difference taught them they were biologically superior as well. In turn, scientific racism helped legitimate and justify the tremendous growth of slavery that occurred during the eighteenth century. If one "race" of humans was fundamentally different and inferior, its members could be seen as particularly fit for enslavement.

Racist ideas did not go unchallenged. *Encyclopedia* editor Denis Diderot penned a scathing critique of European arrogance and exploitation in the voice of Tahitian villagers. (See "Listening to the Past: Denis Diderot's 'Supplement to Bougainville's Voyage,'" page 508.) Scottish philosopher James Beattie (1735–1803) responded directly to claims of white superiority by pointing out that Europeans had started out as savage as nonwhites and that many non-European peoples in the Americas, Asia, and Africa had achieved high levels of civilization. German thinker Johann Gottfried von Herder (1744–1803) criticized Kant, arguing that humans could not be classified into races based on skin color and that each culture was as intrinsically worthy as any other.

Scholars are only at the beginning of efforts to understand links between Enlightenment ideas about race and its notions of equality, progress, and reason. There are clear parallels, though, between the use of science to propagate racial hierarchies and its use to defend social inequalities between men and women. Swiss philosopher Jean-Jacques

*Encyclopedia* Image of the Cotton Industry This romanticized image of slavery in the West Indies cotton industry was published in Diderot and d'Alembert's *Encyclopedia*. It shows enslaved men, at right, gathering and picking over cotton bolls, while the woman at left mills the bolls to remove their seeds. The *Encyclopedia* presented mixed views on slavery; one article described it as "indispensable" to economic development, while others argued passionately for the natural right to freedom of all mankind. (Courtesy, Dover Publications)

CHAPTER LOCATOR | How did European views of nature change in this period? | What were the core principles of the Enlightenment? | What did enlightened absolutism mean?

507

# LISTENING TO THE PAST

## Denis Diderot's "Supplement to Bougainville's Voyage"

*Denis Diderot (1713–1784) was born in a provincial town in eastern France and educated in Paris. Rejecting careers in the church and the law, he devoted himself to literature and philosophy. In 1749, sixty years before Charles Darwin's birth, Diderot was jailed by Parisian authorities for publishing an essay questioning God's role in the creation and suggesting the autonomous evolution of species. Following these difficult beginnings, Diderot's editorial work and writing on the* Encyclopedia *were the crowning intellectual achievements of his life and, according to some, of the Enlightenment itself.*

*Like other philosophes, Diderot employed numerous genres to disseminate Enlightenment thought, ranging from scholarly articles in the* Encyclopedia, *to philosophical treatises, novels, plays, book reviews, and erotic stories. His "Supplement to Bougainville's Voyage" (1772) was a fictional account of a European voyage to Tahiti inspired by the writings of traveler Louis-Antoine de Bougainville. In this passage, Diderot expresses his own loathing of colonial conquest and exploitation through the voice of an elderly Tahitian man. The character's praise for his own culture allows Diderot to express his Enlightenment idealization of "natural man," free from the vices of civilized societies.*

❝ He was the father of a numerous family. At the time of the Europeans' arrival, he cast upon them a look that was filled with scorn, though it revealed no surprise, no alarm and no curiosity. They approached him; he turned his back on them and retired into his hut. His thoughts were only too well revealed by his silence and his air of concern, for in the privacy of his thoughts he groaned inwardly over the happy days of his people, now gone forever. At the moment of Bougainville's departure, when all the natives ran swarming onto the beach, tugging at his clothing and throwing their arms around his companions and weeping, the old man stepped forward and solemnly spoke:

"Weep, wretched Tahitians, weep — but rather for the arrival than for the departure of these wicked and grasping men! The day will come when you will know them for what they are. Someday they will return, bearing in one hand that piece of wood you see suspended from this one's belt and in the other the piece of steel that hangs at the side of his companions. They will load you with chains, slit your throats and enslave you to their follies and vices. Someday you will be slaves to them, you will be as corrupt, as vile, as wretched as they are. . . ."

Then, turning to Bougainville, he went on: "And you, leader of these brigands who obey you, take your vessel swiftly from our shores. We are innocent and happy, and you can only spoil our happiness. We follow the pure instinct of nature, and you have tried to efface her imprint from our hearts. Here all things are for all, and you have preached to us I know not what distinctions between mine and thine. . . .

". . . You are not slaves; you would suffer death rather than be enslaved, yet you want to make slaves of us! Do you believe, then, that the Tahitian does not know how to die in defense of his liberty? This Tahitian, whom you want to treat as a chattel, as a dumb animal — this Tahitian is your brother. You are both children of Nature — what right do you have over him that he does not have over you?

"You came; did we attack you? Did we plunder your vessel? Did we seize you and expose you to the arrows of our enemies? Did we force you to work in the fields alongside our beasts of burden? We respected our own image in you. Leave us our own customs, which are wiser and more decent than yours. We have no wish to barter what you call our ignorance for your useless knowledge. We possess already all that is good or necessary for our existence. Do we merit your scorn because we have not been

Rousseau used women's "natural" passivity to argue for their passive role in society, just as other thinkers used non-Europeans' "natural" inferiority to defend slavery and colonial domination. The new powers of science and reason were thus marshaled to imbue traditional stereotypes with the force of natural law.

## Late Enlightenment

After about 1770 a number of thinkers and writers began to attack the Enlightenment's faith in reason, progress, and moderation. The most famous of these was the Swiss Jean-Jacques Rousseau (1712–1778). Like other Enlightenment thinkers, Rousseau was passionately committed to individual freedom. Unlike them, however, he attacked rationalism and civilization as destroying, rather than liberating, the individual. Warm, spontaneous

able to create superfluous wants for ourselves? When we are hungry, we have something to eat; when we are cold, we have clothing to put on. You have been in our huts—what is lacking there, in your opinion? You are welcome to drive yourselves as hard as you please in pursuit of what you call the comforts of life, but allow sensible people to stop when they see they have nothing to gain but imaginary benefits from the continuation of their painful labors. If you persuade us to go beyond the bounds of strict necessity, when shall we come to the end of our labor? When shall we have time for enjoyment? We have reduced our daily and yearly labors to the least possible amount, because to us nothing seemed more desirable than leisure. Go and bestir yourselves in your own country; there you may torment yourselves as much as you like; but leave us in peace, and do not fill our heads with a hankering after your false needs and imaginary virtues." 〞

**Source:** From Denis Diderot, *Supplement to Bougainville's Voyage*, edited by Jacques Barzun (Upper Saddle River, N.J.: Prentice-Hall, 1965. © 2010 by Jacques Barzun. All rights reserved, c/o Writers Representatives LLC, New York, NY, 10011, permissions@writersrep.com.

## QUESTIONS FOR ANALYSIS

1. On what grounds does the speaker argue for the Tahitians' basic equality with the Europeans?
2. What is the good life according to the speaker, and how does it contrast with the European way of life? Which do you think is the better path?
3. In what ways could Diderot's thoughts here be seen as representative of Enlightenment ideas? Are there ways in which they are not?
4. How realistic do you think this account is? Does it matter? How might defenders of colonial expansion respond to Diderot's criticism?

This image depicts the meeting of French explorer Louis-Antoine de Bougainville with Tahitians in April 1768. Of his stay on the island, Bougainville wrote: "I felt as though I had been transported to the Garden of Eden. . . . Everywhere reigned hospitality, peace, joy, and every appearance of happiness." Diderot's philosophical tract was a fictional sequel to Bougainville's account. (Unknown artist, Tahitians presenting fruit to Bougainville attended by his officers. PIC T2996 NK5066 LOC7321, National Library of Australia)

feeling had to complement and correct cold intellect. Moreover, the basic goodness of the individual and the unspoiled child had to be protected from the cruel refinements of civilization. Rousseau's ideals greatly influenced the early romantic movement, which rebelled against the culture of the Enlightenment in the late eighteenth century.

Rousseau also called for a rigid division of gender roles. According to Rousseau, women and men were radically different beings. Destined by nature to assume a passive role in sexual relations, women should also be passive in social life. Women's love for displaying themselves in public, attending salons, and pulling the strings of power was unnatural and had a corrupting effect on both politics and society. Rousseau thus rejected the sophisticated way of life of Parisian elite women. His criticism led to broader calls for privileged women to renounce their frivolous ways and stay at home to care for their children.

CHAPTER LOCATOR | How did European views of nature change in this period? | **What were the core principles of the Enlightenment?** | What did enlightened absolutism mean?

509

Rousseau's contribution to political theory in *The Social Contract* (1762) drew less attention at first but proved to be highly significant. His contribution was based on two fundamental concepts: the general will and popular sovereignty. According to Rousseau, the general will is sacred and absolute, reflecting the common interests of all the people, who have displaced the monarch as the holder of sovereign power. The general will is not necessarily the will of the majority, however. At times the general will may be the authentic, long-term needs of the people as correctly interpreted by a farseeing minority. Little noticed before the French Revolution, Rousseau's concept of the general will appealed greatly to democrats and nationalists after 1789. Rousseau was both one of the most influential voices of the Enlightenment and, in his rejection of rationalism and social discourse, a harbinger of reaction against Enlightenment ideas.

As the reading public developed, it joined forces with the philosophes to call for the autonomy of the printed word. Immanuel Kant (1724–1804), a professor in East Prussia and the greatest German philosopher of his day, posed the question of the age when he published a pamphlet in 1784 entitled *What Is Enlightenment?* Kant answered, "*Sapere Aude* (dare to know)! 'Have the courage to use your own understanding' is therefore the motto of enlightenment." He argued that if serious thinkers were granted the freedom to exercise their reason publicly in print, enlightenment would almost surely follow. Kant was no revolutionary; he also insisted that in their private lives, individuals must obey all laws, no matter how unreasonable, and should be punished for "impertinent" criticism. Kant thus tried to reconcile absolute monarchical authority with a critical public sphere. This balancing act characterized experiments with "enlightened absolutism" in the eighteenth century.

## ▼ What did enlightened absolutism mean?

How did the Enlightenment influence political developments? To this important question there is no easy answer. Most Enlightenment thinkers outside of England and the Netherlands, especially in central and eastern Europe, believed that political change could best come from above—from the ruler—rather than from below. Royal absolutism was a fact of life. Therefore, the philosophes and their sympathizers realistically concluded that a benevolent absolutism offered the best opportunities for improving society.

Many government officials were interested in philosophical ideas. Their daily involvement in complex affairs of state made them naturally attracted to ideas for improving human society. Encouraged and instructed by these officials, some absolutist rulers tried to reform their governments in accordance with enlightenment ideals—what historians have often called the enlightened absolutism of the later eighteenth century. The most influential of the new-style monarchs were in Prussia, Russia, and Austria. Their example illustrates both the achievements and the great limitations of enlightened absolutism.

**enlightened absolutism** Term coined by historians to describe the rule of eighteenth-century monarchs who, without renouncing their own absolute authority, adopted Enlightenment ideals of rationalism, progress, and tolerance.

### Frederick the Great of Prussia

Frederick II (r. 1740–1786), commonly known as Frederick the Great, built masterfully on the work of his father, Frederick William I (see Chapter 16). Although in his youth he embraced culture and literature rather than the life of the barracks championed by his father, by the time he came to the throne Frederick was determined to use the army that his father had left him.

When the young Maria Theresa of Austria inherited the Habsburg dominions upon the death of her father Charles VI, Frederick pounced. He invaded her rich, mainly German province of Silesia (sigh-LEE-zhuh), defying solemn Prussian promises to respect the Pragmatic Sanction, a diplomatic agreement that had guaranteed Maria Theresa's

**The War of Austrian Succession, 1740–1748**

Legend:
- Prussia, 1740
- Prussian gains, 1742
- Austria, 1740
- Boundary of the Holy Roman Empire

Königsberg
Berlin
POLAND
SILESIA
Prague
Vienna
AUSTRIA
HUNGARY

succession. In 1742, as other greedy powers vied for her lands in the European War of the Austrian Succession (1740–1748), Maria Theresa was forced to cede almost all of Silesia to Prussia. In one stroke Prussia had doubled its population to 6 million people and become a European Great Power.

Though successful in 1742, Frederick had to fight against great odds to save Prussia from total destruction after the on-going competition between Britain and France for colonial empire brought another great conflict in 1756. Maria Theresa, seeking to regain Silesia, formed an alliance with the leaders of France and Russia. The aim of the alliance during the resulting Seven Years' War (1756–1763) was to conquer Prussia and divide up its territory. In the end Frederick was miraculously saved: Peter III came to the Russian throne in 1762 and called off the attack against Frederick, whom he greatly admired.

The terrible struggle of the Seven Years' War tempered Frederick's interest in territorial expansion and brought him to consider how more humane policies for his subjects might also strengthen the state. Thus he tolerantly allowed his subjects to believe as they wished in religious and philosophical matters. He promoted the advancement of knowledge, improving his country's schools and permitting scholars to publish their findings. Moreover, Frederick tried to improve the lives of his subjects more directly. As he wrote his friend Voltaire, "I must enlighten my people, cultivate their manners and morals, and make them as happy as human beings can be, or as happy as the means at my disposal permit."

The legal system and the bureaucracy were Frederick's primary tools. Prussia's laws were simplified, torture of prisoners was abolished, and judges decided cases quickly and impartially. Prussian officials became famous for their hard work and honesty. After the Seven Years' War ended in 1763, Frederick's government energetically promoted the reconstruction of agriculture and industry in his war-torn country.

Frederick's dedication to high-minded government went only so far, however. While he condemned serfdom in the abstract, he accepted it in practice and did not free the serfs on his own estates. He accepted and extended the privileges of the nobility, who remained the backbone of the army and the entire Prussian state. In reforming Prussia's bureaucracy, Frederick drew on the principles of cameralism, the German science of public administration that emerged in the decades following the Thirty Years' War. Influential throughout the German lands, cameralism held that monarchy was the best of all forms of government, that all elements of society should be placed at the service of the state, and that, in turn, the state should make use of its resources and authority to improve society.

**cameralism** View that monarchy was the best form of government, that all elements of society should serve the monarch, and that, in turn, the state should use its resources and authority to increase the public good.

## Catherine the Great of Russia

Catherine the Great of Russia (r. 1762–1796) was one of the most remarkable rulers of her age, and the French philosophes adored her. Catherine was a German princess from Anhalt-Zerbst (AHN-hahlt ZEHRBST), an insignificant principality sandwiched between Prussia and Saxony. Her father commanded a regiment of the Prussian army, but her mother was related to the Romanovs of Russia.

At the age of fifteen Catherine's Romanov connection made her a suitable bride for the heir to the Russian throne. When her husband Peter III came to power during the Seven Years' War, his decision to withdraw Russian troops from the coalition against

CHAPTER LOCATOR | How did European views of nature change in this period? | What were the core principles of the Enlightenment? | What did enlightened absolutism mean?

**511**

**Catherine the Great** Strongly influenced by the Enlightenment, Catherine the Great cultivated the French philosophes and instituted moderate reforms, only to reverse them in the aftermath of Pugachev's rebellion. This equestrian portrait now hangs above her throne in the palace throne room in St. Petersburg. (Musée des Beaux-Arts, Chartres/The Bridgeman Art Library)

Prussia alienated the army. Catherine profited from his unpopularity to form a conspiracy to depose her husband. In 1762 Catherine's lover Gregory Orlov and his three brothers murdered Peter, and the German princess became empress of Russia.

Never questioning that absolute monarchy was the best form of government, Catherine set out to rule in an enlightened manner. She had three main goals. First, she worked hard to continue Peter the Great's effort to bring the culture of western Europe to Russia (see Chapter 16). To do so, she imported Western architects, sculptors, musicians, and intellectuals. She bought masterpieces of Western art and patronized the philosophes. Moreover, this intellectual ruler, who wrote plays and loved good talk, set the tone for the entire Russian nobility. Peter the Great westernized Russian armies, but it was Catherine who westernized the imagination of the Russian nobility.

Catherine's second goal was domestic reform, and she began her reign with sincere and ambitious projects. In 1767 she appointed a special legislative commission to prepare a new law code. This project was never completed, but Catherine did restrict the practice of torture and allowed limited religious toleration. She also tried to improve education and strengthen local government. The philosophes applauded these measures and hoped more would follow.

Such was not the case. In 1773 a common Cossack soldier named Emelian Pugachev (PYOO-gah-chehv) sparked a gigantic uprising of serfs. Proclaiming himself the true tsar, Pugachev issued orders abolishing serfdom, taxes, and army service. Thousands joined his cause, slaughtering landlords and officials over a vast area of southwestern Russia. Pugachev's untrained forces eventually proved no match for Catherine's noble-led army, and Pugachev was captured and executed.

Pugachev's rebellion put an end to any intentions Catherine might have had about reforming the system. The peasants were clearly dangerous, and her empire rested on the support of the nobility. After 1775 Catherine gave the nobles absolute control of their serfs, and she extended serfdom into new areas. In 1785 she formalized the nobility's privileged position, freeing nobles forever from taxes and state service. Under Catherine the Russian nobility attained its most exalted position, and serfdom entered its most oppressive phase.

Catherine's third goal was territorial expansion, and in this respect she was extremely successful. Her armies subjugated the last descendants of the Mongols and the Crimean Tartars and began the conquest of the Caucasus (KAW-kuh-suhs). Her greatest coup was the partition of Poland (Map 17.1). When, between 1768 and 1772, Catherine's armies scored unprecedented victories against the Turks and thereby threatened to disturb the balance of power between Russia and Austria in eastern Europe, Frederick of Prussia came forward with a deal. He proposed that Turkey be let off easily and that Prussia, Austria, and Russia each compensate itself by taking a slice of Polish territory. The first partition of Poland took place in 1772. Subsequent partitions in 1793 and 1795 gave away the rest of Polish territory, and Poland vanished from the map.

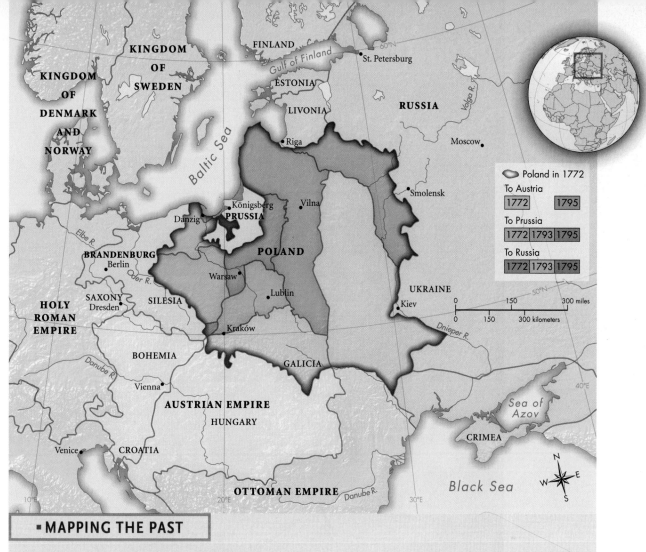

## Map 17.1 The Partition of Poland, 1772–1795

In 1772 war between Russia and Austria threatened over Russian gains from the Ottoman Empire. To satisfy desires for expansion without fighting, Prussia's Frederick the Great proposed that parts of Poland be divided among Austria, Prussia, and Russia. In 1793 and 1795 the three powers partitioned the remainder, and the ancient republic of Poland vanished from the map.

**ANALYZING THE MAP** Of the three powers that divided the kingdom of Poland, which benefited the most? How did the partition affect the geographical boundaries of each state, and what was the significance? What border with the former Poland remained unchanged? Why do you think this was the case?

**CONNECTIONS** Why was Poland vulnerable to partition in the latter half of the eighteenth century? What does it say about European politics at the time that a country could simply cease to exist on the map? Could that happen today?

To complete this activity online, go to the Online Study Guide at bedfordstmartins.com/mckaywestunderstanding.

## The Austrian Habsburgs

Maria Theresa (r. 1740–1780) of Austria also set out to reform her nation, although traditional power politics was a more important motivation for her than were Enlightenment teachings. Maria Theresa was a remarkable but old-fashioned absolutist. Her more radical son, Joseph II (r. 1780–1790), drew on Enlightenment ideals, earning the title of "revolutionary emperor."

CHAPTER LOCATOR | How did European views of nature change in this period? | What were the core principles of the Enlightenment? | What did enlightened absolutism mean?

513

**Maria Theresa** The empress and her husband pose with eleven of their sixteen children at Schönbrunn palace in this family portrait by court painter Martin Meytens (1695–1770). Joseph, the heir to the throne, stands at the center of the star on the floor. Wealthy women often had very large families, in part because they, unlike poor women, seldom nursed their babies. (Réunion des Musées Nationaux/Art Resource, NY)

Emerging from the long War of the Austrian Succession in 1748 with the loss of Silesia, Maria Theresa was determined to introduce reforms that would make the state stronger and more efficient. First, she introduced measures aimed at limiting the papacy's political influence in her realm. Second, a whole series of administrative reforms strengthened the central bureaucracy, smoothed out some provincial differences, and revamped the tax system, taxing even the lands of nobles, previously exempt from taxation. Third, the government sought to improve the lot of the agricultural population, cautiously reducing the power of lords over their hereditary serfs and their partially free peasant tenants.

Coregent with his mother from 1765 onward and a strong supporter of change, Joseph II moved forward rapidly when he came to the throne in 1780. Most notably, Joseph abolished serfdom in 1781, and in 1789 he decreed that peasants could pay landlords in cash rather than through compulsory labor on their land. This measure was rejected not only by the nobility but also by the peasants it was intended to help, because they lacked the necessary cash. When Joseph died prematurely at forty-nine, the entire Habsburg empire was in turmoil. His brother Leopold II (r. 1790–1792) canceled Joseph's radical edicts in order to re-establish order.

Despite differences, Joseph II and the other eastern European absolutists of the later eighteenth century combined old-fashioned state-building with the culture and critical thinking of the Enlightenment. In doing so, they succeeded in expanding the role of the state in the life of society. Their failure to implement policies we would recognize as humane and enlightened—such as abolishing serfdom—may reveal inherent limitations in Enlightenment thinking about equality and social justice, rather than in their execution of Enlightenment programs. The fact that leading philosophes supported rather than criticized eastern rulers' policies suggests some of the blinders of the era.

## Jewish Life and the Limits of Enlightened Absolutism

Perhaps the best example of the limitations of enlightened absolutism are the debates surrounding the possible emancipation of the Jews. Europe's small Jewish populations lived under highly discriminatory laws. For the most part, Jews were confined to tiny, overcrowded ghettos, were excluded by law from most business and professional activities, and could be ordered out of a kingdom at a moment's notice. Still, a very few did manage to succeed and to obtain the right of permanent settlement, usually by performing some special service for the state.

In the eighteenth century, an Enlightenment movement known as the Haskalah emerged from within the European Jewish community, led by the Prussian philosopher Moses Mendelssohn (MEN-dul-suhn) (1729–1786). (See "Individuals in Society: Moses Mendelssohn and the Jewish Enlightenment," page 516.) Christian and Jewish Enlightenment philosophers, including Mendelssohn, began to advocate for freedom and civil rights for European Jews. In an era of reason, tolerance, and universality, they argued, restrictions on religious grounds could not stand.

**Haskalah** The Jewish Enlightenment of the second half of the eighteenth century, led by the Prussian philosopher Moses Mendelssohn.

Arguments for tolerance won some ground. The British Parliament passed a law allowing naturalization of Jews in 1753, but later repealed the law due to public outrage. The most progressive reforms took place under Austrian emperor Joseph II. His liberal edicts included measures intended to integrate Jews more fully into society, including eligibility for military service, admission to higher education and artisanal trades, and removal of requirements for special clothing or emblems. Welcomed by many Jews, these reforms raised fears among traditionalists of assimilation into the general population.

**The Pale of Settlement, 1791**

Many monarchs refused to entertain the idea of emancipation. Although he permitted freedom of religion to his Christian subjects, Frederick the Great of Prussia firmly opposed any general emancipation for the Jews. Catherine the Great, who acquired most of Poland's large Jewish population when she annexed part of that country in the late eighteenth century, similarly refused. In 1791 she established the Pale of Settlement, a territory including parts of modern-day Poland, Latvia, Lithuania, Ukraine, and Belorussia, in which most Jews were required to live.

The first European state to remove all restrictions on the Jews was France under the French Revolution. Over the next hundred years, Jews gradually won full legal and civil rights throughout the rest of western Europe. Emancipation in eastern Europe took even longer and aroused more conflict and violence.

CHAPTER LOCATOR | How did European views of nature change in this period? | What were the core principles of the Enlightenment? | What did enlightened absolutism mean?

515

# INDIVIDUALS IN SOCIETY

## Moses Mendelssohn and the Jewish Enlightenment

**IN 1743 A SMALL, HUMPBACKED JEWISH BOY WITH** a stammer left his poor parents in Dessau (DEH-sow) in central Germany and walked eighty miles to Berlin, the capital of Frederick the Great's Prussia. According to one story, when the boy reached the Rosenthaler (ROH-zuhn-tah-luhr) Gate, the only one through which Jews could pass, he told the inquiring watchman that his name was Moses and that he had come to Berlin "to learn." The watchman laughed and waved him through. "Go Moses, the sea has opened before you."*

In Berlin the young Mendelssohn studied Jewish law and eked out a living copying Hebrew manuscripts in a beautiful hand. But he was soon fascinated by an intellectual world that had been closed to him in the Dessau ghetto. There, like most Jews throughout central Europe, he had spoken Yiddish — a mixture of German, Polish, and Hebrew. Now, working mainly on his own, he mastered German; he learned Latin, Greek, French, and English; and he studied mathematics and Enlightenment philosophy. Word of his exceptional abilities spread in Berlin's Jewish community (the dwelling of 1,500 of the city's 100,000 inhabitants). He began tutoring the children of a wealthy Jewish silk merchant, and he soon became the merchant's clerk and later his partner. But his great passion remained the life of the mind and the spirit, which he avidly pursued in his off hours.

Gentle and unassuming in his personal life, Mendelssohn was a bold thinker. Reading eagerly in Western philosophy since antiquity, he was, as a pious Jew, soon convinced that Enlightenment teachings need not be opposed to Jewish thought and religion. He concluded that reason could complement and strengthen religion, although each would retain its integrity as a separate sphere.† Developing his idea in his first great work, "On the Immortality of the Soul" (1767), Mendelssohn used the neutral setting of a philosophical dialogue between Socrates and his followers in ancient Greece to argue that the human soul lived forever. In refusing to bring religion and critical thinking into conflict, he was strongly influenced by contemporary German philosophers who argued similarly on behalf of Christianity. He reflected the way the German Enlightenment generally supported established religion, in contrast to the French Enlightenment, which attacked it.

Mendelssohn's treatise on the human soul captivated the educated German public, which marveled that a Jew could have written a philosophical masterpiece. In the excitement, a Christian zealot named Lavater challenged Mendelssohn in a pamphlet to accept Christianity or to demonstrate how the Christian faith was not "reasonable." Replying politely but passionately, the Jewish philosopher affirmed that his studies had only strengthened him in his faith, although he did not seek to convert anyone not born into Judaism. Rather, he urged toleration in religious matters and spoke up courageously against Jewish oppression.

Orthodox Jew and German philosophe, Moses Mendelssohn serenely combined two very different worlds. He built a bridge from the ghetto to the dominant culture over which many Jews would pass, including his novelist daughter Dorothea and his famous grandson, the composer Felix Mendelssohn.

### QUESTIONS FOR ANALYSIS

1. How did Mendelssohn seek to influence Jewish religious thought in his time?
2. How do Mendelssohn's ideas compare with those of the French Enlightenment?

*H. Kupferberg, *The Mendelssohns: Three Generations of Genius* (New York: Charles Scribner's Sons, 1972), p. 3.

†D. Sorkin, *Moses Mendelssohn and the Religious Enlightenment* (Berkeley: University of California Press, 1996), pp. 8 ff.

**Lavater (right) attempts to convert Mendelssohn, in a painting of an imaginary encounter by Moritz Oppenheim.** (Collection of the Judah L. Magnes Museum, Berkeley)

# ← LOOKING BACK LOOKING AHEAD →

HAILED AS THE ORIGINS of modern thought, the scientific revolution must also be seen as a product of its past. Medieval universities gave rise to important new scholarship, and the ambition and wealth of Renaissance patrons nurtured intellectual curiosity. Religious faith also impacted the scientific revolution, inspiring thinkers to understand the glory of God's creation, while bringing censure and personal tragedy to others. Natural philosophers following Copernicus pioneered new methods of observing and explaining nature while drawing on centuries-old traditions of astrology, alchemy, and magic.

The Enlightenment ideas of the eighteenth century were a similar blend of past and present; they could serve as much to bolster authoritarian regimes as to inspire revolutionaries to fight for individual rights and liberties. Although the Enlightenment fostered critical thinking about everything from science to religion, the majority of Europeans, including many prominent thinkers, remained devout Christians.

The achievements of the scientific revolution and the Enlightenment are undeniable. Key Western values of rationalism, human rights and open-mindedness were born from these movements. With their new notions of progress and social improvement, Europeans would embark on important revolutions in industry and politics in the century that followed. Nonetheless, others have seen a darker side. For these critics, the mastery over nature permitted by the scientific revolution now threatens to overwhelm the earth's fragile equilibrium, and the Enlightenment belief in the universal application of reason can lead to arrogance and intolerance, particularly intolerance of other people's spiritual, cultural, and political values. Such vivid debate about the legacy of these intellectual and scientific developments testifies to their continuing importance in today's world. ∎

- **For a list of suggested readings for this chapter, visit** *bedfordstmartins.com/mckaywestunderstanding*.

- **For primary sources from this period, see** *Sources of Western Society*, Second Edition.

- **For Web sites, images, and documents related to topics in this chapter, see Make History at** *bedfordstmartins.com/mckaywestunderstanding*.

CHAPTER LOCATOR | How did European views of nature change in this period? | What were the core principles of the Enlightenment? | What did enlightened absolutism mean?

517

# ▪ Chapter 17 Study Guide

Online Study Guide
bedfordstmartins.com/mckaywestunderstanding

## Step 1

**GETTING STARTED** Below are basic terms about this period in the history of Western civilization. Can you identify each term below and explain why it matters? To do this exercise online, go to bedfordstmartins.com/mckaywestunderstanding.

| TERMS | WHO (OR WHAT) AND WHEN | WHY IT MATTERS |
|---|---|---|
| natural philosophy, p. 490 | | |
| Copernican hypothesis, p. 492 | | |
| experimental method, p. 494 | | |
| law of inertia, p. 494 | | |
| law of universal gravitation, p. 495 | | |
| empiricism, p. 495 | | |
| Cartesian dualism, p. 496 | | |
| Enlightenment, p. 498 | | |
| rationalism, p. 499 | | |
| philosophes, p. 500 | | |
| reading revolution, p. 504 | | |
| salons, p. 505 | | |
| rococo, p. 505 | | |
| public sphere, p. 505 | | |
| enlightened absolutism, p. 510 | | |
| cameralism, p. 511 | | |
| Haskalah, p. 515 | | |

## Step 2

**MOVING BEYOND THE BASICS** The exercise below requires a more advanced understanding of the chapter material. Examine the contributions of key figures of the scientific revolution by filling in the chart below with descriptions of the major contributions of key people. Be sure to include both concrete discoveries and contributions to the development of the scientific method. When you are finished, consider the following questions: How did these thinkers build off of each other's discoveries and insights? What common goals did they share? To do this exercise online, go to bedfordstmartins.com/mckaywestunderstanding.

| | DISCOVERIES AND CONTRIBUTIONS |
|---|---|
| Nicolaus Copernicus | |
| Tycho Brahe | |
| Johannes Kepler | |
| Francis Bacon | |
| René Descartes | |
| Galileo Galilei | |
| Isaac Newton | |

**PUTTING IT ALL TOGETHER** Now that you've reviewed key elements of the chapter, take a step back and try to see the big picture. Remember to use specific examples from the chapter in your answers. To do this exercise online, go to bedfordstmartins.com/mckaywestunderstanding.

### THE SCIENTIFIC REVOLUTION

- What was revolutionary about the scientific revolution? How did the study of nature in the sixteenth century differ from the study of nature in the Middle Ages?

- How did Newton's ideas build on the contributions of his predecessors? Is it fair to describe his work as the culmination of the scientific revolution? Why or why not?

- How did religious belief both stimulate and hinder scientific inquiry?

### THE ENLIGHTENMENT

- How did the scientific revolution contribute to the emergence of the Enlightenment? What new ideas about the power and potential of human reason were central to both developments?

- In what ways did the Enlightenment influence eighteenth-century European society and politics? In what ways was its influence limited?

- How did Enlightenment thinkers deal with issues of gender and race? What does this tell us about the nature of the Enlightenment?

### ENLIGHTENED ABSOLUTISM

- Why did many Enlightenment thinkers see absolute monarchy as a potential force for good? What light do the political views of the philosophes shed on the nature and limits of Enlightenment thinking?

- How did Enlightenment ideas contribute to the expansion of the role of the state in central and eastern European society? What existing social and economic structures were least susceptible to enlightened reform? Why?

■ **In Your Own Words** Imagine that you must explain Chapter 17 to someone who hasn't read it. What would be the most important points to include and why?

# 18

# The Expansion of Europe

## 1650–1800

Absolutism and aristocracy, a combination of raw power and elegant refinement, were a world apart from the common people. For most people in the eighteenth century, life remained a struggle with poverty and uncertainty, with the landlord and the tax collector. In 1700 peasants on the land and artisans in their shops lived little better than had their ancestors in the Middle Ages, primarily because European societies still could not produce very much as measured by modern standards. Despite the hard work of ordinary men and women, there was seldom enough good food, warm clothing, and decent housing. The idea of progress, of substantial improvement in the lives of great numbers of people, was still the dream of only a small elite in fashionable salons.

Yet the economic basis of European life was beginning to change. In the course of the eighteenth century, the European economy emerged from the long crisis of the seventeenth century, responded to challenges, and began to expand once again. Population resumed its growth, while colonial empires developed and colonial elites prospered. Some areas were more fortunate than others. The rising Atlantic powers—Holland, France, and above all England—and their colonies led the way. The expansion of agriculture, industry, trade, and population marked the beginning of a surge comparable to that of the eleventh- and twelfth-century springtime of European civilization. But this time, broadly based expansion was not cut short by plague and famine. This time the response to new challenges led toward one of the most influential developments in human history, the Industrial Revolution, considered in Chapter 21. ■

**Life in the Expanding Europe of the Eighteenth Century.** The activities of the bustling cosmopolitan port of Marseilles were common to ports across Europe in the eighteenth century. Here a wealthy Frenchwoman greets a group of foreign merchants, while dockhands struggle to shift their heavy loads. (Musée de la Marine, Paris/Gianni Dagli Orti/The Art Archive)

# Chapter Preview

▶ **How did European agriculture change between 1650 and 1800?**

▶ **Why did the population rise in the eighteenth century?**

▶ **What led to the growth of rural industry?**

▶ **What were guilds and why were they controversial?**

▶ **What role did colonial markets play in Europe's development?**

# ▼ How did European agriculture change between 1650 and 1800?

At the end of the seventeenth century the economy of Europe was agrarian. At least 80 percent of western Europeans drew their livelihoods from agriculture. In eastern Europe the percentage was considerably higher. Men and women were tied to the land, plowing fields and sowing seed, reaping harvests and storing grain. Yet even in a rich agricultural region such as the Po Valley in northern Italy, by modern standards, output was distressingly low.

In most regions of Europe in the sixteenth and seventeenth centuries, climatic conditions produced poor or disastrous harvests every eight or nine years. Unbalanced and inadequate food in famine years made people extremely susceptible to illnesses such as influenza and smallpox. As a result, in famine years the number of deaths soared far above normal. A third of a village's population might disappear in a year or two. But new developments in agricultural technology and methods gradually brought an end to the ravages of hunger in western Europe.

## The Legacy of the Open-Field System

Why, in the late seventeenth century, did Europeans produce barely enough food to survive? The answer lies in the pattern of farming that had developed in the Middle Ages. From the Middle Ages up to the seventeenth century, much of Europe was farmed through the open-field system. The land to be cultivated was divided into several large fields, which were in turn cut up into long, narrow strips. The fields were open, and the strips were not enclosed into small plots by fences or hedges. The whole peasant village followed the same pattern of plowing, sowing, and harvesting in accordance with tradition and the village leaders.

The ever-present problem was soil exhaustion. Wheat planted year after year in a field will deplete nitrogen in the soil. Since the supply of manure for fertilizer was limited, the only way for the land to recover was to lie fallow for a period of time. Clover and other annual grasses that grew in unplanted fields restored nutrients to the soil and also provided food for livestock. In the early Middle Ages a year of fallow was alternated with a year of cropping; then three-year rotations were introduced, especially on more fertile lands. On each strip of land, a year of wheat or rye was followed by a year of oats or beans and only then by a year of fallow. The three-year system was an important achievement because cash crops could be grown two years out of three, rather than only one year in two.

Traditional village rights reinforced communal patterns of farming. In addition to rotating field crops in a uniform way, villages maintained open meadows for hay and natural pasture. In many places the harvest was followed by a brief period, also established by tradition, for the gleaning of grain. In this process, poor women would go through the fields picking up the few single grains that had fallen to the ground in the course of the harvest. Many villages were surrounded by woodlands, also held in common, which provided essential firewood, building materials, and nutritional roots and berries.

In the age of absolutism and nobility, the state and landlords continued to levy heavy taxes and high rents, thereby stripping peasants of much of their meager earnings. Generally speaking, the peasants of eastern Europe were worse off. As we saw in Chapter 16, they were serfs bound to their lords in hereditary service. In much of eastern Europe, working five or six days per week on the lord's land for no pay was not uncommon.

Social conditions were better in western Europe, where peasants were generally free from serfdom. In France, western Germany, England, and the Low Countries (modern-day Belgium and the Netherlands), they owned land and could pass it on to their chil-

Chapter 18
**The Expansion of Europe**
**522** 1650–1800

CHAPTER LOCATOR | How did European agriculture change between 1650 and 1800?

dren. Yet life in the village was unquestionably hard, and poverty was the great reality for most people. Owning only a portion of the land that they worked (the village lord typically owned as much as half), poor peasants were forced to seek wages in a variety of jobs in order to eke out a living.

## The Agricultural Revolution

One way for European peasants to improve their difficult position was to revolt and take land from those who owned it but did no labor. Yet the social and political conditions that sustained the ruling elites were deeply rooted, and powerful forces stood ready to crush protest. Only with the coming of the French Revolution in 1789 were European peasants, mainly in France, able to improve their position by means of radical mass action. Technological progress offered another possibility. If peasants (and their noble landlords) could replace the idle fallow with crops, they could greatly increase the land under cultivation. So remarkable were the possibilities and the results that historians have often spoken of the progressive elimination of the fallow, which occurred gradually throughout Europe from about 1650 to 1850, as an agricultural revolution.

Because grain crops exhaust the soil and make fallowing necessary, the secret to eliminating the fallow lies in alternating grain with nitrogen-storing crops. The most important of these land-reviving crops are peas and beans, root crops such as turnips and potatoes, and clovers and grasses. As the eighteenth century went on, the number of crops that were systematically rotated grew. New patterns of organization allowed some farmers to develop increasingly sophisticated patterns of crop rotation to suit different kinds of soils and continual experimentation, fueled by developments in the scientific revolution (see Chapter 17), led to more methodical farming.

Improvements in farming had multiple effects. The new crops made ideal feed for animals; with more fodder, hay, and root crops for the winter months, peasants and larger farmers could build up their herds of cattle and sheep. More animals meant more meat and better diets. More animals also meant more manure for fertilizer and therefore more grain.

Advocates of the new crop rotations, who included an emerging group of experimental scientists, some government officials, and a few big landowners, believed that new methods were impossible within the traditional framework of open fields and common rights. They argued that innovating agriculturalists needed to enclose and consolidate their scattered holdings into compact, fenced-in fields in order to farm more effectively. In doing so, the innovators also needed to enclose their individual shares of a village's natural pastureland, the common. According to proponents of this movement, known as enclosure, a revolution in village life and organization was the necessary price of technical progress.

That price seemed too high to many poor rural people who had small, inadequate holdings or very little land at all. Poor peasants used commonly held pastureland to graze livestock, and marshlands or forest outside the village as a source for foraged goods that could make the difference between survival and famine in harsh times. Thus, when the small landholders and the village poor could effectively oppose the enclosure of the

## Chapter Chronology

| | |
|---|---|
| 1650–1850 | Agricultural revolution |
| 1651–1663 | British Navigation Acts |
| 1652–1674 | Anglo-Dutch wars |
| 1700–1790 | Height of Atlantic slave trade; expansion of rural industry in Europe |
| 1701–1763 | British and French mercantilist wars of empire |
| 1720–1722 | Last outbreak of bubonic plague in Europe |
| 1720–1789 | Growth of European population |
| 1756–1763 | Seven Years' War |
| 1760–1815 | Height of parliamentary enclosure in England |
| 1763 | Treaty of Paris; France cedes its possessions in India and North America |
| 1770 | James Cook claims the east coast of Australia for England |
| 1776 | Smith, *Inquiry into the Nature and Causes of the Wealth of Nations* |
| 1805 | British takeover of India complete |
| 1807 | British slave trade abolished |

**agricultural revolution** The period in Europe from the mid-seventeenth through the mid-nineteenth centuries during which great agricultural progress was made and the fallow, or idling of a field to replenish nutrients, was gradually eliminated.

**enclosure** The movement to fence in fields in order to farm more effectively, at the expense of poor peasants who relied on common fields for farming and pasture.

Why did the population rise in the eighteenth century?

What led to the growth of rural industry?

What were guilds and why were they controversial?

What role did colonial markets play in Europe's development?

523

**Enclosure Mapmakers in Henlow, England** This rare image shows the process of making new maps to document the enclosure of fields in England. Drawn on the enclosure map for Henlow, Bedfordshire, around 1795, the scene shows a surveyor and his assistants at work. (Bedford and Luton Archives Service, Bedfordshire, UK)

open fields and the common lands, they did so. In many countries they found allies among the larger, predominately noble landowners who were also wary of enclosure because it required large investments in purchasing and fencing land and thus posed risks for them as well.

The old system of unenclosed open fields and the new system of continuous rotation coexisted in Europe for a long time. Open fields could still be found in much of France and Germany as late as the nineteenth century. Throughout the end of the eighteenth century, the new system of enclosure was extensively adopted only in the Low Countries and England.

## The Leadership of the Low Countries and England

The new methods of the agricultural revolution originated in the Low Countries. Seventeenth-century republican Holland, already the most advanced country in Europe in many areas of human endeavor (see Chapter 16), led the way. By the middle of the seventeenth century intensive farming was well established, and the innovations of enclosed fields, continuous rotation, heavy manuring, and a wide variety of crops were all present. Agriculture was highly specialized and commercialized.

One reason for early Dutch leadership in farming was that the area was one of the most densely populated in Europe. In order to feed themselves and provide employment, the Dutch were forced at an early date to seek maximum yields from their land and to increase the cultivated area through the draining of marshes and swamps. The pressure of population was connected with the second cause: the growth of towns and cities. Stimu-

Chapter 18
**The Expansion of Europe**
**1650–1800**

524

CHAPTER LOCATOR | How did European agriculture change between 1650 and 1800?

*The Vegetable Market,* 1662 The wealth and well-being of the industrious, capitalistic Dutch shine forth in this winsome market scene by Dutch artist Hendrick Sorgh. The market woman's baskets are filled with delicious fresh produce that ordinary citizens can afford—eloquent testimony to the responsive, enterprising character of Dutch agriculture. (Rijksmuseum, Amsterdam)

lated by commerce and overseas trade, Amsterdam grew from thirty thousand to two hundred thousand inhabitants in the seventeenth century. The growing urban population provided Dutch peasants with markets for all they could produce and allowed each region to specialize in what it did best.

The English learned much from the Dutch example. Drainage and water control were one subject in which they received instruction. In the first half of the seventeenth century Dutch experts made a great contribution to draining the extensive marshes, or fens, of England. The most famous of these Dutch engineers, Cornelius Vermuyden, directed one large drainage project in Yorkshire and another in Cambridgeshire. In the Cambridge fens, Vermuyden and his Dutch workers eventually reclaimed forty thousand acres, which were then farmed intensively in the Dutch manner.

Jethro Tull (1674–1741) was an important English innovator. A true son of the early Enlightenment, Tull adopted a critical attitude toward accepted ideas about farming and tried to develop better methods through empirical research. He was especially enthusiastic about using horses, rather than slower-moving oxen, for plowing. He also advocated sowing seed with drilling equipment rather than scattering it by hand. Drilling distributed seed in an even manner and at the proper depth. There were also improvements in livestock, achieved through selective breeding for desirable characteristics.

By the mid-eighteenth century English agriculture was in the process of a long but radical transformation. The eventual result was that by 1870 English farmers were producing 300 percent more food than they had produced in 1700, even though the number of people working the land had increased by only 14 percent. Growth in production was achieved in part by land enclosures. About half the farmland in England was enclosed through private initiatives prior to 1700. From the 1760s to the end of the Napoleonic era in 1815, a series of acts of Parliament enclosed most of the remaining common land.

By eliminating common rights and greatly reducing the access of poor men and women to the land, the eighteenth-century enclosure movement marked the completion of two

Why did the population rise in the eighteenth century?

What led to the growth of rural industry?

What were guilds and why were they controversial?

What role did colonial markets play in Europe's development?

proletarianization The transformation of large numbers of small peasant farmers into landless rural wage earners.

major historical developments in England—the rise of market-oriented estate agriculture and the emergence of a landless rural proletariat. By the early nineteenth century a tiny minority of English and Scottish landowners held most of the land and pursued profits aggressively, leasing their holdings through agents at competitive prices to middle-size farmers, who relied on landless laborers for their workforce. In no other European country had this proletarianization (proh-luh-tay-ree-uh-nuh-ZAY-shun)—this transformation of large numbers of small peasant farmers into landless rural wage earners—gone so far. England's village poor found the cost of change heavy and unjust.

▼ # Why did the population rise in the eighteenth century?

Another factor that affected the existing order of life and forced economic changes in the eighteenth century was the beginning of the population explosion. Explosive growth continued in Europe until the twentieth century, by which time it was affecting non-western areas of the globe. In this section we examine the causes of the population growth; the following section considers how the challenge of more mouths to feed and more hands to employ affected the European economy.

## Long-standing Obstacles to Population Growth

Until 1700 the total population of Europe grew slowly much of the time, and it followed an irregular cyclical pattern. This cyclical pattern had a great influence on many aspects of social and economic life. The Black Death caused a sharp drop in population and food prices after 1350 and also created a labor shortage throughout Europe. Some economic historians calculate that for many common people in western Europe, the later Middle Ages was an era of exceptional well-being.

But this well-being eroded in the course of the sixteenth century. The second great surge of population growth outstripped the growth of agricultural production after about 1500. There was less food per person, and food prices rose more rapidly than wages, a development intensified by the inflow of precious metals from the Americas (see Chapter 15) and a general, if uneven, European price revolution. The result was a substantial decline in living standards throughout Europe. By 1600 the pressure of population on resources was severe in much of Europe, and widespread poverty was an undeniable reality.

For this reason, population growth slowed and stopped in seventeenth-century Europe. Births and deaths, fertility and mortality, were in a crude but effective balance. The population grew modestly in normal years at a rate of perhaps 0.5 to 1 percent, or enough to double the population in 70 to 140 years.

Although population growth of even 1 percent per year seems fairly modest, it will produce a very large increase over a long period: in three hundred years it will result in sixteen times as many people. Yet such gigantic increases did not occur in agrarian Europe. In certain abnormal years and tragic periods—the Black Death was only the most extreme example—many more people died than were born, and total population fell sharply, even catastrophically. A number of years of modest growth would then be necessary to make up for those who had died in an abnormal year. Such increases in deaths occurred periodically in the seventeenth century on a local and regional scale, and these demographic crises combined to check the growth of population until after 1700.

The grim reapers of demographic crisis were famine, epidemic disease, and war. Famine, the inevitable result of low yields and periodic crop failures, was particularly murder-

Chapter 18
The Expansion of Europe
1650–1800

526

CHAPTER LOCATOR | How did European agriculture change between 1650 and 1800?

ous because it was accompanied by disease. Famine stunned and weakened a population, and disease finished it off. Disease, as the example of the Black Death illustrates, could also ravage the population independently of famine.

The indirect effects of war were even more harmful than the organized killing. Armies passed all manner of contagious diseases throughout the countryside. Armies also requisitioned scarce food supplies and disrupted the agricultural cycle while battles destroyed precious crops and farmlands. The Thirty Years' War witnessed all possible combinations of distress. The number of inhabitants in the German states alone declined by more than two-thirds in some large areas and by at least one-third almost everywhere else.

## The New Pattern of the Eighteenth Century

In the eighteenth century the population of Europe began to grow markedly. This increase in numbers occurred in all regions of Europe. The size of the European population grew steadily from 1720 to 1789, with especially dramatic increases after about 1750 (Figure 18.1).

What caused this population growth? In some areas women had more babies than before because new opportunities for employment in rural industry (see page 528) allowed them to marry at an earlier age. But the basic cause of European population increase as a whole was a decline in mortality—fewer deaths.

One of the primary reasons behind this decline was the mysterious disappearance of the bubonic plague. Following the Black Death in the fourteenth century, plagues had remained part of the European experience all the way through the first two decades of the eighteenth century, striking again and again with savage force, particularly in towns. Exactly why plague disappeared is unknown. Stricter measures of quarantine in Mediterranean ports and along the Austrian border with Turkey helped by carefully isolating human carriers of plague. Chance and plain good luck were probably just as important.

Advances in medical knowledge did not contribute much to reducing the death rate in the eighteenth century. The most important advance in preventive medicine in this period was inoculation against smallpox, and this great improvement was long confined mainly to England, probably doing little to reduce deaths throughout Europe until the latter part of the century. However, improvements in the water supply and sewage, which were frequently promoted by strong absolutist monarchies, resulted in somewhat better public health and helped reduce such diseases as typhoid and typhus in some urban areas of western Europe. Improvements in water supply and the drainage of swamps also reduced Europe's large insect population, including disease-carrying flies and mosquitoes. Thus early public health measures helped the decline in mortality that began with the disappearance of plague and continued into the early nineteenth century.

Human beings also became more successful in their efforts to safeguard the supply of food. The eighteenth century was a time of considerable canal and road building in western Europe. These advances in transportation, which were also among the more positive aspects of strong absolutist states, lessened the impact of local crop failure and

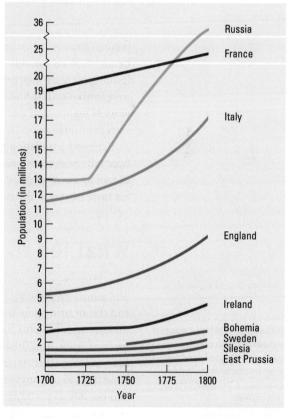

**Figure 18.1** **The Increase of Population in Europe in the Eighteenth Century** Population grew across Europe in the eighteenth century, though the most dramatic increases occurred after 1750. Russia experienced the largest increase and emerged as Europe's most populous state as natural increase was complemented by growth from territorial expansion.

Why did the population rise in the eighteenth century?

What led to the growth of rural industry?

What were guilds and why were they controversial?

What role did colonial markets play in Europe's development?

The Plague at Marseilles The bishop of Marseilles blesses victims of the plague that overwhelmed Marseilles in 1720. Some hundred thousand people died in the outbreak, which was the last great episode of plague in western Europe. (Louvre/Réunion des Musées Nationaux/Art Resource, NY)

famine. Emergency supplies could be brought in, and localized starvation became less frequent. Wars became less destructive than in the seventeenth century and spread fewer epidemics. Nutritious new foods, particularly the potato from South America, were introduced. In short, population grew in the eighteenth century primarily because years of higher than average death rates were less catastrophic. Famines, epidemics, and wars continued to occur and to affect population growth, but their severity moderated.

Renewed population growth in the eighteenth century intensified the imbalance between the number of people and the economic opportunities available to them. At a time of rapidly rising population, improvements in agricultural efficiency lessened the need for rural laborers. The rural poor were forced to look for new ways to make a living.

## ▼ What led to the growth of rural industry?

The growth of population increased the number of rural workers with little or no land, and this in turn contributed to the development of industry in rural areas. The poor in the countryside increasingly needed to supplement their agricultural earnings with other types of work, and urban capitalists were eager to employ them, often at lower wages than urban workers received. Cottage industry, which consisted of manufacturing with hand tools in peasant cottages and work sheds, grew markedly in the eighteenth century and became a crucial feature of the European economy.

**cottage industry** A stage of industrial development in which rural workers used hand tools in their homes to manufacture goods on a large scale for sale in a market.

**putting-out system** The eighteenth-century system of rural industry in which a merchant loaned raw materials to cottage workers, who processed them and returned the finished products to the merchant.

### The Putting-Out System

Cottage industry was often organized through the putting-out system. The two main participants in the putting-out system were the merchant capitalist and the rural worker. In this system, the merchant loaned, or "put out," raw materials to cottage workers,

Chapter 18
**The Expansion of Europe**
**528** 1650–1800

CHAPTER LOCATOR | How did European agriculture change between 1650 and 1800?

**The Weaver's Repose** This painting by Decker Cornelis Gerritz (1594–1637) captures the pleasure of release from long hours of toil in cottage industry. The loom realistically dominates the cramped living space and the family's modest possessions. (Musées Royaux des Beaux-Arts, Brussels. Copyright A.C.I.)

who processed the raw materials in their own homes and returned the finished products to the merchant. As industries grew in scale and complexity, production was often broken into many stages. For example, a merchant would provide raw wool to one group of workers for spinning into thread. He would then pass the thread to another group of workers to be bleached, to another for dying, and to another for weaving into cloth. The merchant paid outworkers by the piece and proceeded to sell the finished product to regional, national, or international markets.

The putting-out system grew because it had competitive advantages. Underemployed labor was abundant, and poor peasants and landless laborers would work for low wages. Since production in the countryside was unregulated, workers and merchants could change procedures and experiment as they saw fit. Because workers did not need to meet rigid guild standards, cottage industry became capable of producing many kinds of goods. Although luxury goods for the rich, such as exquisite tapestries and fine porcelain, demanded special training, close supervision, and centralized workshops, the limited skills of rural industry were sufficient for everyday articles.

Rural manufacturing did not spread across Europe at an even rate. It developed most successfully in England, particularly for the spinning and weaving of woolen cloth. By 1500 half of England's textiles were being produced in the countryside. By 1700 English industry was generally more rural than urban and heavily reliant on the putting-out system. Most continental countries, with the exception of Flanders and the Netherlands, developed rural industry more slowly. The latter part of the eighteenth century witnessed a remarkable expansion of rural industry in certain densely populated regions of continental Europe (Map 18.1).

## The Lives of Rural Textile Workers

Until the nineteenth century, the industry that employed the most people in Europe was textiles. The making of linen, woolen, and eventually cotton cloth was the typical activity of cottage workers engaged in the putting-out system. A look inside the cottage of the English weaver illustrates a way of life as well as an economic system. The rural worker

Why did the population rise in the eighteenth century?

**What led to the growth of rural industry?**

What were guilds and why were they controversial?

What role did colonial markets play in Europe's development?

529

Persons per square mile
- More than 100
- 50 to 100
- Fewer than 50
- Textile production
- Metal production
- *Wool* Main textile product

## ▪ MAPPING THE PAST

## Map 18.1 Industry and Population in Eighteenth-Century Europe

The growth of cottage manufacturing in rural areas helped country people increase their income and contributed to population growth. The putting-out system began in England, and much of the work was in the textile industry. Cottage industry was also strong in the Low Countries (modern-day Belgium and Holland).

**ANALYZING THE MAP** What does this map suggest about the relationship between population density and the growth of textile production? What geographical characteristics seem to have played a role in encouraging this industry?

**CONNECTIONS** How would you account for the distribution of each type of cloth across Europe? Did metal production draw on different demographic and geographical conditions? Why do you think this was the case?

To complete this activity online, go to the Online Study Guide at bedfordstmartins.com/mckaywestunderstanding.

lived in a small cottage with tiny windows and little space. The cottage was often a single room that served as workshop, kitchen, and bedroom. There were only a few pieces of furniture, of which the weaver's loom was by far the largest and most important.

Handloom weaving was a family enterprise. All members of the family helped in the work. Operating the loom was considered a man's job, reserved for the male head of the family. Women and children worked at auxiliary tasks; they prepared the warp (vertical) threads and mounted them on the loom, wound threads on bobbins for the weft (horizontal) threads, and sometimes operated the warp frame while the father passed the shuttle.

The work of four or five spinners was needed to keep one weaver steadily employed. Since the weaver's family usually could not produce enough thread, alternate sources of

Chapter 18
The Expansion of Europe
1650–1800

530

CHAPTER LOCATOR

How did European agriculture change between 1650 and 1800?

labor were needed. Merchants turned to the wives and daughters of agricultural workers, who took on spinning work in their spare time. In England, many widows and single women also became "spinsters," so many in fact that the word became a synonym for an unmarried woman. In parts of Germany, spinning employed whole families and was not reserved for women. As the industry expanded and merchants covered ever greater distances in search of workers, they sometimes turned to local shopkeepers to manage the spinners in their villages.

Relations between workers and employers were often marked by sharp conflict. (See "Listening to the Past: Contrasting Views on the Effects of Rural Industry," page 532.) There were constant disputes over the weights of materials and the quality of finished work. Merchants accused workers of stealing raw materials, and weavers complained that merchants delivered underweight bales.

Conditions were particularly hard for female workers. While men could earn decent wages through long hours of arduous labor, women's wages were always terribly low. A single or widowed spinner faced a desperate struggle with poverty. Any period of illness or unemployment could spell disaster for her and her children.

From the merchant capitalist's point of view, the problem was not low wages but the control of rural labor. Scattered across the countryside, cottage workers were difficult to supervise and direct. Moreover, the pace of their work depended on the agricultural calendar. In spring and late summer planting and haymaking occupied all hands in the rural village, leading to shortages in the supply of thread. Merchants, whose livelihood depended on their ability to meet orders on time, bitterly resented their lack of control over rural labor. They accused workers—especially female spinners—of laziness, drunkenness, and immorality. If workers failed to produce enough thread, they reasoned, it must be because their wages were too high and they had little incentive to work.

Merchants thus insisted on maintaining the lowest possible wages to force the "idle" poor into productive labor. They also lobbied for, and obtained, new police powers over workers. Imprisonment and public whipping became common punishments for pilfering small amounts of yarn or cloth. For poor workers, their right to hold on to the bits and pieces left over in the production process was akin to the traditional peasant right of gleaning in common lands. With progress came the loss of traditional safeguards for the poor.

## The Industrious Revolution

One scholar has used the term industrious revolution to summarize the social and economic changes taking place in Europe in the late seventeenth and early eighteenth centuries.[1] This occurred as households in northwestern Europe reduced leisure time, stepped up the pace of work, and, most importantly, redirected the labor of women and children away from the production of goods for household consumption and toward wage work. In the countryside, the spread of cottage industry can be seen as one manifestation of the industrious revolution, while in the cities there was a rise in female employment outside the home (see page 535). By working harder and increasing the number of wageworkers, rural and urban households could purchase more goods, even in a time of stagnant or falling wages.

The effect of these changes is still debated. While some scholars lament the encroachment of longer work hours and stricter discipline, others insist that poor families made decisions based on their own self-interests. With more finished goods becoming available at lower prices, households sought cash income to participate in an emerging consumer economy.

The role of women and girls in this new economy is particularly controversial. When women entered the labor market, they almost always worked at menial, tedious jobs for very low wages. Yet when women earned their own wages, they also seem to have taken

**industrious revolution** The shift that occurred as families in northwestern Europe focused on earning wages instead of producing goods for household consumption; this reduced their economic self-sufficiency but increased their ability to purchase consumer goods.

Why did the population rise in the eighteenth century?

**What led to the growth of rural industry?**

What were guilds and why were they controversial?

What role did colonial markets play in Europe's development?

531

## Contrasting Views on the Effects of Rural Industry

*English commentators quickly noted the effects of rural industry on families and daily life. Some were greatly impressed by the rise in living standards made possible by the putting-out system, while others noted the rising economic inequality between merchant and workers and the power the former acquired over the latter. In the first excerpt, novelist and economic writer Daniel Defoe enthusiastically praises cottage industry. He notes that the labor of women and children in spinning and weaving brought in as much or more income than the man's agricultural work, allowing the family to eat well and be warmly clothed. It is interesting to note that Defoe assumes a rural world in which the process of enclosure is complete; poor men do not own their own land, but toil as wage laborers on the land of others. He also offers one explanation for the increasing use of Africans as slaves in British colonies: reliable wages from cottage industry meant that the English poor did not have to "sell themselves to the Plantations," thus leading plantation owners to seek other sources of labor.*

*The second source is a popular song written around 1700. Couched in the voice of the ruthless cloth merchant, it expresses the bitterness and resentment textile workers felt against the employers. One can imagine a group of weavers gathered together at the local tavern singing their protest on a rare break from work.*

### Daniel Defoe, *A Plan of the English Commerce.*

*Being a compleat prospect of the trade of this nation, as well the home trade as the foreign,* 1728

❝ [A] poor labouring man that goes abroad to his Day Work, and Husbandry, Hedging, Ditching, Threshing, Carting, &c. and brings home his Week's Wages, suppose at eight Pence to twelve Pence a Day, or in some Counties less; if he has a Wife and three or four Children to feed, and who get little or nothing for themselves, must fare hard, and live poorly; 'tis easy to suppose it must be so.

But if this Man's Wife and Children can at the same Time get Employment, if at next Door, or at the next Village there lives a Clothier, or a Bay Maker, or a stuff or Drugget Weaver;* the Manufacturer sends the poor Woman combed Wool, or carded Wool every Week to spin, and she gets eight Pence or nine Pence a day at home; the Weaver sends for her two little Children, and they work by the Loom, winding, filling quills, &c. and the two bigger Girls spin at home with their Mother, and these earn three Pence or four Pence a Day each: So that put it together, the Family at Home gets as much as the Father gets Abroad, and generally more.

This alters the Case extremely, the Family feels, it, they all feed better, are cloth'd warmer, and do not so easily nor so often fall into Misery and Distress; the Father gets them Food, and the Mother gets them Clothes; and as they grow, they do not run away to be Footmen

and Soldiers, Thieves and Beggars or sell themselves to the Plantations to avoid the Gaol and the Gallows, but have a Trade at their Hands, and every one can get their Bread.

N.B. I once went through a large populous manufacturing Town in England, and observ'd, that an Officer planted there, with a Serjeant and two Drums, had been beating up a long Time and could get no Recruits, except two or three Sots. . . . Enquiring the Reason of it, an honest Clothier of the Town answered me effectually thus, *The Case is plain,* says he, thus there is at this Time a brisk Demand for Goods, we have 1100 Looms, *added he,* in this Town and the Villages about it and not one of them want Work; and there is not a poor Child in the Town of above four Years old, but can earn his Bread; besides, there being so good a Trade at this Time, causes us to advance Wages a little and the Weaver and the Spinner get more than they used to do; and while it is so, they may beat the Heads of their Drums out, if they will, they'll get no Soldiers here. ❞

### Anonymous, "The Clothier's Delight"

*Or the rich Men's Joy, and the poor Men's Sorrow, wherein is exprest the Craftiness and Subtility of many Clothiers in England, by beating down their Workmen's Wages,* ca. 1700

❝ Of all sorts of callings that in England be
There is none that liveth so gallant as we;
Our trading maintains us as brave as a knight,
We live at our pleasure and take our delight;
We heapeth up richest treasure great store
Which we get by griping and grinding the poor.
   And this is a way for to fill up our purse
   Although we do get it with many a curse.

Throughout the whole kingdom, in country and town,
There is no danger of our trade going down,
So long as the Comber can work with his comb,
And also the Weaver weave with his lomb;
The Tucker and Spinner that spins all the year,
We will make them to earn their wages full dear.
   And this is a way, etc.

And first for the Combers, we will bring them down,
From eight groats a score until half a crown;
If at all they murmur and say 'tis too small
We bid them choose whether they will work at all.
We'll make them believe that trading is bad
We care not a pin, though they are n'er so sad.
   And this is a way, etc.

We'll make the poor Weavers work at a low rate,
We'll find fault where there's no fault, and so we will bate;

If trading grows dead, we will presently show it,
But if it grows good, they shall never know it;
We'll tell them that cloth beyond sea will not go,
We care not whether we keep clothing or no.
    And this is a way, etc.

Then next for the Spinners we shall ensue;
We'll make them spin three pound instead of two;
When they bring home their work unto us, they
    complain
And say that their wages will not
    them maintain;
But that if an ounce of weight
    they do lack,
Then for to bate threepence we
    will not be slack.
    And this is a way, etc.

But if it holds weight, then their
    wages they crave,
We have got no money, and what's
    that you'd have?
We have bread and bacon and butter
    that's good,
With oatmeal and salt that is
    wholesome for food;
We have soap and candles whereby to
    give light,
That you may work by them so long as
    you have sight.
    And this is a way, etc.

. . .

And thus, we do gain our wealth and estate
By many poor men that work early and late;
If it were not for those that labour so hard,
We might go and hang ourselves without regard;
The combers, the weavers, the tuckers also,
With the spinners that work for wages full low,
By these people's labour we fill up our purse,
Although we do get it with many a curse. 🗩

**Sources:** Daniel Defoe, *A Plan of the English Commerce. Being a compleat prospect of the trade of this nation, as well the home trade as the foreign.* London, 1728, pp. 90–91; Paul Mantoux and Marjorie Vernon, eds., *The Industrial Revolution in the Eighteenth Century: An Outline of the Beginnings of the Modern Factory System in England,* (1928; Taylor and Francis, 2006), pp. 76–77.

## QUESTIONS FOR ANALYSIS

1. What division of labor in the textile industry does Defoe describe? How does this division of labor resemble or differ from the household in which you grew up?

2. On what basis are wages paid, and what strategies do merchants use to keep wages down, according to "The Clothier's Delight"? How are they able to impose such strategies on workers?

3. How do you reconcile the difference of opinion between the two sources? Was one right and the other wrong, or could a more complex analysis be true?

*Bay, stuff, and drugget were types of coarse woolen cloth typical of the inexpensive products of rural weaving.

This spinning wheel was powered by the spinner's foot by means of the treadle, which was connected to the wheel by a rod and crankshaft. Purchasing a spinning wheel, which cost a few days of a laborer's wage, allowed rural women and children to generate precious supplemental income in the off-season. The work was relatively slow, however, and thread from four or five wheels was required to supply one weaver. (Science and Society Picture Library/SuperStock)

Why did the population rise in the eighteenth century?

**What led to the growth of rural industry?**

What were guilds and why were they controversial?

What role did colonial markets play in Europe's development?

533

**The Linen Industry in Ireland** Many steps went into making textiles. Here the women are beating away the woody part of the flax plant so that the man can comb out the soft part. The combed fibers will then be spun into thread and woven into cloth by this family enterprise. The increased labor of women and girls in the late seventeenth century helped produce an industrious revolution. (Victoria & Albert Museum, London/Eileen Tweedy/The Art Archive)

on a proportionately greater role in household decision making. Most of their scant earnings went for household necessities, but there were sometimes a few shillings left for a few ribbons or a new pair of stockings. Women's use of their surplus income thus helped spur the rapid growth of the textile industries in which they labored so hard.

These new sources and patterns of labor established important foundations for the Industrial Revolution of the late eighteenth and nineteenth centuries. They created households in which all members worked for wages rather than in a united family business and in which consumption relied on market-produced rather than homemade goods. It was not until the mid-nineteenth century, with rising industrial wages, that a new model emerged in which the male "breadwinner" was expected to earn enough to support the whole family and women and children were relegated back to the domestic sphere. With women estimated to compose 39 percent of the global workforce, today's world is experiencing a second industrious revolution in a similar climate of stagnant wages and increased demand for consumer goods.[2]

## ▼ What were guilds and why were they controversial?

**guild system** The organization of artisanal production into trade-based associations, or guilds, each of which received a monopoly over its trade and the right to train apprentices and hire workers.

One consequence of the growth of rural industry was an undermining of the traditional guild system that protected urban artisans. Guilds continued to dominate production in towns and cities, providing their masters with economic privileges as well as a proud social identity, but they increasingly struggled against competition from rural workers. Meanwhile, those excluded from guild membership—women, day laborers, Jews, and foreigners—worked on the margins of the urban economy.

**Chapter 18**
**The Expansion of Europe**
**534**      **1650–1800**

CHAPTER LOCATOR | How did European agriculture change between 1650 and 1800?

In the second half of the eighteenth century, critics attacked the guilds as outmoded institutions that obstructed technical progress and innovation. Until recently, most historians repeated that view. An ongoing reassessment of guilds now emphasizes their ability to adapt to changing economic circumstances.

## Urban Guilds

Originating around 1200 during the economic boom of the Middle Ages, the guild system reached its peak in most of Europe in the seventeenth and eighteenth centuries. During this period, urban guilds grew dramatically in number in cities and towns across Europe. In this period, the number of guilds in the city of Paris grew from 60 in 1672 to 129 in 1691.

European guild masters occupied the summit of the world of work. Each guild received a detailed set of privileges from the government, including exclusive rights to produce and sell certain goods, access to restricted markets in raw materials, and the rights to train apprentices, hire workers, and open shops. Guilds also served social and religious functions, providing a locus of sociability and group identity to the middling classes of European cities.

To ensure there was enough work to go around, guilds jealously restricted their membership to local men who had several years of work experience, paid stiff membership fees, and completed a masterpiece. They also favored family connections. Masters' sons enjoyed automatic access to their fathers' guilds, while outsiders were often barred from entering. Thus, most urban men and women worked in non-guild trades as domestic servants, as manual laborers, and as vendors of food, used clothing, and other goods.

The guilds' ability to enforce their rigid barriers varied a great deal across Europe. In England, national regulations superseded guild regulations, sapping their importance. In France, the Crown developed an ambiguous attitude toward guilds, relying on them for taxes and enforcement of quality standards, yet allowing non-guild production to flourish in the countryside in the 1760s, and even in some urban neighborhoods. The German guilds were perhaps the most powerful in Europe, and the most conservative. Journeymen in German cities, with their masters' support, violently protested the encroachment of non-guild workers.

At the same time that cottage industry began to infringe on the livelihoods of urban artisans, new Enlightenment ideals called into question the very existence of the guild system. Eighteenth-century critics of guilds derided them as outmoded and exclusionary institutions that obstructed technical innovation and progress.

Although many historians have repeated these charges, more recent scholarship has emphasized the flexibility and adaptability of the guild system and its vitality through the eighteenth century. Guild masters adopted new technologies and found creative ways to circumvent impractical rules. Instead of reviling non-guild workers, some masters gave them piecework or even formed partnerships with them. For many merchants and artisans, economic regulation did not hinder commerce but instead fostered the confidence necessary to stimulate it. In an economy with few banks or credit institutions, knowing that a guild had examined a master's qualifications and regularly inspected his shop helped potential buyers trust the goods they purchased.

Moreover, some guilds were accessible to women in Paris and a handful of other European cities. Most involved needlework and textiles, occupations that were considered appropriate for women. In 1675 seamstresses gained a new all-female guild in Paris, and soon seamstresses joined tailors' guilds in parts of France, England, and the Netherlands. In the same period new vocational training programs were established for poor girls in many European cities. By the mid-eighteenth century male masters began to hire more female workers, often in defiance of their own guild statutes.

Why did the population rise in the eighteenth century?

What led to the growth of rural industry?

What were guilds and why were they controversial?

What role did colonial markets play in Europe's development?

535

**Guild Procession in Seventeenth-Century Brussels** Guilds played an important role in the civic life of the early modern city. They collected taxes from their members, imposed quality standards and order on the trades, and represented the interests of commerce and industry to the government. In return, they claimed exclusive monopolies over their trades and the right to govern their own affairs. Guilds marched in processions like the one shown here at important city events, proudly displaying their corporate insignia. (Victoria & Albert Museum, London/Art Resource, NY)

## Adam Smith and Economic Liberalism

The impact of new patterns of labor inspired comment and controversy. One of the best-known critics of government regulation of trade or industry was Adam Smith (1723–1790), a professor of philosophy and a leading figure of the Scottish Enlightenment. Smith developed the general idea of freedom of enterprise and established the basis for modern economics in his groundbreaking work, *Inquiry into the Nature and Causes of the Wealth of Nations* (1776). Smith criticized guilds, or corporations, for their stifling and outmoded restrictions, a critique he extended to all state-approved monopolies and privileged companies. Far preferable was free competition, which would best protect consumers from price gouging and give all citizens a fair and equal right to do what they did best.

In keeping with his deep-seated fear of political oppression and with the "system of natural liberty" that he advocated, Smith argued that government should limit itself to "only three duties": it should provide a defense against foreign invasion, maintain civil order with courts and police protection, and sponsor certain indispensable public works and institutions that could never adequately profit private investors. He believed that the pursuit of self-interest in a competitive market would be sufficient to improve the living conditions of citizens, a view that quickly emerged as the classic argument for economic liberalism.

Many artisans welcomed the eighteenth century economic liberalization that came with Smith, the Enlightenment, and the French Revolution, but some continued to up-

**economic liberalism** A belief in free trade and competition based on Adam Smith's argument that the invisible hand of free competition would benefit all individuals, rich and poor.

Chapter 18
**The Expansion of Europe**
536    1650–1800

CHAPTER LOCATOR    How did European agriculture change between 1650 and 1800?

hold the ideals of the guilds. In parts of Germany guilds persisted until the second half of the nineteenth century. Clandestine journeymen's associations in France survived into the nineteenth century. Skilled artisans across Europe espoused the values of hand craftsmanship and limited competition in contrast to the proletarianization and loss of skills they endured in mechanized production. Nevertheless, by the middle of the nineteenth century economic deregulation was championed by most European governments and elites.

In the nineteenth and twentieth centuries Smith was often seen as an advocate of unbridled capitalism, but his ideas were considerably more complex. In his own mind, Smith spoke for truth, not for special interests. Unlike many disgruntled merchant capitalists, he applauded the modest rise in real wages of British workers in the eighteenth century and went on to say that "No society can surely be flourishing and happy, of which the far greater part of the members are poor and miserable." Quite realistically, Smith concluded that employers were "always and everywhere in a sort of tacit, but constant and uniform combination, not to raise the wages of labour above their actual rate" and sometimes entered "into particular combinations to sink the wages even below this rate." He also deplored the deadening effects of the division of labor and called for government intervention to raise workers' living standards.[3]

## ▼ What role did colonial markets play in Europe's development?

In addition to agricultural improvement, population pressure, and growing cottage industry, the expansion of Europe in the eighteenth century was characterized by the increase of world trade. In the eighteenth century Spain and Portugal revitalized their empires and began drawing more wealth from renewed colonial development. Yet once again the countries of northwestern Europe—the Netherlands, France, and above all Great Britain—benefited most. The Atlantic economy that these countries developed from 1650 to 1790 would prove crucial in the building of a global economy.

### Mercantilism and Colonial Wars

Britain's commercial leadership in the eighteenth century had its origins in the mercantilism of the seventeenth century (see Chapter 16). Eventually eliciting criticism from Enlightenment thinker Adam Smith and other proponents of free trade in the late eighteenth century, European mercantilism was a system of economic regulations aimed at increasing the power of the state. As practiced by a leading advocate such as Colbert under Louis XIV, mercantilism aimed particularly at creating a favorable balance of foreign trade in order to increase a country's stock of gold. A country's gold holdings served as an all-important treasure chest that could be opened periodically to pay for war in a violent age.

In England the desire to increase both military power and private wealth resulted in the mercantile system of the Navigation Acts. Oliver Cromwell established the first of these laws in 1651, and the restored monarchy of Charles II extended them in 1660 and 1663. The acts required that most goods imported from Europe into England and Scotland (Great Britain after 1707) be carried on British-owned ships with British crews or on ships of the country producing the article. Moreover, these laws gave British merchants and shipowners a virtual monopoly on trade with British colonies. The colonists were required to ship their products on British (or American) ships and to buy almost all European goods from Britain. It was believed that these economic regulations would

**Navigation Acts** A series of English laws that controlled the import of goods to Britain and British colonies.

eliminate foreign competition, thereby helping British merchants and workers as well as colonial plantation owners and farmers. It was hoped, too, that the emerging British Empire would develop a shipping industry with a large number of experienced seamen who could serve when necessary in the Royal Navy.

The Navigation Acts were a form of economic warfare. Their initial target was the Dutch, who were far ahead of the English in shipping and foreign trade in the mid-seventeenth century (see Chapter 16). In conjunction with three Anglo-Dutch wars between 1652 and 1674, the Navigation Acts seriously damaged Dutch shipping and commerce. The British seized the thriving Dutch colony of New Amsterdam in 1664 and renamed it New York. By the late seventeenth century the Netherlands was falling behind England in shipping, trade, and colonies. Thereafter France stood clearly as England's most serious rival in the competition for overseas empire. Rich in natural resources, with a population three or four times that of England, continental Europe's leading military power was already building a powerful fleet and a worldwide system of rigidly monopolized colonial trade. Thus from 1701 to 1763 Britain and France were locked in a series of wars to decide, in part, which nation would become the leading maritime power and claim the profits of Europe's overseas expansion (Map 18.2).

The first round was the War of the Spanish Succession (see Chapter 16), which started in 1701 when Louis XIV accepted the Spanish crown willed to his grandson. Besides upsetting the continental balance of power, a union of France and Spain threatened to encircle and destroy the British colonies in North America (see Map 18.2). Defeated by a great coalition of states after twelve years of fighting, Louis XIV was forced in the Peace of Utrecht (YOO-trehkt) in 1713 to cede its North American holdings in Newfoundland, Nova Scotia, and the Hudson Bay territory to Britain. Spain was compelled to give Britain control of its West African slave trade and to let Britain send one ship of merchandise into the Spanish colonies annually.

Conflict continued among the European powers over both domestic and colonial affairs. The War of the Austrian Succession (1740–1748), which started when Frederick the Great of Prussia seized Silesia from Austria's Maria Theresa (see Chapter 17), gradually became a world war that included Anglo-French conflicts in India and North America. The war ended as an inconclusive standoff, but it helped set the stage for the Seven Years' War (1756–1763). In central Europe, Austria's Maria Theresa sought to win back Silesia and crush Prussia, thereby re-establishing the Habsburgs' traditional leadership in German affairs. She almost succeeded in her goals, but Prussia survived with its boundaries intact.

Inconclusive in Europe, the Seven Years' War was the decisive round in the Franco-British competition for colonial empire. The fighting began in North America. The population of New France was centered in Quebec and along the St. Lawrence River, but French soldiers and Canadian fur traders had also built forts and trading posts along the Great Lakes, through the Ohio country, and down the Mississippi to New Orleans (Map 18.3). Allied with many Native American tribes, the French built more forts in 1753 in what is now western Pennsylvania to protect their claims. The following year a Virginia force attacked a small group of French soldiers, and soon the war to conquer Canada was on.

French and Canadian forces under the marquis de Montcalm fought well and scored major victories until 1758. Then, led by their new chief minister, William Pitt, the British diverted men and money from the war in Europe, using superior sea power to destroy the French fleet and choke off French commerce around the world. In 1759 a combined British naval and land force laid siege to Quebec, defeating Montcalm's army in a battle that sealed the fate of France in North America.

British victory on all colonial fronts was ratified in the 1763 Treaty of Paris. France lost its remaining possessions on mainland North America. Canada and all French territory east of the Mississippi River passed to Britain, and France ceded Louisiana to Spain

**Treaty of Paris** The treaty that ended the Seven Years' War in Europe and the colonies in 1763 and ratified British victory on all colonial fronts.

Chapter 18
**The Expansion of Europe**
538    1650–1800

CHAPTER LOCATOR    How did European agriculture change between 1650 and 1800?

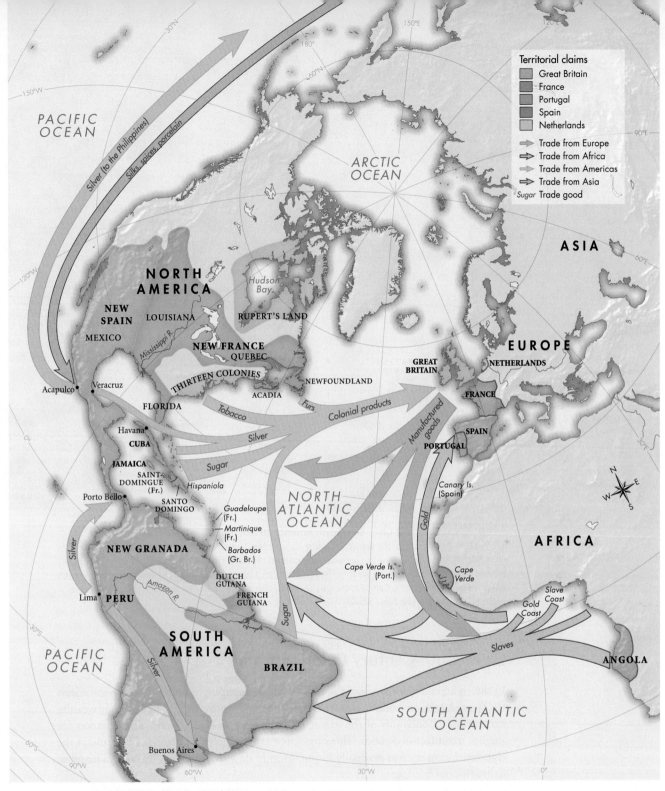

**Territorial claims**
- Great Britain
- France
- Portugal
- Spain
- Netherlands

➡ Trade from Europe
➡ Trade from Africa
➡ Trade from Americas
➡ Trade from Asia
*Sugar* Trade good

PACIFIC OCEAN

Silver (to the Philippines)

Silks, spices, porcelain

ARCTIC OCEAN

ASIA

NORTH AMERICA

NEW SPAIN

LOUISIANA

Hudson Bay

RUPERT'S LAND

EUROPE

MEXICO

Mississippi R.

NEW FRANCE
QUEBEC

GREAT BRITAIN

NETHERLANDS

Acapulco    Veracruz

THIRTEEN COLONIES

NEWFOUNDLAND

FRANCE

FLORIDA

ACADIA

Tobacco

Furs

Colonial products

SPAIN

Manufactured goods

PORTUGAL

Havana

Silver

CUBA

Gold

Canary Is.
(Spain)

JAMAICA
SAINT-DOMINGUE
(Fr.)

Sugar

Hispaniola

Porto Bello

SANTO DOMINGO

Guadeloupe
(Fr.)

NORTH ATLANTIC OCEAN

Martinique
(Fr.)

AFRICA

NEW GRANADA

Amazon R.

Barbados
(Gr. Br.)

DUTCH GUIANA

FRENCH GUIANA

Cape Verde Is.
(Port.)

Cape Verde

Slave Coast

Gold Coast

Lima    PERU

Silver

Sugar

Slaves

ANGOLA

SOUTH AMERICA

BRAZIL

PACIFIC OCEAN

Silver

SOUTH ATLANTIC OCEAN

Buenos Aires

**Map 18.2  The Atlantic Economy in 1701** The growth of trade encouraged both economic development and military conflict in the Atlantic basin. Four continents were linked together by the exchange of goods and slaves.

as compensation for Spain's loss of Florida to Britain. France also gave up most of its holdings in India, opening the way to British dominance on the subcontinent. By 1763 British naval power, built in large part on the rapid growth of the British shipping industry after the passage of the Navigation Acts, had triumphed decisively: Britain had realized its goal of monopolizing a vast trading and colonial empire.

Why did the population rise in the eighteenth century?

What led to the growth of rural industry?

What were guilds and why were they controversial?

What role did colonial markets play in Europe's development?

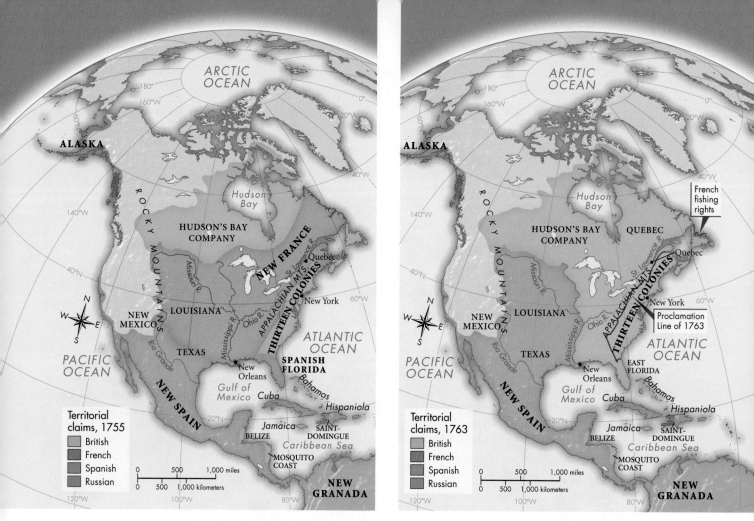

**Map 18.3 European Claims in North America Before and After the Seven Years' War, 1755–1763** As a result of the war, France lost its vast territories. In an effort to avoid costly conflicts with Native Americans living in the newly conquered territory, the British government in 1763 prohibited colonists from settling west of the Appalachian Mountains. One of the few remaining French colonies in the Americas, Saint-Domingue (on the island of Hispaniola) was the most profitable plantation colony in the New World.

## Eighteenth-Century Colonial Trade

In the eighteenth century, stimulated by trade and empire building, London grew into the West's largest and richest city. Above all, the rapidly growing and increasingly wealthy agricultural populations of the mainland colonies provided an expanding market for English manufactured goods. This situation was extremely fortunate, for England in the eighteenth century was gradually losing, or only slowly expanding, its sales to many of its traditional European markets.

English exports of manufactured goods to the Atlantic economy came to the rescue. Sales to the mainland colonies of North America and the West Indian sugar islands—with an important assist from West Africa and Latin America—soared from £500,000 to £4.0 million (Figure 18.2). Exports to England's other colonies in Ireland and India also rose substantially in the eighteenth century. Thus, the mercantilist system achieved remarkable success for England in the eighteenth century, and by the 1770s England stood on the threshold of the epoch-making industrial changes that would become known as the Industrial Revolution.

**540**    Chapter 18   **The Expansion of Europe**   1650–1800

CHAPTER LOCATOR    How did European agriculture change between 1650 and 1800?

Although they lost many possessions to the English, the French still profited enormously from colonial trade. The colonies of Saint-Domingue (modern-day Haiti), Martinique, and Guadeloupe remained in French hands. They provided immense fortunes in plantation agriculture and slave trading during the second half of the eighteenth century. The wealth generated from colonial trade fostered the confidence of the merchant classes in Paris, Bordeaux, and other large cities, and merchants soon joined other elite groups clamoring for more political power.

The third major player in the Atlantic economy, Spain, also saw its colonial fortunes improve during the eighteenth century. Not only did it gain Louisiana from France in 1763, but its influence expanded westward all the way to northern California through the efforts of Spanish missionaries and ranchers. Its mercantilist goals were boosted by a recovery in silver production, which had dropped significantly in the seventeenth century.

Silver mining also stimulated food production for the mining camps, and wealthy Spanish landowners developed a system of **debt peonage** (PEE-uh-nihj) to keep indigenous workers on their estates. Under this system, which was similar to serfdom, a planter or rancher would keep workers in perpetual debt bondage by advancing them food, shelter, and a little money.

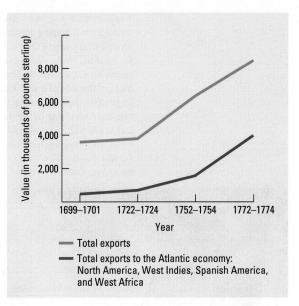

**Figure 18.2** **Exports of English Manufactured Goods, 1700–1774** While trade between England and Europe stagnated after 1700, English exports to Africa and the Americas boomed and greatly stimulated English economic development. (Source: Data from R. Davis, "English Foreign Trade, 1700–1774," *Economic History Review*, 2d ser., 15 [1962]: 302–303.)

## The Atlantic Slave Trade

As the volume of transatlantic trade increased, the four continents bordering the ocean were increasingly drawn into an integrated economic system. At the core of this Atlantic world was the Atlantic slave trade. The forced migration of millions of Africans was a key element in the Atlantic system and western European economic expansion throughout the eighteenth century. The brutal practice intensified dramatically after 1700 and especially after 1750 with the growth of trade and demand for slave-produced goods like sugar and cotton. According to the most authoritative source, European traders purchased and shipped 6.5 million African slaves across the Atlantic between 1701 and 1800—more than half of the estimated total of 12.5 million Africans transported between 1450 and 1900, of whom 15 percent died in procurement and transit.[4]

**debt peonage** A form of serfdom that allowed a planter or rancher to keep his workers or slaves in perpetual debt bondage by periodically advancing food, shelter, and a little money.

**Atlantic slave trade** The forced migration of Africans across the Atlantic for slave labor on plantations and in other industries; the trade reached its peak in the eighteenth century and ultimately involved more than twelve million Africans.

**Plantation Zones, ca. 1700**

The rise of plantation agriculture was responsible for the tremendous growth of the slave trade. Among all European colonies, the plantations of Portuguese Brazil received by far the largest number of enslaved Africans over the entire period of the slave trade—45 percent of the total. Another 45 percent were divided among the many Caribbean colonies. The colonies of mainland North America took only 3 percent of slaves arriving from Africa, relying mostly on natural growth of the enslaved population.

Eighteenth-century intensification of the slave trade resulted in fundamental changes in its organization. After 1700, European governments and ship captains cut back on fighting among themselves and concentrated on commerce.

Why did the population rise in the eighteenth century?

What led to the growth of rural industry?

What were guilds and why were they controversial?

What role did colonial markets play in Europe's development?

**The Atlantic Slave Trade** This engraving from 1814 shows traders leading a group of slaves to the West African coast, where they will board ships to cross the Atlantic. Many slaves died enroute or arrived greatly weakened and ill. The newspaper advertisement of the sale of a ship's cargo of slaves in Charleston, South Carolina, promises "fine, healthy negroes," testifying to the dangers of the crossing and to the frequency of epidemic diseases like smallpox. (engraving: Bibliothèque de l'Arsenal, Paris/ Archives Charmet/The Bridgeman Art Library; advertisement: The Granger Collection, NY)

TO BE SOLD on board the Ship *Bance-Yland*, on tuesday the 6th of *May* next, at *Afhley-Ferry*; a choice cargo of about 250 fine healthy

NEGROES,

juft arrived from the Windward & Rice Coaft. —The utmoft care has already been taken, and fhall be continued, to keep them free from the leaft danger of being infected with the SMALL-POX, no boat having been on board, and all other communication with people from *Charles-Town* prevented.

*Auftin, Laurens, & Appleby.*

*N. B.* Full one Half of the above Negroes have had the SMALL-POX in their own Country.

They generally adopted the shore method of trading, which was less expensive than maintaining fortified trading posts. Under this system, European ships sent boats ashore or invited African dealers to bring traders and slaves out to their ships. This method allowed ships to move easily along the coast from market to market and to depart more quickly for the Americas.

Some African merchants and rulers who controlled exports profited from the greater demand for slaves. But generally such economic returns did not spread very far, and the negative consequences of the expanding slave trade predominated. Wars among African states to obtain salable captives increased, and leaders used slave profits to purchase more arms than textiles and consumer goods. While the populations of Europe and Asia grew substantially in the eighteenth century, the population of Africa stagnated or possibly declined.

Most Europeans did not personally witness the horrors of the slave trade between Africa and the Americas, and until the early part of the eighteenth century, they considered the African slave trade a legitimate business. But as details of the plight of slaves became known, a campaign to abolish slavery developed in Britain. In the late 1780s the abolition campaign grew into a mass movement of public opinion, the first in British history. British women were prominent in this movement. In 1807 Parliament abolished

Chapter 18
**The Expansion of Europe**
542          1650–1800

CHAPTER LOCATOR          How did European agriculture change between 1650 and 1800?

**Slaves Harvesting Sugar Cane** In this 1828 print a long line of hard-working slaves systematically harvests the ripe cane on the island of Antigua, while on the right more slaves load cut cane into wagons for refining at the plantation's central crushing mill. The manager on horseback may be ordering the overseer to quicken the work pace, always brutal and unrelenting at harvest time. Slave labor made high-intensity capitalist production of sugar possible in the Americas. (John Carter Brown Library at Brown University)

the British slave trade, although slavery continued in British colonies and the Americas for decades.

## Identities and Communities of the Atlantic World

Not only slaves and commodities but also free people and ideas circulated through the eighteenth-century Atlantic world. As contacts among the Atlantic coasts of the Americas, Africa, and Europe became more frequent, and as European settlements grew into well-established colonies, new identities and communities emerged.

The term *Creole* referred to people of Spanish ancestry born in the Americas. Wealthy Creoles and their counterparts throughout the Atlantic colonies prided themselves on following European ways of life. Over time, however, the colonial elite came to feel that their circumstances gave them different interests and characteristics from those of their home population. As one observer explained, "a turn of mind peculiar to the planter, occasioned by a physical difference of constitution, climate, customs, and education, tends . . . to repress the remains of his former attachment to his native soil."[5] Creole traders and planters increasingly resented the regulations and taxes imposed by colonial bureaucrats.

Not all Europeans in the colonies were wealthy. Numerous poor or middling whites worked as clerks, shopkeepers, craftsmen, and plantation managers. Whether rich or poor, however, white Europeans usually made up a small proportion of the population. Since most European migrants were men, much of the population of the Atlantic world descended from unions—forced or through choice—of European men and indigenous

Why did the population rise in the eighteenth century?

What led to the growth of rural industry?

What were guilds and why were they controversial?

What role did colonial markets play in Europe's development?

543

or African women (see Chapter 15). Colonial attempts to classify and systematize racial categories greatly influenced developing Enlightenment thought on racial difference (see Chapter 17).

Mixed-race populations sometimes rose to the colonial elite. The Spanish conquistadors often consolidated their power through marriage to the daughters of local rulers, and their descendants were among the most powerful inhabitants of Spanish America.

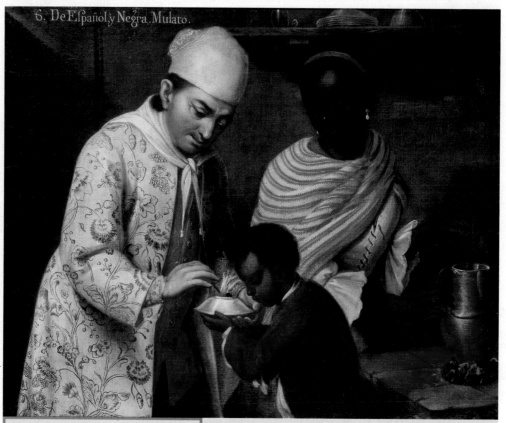

6. De Español y Negra, Mulato.

## ▪ PICTURING THE PAST

### Mulatto Painting

The caption in the upper left corner of this mid-eighteenth-century painting identifies the family as being composed of a Spanish father and a black mother, whose child is described as "mulatto." The painting was number six in a series of sixteen images by the painter Jose de Alcibar, each showing a different racial and ethnic combination. The series belonged to a popular genre in the Spanish Americas known as *castas* paintings, which commonly depicted sixteen different forms of racial mixing.

(Attrib. Jose de Alcibar, 6, *De Espanol y Negra, Mulato*, ca. 1760–1770. Denver Art Museum: Collection of Frederick and Jan Mayer. Photography provided by the Denver Art Museum)

**ANALYZING THE IMAGE** How would you characterize the relations among mother, father, and child as shown in this painting? Does the painter suggest power relations within the family? What attitude does the painter seem to have toward the family?

**CONNECTIONS** Why do you think such paintings were so popular? Who do you think the audience might have been, and why would viewers be fascinated by such images?

To complete this activity online, go to the Online Study Guide at bedfordstmartins.com/mckaywestunderstanding.

Chapter 18
The Expansion of Europe
**544** 1650–1800

CHAPTER LOCATOR | How did European agriculture change between 1650 and 1800?

In the Spanish and French Caribbean, as in Brazil, many masters acknowledged and freed their mixed-race children, leading to sizable populations of free people of color. Advantaged by their fathers, some became wealthy land and slave owners in their own right. In the British colonies of the Caribbean and the southern mainland, by contrast, masters tended to leave their mixed-race progeny in slavery, maintaining a stark discrepancy between free whites and enslaved people of color.[6] British colonial law forbade marriage between Englishmen and women and Africans or Native Americans.

The identities inspired by racial and ethnic mixing were equally complex. Colonial elites became "Americanized" by adopting native foods and sought relief from tropical disease in native remedies. Some mixed-race people sought to enter Creole society and obtain its many official and unofficial privileges by passing as white. Where they existed in any number, though, free people of color established their own social hierarchies based on wealth, family connections, occupation, and skin color. (See "Individuals in Society: Olaudah Equiano," page 546.)

Converting indigenous people to Christianity was a key ambition for all European powers in the New World. Jesuits, Franciscans, Dominicans, and other religious orders established Catholic missions throughout Spanish, Portuguese, and French colonies. Rather than a straightforward imposition of Christianity, conversion entailed a complex process of cultural exchange. Catholic friars were among the first Europeans to seek understanding of native cultures and languages as part of their effort to render Christianity comprehensible to indigenous people. In turn, Christian ideas and practices in the New World took on a distinctive character. For example, a sixteenth-century apparition of the Virgin Mary in Mexico City, known as the Virgin of Guadalupe, became a central icon of Spanish-American Catholicism.

Missionaries' success in the New World varied over time and space. In Central and South America, large-scale conversion forged enduring Catholic cultures in Portuguese and Spanish colonies. Conversion efforts in North America were less effective due to the scattered nature of settlement and the lesser integration of native people into the colonial community. On the whole, Protestants were less active as missionaries in this period.

The practice of slavery reveals important limitations on efforts to spread Christianity. Slave owners often refused to baptize their slaves in case baptism would confer additional rights upon them. In some areas, particularly among the mostly African-born slaves of the Caribbean, elements of African religious belief and practice endured, often incorporated with Christian traditions.

Restricted from owning land and holding many occupations in Europe, Jews were eager participants in the new Atlantic economy and established a network of mercantile communities along its trade routes. As in the Old World, Jews in European colonies faced discrimination. Jews were considered to be white Europeans and thus ineligible to be slaves, but they did not enjoy equal status with Christians. The status of Jews adds one more element to the complexity of Atlantic identities.

## Trade and Empire in Asia and the Pacific

As the Atlantic economy took shape, Europeans continued to vie for dominance in the Asian trade. Between 1500 and 1600 the Portuguese had become major players in the Indian Ocean trading world, eliminating Venice as Europe's chief supplier of spices and other Asian luxury goods. The Portuguese dominated but did not fundamentally alter the age-old pattern of Indian Ocean trade, which involved merchants from many areas as more or less autonomous players. This situation changed radically with the intervention of the Dutch and then the English (see Chapter 15).

Formed in 1602, the Dutch East India Company had taken control of the Portuguese spice trade in the Indian Ocean, with the port of Batavia (Jakarta) in Java as its center of operations. Within a few decades they had expelled the Portuguese from Ceylon and

Why did the population rise in the eighteenth century?    What led to the growth of rural industry?    What were guilds and why were they controversial?    **What role did colonial markets play in Europe's development?**

545

# INDIVIDUALS IN SOCIETY

## Olaudah Equiano

**THE SLAVE TRADE WAS A MASS MIGRATION** involving millions of human beings. It was also the sum of individual lives spent partly or entirely in slavery. Although most of the individuals remain hidden to us, Olaudah Equiano (1745–1797) is an important exception. According to his autobiography, Equiano was born in Benin (modern Nigeria) of Ibo ethnicity. His father, one of the village elders (or chieftains), presided over a large household that included "many slaves," prisoners captured in local wars. All people, slave and free, shared in the cultivation of family lands. One day when all the adults were in the fields, two strange men and a woman broke into the family compound, kidnapped the eleven-year-old boy and his sister, tied them up, and dragged them into the woods. Brother and sister were separated, and Olaudah was sold several times to various dealers before reaching the coast. As it took six months to walk there, his home must have been far inland.

The slave ship and the strange appearance of the white crew terrified the boy. Much worse was the long voyage from Benin to Barbados in the Caribbean, as Equiano later recounted. "The stench of the [ship's] hold . . . became absolutely pestilential . . . [and] brought on a sickness among the slaves, of which many died. . . . The shrieks of the women and the groans of the dying rendered the whole a scene of horror almost inconceivable." Placed on deck with the sick and dying, Equiano saw two and then three of his "enchained countrymen" escape somehow through the nettings and jump into the sea, "preferring death to such a life of misery."*

Equiano's new owner, an officer in the Royal Navy, took him to England and saw that the lad received some education. Engaged in bloody action in Europe for almost four years as a captain's boy in the Seven Years' War, Equiano hoped that his loyal service and Christian baptism would help secure his freedom. He also knew that slavery was generally illegal in England. But his master deceived him. Docking in London, the slave owner and his accomplices forced a protesting and heartbroken Equiano onto a ship bound for the Caribbean.

There he was sold to Robert King, a Quaker merchant from Philadelphia who dealt in sugar and rum. Equiano developed his mathematical skills, worked hard to please as a clerk in King's warehouse, and became first mate on one of King's ships. Allowed to trade on the side for his own profit, Equiano amassed capital, repaid King his original purchase price, and received his deed of manumission, authorizing his freedom, at the age of twenty-one. King urged his talented former slave to stay on as a business partner, but Equiano hated the limitations and dangers of black freedom in the colonies—he was almost kidnapped back into slavery while loading a ship in Georgia—and could think only of England. Settling in London, Equiano studied, worked as a hairdresser, and went to sea periodically as a merchant seaman. He developed his ardent Christian faith and

---

other East Indian islands. Unlike the Portuguese, the Dutch transformed the Indian Ocean trading world. Whereas East Indian states and peoples maintained independence under the Portuguese, the Dutch established outright control and reduced them to dependents.

After these successes, the Dutch hold in Asia faltered in the eighteenth century due to the company's failure to diversify to meet changing consumption patterns. Fierce competition from its main rival, the English East India Company (established 1600), also severely undercut Dutch trade.

Britain initially struggled for a foothold in Asia. With the Dutch monopolizing the Indian Ocean, the British turned to India. Throughout the seventeenth century the British East India Company relied on trade concessions from the powerful Mughal emperor, who granted only piecemeal access to the subcontinent. Finally, in 1716 the Mughals conceded empire-wide trading privileges. To further their economic interests, British East India Company agents in-

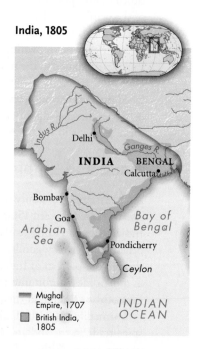

**India, 1805**

Delhi
Indus R.
Ganges R.
**INDIA**   **BENGAL**
Calcutta
Bombay
Goa
Arabian Sea
Bay of Bengal
Pondicherry
Ceylon

█ Mughal Empire, 1707
▨ British India, 1805

INDIAN OCEAN

Chapter 18
**The Expansion of Europe**
1650–1800

546

CHAPTER LOCATOR | How did European agriculture change between 1650 and 1800?

became a leading member of London's sizable black community.

Equiano loathed the brutal slavery and the vicious exploitation that he saw in the West Indies and Britain's mainland colonies. A complex and sophisticated man, he also respected the integrity of Robert King and admired British navigational and industrial technologies. He encountered white oppressors and made white friends. He once described himself as "almost an Englishman." In the 1780s he joined with white and black activists in the antislavery campaign and wrote *The Interesting Narrative of the Life of Olaudah Equiano Written by Himself*, a well-documented autobiographical indictment of slavery. Above all, he urged Christians to live by the principles they professed and to treat Africans equally as free human beings and children of God. With the success of his widely read book, he carried his message to large audiences across Britain and Ireland and inspired the growing movement to abolish slavery.

Recently, scholars have unearthed contemporary documents in which Equiano gave an American, rather than African, birthplace.† This discovery has raised controversy about the authenticity of parts of his autobiography; whatever his place of birth, Equiano's account of the Middle Passage was certainly based on discussions with many fellow slaves even if not on his own experience.

## QUESTIONS FOR ANALYSIS

1. What aspects of Olaudah Equiano's life as a slave were typical? What aspects were atypical?
2. Describe Equiano's culture and personality. What aspects are most striking? Why?

*Olaudah Equiano, *The Interesting Narrative of the Life of Olaudah Equiano Written by Himself*, ed. with an introduction by Robert J. Allison (Boston: Bedford Books, 1995), pp. 56–57. Recent scholarship has re-examined Equiano's life and thrown some details of his identity into question.

†Vincent Carretta, "Olaudah Equiano or Gustavus Vassa? New Light on an Eighteenth-Century Question of Identity," *Slavery and Abolition* 20, 3 (December 1999): 96–105.

**Olaudah Equiano, in an engraving from his autobiography.** (National Portrait Gallery, Smithsonian Institution/Art Resource, NY)

creasingly intervened in local affairs and made alliances or waged war against Indian princes.

Britain's great rival for influence in India was France. During the War of the Austrian Succession, British and French forces in India supported opposing rulers in local power struggles. Their rivalry was finally resolved by the Treaty of Paris, which granted virtually all of France's possessions in India to the British. With the elimination of their rival, British ascendancy in India accelerated. In 1764 company forces defeated the Mughal emperor, leaving him on the throne as a ruler in title only. By about 1805 the British had overcome vigorous Indian resistance to gain economic and political dominance of much of the subcontinent.

The late eighteenth century also witnessed the beginning of British settlement of the continent of Australia. Captain James Cook claimed the east coast of Australia for England in 1770, naming it New South Wales. The first colony was established there in the late 1780s, relying on the labor of convicted prisoners forcibly transported from Britain. Settlement of the western portion of the continent followed in the 1790s. The first colonies struggled for survival and, after an initial period of friendly relations, soon aroused the hostility and resistance of Aboriginal peoples. Cook himself was killed by islanders in Hawaii in 1779, having charted much of the Pacific Ocean for the first time.

Why did the population rise in the eighteenth century?

What led to the growth of rural industry?

What were guilds and why were they controversial?

What role did colonial markets play in Europe's development?

547

**The British in India, ca. 1785** This Indian miniature shows the wife (center) of a British officer attended by many Indian servants. A British merchant (left) awaits her attention. The picture reflects the luxurious lifestyle of the British elite in India, many members of which returned home with colossal fortunes. (Scala/Art Resource, NY)

The rising economic and political power of Europeans in this period drew on the connections they established between the Asian and Atlantic trade worlds. An outstanding example is the trade in cowry shells. These seashells, originating in the Maldive Islands in the Indian Ocean, were used as a form of currency in West Africa. European traders obtained them in Asia, packing them alongside porcelains, spices, and silks for the journey home. The cowries were then brought from European ports to the West African coast to be traded for slaves. Indian textiles were also prized in Africa and played a similar role in exchange. Thus, the trade of the Atlantic was inseparable from Asian commerce, and Europeans were increasingly found dominating commerce in both worlds.

Chapter 18
**The Expansion of Europe**
**548** 1650–1800

CHAPTER LOCATOR | How did European agriculture change between 1650 and 1800?

# ← LOOKING BACK LOOKING AHEAD →

BY THE TURN OF THE EIGHTEENTH CENTURY, western Europe had begun to shake off the effects of long decades of famine, disease, warfare, economic depression, and demographic stagnation. The eighteenth century witnessed a breakthrough in agricultural production that, along with improved infrastructure and the retreat of epidemic disease, contributed to a substantial increase in population. One crucial catalyst for agricultural innovation was the scientific revolution, which provided new tools of empirical observation and experimentation. The Enlightenment as well, with its emphasis on progress and public welfare, convinced government officials, scientists, and informed landowners to seek better solutions to old problems. By the end of the century, industry and trade also attracted enlightened commentators who advocated free markets and less government control. Modern political economy is thus one more legacy of the Enlightenment.

As the era of European exploration and conquest gave way to colonial empire-building, the eighteenth century witnessed increased consolidation of global markets and bitter competition among Europeans for the spoils of empire. From its slow inception in the mid-fifteenth century, the African slave trade reached brutal heights in the second half of the eighteenth century. The eighteenth-century Atlantic world thus tied the shores of Europe, the Americas, and Africa in a web of commercial and human exchange that also had strong ties with the Pacific and the Indian Ocean.

The new dynamics of the eighteenth century prepared the way for world-shaking changes. Population growth and rural industry began to undermine long-standing traditions of daily life in western Europe. The transformed families of the industrious revolution developed not only new habits of work, but also a new sense of confidence in their abilities. By the 1770s England was approaching an economic breakthrough as fully significant as the great political upheaval destined to develop shortly in neighboring France. In the same period, the first wave of resistance to European domination rose up in the colonies. The great revolutions of the late eighteenth century would change the world forever. ∎

- **For a list of suggested readings for this chapter, visit** *bedfordstmartins.com/mckaywestunderstanding*.

- **For primary sources from this period, see** *Sources of Western Society*, Second Edition.

- **For Web sites, images, and documents related to topics in this chapter, see Make History at** *bedfordstmartins.com/mckaywestunderstanding*.

Why did the population rise in the eighteenth century?

What led to the growth of rural industry?

What were guilds and why were they controversial?

**What role did colonial markets play in Europe's development?**

## Step 1

**GETTING STARTED** Below are basic terms about this period in the history of Western civilization. Can you identify each term below and explain why it matters? To do this exercise online, go to bedfordstmartins.com/mckaywestunderstanding.

| TERMS | WHO (OR WHAT) AND WHEN | WHY IT MATTERS |
|---|---|---|
| agricultural revolution, p. 523 | | |
| enclosure, p. 523 | | |
| proletarianization, p. 526 | | |
| cottage industry, p. 528 | | |
| putting-out system, p. 528 | | |
| industrious revolution, p. 531 | | |
| guild system, p. 534 | | |
| economic liberalism, p. 536 | | |
| Navigation Acts, p. 537 | | |
| Treaty of Paris, p. 538 | | |
| debt peonage, p. 541 | | |
| Atlantic slave trade, p. 541 | | |

## Step 2

**MOVING BEYOND THE BASICS** The exercise below requires a more advanced understanding of the chapter material. Examine the connections between the major social and economic developments of the seventeenth and eighteenth centuries by describing the causes and consequences of the agricultural revolution, the eighteenth-century population explosion, and the growth of rural industry. When you are finished, consider the following questions: How did the agricultural revolution contribute to population growth in the eighteenth century? Why did some parts of Europe see greater changes in the rural economy? To do this exercise online, go to bedfordstmartins.com/mckaywestunderstanding.

| PHASE | CAUSES | CONSEQUENCES |
|---|---|---|
| Agricultural Revolution | | |
| Population Growth | | |
| Growth of Rural Industry | | |

## Step 3

## PUTTING IT ALL TOGETHER Now that you've reviewed key elements of the chapter, take a step back and try to see the big picture. Remember to use specific examples from the chapter in your answers. To do this exercise online, go to bedfordstmartins.com/mckaywestunderstanding.

### THE AGRICULTURAL REVOLUTION

- What was revolutionary about the agricultural revolution?

- Why did the Low Countries and England lead the way in agricultural innovation? How did their strong commercial and mercantile traditions contribute in this context?

### POPULATION GROWTH

- Compare and contrast European demographic patterns before and after 1700. How would you explain the major differences you note?

- What were the most important consequences of population growth in the eighteenth century? How did population growth change the European economy?

### ECONOMIC CHANGE

- How did the production of textiles change over the course of the eighteenth century? What larger trends were reflected in these changes?

- What is meant by the term "industrious revolution"? What developments does this term aim to summarize?

- What role did guilds play in the urban economy? Why did some eighteenth-century observers see guilds as obstacles to progress and innovation?

### EUROPE AND THE GLOBAL ECONOMY

- How did European nations define their economic interests? How did such definitions shape European policies and actions overseas?

- What role did slavery play in the Atlantic economy? How did slavery shape emerging colonial communities? How did it shape social and economic developments in Europe?

■ **In Your Own Words** Imagine that you must explain Chapter 18 to someone who hasn't read it. What would be the most important points to include and why?

# 19

# The Changing Life of the People

## 1700–1800

The discussion of agriculture and industry in the last chapter showed the common people at work, straining to make ends meet within the larger context of population growth, gradual economic expansion, and ferocious political competition at home and overseas. This chapter shows us how that world of work was embedded in a rich complex of family organization, community practices, everyday experiences, and collective attitudes. As with the economy, traditional habits and practices of daily life changed considerably over the eighteenth century. Change was particularly dramatic in the growing cities of northwestern Europe, where traditional social controls were undermined by the anonymity and increased social interaction of the urban setting.

Historians have intensively studied many aspects of popular life, including marriage patterns and family size, childhood and education, nutrition, health care, and religious worship. Uncovering the life of the common people has been a formidable challenge because they left few written records and regional variations abounded. Yet imaginative research has resulted in major findings and much greater knowledge. It is now possible to follow the common people into their homes, workshops, churches, and taverns and to ask, "What were the everyday experiences of ordinary people, and how did they change over the eighteenth century?" ■

**Life in the Eighteenth Century.** The huge fresh-food market known as Les Halles was the pulsing heart of eighteenth-century Paris. Here, peddlers offer food and drink to the men and women of the market, many of whom had arrived in the predawn hours to set up their stalls. (akg-images)

# Chapter Preview

▶ How did family life change in the eighteenth century?

▶ How did attitudes toward child rearing change in this period?

▶ How and why did popular culture change during this period?

▶ What role did religion play in eighteenth-century society?

▶ How did medicine evolve in the eighteenth century?

## ▼ How did family life change in the eighteenth century?

The basic unit of social organization is the family. Within the structure of the family human beings love, mate, and reproduce. It is primarily the family that teaches the child, imparting values and customs that condition an individual's behavior for a lifetime. The family is also an institution woven into the web of history. It evolves and changes, assuming different forms in different times and places. The eighteenth century witnessed such an evolution, as patterns of marriage shifted and individuals adapted and conformed to the new and changing realities of the family unit.

### Late Marriage and Nuclear Families

The three-generation extended family was a rarity in western and central Europe by 1700. Indeed, the extended family may never have been common in Europe, although it is hard to know about the early Middle Ages because very few records survive. When young European couples married, they normally established their own households and lived apart from their parents, much like the nuclear families (a family group consisting of parents and their children with no other relatives) common in America today.

Young Serving Girl Increased migration to urban areas in the eighteenth century contributed to a loosening of traditional morals and soaring illegitimacy rates. Young women who worked as servants or shopgirls could not be supervised as closely as those who lived at home. The themes of seduction, fallen virtue, and familial conflict were popular in eighteenth-century art, such as in this painting by Pietro Longhi (1702–1785). (Cameraphoto Arte, Venice/Art Resource, NY)

Most people did not marry young in the seventeenth and eighteenth centuries. The average person married surprisingly late. Studies of England and France in the seventeenth and eighteenth centuries show that both men and women married for the first time at an average age of twenty-five to twenty-seven. Ten to 20 percent of men and women never married at all.

Why was marriage delayed? The main reason was that couples normally did not marry until they could start an independent household and support themselves and their future children. Peasants often needed to wait until the father's death to inherit land and marry. In the towns, men and women worked to accumulate enough savings to start a small business and establish their own home. Laws and tradition also limited early marriage. In some areas couples needed the legal permission or tacit approval of the local lord or landowner in order to marry. Poor couples had particular difficulty securing the approval of local officials, who believed that freedom to marry for the lower classes would result in more landless paupers, more abandoned children, and more money for welfare. Village elders often agreed.

The custom of late marriage combined with the nuclear-family household distinguished European society from other areas of the world. It

Chapter 19
The Changing Life of the People
1700–1800

554

CHAPTER LOCATOR | How did family life change in the eighteenth century?

seems likely that the economic advantage early modern Europe acquired relative to other world regions derived in large part from this marriage pattern. Late marriage joined a mature man and a mature woman—two adults who had already accumulated social and economic capital and could transmit self-reliance and skills to the next generation. This marriage pattern also favored a greater degree of equality between husband and wife.

## Work Away from Home

Many young people worked within their families until they could start their own households. Boys plowed and wove; girls spun and tended the cows. Many others left home to work elsewhere. In the trades, a lad would enter apprenticeship around age sixteen and finish in his late teens or early twenties. During that time he would not be permitted to marry. An apprentice from a rural village would typically move to a city or town to learn a trade. If he was lucky and had connections, he might eventually be admitted to a guild and establish his economic independence. Many poor families could not afford apprenticeships for their sons. Without craft skills, these youths drifted from one low-paying job to another. They were always subject to economic fluctuations and unemployment.

Many adolescent girls also left their families to work. The range of opportunities open to them was more limited, however. Apprenticeship was sometimes available with mistresses in traditionally female occupations like seamstress, linen draper, or midwife. With the growth in production of finished goods for the emerging consumer economy during the eighteenth century (see Chapter 18), demand rose for skilled female labor and, with it, greater opportunities for women. Even male guildsmen hired girls and women, despite guild restrictions.

Service in another family's household was by far the most common job for girls, and even middle-class families often sent their daughters into service. Constantly under the eye of her mistress, the servant girl had many tasks—cleaning, shopping, cooking, child care. Often the work was endless, for there were few laws to limit exploitation. Court records are full of servant girls' complaints of physical mistreatment by their mistresses.

In theory, domestic service offered a young girl protection and security in a new family. But in practice she was often the easy prey of a lecherous master or his sons or friends. If the girl became pregnant, she could be fired without notice and thrown out in disgrace. Many families could not or would not accept such a girl back into the home. Forced to make their own way, they had no choice but to turn to a harsh life of prostitution and petty thievery (see page 557). "What are we?" exclaimed a bitter Parisian prostitute. "Most of us are unfortunate women, without origins, without education, servants and maids for the most part."[1]

## Premarital Sex and Community Controls

Ten years between puberty and marriage was a long time for sexually mature young people to wait. Many unmarried couples satisfied their sexual desires with fondling and petting. Others went further and engaged in premarital intercourse. Those who did so risked pregnancy and the stigma of illegitimate birth. Birth control was not unknown in Europe before the nineteenth century, but it was primitive and unreliable. Condoms were expensive and mainly used by aristocratic libertines and by prostitutes. The most

# Chapter Chronology

| 1717 | Elementary school attendance mandatory in Prussia |
| 1750–1791 | John Wesley preaches revival in England |
| 1750–1850 | Illegitimacy explosion |
| 1757 | Madame du Coudray, *Manual on the Art of Childbirth* |
| 1762 | Jean-Jacques Rousseau advocates more attentive child care in *Emile* |
| 1763 | Louis XV orders Jesuits out of France |
| 1774 | Elementary school attendance mandatory in Austria |
| 1776 | Thomas Paine, *Common Sense* |
| 1796 | Jenner performs first smallpox vaccination |

How did attitudes toward child rearing change in this period?

How and why did popular culture change during this period?

What role did religion play in eighteenth-century society?

How did medicine evolve in the eighteenth century?

**The Village Wedding** The spirited merrymaking of a peasant wedding was a popular theme of European artists in the eighteenth century. Given the harsh conditions of life, a wedding provided a treasured moment of feasting, dancing, and revelry. With the future of the village at stake, the celebration of marriage was a public event. (Private Collection/The Bridgeman Art Library)

common method of contraception was coitus interruptus—withdrawal by the male before ejaculation.

Did the combination of sexual activity and lack of reliable contraception mean that late marriage in preindustrial Europe went hand in hand with many illegitimate children? For most of western and central Europe until at least 1750, the answer is no. English parish registers seldom listed more than one illegitimate child out of every twenty children baptized. Some French parishes in the seventeenth century had extraordinarily low rates of illegitimacy, with less than 1 percent of babies born out of wedlock. Illegitimate babies were apparently a rarity, at least as far as the official church records are concerned.

Where collective control over sexual behavior among youths failed, community pressure to marry often prevailed. Studies of regions of France and England show that around 20 percent of children were conceived before the couple was married, but less than 5 percent were born out of wedlock.[2] No doubt many of these couples were already engaged, or at least in a committed relationship, before they entered into intimate relations, and pregnancy simply set the marriage date once and for all.

The combination of low rates of illegitimate birth with large numbers of pregnant brides reflects the powerful community controls of the traditional village, particularly the open-field village, with its pattern of cooperation and common action. Irate parents, anxious village elders, indignant priests, and stern landlords all combined to pressure

**community controls** A pattern of cooperation and common action in a traditional village that sought to uphold the economic, social, and moral stability of the closely knit community.

Chapter 19
**The Changing Life of the People**
**556** 1700–1800

CHAPTER LOCATOR | How did family life change in the eighteenth century?

young people who wavered about marriage in the face of unexpected pregnancies. In the countryside these controls meant that premarital sex was not entered into lightly and that it was generally limited to those contemplating marriage.

The concerns of the village and the family weighed heavily on couple's lives after marriage as well. Whereas uninvolved individuals today try to stay out of the domestic disputes of their neighbors, the people in peasant communities gave such affairs loud and unfavorable publicity either at the time or during the carnival season (see page 565). Relying on degrading public rituals, the young men of the village would typically gang up on their victim and force him or her to sit astride a donkey facing backward and holding up the donkey's tail. They would parade the overly brutal spouse-beater or the adulterous couple around the village, loudly proclaiming the offender's misdeeds. The donkey ride and other colorful humiliations were common punishments throughout much of Europe. They epitomized the community's effort to police personal behavior and maintain moral standards.

## New Patterns of Marriage and Illegitimacy

In the second half of the eighteenth century, long-standing patterns of marriage and illegitimacy shifted dramatically. One important change was a rise in young people's ability to choose partners for themselves, rather than following the economic or social interests of their families. This change occurred because social and economic transformations made it harder for families and communities to supervise their behavior. More youths in the countryside worked for their own wages, rather than on a family farm, and their economic autonomy translated into increased freedom of action. Moreover, many youths joined the flood of migrants to the cities, either with their families or in search of work on their own. Urban life provided young people with more social contacts and less social control.

One less positive outcome of loosening social control was an illegitimacy explosion. Why did the number of illegitimate births skyrocket? One reason was a rise in sexual activity among young people. The loosened social controls that gave young people more choice in marriage also provided them with more opportunities to yield to the attraction of the opposite sex. As in previous generations, many of the young couples who engaged in sexual activity intended to marry. In one medium-size French city in 1787–1788, the great majority of unwed mothers stated that sexual intimacy had followed promises of marriage.

The problem for young women who became pregnant was that fewer men followed through on their promises. The second half of the eighteenth century witnessed sharply rising prices for food, homes, and other necessities of life. Wages rose too, but not enough to offset price increases. Many men were no doubt sincere in their proposals, but their lives were insecure, and they hesitated to take on the burden of a wife and child. Thus, while some happy couples benefited from matches of love rather than convenience, in many cases the intended marriage did not take place. The romantic, yet practical dreams and aspirations of young people were frustrated by low wages, inequality, and changing economic and social conditions. Old patterns of marriage and family were breaking down. Only in the late nineteenth century would more stable patterns reappear.

## Sex on the Margins of Society

Not all sex acts took place between men and women hopeful of marriage. Prostitution offered both single and married men an outlet for sexual desire. After a long period of relative tolerance, prostitutes encountered increasingly harsh and repressive laws in the sixteenth and early seventeenth centuries as officials across Europe began to close licensed brothels and declare prostitution illegal.

**illegitimacy explosion** The sharp increase in out-of-wedlock births that occurred in Europe between 1750 and 1850, caused by low wages and the breakdown of community controls.

How did attitudes toward child rearing change in this period?

How and why did popular culture change during this period?

What role did religion play in eighteenth-century society?

How did medicine evolve in the eighteenth century?

557

Despite this repression, prostitution continued to flourish in the eighteenth century. Most prostitutes were working women who turned to the sex trade when confronted with unemployment or seasonal shortages of work. Such women did not become social pariahs, but retained ties with the communities of laboring poor to which they belonged. If caught by the police, however, they were liable to imprisonment or banishment. Farther up the social scale were courtesans whose wealthy protectors provided apartments, servants, clothing, and cash. After a brilliant, but brief, career, an aging courtesan faced with the loss of her wealthy client could descend once more to streetwalking.

Relations between individuals of the same sex attracted even more condemnation than prostitution, since they defied the Bible's limitation of sex to the purposes of procreation. Male same-sex relations were prohibited by law in most European states, under pain of death. Such laws, however, were enforced unevenly, most strictly in Spain and far less so in the Scandinavian countries and Russia.[3] Protected by their status, nobles and royals sometimes openly indulged their same-sex passions, which were accepted as long as they married and produced legitimate heirs. In the late seventeenth century new male homosexual subcultures began to emerge in Paris, Amsterdam, and London, with their own slang, meeting places, and styles of dress.

Same-sex relations existed among women as well, but they attracted less anxiety and condemnation than those among men. Some women were prosecuted for "unnatural" relations; others attempted to escape the narrow confines imposed on them by dressing as men. Cross-dressing women occasionally snuck into the armed forces, such as Ulrika Elenora Stålhammar, who served as a man in the Swedish army for thirteen years and married a woman. After confessing her transgressions, she was sentenced to a lenient one-month imprisonment.[4] The beginnings of a distinctive lesbian subculture appeared in London at the end of the eighteenth century.

Across the early modern period, traditional tolerance for sexual activities outside of heterosexual marriage—be they sex with prostitutes or same-sex relations among high class men—began to fade. This process accelerated in the eighteenth century, as Enlightenment critics attacked court immorality and preached virtue and morality for middle-class men, who should prove their worthiness to take over the reins of power.

## ▼ How did attitudes toward child rearing change in this period?

On the whole, European women married late, but then began bearing children rapidly. If a woman married before she was thirty, and if both she and her husband lived to fifty, she would most likely give birth to six or more children. Infant mortality was extremely high by modern standards, and many women died in childbirth due to limited medical knowledge and techniques.

For those children who did survive, new Enlightenment ideals in the latter half of the century stressed the importance of parental nurturing. New worldviews also led to an increase in elementary schools throughout Europe, but despite the efforts of enlightened absolutists and religious institutions, formal education played only a modest role in the lives of ordinary children.

### Child Care and Nursing

Newborns entered a dangerous world. They were vulnerable to infectious diseases, and many babies died of dehydration brought about by diarrhea. Of those who survived infancy, many more died in childhood. Childbirth was also dangerous. Women who bore

Chapter 19
**The Changing Life of the People**
1700–1800

558

CHAPTER LOCATOR | How did family life change in the eighteenth century?

six children faced a cumulative risk of dying in childbirth a thousand times as great as the risk in Europe today.[5] They died from blood loss and shock during delivery and from infections caused by unsanitary conditions.

In the countryside, women of the lower classes generally breast-fed their infants for two years or more. Although not a foolproof means of birth control, breast-feeding decreases the likelihood of pregnancy by delaying the resumption of ovulation. By nursing their babies, women limited their fertility and spaced their children two or three years apart. Nursing also saved lives: breast-fed infants received precious immunity-producing substances and were more likely to survive than those who were fed other food.

Women of the aristocracy and upper middle class seldom nursed their own children. Instead, they hired live-in wet nurses to suckle their children. Working women in the cities also relied on wet nurses because they needed to earn a living. Unable to afford live-in wet nurses, they often turned to the cheaper services of women in the countryside. Rural wet-nursing was a widespread business in the eighteenth century, conducted within the framework of the putting-out system.

**wet-nursing** A widespread and flourishing business in the eighteenth century in which women were paid to breast-feed other women's babies.

In the second half of the eighteenth century critics mounted a harsh attack against wet-nursing. Enlightenment thinkers proclaimed that wet-nursing was robbing European society of reaching its full potential. They were convinced, incorrectly, that the population was declining (in fact it was rising, but they lacked accurate population data) and blamed this decline on women's failure to nurture their children properly. Some also railed against practices of contraception and masturbation, which they believed were robbing their nations of potential children. Despite these complaints, many women had no choice but to rely on wet nurses until the late-nineteenth-century introduction of sterilized cows' milk and artificial nipples.

**Arrival of the Wet Nurses** Wet-nursing was big business in eighteenth-century France, particularly in Paris and the north. Here, rural wet nurses bring their charges back to the city to be reunited with their families after around two years of care. These children were lucky survivors of a system that produced high mortality rates. (Réunion des Musées Nationaux/Art Resource, NY)

How did attitudes toward child rearing change in this period?

How and why did popular culture change during this period?

What role did religion play in eighteenth-century society?

How did medicine evolve in the eighteenth century?

559

## Foundlings and Infanticide

The young woman who could not provide for an unwanted child had few choices, especially if she had no prospect of marriage. Abortions were illegal, dangerous, and apparently rare. In desperation, some women, particularly in the countryside, hid unwanted pregnancies, delivered in secret, and smothered their newborn infants. If discovered, infanticide (ihn-FAN-tuh-sighd) was punishable by death.

Women in cities had more choices to dispose of babies they could not support. Foundling homes (orphanages) first took hold in Italy, Spain, and Portugal in the sixteenth century, spreading to France in 1670 and the rest of Europe in the following decades. As new homes were established and old ones expanded, the number of foundlings being cared for surged. By the end of the century European foundling hospitals were admitting annually about one hundred thousand abandoned children, nearly all of them infants.

Across Europe, foundling homes emerged as a favorite charity of the rich and powerful. At their best, eighteenth-century foundling homes were a good example of Christian charity and social concern in an age of great poverty and inequality. Yet the foundling home was no panacea. By the 1770s one-third of all babies born in Paris were being immediately abandoned to foundling homes by their mothers. Many were the offspring of single women, the result of the illegitimacy explosion of the second half of the eighteenth century. But fully one-third of all the foundlings were abandoned by married couples too poor to feed another child.[6]

Great numbers of babies entered foundling homes, but few left. Even in the best of these homes, 50 percent of the babies normally died within a year. In the worst, fully 90 percent did not survive.[7] They succumbed to long journeys over rough roads, neglect by their wet nurses, and customary childhood illnesses. So great were the losses that some contemporaries called the foundling hospitals "legalized infanticide."

##  Attitudes Toward Children

What were the typical circumstances of children's lives? The topic of parental attitudes toward children in the early modern period remains controversial. Some scholars have claimed that parents did not risk forming emotional attachments to young children because of high mortality rates. With a reasonable expectation that a child might die, some scholars believe, parents maintained an attitude of indifference, if not downright negligence.

Contemporaries were well aware of the dangers of childhood and of the high mortality rates. The great eighteenth-century English historian Edward Gibbon (1737–1794) wrote, with some exaggeration, that "the death of a new born child before that of its parents may seem unnatural but it is a strictly probable event, since of any given number the greater part are extinguished before the ninth year, before they possess the faculties of the mind and the body."

Emotional prudence could lead to emotional distance. The French essayist Michel de Montaigne, who lost five of his six daughters in infancy, wrote, "I cannot abide that passion for caressing new-born children, which have neither mental activities nor recognisable bodily shape by which to make themselves loveable and I have never willingly suffered them to be fed in my presence."[8] In contrast to this harsh picture, however, historians have drawn ample evidence from diaries, letters, and family portraits that many parents did cherish their children and suffered greatly when they died. The English poet Ben Jonson wrote movingly in "On My First Son" of the death of his six-year-old son Benjamin in 1603:

*Farewell, thou child of my right hand, and joy;*
*My sin was too much hope of thee, loved boy.*

Chapter 19
**The Changing Life of the People**
**560**   1700–1800

CHAPTER LOCATOR | How did family life change in the eighteenth century?

*The First Step of Childhood* This tender snapshot of a baby's first steps toward an adoring mother exemplifies new attitudes toward children and raising them ushered in by the Enlightenment. Authors like Jean-Jacques Rousseau encouraged elite mothers like the one pictured here to take a more personal interest in raising their children, instead of leaving them in the hands of indifferent wet nurses and nannies. Many women responded eagerly to this call, and the period saw a more sentimentalized view of childhood and family life. (Erich Lessing/Art Resource, NY)

*Seven years thou wert lent to me, and I thee pay,*
*Exacted by thy fate, on the just day.*

Discipline of children was often severe. The axiom "Spare the rod and spoil the child" seems to have been coined in the mid-seventeenth century. Susannah Wesley (1669–1742), mother of John Wesley, the founder of Methodism (see page 574), agreed. According to her, the first task of a parent toward her children was "to conquer the will, and bring them to an obedient temper."

The Enlightenment produced an enthusiastic new discourse about childhood and child rearing. Starting around 1760 critics called for greater tenderness toward children and proposed imaginative new teaching methods. In addition to supporting foundling homes and urging women to nurse their babies, these new voices ridiculed the practice of swaddling babies and using rigid whale-boned corsets to mold children's bones. Instead of dressing children in miniature versions of adult clothing, critics called for loose and comfortable clothing to allow freedom of movement. These voices belonged to the overall Enlightenment celebration of nature and the natural laws that should guide human behavior. For Enlightenment thinkers, the best hopes for creating a new society, untrammeled by the prejudices of the past, lay in a radical reform of child-rearing techniques.

How did attitudes toward child rearing change in this period?　　How and why did popular culture change during this period?　　What role did religion play in eighteenth-century society?　　How did medicine evolve in the eighteenth century?

561

One of the century's most influential works on child rearing was Jean-Jacques Rousseau's *Emile or On Education* (1762), which fervently advocated breast-feeding and natural dress. Rousseau argued that boys' education should include plenty of fresh air and exercise and that they should be taught practical craft skills in addition to book learning. Rousseau insisted that girls' education focus on their future domestic responsibilities. For Rousseau, women's "nature" destined them solely for a life of marriage and child rearing. The ideas of Rousseau and other reformers became extremely popular and helped foster more sentimental attitudes toward children.

## The Spread of Elementary Schools

The availability of education outside the home gradually increased over the early modern period. The wealthy led the way in the sixteenth century with special colleges, often run by Jesuits in Catholic areas. Schools charged specifically with educating children of the common people began to appear in the second half of the seventeenth century. Such schools specialized in teaching six- to twelve-year-old children basic literacy, religion, and perhaps some arithmetic for the boys and needlework for the girls. The number of such schools expanded in the eighteenth century, although they were never sufficient to educate the mass of the population.

Religious faith played an important role in the spread of education. From the middle of the seventeenth century, Presbyterian Scotland was convinced that the path to salvation lay in careful study of the Scriptures, and it established an effective network of parish schools for rich and poor alike. The Church of England and the dissenting congregations — Puritans, Presbyterians, Quakers, and so on — established "charity schools" to instruct poor children. The first proponents of universal education, in Prussia, were inspired by the Protestant idea that every believer should be able to read the Bible and by the new idea of a population capable of effectively serving the state. As early as 1717 Prussia made attendance at elementary schools compulsory for boys and girls, albeit only in areas where schools already existed.[9]

Catholic states pursued their own programs of popular education. In the 1660s France began setting up charity schools to teach poor children their catechism and prayers as well as reading and writing. Enthusiasm for popular education was even greater in the Habsburg Empire, inspired by the expansion of schools in rival German states. In 1774 Maria Theresa issued her own compulsory education edict, imposing five hours of school, five days a week, for all children aged six to twelve.[10] Across Europe some elementary education was becoming a reality, and schools were of growing significance in the life of the child.

## ▼ How and why did popular culture change during this period?

Because of the new efforts in education, basic literacy was growing among the popular classes, whose reading habits centered primarily on religious material, but who also began to incorporate more practical and entertaining literature. In addition to reading, people of all classes enjoyed a range of leisure activities including storytelling, fairs, festivals, and sports.

One of the most important developments in European society in the eighteenth century was the emergence of a fledgling consumer culture. Much of the expansion took place among the upper and upper-middle classes, but a boom in cheap reproductions of luxury items also permitted people of modest means to participate. From food to ribbons and

Chapter 19
**The Changing Life of the People**
**562** 1700–1800

CHAPTER LOCATOR | How did family life change in the eighteenth century?

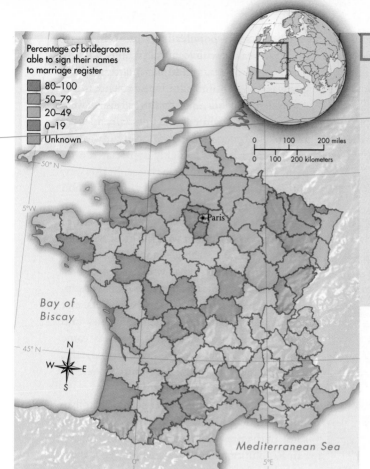

Percentage of bridegrooms able to sign their names to marriage register
- 80–100
- 50–79
- 20–49
- 0–19
- Unknown

■ MAPPING THE PAST

**Map 19.1 Literacy in France, ca. 1789**
Literacy rates increased, but they still varied widely between and within states in eighteenth-century Europe.

**ANALYZING THE MAP** What trends in French literacy rates does this map reveal? Which regions seem to be ahead? How would you account for the regional variations?

**CONNECTIONS** Note the highly variable nature of literacy rates across the country. Why might the rate of literacy be higher closer to the capital city of Paris? Why would some areas have low rates?

To complete this activity online, go to the Online Study Guide at bedfordstmartins.com/mckaywestunderstanding.

from coal stoves to umbrellas, the material worlds of city dwellers grew richer and more diverse. This "consumer revolution," as it has been called, created new expectations for comfort, hygiene, and self-expression in daily life, thus dramatically changing European life in the eighteenth century.

## Popular Literature

The surge in childhood education in the eighteenth century led to a remarkable growth in basic literacy between 1600 and 1800. Whereas in 1600 only one male in six was barely literate in France and Scotland, and one in four in England, by 1800 almost nine out of ten Scottish males, two out of three French males (Map 19.1), and more than half of English males were literate. In all three countries, the bulk of the jump occurred in the eighteenth century. Women were also increasingly literate, although they lagged behind men.

The growth in literacy promoted growth in reading. While the Bible remained the overwhelming favorite, especially in Protestant countries, short pamphlets known as chapbooks were the staple of popular literature. Printed on the cheapest paper, many chapbooks featured Bible stories, prayers, devotions, and the lives of saints and exemplary Christians.

Entertaining, often humorous stories formed a second element of popular literature. Fairy tales, medieval romances, true crime stories, and fantastic adventures were all widely read. These tales presented a world of danger and magic, of supernatural powers, fairy godmothers, and evil trolls, that provided a temporary flight from harsh everyday reality. They also contained nuggets of ancient folk wisdom, counseling prudence in a world full of danger and injustice.

| How did attitudes toward child rearing change in this period? | **How and why did popular culture change during this period?** | What role did religion play in eighteenth-century society? | How did medicine evolve in the eighteenth century? |

*Young Woman Reading a Letter* Literacy rates for men and women rose substantially during the eighteenth century. The novel also emerged as a new literary genre in this period. With its focus on emotions, love, and family melodrama, the novel was seen as a particularly feminine genre, and it allowed women writers more access to publication. Writing and reading letters were also associated with women. Some contemporaries worried that women's growing access to reading and writing would excite their imaginations and desires, leading to moral dissolution. (Réunion des Musées Nationaux/ Art Resource, NY)

Finally, some popular literature was highly practical, dealing with rural crafts, household repairs, useful plants, and similar matters. Much lore was stored in almanacs, where calendars listing secular, religious, and astrological events were mixed with agricultural schedules, arcane facts, and jokes. The almanac was universal, was not controversial, and was highly appreciated even by many in the comfortable classes. In this way, elites still shared some elements of a common culture with the masses.

While it is safe to say that the vast majority of ordinary people did not read the great works of the Enlightenment, that does not mean they were immune to the ideas. Urban working people were exposed to new ideas through rumors and gossip. They also had access to cheap pamphlets that helped translate Enlightenment critiques into ordinary language. Servants, who usually came from rural areas and traveled home periodically, were well situated to transmit ideas from educated employers to the village.

Certainly some ordinary people did assimilate Enlightenment ideals. Thomas Paine, author of some of the most influential texts of the American Revolution, was an English corset-maker's son who left school at age twelve and carried on his father's trade before immigrating to the colonies. His 1776 pamphlet *Common Sense* attacked the weight of custom and the evils of government against the natural society of men. This text, which sold 120,000 copies in its first months of publication, is vivid proof of working people's ability to receive Enlightenment ideas.

## Leisure and Recreation

Despite the spread of literacy, the culture of the village remained largely oral rather than written. In the winter months, peasant families gathered around the fireplace to talk, sing, tell stories, do craftwork, and keep warm. In some parts of Europe, women would gather together in someone's cottage to socialize. Sometimes a few young men would be invited so that the daughters (and mothers) could size up potential suitors in a supervised atmosphere. A favorite recreation of men was drinking and talking in public places, and it was a sorry village that had no tavern.

Towns and cities offered a wider range of amusements, including pleasure gardens, theaters, and lending libraries. Urban fairs featured food, acrobats, freak shows, and conjuring acts. Leisure activities were another form of consumption marked by growing commercialization. For example, commercial, profit-oriented spectator sports emerged in this period, such as horse races, boxing matches, and bullfights.

**Blood sports**, such as bullbaiting and cockfighting, also remained popular. In bullbaiting, the bull, usually staked on a chain in the courtyard of an inn, was attacked by ferocious dogs for the amusement of the innkeeper's clients. In cockfighting, two roosters, carefully trained by their owners and armed with razor-sharp steel spurs, slashed and

**blood sports** Popular with the eighteenth-century European masses, events such as bullbaiting and cockfighting that involved inflicting violence and bloodshed on animals.

Chapter 19
**The Changing Life of the People**
**564**　1700–1800

CHAPTER LOCATOR | How did family life change in the eighteenth century?

**A Boxing Match** The eighteenth century witnessed a rise in commercial sporting events and other leisure activities. Here two men spar in a boxing match staged in London for the entertainment of the gathered crowd. The popularity of boxing rose among wealthy spectators in the eighteenth century as bearbaiting and bullbaiting were increasingly condemned as excessively brutal. In the early years, female boxers were as popular as men. (Bildarchiv Preussischer Kulturbesitz/Art Resource, NY)

clawed each other in a small ring in a fight to the death. An added attraction of cockfighting was that spectators could bet on the combat and its uncertain outcome.

Popular recreation merged with religious celebration in a variety of festivals and processions throughout the year. The most striking display of these religiously inspired events was **carnival**, a time of reveling and excess in Catholic Europe, especially in Mediterranean countries. Carnival preceded Lent — the forty days of fasting and penitence before Easter — and for a few exceptional days a wild release of drinking, masquerading, and dancing reigned. Moreover, a combination of plays, processions, and raucous spectacles turned the established order upside down. Peasants dressed as nobles and men as women, and rich masters waited on their servants at the table. This annual holiday gave people a much appreciated chance to release their pent-up frustrations and aggressions before life returned to the usual pattern of hierarchy and hard work.

In trying to place the vibrant popular culture of the common people in broad perspective, historians have stressed the growing criticism levied against it by the educated elites in the second half of the eighteenth century. These elites, which had previously shared the enthusiasm for popular entertainments, now tended to see superstition, sin, disorder, and vulgarity.[11] The resulting attack on popular culture, which was tied to the clergy's efforts to eliminate paganism and superstition, was intensified as an educated public embraced the critical worldview of the Enlightenment.

**carnival** The few days of revelry in Catholic countries that preceded Lent and that included drinking, masquerading, dancing, and rowdy spectacles that turned the established order upside down.

How did attitudes toward child rearing change in this period?

**How and why did popular culture change during this period?**

What role did religion play in eighteenth-century society?

How did medicine evolve in the eighteenth century?

565

# New Foods and Appetites

At the beginning of the eighteenth century, ordinary men and women depended on grain as fully as they had in the past. Bread was quite literally the staff of life. Peasants in the Beauvais region of France ate two pounds of bread a day. Even peasants normally needed to buy some grain for food, and, in full accord with landless laborers and urban workers, they believed in the moral economy and the just price. That is, they believed that prices should be "fair," protecting both consumers and producers, and that just prices should be imposed by government decree if necessary. When prices rose above this level, they often took action in the form of bread riots (see Chapter 16).

The rural poor also ate a fair quantity of vegetables. Peas and beans were probably the most common. In most regions other vegetables appeared on the tables of the poor in season, primarily cabbages, carrots, and wild greens. Fruit was mostly limited to the summer months. Too precious to drink, milk was used to make cheese and butter, which peasants sold in the market to earn cash for taxes and land rents.

The common people of Europe ate less meat in 1700 than in 1500 because their general standard of living had declined and meat was more expensive. Moreover, harsh laws in most European countries reserved the right to hunt and eat game to nobles and large landowners. Few laws were more bitterly resented—or more frequently broken—by ordinary people than those governing hunting.

The diet of small traders and artisans—the people of the towns and cities—was less monotonous than that of the peasantry. Markets provided a substantial variety of meats, vegetables, and fruits, although bread and beans still formed the bulk of such families' diets. Not surprisingly, the diet of the rich was quite different from that of the poor. The upper classes were rapacious carnivores, and a truly elegant dinner consisted of an abundance of rich meat and fish dishes, complemented with sweets, cheeses, and nuts of all kinds. During such dinners, it was common to spend five or more hours at table, eating and drinking and enjoying the witty banter of polite society.

Patterns of food consumption changed markedly as the century progressed. Because of a growth of market gardening, a greater variety of vegetables appeared in towns and cities. This was particularly the case in the Low Countries and England, which pioneered new methods of farming. Introduced into Europe from the Americas—along with corn, squash, tomatoes, and many other useful plants—the potato provided an excellent new food source. Containing a good supply of carbohydrates, calories, and vitamins A and C, the potato offset the lack of vitamins from unavailable green vegetables in the poor person's winter and early-spring diet, and it provided a much higher caloric yield than grain for a given piece of land. In the course of the eighteenth century the large towns and cities of maritime Europe also began to receive semitropical fruits, such as oranges and lemons, from Portugal and the West Indies, but they remained expensive.

The most remarkable dietary change in the eighteenth century was in the consumption of sugar and tea. No other commodities grew so quickly in popularity. Previously expensive and rare luxury items, they became dietary staples for people of all social classes. This was possible, in part, because of the steady drop in prices created by the expansion of colonial slave labor in the New World. Other colonial goods also became important items of daily consumption, including coffee, tobacco, and chocolate.

Why were colonial products so popular? Part of the motivation for consuming these products was a desire to emulate the luxurious lifestyles of the elite. Having seen pictures of or read about the fine lady's habit of "tea time" or the gentleman's appreciation for a pipe, common Europeans sought to experience these pleasures for themselves. Moreover, the quickened pace of work in the eighteenth century created new needs for stimulants among working people. (See "Listening to the Past: Louis-Sébastien Mercier, A Day in

Chapter 19
**The Changing Life of the People**
**566** 1700–1800

CHAPTER LOCATOR | How did family life change in the eighteenth century?

**Chocolate Drinking** This Spanish tile from 1710 illustrates the new practice of preparing and drinking hot chocolate. Originating in the New World, chocolate was one of the many new foods imported to Europe in the wake of the voyages of discovery. The first Spanish chocolate mills opened in the mid-seventeenth century, and consumption of chocolate rapidly increased. The inclusion of this tile in the decoration of a nobleman's house testifies to public interest in the new drink. (Courtesy, Museu de Ceramica. Photo: Guillem Fernandez-Huerta)

the Life of Paris," page 568.) Whereas the gentry took tea as a leisurely and genteel ritual, the lower classes usually drank tea at work to fight monotony or fatigue. With the widespread adoption of these products, working people in Europe became increasingly dependent on faraway colonial economies and slave labor. Their understanding of daily necessities and how to procure those necessities shifted definitively, linking them to global trade networks beyond their ability to shape or control.

## Toward a Consumer Society

Along with foodstuffs, all manner of other goods increased in variety and number in the eighteenth century. This proliferation led to a growth in consumption and new attitudes toward consumer goods so wide-ranging that some historians have referred to an eighteenth-century consumer revolution.[12] The result of this revolution was the birth of a new type of society in which people derived their self-identity as much from their consuming practices as from their working lives and place in the production process. As people were provided the opportunity to pick and choose among a new variety of consumer goods, new notions of individuality and self-expression developed. The full emergence of a consumer society did not take place until much later, but its roots lie in the eighteenth century.

Increased demand for consumer goods was not merely an innate response to increased supply. Eighteenth-century merchants pioneered new techniques to incite demand: they initiated marketing campaigns, opened fancy boutiques with large windows, and advertised the patronage of royal princes and princesses. By diversifying their product lines

**consumer revolution** The wide-ranging growth in consumption and new attitudes toward consumer goods that emerged in the cities of northwestern Europe in the second half of the eighteenth century.

How did attitudes toward child rearing change in this period?

**How and why did popular culture change during this period?**

What role did religion play in eighteenth-century society?

How did medicine evolve in the eighteenth century?

**567**

# LISTENING TO THE PAST

## Louis-Sébastien Mercier, A Day in the Life of Paris

*Louis-Sébastien Mercier (1740–1814) was the best chronicler of everyday life in eighteenth-century Paris. His masterpiece was the* Tableau de Paris *(1781–1788), a multivolume work composed of 1,049 chapters that covered subjects ranging from convents to cafés, bankruptcy to booksellers, the latest fashions to royal laws. As this excerpt demonstrates, he aimed to convey the infinite diversity of people, places, and things he saw around him, and in so doing he left future generations a precious record of the changing dynamics of Parisian society in the second half of the eighteenth century.*

*Mercier's family belonged to the respectable artisan classes. This middling position ideally suited Mercier for observing the extremes of wealth and poverty around him. Although these volumes contain many wonderful glimpses of daily life, they should not be taken for an objective account. Mercier brought his own moral and political sensibilities, influenced by Jean-Jacques Rousseau, to the task.*

## Chapter 39: How the Day Goes

❝ It is curious to see how, amid what seems perpetual life and movement, certain hours keep their own characteristics, whether of bustle or of leisure. Every round of the clock-hand sets another scene in motion, each different from the last, though all about equal in length. Seven o'clock in the morning sees all the gardeners, mounted on their nags and with their baskets empty, heading back out of town again. No carriages are about, and not a presentable soul, except a few neat clerks hurrying to their offices. Nine o'clock sets all the barbers in motion, covered from head to foot with flour—hence their soubriquet of "whitings"*—wig in one hand, tongs in the other. Waiters from the lemonade-shops are busy with trays of coffee and rolls, breakfast for those who live in furnished rooms. . . . An hour later the Law comes into action; a black cloud of legal practitioners and hangers-on descend upon the Châtelet,† and the other courts; a procession of wigs and gowns and briefbags, with plaintiffs and defendants at their heels. Midday is the stockbrokers' hour, and the idlers'; the former hurry off to the Exchange, the latter to the Palais-Royal.‡ The Saint-Honoré§ quarter, where all the financiers live, is at its busiest now, its streets are crowded with the customers and clients of the great.

At two o'clock those who have invitations to dine set out, dressed in their best, powdered, adjusted, and walking on tiptoe not to soil their stockings. All the cabs are engaged, not one is to be found on the rank; there is a good deal of competition for these vehicles, and you may see two would-be passengers jumping into a cab together from different sides, and furiously disputing which was first. . . .

Three o'clock and the streets are not so full; everyone is at dinner; there is a momentary calm, soon to be broken, for at five fifteen the din is as though the gates of hell were opened, the streets are impass-able with traffic going all ways at once, towards the playhouses or the public gardens. Cafés are at their busiest.

Towards seven the din dies down, everywhere and all at once. You can hear the cab-horses' hoofs pawing the stones as they wait—in vain. It is as though the whole town were gagged and bound, suddenly, by an invisible hand. This is the most dangerous time of the whole day for thieves and such, especially towards autumn when the days begin to draw in; for the watch is not yet about, and violence takes its opportunity.

Night falls; and, while scene-shifters set to work at the play-houses, swarms of other workmen, carpenters, masons and the like, make their way towards the poorer quarters. They leave white footprints from the plaster on their shoes, a trail that any eye can follow. They are off home, and to bed, at the hour which finds elegant ladies sitting down to their dressing-tables to prepare for the business of the night.

At nine this begins; they all set off for the play. Houses tremble as the coaches rattle by, but soon the noise ceases; all the fine ladies are making their evening visits, short ones, before supper. Now the prostitutes begin their night parade, breasts uncovered, heads tossing, colour high on their cheeks, and eyes as bold as their hands. These creatures, careless of the light from shop-windows and street lamps, follow and accost you, trailing through the mud in their silk stockings and low shoes, with words and gestures well matched for obscenity. . . .

By eleven, renewed silence. People are at supper, private people, that is; for the cafés begin at this hour to turn out their patrons, and to send the various idlers and workless and poets back to their garrets for the night. A few prostitutes still linger, but they have to use more circumspection, for the watch is about, patrolling the streets, and this is the hour when they "gather 'em in"; that is the traditional expression.

A quarter after midnight, a few carriages make their way home, taking the non–card players back to bed. These lend the town a sort of transitory life; the tradesman wakes out of his first sleep at the sound of them, and turns to his wife, by no means unwilling. More than one young Parisian must owe his existence to this sudden passing rattle of wheels. . . .

At one in the morning six thousand peasants arrive, bringing the town's provision of vegetables and fruits and flowers, and make straight for the Halles**;. . . . As for the market itself, it never sleeps. . . . Perpetual noise, perpetual motion, the curtain never rings down on the enormous stage; first come the fishmongers, and after these the egg-dealers, and after these the retail buyers; for the Halles keep all the other markets

Chapter 19
**The Changing Life of the People**

568        1700–1800

CHAPTER LOCATOR | How did family life change in the eighteenth century?

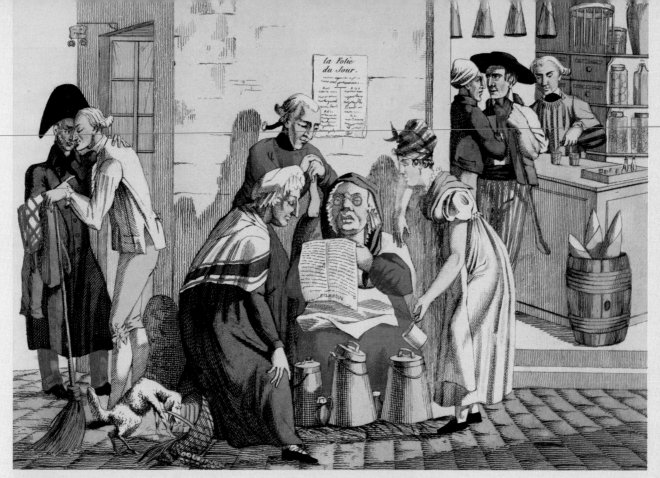

In this Parisian street scene, a milk seller doubles as a provider of news, reading a hand-printed news sheet to a small gathering. Gossip, rumor, and formal or informal newspapers, like the one pictured here, ensured that information traversed the city at astonishing speeds. (Musée de la Ville de Paris, Musée Carnavalet, Paris/Lauros/Giraudon/The Bridgeman Art Library)

of Paris going; they are the warehouses whence these draw their supplies. The food of the whole city is shifted and sorted in high-piled baskets; you may see eggs, pyramids of eggs, moved here and there, up steps and down, in and out of the throngs, miraculous; not one is ever broken. . . .

This impenetrable din contrasts oddly with the sleeping streets, for at that hour none but thieves and poets are awake.

Twice a week, at six, those distributors of the staff of life, the bakers of Gonesse,†† bring in an enormous quantity of loaves to the town, and may take none back through the barriers. And at this same hour work-men take up their tools, and trudge off to their day's labour. Coffee with milk is, unbelievably, the favoured drink among these stalwarts nowadays. . . .

So coffee-drinking has become a habit, and one so deep-rooted that the working classes will start the day on nothing else. It is not costly, and has more flavour to it, and more nourishment too, than any-thing else they can afford to drink; so they consume immense quantities, and say that if a man can only have coffee for breakfast it will keep him going till nightfall. 𝄞

**Source:** Excerpt from *Panorama of Paris: Selections from "Le Tableau de Paris,"* by Louis Sébastien Mercier, based on the translation by Helen Simpson, edited with a new preface and translations by Jeremy D. Popkin. Copyright © 1999 The Pennsylvania State University. Reprinted by permission of Penn State Press.

## QUESTIONS FOR ANALYSIS

1. What different social groups does Mercier describe in Paris? Does he approve or disapprove of Parisian society as he describes it?
2. How do the social classes described by Mercier differ in their use of time, and why? Do you think the same distinctions exist today?
3. What evidence of the consumer revolution can you find in Mercier's account? How do the goods used by eighteenth-century Parisians compare to the ones you use in your life today?

*Small fish typically rolled in flour and fried.
†The main criminal court of Paris.
‡A garden surrounded by arcades with shops and cafés.
§A fashionable quarter for the wealthy.
**The city's central wholesale food market.
††A suburb of Paris, famous for the excellent bread baked there.

How did attitudes toward child rearing change in this period?

How and why did popular culture change during this period?

What role did religion play in eighteenth-century society?

How did medicine evolve in the eighteenth century?

## The Fashion Merchant

Well-to-do women spent their mornings preparing their toilettes and receiving visits from close friends and purveyors of various goods and services. In this 1746 painting by François Boucher, a leisured lady has just been coiffed by her hairdresser. Wearing the cape she donned to protect her clothing from the hair powder, she receives a fashion merchant, who displays an array of ribbons and other baubles. (Photos 12.com — ARJ)

**ANALYZING THE IMAGE** In this painting, which woman is the fashion merchant and which is her client? What are they doing at the moment the picture is painted? How would you characterize the relationship between the two women in this painting?

**CONNECTIONS** In what ways does the fashion merchant's attire provide evidence of the consumer revolution of the eighteenth century? Compare this image to the painting of the serving girl (page 554). What contrasting images of the working woman do these two images present?

To complete this activity online, go to the Online Study Guide at bedfordstmartins.com/mckaywestunderstanding.

and greatly accelerating the turnover of styles, they seized the reins of fashion from the courtiers who had earlier controlled it. Instead of setting new styles, duchesses and marquises now bowed to the dictates of fashion merchants. (See "Individuals in Society: Rose Bertin, 'Minister of Fashion,'" page 571.) Fashion also extended beyond court circles to touch many more items and social groups.

Clothing was one of the chief indicators of the growth of consumerism. Shrewd entrepreneurs made fashionable clothing seem more desirable, while legions of women entering the textile and needle trades made it ever cheaper. As a result, eighteenth-century western Europe witnessed a dramatic rise in the consumption of clothing, particularly in large cities. Colonial economies again played an important role lowering the cost of materials, such as cotton and vegetable dyes, largely due to the unpaid toil of enslaved Africans. Cheaper copies of elite styles made it possible for working people to aspire to follow fashion for the first time.

The spread of fashion was primarily a female phenomenon. Parisian women significantly out-consumed men, acquiring larger and more expensive wardrobes than those of their husbands, brothers, and fathers. This was true across the social spectrum; in ribbons, shoes, gloves, and lace, European working women reaped in the consumer revolution what they had sown in the industrious revolution (see Chapter 18). There were also new gender distinctions in dress. Previously, noblemen vied with noblewomen in the magnificence and ostentation of their apparel; by the end of the eighteenth century men were wearing early versions of the plain dark suit that remains standard male formal

Chapter 19
**The Changing Life of the People**
1700–1800

570

CHAPTER LOCATOR | How did family life change in the eighteenth century?

**This portrait of Rose Bertin was painted at the height of her popularity in 1780.** (Jean-Francois Janinet, French, 1752–1814, *Mademoiselle Bertin*, n.d., engraving on paper, 155 × 135 mm [image/plate]; 120 × 105 mm [primary support]; 280 × 215 mm [secondary support], Celia Culver Gilbert Memorial Collection, 1924.1309, The Art Institute of Chicago. Photography © The Art Institute of Chicago)

**ONE DAY IN 1779, AS THE FRENCH ROYAL FAMILY** rode in a carriage through the streets of Paris, Queen Marie-Antoinette noticed her fashion merchant, Rose Bertin, observing the royal procession. "Ah! there is mademoiselle Bertin," the queen exclaimed, waving her hand. Bertin responded with a curtsey. The king then stood and greeted Bertin, followed by the royal family and their entourage.* The incident shocked the public, for no common merchant had ever received such homage from royalty.

Bertin had come a long way from her humble beginnings. Born in 1747 to a poor family in northern France, she moved to Paris in the 1760s to work as a shop assistant. Bertin eventually opened her own boutique on the fashionable rue Saint-Honoré. In 1775 Bertin received the highest honor of her profession when she was selected by Marie-Antoinette as one of her official purveyors.

Based on the queen's patronage, and riding the wave of the new consumer revolution, Bertin became one of the most successful entrepreneurs in Europe. Bertin established not only a large clientele, but also a reputation for arrogance. She refused to work for non-noble customers, claiming that the orders of the queen and her court claimed all her attention. She astounded courtiers by referring to her "work" with the queen, as though the two were collaborators rather than absolute monarch and lowly subject. Bertin's close relationship with Marie-Antoinette and the fortune the queen spent on her wardrobe

hurt the royal family's image. One journalist derided Bertin as a "minister of fashion," whose influence outstripped that of all the others in royal government.

In January 1787 rumors spread through Paris that Bertin had filed for bankruptcy with debts of 2 to 3 million livres (a worker's annual salary was around 200 livres). Despite her notoriously high prices and rich clients, this news did not shock Parisians, because the nobility's reluctance to pay its debts was equally well known. Bertin somehow held on to her business. Some said she had spread the bankruptcy rumors herself to shame the court into paying her bills.

Bertin remained loyal to the crown during the tumult of the French Revolution and sent dresses to the queen even after the arrest of the royal family. Fearing for her life, she left France for Germany in 1792 and continued to ply her profession in exile. She returned to France in 1800 and died in 1813, one year before the restoration of the Bourbon monarchy might have renewed her acclaim.†

Rose Bertin scandalized public opinion with her self-aggrandizement and ambition, yet history was on her side. She was the first celebrity fashion stylist and one of the first self-made career women to rise from obscurity to fame and fortune based on her talent, taste, and hard work. Her legacy remains in the exalted status of today's top fashion designers and in the dreams of small-town girls to make it in the big city.

### QUESTIONS FOR ANALYSIS

1. Why was the relationship between Queen Marie-Antoinette and Rose Bertin so troubling to public opinion? Why would relations between a queen and a fashion merchant have political implications?
2. Why would someone who sold fashionable clothing and accessories rise to such a prominent position in business and society? What makes fashion so important in the social world?

*Mémoires secrets pour servir à l'histoire de la république des lettres en France*, vol. 13, 299, 5 mars 1779 (London: John Adamson, 1785).

†On Rose Bertin, see Clare Haru Crowston, "The Queen and Her 'Minister of Fashion': Gender, Credit and Politics in Pre-Revolutionary France," *Gender and History* 14, 1 (April 2002): 92–116.

How did attitudes toward child rearing change in this period?

How and why did popular culture change during this period?

What role did religion play in eighteenth-century society?

How did medicine evolve in the eighteenth century?

571

wear in the West. This was one more aspect of the increasingly rigid differences drawn between appropriate male and female behavior.

Changes in outward appearances were reflected in inner spaces as new attitudes about privacy and intimate life also emerged. In 1700 the cramped home of a modest family consisted of a few rooms, each of which had multiple functions. The same room was used for sleeping, receiving friends, and working. In the eighteenth century rents rose sharply, making it impossible to gain more space, but families began attributing specific functions to specific rooms. They also began to erect inner barriers within the home to provide small niches in which individuals could seek privacy.

New levels of comfort and convenience accompanied this trend toward more individualized ways of life. In 1700 a meal might be served in a common dish, with each person dipping his or her spoon into the pot. By the end of the eighteenth century even humble households contained a much greater variety of cutlery and dishes, making it possible for each person to eat from his or her own plate. More books and prints, which also proliferated at lower prices, decorated the shelves and walls. Improvements in glassmaking provided more transparent glass, which allowed daylight to penetrate into gloomy rooms. Cold and smoky hearths were increasingly replaced by more efficient and cleaner coal stoves. Rooms were warmer, better lit, more comfortable, and more personalized.

**The Consumer Revolution** From the mid-eighteenth century on, the cities of western Europe witnessed a new proliferation of consumer goods. Items once limited to the wealthy few—such as fans, watches, snuffboxes, umbrellas, ornamental containers (right), and teapots—were now reproduced in cheaper versions for middling and ordinary people. The fashion for wide hoopskirts was so popular that the armrests on the chairs of the day, known as Louis XV chairs (left), were specially designed to accommodate them. (jar: Victoria & Albert Museum, London/The Bridgeman Art Library; chair: Louvre/Réunion des Musées Nationaux/Art Resource, NY)

Chapter 19
**The Changing Life of the People**
1700–1800

572

CHAPTER LOCATOR | How did family life change in the eighteenth century?

The scope of the new consumer economy should not be exaggerated. These developments were concentrated in large cities in northwestern Europe and in the colonial cities of North America. Even in these centers the elite benefited the most from new modes of life. This was not yet the society of mass consumption that emerged toward the end of the nineteenth century with the full expansion of the Industrial Revolution. The eighteenth century did, however, lay the foundations for one of the most distinctive features of modern Western life: societies based on the consumption of goods and services obtained through the market in which individuals form their identities and self-worth through the goods they consume.

# ▼ What role did religion play in eighteenth-century society?

Though the critical spirit of the Enlightenment made great inroads in the eighteenth century, the majority of ordinary men and women, especially those in rural areas, remained committed Christians. Religious faith promised salvation, and it gave comfort in the face of sorrow and death. Religion also remained strong because it was embedded in local traditions and everyday social experience.

Yet the popular religion of village Europe was also enmeshed in a larger world of church hierarchies and state power. These powerful outside forces sought to regulate religious life at the local level. Their efforts created tensions that helped set the scene for vigorous religious revivals in Protestant Germany and England as well as in Catholic France. Tensions arose between authorities and the people as powerful elites began to criticize many popular religious practices that their increasingly rationalistic minds deemed foolish and superstitious.

## Church Hierarchy

As in the Middle Ages, the local parish church remained the focal point of religious devotion and community cohesion. Neighbors came together in church for services, baptisms, marriages, funerals, and special events. Priests and parsons kept the community records of births, deaths, and marriages. They distributed charity and looked after orphans. They also provided primary education to the common people. Thus the parish church was woven into the very fabric of community life.

While the parish church remained central to the community, it was also subject to greater control from the state. In Protestant areas princes and monarchs headed the official church, and they regulated their "territorial churches" strictly, selecting personnel and imposing rules. By the eighteenth century the radical ideas of the Reformation had resulted in another version of church bureaucracy.

Catholic monarchs in this period also took greater control of religious matters in their kingdoms, weakening papal authority. Spain took firm control of ecclesiastical appointments. Papal proclamations could not even be read in Spanish churches without prior approval from the government. Spain also asserted state control over the Spanish Inquisition, which pursued heresy as an independent agency under Rome's direction and went far toward creating a "national" Catholic Church, as France had done earlier.

A more striking indication of state power and papal weakness was the fate of the Society of Jesus, or Jesuits. The Jesuits were extraordinary teachers, missionaries, and agents of the papacy. In many Catholic countries they exercised tremendous political influence, holding high government positions and educating the nobility in their colleges. Yet by playing politics so effectively, the Jesuits eventually elicited a broad coalition of enemies.

How did attitudes toward child rearing change in this period?

How and why did popular culture change during this period?

**What role did religion play in eighteenth-century society?**

How did medicine evolve in the eighteenth century?

573

Bitter controversies led Louis XV to order the Jesuits out of France in 1763 and to confiscate their property. France and Spain then pressured Rome to dissolve the Jesuits completely. In 1773 a reluctant pope caved in, although the order was revived after the French Revolution.

Some Catholic rulers also believed that the clergy in monasteries and convents should make a more practical contribution to social and religious life. Austria, a leader in controlling the church (see Chapter 17) and promoting primary education, showed how far the process could go. Maria Theresa began by sharply restricting entry into "unproductive" orders. In his Edict on Idle Institutions, her successor, Joseph II, abolished contemplative orders, henceforth permitting only orders that were engaged in teaching, nursing, or other practical work. The state expropriated the dissolved monasteries and used their wealth for charitable purposes and higher salaries for ordinary priests. Joseph II also issued edicts of religious tolerance, including for Jews, making Austria one of the first European states to lift centuries-old restrictions on its Jewish population.

## Protestant Revival

By the late seventeenth century the vast reforms of the Protestant Reformation were complete and had been widely adopted in most Protestant churches. Medieval practices of idolatry, saint worship, and pageantry were abolished; stained glass windows were smashed and murals whitewashed. Yet many official Protestant churches had settled into a smug complacency. This, along with the growth of state power and bureaucracy in local parishes threatened to eclipse one of the Reformation's main goals — to bring all believers closer to God.

In this context, a Protestant revival began in Germany in the late seventeenth century. It was known as **Pietism** (PIGH-uh-tih-zum), and three aspects helped explain its powerful appeal. First, Pietism called for a warm, emotional religion that everyone could experience. Enthusiasm — in prayer, in worship, in preaching, in life itself — was the key concept. "Just as a drunkard becomes full of wine, so must the congregation become filled with spirit," declared one exuberant writer. Another said simply, "The heart must burn."[13]

Second, Pietism reasserted the earlier radical stress on the priesthood of all believers, thereby reducing the gulf between official clergy and Lutheran laity. Bible reading and study were enthusiastically extended to all classes, and this provided a powerful spur for popular literacy as well as individual religious development (see page 563). Pietists were largely responsible for the educational reforms implemented by Prussia in the early eighteenth century. Finally, Pietists believed in the practical power of Christian rebirth in everyday affairs. Reborn Christians were expected to lead good, moral lives and to come from all social classes.

Pietism soon spread through the German-speaking lands and to Scandinavia. It also had a major impact on John Wesley (1703–1791), who served as the catalyst for popular religious revival in England. Wesley came from a long line of ministers, and when he went to Oxford University to prepare for the clergy, he organized a Holy Club for similarly minded students, who were soon known contemptuously as **Methodists** because they were so methodical in their devotion. Yet like the young Martin Luther, Wesley remained intensely troubled about his own salvation even after his ordination as an Anglican priest in 1728.

Wesley's anxieties related to grave problems of the faith in England. The government shamelessly used the Church of England to provide favorites with high-paying jobs. Both church and state officials failed to respond to the spiritual needs of the people, abandoning the construction of new churches while the population grew, and in many parishes there was a shortage of pews. Services and sermons had settled into an uninspiring routine. Moreover, Enlightenment skepticism was making inroads among the educated classes, and deism — a belief in God but not in organized religion — was becoming popu-

**Pietism** A Protestant revival movement in early-eighteenth-century Germany and Scandinavia that emphasized a warm and emotional religion, the priesthood of all believers, and the power of Christian rebirth in everyday affairs.

**Methodists** Members of a Protestant revival movement started by John Wesley, so called because they were so methodical in their devotion.

Chapter 19
**The Changing Life of the People**
**574**    1700–1800

CHAPTER LOCATOR | How did family life change in the eighteenth century?

lar. Some bishops and church leaders seemed to believe that doctrines such as the virgin birth were little more than elegant superstitions.

Spiritual counseling from a sympathetic Pietist minister from Germany prepared Wesley for a mystical, emotional "conversion" he experienced in 1738 while attending a religious meeting. While listening to a speaker at the meeting, Wesley suddenly felt a new and profound faith in Christ. Wesley's emotional experience resolved his intellectual doubts. Moreover, he was convinced that any person, no matter how poor or uneducated, might have a similarly heartfelt conversion and gain the same blessed assurance. He took the good news to the people, traveling some 225,000 miles by horseback and preaching more than forty thousand sermons between 1750 and 1790. Since existing churches were often overcrowded and the church-state establishment was hostile, Wesley preached in open fields to large gatherings. Of critical importance was Wesley's rejection of Calvinist predestination—the doctrine of salvation granted to only a select few. Instead, he preached that all men and women who earnestly sought salvation might be saved. It was a message of hope and joy, of free will and universal salvation.

Wesley's ministry won converts, formed Methodist cells, and eventually resulted in a new denomination. And just as Wesley had been inspired by the Pietist revival in Germany, so evangelicals in the Church of England and the old dissenting groups now followed Wesley's example of preaching to all people, giving impetus to an even broader awakening among the lower classes. Thus, in Protestant countries religion continued to be a vital force in the lives of the people.

**Hogarth's Satirical View of the Church** William Hogarth (1697–1764) was one of the foremost satirical artists of his day. This image mocks a London Methodist meeting, where the congregation swoons in enthusiasm over the preacher's sermon. The woman in the foreground giving birth to rabbits refers to a hoax perpetrated in 1726 by a servant named Mary Tofts; the gullibility of those who believed Tofts is likened to that of the Methodist congregation. (HIP/Art Resource, NY)

## Catholic Piety

Religion also flourished in Catholic Europe around 1700, but there were important differences from Protestant practice. First, the visual contrast was striking; baroque art still lavished rich figures and images on Catholic churches, just as most Protestants had removed theirs during the Reformation. Moreover, people in Catholic Europe on the whole participated more actively in formal worship than did Protestants. More than 95 percent of the population probably attended church for Easter communion, the climax of the religious year.

The tremendous popular strength of religion in Catholic countries can in part be explained by the church's integral role in community life and popular culture. Thus, although Catholics reluctantly confessed their sins to priests, they enthusiastically joined together in religious festivals to celebrate the passage of the liturgical year. Moreover, each parish had its own saints' days, processions, and pilgrimages. Led by its priest, a congregation might march around the village or across the countryside to a local shrine. Before each procession or feast day, the priest explained its religious significance to kindle

How did attitudes toward child rearing change in this period?   How and why did popular culture change during this period?   **What role did religion play in eighteenth-century society?**   How did medicine evolve in the eighteenth century?

575

group piety. Processions were also folklore and tradition, an escape from work, and a form of recreation. The Reformation had largely eliminated such festivities in Protestant areas.

**Jansenism** A sect of Catholicism originating with Cornelius Jansen that emphasized the heavy weight of original sin and accepted the doctrine of predestination; it was outlawed as heresy by the pope.

Catholicism had its own version of the Pietist revivals that shook Protestant Europe. Jansenism originated with Cornelius Jansen (1585–1638), bishop of Ypres in the Spanish Netherlands, who called for a return to the austere early Christianity of Saint Augustine. In contrast to the worldly Jesuits, Jansen emphasized the heavy weight of original sin and accepted the doctrine of predestination. Although outlawed by papal and royal edicts as Calvinist heresy, Jansenism attracted Catholic followers eager for religious renewal, particularly among the French. Many members of France's urban elite, especially judicial nobles and some parish priests, became known for their Jansenist piety and spiritual devotion. Such stern religious values encouraged the judiciary's increasing opposition to the French monarchy in the second half of the eighteenth century.

Among the urban poor, a different strain of Jansenism took hold. Prayer meetings brought men and women together in ecstatic worship, and some participants fell into convulsions and spoke in tongues. The police of Paris posted spies to report on such gatherings and conducted mass raids and arrests.

### Marginal Beliefs and Practices

In the countryside, many peasants continued to hold religious beliefs that were marginal to the Christian faith altogether, often of obscure or even pagan origin. On the Feast of Saint Anthony, for example, priests were expected to bless salt and bread for farm animals to protect them from disease. Catholics believed that saints' relics could bring fortune or attract lovers, and there were healing springs for many ailments. The ordinary person combined strong Christian faith with a wealth of time-honored superstitions.

Inspired initially by the fervor of the Reformation era, then by the critical rationalism of the Enlightenment, religious and secular authorities sought increasingly to "purify" popular spirituality. The severity of the attack on popular belief varied widely by country and region. Where authorities pursued purification vigorously, as in Austria under Joseph II, pious peasants saw only an incomprehensible attack on age-old faith and drew back in anger. Their reaction dramatized the growing tension between the attitudes of educated elites and the common people.

It was in this era of growing intellectual disdain for popular beliefs that the persecution of witches slowly came to an end across Europe. Common people in the countryside continued to fear the devil and his helpers, but the elite increasingly dismissed such fears and refused to prosecute suspected witches. The last witch was executed in England in 1682, the same year France prohibited witchcraft trials. By the late eighteenth century most European states and their colonies had followed suit.

## ▼ How did medicine evolve in the eighteenth century?

Although significant breakthroughs in medical science would not come until the late nineteenth century, the Enlightenment's growing focus on discovering the laws of nature and on human problems did give rise to a great deal of research and experimentation in the 1700s. Medical practitioners greatly increased in number, although their techniques did not differ much from those of previous generations. Care of the sick in this era was the domain of several competing groups: faith healers, apothecaries (pharmacists), physicians, surgeons, and midwives. From the Middle Ages through the seventeenth century,

Chapter 19
**The Changing Life of the People**
**576**   1700–1800

CHAPTER LOCATOR   | How did family life change in the eighteenth century?

both men and women were medical practitioners. However, since women were generally denied admission to medical colleges and lacked the diplomas necessary to practice, the range of medical activities open to them was restricted. In the eighteenth century women's traditional roles as midwives and healers eroded even further.

## Faith Healing and General Practice

In the course of the eighteenth century, faith healers remained active. They and their patients believed that evil spirits caused disease by lodging in people and that the proper treatment was to exorcise, or drive out, the offending devil. This demonic view of disease was strongest in the countryside, where popular belief placed great faith in the healing power of religious relics, prayer, and the laying on of hands.

In the larger towns and cities, apothecaries sold herbs, drugs, and patent medicines for every conceivable "temperament and distemper." Like all varieties of medical practitioners, apothecaries advertised their wares, their high-class customers, and their miraculous cures in newspapers and commercial circulars. Medicine, like food and fashionable clothing, thus joined the era's new commercial culture.

**An Eighteenth-Century Pharmacy** In this lively painting a woman consults an apothecary (in the elegant red suit) while his assistants assemble drugs for new prescriptions. By 1700 apothecaries had emerged as a separate group of state-licensed medical professionals. They drew on published lists and books describing the properties and dosages of their concoctions, but there were many different "recipes" and trade secrets. (Civico Museo Bibliograco Musicale, Bologna, Italy/The Bridgeman Art Library)

Physicians, who were invariably men, were apprenticed in their teens to practicing physicians for several years of on-the-job training. This training was then rounded out with hospital work or some university courses. Because such prolonged training was expensive, physicians came mainly from prosperous families, and they usually concentrated on urban patients from similar social backgrounds.

Physicians in the eighteenth century were increasingly willing to experiment with new methods, but time-honored practices lay heavily on them. Like apothecaries, they laid great stress on purging, and bloodletting was still considered a medical cure-all.

## Surgery

Long considered to be craftsmen comparable to butchers and barbers, surgeons began studying anatomy seriously and improved their art in the eighteenth century. The eighteenth-century surgeon (and patient) labored in the face of incredible difficulties. Almost all operations were performed without painkillers, for the anesthesia of the day was hard to control and too dangerous for general use. Many patients died from the agony and shock of such operations. Surgery was also performed in utterly unsanitary conditions, for there was no knowledge of bacteriology and the nature of infection. The simplest wound treated by a surgeon could fester and lead to death.

How did attitudes toward child rearing change in this period?

How and why did popular culture change during this period?

What role did religion play in eighteenth-century society?

How did medicine evolve in the eighteenth century?

577

## Midwifery

Midwives continued to deliver the overwhelming majority of babies throughout the eighteenth century. Trained initially by another woman practitioner—and regulated by a guild in many cities—the midwife primarily assisted in labor and delivering babies. She also treated female problems, such as irregular menstrual cycles, breast-feeding difficulties, infertility, and venereal disease, and ministered to small children.

The midwife orchestrated labor and birth in a woman's world, where friends and relatives assisted the pregnant woman in the familiar surroundings of her own home. The male surgeon (and the husband) rarely entered this female world, because most births, then as now, were normal and spontaneous. After the invention of forceps became publicized in 1734, surgeon-physicians used their monopoly over this and other instruments to seek lucrative new business. Attacking midwives as ignorant and dangerous, they sought to undermine faith in

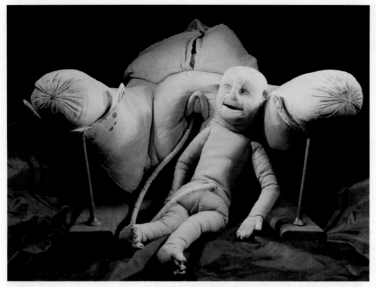

**Du Coudray's Life-Size Model for Simulating Childbirth** One of the pioneers of modern midwifery, Madame Angelique Marguerite Le Boursier du Coudray underwent a rigorous three-year apprenticeship and was a member of the Parisian surgeons' guild. After training rural midwives in the French province of Auvergne, in 1757, she published her *Manual on the Art of Childbirth*. In 1759, the French government authorized her to carry her instruction "throughout the realm," a move that may well have contributed to the decline in infant mortality in France. (Musée Flaubert d'histoire de la médecine, Rouen)

midwives and persuaded growing numbers of wealthy women of the superiority of their services.

Research suggests that women practitioners successfully defended much but not all of their practice in the eighteenth century. One enterprising French midwife, Madame du Coudray, wrote a widely used textbook, *Manual on the Art of Childbirth* (1757). She then secured royal financing for her campaign to teach better birthing techniques to village midwives. Du Coudray traveled all over France using a life-size model of the female body and fetus to help teach illiterate women.

## The Conquest of Smallpox

Experimentation and the intensified search for solutions to human problems led to some real advances in medicine after 1750. The eighteenth century's greatest medical triumph was the eradication of smallpox. With the progressive decline of bubonic plague, smallpox became the most terrible of the infectious diseases, and it is estimated that 60 million Europeans died of it in the eighteenth century.

The first step in the conquest of this killer in Europe came in the early eighteenth century. An English aristocrat, Lady Mary Wortley Montagu, learned about smallpox inoculation in the Muslim lands of western Asia while her husband was serving as British ambassador to the Ottoman Empire. She was instrumental in spreading the practice in England after her return in 1722. But inoculation was risky and was widely condemned because about one person in fifty died from it. In addition, people who had been inoculated were infectious and often spread the disease.

While the practice of inoculation with the smallpox virus was refined over the century, the crucial breakthrough was made by Edward Jenner (1749–1823), a talented country doctor. His starting point was the countryside belief that dairy maids who had contracted cowpox did not get smallpox. Cowpox produces sores that resemble those of smallpox, but the disease is mild and is not contagious.

Chapter 19
**The Changing Life of the People**
**578** 1700–1800

CHAPTER LOCATOR | How did family life change in the eighteenth century?

For eighteen years Jenner carefully collected data. Finally, in 1796 he performed his first vaccination on a young boy using matter taken from a milkmaid with cowpox. After performing more successful vaccinations, Jenner published his findings in 1798. The new method of treatment spread rapidly, and smallpox soon declined to the point of disappearance in Europe and then throughout the world.

# ← LOOKING BACK  LOOKING AHEAD →

THE FUNDAMENTAL PATTERNS OF LIFE in early modern Europe remained very much the same up to the eighteenth century. The vast majority of people lived in the countryside and followed age-old rhythms of seasonal labor in the fields and farmyard. Community ties were close in small villages, where the struggle to prevail over harsh conditions called on all hands to work together and to pray together. The daily life of a peasant in 1700 would have been familiar to his ancestors in the 1400s. Indeed, the three orders of society enshrined in medieval social hierarchy were binding legal categories in France up to 1789.

And yet, the economic changes inaugurated in the late seventeenth century— enclosure, cottage industry, the industrious revolution, and colonial expansion— contributed to the profound social and cultural transformation of daily life in eighteenth-century Europe. Men and women of the laboring classes, especially in the cities, experienced change in many facets of their daily lives: in loosened community controls over sex and marriage, rising literacy rates, new goods and ways of utilizing space, and a wave of religious piety that challenged traditional orthodoxies. Both their age-old cultural practices and new religious fervor were met with mounting disbelief and ridicule by the educated classes in a period of increased distance between popular and elite culture.

Economic, social, and cultural change would culminate in the late eighteenth century with the outbreak of revolution in the Americas and Europe. Initially led by the elite, political upheavals relied on the enthusiastic participation of the poor and their desire for greater inclusion in the life of the nation. Such movements also encountered resistance from the common people when revolutionaries trampled on their religious sentiments and practices. For many observers, contemporaries and historians alike, the transformations of the eighteenth century constituted a fulcrum between the old world of hierarchy and tradition and the modern world with its claims to equality and freedom. ■

- **For a list of suggested readings for this chapter, visit** *bedfordstmartins.com/mckaywestunderstanding.*

- **For primary sources from this period, see** *Sources of Western Society,* Second Edition.

- **For Web sites, images, and documents related to topics in this chapter, see Make History at** *bedfordstmartins.com/mckaywestunderstanding.*

| How did attitudes toward child rearing change in this period? | How and why did popular culture change during this period? | What role did religion play in eighteenth-century society? | How did medicine evolve in the eighteenth century? |
|---|---|---|---|

# Chapter 19 Study Guide

Online Study Guide
bedfordstmartins.com/mckaywestunderstanding

## Step 1

**GETTING STARTED** Below are basic terms about this period in the history of Western civilization. Can you identify each term below and explain why it matters? To do this exercise online, go to bedfordstmartins.com/mckaywestunderstanding.

| TERMS | WHO (OR WHAT) AND WHEN | WHY IT MATTERS |
|---|---|---|
| community controls, p. 556 | | |
| illegitimacy explosion, p. 557 | | |
| wet-nursing, p. 559 | | |
| blood sports, p. 564 | | |
| carnival, p. 565 | | |
| just price, p. 566 | | |
| consumer revolution, p. 567 | | |
| Pietism, p. 574 | | |
| Methodists, p. 574 | | |
| Jansenism, p. 576 | | |

## Step 2

**MOVING BEYOND THE BASICS** The exercise below requires a more advanced understanding of the chapter material. Examine the major trends in European social and cultural life that culminated in the emergence of new social and cultural patterns in the nineteenth century by filling in the chart below with descriptions of social and cultural developments in four key areas: marriage and family life, childhood and education, popular culture and consumerism, and religious life. When you are finished, consider the following questions: How did the relationship between the individual and the community change in the eighteenth century? How did the demographic and economic developments you studied in Chapter 18 shape the social and cultural developments you learned about in this chapter? To do this exercise online, go to bedfordstmartins.com/mckaywestunderstanding.

| | DEVELOPMENTS |
|---|---|
| Marriage and Family Life | |
| Childhood and Education | |
| Popular Culture and Consumerism | |
| Religious Life | |

**PUTTING IT ALL TOGETHER** Now that you've reviewed key elements of the chapter, take a step back and try to see the big picture. Remember to use specific examples from the chapter in your answers. To do this exercise online, go to bedfordstmartins.com/mckaywestunderstanding.

### MARRIAGE, CHILDREN, AND FAMILY

- What role did communities play in shaping marriage patterns and family life?
- How did social and economic changes contribute to new patterns of marriage and illegitimacy in the eighteenth century?
- Why was childhood so dangerous in the eighteenth century? How did the dangers of childhood shape parental attitudes toward children?
- How and why did attitudes toward education change in the eighteenth century? Why did states become more involved in education?

### POPULAR CULTURE AND CONSUMERISM

- Compare and contrast seventeenth and eighteenth century popular culture. How did increasing literacy contribute to the changes you note?
- What explains the growth of consumer culture in the eighteenth century? How did the emergence of a culture of consumption change notions of individuality and self-expression?

### RELIGIOUS AUTHORITY AND BELIEFS

- What role did the state play in eighteenth-century religion? How would you characterize church-state relations in the eighteenth century?
- What light do the religious revivals of the eighteenth century shed on the values, beliefs, and aspirations of eighteenth-century Europeans?

### MEDICAL PRACTICE

- Who practiced medicine in the eighteenth century? What role did social background play in determining which practitioners treated which patients?
- What advances were made in European medicine in the eighteenth century? What contributions, if any, did these advances make to the general health of the European population?

■ **In Your Own Words** Imagine that you must explain Chapter 19 to someone who hasn't read it. What would be the most important points to include and why?

# 20
# The Revolution in Politics

## 1775–1815

The last years of the eighteenth century were a time of great upheaval as a series of revolutions and wars challenged the old order of monarchs and aristocrats. The ideas of freedom and equality, ideas that have not stopped shaping the world since that era, flourished and spread. The revolutionary era began in North America in 1775. Then in 1789 France, the most populous country in western Europe and a center of culture and intellectual life, became the leading revolutionary nation. It established first a constitutional monarchy, then a radical republic, and finally a new empire under Napoleon that would last until 1815. During this period of constant domestic turmoil, French armies violently exported revolution beyond the nation's borders, eager to establish new governments throughout much of Europe. Inspired both by the ideals of the Revolution on the continent and by internal colonial conditions, the slaves of Saint-Domingue rose up in 1791. Their rebellion would eventually lead to the creation of the new independent nation of Haiti in 1804. In Europe and its colonies abroad, the world of modern politics was born. ■

**Life in Revolutionary France.** On the eve of the French Revolution, angry crowds like this one gathered in Paris to protest the high-handed actions of the royal government. Throughout the Revolution, decisive events took place in the street as much as in the chambers of the National Assembly. (Musée de la Ville de Paris, Musée Carnavalet, Paris/Lauros/Giraudon/The Bridgeman Art Library)

# Chapter Preview

▶ What were the origins of the French Revolution?

▶ What forces shaped the Revolution between 1789 and 1791?

▶ Why did the Revolution take a radical turn after 1791?

▶ What led to the rise and fall of Napoleon?

# ▼ What were the origins of the French Revolution?

The origins of the French Revolution are complex, involving numerous interrelated factors. These include deep social changes in France, a long-term political crisis that eroded monarchical legitimacy, the practical and ideological effects of the American Revolution, the impact of new political ideas derived from the Enlightenment, and, perhaps most important, a financial crisis created by France's participation in expensive overseas wars.

## Legal Orders and Social Reality

**estates** The three legal categories, or orders, of France's inhabitants: the clergy, the nobility, and everyone else.

France's 25 million inhabitants were legally divided into three orders, or estates—the clergy, the nobility, and everyone else. As the nation's first estate, the clergy numbered about one hundred thousand and had important privileges. It owned about 10 percent of the land and paid only a "voluntary gift," rather than regular taxes, to the government every five years. Moreover, the church levied a property tax (tithe) on landowners.

The second estate consisted of some four hundred thousand nobles. Nobles owned about 25 percent of the land in France outright, and they too were lightly taxed. Moreover, nobles continued to enjoy certain manorial rights, or privileges of lordship, that dated back to medieval times. These included exclusive rights to hunt and fish, village monopolies on baking bread and pressing grapes for wine, fees for justice, and a host of other honorific privileges.

Everyone else—nearly 98 percent of the population—was a commoner, legally a member of the third estate. A few commoners—prosperous merchants, lawyers, and officials—were well educated and rich. Yet the vast majority of the third estate consisted of peasants, rural agricultural workers, urban artisans, and unskilled day laborers. Thus the third estate was a conglomeration of very different social groups united only by their shared legal status.

In discussing the origins of the French Revolution, historians long focused on growing tensions between the nobility and the comfortable members of the third estate, the bourgeoisie (boorzh-wah-ZEE) or upper middle class. Increasing in size, wealth, culture, and self-confidence, this rising bourgeoisie became progressively exasperated by feudal laws restraining the economy and by the pretensions of a nobility that was closing ranks against middle-class aspirations. As a result, the French bourgeoisie eventually rose up to lead the entire third estate in a great social revolution that destroyed feudal privileges and established a capitalist order based on individualism and a market economy.

In the last thirty years, the French Revolution's origins have been subject to what historians refer to as revisionism, or new interpretations. Above all, revisionist historians have questioned the existence of growing social conflict between a progressive capitalistic bour-

**The Three Estates** In this political cartoon from 1789 a peasant of the third estate struggles under the weight of a happy clergyman and a plumed nobleman. The caption—"Let's hope this game ends soon"—sets forth a program of reform that any peasant could understand. (Réunion des Musées Nationaux/Art Resource, NY)

A FAUT ESPERER Q'EU JEU LA FINIRA BEN TOT.

*l'tuteur en Campagne Ap. 1789.*

geoisie and a reactionary feudal nobility in eighteenth-century France. Instead, they see both bourgeoisie and nobility as highly fragmented. The ancient sword nobility, for example, made up of people who descended from the oldest noble families, was separated by differences in wealth, education, and worldview from the newer robe nobility, people who acquired noble titles through service in the royal administration and judiciary. Differences within the bourgeoisie—between wealthy financiers and local lawyers, for example—were no less profound. Rather than standing as unified blocs against each other, nobility and bourgeoisie formed two parallel social ladders increasingly linked together at the top by wealth, marriage, and Enlightenment culture.

Revisionist historians note that the nobility and the bourgeoisie were not really at odds in the economic sphere. The ideal of the merchant capitalist was to gain enough wealth to retire from trade, purchase an estate, and live nobly as a large landowner. At the same time, wealthy nobles often acted as aggressive capitalists, investing especially in mining, metallurgy, and foreign trade. In addition, until the Revolution actually began, key sections of the nobility were liberal and generally joined the bourgeoisie in opposition to the government.

Revisionists have clearly shaken the belief that the bourgeoisie and the nobility were inevitably locked in growing conflict before the Revolution. Yet they also make clear that the Old Regime had ceased to correspond with social reality by the 1780s. Legally, society was still based on rigid orders inherited from the Middle Ages, but in reality those distinctions were often blurred.

An upper echelon of aristocratic and bourgeois notables saw itself as an educated elite that stood well above the common masses, united in its frustration with a bureaucratic monarchy that continued to claim the right to absolute power. Meanwhile, for France's laboring poor—the vast majority of the population—traditions remained strong and life itself remained a struggle.

## The Crisis of Political Legitimacy

Overlaying these social changes was a structural deadlock in France's tax system and the century-long political and fiscal struggle between the monarchy and its opponents sparked by the expenses of a series of foreign wars. When Louis XIV died in 1715 and was succeeded by his five-year-old great-grandson, Louis XV (r. 1715–1774), the system of absolutist rule was challenged. Under the young monarch's regent, the duke of Orléans (1674–1723), a number of institutions retrieved powers they had lost under Louis XIV. Most important, the high courts of France—the parlements—regained their ancient right to evaluate royal decrees publicly in writing before they were registered and given the force of law. The magistrates of the parlements were leaders of the robe nobility. By allowing a well-entrenched and highly articulate branch of the nobility to evaluate the king's decrees before they became law, the duke of Orléans sanctioned a counterweight to absolute power.

These implications became clear when the heavy expenses of war in the eighteenth century proved unbearable for the state treasury. The War of the Austrian Succession (see

CHAPTER LOCATOR    What were the origins of the French Revolution?    What forces shaped the Revolution between 1789 and 1791?    Why did the Revolution take a radical turn after 1791?    What led to the rise and fall of Napoleon?

585

Chapter 17) plunged France into financial crisis and pushed the state to attempt a reform of the tax system. In 1748 Louis XV's finance minister decreed a 5 percent income tax on every individual regardless of social status. The result was a vigorous protest from those previously exempt from taxation—the nobility, the clergy, towns, and some wealthy bourgeoisie—led by the influential Parlement of Paris. The monarchy retreated; the new tax was dropped.

Following the disastrously expensive Seven Years' War (see Chapter 18), the conflict re-emerged. The government tried to maintain emergency taxes after the war ended; the Parlement of Paris protested and even challenged the basis of royal authority, claiming that the king's power had to be limited to protect liberty. Once again the government caved in and withdrew the taxes. The judicial opposition then asserted that the king could not levy taxes without the consent of the Parlement of Paris.

In 1768, after years of attempted compromise, Louis appointed a tough career official named René de Maupeou (moh-POO) as chancellor and ordered him to crush the judicial opposition. Maupeou abolished the existing parlements and exiled the members of the Parlement of Paris to the provinces. He created new and docile parlements of royal officials, known as the Maupeou parlements, and he began once again to tax the privileged groups. Public opinion as a whole sided with the old parlements, however, and there was widespread criticism of "royal despotism."

Learned dissent was accompanied by scandalous libels. Kings had always maintained mistresses, who were invariably chosen from the court nobility. Louis XV broke that pattern with Madame de Pompadour, daughter of a disgraced bourgeois financier. As the king's favorite mistress from 1745 to 1750, Pompadour exercised tremendous influence that continued even after their love affair ended. Pompadour's modest birth and hidden political influence generated a stream of resentful and illegal pamphleteering.

After Pompadour was replaced by a common prostitute, the stream of scandalmongering became a torrent. Lurid and pornographic depictions of the court ate away at the foundations of royal authority. The king was being stripped of the aura of being God's anointed on earth (a process called *desacralization*) and was being reinvented in the popular imagination as a degenerate.

Despite the progressive desacralization (dee-SAY-kruh-ligh-ZAY-shun) of the monarchy, Louis XV would probably have prevailed had he lived longer, but he died in 1774. The new king, Louis XVI (r. 1774–1792), was a shy twenty-year-old with good intentions. Taking the throne, he is reported to have said, "What I should like most is to be loved."[1] The eager-to-please monarch yielded to France's educated elite, dismissing chancellor Maupeou and repudiating his work. Louis also waffled on the economy, dismissing controller-general Turgot when his attempts to liberalize the economy drew fire. A weakened but unreformed monarchy now faced a judicial opposition that claimed to speak for the entire French nation.

## The American Revolution and Its Impact

Coinciding with the first years of Louis XVI's reign, the American Revolution had an enormous impact on France in both practical and ideological terms. French expenses to support the colonists bankrupted the Crown, while the ideals of liberty and equality provided inspiration for political reform.

Like the French Revolution, the American Revolution had its immediate origin in struggles over increased taxes. The high cost of the Seven Years' War doubled the British national debt. When the government tried to recoup some of the losses by increasing taxes in the colonies in 1765, the colonists reacted with anger. The key questions were political rather than economic. To what extent could the home government assert its power while limiting the authority of colonial legislatures and their elected representatives? The British government asserted that Americans were represented in Parliament, albeit indirectly (like most British people themselves), and that the absolute supremacy of Parliament throughout the empire could not be questioned. Many Americans felt otherwise.

In 1773 the dispute over taxes and representation flared up again after the British government awarded a monopoly on Chinese tea to the East India Company, suddenly excluding colonial merchants from a lucrative business. In response, Boston men disguised as Indians held a "tea party" and threw the company's tea into the harbor. This led to extreme measures. The so-called Coercive Acts closed the port of Boston, curtailed local elections, and greatly expanded the royal governor's power. County conventions in Massachusetts protested vehemently and other colonial assemblies joined in the denunciations.

Both the British Parliament and the First Continental Congress, which met in September 1774 in Philadelphia, rejected compromise. In April 1775 fighting began at Lexington and Concord. Some colonists remained loyal to the Crown; large numbers of these Loyalists emigrated to the northern colonies of Canada.

On July 4, 1776, the Second Continental Congress adopted the Declaration of Independence. Written by Thomas Jefferson, it listed the tyrannical acts committed by George III (r. 1760–1820) and proclaimed the natural rights of mankind and the sovereignty of the American states. The Declaration of Independence in effect universalized the traditional rights of English people and made them the rights of all mankind.

**Toward Revolution in Boston** The Boston Tea Party was only one of many angry confrontations between British officials and Boston patriots. On January 27, 1774, an angry crowd seized a British customs collector and tarred and feathered him. This English cartoon from 1774 satirizes the event. What does the noose in the "liberty tree" suggest about the cartoonist's view of these events? (The Granger Collection, NY)

The European powers closely followed the course of the American Revolution. The French wanted revenge for the humiliating defeats of the Seven Years' War. They supplied the rebels with guns and gunpowder. By 1777 French volunteers were arriving in Virginia, including the marquis de Lafayette (1757–1834), who became one of George Washington's most trusted generals. In 1778 the French government offered a formal alliance to the Americans and in 1779 and 1780 the Spanish and Dutch declared war on Britain. Catherine the Great of Russia helped organize the League of Armed Neutrality in order to protect neutral shipping rights, which Britain refused to recognize.

Thus by 1780 Great Britain was engaged in an imperial war against most of Europe as well as against the thirteen colonies. In these circumstances, and in the face of severe reverses, a new British government decided to cut its losses. By the Treaty of Paris in 1783, Britain recognized the independence of the thirteen colonies and ceded all its territory between the Allegheny Mountains and the Mississippi River to the Americans.

No country felt the consequences of the American Revolution more directly than France. Hundreds of French officers served in America and were inspired by the experience, the marquis de Lafayette chief among them. French intellectuals engaged in passionate analysis of the new federal Constitution — ratified in 1789 — as well as the constitutions of the various states of the new United States. Perhaps more important, the expenses of supporting America's revolutionary forces provided the last nail in the coffin for the French treasury.

CHAPTER LOCATOR | What were the origins of the French Revolution? | What forces shaped the Revolution between 1789 and 1791? | Why did the Revolution take a radical turn after 1791? | What led to the rise and fall of Napoleon?

587

## Financial Crisis

The French Revolution thus had its immediate origins in the king's financial difficulties. Thwarted in its efforts to raise revenues by reforming the tax system, the government was forced to finance all of its enormous expenditures during the American war with borrowed money. As a result, the national debt and the annual budget deficit soared. By the 1780s fully 50 percent of France's annual budget went for interest payments on the debt.

Faced with imminent financial disaster in 1786, the royal government had no alternative but to try to increase taxes. Since France's tax system was unfair and out-of-date, increased revenues were possible only through fundamental reform. In 1787 Louis XVI's minister of finance proposed to impose a general tax on all landed property as well as to form provincial assemblies to help administer the tax, and he convinced the king to call an Assembly of Notables to gain support for the idea. The notables, who were mainly important noblemen and high-ranking clergy, insisted that such sweeping tax changes required the approval of the Estates General, the representative body of all three estates, which had not met since 1614.

In an attempt to reassert his authority, the king dismissed the notables and established new taxes by decree. The judges of the Parlement of Paris promptly declared the royal initiative null and void. When the king tried to exile the judges, a tremendous wave of protest swept the country. Finally, in July 1788, Louis XVI bowed to public opinion and called for a spring session of the Estates General.

**Estates General** A legislative body in prerevolutionary France made up of representatives of each of the three classes, or estates; it was called into session in 1789 for the first time since 1614.

# What forces shaped the Revolution between 1789 and 1791?

The process of electing delegates and formulating grievances for the Estates General politicized the French as no event in their prior history had done. As delegates at Versailles struggled over who truly represented the nation, the common people of France took matters into their own hands, rising up against noble lords and even reaching out to the royal family in their demands for change. Meanwhile, the complex slave society of colonial Saint-Domingue was rocked by conflicting political aspirations inspired by events in Paris.

## The Formation of the National Assembly

Once Louis had agreed to hold the Estates General, the three orders — clergy, nobility, and commoners — separately elected delegates in each electoral district and prepared their own lists of grievances. The process of drafting their complaints unleashed a flood of debate and discussion across France.

Results of the elections reveal the political loyalties and mindsets of each estate on the eve of the Revolution. The local assemblies of the clergy elected mostly parish priests rather than church leaders, demonstrating their dissatisfaction with the church hierarchy. The nobility voted in a majority of conservatives, primarily from the provinces, where nobles were less wealthy and more numerous. Nonetheless, fully one-third of noble representatives were liberals committed to major changes. Members of the third estate elected primarily lawyers and government officials to represent them, with few delegates representing business or the poor.

The petitions for change coming from the three estates showed a surprising degree of consensus about the issues at stake. There was general agreement that royal absolutism should give way to a constitutional monarchy in which laws and taxes would require the

**The Tennis Court Oath, June 20, 1789** Painted two years after the event shown, this dramatic painting by Jacques-Louis David depicts a crucial turning point in the early days of the Revolution. On June 20 delegates of the third estate arrived at their meeting hall in the Versailles palace to find the doors closed and guarded. Fearing the king was about to dissolve their meeting by force, the deputies reassembled at a nearby indoor tennis court and swore a solemn oath not to disperse until they had been recognized as the National Assembly. (Musée de la Ville de Paris, Musée Carnavalet, Paris/Lauros/Giraudon/The Bridgeman Art Library)

consent of the Estates General in regular meetings. All agreed that individual liberties would have to be guaranteed by law and that economic regulations should be loosened.

On May 5, 1789, the twelve hundred delegates of the three estates gathered in Versailles for the opening session of the Estates General. Despite widespread hopes for serious reform, the Estates General was almost immediately deadlocked due to arguments about voting procedures. Controversy had begun during the electoral process, when the government confirmed that, following precedent, each estate should meet and vote separately. During the lead-up to the Estates General, critics demanded a single assembly dominated by the third estate. In his famous pamphlet *What Is the Third Estate?* the abbé Emmanuel Joseph Sieyès (himself a member of the first estate) argued that the nobility was a tiny overprivileged minority and that the neglected third estate constituted the true strength of the French nation. (See "Listening to the Past: Abbé de Sieyès, *What Is the Third Estate?*" page 590.) The government conceded that the third estate should have as many delegates as the clergy and the nobility combined, but then rendered this act meaningless by upholding voting by separate order. Reform-minded critics saw fresh evidence of an aristocratic conspiracy.

The issue came to a head in June 1789 when the delegates of the third estate refused to transact any business until the king ordered the clergy and nobility to sit with them in a single body. Finally, after six weeks, a few parish priests began to go over to the third estate, which on June 17 voted to call itself the **National Assembly**. On June 20 the delegates of the third estate, excluded from their hall because of "repairs," moved to a large indoor tennis court where they swore the famous Oath of the Tennis Court, pledging not to disband until they had written a new constitution.

**National Assembly** The first French revolutionary legislature, made up primarily of representatives of the third estate and a few from the nobility and clergy, in session from 1789 to 1791.

CHAPTER LOCATOR | What were the origins of the French Revolution? | **What forces shaped the Revolution between 1789 and 1791?** | Why did the Revolution take a radical turn after 1791? | What led to the rise and fall of Napoleon?

589

*In the flood of pamphlets that appeared after Louis XVI's call for a meeting of the Estates General, the most influential was written in 1789 by a Catholic priest named Emmanuel Joseph Sieyès. In* What Is the Third Estate? *the abbé Sieyès vigorously condemned the system of privilege that lay at the heart of French society. The term* privilege *combined the Latin words for "private" and "law." In Old Regime France, no one set of laws applied to all; over time, the monarchy had issued a series of particular laws, or privileges, that enshrined special rights and entitlements for select individuals and groups. Noble privileges were among the weightiest.*

*Sieyès rejected this entire system of legal and social inequality. Deriding the nobility as a foreign parasite, he argued that the common people of the third estate, who did most of the work and paid most of the taxes, constituted the true nation. His pamphlet galvanized public opinion and played an important role in convincing representatives of the third estate to proclaim themselves a "National Assembly" in June 1789. Sieyès later helped bring Napoleon Bonaparte to power, abandoning the radicalism of 1789 for an authoritarian regime.*

**❝** 1.  What is the Third Estate? Everything.
2.  What has it been until now in the political order? Nothing.
3.  What does it want? To become something.

. . . What is a Nation? A body of associates living under a *common* law and represented by the same *legislature.*

Is it not more than certain that the noble order has privileges, exemptions, and even rights that are distinct from the rights of the great body of citizens? Because of this, it [the noble order] does not belong to the common order, it is not covered by the law common to the rest. Thus its civil rights already make it a people apart inside the great Nation. It is truly *imperium in imperio* [a law unto itself].

As for its *political* rights, the nobility also exercises them separately. It has its own representatives who have no mandate from the people. Its deputies sit separately, and even when they assemble in the same room with the deputies of the ordinary citizens, the nobility's representation still remains essentially distinct and separate: it is foreign to the Nation by its very principle, for its mission does not emanate from the people, and by its purpose, since it consists in defending, not the general interest, but the private interests of the nobility.

The Third Estate therefore contains everything that pertains to the Nation and nobody outside of the Third Estate can claim to be part of the Nation. What is the Third Estate? EVERYTHING . . . .

By Third Estate is meant the collectivity of citizens who belong to the common order. Anybody who holds a legal privilege of any kind leaves that common order, stands as an exception to the common law, and in consequence does not belong to the Third Estate. . . . It is certain that the moment a citizen acquires privileges contrary to common law, he no longer belongs to the common order. His new interest is opposed to the general interest; he has no right to vote in the name of the people. . . .

In vain can anyone's eyes be closed to the revolution that time and the force of things have brought to pass; it is none the less real. Once upon a time the Third Estate was in bondage and the noble order was everything that mattered. Today the Third is everything and nobility but a word. Yet under the cover of this word a new and intolerable aristocracy has slipped in, and the people has every reason to no longer want aristocrats. . . .

What is the will of a Nation? It is the result of individual wills, just as the Nation is the aggregate of the individuals who compose it. It is impossible to conceive of a legitimate association that does not have

---

The king's response to this crucial challenge to his authority was disastrously ambivalent. On June 23 he made a conciliatory speech to a joint session in which he urged reforms, and four days later he ordered the three estates to meet together. At the same time, Louis apparently followed the advice of relatives and court nobles who urged him to dissolve the National Assembly by force. The king called an army of eighteen thousand troops toward the capital, and on July 11 he dismissed his finance minister and other more liberal ministers. It appeared that the monarchy was prepared to renege on its promises for reform and to use violence to restore its control.

## The Storming of the Bastille

While delegates at Versailles were pressing for political rights, economic hardship gripped the common people. A poor grain harvest in 1788 had caused the price of bread to soar.

This bust, by the sculptor Pierre Jean David d'Angers, shows an aged and contemplative Sieyès reflecting, perhaps, on his key role in the outbreak and unfolding of the Revolution. (Erich Lessing/Art Resource, NY)

for its goal the common security, the common liberty, in short, the public good. No doubt each individual also has his own personal aims. He says to himself, "protected by the common security, I will be able to peacefully pursue my own personal projects, I will seek my happiness where I will, assured of encountering only those legal obstacles that society will prescribe for the common interest, in which I have a part, and with which my own personal interest is so usefully allied." . . .

Advantages which differentiate citizens from one another lie outside the purview of citizenship. Inequali-ties of wealth or ability are like the inequalities of age, sex, size, etc. In no way do they detract from the *equality* of citizenship. These individual advantages no doubt benefit from the protection of the law; but it is not the legislator's task to create them, to give privileges to some and refuse them to others. The law grants nothing; it protects what already exists until such time that what exists begins to harm the common interest. These are the only limits on individual freedom. I imagine the law as being at the center of a large globe; we the citizens without exception, stand equidistant from it on the surface and occupy equal places; all are equally dependent on the law, all present it with their liberty and their property to be protected; and this is what I call the *common rights* of citizens, by which they are all alike. All these individuals communicate with each other, enter into contracts, negotiate, always under the common guarantee of the law. If in this general activity somebody wishes to get control over the person of his neighbor or usurp his property, the common law goes into action to repress this criminal attempt and puts everyone back in their place at the same distance from the law. . . .

It is impossible to say what place the two privileged orders [the clergy and the nobility] ought to occupy in the social order: this is the equivalent of asking what place one wishes to assign to a malignant tumor that torments and undermines the strength of the body of a sick person. It must be *neutralized*. We must re-establish the health and working of all organs so thoroughly that they are no longer susceptible to these fatal schemes that are capable of sapping the most essential principles of vitality.

**Source:** *The French Revolution and Human Rights: A Brief Documentary History*, pp. 65, 67, 68–70, edited, translated, and with an introduction by Lynn Hunt. © 1996 by Bedford Books of St. Martin's Press.

### QUESTIONS FOR ANALYSIS

1. What criticism of noble privileges does Sieyès offer? Why does he believe nobles are "foreign" to the nation?
2. How does Sieyès define the nation, and why does he believe that the third estate constitutes the nation?
3. What relationship between citizens and the law does Sieyès envision? What limitations on the law does he propose?

With food so expensive and with so much uncertainty, the demand for manufactured goods collapsed. Many thousands of artisans and small traders were thrown out of work and bread riots broke out in Paris and the surrounding area in late April and May.

Against this background of political and economic crisis, the people of Paris entered decisively onto the revolutionary stage. They believed that they should have steady work and enough bread at fair prices to survive. They also feared that the dismissal of the king's moderate finance minister would put them at the mercy of aristocratic landowners and grain speculators. At the beginning of July, knowledge spread of the massing of troops near Paris. On July 13, 1789, the people began to seize arms for the defense of the city, and on July 14 several hundred people marched to the Bastille (ba-STEEL) to search for weapons and gunpowder.

The Bastille, once a medieval fortress, was a royal prison. The governor of the fortress-prison refused to hand over the powder, panicked, and ordered his men to resist; the

CHAPTER LOCATOR | What were the origins of the French Revolution? | What forces shaped the Revolution between 1789 and 1791? | Why did the Revolution take a radical turn after 1791? | What led to the rise and fall of Napoleon?

591

guards killed ninety-eight people attempting to enter. The Parisians brought in cannons to batter the main gate, and fighting continued until the prison surrendered. The next day a committee of citizens appointed the marquis de Lafayette commander of the city's armed forces.

The popular uprising forestalled the king's attempt to reassert his authority. On July 17 Louis announced the reinstatement of his liberal finance minister and the withdrawal of troops from Paris. The National Assembly was now free to continue its work without the threat of royal military intervention.

## Peasant Revolt and the Rights of Man

Just as the laboring poor of Paris had been roused to a revolutionary fervor, the struggling French peasantry had also reached its boiling point. In the summer of 1789, throughout France peasants began to rise in insurrection against their lords, ransacking manor houses and burning feudal documents that recorded their obligations. In some areas peasants reinstated traditional village practices, undoing recent enclosures and reoccupying old common lands. They seized forests, and taxes went unpaid. Fear of marauders and vagabonds hired by vengeful landlords—called the Great Fear by contemporaries—seized the rural poor and fanned the flames of rebellion.

**Great Fear** The fear of noble reprisals against peasant uprisings that seized the French countryside and led to further revolt.

Faced with chaos, the National Assembly responded to peasant demands with a surprise maneuver on the night of August 4, 1789. By a decree of the assembly, all the old noble privileges—peasant serfdom where it still existed, exclusive hunting rights, fees for justice, village monopolies, the right to make peasants work on the roads, and a host of other dues—were abolished along with the tithes paid to the church. From this point on, French peasants would seek mainly to protect and consolidate this victory.

Having granted new rights to the peasantry, the National Assembly moved forward with its mission of reform. On August 27, 1789, it issued the Declaration of the Rights of Man and of the Citizen, which stated, "Men are born and remain free and equal in rights." This clarion call of the liberal revolutionary ideal guaranteed equality before the law, representative government, and individual freedom. This revolutionary credo, only two pages long, was disseminated throughout France and Europe and around the world.

**The Great Fear, 1789**

## Parisian Women March on Versailles

The National Assembly's declaration had little practical effect for the poor and hungry people of Paris, where a revolutionary spirit continued to smolder. The economic crisis in the city worsened after the fall of the Bastille, as aristocrats fled the country and the luxury market collapsed. Foreign markets also shrank in the aftermath of the crisis, and unemployment among the urban working class grew. In addition, women—the traditional managers of food and resources in poor homes—could no longer look to the church, which had been stripped of its tithes, for aid.

On October 5 some seven thousand women marched the twelve miles from Paris to Versailles to demand action. This great crowd, "armed with scythes, sticks and pikes," invaded the National Assembly. Interrupting a delegate's speech, an old woman defiantly shouted into the debate, "Who's that talking down there? Make the chatterbox shut up. That's not the point: the point is that we want bread."[2] Hers was the genuine voice of the people, essential to any understanding of the French Revolution.

*a Versaille a Versaille.* du 5. Octobre 1789.

**The Women of Paris March to Versailles** On October 5, 1789, a large group of poor Parisian women marched to Versailles to protest the price of bread. The angry women forced the royal family to return with them and to live in Paris, rather than remain isolated from their subjects at court. (Erich Lessing/Art Resource, NY)

The women invaded the royal apartments, killed some of the royal bodyguards, and searched for the queen, Marie Antoinette, who was widely despised for her frivolous and supposedly immoral behavior. "We are going to cut off her head, tear out her heart, fry her liver, and that won't be the end of it," they shouted. Lafayette and the National Guard intervened to save the royal family but the only way to calm the disorder was for the king to live in Paris, closer to his people, as the crowd demanded.

## A Constitutional Monarchy and Its Challenges

The day after the women's march on Versailles, the National Assembly followed the king to Paris, and the next two years, until September 1791, saw the consolidation of the liberal revolution. Under middle-class leadership, the National Assembly abolished the French nobility as a legal order and established a **constitutional monarchy**, which Louis XVI reluctantly agreed to accept in July 1790. The king remained the head of state, but all lawmaking power now resided in the National Assembly, elected by the wealthiest half of French males. New laws broadened women's rights to seek divorce, to inherit property, and to obtain financial support for illegitimate children from fathers, but women were not allowed to hold political office or even vote.

This decision was attacked by a small number of men and women who believed that the rights of man should be extended to all French citizens. Olympe de Gouges (1748–1793), a self-taught writer and woman of the people, protested the evils of slavery as well as the injustices done to women. In September 1791 she published her "Declaration of the Rights of Woman." De Gouges's pamphlet echoed its famous predecessor, the "Declaration of the Rights of Man and of the Citizen," proclaiming, "Woman is born free and remains equal to man in rights." Her position found little sympathy among leaders of the revolution.

In addition to ruling on women's rights, the National Assembly replaced the complicated patchwork of historic provinces with eighty-three departments of approximately

**constitutional monarchy**
A form of government in which the king retains his position as head of state, while the authority to tax and make new laws resides in an elected body.

CHAPTER LOCATOR | What were the origins of the French Revolution? | **What forces shaped the Revolution between 1789 and 1791?** | Why did the Revolution take a radical turn after 1791? | What led to the rise and fall of Napoleon?

593

**Village Festival in Honor of Old Age, 1795** The French Revolution inaugurated many new civic festivals in an attempt to erase memories of the Catholic holidays and feast days of the prerevolutionary era. As in bygone days, the new festivals, like this one honoring village elders, included dancing, drinking, and courting among the young couples of the village. Many people, however, especially in rural France, missed the religious tenor of prerevolutionary holidays. (Bibliothèque nationale de France/Archives Charmet/The Bridgeman Art Library)

equal size. Monopolies, guilds, and workers' associations were prohibited, and barriers to trade within France were abolished in the name of economic liberty. Thus the National Assembly applied the spirit of the Enlightenment in a thorough reform of France's laws and institutions.

The National Assembly also imposed a radical reorganization on the country's religious life. It granted religious freedom to the small minority of French Jews and Protestants. In November 1789 it nationalized the Catholic Church's property and abolished monasteries. The government used all former church property as collateral to guarantee a new paper currency, the assignats (A-sihg-nat), and then sold the property in an attempt to put the state's finances on a solid footing. Although the land was sold in large blocks, peasants eventually purchased much when it was subdivided, strengthening their attachment to the new revolutionary order in the countryside.

Imbued with the rationalism and skepticism of the eighteenth-century philosophes (see Chapter 17), many delegates distrusted popular piety and "superstitious religion." Thus in July 1790, with the Civil Constitution of the Clergy, they established a national church with priests chosen by voters. The National Assembly then forced the Catholic clergy to take a loyalty oath to the new government. The pope formally condemned this attempt to subjugate the church, and only half the priests of France swore the oath. Many sincere Christians, especially those in the countryside, were upset by these changes in the religious order. The attempt to remake the Catholic Church, like the abolition of guilds and workers' associations, sharpened the conflict between the educated classes and the common people that had been emerging in the eighteenth century.

## Revolutionary Aspirations in Saint-Domingue

On the eve of the Revolution, Saint-Domingue—the most profitable of all Caribbean colonies—was even more rife with social tensions than France itself. The island was inhabited by a variety of social groups who resented and mistrusted one another. The European population included French colonial officials, wealthy plantation owners and merchants, and poor immigrants. Greatly outnumbering the white population were the colony's five hundred thousand slaves, along with a sizable population of free people of African and mixed African and European descent. Members of this last group referred to themselves as "free coloreds" or free people of color.

The 1685 *Code Noir* (Black Code) that set the parameters of French slavery had granted free people of color the same legal status as whites: they could own property, live where they wished, and pursue any education or career they desired. From the 1760s on, however, colonial administrators began rescinding these rights, and by the time of the Revolution, many aspects of free coloreds' lives were ruled by discriminatory laws.

The political and intellectual turmoil of the 1780s, with its growing rhetoric of "liberty, equality, and fraternity," raised new challenges and possibilities for each of these groups. For slaves, news of abolitionist movements in France led to hopes that the mother country might grant them freedom. Free people of color looked to reforms in Paris as

**Saint-Domingue Slave Life** Although the brutal conditions of plantation slavery left little time or energy for leisure, slaves on Saint-Domingue took advantage of their day of rest on Sunday to engage in social and religious activities. The law officially prohibited slaves of different masters from mingling together, but such gatherings were often tolerated if they remained peaceful. This image depicts a fight between two slaves, precisely the type of unrest and violence feared by authorities. (Musée du Nouveau Monde, La Rochelle/Photos12.com—ARJ)

CHAPTER LOCATOR | What were the origins of the French Revolution? | **What forces shaped the Revolution between 1789 and 1791?** | Why did the Revolution take a radical turn after 1791? | What led to the rise and fall of Napoleon?

595

a means of gaining political enfranchisement and reasserting equal status with whites. The white elite, not surprisingly, saw matters very differently. Infuriated by talk of abolition and determined to protect their way of life, they looked to revolutionary ideals of representative government for the chance to gain control of their own affairs, as had the American colonists before them.

The National Assembly frustrated the hopes of all these groups. Cowed by colonial representatives who claimed that support for free people of color would result in slave insurrection and independence, the Assembly refused to extend French constitutional safeguards to the colonies. After dealing this blow to the aspirations of slaves and free coloreds, the committee also reaffirmed French monopolies over colonial trade, thereby angering planters as well.

In July 1790 Vincent Ogé (aw-ZHAY), a free man of color, returned to Saint-Domingue from Paris determined to redress these issues. He raised an army of several hundred and sent letters to the new Provincial Assembly of Saint-Domingue demanding political rights for all free citizens. After initial victories, his army was defeated, and Ogé himself was tortured and executed by colonial officials. In May 1791, in an attempt to respond to what it perceived as partly justified grievances, the National Assembly granted political rights to free people of color born to two free parents who possessed sufficient property. When news of this legislation arrived in Saint-Domingue, the white elite was furious, and the colonial governor refused to enact it. Violence now erupted between groups of whites and free coloreds in parts of the colony.

## ▼ Why did the Revolution take a radical turn after 1791?

When Louis XVI accepted the National Assembly's constitution in September 1791, a young provincial lawyer and delegate named Maximilien Robespierre (1758–1794) concluded that "The Revolution is over." Robespierre was right in the sense that the most constructive and lasting reforms were in place. Yet he was wrong in the sense that a much more radical stage lay ahead.

### Foreign Reactions to the Revolution

The outbreak and progress of revolution in France produced great excitement and a sharp division of opinion in Europe and the United States. Liberals and radicals saw a mighty triumph of liberty over despotism. On the other hand, conservative leaders such as British statesman Edmund Burke (1729–1797) were troubled by the aroused spirit of reform. In 1790 Burke published *Reflections on the Revolution in France*, in which he defended inherited privileges. He glorified Britain's unrepresentative Parliament and predicted that reform like that occurring in France would lead only to chaos and tyranny.

One passionate rebuttal to Burke came from a young writer in London, Mary Wollstonecraft (1759–1797). Incensed by Burke's book, Wollstonecraft (WOOL-stuhn-kraft) immediately wrote a blistering, widely read attack, *A Vindication of the Rights of Man* (1790). Two years later, she published her masterpiece, *A Vindication of the Rights of Woman* (1792). Like de Gouges one year before her, Wollstonecraft demanded equal rights for women. She advocated rigorous coeducation, which would make women better wives and mothers, good citizens, and economically independent. Wollstonecraft's analysis testifies to the power of the Revolution to excite and inspire outside of France.

The kings and nobles of continental Europe, who had at first welcomed the revolution in France as weakening a competing power, began to feel as threatened by its mes-

**The Capture of Louis XVI, June 1791** This painting commemorates the midnight arrest of Louis XVI and the royal family as they tried to flee France in disguise and reach counter-revolutionaries in the Austrian Netherlands. Recognized and stopped at Varennes, just forty miles from the border, the king still nearly succeeded, telling municipal officers that dangerous mobs controlled Paris and securing promises of safe passage. But within hours the local leaders reversed themselves, and by morning Louis XVI was headed back to Paris. (Bibliothèque nationale de France)

sage. In June 1791 Louis XVI and Marie Antoinette were arrested and returned to Paris after trying unsuccessfully to slip out of France. For supporters of the Revolution, the attempted flight was proof that the king's professed acceptance of the constitution was a sham and that he was a traitor intent on procuring foreign support for an invasion of France. The arrest of a crowned head of state led the monarchs of Austria and Prussia to issue the Declaration of Pillnitz two months later. The Declaration professed the rulers' willingness to intervene in France to restore Louis XVI's monarchical rule if necessary. It was expected to have a sobering effect on revolutionary France without causing war.

But the crowned heads of Europe misjudged the situation in France. The new representative body that convened in Paris in October 1791, called the Legislative Assembly, had completely new delegates and a different character. The great majority of the legislators were still prosperous, well-educated middle-class men, but they were younger and less cautious than their predecessors. Many of the deputies belonged to the political Jacobin (JA-kuh-bihn) club. Such clubs had proliferated in Parisian neighborhoods since the beginning of the Revolution, drawing men and women to debate the political questions of the day.

## The Outbreak of War

The new representatives to the Assembly reacted with patriotic fury to the Declaration of Pillnitz. If the kings of Europe were attempting to incite war against France, then "we will incite a war of people against kings. . . . Ten million Frenchmen, kindled by the fire of liberty, armed with the sword, with reason, with eloquence would be able to

CHAPTER LOCATOR | What were the origins of the French Revolution? | What forces shaped the Revolution between 1789 and 1791? | **Why did the Revolution take a radical turn after 1791?** | What led to the rise and fall of Napoleon?

597

change the face of the world and make the tyrants tremble on their thrones."[3] In April 1792 France declared war on Francis II, the Habsburg monarch.

France's crusade against tyranny went poorly at first. Prussian forces joined Austria against the French, who broke and fled at their first military encounter with this First Coalition. The road to Paris lay open, and it is possible that only conflict between the eastern monarchs over the division of Poland (see Chapter 17) saved France from an early and total defeat.

The Assembly declared the country in danger, and volunteers rallied to the capital. In this wartime atmosphere, rumors of treason by the king and queen spread in Paris. On August 10, 1792, a revolutionary crowd attacked the royal palace at the Tuileries (TWEE-luh-reez), while the king and his family fled for their lives to the nearby Legislative Assembly. Rather than offering refuge, the Assembly suspended the king from all his functions, imprisoned him, and called for a new National Convention to be elected by universal male suffrage.

## The Second Revolution

**second revolution** From 1792 to 1795, the second phase of the French Revolution, during which the fall of the French monarchy introduced a rapid radicalization of politics.

**Jacobin club** A political club in revolutionary France whose members were well-educated radical republicans.

**Girondists** A moderate group that fought for control of the French National Convention in 1793.

**the Mountain** Led by Robespierre, the French National Convention's radical faction, which seized legislative power in 1793.

The fall of the monarchy marked a rapid radicalization of the Revolution, a phase that historians often call the second revolution. In late September 1792 the new, popularly elected National Convention proclaimed France a republic, a nation in which the people, instead of a monarch, held sovereign power.

All the members of the National Convention were republicans, and at the beginning almost all belonged to the Jacobin club of Paris. But the Jacobins themselves were increasingly divided into two bitterly competitive groups—the Girondists (juh-RAHN-dihsts) and the Mountain, led by Robespierre and another young lawyer, Georges Jacques Danton.

This division emerged clearly after the National Convention overwhelmingly convicted Louis XVI of treason. The Girondists accepted his guilt but did not wish to put the king to death. By a narrow majority, the Mountain carried the day, and Louis was executed on January 21, 1793, on the newly invented guillotine. But both the Girondists and the Mountain were determined to continue the "war against tyranny." The Prussians had been stopped at the Battle of Valmy on September 20, 1792, one day before the republic was proclaimed. French armies then invaded Savoy and captured Nice, moved into the German Rhineland, and by November 1792 were occupying the entire Austrian Netherlands (modern-day Belgium).

Everywhere they went, French armies of occupation chased the princes, abolished feudalism, and found support among some peasants and middle-class people. But the French armies also lived off the land, requisitioning food and supplies and plundering local treasures. The liberators looked increasingly like foreign invaders. International tensions mounted. In February 1793 the National Convention, at war with Austria and Prussia, declared war on Britain, Holland, and Spain as well. Republican France was now at war with almost all of Europe.

Groups within France added to the turmoil. Peasants in western France revolted against being drafted into the army, with the Vendée region of Brittany emerging as the epicenter of revolt. Devout Catholics, royalists, and foreign agents encouraged their rebellion, and the counter-revolutionaries recruited veritable armies to fight for their cause.

In March 1793 the National Convention was locked in a life-and-death political struggle between members of the Mountain and the more moderate Girondists. With the

Areas of Insurrection, 1793

- Vendée Rebellion
- Counter-revolutionary insurrections

middle-class delegates so bitterly divided, the laboring poor of Paris once again emerged as the decisive political factor. The laboring poor and the petty traders were often known as the sans-culottes (sanz-koo-LAHT, "without breeches") because their men wore trousers instead of the knee breeches of the aristocracy and the solid middle class. They demanded radical political action to guarantee them their daily bread. The Mountain, sensing an opportunity to outmaneuver the Girondists, joined with sans-culottes activists to engineer a popular uprising. On June 2, 1793, armed sans-culottes invaded the Convention and forced deputies to arrest twenty-nine Girondist deputies for treason. All power passed to the Mountain.

The Convention also formed the Committee of Public Safety in April 1793 to deal with the threats from within and outside France. The committee, which Robespierre led, was given dictatorial power to deal with the national emergency. Moderates in

**sans-culottes** The laboring poor of Paris, so called because the men wore trousers instead of the knee breeches of the aristocracy and middle class; the word came to refer to the militant radicals of the city.

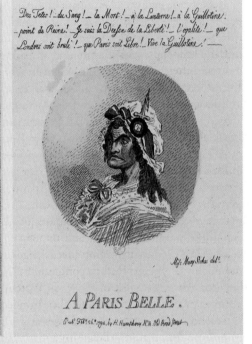

A PARIS BELLE.

### ▪ PICTURING THE PAST

### Contrasting Visions of the Sans-Culottes

These two images offer profoundly different representations of a sans-culotte woman. The image on the left was created by a French artist, while the image on the right is English. The French words above the image on the right read in part, "Heads! Blood! Death! . . . I am the Goddess of Liberty! . . . Long Live the Guillotine!" (Bibliothèque nationale de France)

**ANALYZING THE IMAGE** How would you describe the woman on the left? What qualities does the artist seem to ascribe to her, and how do you think these qualities relate to the sans-culottes and the Revolution? How would you characterize the facial expression and attire of the woman on the right? How does the inclusion of the text contribute to your impressions of her?

**CONNECTIONS** What does the contrast between these two images suggest about differences between French and English perceptions of the sans-culottes and of the French Revolution? Why do you think the artists have chosen to depict women?

To complete this activity online, go to the Online Study Guide at bedfordstmartins.com/ mckaywestunderstanding.

CHAPTER LOCATOR | What were the origins of the French Revolution? | What forces shaped the Revolution between 1789 and 1791? | **Why did the Revolution take a radical turn after 1791?** | What led to the rise and fall of Napoleon?

599

leading provincial cities revolted against the committee's power and demanded a decentralized government. Counter-revolutionary forces in the Vendée won significant victories, and the republic's armies were driven back on all fronts. By July 1793 only the areas around Paris and on the eastern frontier were firmly held by the central government. Defeat seemed imminent.

## Total War and the Terror

A year later, in July 1794, the central government had reasserted control over the provinces. In addition, the Austrian Netherlands and the Rhineland were once again in the hands of conquering French armies, and the First Coalition of Austria and Prussia was falling apart. This remarkable change of fortune was due to the revolutionary government's success in harnessing the explosive forces of a planned economy, revolutionary terror, and modern nationalism in a total war effort.

Robespierre and the Committee of Public Safety advanced on several fronts in 1793 and 1794, seeking to impose republican unity across the nation. First, they collaborated with the sans-culottes, who retained the common people's faith in fair prices and a moral economic order and who distrusted most wealthy capitalists and all aristocrats. Thus in September 1793 Robespierre and his coworkers established a planned economy with egalitarian social overtones. Rather than let supply and demand determine prices, the government set maximum allowable prices for key products. Though the state was too weak to enforce all its price regulations, it did fix the price of bread in Paris at levels the poor could afford. The people were also put to work, mainly producing arms and munitions for the war effort. The government told craftsmen what to produce, nationalized many small workshops, and requisitioned raw materials and grain. The second revolution and the ascendancy of the sans-culottes had produced an embryonic emergency socialism, which thoroughly frightened Europe's propertied classes and greatly influenced the subsequent development of socialist ideology (see Chapter 22).

Second, while radical economic measures supplied the poor with bread and the armies with weapons, the **Reign of Terror** (1793–1794) solidified the home front. Special revolutionary courts responsible only to Robespierre's Committee of Public Safety tried "enemies of the nation" for political crimes. Some forty thousand French men and women were executed or died in prison. Robespierre's Reign of Terror was and is one of the most controversial phases of the French Revolution. Presented

**Reign of Terror** The period from 1793 to 1794 during which Robespierre's Committee of Public Safety tried and executed thousands suspected of treason and a new revolutionary culture was imposed.

**The Guillotine** Prior to the French Revolution, methods of execution included hanging and being broken at the wheel. Only nobles enjoyed the privilege of a relatively swift and painless death by decapitation, delivered by an executioner's ax. The guillotine, a model of which is shown here, was devised by French revolutionaries as a humane and egalitarian form of execution. Ironically, due to the mass executions under the Terror, it is now seen instead as a symbol of revolutionary cruelty. (Musée de la Ville de Paris, Musée Carnavalet, Paris/Lauros/Giraudon/The Bridgeman Art Library)

as a necessary measure to save the republic, the Terror was a weapon directed against all suspected of opposing the revolutionary government. As Robespierre himself put it, "Terror is nothing more than prompt, severe inflexible justice."[4] For many Europeans of the time, however, the Reign of Terror represented a frightening perversion of the ideals of 1789.

In their efforts to impose unity, the Jacobins took actions to suppress women's participation in political debate, which they perceived as disorderly and a distraction from women's proper place in the home. On October 30, 1793, the National Convention declared that "The clubs and popular societies of women, under whatever denomination are prohibited." Among those convicted of sedition was writer Olympe de Gouges, who was sent to the guillotine in November 1793.

Beyond imposing political unity by force, the program of the Terror also included efforts to bring the revolution into all aspects of everyday life. The government sponsored revolutionary art and songs as well as a new series of secular holidays and open-air festivals to celebrate republican virtue and a love of nation. They attempted to rationalize French daily life by adopting the decimal system for weights and measures and a new calendar based on ten-day weeks. An important element of this cultural revolution was the campaign of **dechristianization**, which aimed to eliminate Catholic symbols and beliefs. Fearful of the hostility aroused in rural France, Robespierre called for a halt to dechristianization measures in mid-1794.

**dechristianization** Campaign to eliminate Christian faith and practice in France undertaken by the revolutionary government.

The third and perhaps most decisive element in the French republic's victory over the First Coalition was its ability to draw on the power of patriotic dedication to a national state and a national mission. An essential part of modern nationalism, which would fully emerge throughout Europe in the nineteenth century, this commitment was something new in history. With a common language and a common tradition newly reinforced by the ideas of popular sovereignty and democracy, large numbers of French people were stirred by a common loyalty. They developed an intense emotional commitment to the defense of the nation, and they saw the war as a life-and-death struggle between good and evil.

The all-out mobilization of French resources under the Terror combined with the fervor of modern nationalism to create an awesome fighting machine. After August 1793 all unmarried young men were subject to the draft, and by January 1794 French armed forces outnumbered their enemies almost four to one. Well-trained, well-equipped, and constantly indoctrinated, the enormous armies of the republic were led by young, impetuous generals. These generals often had risen from the ranks, and they personified the opportunities the Revolution offered gifted sons of the people. Following orders from Paris to attack relentlessly, French generals used mass assaults at bayonet point to overwhelm the enemy. By spring 1794 French armies were victorious on all fronts. The republic was saved.

## Revolution in Saint-Domingue

Just as the sans-culottes helped push forward more radical reforms in France, the second stage of revolution in Saint-Domingue also resulted from decisive action from below. In August 1791 slaves, who had been witnesses to the confrontation between whites and free coloreds for over a year, took events into their own hands. Groups of slaves held a series of nighttime meetings to plan a mass insurrection.

Revolts began on a few plantations on the night of August 22. Within a few days the uprising had swept much of the northern plain, creating a slave army estimated at around 2,000 individuals. By August 27 it was described by one observer as "10,000 strong, divided into 3 armies, of whom 700 or 800 are on horseback, and tolerably well-armed." During the next month slaves attacked and destroyed hundreds of sugar and coffee plantations.

CHAPTER LOCATOR | What were the origins of the French Revolution? | What forces shaped the Revolution between 1789 and 1791? | **Why did the Revolution take a radical turn after 1791?** | What led to the rise and fall of Napoleon?

601

# ▪ The French Revolution

## NATIONAL ASSEMBLY (1789–1791)

| | |
|---|---|
| **May 5, 1789** | Estates General meets at Versailles |
| **June 17, 1789** | Third estate declares itself the National Assembly |
| **June 20, 1789** | Oath of the Tennis Court |
| **July 14, 1789** | Storming of the Bastille |
| **July–August 1789** | Great Fear |
| **August 4, 1789** | Abolishment of feudal privileges |
| **August 27, 1789** | Declaration of the Rights of Man and of the Citizen |
| **October 5, 1789** | Women march on Versailles; royal family returns to Paris |
| **November 1789** | National Assembly confiscates church lands |
| **July 1790** | Civil Constitution of the Clergy establishes a national church; Louis XVI agrees to constitutional monarchy |
| **June 1791** | Royal family arrested while fleeing France |
| **August 1791** | Declaration of Pillnitz; slave insurrections in Saint-Domingue |

## LEGISLATIVE ASSEMBLY (1791–1792)

| | |
|---|---|
| **April 1792** | France declares war on Austria; enfranchisement of free people of color |
| **August 1792** | Mob attacks the palace, and Legislative Assembly takes Louis XVI prisoner |

## NATIONAL CONVENTION (1792–1795)

| | |
|---|---|
| **September 1792** | September Massacres; National Convention abolishes monarchy and declares France a republic |
| **January 1793** | Louis XVI executed |
| **February 1793** | France declares war on Britain, Holland, and Spain; revolts take place in some provinces |
| **March 1793** | Struggle between Girondists and the Mountain |
| **April 1793** | Creation of the Committee of Public Safety |
| **June 1793** | Arrest of Girondist leaders |
| **September 1793** | Price controls are instituted; British troops invade Saint-Domingue |
| **October 1793** | National Convention bans women's political societies |
| **1793–1794** | Reign of Terror |
| **February 1794** | Abolishment of slavery in all French territories |
| **Spring 1794** | French armies victorious on all fronts |
| **July 1794** | Robespierre executed; Thermidorian reaction begins |

## THE DIRECTORY (1795–1799)

| | |
|---|---|
| **1795** | Economic controls abolished; suppression of sans-culottes begins |
| **1796** | France regains control of Saint-Domingue under Toussaint L'Ouverture |
| **1799** | Napoleon seizes power |

On April 4, 1792, as war loomed with the European states, the National Assembly issued a decree enfranchising all free blacks and free people of color. The Assembly hoped this measure would win the loyalty of free blacks and their aid in defeating the slave rebellion.

Warfare in Europe soon spread to Saint-Domingue (Map 20.1), adding another complicating factor to its domestic conflicts. Since the beginning of the slave insurrection, the Spanish in neighboring Santo Domingo had supported rebel slaves, and in early 1793 they began to bring slave leaders and their soldiers into the Spanish army. Toussaint L'Ouverture (TOO-sa LOO-vair-toor) (1743–1803), a freed slave who had joined the revolt, was named a Spanish officer. In September the British navy also blockaded the colony, and invading British troops captured French territory on the island. For the Spanish and British, revolutionary chaos provided a tempting opportunity to capture a profitable colony.

Desperate for forces to oppose France's enemies, the commissioners sent by the newly elected National Convention promised freedom to slaves who fought for France. By October 1793 they had abolished slavery throughout the colony. On February 4, 1794, the Convention ratified the abolition of slavery and extended it to all French territories, including the Caribbean colonies of Martinique and Guadeloupe.

The tide of battle began to turn when Toussaint L'Ouverture switched sides, bringing his military and political skills, along with four thousand well-trained soldiers, to support the French war effort. By 1796 the French had gradually regained control of the colony, and L'Ouverture had emerged as the key leader of the combined slave and free colored forces. In May 1796 he was named commander of the western province of Saint-Domingue. The increasingly conservative nature of the French government during the

**Map 20.1 The War of Haitian Independence, 1791–1804** Neighbored by the Spanish colony of Santo Domingo, Saint-Domingue was the most profitable European colony in the Caribbean. In 1770 the French transferred the capital from Le Cap to Port-au-Prince. Slave revolts erupted in the north near Le Cap in 1791. Port-au-Prince became capital of the newly independent Haiti in 1804.

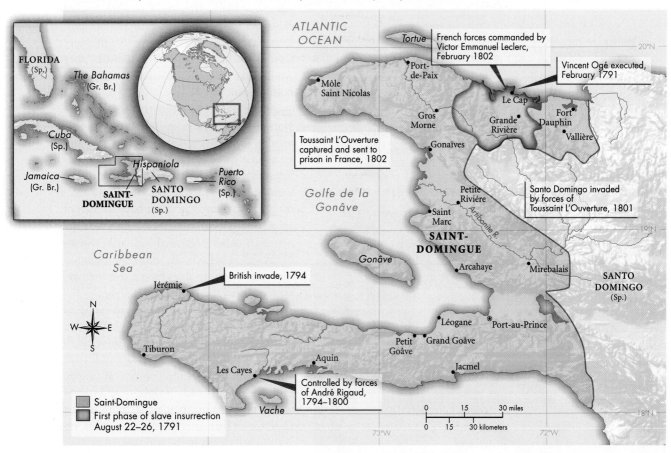

CHAPTER LOCATOR | What were the origins of the French Revolution? | What forces shaped the Revolution between 1789 and 1791? | **Why did the Revolution take a radical turn after 1791?** | What led to the rise and fall of Napoleon?

Thermidorian reaction, however, threatened to undo the gains made by former slaves and free people of color.

## The Thermidorian Reaction and the Directory

The success of the French armies led Robespierre and the Committee of Public Safety to relax the emergency economic controls, but they extended the political Reign of Terror. In March 1794, Robespierre's Terror wiped out many of his critics. Two weeks later, Robespierre sent long-standing collaborators, including Danton, to the guillotine. A group of radicals and moderates in the Convention, knowing that they might be next, organized a conspiracy. They howled down Robespierre when he tried to speak to the National Convention on July 27, 1794—a date known as "9 Thermidor" according to France's newly adopted republican calendar. The next day it was Robespierre's turn to be guillotined.

As Robespierre's closest supporters followed their leader to the guillotine, France experienced a thorough reaction to the despotism of the Reign of Terror. In a general way, this Thermidorian reaction recalled the early days of the Revolution. The respectable middle-class lawyers and professionals who had led the liberal revolution of 1789 reasserted their authority. In 1795 the National Convention abolished many of the radicals' economic controls, let prices rise sharply, and severely restricted the local political organizations in which the sans-culottes had their strength.

**Thermidorian reaction**
A reaction to the violence of the Reign of Terror in 1794, resulting in the execution of Robespierre and the loosening of economic controls.

The collapse of economic controls, coupled with runaway inflation, hit the working poor very hard. After the Convention used the army to suppress the sans-culottes' protests, the urban poor lost their revolutionary fervor. Excluded and disillusioned, they would have little interest in and influence on politics until 1830.

As for the middle-class members of the National Convention, in 1795 they wrote yet another constitution that they believed would guarantee their economic position and political supremacy. As in previous elections, the mass of the population voted only for electors, whose number was cut back to men of substantial means. Electors then elected the members of a reorganized legislative assembly as well as key officials throughout France. The new assembly also chose a five-man executive called the Directory.

The Directory continued to support French military expansion abroad. War was no longer so much a crusade as a response to economic problems. Large, victorious French armies reduced unemployment at home. However, the French people quickly grew weary of the unprincipled actions of the Directory. This general dissatisfaction revealed itself clearly in the national elections of 1797, which returned a large number of con-

**The Execution of Robespierre** Completely wooden except for the heavy iron blade, the guillotine was painted red for Robespierre's execution, a detail not captured in this black and white engraving of the 1794 event. Large crowds witnessed the execution in a majestic public square in central Paris, then known as the Place de la Revolution and now called the Place de la Concorde (Harmony Square). (Snark/Art Resource, NY)

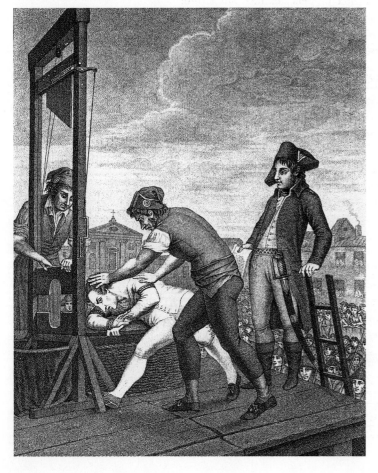

servative and even monarchist deputies who favored peace at almost any price. The members of the Directory, fearing for their skins, used the army to nullify the elections and began to govern dictatorially. Two years later Napoleon Bonaparte ended the Directory in a coup d'état (koo day-TAH) and substituted a strong dictatorship for a weak one.

# ▼ What led to the rise and fall of Napoleon?

For almost fifteen years, from 1799 to 1814, France was in the hands of a keen-minded military dictator of exceptional ability. Napoleon Bonaparte (1769–1821) realized the need to put an end to civil strife in France in order to create unity and consolidate his rule. And he did. But Napoleon saw himself as a man of destiny, and the glory of war and the dream of universal empire proved irresistible.

## Napoleon's Rule of France

Born in Corsica into an impoverished noble family in 1769, Napoleon left home and became a lieutenant in the French artillery in 1785. After a brief and unsuccessful adventure fighting for Corsican independence in 1789, he returned to France as a French patriot and a revolutionary. Rising rapidly in the new army, Napoleon was placed in command of French forces in Italy and won brilliant victories there in 1796 and 1797. His next campaign, in Egypt, was a failure, but Napoleon returned to France before the fiasco was generally known, and his reputation remained intact.

Napoleon soon learned that some prominent members of the legislature were plotting against the Directory. The dissatisfaction of these plotters stemmed not so much from the fact that the Directory was a dictatorship as from the fact that it was a weak dictatorship. Ten years of upheaval and uncertainty had made firm rule much more appealing than liberty and popular politics to these disillusioned revolutionaries.

The plotters wanted a strong military ruler. The flamboyant thirty-year-old Napoleon, nationally revered for his heroism, was ideal. Thus the conspirators and Napoleon organized a takeover. On November 9, 1799, they ousted the Directors, and the following day soldiers disbanded the legislature. Napoleon was named first consul of the republic, and a new constitution consolidating his position was overwhelmingly approved in a plebiscite (a one-time vote by all French men) in December 1799.

The essence of Napoleon's domestic policy was to use his popularity and charisma to maintain order and end civil strife. He did so by working out unwritten agreements with powerful groups in France whereby the groups received favors in return for loyal service. Napoleon's bargain with the middle class was codified in the famous Civil Code of March 1804, also known as the **Napoleonic Code**, which reasserted two of the fundamental principles of the revolution of 1789: equality of all male citizens before the law, and absolute security of wealth and private property.

At the same time, Napoleon built on the bureaucracy inherited from the Revolution and the Old Regime to create a thoroughly centralized state. He consolidated his rule by recruiting disillusioned revolutionaries for the network of government officials that depended on him and came to serve him well. Nor were members of the old nobility slighted. In 1800 and again in 1802 Napoleon granted amnesty to one hundred thousand émigrés on the condition that they return to France and take a loyalty oath. Members of this returning elite soon occupied many high posts in the expanding centralized state.

Napoleon applied his diplomatic skills to healing the Catholic Church in France so that it could serve as a bulwark of social stability. Napoleon and Pope Pius VII (pontificate 1800–1823) signed the Concordat (kuhn-KOHR-dat) of 1801. The pope gained the

**Napoleonic Code** French civil code promulgated in 1804 that reasserted the 1789 principles of the equality of all male citizens before the law and the absolute security of wealth and private property as well as restricting rights accorded to women by previous revolutionary laws.

CHAPTER LOCATOR | What were the origins of the French Revolution? | What forces shaped the Revolution between 1789 and 1791? | Why did the Revolution take a radical turn after 1791? | **What led to the rise and fall of Napoleon?**

**605**

right for French Catholics to practice their religion freely, but Napoleon gained political power: his government now nominated bishops, paid the clergy, and exerted great influence over the church in France. The domestic reforms of Napoleon's early years were his greatest achievement. Much of his legal and administrative reorganization has survived in France to this day. More generally, Napoleon's domestic initiatives gave the great majority of French people a sense of stability and national unity.

Order and unity had a price: authoritarian rule. Women, who had often participated in revolutionary politics without having legal equality, lost many of the gains they made in the 1790s. Under the new Napoleonic Code, women were dependents of either their fathers or their husbands, and they could not make contracts or have bank accounts in their own names. Napoleon aimed at re-establishing a family monarchy, where the power of the husband and father was as absolute over the wife and the children as that of Napoleon was over his subjects.

Free speech and freedom of the press were curtailed. By 1811 only four newspapers were left, and they were little more than organs of government propaganda. The occasional elections were a farce. Later laws prescribed harsh penalties for political offenses, and people were watched carefully under an efficient spy system. After 1810 political suspects were held in state prisons, as they had been during the Terror.

## Napoleon's Expansion in Europe

After coming to power in 1799 Napoleon sent peace feelers to Austria and Great Britain, the two remaining members of the Second Coalition that had been formed against France in 1798. When these overtures were rejected, French armies led by Napoleon decisively defeated the Austrians. Military victory was capped by peace treaties with Austria in 1801 and Britain in 1802 and the acknowledgment by those two powers of an expanded France.

In 1802 Napoleon was secure but driven to expand his power. Aggressively redrawing the map of Germany so as to weaken Austria and encourage the secondary states of southwestern Germany to side with France, Napoleon tried to restrict British trade with all of Europe. He then plotted to attack Great Britain, but his Mediterranean fleet was destroyed by Lord Nelson at the Battle of Trafalgar on October 21, 1805. Renewed fighting had its advantages, however, for the first consul used the wartime atmosphere to have himself proclaimed emperor in late 1804.

Austria, Russia, and Sweden joined with Britain to form the Third Coalition against France shortly before the Battle of Trafalgar. Yet the Austrians and the Russians were no match for Napoleon, who scored a brilliant victory over them at the Battle of Austerlitz in December 1805. Russia decided to pull back, and Austria accepted large territorial losses in return for peace as the Third Coalition collapsed.

Napoleon then proceeded to reorganize the German states to his liking. In 1806 he abolished many of the tiny German states as well as the Holy Roman Empire and established by decree the German Confederation of the Rhine, a union of fifteen German states minus Austria, Prussia, and Saxony. Naming himself "protector" of the confederation, Napoleon firmly controlled western Germany.

Napoleon's intervention in German affairs alarmed the Prussians, who mobilized their armies. Napoleon attacked and won two more brilliant victories in October 1806 at Jena and Auerstädt, where the Prussians were outnumbered two to one. The war with Prussia, now joined by Russia,

**German Confederation of the Rhine, 1806**

continued into the following spring. After Napoleon's larger armies won another victory, Alexander I of Russia was ready to negotiate the peace. In the treaties of Tilsit in 1807, Prussia lost half of its population, while Russia accepted Napoleon's reorganization of western and central Europe and promised to enforce Napoleon's economic blockade against British goods.

## The War of Haitian Independence

In the midst of these victories, Napoleon was forced to accept defeat overseas. With Toussaint L'Ouverture acting increasingly as an independent ruler of the western province of Saint-Domingue, another general, André Rigaud, set up his own government in the southern peninsula. Tensions mounted between L'Ouverture and Rigaud. While L'Ouverture was a freed slave of African descent, Rigaud belonged to the free colored elite. This elite resented the growing power of former slaves like L'Ouverture, who in turn accused them of adopting the racism of white settlers. Civil war broke out between the two sides in 1799 when L'Ouverture's forces, led by his lieutenant Jean Jacques Dessalines, invaded the south. Victory over Rigaud gave L'Ouverture control of the entire colony. (See "Individuals in Society: Toussaint L'Ouverture," page 608.)

This victory was soon challenged by Napoleon, who had his own plans for using profits from Caribbean plantations, where he intended to re-establish slavery, as a basis for expanding French power. Napoleon ordered his brother-in-law, General Charles-Victor-Emmanuel Leclerc, to lead an expedition to the island to crush the new regime.

In 1802 Leclerc landed in Saint-Domingue. Although Toussaint L'Ouverture cooperated with the French and turned his army over to them, he was arrested and deported to France, along with his family, where he died in 1803. Jean Jacques Dessalines united the resistance under his command and led it to a crushing victory over the French forces. On January 1, 1804, Dessalines formally declared the independence of Saint-Domingue and the creation of the new sovereign nation of Haiti, the name used by the pre-Columbian inhabitants of the island.

Haiti, the second independent state in the Americas and the first in Latin America, was thus born from the first successful large-scale slave revolt in history. Fearing the spread of slave rebellion to the United States, President Thomas Jefferson refused to recognize Haiti. Both the American and the French Revolutions thus exposed their limits by acting to protect economic interests at the expense of revolutionary ideals of freedom and equality. Yet, Haitian independence had fundamental repercussions for world history, helping spread the idea that liberty, equality, and fraternity must apply to all people.

## The Grand Empire and Its End

Napoleon resigned himself to the loss of Saint-Domingue, but he still maintained imperial ambitions in Europe. Increasingly, he saw himself as the emperor of Europe, not just of France. The so-called Grand Empire he built had three parts. The core was an ever-expanding France, which by 1810 included Belgium, Holland, parts of northern Italy, and much German territory on the east bank of the Rhine. The second part consisted of a number of dependent satellite kingdoms. The third part comprised the independent but allied states of Austria, Prussia, and Russia. After 1806 both satellites and allies were expected to support Napoleon's Continental System, a blockade in which no ship coming from Britain or her colonies was allowed to dock at any port controlled by the French. It was intended to halt all trade between Britain and continental Europe, thereby destroying the British economy and its military force.

The impact of the Grand Empire on the peoples of Europe was considerable. In the areas incorporated into France and in the satellites (Map 20.2), Napoleon abolished feudal dues and serfdom. Yet Napoleon had to put the interests of France first in order to

**Grand Empire** The empire over which Napoleon and his allies ruled, encompassing virtually all of Europe except Great Britain and Russia.

**Continental System** A blockade imposed by Napoleon to halt all trade between continental Europe and Britain, thereby weakening the British economy and military.

CHAPTER LOCATOR | What were the origins of the French Revolution? | What forces shaped the Revolution between 1789 and 1791? | Why did the Revolution take a radical turn after 1791? | What led to the rise and fall of Napoleon?

607

# INDIVIDUALS IN SOCIETY

## Toussaint L'Ouverture

**LITTLE IS KNOWN OF THE EARLY LIFE** of Saint-Domingue's brilliant military and political leader Toussaint L'Ouverture. He was born in 1743 on a plantation outside Le Cap owned by the Count de Bréda. According to tradition, L'Ouverture was the eldest son of a captured African prince from modern-day Benin. Toussaint Bréda, as he was then called, occupied a privileged position among slaves. Instead of performing backbreaking labor in the fields, he served his master as a coachman and livestock keeper. He also learned to read and write French and some Latin, but he was always more comfortable with the Creole dialect.

During the 1770s the plantation manager emancipated L'Ouverture, who subsequently leased his own small coffee plantation, worked by slaves. He married Suzanne Simone, who already had one son, and the couple had another son during their marriage. In 1791 he joined the slave uprisings that swept Saint-Domingue, and he took on the *nom de guerre* ("war name") "L'Ouverture," meaning "the opening." L'Ouverture rose to prominence among rebel slaves allied with Spain and by early 1794 controlled his own army. A devout Catholic who led a frugal and ascetic life, L'Ouverture impressed others with his enormous physical energy, intellectual acumen, and air of mystery. In 1794 he defected to the French side and led his troops to a series of victories against the Spanish. In 1795 the National Convention promoted L'Ouverture to brigadier general.

Over the next three years L'Ouverture successively eliminated rivals for authority on the island. First he freed himself of the French commissioners sent to govern the colony. With a firm grip on power in the northern province, L'Ouverture defeated General André Rigaud in 1800 to gain control in the south. His army then marched on the capital of Spanish Santo Domingo on the eastern half of the island, meeting little resistance. The entire island of Hispaniola was now under his command.

With control of Saint-Domingue in his hands, L'Ouverture was confronted with the challenge of building a post-emancipation society, the first of its kind. The task was made even more difficult by the chaos wreaked by war, the destruction of plantations, and bitter social and racial tensions. For L'Ouverture the most pressing concern was to re-establish the plantation economy. Without revenue to pay his army, the gains of the rebellion could be lost. He therefore encouraged

**Equestrian portrait of Toussaint L'Ouverture.** (Réunion des Musées Nationaux/Art Resource, NY)

white planters to return and reclaim their property. He also adopted harsh policies toward former slaves, forcing them back to their plantations and restricting their ability to acquire land. When they resisted, he sent troops across the island to enforce submission. L'Ouverture's 1801 constitution reaffirmed his draconian labor policies and named L'Ouverture governor for life, leaving Saint-Domingue as a colony in name alone. In June 1802 French forces arrested L'Ouverture and jailed him at Fort de Joux in France's Jura Mountains near the Swiss border. L'Ouverture died of pneumonia on April 7, 1803. It was left to his lieutenant, Jean Jacques Dessalines, to win independence for the new Haitian nation.

## QUESTIONS FOR ANALYSIS

1. Toussaint L'Ouverture was both slave and slave owner. How did each experience shape his life and actions?
2. What did Toussaint L'Ouverture and Napoleon Bonaparte have in common? How did they differ?

safeguard his power base. Levying heavy taxes in money and men for his armies, he came to be regarded more as a conquering tyrant than as an enlightened liberator. Thus French rule sparked patriotic upheavals and encouraged the growth of reactive nationalism.

The first great revolt occurred in Spain. In 1808 a coalition of Catholics, monarchists, and patriots rebelled against Napoleon's attempts to make Spain a French satellite. French armies occupied Madrid, but the foes of Napoleon fled to the hills and waged uncompro-

**French empire**
**Dependent states**
**Allied with Napoleon**
**French victory**
**French defeat**

- MAPPING THE PAST

## Map 20.2 Napoleonic Europe in 1812

Only Great Britain remained at war with Napoleon at the height of the Grand Empire. Many British goods were smuggled through Helgoland, a tiny but strategic British possession off the German coast.

**ANALYZING THE MAP** How had the balance of power shifted in Europe from 1715 to 1812? What changed, and what remained the same? What was the impact of Napoleon's wars on Germany and the Italian peninsula?

**CONNECTIONS** Why did Napoleon succeed in achieving vast territorial gains where Louis XIV did not?

To complete this activity online, go to the Online Study Guide at bedfordstmartins.com/mckaywestunderstanding.

mising guerrilla warfare. Spain was a clear warning: resistance to French imperialism was growing.

Yet Napoleon pushed on. In 1810, when the Grand Empire was at its height, Britain still remained at war with France, helping the guerrillas in Spain and Portugal. The Continental System was a failure. Instead of harming Britain, it was France that suffered from Britain's counter-blockade, which created hard times for French artisans and the

CHAPTER LOCATOR | What were the origins of the French Revolution? | What forces shaped the Revolution between 1789 and 1791? | Why did the Revolution take a radical turn after 1791? | **What led to the rise and fall of Napoleon?**

609

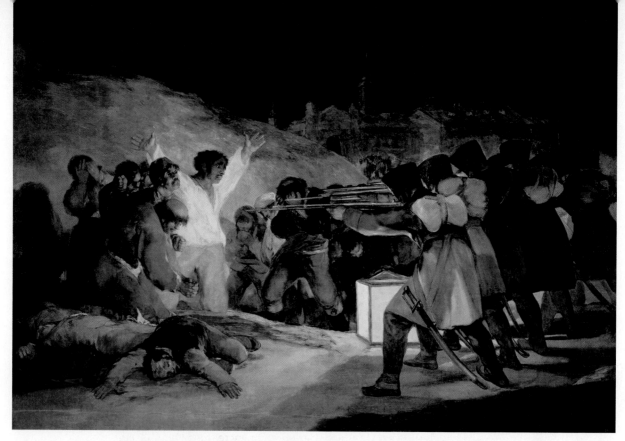

Francisco Goya, *The Third of May 1808* Spanish master Francisco Goya created a passionate and moving indictment of the brutality of war in this painting from 1814, which depicts the close-range execution of Spanish rebels by Napoleon's forces in May 1808. Goya's painting evoked the bitterness and despair of many Europeans who suffered through Napoleon's invasions. (Erich Lessing/Art Resource, NY)

middle class. Perhaps looking for a scapegoat, Napoleon turned on Alexander I of Russia, who in 1811 openly repudiated Napoleon's war of prohibitions against British goods.

Napoleon's invasion of Russia began in June 1812. Originally planning to winter in the Russian city of Smolensk if Alexander did not sue for peace, Napoleon reached Smolensk and recklessly pressed on toward Moscow. The Battle of Borodino that followed was a draw, and the Russians retreated in good order. Alexander ordered the evacuation of Moscow, which the Russians then burned in part, and he refused to negotiate. Finally, after five weeks in the scorched and abandoned city, Napoleon ordered a disastrous retreat. The Russian army, the Russian winter, and starvation cut Napoleon's army to pieces.

Leaving his troops to their fate, Napoleon raced to Paris to raise another army. Possibly he might still have saved his throne if he had been willing to accept a France reduced to its historical size — the proposal offered by Austria's foreign minister, Prince Klemens von Metternich. But Napoleon refused. Austria and Prussia deserted Napoleon and joined Russia and Great Britain in the Treaty of Chaumont in March 1814, by which the four powers pledged allegiance to defeat the French emperor. All across Europe patriots called for a "war of liberation" against Napoleon's oppression. Less than a month later, on April 4, 1814, a defeated Napoleon abdicated his throne. After this unconditional abdication, the victorious allies granted Napoleon the island of Elba off the coast of Italy as his own tiny state.

The allies also agreed to the restoration of the Bourbon dynasty under Louis XVIII (r. 1814–1824) and promised to treat France with leniency in a peace settlement. The new monarch tried to consolidate support among the people by issuing the Constitutional Charter, which accepted many of France's revolutionary changes and guaranteed civil liberties.

Yet Louis XVIII lacked the glory and magnetism of Napoleon. Hearing of political unrest in France and diplomatic tensions in Vienna, Napoleon staged a daring escape from Elba in February 1815. Landing in France, he issued appeals for support and marched on Paris. French officers and soldiers who had fought so long for their emperor responded to the call. Louis XVIII fled, and once more Napoleon took command. But Napoleon's gamble was a desperate long shot, for the allies were united against him. At the end of a frantic period known as the Hundred Days, they crushed his forces at Waterloo, in present-day Belgium, on June 18, 1815, and imprisoned him on the island of St. Helena, off the western coast of Africa. Louis XVIII returned to the throne, and the allies dealt more harshly with the French. As for Napoleon, he took revenge by writing his memoirs, nurturing the myth that he had been Europe's revolutionary liberator, a hero whose work had been undone by oppressive reactionaries.

# ← LOOKING BACK **LOOKING AHEAD** →

UNTIL 1789 the medieval ordering of French society into three estates remained in force, and the king, claiming to embody the nation in his person by the grace of God, continued to rule absolutely. Yet monumental changes had occurred over the eighteenth century as population grew, urbanization spread, and literacy increased (see Chapter 19). Enlightenment ideals influenced members of all three estates, who increasingly questioned the power of the monarchy and the rigid structure of society. As the sacred aura of the monarchy diminished, the royal government became increasingly incapable of resolving the urgent financial and political crises of the Old Regime. Exactly who should have the power, however, and how France should be governed, were questions that had many conflicting answers and resulted in decades of war and instability.

The age of revolution both drew on and affected European colonies in the Americas. The high stakes of colonial empire had heightened competition among European states, leading to a series of wars that generated crushing costs for overburdened treasuries. As was the case for the British in their North American colonies, the desperate need for new taxes weakened the French state and opened the door to revolution. In turn, the ideals of the French Revolution inspired slaves and free people of color in Saint-Domingue, thus opening the promise of liberty, equality, and fraternity to people of all races.

Nineteenth- and early-twentieth-century Europe experienced periodic convulsions of revolution as successive generations struggled over political rights first proclaimed by the generation of 1789. Meanwhile, as dramatic events unfolded in France, a parallel revolution had gathered steam across the Channel. This was the British Industrial Revolution, originating around 1750 and accelerating through the end of the eighteenth century. After 1815 the twin forces of industrialization and democratization would combine to create the modern nation-states of Europe. ▪

- **For a list of suggested readings for this chapter, visit** *bedfordstmartins.com/mckaywestunderstanding*.

- **For primary sources from this period, see** *Sources of Western Society*, Second Edition.

- **For Web sites, images, and documents related to topics in this chapter, see Make History at** *bedfordstmartins.com/mckaywestunderstanding*.

CHAPTER LOCATOR | What were the origins of the French Revolution? | What forces shaped the Revolution between 1789 and 1791? | Why did the Revolution take a radical turn after 1791? | **What led to the rise and fall of Napoleon?**

611

# Chapter 20 Study Guide

Online Study Guide
bedfordstmartins.com/mckaywestunderstanding

## Step 1

**GETTING STARTED** Below are basic terms about this period in the history of Western civilization. Can you identify each term below and explain why it matters? To do this exercise online, go to bedfordstmartins.com/mckaywestunderstanding.

| TERMS | WHO (OR WHAT) AND WHEN | WHY IT MATTERS |
|---|---|---|
| estates, p. 584 | | |
| Estates General, p. 588 | | |
| National Assembly, p. 589 | | |
| Great Fear, p. 592 | | |
| constitutional monarchy, p. 593 | | |
| second revolution, p. 598 | | |
| Jacobin club, p. 598 | | |
| Girondists, p. 598 | | |
| the Mountain, p. 598 | | |
| sans-culottes, p. 599 | | |
| Reign of Terror, p. 600 | | |
| dechristianization, p. 601 | | |
| Thermidorian reaction, p. 604 | | |
| Napoleonic Code, p. 605 | | |
| Grand Empire, p. 607 | | |
| Continental System, p. 607 | | |

## Step 2

**MOVING BEYOND THE BASICS** The exercise below requires a more advanced understanding of the chapter material. Examine the four main phases of the French Revolution by filling in the chart below with descriptions of the leaders and key groups that shaped important developments, the policies and reforms initiated during the phase, and the groups that gained and lost the most as a result of those policies. When you are finished, consider the following question: What were the successes and failures of each phase of the Revolution? To do this exercise online, go to bedfordstmartins.com/mckaywestunderstanding.

| PHASE | LEADERS AND KEY GROUPS | POLICIES AND REFORMS | WINNERS AND LOSERS |
|---|---|---|---|
| The First Revolution: 1789–1791 | | | |
| The Second Revolution: 1791–1794 | | | |
| The Directory: 1794–1799 | | | |
| Napoleonic France: 1799–1815 | | | |

## Step 3 ▷ PUTTING IT ALL TOGETHER

Now that you've reviewed key elements of the chapter, take a step back and try to see the big picture. Remember to use specific examples from the chapter in your answers. To do this exercise online, go to bedfordstmartins.com/mckaywestunderstanding.

### BACKGROUND TO REVOLUTION

- How did the French crown's fiscal problems lead to a political crisis in 1789? Is it fair to say that problems with government finances *caused* the French Revolution? Why or why not?

- In your opinion, what role, if any, did social tensions play in bringing about the French Revolution? What evidence can you present to support your position?

### POLITICS AND THE PEOPLE, 1789–1791

- How did the people of Paris see France's problems in the late 1780s and early 1790s? How might the view of the average Parisian have differed from that of the early leaders of the Revolution?

- How did the people of Saint-Domingue react to the news of revolution in France? How would you explain their reaction? How did the French Revolution contribute to increasing social and political tensions in Saint-Domingue?

### TOTAL WAR AND REPUBLICAN FRANCE, 1791–1799

- How was violence used as a political tool during the period of the Second Revolution? What justifications were offered for its use? In your opinion, how valid were these justifications?

- How did war and the threat of war shape the course of the Revolution between 1791 and 1799?

### THE NAPOLEONIC ERA, 1799–1815

- Should Napoleon be considered a "revolutionary"? Why or why not?

- Why was Napoleon driven to create a French Empire in Europe? To what degree did his popularity depend on military victories? Could he have made peace with the rest of Europe if he had wanted to?

■ **In Your Own Words**  Imagine that you must explain Chapter 20 to someone who hasn't read it. What would be the most important points to include and why?

# 21

# The Revolution in Energy and Industry

## ca. 1780–1850

While the revolution in France was opening a new political era, another revolution was beginning to transform economic and social life. The Industrial Revolution began in Great Britain around the 1780s and started to influence continental Europe after 1815. Some historians see industrial development as basically moderate and evolutionary, but it was rapid and brought about numerous radical changes. Quite possibly only the development of agriculture during Neolithic times had a comparable impact and significance.

The Industrial Revolution profoundly modified much of human experience. It changed patterns of work, transformed the social class structure and the way people thought about class, and eventually altered the international balance of political power. The Industrial Revolution also helped ordinary people gain a higher standard of living as the widespread poverty of the preindustrial world was gradually reduced.

Unfortunately, the improvement in the European standard of living was limited until about 1850 for at least two reasons. First, even in Britain, only a few key industries experienced a technological revolution. Many more industries continued to use old methods, especially on the continent, and this held down the increase in total production. Second, the increase in total population, which began in the eighteenth century (see Chapter 18), continued across Europe as the era of the Industrial Revolution unfolded. The rapid growth in population threatened to eat up the growth in production and to leave most individuals poorer than ever. As a consequence, rapid population growth provided a somber background for European industrialization and made the wrenching transformation all the more difficult. ■

**Life in the Industrial Revolution.** This realistic painting from mid-nineteenth-century northern England shows women textile workers as they relax and socialize on their lunch break. Most of the workers are young and probably unmarried. (© Manchester Art Gallery, UK/The Bridgeman Art Library)

# Chapter Preview

▶ **How did the Industrial Revolution develop in Britain?**

▶ **How did continental Europe industrialize after 1815?**

▶ **What were the social consequences of industrialization?**

# ▼ How did the Industrial Revolution develop in Britain?

The Industrial Revolution began in Great Britain. The transformation in industry was something new in history, and it was quite unplanned. With no models to copy and no idea of what to expect, Britain had to pioneer not only in industrial technology but also in social relations and urban living. Just as France was the trailblazer in political change, Britain was the leader in economic development, and it must therefore command special attention.

## Eighteenth-Century Origins

Scholars generally agree that industrial changes grew out of a long process of development. The expanding Atlantic economy of the eighteenth century served mercantilist Britain well. The colonial empire that Britain aggressively built, augmented by a strong position in Latin America and in the African slave trade, provided a growing market for British manufactured goods.

Agriculture also played a central role in bringing about the Industrial Revolution in Britain. English farmers were second only to the Dutch in productivity in 1700, and they were continually adopting new methods of farming. The result, especially before 1760, was a period of bountiful crops and low food prices. The ordinary English family did not have to spend almost everything it earned just to buy bread. Thus the family could spend more on manufactured goods. Moreover, in the eighteenth century the members of the average British family were redirecting their labor away from unpaid work for household consumption toward work for wages that they could spend on goods, a trend reflecting the increasing commercialization of the entire European economy (see Chapter 18).

As manufacturing expanded to supply both foreign and British customers, the domestic market for raw materials was well-positioned to meet the growing demands of manufacturers. In an age when it was much cheaper to ship goods by water than by land, no part of England was more than fifty miles from navigable water. Beginning in the 1770s, a canal-building boom enhanced this advantage. Rivers and canals provided easy movement of England's and Wales's enormous deposits of iron and coal, resources that would be critical raw materials in Europe's early industrial age. Nor were there any tariffs within the country to hinder trade, as there were in France before 1789 and in politically fragmented Germany.

Britain had a host of other assets that helped give rise to its industrial leadership. Unlike eighteenth-century France, Britain had an effective central bank and well-developed credit markets. The monarchy and the aristocratic oligarchy provided stable and predictable government. At the same time, the government let the domestic economy operate with few controls, encouraging personal initiative, technical change, and a free market. Finally, Britain had long had a large class of hired agricultural laborers. Along with cottage workers, these rural wage earners formed a potential industrial labor force for capitalist entrepreneurs.

All these factors combined to initiate the Industrial Revolution. This technical revolution went hand in hand with an impressive quickening in the annual rate of industrial

**Industrial Revolution**
A term first coined in the 1830s to describe the burst of major inventions and economic expansion that took place in certain industries, such as cotton textiles and iron.

Industrial areas
- ■ Coal deposit
- ○ Metal goods
- ■ Woolen cloth
- — Canals, 1800
- — Navigable rivers

SCOTLAND

North Sea

Newcastle

Manchester · Sheffield

Birmingham · Iron
WALES

Iron

Bath · London

Iron

Exeter

English Channel

**Cottage Industry and Transportation in Eighteenth-Century England**

growth in Britain. Whereas industry had grown at only 0.7 percent between 1700 and 1760 (before the Industrial Revolution), it grew at the much higher rate of 3 percent between 1801 and 1831 (when industrial transformation was in full swing).[1]

## The First Factories

The pressure to produce more goods for a growing market was directly related to the first decisive breakthrough of the Industrial Revolution — the creation of the world's first large factories in the British cotton textile industry. Technological innovations in the manufacture of cotton cloth led to a new system of production and social relationships. Although the putting-out system of merchant capitalism (see Chapter 18) was expanding all across Europe in the eighteenth century, this pattern of rural industry was most fully developed in Britain. There, under the pressure of growing demand, the system's limitations began to outweigh its advantages for the first time. This was especially true in the British textile industry after about 1760.

A constant shortage of thread in the textile industry focused attention on ways of improving spinning. After many experiments over a generation, James Hargreaves invented his cotton-spinning jenny about 1765. At almost the same moment, Richard Arkwright invented (or possibly pirated) another kind of spinning machine, the water frame. These breakthroughs produced an explosion in the cotton textile industry in the 1780s. By 1790 the new machines were producing ten times as much cotton yarn as had been made in 1770.

Hargreaves's **spinning jenny** was simple, inexpensive, and powered by hand. Arkwright's **water frame**, however, quickly acquired a capacity of several hundred spindles and demanded much more power — waterpower. The water frame thus required large specialized mills, factories that employed as many as one thousand workers from the very beginning. After 1790, all cotton spinning was gradually concentrated in factories.

The first consequences of these revolutionary developments in the textile industry were more beneficial than is generally believed. Cotton goods became much cheaper, and they were increasingly bought by all classes. Families using cotton in cottage industry were freed from their constant search for adequate yarn from scattered part-time spinners, since all the thread needed could be spun in the cottage on the jenny or obtained from a nearby factory. The wages of weavers, now hard-pressed to keep up with the spinners, rose markedly until about 1792. Weavers were among the best-paid workers in England. As a result, large numbers of agricultural laborers became hand-loom weavers, while mechanics and capitalists sought to invent a power loom to save on labor costs. This Edmund Cartwright achieved in 1785. But the power looms of the factories worked poorly at first, and hand-loom weavers continued to receive good wages until at least 1800.

Unfortunately, working conditions in the early cotton factories were less satisfactory than those of cottage weavers and spinners, and adult workers were reluctant to work in them. Therefore, factory owners often turned to young children who had been abandoned by their parents and put in the care of local parishes. Apprenticed as young as five or six years of age, boy and girl workers were forced by law to labor for their "masters" for as many as fourteen years. Housed, fed, and locked up nightly in factory dormitories, the young workers labored thirteen or fourteen hours a day for little or no pay. Harsh physical punishment maintained brutal discipline.

## Chapter Chronology

| | |
|---|---|
| ca. 1765 | Hargreaves invents spinning jenny; Arkwright creates water frame |
| 1769 | Watt patents modern steam engine |
| 1775–1783 | American Revolution |
| ca. 1780–1850 | Industrial Revolution; population boom in Great Britain |
| 1789–1799 | French Revolution |
| 1799 | Combination Acts passed |
| 1810 | Strike of Manchester cotton spinners |
| 1824 | Combination Acts repealed |
| 1830 | Stephenson's *Rocket*; first important railroad |
| 1830s | Industrial banks in Belgium |
| 1833 | Factory Act |
| 1842 | Mines Act |
| 1851 | Great Exhibition held at Crystal Palace |

**spinning jenny** A simple, inexpensive, hand-powered spinning machine created by James Hargreaves in 1765.

**water frame** A spinning machine created by Richard Arkwright that had a capacity of several hundred spindles and used waterpower; it therefore required a larger and more specialized mill — a factory.

CHAPTER LOCATOR | How did the Industrial Revolution develop in Britain? | How did continental Europe industrialize after 1815? | What were the social consequences of industrialization?

617

**Woman Working a Spinning Jenny** The loose cotton strands on the slanted bobbins shown in this illustration of Hargreave's spinning jenny passed up to the sliding carriage and then on to the spindles in back for fine spinning. The worker, almost always a woman, regulated the sliding carriage with one hand, and with the other she turned the crank on the wheel to supply power. By 1783 one woman could spin by hand a hundred threads at a time. (Mary Evans Picture Library/The Image Works)

The creation of the world's first modern factories in the British cotton textile industry in the 1770s and 1780s, which grew out of the putting-out system of cottage production, was a major historical development. Both symbolically and substantially, the big new cotton mills marked the beginning of the Industrial Revolution in Britain. By 1831 the largely mechanized cotton textile industry accounted for fully 22 percent of the country's entire industrial production.

## The Problem of Energy

Human beings have long used their toolmaking abilities to construct machines that convert one form of energy into another for their own benefit. In the medieval period, people began to develop water mills to grind their grain and windmills to pump water and drain swamps. More efficient use of water and wind in the sixteenth and seventeenth centuries enabled human beings to accomplish more. Nevertheless, even into the eighteenth century, society continued to rely mainly on wood for energy, and human beings and animals continued to perform most work. This dependence meant that Western civilization remained poor in energy and power.

The shortage of energy had become particularly severe in Britain by the eighteenth century. Wood, a basic raw material and the primary source of heat for all homes and industries, was in ever-shorter supply. Processed wood (charcoal) was the fuel that was mixed with iron ore in the blast furnace to produce pig iron. The iron industry's appetite for wood was enormous, and by 1740 the British iron industry was stagnating.

## The Steam Engine Breakthrough

As this early energy crisis grew worse, Britain looked to coal as an alternative to its vanishing wood. Coal was first used in Britain in the late Middle Ages as a source of heat. By 1640 most homes in London were heated with coal, and it was also used in industry to provide heat for making beer, glass, soap, and other products. The breakthrough came when industrialists began to use coal to produce mechanical energy and to power machinery.

As more coal was produced, mines were dug deeper and deeper, and they were constantly filling with water. Mechanical pumps, usually powered by animals walking in circles at the surface, had to be installed. Such power was expensive and bothersome. In an attempt to overcome these disadvantages, Thomas Savery in 1698 and Thomas Newcomen in 1705 invented the first primitive steam engines. Both engines burned coal to produce steam, which was then used to operate a pump.

In 1763 a gifted young Scot named James Watt (1736–1819) was called on to repair a Newcomen engine. After a series of observations, Watt saw that the Newcomen engine could be improved by adding a separate condenser. This invention, patented in 1769, greatly increased the efficiency of the steam engine.

To invent something is one thing; to make it a practical success is quite another. Watt needed skilled workers, precision parts, and capital, and the relatively advanced nature of the British economy proved essential. A partnership in 1775 with Matthew Boulton, a wealthy English industrialist, provided Watt with adequate capital and exceptional skills in salesmanship that equaled those of the renowned pottery king, Josiah Wedgwood.

**steam engines** A breakthrough invention by Thomas Savery in 1698 and Thomas Newcomen in 1705 that burned coal to produce steam, which was then used to operate a pump; the early models were superseded by James Watt's more efficient steam engine, patented in 1769.

**James Nasmyth's Mighty Steam Hammer** Nasmyth's invention was the forerunner of the modern pile driver, and its successful introduction in 1832 epitomized the rapid development of steam power technology in Britain. In this painting by the inventor himself, workers manipulate a massive iron shaft being hammered into shape at Nasmyth's foundry near Manchester. (Science & Society Picture Library, London)

CHAPTER LOCATOR | How did the Industrial Revolution develop in Britain? | How did continental Europe industrialize after 1815? | What were the social consequences of industrialization?

**619**

(See "Individuals in Society: Josiah Wedgwood," page 622.) In the craft tradition of locksmiths, tinsmiths, and millwrights, Watt found mechanics who could install, regulate, and repair his sophisticated engines. From ingenious manufacturers such as the cannon maker John Wilkinson, Watt was gradually able to purchase precision parts. By the late 1780s, the firm of Boulton and Watt had made the steam engine a practical and commercial success in Britain.

The steam engine of Watt and his followers was the Industrial Revolution's most fundamental advance in technology. For the first time in history, humanity had, at least for a few generations, almost unlimited power at its disposal. Inventors and engineers could devise and implement all kinds of power equipment to aid people in their work, and abundance was at least a possibility for ordinary men and women.

The steam engine was quickly put to use in several industries in Britain, including mining and textiles. Steam power promoted important breakthroughs in other industries. The British iron industry was radically transformed. The use of steam-driven bellows in blast furnaces helped iron makers switch over from limited charcoal to unlimited coke (which is made from coal) in the smelting of pig iron after 1770. In the 1780s, Henry Cort developed the puddling furnace, which allowed pig iron to be refined in turn with coke. Cort also developed steam-powered rolling mills, which were capable of spewing out finished iron in every shape and form. The economic consequence of these technical innovations was a great boom in the British iron industry. In 1740 annual British iron production was only 17,000 tons. With the spread of coke smelting and the impact of Cort's inventions, production had reached 260,000 tons by 1806. In 1844 Britain produced 3 million tons of iron. Once scarce and expensive, iron became the cheap, basic, indispensable building block of the economy.

*Rocket* The name given to George Stephenson's effective locomotive that was first tested in 1830 on the Liverpool and Manchester Railway at 16 miles per hour.

## The Coming of the Railroads

The coal industry had long been using plank roads and rails to move coal wagons within mines and at the surface. Rails reduced friction and allowed a horse or a human being to pull a heavier load. Thus once a rail capable of supporting a heavy locomotive was developed in 1816, all sorts of experiments with steam engines on rails went forward. In 1825 after ten years of work, George Stephenson built an effective locomotive. In 1830 his *Rocket* sped down the track of the just-completed Liverpool and Manchester Railway at sixteen miles per hour. The line from Liverpool to Manchester was a financial as well as a technical success, and many private companies were quickly organized to build more rail lines. Within twenty years, they had completed the main trunk lines of Great Britain (Map 21.1). Other countries were quick to follow.

The significance of the railroad was tremendous. It dramatically reduced the cost and uncertainty of shipping freight overland. This advance had many economic consequences. Previously, markets had tended to be small and local; as the barrier of high transportation costs was lowered, markets became larger and even nationwide. Larger markets encouraged larger fac-

### Map 21.1 The Industrial Revolution in England, ca. 1850

Industry concentrated in the rapidly growing cities of the north and the center of England, where rich coal and iron deposits were close to one another.

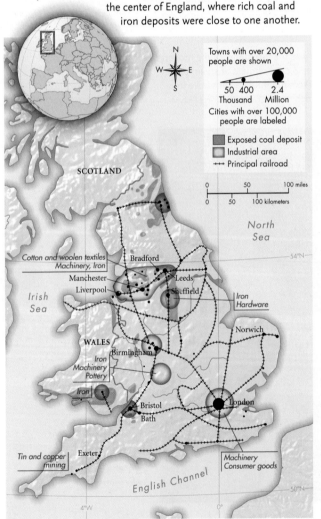

Towns with over 20,000 people are shown

50 400 2.4
Thousand Million
Cities with over 100,000 people are labeled

Exposed coal deposit
Industrial area
Principal railroad

620

Chapter 21
The Revolution in Energy and
Industry • ca. 1780–1850

**The New World of Speed** A colorful timetable poster lists the trains from London to Folkstone, the English Channel's gateway port to the European continent, and proudly proclaims a speedy journey. Tunneling through hills and spanning rivers with bridges, railroad construction presented innumerable challenges and required enormous amounts of capital and labor. (Private Collection/The Bridgeman Art Library)

tories with more sophisticated machinery in a growing number of industries. Such factories could make goods more cheaply and gradually subjected most cottage workers and many urban artisans to severe competitive pressures. In all countries, the construction of railroads created a strong demand for unskilled labor and contributed to the growth of a class of urban workers.

## Industry and Population

In 1851 London hosted an industrial fair called the Great Exhibition in the newly built **Crystal Palace**. For visitors, one fact stood out: Britain was the "workshop of the world." Britain alone produced two-thirds of the world's coal and more than one-half of its iron and cotton cloth. More generally, in 1860 Britain produced 20 percent of the entire world's output of industrial goods, whereas it had produced only about 2 percent of the world total in 1750.[2] Experiencing revolutionary industrial change, Britain became the first industrial nation (see Map 21.1).

As the British economy significantly increased its production of manufactured goods, the gross national product (GNP) rose roughly fourfold at constant prices between 1780 and 1851. At the same time, the population of Britain boomed, growing from about 9 million in 1780 to almost 21 million in 1851. Thus growing numbers consumed much of the increase in total production. Although the question is still debated, many economic historians now believe that rapid population growth in Great Britain was not harmful because it facilitated industrial expansion. More people meant a more mobile labor

**Crystal Palace** The location of the Great Exhibition in 1851 in London, an architectural masterpiece made entirely of glass and iron.

**Lid to a Souvenir Pot Showing the Crystal Palace** More than 6 million visitors from all over Europe visited the Crystal Palace Exhibition in 1851 where they bought millions of souvenirs picturing the glass-and-iron building. This depiction brightened the lid of a ceramic pot. (Fitzwilliam Museum, Cambridge University, UK/Bridgeman Giraudon/The Bridgeman Art Library)

CHAPTER LOCATOR | How did the Industrial Revolution develop in Britain? | How did continental Europe industrialize after 1815? | What were the social consequences of industrialization?

621

# INDIVIDUALS IN SOCIETY

## Josiah Wedgwood

**AS THE MAKING OF CLOTH AND IRON** was revolutionized by technical change and factory organization, so too were the production and consumption of pottery. Acquiring beautiful tableware became a craze for eighteenth-century consumers, and continental monarchs often sought prestige in building royal china works. But the grand prize went to Josiah Wedgwood, who wanted to "astonish the world."

The twelfth child of a poor potter, Josiah Wedgwood (1730–1795) grew up in the pottery district of Staffordshire in the English Midlands, where many tiny potteries made simple earthenware utensils for sale in local markets. Growing up as an apprentice in the family business inherited by his oldest brother, Wedgwood struck off on his own in 1752. Soon manager of a small pottery, Wedgwood learned that new products recharged lagging sales. Studying chemistry and determined to succeed, Wedgwood spent his evenings experimenting with different chemicals and firing conditions.

In 1759, after five years of tireless efforts, Wedgwood perfected a beautiful new green glaze. Now established as a master potter, he opened his own factory and began manufacturing teapots and tableware finished in his green and other unique glazes, or adorned with printed scenes far superior to those being produced by competitors. Wedgwood's products caused a sensation among consumers, and his business quickly earned substantial profits. Subsequent breakthroughs, including ornamental vases imitating classical Greek models and jasperware for jewelry, contributed greatly to Wedgwood's success.

Josiah Wedgwood perfected jasperware, a fine-grained pottery usually made in "Wedgwood blue" with white decoration. This elegant cylindrical vase (opposite), decorated in the form of a miniature Roman household altar, was destined for the luxury market. (portrait: Down House, Downe, Kent, © English Heritage Photo Library/The Bridgeman Art Library; vase: Image copyright © The Metropolitan Museum of Art/Art Resource, NY)

Competitors were quick to copy Wedgwood's new products and sell them at lower prices. Thus Wedgwood and his partner Thomas Bentley sought to cultivate an image of superior fashion, taste, and quality in order to develop and maintain a dominant market position. They did this by first capturing the business of the trend-setting elite. In one brilliant

force, with a wealth of young workers in need of employment and ready to go where the jobs were.

Contemporaries were much less optimistic. In his *Essay on the Principle of Population* (1798), Thomas Malthus (1766–1834) examined the dynamics of human populations. Since, in his opinion, population would always tend to grow faster than the food supply, Malthus concluded that the only hope of warding off such "positive checks" to population growth as war, famine, and disease was "prudential restraint." That is, young men and women had to limit the growth of population by marrying late in life. But Malthus was not optimistic about this possibility. The powerful attraction of the sexes would cause most people to marry early and have many children.

Economist David Ricardo (1772–1823) spelled out the pessimistic implications of Malthus's thought. Ricardo's depressing iron law of wages posited that because of the pressure of population growth, wages would always sink to subsistence level. That is, wages would be just high enough to keep workers from starving.

Malthus, Ricardo, and their followers were proved wrong—in the long run. However, until the 1820s, or even the 1840s, contemporary observers might reasonably have concluded that the economy and the total population were racing neck and neck, with

**iron law of wages** Theory proposed by English economist David Ricardo suggesting that the pressure of population growth prevents wages from rising above the subsistence level.

coup the partners first sold a very large cream-colored dinner set to Britain's queen, which they quickly christened "Queen's ware" and sold as a very expensive, must-have luxury to English aristocrats. Equally brilliant was Bentley's suave expertise in the elegant London showroom selling Wedgwood's imitation Greek vases, which became the rage after the rediscovery of Pompeii and Herculaneum in the mid-eighteenth century.

Above all, once Wedgwood had secured his position as the luxury market leader, he was able to successfully extend his famous brand to the growing middle class, capturing an enormous mass market for his "useful ware." Thus when sales of a luxury good grew "stale," Wedgwood made tasteful modifications and sold it to the middling classes for twice the price his competitors could charge. This unbeatable combination of mass appeal and high prices all across Europe brought Wedgwood great fame and enormous wealth.

A workaholic with an authoritarian streak, Wedgwood contributed substantially to the development of the factory system. In 1769, he opened a

model factory on a new canal he had promoted. With two hundred workers in several departments, Wedgwood exercised tremendous control over his workforce, imposing fines for many infractions, such as being late, drinking on the job, or wasting material. He wanted, he said, to create men who would be like "machines" that "cannot err." Yet Wedgwood also recognized the value in treating workers well. He championed a division of labor that made most workers specialists who received ongoing training. He also encouraged employment of family groups, who were housed in company row houses with long narrow backyards suitable for raising vegetables and chickens. Paying relatively high wages and providing pensions and some benefits, Wedgwood developed a high-quality labor force that learned to accept his rigorous discipline and carried out his ambitious plans.

**QUESTIONS FOR ANALYSIS**

1. How and why did Wedgwood succeed?
2. Was Wedgwood a good boss or a bad one? Why?
3. How did Wedgwood exemplify the new class of factory owners?

the outcome very much in doubt. There was another problem as well. Perhaps workers, farmers, and ordinary people did not get their rightful share of the new wealth. Perhaps only the rich got richer, while the poor got poorer or made no progress. We will turn to this great issue after looking at the process of industrialization in continental countries.

## ▼ How did continental Europe industrialize after 1815?

The new technologies developed in the British Industrial Revolution were adopted slowly in continental Europe. Yet by the end of the nineteenth century, several European countries as well as the United States had also industrialized their economies to a considerable but variable degree. This meant that the process of Western industrialization proceeded gradually, with uneven jerks and with national and regional variations.

CHAPTER LOCATOR | How did the Industrial Revolution develop in Britain? | **How did continental Europe industrialize after 1815?** | What were the social consequences of industrialization?

623

## National Variations

Comparative data on industrial production in different countries over time help give us an overview of what happened. One set of data, the work of a Swiss scholar, compares the level of industrialization on a per capita basis in several countries from 1750 to 1913. These data are far from perfect, but they reflect basic trends and are presented in Table 21.1 for closer study.

Table 21.1 presents a per capita comparison of levels of industrialization—a comparison of how much industrial product was produced, on average, for each person in a given country in a given year. Therefore, all the numbers in Table 21.1 are expressed in terms of a single index number of 100, which equals the per capita level of industrial goods in Great Britain (and Ireland) in 1900. Every number in the table is thus a percentage of the 1900 level in Britain and is directly comparable with other numbers. The countries are listed in roughly the order that they began to use large-scale, power-driven technology.

What does this overview of European industrialization tell us? First, one sees in the first column that in 1750 all countries were fairly close together. Second, the column headed 1800 shows that Britain had opened up a noticeable lead over all continental countries by 1800, and that gap progressively widened as the British Industrial Revolution accelerated to 1830 and reached full maturity by 1860.

Third, variations in the timing and in the extent of industrialization in the continental powers and the United States are also apparent. Belgium, achieving independence from the Netherlands in 1831 and rich in iron and coal, led in adopting Britain's new technology, and it experienced a truly revolutionary surge between 1830 and 1860. France developed factory production more gradually, and most historians now detect no burst in French mechanization and no acceleration in the growth of overall industrial output that may accurately be called revolutionary. They stress instead France's relatively good pattern of early industrial growth. In general, eastern and southern Europe began the process of modern industrialization later than northwestern and central Europe. Nevertheless, these regions made real progress in the late nineteenth century, as growth after 1880 in Austria-Hungary, Italy, and Russia suggests.

Finally, the late but substantial industrialization in eastern and southern Europe meant that all European states (as well as the United States, Canada, and Japan) managed to raise per capita industrial levels in the nineteenth century. These continent-wide increases

| ■ TABLE 21.1 Per Capita Levels of Industrialization, 1750–1913 | | | | | | | |
|---|---|---|---|---|---|---|---|
| | **1750** | **1800** | **1830** | **1860** | **1880** | **1900** | **1913** |
| **Great Britain** | 10 | 16 | 25 | 64 | 87 | 100 | 115 |
| **Belgium** | 9 | 10 | 14 | 28 | 43 | 56 | 88 |
| **United States** | 4 | 9 | 14 | 21 | 38 | 69 | 126 |
| **France** | 9 | 9 | 12 | 20 | 28 | 39 | 59 |
| **Germany** | 8 | 8 | 9 | 15 | 25 | 52 | 85 |
| **Austria-Hungary** | 7 | 7 | 8 | 11 | 15 | 23 | 32 |
| **Italy** | 8 | 8 | 8 | 10 | 12 | 17 | 26 |
| **Russia** | 6 | 6 | 7 | 8 | 10 | 15 | 20 |
| **China** | 8 | 6 | 6 | 4 | 4 | 3 | 3 |
| **India** | 7 | 6 | 6 | 3 | 2 | 1 | 2 |

Note: All entries are based on an index value of 100, equal to the per capita level of industrialization in Great Britain in 1900. Data for Great Britain includes Ireland, England, Wales, and Scotland.

**Source:** P. Bairoch, "International Industrialization Levels from 1750 to 1980," *Journal of European Economic History* 11 (Spring 1982): 294, U.S. Journals at Cambridge University Press.

stood in stark contrast to the large and tragic decreases that occurred at the same time in many non-Western countries, most notably in China and India. European countries industrialized to a greater or lesser extent even as most of the non-Western world deindustrialized. Thus differential rates of wealth- and power-creating industrial development, which heightened disparities within Europe, also greatly magnified existing inequalities between Europe and the rest of the world. We shall return to this momentous change in world economic relationships in Chapter 25.

## The Challenge of Industrialization

The different patterns of industrial development suggest that the process of industrialization was far from automatic. To be sure, throughout Europe the eighteenth century was an era of agricultural improvement, population increase, expanding foreign trade, and growing cottage industry. Thus when the pace of British industry began to accelerate in the 1780s, continental businesses began to adopt the new methods as they proved their profitability. British industry enjoyed clear superiority, but at first the continent was close behind.

By 1815, however, the situation was quite different. No wars in the early industrial period had been fought on British soil, so Britain did not experience nearly as much physical destruction or economic dislocation as the continent did. Rather, British industry maintained the momentum of the 1780s and continued to grow and improve between 1789 and 1815. On the continent, by contrast, the upheavals that began with the French Revolution disrupted trade, created runaway inflation, and fostered social anxiety. War severed normal communications between Britain and the continent, severely handicapping continental efforts to use new British machinery and technology. Thus France and the rest of Europe were further behind Britain in 1815 than in 1789.

This widening gap made it more difficult, if not impossible, for other countries to follow the British pattern in energy and industry after peace was restored in 1815. Above all, in the newly mechanized industries, British goods were being produced very economically, and these goods had come to dominate world markets completely. In addition, British technology had become so advanced and complicated that very few engineers or skilled technicians outside England understood it. Moreover, the technology of steam power had grown much more expensive. It involved large investments in the iron and coal industries and, after 1830, required the existence of railroads. Continental business people had great difficulty finding the large sums of money the new methods demanded, and there was a shortage of laborers accustomed to working in factories. All these disadvantages slowed the spread of modern industry (Map 21.2).

After 1815, however, continental countries had at least three important advantages. First, most continental countries had a rich tradition of putting-out enterprise, merchant capitalists, and skilled urban artisans (see Chapter 18). Such a tradition gave continental firms the ability to adapt and survive in the face of new market conditions. Second, continental capitalists did not need to develop their own advanced technology. Instead, they could simply "borrow" the new methods developed in Great Britain, as well as engineers and some of the financial resources these countries lacked. European countries such as France and Russia also had a third asset that many non-Western areas lacked in the nineteenth century. They had strong independent governments that did not fall under foreign political control. These governments would eventually use the power of the state to promote industry and catch up with Britain.

## Agents of Industrialization

The British realized the great value of their technical discoveries and tried to keep their secrets to themselves. Many talented, ambitious workers, however, slipped out of the country illegally and introduced the new methods abroad.

CHAPTER LOCATOR | How did the Industrial Revolution develop in Britain? | **How did continental Europe industrialize after 1815?** | What were the social consequences of industrialization?

625

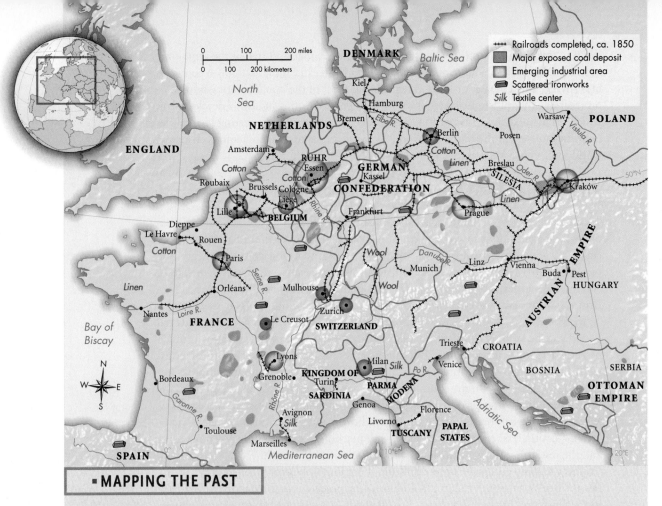

## ▪ MAPPING THE PAST

## Map 21.2 Continental Industrialization, ca. 1850

Although continental countries were beginning to make progress by 1850, they still lagged far behind Britain. For example, continental railroad building was still in an early stage, whereas the British rail system was essentially complete (see Map 21.1). Coal played a critical role in nineteenth-century industrialization both as a power source for steam engines and as a raw material for making iron and steel.

**ANALYZING THE MAP** Locate the major exposed (that is, known) coal deposits in 1850. Which countries and areas appear rich in coal resources, and which appear poor? Is there a difference between northern and southern Europe?

**CONNECTIONS** What is the relationship between known coal deposits and emerging industrial areas in continental Europe? In England (Map 21.1)?

To complete this activity online, go to the Online Study Guide at bedfordstmartins.com/mckaywestunderstanding.

One such man was William Cockerill, a Lancashire carpenter. He and his sons began building cotton-spinning equipment in French-occupied Belgium in 1799. In 1817 the most famous son, John Cockerill, built a large industrial enterprise in Liège in southern Belgium, which produced machinery, steam engines, and then railway locomotives. He also established modern ironworks and coal mines.

Cockerill's plants in the Liège area became centers for the gathering and transmitting of industrial information across Europe. Many skilled British workers came to work for Cockerill, and some went on to found their own companies throughout Europe. Newcomers brought the latest industrial plans and secrets from Britain.

Thus British technicians and skilled workers were a powerful force in the spread of early industrialization. A second aspect of industrialization were talented entrepreneurs such as Fritz Harkort, a pioneer in the German machinery industry. Harkort concluded that Germany had to match all these English achievements as quickly as possible. Setting up shop in the Ruhr Valley, Harkort felt an almost religious calling to build steam engines.

Lacking skilled laborers, Harkort turned to England for experienced, though expensive, mechanics. Getting materials was also difficult. He had to import the thick iron boilers that he needed from England at great cost. In spite of all these problems, Harkort succeeded in building and selling engines. His ambitious efforts over sixteen years also resulted in large financial losses for himself and his partners, and in 1832 he was forced out of his company by his financial backers, who cut back operations to reduce losses. His career illustrates both the great efforts of a few important business leaders to duplicate the British achievement and the difficulty of the task.

Entrepreneurs like Harkort were obviously exceptional. Most continental businesses adopted factory technology slowly, and handicraft methods lived on. Indeed, continental industrialization usually brought substantial but uneven expansion of the handicraft industry in both rural and urban areas for a time. Artisan production of luxury items grew in France as the rising income of the international middle class created increased foreign demand.

## Government Support and Corporate Banking

Another major force in continental industrialization was government, which often helped business people in continental countries to overcome some of their difficulties. Tariff protection was one such support, and it proved quite important. For example, after Napoleon's wars ended in 1815, France was suddenly flooded with cheaper and better British goods. The French government responded by laying high tariffs on many British imports in order to protect the French economy. After 1815 continental governments bore the cost of building roads and canals to improve transportation. They also bore to a significant extent the cost of building railroads. Belgium led the way in the 1830s and 1840s. Built rapidly as a unified network, Belgium's state-owned railroads stimulated the development of heavy industry and made the country an early industrial leader.

The Prussian government provided another kind of invaluable support. It guaranteed that the state treasury would pay the interest and principal on railroad bonds if the closely regulated private companies in Prussia were unable to do so. In France the state shouldered all the expense of acquiring and laying roadbed, including bridges and tunnels. In short, governments helped pay for railroads, the all-important leading sector in continental industrialization.

The career of German journalist and thinker Friedrich List (1789–1846) reflects government's greater role in industrialization on the continent than in England. List considered the growth of modern industry of the utmost importance because manufacturing was a primary means of increasing people's well-being and relieving their poverty. Moreover, List was a dedicated nationalist. He wrote that the "wider the gap between the backward and advanced nations becomes, the more dangerous it is to remain behind." To promote industry was to defend the nation.

The practical policies that List focused on were railroad building and the tariff. List supported the formation of a customs union, or *Zollverein* (TSOL-feh-rign), among the separate German states. Such a tariff union came into being in 1834, allowing goods to move between the German member states without tariffs, while erecting a single uniform tariff against other nations. List wanted a high protective tariff, which would encourage infant industries, allowing them to develop and eventually hold their own against their more advanced British counterparts. He denounced the British doctrine of free trade as part of Britain's attempt to dominate the entire world. By the 1840s List's economic nationalism, designed to protect and develop the national economy, had become increasingly popular in Germany and elsewhere.

**tariff protection** A government's way of supporting and aiding its own economy by laying high taxes on imported goods from other countries, as when the French responded to cheaper British goods flooding their country by imposing high tariffs on some imported products.

**economic nationalism** Policies aimed at protecting and developing a country's economy.

CHAPTER LOCATOR | How did the Industrial Revolution develop in Britain? | **How did continental Europe industrialize after 1815?** | What were the social consequences of industrialization?

627

**A German Ironworks, 1845** The Borsig ironworks in Berlin mastered the new British method of smelting iron ore with coke. Germany, and especially the state of Prussia, was well endowed with both iron and coal, and the rapid exploitation of these resources after 1840 transformed a poor agricultural country into an industrial powerhouse. (akg-images)

Finally, banks, like governments, also played a larger and more creative role on the continent than in Britain. Previously, almost all banks in Europe had been private. Because of the possibility of unlimited financial loss, the partners of private banks tended to be quite conservative and were content to deal with a few rich clients and a few big merchants. They generally avoided industrial investment as being too risky.

In the 1830s, two important Belgian banks pioneered in a new direction. They received permission from the growth-oriented government to establish themselves as corporations enjoying limited liability. That is, stockholders could now lose only their original investments in the bank's common stock, and they could not be forced by the courts to pay for any additional losses out of other property they owned if the bank went bankrupt. Limited liability helped these Belgian banks attract investors. They mobilized impressive resources for investment in big companies, became industrial banks, and successfully promoted industrial development.

Similar corporate banks became important in France and Germany in the 1850s and 1860s. Usually working in collaboration with governments, corporate banks established and developed many railroads and many companies working in heavy industry, which were also increasingly organized as limited liability corporations.

The combined efforts of skilled workers, entrepreneurs, governments, and industrial banks meshed successfully between 1850 and the financial crash of 1873. In Belgium, Germany, and France, key indicators of modern industrial development—such as railway mileage, iron and coal production, and steam-engine capacity—increased at average annual rates of 5 to 10 percent. As a result, rail networks were completed in western and much of central Europe, and the leading continental countries mastered the industrial technologies that had first been developed in Great Britain. In the early 1870s, Britain was still Europe's most industrial nation, but a select handful of countries were closing the gap that had been opened up by the Industrial Revolution.

# ▼ What were the social consequences of industrialization?

Industrial development brought new social relations and intensified long-standing problems between capital and labor in both urban workshops and cottage industry (see Chapter 18). A new group of factory owners and industrial capitalists arose. These men and women and their families strengthened the wealth and size of the middle class, which had previously been made up mainly of merchants and professional people. Modern industry also created a much larger group, the factory workers.

The growth of new occupational groups in industry stimulated new thinking about social relations. Often combined with reflections on the French Revolution, this thinking led to the development of a new overarching interpretation—a new paradigm—regarding social relationships. Briefly, this paradigm argued, with considerable success, that individuals were members of economically determined classes that had conflicting interests. Accordingly, the comfortable, well-educated "public" of the eighteenth century came increasingly to see itself as the middle class (or the middle classes), and the "people" gradually transformed themselves into the modern working class (or working classes). And if the new class interpretation was more of a deceptive simplification than a fundamental truth for some critics, it appealed to many because it seemed to explain what was happening. Therefore, conflicting classes existed, in part, because many individuals came to believe they existed and developed an appropriate sense of class feeling—what Marxists call **class-consciousness**.

> **class-consciousness** An individual's sense of class differentiation.

## The New Class of Factory Owners

Early industrialists operated in a highly competitive economic system. There were countless production problems, and success and large profits were by no means certain. Manufacturers therefore waged a constant battle to cut their production costs and stay afloat. Much of the profit had to go back into the business for new and better machinery.

Most early industrialists drew upon their families and friends for labor and capital, but they came from a variety of backgrounds. Many, such as Harkort, were from well-established merchant families with a rich network of contacts and support. Others, such as Watt, Wedgwood, and Cockerill, were of modest means, especially in the early days. Artisans and skilled workers of exceptional ability had unparalleled opportunities. Members of ethnic and religious groups who had been discriminated against in the traditional occupations controlled by the landed aristocracy jumped at the new chances and often helped each other. Scots, Quakers, and other Protestant dissenters were tremendously important in Britain; Protestants and Jews dominated banking in Catholic France.

As factories and firms grew larger, opportunities declined, at least in well-developed industries. It became considerably harder for a gifted but poor young mechanic to start a small enterprise and end up as a wealthy manufacturer. In Britain by 1830 and in France and Germany by 1860, leading industrialists were more likely to have inherited their well-established enterprises, and they were financially much more secure than their struggling parents had been. They also had a greater sense of class-consciousness; they were fully aware that ongoing industrial development had widened the gap between themselves and their workers.

The wives and daughters of successful businessmen also found fewer opportunities for active participation in Europe's increasingly complex business world. Rather than contributing as vital partners in a family-owned enterprise, as so many middle-class women had done, these women were increasingly valued for their ladylike gentility. By 1850 some influential women writers and most businessmen assumed that middle-class wives and

CHAPTER LOCATOR | How did the Industrial Revolution develop in Britain? | How did continental Europe industrialize after 1815? | **What were the social consequences of industrialization?**

**629**

### Ford Maddox Brown, *Work*

This midcentury painting provides a rich and realistic visual representation of the new concepts of social class that became common by 1850.

(Birmingham Museums and Art Gallery/The Bridgeman Art Library)

**ANALYZING THE IMAGE**  Describe the different types of work shown. What different social classes are depicted, and what kinds of work (or leisure) are the members of the different social classes engaged in?

**CONNECTIONS**  What does this painting and Ford's title for it (*Work*) suggest about the artist's opinion of the work of common laborers?

To complete this activity online, go to the Online Study Guide at bedfordstmartins.com/ mckaywestunderstanding.

daughters should steer clear of work in offices and factories. Rather, a middle-class lady should concentrate on her proper role as wife and mother, preferably in an elegant residential area far removed from ruthless commerce and the volatile working class.

## The New Factory Workers

The social consequences of the Industrial Revolution have long been hotly debated. The condition of British workers during the transformation has always generated the most controversy among historians because Britain was the first country to industrialize and because the social consequences seemed harshest there.

From the beginning, the Industrial Revolution in Britain had its critics. Among the first were the romantic poets. William Blake (1757–1827) called the early factories "satanic mills" and protested against the hard life of the London poor. William Wordsworth (1770–1850) lamented the destruction of the rural way of life and the pollution of the land and water. Some handicraft workers smashed the new machines, which they believed were putting them out of work—notably the Luddites, who attacked whole factories in northern England in 1812 and after. Doctors and reformers wrote of problems in the factories and new towns, while Malthus and Ricardo concluded that workers would earn only enough to stay alive.

This pessimistic view was accepted and reinforced by Friedrich Engels (1820–1895), the future revolutionary and colleague of Karl Marx. After studying conditions in northern England, this young middle-class German published in 1844 *The Condition of the Working Class in England*, a blistering indictment of the middle classes. "At the bar of world opinion," he wrote, "I charge the English middle classes with mass murder, wholesale robbery, and all the other crimes in the calendar." The new poverty of industrial workers was worse than the old poverty of cottage workers and agricultural laborers, according to Engels. The culprit was industrial capitalism, with its relentless competition and constant technical change.

Meanwhile, other observers believed that conditions were improving for the working people. Andrew Ure (yoo-RAY) wrote in 1835 in his study of the cotton industry that conditions in most factories were not harsh and were even quite good. Edwin Chadwick, a government official well acquainted with the problems of the working population, concluded that the "whole mass of the laboring community" was increasingly able "to buy more of the necessities and minor luxuries of life."[3] Nevertheless, those who thought conditions were getting worse for working people were probably in the majority.

In an attempt to go beyond the contradictory judgments of contemporaries, some historians have looked at different kinds of sources. Statistical evidence is one such source. Scholarly statistical studies have weakened the idea that the condition of the working class got much worse with industrialization. But the most recent scholarship also confirms the view that the early years of the Industrial Revolution were hard ones for British workers. There was little or no increase in the purchasing power of the average British worker from about 1780 to about 1820. Only after 1820, and especially after 1840, did real wages rise substantially, so that the average worker earned and consumed roughly 50 percent more in real terms in 1850 than in 1770.[4] In short, there was considerable economic improvement for workers throughout Great Britain by 1850, but that improvement was hard won and slow in coming.

This important conclusion must be qualified, however. First, the hours in the average workweek increased. Thus, to a large extent, workers earned more simply because they worked more. Indeed, in England nonagricultural workers labored about 250 days per year in 1760 as compared to 300 days per year in 1830, while the normal workday remained an exhausting eleven hours throughout the entire period. In 1760 nonagricultural workers still observed many religious and public holidays by not working, and many workers took Monday off. These days of leisure and relaxation declined rapidly after 1760, and by 1830 nonagricultural workers had joined landless agricultural laborers in toiling six rather than five days a week.[5]

Second, the wartime decline in the average worker's real wages and standard of living from 1792 to 1815 had a powerful negative impact on workers. These difficult war years, with more unemployment and sharply higher prices for bread, were formative years for the new factory labor force, and they colored the early experience of modern industrial life in somber tones.

Another way to consider the workers' standard of living is to look at the goods that they purchased. Again the evidence is somewhat contradictory. Speaking generally, workers ate somewhat more food of higher nutritional quality as the Industrial Revolution progressed. Diets became more varied; people ate more potatoes, dairy products, fruits, and vegetables. Clothing improved, but housing for working people probably deteriorated somewhat. In short, per capita use of specific goods supports the position that the standard of living of the working classes rose, at least moderately, after the long wars with France.

**Luddites** Group of handicraft workers who attacked whole factories in northern England in 1812 and after, smashing the new machines that they believed were putting them out of work.

CHAPTER LOCATOR | How did the Industrial Revolution develop in Britain? | How did continental Europe industrialize after 1815? | **What were the social consequences of industrialization?**

**631**

## Work in Early Factories

What about working conditions? Did workers eventually earn more only at the cost of working longer and harder? Were workers exploited harshly by the new factory owners?

The first factories were cotton mills, which began functioning in the 1770s along fast-running rivers and streams and were often located in sparsely populated areas. Cottage workers in the vicinity, accustomed to the putting-out system, were reluctant to work in the new factories even when they received relatively good wages because factory work was unappealing. In the factory, workers had to keep up with the machine and follow its relentless tempo. Moreover, they had to show up every day, on time, and work long, monotonous hours under the constant supervision of demanding overseers, and they were punished systematically if they broke the work rules.

Cottage workers were not used to that kind of life and discipline. All members of the family worked hard and long, but in spurts, setting their own pace. They could interrupt their work when they wanted to. Women and children could break up their long hours of spinning with other tasks. On Saturday afternoon the head of the family delivered the week's work to the merchant manufacturer and got paid. Saturday night was a time of relaxation and drinking, especially for the men.

Also, early factories resembled English poorhouses, where totally destitute people went to live at public expense. Some poorhouses were industrial prisons, where the inmates had to work in order to receive their food and lodging. The similarity between large brick factories and large stone poorhouses increased the cottage workers' fear of factories and their hatred of factory discipline. It was cottage workers' reluctance to work in factories that prompted the early cotton mill owners to turn to abandoned and pauper children

**Workers at a Large Cotton Mill** This 1833 engraving shows adult women operating power looms under the supervision of a male foreman, and it accurately reflects both the decline of family employment and the emergence of a gender-based division of labor in many English factories. The jungle of belts and shafts connecting the noisy looms to the giant steam engine on the ground floor created a constant din. (Time Life Pictures/Getty Images)

for their labor. As we have seen, these owners contracted with local officials to employ large numbers of these children, who had no say in the matter. In the eighteenth century, semi-forced child labor seemed necessary and was socially accepted. From our modern point of view, it was cruel exploitation and a blot on the record of the new industrial system.

## Working Families and Children

By the 1790s the early pattern was rapidly changing. The use of pauper apprentices was in decline, and in 1802 it was forbidden by Parliament. Many more textile factories were being built, mainly in urban areas, where they could use steam power rather than waterpower and attract a workforce more easily than in the countryside. As a result, people came from near and far to work in the cities, both as factory workers and as laborers, builders, and domestic servants. Yet as they took these new jobs, working people did not simply give in and accept the highly disciplined system of labor. Rather, they helped modify the system by carrying over old, familiar working traditions.

For one thing, workers often came to the mills and the mines as family units. This was how they had worked on farms and in the putting-out system. The mill or mine owner bargained with the head of the family and paid him or her for the work of the whole family. The preservation of the family as an economic unit in the factories from the 1790s on made the new surroundings more tolerable, both in Great Britain and in other countries, during the early stages of industrialization. Parents disciplined their children, making firm measures socially acceptable, and directed their upbringing. The presence of the whole family meant that children and adults worked the same long hours (twelve-hour shifts were normal in cotton mills in 1800). Adult workers were not particularly interested in limiting the minimum working age or hours of their children as long as family members worked side by side. Only when technical changes threatened to place control and discipline in the hands of impersonal managers and overseers did adult workers protest against inhuman conditions in the name of their children.

Some enlightened employers and social reformers in Parliament definitely felt otherwise. They argued that more humane standards were necessary, and they used widely circulated parliamentary reports to influence public opinion. For example, Robert Owen (1771–1858), a successful manufacturer in Scotland, testified in 1816 before an investigating committee on the basis of his experience. He argued that employing children under ten years of age as factory workers was "injurious to the children, and not beneficial to the proprietors."[6] Workers also provided graphic testimony at such hearings as the reformers pressed Parliament to pass corrective laws. They scored some important successes.

Their most significant early accomplishment was the Factory Act of 1833. It limited the factory workday for children between nine and thirteen to eight hours and that of adolescents between fourteen and eighteen to twelve hours. Children under nine were to be enrolled in the elementary schools that factory owners were required to establish. The employment of children declined rapidly. Thus the Factory Act broke the pattern of whole families working together in the factory because efficiency required standardized shifts for all workers.

Ties of blood and kinship were important in other ways in Great Britain in the formative years between about 1790 and 1840. Many manufacturers and builders hired workers through subcontractors. They paid the subcontractors on the basis of what the subcontractors and their crews produced. Subcontractors in turn hired and fired their own workers, many of whom were friends and relations. The subcontractor might be as harsh as the greediest capitalist, but the relationship between subcontractor and work crew was close and personal. This kind of personal relationship had traditionally existed in cottage industry and in urban crafts, and it was more acceptable to many workers than impersonal factory discipline.

**Factory Act of 1833** English law that led to a sharp decline in the employment of children by limiting the hours that children over age nine could work and requiring younger children to attend factory-run elementary schools.

CHAPTER LOCATOR | How did the Industrial Revolution develop in Britain? | How did continental Europe industrialize after 1815? | What were the social consequences of industrialization?

633

Ties of kinship were particularly important for newcomers, who often traveled great distances to find work. Many urban workers in Great Britain were from Ireland. Forced out of rural Ireland by population growth and deteriorating economic conditions from 1817 on, Irish in search of jobs took what they could get. As early as 1824, most of the workers in the Glasgow cotton mills were Irish; in 1851 one-sixth of the population of Liverpool was Irish. Like many other immigrant groups held together by ethnic and religious ties, the Irish worked together, formed their own neighborhoods, and not only survived but also thrived.

## The Sexual Division of Labor

The era of the Industrial Revolution witnessed major changes in the sexual division of labor. In preindustrial Europe most people generally worked in family units. By tradition, certain jobs were defined by gender, but many tasks might go to either sex. Family employment carried over into early factories and subcontracting, but by the 1830s it was collapsing as child labor was restricted and new attitudes emerged. A different sexual division of labor gradually arose to take its place. By 1850 the man was emerging as the family's primary wage earner, while the married woman found only limited job opportunities. Generally denied good jobs at good wages in the growing urban economy, women were expected to concentrate on housework, raising the children, and some craftwork at home.

**separate spheres** A gender division of labor with the wife at home as mother and homemaker and the husband as wage earner.

This new pattern of separate spheres, which will be considered further in Chapter 23, had several aspects. First, all studies agree that married women from the working classes were much less likely to work full-time for wages outside the house after the first child arrived, although they often earned small amounts doing putting-out handicrafts at home and taking in boarders. Second, when married women did work for wages outside the house, they usually came from the poorest families, where the husbands were poorly paid, sick, unemployed, or missing. Third, these poor married or widowed women were joined by legions of young unmarried women, who worked full-time but only in certain jobs, of which textile factory work, laundering, and domestic service were particularly important. Fourth, all women were generally confined to low-paying, dead-end jobs. Evolving gradually, but largely in place by 1850, the new sexual division of labor in Britain constituted a major development in the history of women and of the family.

If the reorganization of paid work along gender lines is widely recognized, there is no agreement on its causes. One school of scholars sees little connection with industrialization and finds the answer in the deeply ingrained sexist attitudes that predated the economic transformation. These scholars stress the role of male-dominated craft unions in denying working women access to good jobs and relegating them to unpaid housework. Other scholars, stressing that the gender roles of women and men can vary enormously with time and culture, look more to a combination of economic and biological factors in order to explain the emergence of a sex-segregated division of labor.

Three ideas stand out in this more recent interpretation. First, the new and unfamiliar discipline of the clock and the machine was especially hard on married women of the laboring classes. Above all, relentless factory discipline conflicted with child care in a way that labor on the farm or in the cottage had not.

Second, running a household in conditions of primitive urban poverty was an extremely demanding job in its own right. There were no supermarkets or public transportation. Shopping and feeding the family constituted a never-ending challenge. Yet another brutal job outside the house—a "second shift"—had limited appeal for the average married woman from the working class. Thus many women might well have accepted the emerging division of labor as the best available strategy for family survival in the industrializing society.[7]

Third, why were the young, generally unmarried women who did work for wages outside the home segregated and confined to certain "women's jobs"? No doubt the desire of males to monopolize the best opportunities and hold women down provides part of the answer. Yet as some feminist scholars have argued, sex-segregated employment was also a collective response to the new industrial system. Previously, at least in theory, young people worked under a watchful parental eye. The growth of factories and mines brought unheard-of opportunities for girls and boys to mix on the job, free of familial supervision. Such opportunities led to more unplanned pregnancies and fueled the illegitimacy explosion that had begun in the late eighteenth century and that gathered force until at least 1850 (see Chapter 19). Thus segregation of jobs by gender was partly an effort by older people to help control the sexuality of working-class youths.

Investigations into the British coal industry before 1842 provide a graphic example of this concern. (See "Listening to the Past: The Testimony of Young Mine Workers," page 636.) The middle-class men leading the inquiry, who expected their daughters and wives to pursue ladylike activities, often failed to appreciate the physical effort of the girls and women who dragged with belt and chain the heavy carts of coal along narrow underground passages. But they professed horror at the sight of girls and women working without shirts, which was a common practice because of the heat, and they quickly assumed the prevalence of licentious sex with the male miners, who also wore very little clothing. In fact, most girls and married women worked for related males in a family unit that provided considerable protection and restraint. Yet many witnesses from the working class also believed that "blackguardism and debauchery" were common and that "they are best out of the pits, the lasses." The Mines Act of 1842 prohibited underground work for all women and girls as well as for boys under ten.

Some women who had to support themselves protested against being excluded from coal mining, which paid higher wages than most other jobs open to working-class women. But provided they were part of families that could manage economically, the girls and the women who had worked underground were generally pleased with the law. In explaining her satisfaction in 1844, one mother of four provided real insight into why many married working women accepted the emerging sexual division of labor:

> *While working in the pit I was worth to my [miner] husband seven shillings a week, out of which we had to pay 2½ shillings to a woman for looking after the younger children. I used to take them to her house at 4 o'clock in the morning, out of their own beds, to put them into hers. Then there was one shilling a week for washing; besides, there was mending to pay for, and other things. The house was not guided. The other children broke things; they did not go to school when they were sent; they would be playing about, and get ill-used by other children, and their clothes torn. Then when I came home in the evening, everything was to do after the day's labor, and I was so tired I had no heart for it; no fire lit, nothing cooked, no water fetched, the house dirty, and nothing comfortable for my husband. It is all far better now, and I wouldn't go down again.*[8]

## The Early Labor Movement in Britain

Many kinds of employment changed slowly during and after the Industrial Revolution in Great Britain. In 1850 more British people still worked on farms than in any other occupation. The second-largest occupation was domestic service, with more than one million household servants, 90 percent of whom were women. Thus many old, familiar jobs outside industry lived on and provided alternatives for individual workers. This helped ease the transition to industrial civilization.

Within industry itself, the pattern of artisans working with hand tools in small shops remained unchanged in many trades, even as others were revolutionized by technological

**Mines Act of 1842** English law prohibiting underground work for all women and girls as well as for boys under ten.

CHAPTER LOCATOR | How did the Industrial Revolution develop in Britain? | How did continental Europe industrialize after 1815? | What were the social consequences of industrialization?

635

## The Testimony of Young Mine Workers

*The use of child labor in British industrialization quickly attracted the attention of humanitarians and social reformers. This interest led to investigations by parliamentary commissions, which resulted in laws limiting the hours and the ages of children working in large factories. Designed to build a case for remedial legislation, parliamentary inquiries gave large numbers of workers a rare chance to speak directly to contemporaries and to historians.*

*The moving passages that follow are taken from testimony gathered in 1841 and 1842 by the Ashley Mines Commission. Interviewing employers and many male and female workers, the commissioners focused on the physical condition of the youth and on the sexual behavior of workers far underground. The subsequent Mines Act of 1842 sought to reduce immoral behavior and sexual bullying by prohibiting underground work for all women and girls (and for boys younger than ten).*

### Mr. Payne, coal master

❝ That children are employed generally at nine years old in the coal pits and sometimes at eight. In fact, the smaller the vein of coal is in height, the younger and smaller are the children required; the work occupies from six to seven hours per day in the pits; they are not ill-used or worked beyond their strength; a good deal of depravity exists but they are certainly not worse in morals than in other branches of the Sheffield trade, but upon the whole superior; the morals of this district are materially improving; Mr. Bruce, the clergyman, has been zealous and active in endeavoring to ameliorate their moral and religious education. . . . ❞

### Ann Eggley, hurrier, 18 years old

❝ I'm sure I don't know how to spell my name. We go at four in the morning, and sometimes at half-past four. We begin to work as soon as we get down. We get out after four, sometimes at five, in the evening. We work the whole time except an hour for dinner, and sometimes we haven't time to eat. I hurry [move coal wagons underground] by myself, and have done so for long. I know the corves [small coal wagons] are very heavy, they are the biggest corves anywhere about. The work is far too hard for me; the sweat runs off me all over sometimes. I am very tired at night. Sometimes when we get home at night we have not power to wash us, and then we go to bed. Sometimes we fall asleep in the chair. Father said last night it was both a shame and a disgrace for girls to work as we do, but there was naught else for us to do. I began to hurry when I was seven and I have been hurrying ever since. I have been 11 years in the pits. The girls are always tired. I was poorly twice this winter; it was with headache. I hurry for Robert Wiggins; he is not akin to me. . . . We don't always get enough to eat and drink, but we get a good supper. I have known my father go at two in the morning to work . . . and he didn't come out till four. I am quite sure that we work constantly 12 hours except on Saturdays. We wear trousers and our shifts in the pit and great big shoes clinkered and nailed. The girls never work naked to the waist in our pit. The men don't insult us in the pit. The conduct of the girls in the pit is good enough sometimes and sometimes bad enough. I never went to a day-school. I went a little to a Sunday-school, but I soon gave it over. I thought it too bad to be confined both Sundays and week-days. I walk about and get the fresh air on Sundays. I have not learnt to read. I don't know my letters. I never learnt naught. I never go to church or chapel; there is no church or chapel at Gawber, there is none nearer than a mile. . . . I have never heard that a good man came into the world who was God's son to save sinners. I never heard of Christ at all. Nobody has ever told me about him, nor have my father and mother ever taught me to pray. I know no prayer; I never pray. ❞

### Patience Kershaw, aged 17

❝ My father has been dead about a year; my mother is living and has ten children, five lads and five lasses; the oldest is about thirty, the youngest is four; three lasses go to mill; all the lads are colliers, two getters and three hurriers; one lives at home and does nothing; mother does nought but look after home.

change. For example, the British iron industry was completely dominated by large-scale capitalist firms by 1850. Many large ironworks had more than one thousand people on their payrolls. Yet the firms that fashioned iron into small metal goods, such as tools, tableware, and toys, employed on average fewer than ten wage workers who used handicraft skills. Only gradually after 1850 did some owners find ways to reorganize some handicraft industries with new machines and new patterns of work. The survival of small workshops gave many workers an alternative to factory employment.

Working-class solidarity and class-consciousness developed in small workshops as well as in large factories. In the northern factory districts, anticapitalist sentiments were fre-

This illustration of a girl dragging a coal wagon was one of several that shocked public opinion and contributed to the Mines Act of 1842. (© British Library Board)

All my sisters have been hurriers, but three went to the mill. Alice went because her legs swelled from hurrying in cold water when she was hot. I never went to day-school; I go to Sunday-school, but I cannot read or write; I go to pit at five o'clock in the morning and come out at five in the evening; I get my breakfast of porridge and milk first; I take my dinner with me, a cake, and eat it as I go; I do not stop or rest any time for the purpose; I get nothing else until I get home, and then have potatoes and meat, not every day meat. I hurry in the clothes I have now got on, trousers and ragged jacket; the bald place upon my head is made by thrusting the corves; my legs have never swelled, but sisters' did when they went to mill; I hurry the corves a mile and more under ground and back; they weigh 300 cwt.;* I hurry 11 a day; I wear a belt and chain at the workings to get the corves out; the putters [miners] that I work for are *naked* except their caps; they pull off all their clothes; I see them at work when I go up; sometimes they beat me, if I am not quick enough, with their hands; they strike me upon my back; the boys take liberties with me, sometimes, they pull me about; I am the only girl in the pit; there are about 20 boys and 15 men; all the men are naked; I would rather work in mill than in coal-pit. "

*An old English unit of weight equaling 112 pounds.

## Isabel Wilson, 38 years old, coal putter

" When women have children thick [fast] they are compelled to take them down early. I have been married 19 years and have had 10 bairns [children]; seven are in life. When on Sir John's work was a carrier of coals, which caused me to miscarry five times from the strains, and was gai [very] ill after each. Putting is no so oppressive; last child was born on Saturday morning, and I was at work on the Friday night.

Once met with an accident; a coal brake my cheek-bone, which kept me idle some weeks. I have wrought below 30 years, and so has the guid man; he is getting touched in the breath now.

None of the children read, as the work is no regular. I did read once, but no able to attend to it now; when I go below lassie 10 years of age keeps house and makes the broth or stir-about. "

**Source:** *Voices of the Industrial Revolution: Selected Readings from the Liberal Economists and Their Critics*, pp. 87–90, edited by J. Bowditch and C. Ramsland. Copyright © 1961, 1989 by the University of Michigan. Reprinted by permission.

### QUESTIONS FOR ANALYSIS

1. How does Payne's testimony compare with that of Ann Eggley and Patience Kershaw?
2. Describe the work of Eggley, Kershaw, and Wilson. What strikes you most about the testimonies of these workers?
3. The witnesses were responding to questions from middle-class commissioners. What did the commissioners seem interested in? Why?

quent by the 1820s. Commenting in 1825 on a strike in the woolen center of Bradford and the support it had gathered from other regions, one paper claimed with pride that "it is all the workers of England against a few masters of Bradford."[9] Modern technology and factory organization had created a few versus the many.

The transformation of some traditional trades by organizational changes, rather than technological innovations, could by themselves also create ill will and class feeling. The classical liberal concept of economic freedom and laissez faire emerged in the late eighteenth century, and it continued to gather strength in the early nineteenth century (see Chapter 22). In 1799 Parliament passed the **Combination Acts**, which outlawed unions

**Combination Acts** English laws passed in 1799 that outlawed unions and strikes, favoring capitalist business people over skilled artisans. Bitterly resented and widely disregarded by many craft guilds, the acts were repealed by Parliament in 1824.

CHAPTER LOCATOR | How did the Industrial Revolution develop in Britain? | How did continental Europe industrialize after 1815? | **What were the social consequences of industrialization?**

637

**Union Membership Certificate** This handsome membership certificate belonged to Arthur Watton, a properly trained and certified papermaker of Kings Norton in Birmingham, England. Members of such unions proudly framed their certificates and displayed them in their homes, showing that they were skilled workers. (Courtesy, Sylvia Waddell)

and strikes. In 1813 and 1814, Parliament repealed the old and often disregarded law of 1563 regulating the wages of artisans and the conditions of apprenticeship. As a result of these and other measures, certain skilled artisan workers, such as boot makers and high-quality tailors, found aggressive capitalists ignoring traditional work rules and trying to flood their trades with unorganized women workers and children to beat down wages.

The capitalist attack on artisan guilds and work rules was bitterly resented by many craft workers, who subsequently played an important part in Great Britain and in other countries in gradually building a modern labor movement. The Combination Acts were widely disregarded by workers. Printers, papermakers, carpenters, tailors, and other such craftsmen continued to take collective action, and societies of skilled factory workers also organized unions. Unions sought to control the number of skilled workers, limit apprenticeship to members' own children, and bargain with owners over wages.

They were not afraid to strike; there was, for example, a general strike of adult cotton spinners in Manchester in 1810. In the face of widespread union activity, Parliament repealed the Combination Acts in 1824, and unions were tolerated, though not fully accepted, after 1825. The next stage in the development of the British trade-union movement was the attempt to create a single large national union. This effort was led not so much by working people as by social reformers such as Robert Owen. Owen, a self-made cotton manufacturer (see page 633), had pioneered in industrial relations by combining firm discipline with concern for the health, safety, and hours of his workers. After 1815 he experimented with cooperative and socialist communities, including one at New Harmony, Indiana. Then in 1834 Owen organized one of the largest and most visionary of the early national unions, the Grand National Consolidated Trades Union.

When Owen's and other grandiose schemes collapsed, the British labor movement moved once again after 1851 in the direction of craft unions. The most famous of these was the Amalgamated Society of Engineers, which represented skilled machinists. These unions won real benefits for members by fairly conservative means and thus became an accepted part of the industrial scene.

British workers also engaged in direct political activity in defense of their own interests. After the collapse of Owen's national trade union, many working people went into the Chartist movement, which sought political democracy. The key Chartist demand—

that all men be given the right to vote—became the great hope of millions of aroused people. Workers were also active in campaigns to limit the workday in factories to ten hours and to permit duty-free importation of wheat into Great Britain to secure cheap bread. Thus working people developed a sense of their own identity and played an active role in shaping the new industrial system. They were neither helpless victims nor passive beneficiaries.

# ← LOOKING BACK LOOKING AHEAD →

ONE POPULAR IDEA in the 1830s, first developed by a French economist, was that Britain had experienced an "industrial revolution" at the same time that France had experienced the French Revolution. One revolution was economic, the other was political; one was ongoing and successful, while the other had failed and come to a definite end in 1815, when Europe's conservative monarchs defeated Napoleon and restored the French kings of the Old Regime.

In fact, in 1815 the French Revolution, like the Industrial Revolution, was an unfinished revolution. Just as Britain was in the midst of its economic transformation and the states of northwestern Europe would begin rapid industrialization only in the 1850s, so too after 1815 were the political conflicts and ideologies of revolutionary France still very much alive. The French Revolution had opened the era of modern political life in Europe. It had brought into existence many of the political forces and ideologies that would interact with industrialization to refashion Europe and create a new urban society. Moreover, in 1815 the unfinished French Revolution carried the very real possibility of renewed political upheaval. This possibility would become dramatic reality in 1848, when political revolutions swept across Europe like a whirlwind. ■

- **For a list of suggested readings for this chapter, visit** *bedfordstmartins.com/mckaywestunderstanding*.

- **For primary sources from this period, see** *Sources of Western Society*, Second Edition.

- **For Web sites, images, and documents related to topics in this chapter, see Make History at** *bedfordstmartins.com/mckaywestunderstanding*.

CHAPTER LOCATOR | How did the Industrial Revolution develop in Britain? | How did continental Europe industrialize after 1815? | What were the social consequences of industrialization?

639

# Chapter 21 Study Guide

Online Study Guide
bedfordstmartins.com/mckaywestunderstanding

## Step 1

**GETTING STARTED** Below are basic terms about this period in the history of Western civilization. Can you identify each term below and explain why it matters? To do this exercise online, go to bedfordstmartins.com/mckaywestunderstanding.

| TERMS | WHO (OR WHAT) AND WHEN | WHY IT MATTERS |
|---|---|---|
| Industrial Revolution, p. 616 | | |
| spinning jenny, p. 617 | | |
| water frame, p. 617 | | |
| steam engines, p. 619 | | |
| *Rocket*, p. 620 | | |
| Crystal Palace, p. 621 | | |
| iron law of wages, p. 622 | | |
| tariff protection, p. 627 | | |
| economic nationalism, p. 627 | | |
| class-consciousness, p. 629 | | |
| Luddites, p. 631 | | |
| Factory Act of 1833, p. 633 | | |
| separate spheres, p. 634 | | |
| Mines Act of 1842, p. 635 | | |
| Combination Acts, p. 637 | | |

## Step 2

**MOVING BEYOND THE BASICS** The exercise below requires a more advanced understanding of the chapter material. Examine the changes in work and home life brought on by the process of industrialization by filling out the chart below with descriptions of key aspects of work and home life for cottage and factory workers. When you are finished, consider the following questions: How did the relationship between home and work life change as industrialization progressed? How did changes in work patterns reshape gender relations? How did industrialization change the way that workers thought about themselves and their communities? To do this exercise online, go to bedfordstmartins.com/mckaywestunderstanding.

| | COTTAGE INDUSTRY | FACTORY WORK |
|---|---|---|
| Nature of Work | | |
| Work Discipline and Pace | | |
| Work and Gender | | |
| Work and Children | | |
| Home Life | | |
| Identity/Class Consciousness | | |

**PUTTING IT ALL TOGETHER** Now that you've reviewed key elements of the chapter, take a step back and try to see the big picture. Remember to use specific examples from the chapter in your answers. To do this exercise online, go to bedfordstmartins.com/mckaywestunderstanding.

### INDUSTRIALIZATION IN CONTINENTAL EUROPE

- Compare and contrast conditions in continental Europe before and after 1815. What made conditions after 1815 more favorable to industrialization than conditions before 1815?

- What role did government play in continental industrialization? How did continental governments work

with private individuals and companies to promote economic development?

### THE INDUSTRIAL REVOLUTION IN BRITAIN

- What advantages help explain Britain's early industrialization? How did those advantages combine to spark the Industrial Revolution?

- How did British innovators solve the eighteenth-century energy crisis? How did their solution help transform the British economy?

### RELATIONS BETWEEN CAPITAL AND LABOR

- How did ideas about "women's work" change as a result of industrialization?

- What is class-consciousness? How did industrialization help produce a new sense among workers of their own social identity?

■ **In Your Own Words** Imagine that you must explain Chapter 21 to someone who hasn't read it. What would be the most important points to include and why?

# 22

# Ideologies and Upheavals

## 1815–1850

The economic and political transformation of modern times began in the late eighteenth century with the Industrial Revolution in England and then the French Revolution. Until about 1815, these economic and political revolutions were separate, involving different countries and activities while proceeding at very different paces. After peace returned in 1815, economic and political changes tended to fuse, reinforcing each other and bringing about what historian Eric Hobsbawm has called the dual revolution. For instance, the growth of the industrial middle class encouraged the drive for representative government, and the demands of the French sans-culottes (laboring poor) in 1793 and 1794 inspired many socialist thinkers. Radical change was eventually a constant, but the particular results varied enormously. In central and eastern Europe especially, the traditional elites—the monarchs, noble landowners, and bureaucrats—proved capable of defending their privileges and eventually used nationalism to respond to the dual revolution and to serve their interests, as we shall see in Chapter 24.

The dual revolution also posed a tremendous intellectual challenge. The meanings of the economic, political, and social changes that were occurring, as well as the ways they would be shaped by human action, were anything but clear. In literature, art, and music, the uncertainty of the era was reflected in the dynamism of the romantic movement. In politics, powerful new ideological forces emerged: a revitalized conservatism and three ideologies of change—liberalism, nationalism, and socialism. All played critical roles in the political and social battles of the era and the great popular upheaval that eventually swept across Europe in the revolutions of 1848. ■

**Life in the Revolutionary Era.** The sight [...] many areas of Europe between 1830 and 1848. Here Louis Philippe, the new [...] people. The three-colored Republican flag he has just accepted goes before him. (L[...])

## Chapter Preview

▶ How was peace restored and maintained after 1815?

▶ What new ideologies emerged to challenge conservatism?

▶ What were the characteristics of the romantic movement?

▶ How and where was conservatism challenged after 1815?

▶ Why did the revolutions of 1848 fail almost completely?

# ▼ How was peace restored and maintained after 1815?

The eventual triumph of revolutionary economic and political forces was by no means certain as the Napoleonic era ended. Quite the contrary. The conservative, aristocratic monarchies of Russia, Prussia, Austria, and Great Britain—the Quadruple Alliance— had finally defeated France and reaffirmed their determination to hold France in line. But many other international questions were outstanding, and the allies agreed to meet at the Congress of Vienna to fashion a general peace settlement.

Most people longed for peace. The great challenge for political leaders in 1814 was to construct a settlement that would last and not sow the seeds of another war. Their efforts were largely successful and contributed to a century unmarred by destructive generalized war (Map 22.1).

**Congress of Vienna** A meeting of the Quadruple Alliance— Russia, Prussia, Austria, and Great Britain—and restoration France to fashion a general peace settlement that began after the defeat of Napoleon's France in 1814.

## The European Balance of Power

With the French agreeing to the restoration of the Bourbon dynasty (see Chapter 20), the allies were lenient toward that nation after Napoleon's abdication. The first Peace of Paris gave France the boundaries it possessed in 1792, which were larger than those of 1789, and France did not have to pay any war reparations.

**Adjusting the Balance** The Englishman on the left uses his money to counterbalance the people that the Prussian and the fat Metternich are gaining in Saxony and Italy. Alexander I sits happily on his prize, Poland. This cartoon captures the essence of how the educated public thought about the balance-of-power diplomacy resulting in the Treaty of Vienna. (Bibliothèque nationale de France)

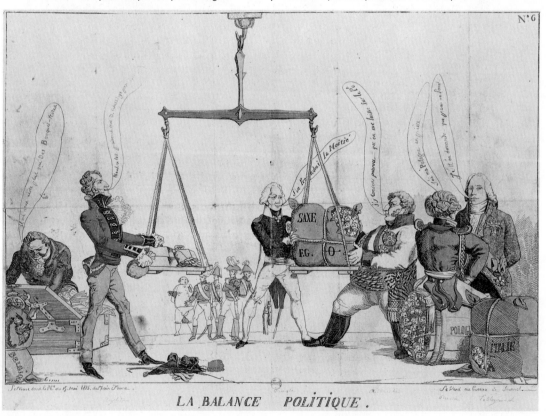

LA BALANCE POLITIQUE.

Chapter 22
Ideologies and Upheavals
644      1815–1850

CHAPTER LOCATOR     How was peace restored and maintained after 1815?

When the four allies of the Quadruple Alliance met together at the Congress of Vienna, they also agreed to raise a number of barriers against renewed French aggression. The Low Countries—Belgium and Holland—were united under an enlarged Dutch monarchy capable of opposing France more effectively. Prussia received considerably more territory on France's eastern border so as to stand as the "sentinel on the Rhine" against France. In these ways, the Quadruple Alliance combined leniency toward France with strong defensive measures.

In their moderation toward France, the allies were motivated by self-interest and traditional ideas about the balance of power. To Klemens von Metternich (MEH-tuhr-nihk) and Robert Castlereagh (KA-suhl-ray), the foreign ministers of Austria and Great Britain, respectively, as well as their French counterpart, Charles Talleyrand, the balance of power meant an international equilibrium of political and military forces that would discourage aggression by any combination of states or, worse, the domination of Europe by any single state.

The Great Powers—Austria, Britain, Prussia, Russia, and France—used the balance of power to settle their own disputes at the Congress of Vienna. There was general agreement among the victors that each of them should receive compensation in the form of territory for their successful struggle against the French. Great Britain had already won colonies and strategic outposts during the long wars. Austria gave up territories in Belgium and southern Germany but expanded greatly elsewhere, taking parts of northern Italy as well as former Polish possessions and new lands on the eastern coast of the Adriatic. Russia added a small Polish kingdom and Prussia took part of Saxony (see Map 22.1).

Unfortunately for France, Napoleon suddenly escaped from the island of Elba (see Chapter 20). Yet the second Peace of Paris, concluded after Napoleon's final defeat at Waterloo in 1815, was still relatively moderate toward France. Louis XVIII was restored to his throne. France lost only a little territory, had to pay an indemnity of 700 million francs, and had to support an army of occupation for five years. The rest of the settlement already concluded at the Congress of Vienna was left intact. The members of the Quadruple Alliance, however, did agree to meet periodically to discuss their common interests and to consider appropriate measures for the maintenance of peace in Europe. This agreement marked the beginning of the European "congress system," which lasted long into the nineteenth century.

## Repressing the Revolutionary Spirit

There was also a domestic political side to the reestablishment of peace. In 1815 under Metternich's leadership, Austria, Prussia, and Russia embarked on a crusade against the ideas and politics of the dual revolution. This crusade lasted until 1848. The first step was the Holy Alliance, formed by Austria, Prussia, and Russia in September 1815. First proposed by Russia's Alexander I, the alliance soon became a symbol of the repression of liberal and revolutionary movements all over Europe.

In 1820 revolutionaries succeeded in forcing the monarchs of Spain and the southern Italian kingdom of the Two Sicilies to grant liberal constitutions against their wills. Calling a conference at Troppau in Austria, Metternich and Alexander I proclaimed the

**dual revolution** A term that historian Eric Hobsbawm used for the economic and political changes that tended to fuse and reinforce each other after 1815.

**Holy Alliance** An alliance formed by the conservative rulers of Austria, Russia, and Prussia in September 1815 that became a symbol of the repression of liberal and revolutionary movements all over Europe.

What new ideologies emerged to challenge conservatism?    What were the characteristics of the romantic movement?    How and where was conservatism challenged after 1815?    Why did the revolutions of 1848 fail almost completely?

**Great Powers**
- Great Britain
- France
- Kingdom of Prussia
- Austrian Empire
- Russian Empire
- — Boundary of the German Confederation

## ▪ MAPPING THE PAST

## Map 22.1  Europe in 1815

In 1815 Europe contained many different states, but after the defeat of Napoleon international politics was dominated by the five Great Powers: Russia, Prussia, Austria, Great Britain, and France. (The number rises to six if one includes the Ottoman Empire.)

**ANALYZING THE MAP**  Trace the political boundaries of each Great Power, and compare their geographical strengths and weaknesses. What territories did Prussia and Austria gain as a result of the war with Napoleon?

**CONNECTIONS**  How did Prussia's and Austria's territorial gains contribute to the balance of power established at the Congress of Vienna? What other factors enabled the Great Powers to achieve such a long-lasting peace?

To complete this activity online, go to the Online Study Guide at bedfordstmartins.com/mckaywestunderstanding.

principle of active intervention to maintain all autocratic regimes whenever they were threatened. Austrian forces then marched into Naples in 1821 and restored Ferdinand I to the throne of the Two Sicilies, while French armies in 1823 likewise restored the Spanish regime.

In the following years, Metternich continued to battle against liberal political change. Metternich's policies dominated not only Austria and the Italian peninsula but also the entire German Confederation, which the peace settlement of Vienna had called into being. The confederation comprised thirty-eight independent German states, including Prussia and Austria (see Map 22.1). It was through the German Confederation that Metternich had the infamous Carlsbad Decrees issued in 1819. These decrees required the thirty-eight German member states to root out subversive ideas in their universities and newspapers. The decrees also established a permanent committee with spies and informers to investigate and punish any liberal or radical organizations.

**1820 Revolts in Spain and Italy**

## Metternich and Conservatism

Born into the middle ranks of the landed nobility of the Rhineland, Prince Klemens von Metternich (1773–1859) was Austrian foreign minister from 1809 to 1848. Metternich had a pessimistic view of human nature, which led him to conclude that strong governments were necessary to protect society from the baser elements of human behavior. Metternich also defended his class and its rights and privileges. The nobility was one of Europe's most ancient institutions, and conservatives regarded tradition as the basic source of human institutions.

Metternich firmly believed that liberalism, as embodied in revolutionary America and France, had been responsible for a generation of war with untold bloodshed and suffering. He blamed liberal middle-class revolutionaries for stirring up the lower classes, which he believed desired nothing more than peace and quiet.

The threat of liberalism appeared doubly dangerous to Metternich because it generally went with national aspirations. Liberals believed that each people, each national group, had a right to establish its own independent government and seek to fulfill its own destiny. The idea of national self-determination was repellent to Metternich because it threatened to destroy the Austrian Empire and revolutionize central Europe.

The Austrian Empire of the Habsburgs was made up of many peoples (Map 22.2). The Germans had long dominated the empire, yet they accounted for only one-fourth of the population. The Magyars (Hungarians), a substantially smaller group, dominated the kingdom of Hungary, though they did not account for a majority of the population in that part of the Austrian Empire.

The Czechs, the third major group, were concentrated in Bohemia and Moravia. There were also large numbers of Italians, Poles, and Ukrainians as well as smaller groups of Slovenes, Croats, Serbs, and Romanians. The various Slavic peoples, together with the Italians and the Romanians, represented a widely scattered and completely divided majority in an empire politically dominated by Germans and Hungarians. Thus the different parts and provinces of the empire differed in languages, customs, and institutions.

The multiethnic state Metternich served was both strong and weak. It was strong because of its large population and vast territories; it was weak because of its many and potentially dissatisfied nationalities. In these circumstances, Metternich virtually had to oppose liberalism and nationalism, for Austria was simply unable to accommodate these ideologies of the dual revolution.

**Carlsbad Decrees** Issued in 1819, these decrees were designed to uphold Metternich's conservatism, requiring the German states to root out subversive ideas and squelch any liberal organizations.

**Map 22.2 Peoples of the Habsburg Monarchy, 1815** The old dynastic state was a patchwork of nationalities. Note the widely scattered pockets of Germans and Hungarians.

**Map legend:**
- Germans
- Magyars (Hungarians)
- Italians
- Romanians
- Poles
- Czechs
- Carpatho-Ukrainians (Ruthians)
- Croats and Serbs
- Slovaks
- Slovenes
- Boundary of the Austrian Empire

## ▼ What new ideologies emerged to challenge conservatism?

In the years following the peace settlement of 1815 intellectuals and social observers sought to understand the revolutionary changes that had occurred and were still taking place. Almost all of these basic ideas were radical. In one way or another, the new ideas rejected conservatism, with its stress on tradition, a hereditary monarchy, a strong and privileged landowning aristocracy, and an official church. Radical thinkers developed and refined alternative visions — alternative ideologies — and tried to convince society to act on them.

### Liberalism and the Middle Class

**liberalism** The principal ideas of this movement were equality and liberty; liberals demanded representative government and equality before the law as well as individual freedoms such as freedom of the press, freedom of speech, freedom of assembly, and freedom from arbitrary arrest.

The principal ideas of liberalism — liberty and equality — were by no means defeated in 1815. First realized successfully in the American Revolution and then achieved in part in the French Revolution, liberalism demanded representative government and equality

Chapter 22
**Ideologies and Upheavals**
**648** 1815–1850

CHAPTER LOCATOR | How was peace restored and maintained after 1815?

before the law. The idea of liberty also meant specific individual freedoms: freedom of the press, freedom of speech, freedom of assembly, and freedom from arbitrary arrest. In Europe only France with Louis XVIII's Constitutional Charter and Great Britain with its Parliament and historic rights of English men and women had realized much of the liberal program in 1815. Even in those countries, liberalism had not fully succeeded.

Liberalism faced more radical ideological competitors in the early nineteenth century. Opponents of liberalism especially criticized its economic principles, which called for unrestricted private enterprise and no government interference in the economy. This philosophy was popularly known as the doctrine of laissez faire (lay-say FEHR). (This form of liberalism is often called "classical" liberalism in the United States in order to distinguish it from modern American liberalism, which usually favors more government programs to meet social needs and to regulate the economy.)

As we saw in Chapter 18 Adam Smith posited the idea of a free economy in 1776 in opposition to mercantilism and its attempt to regulate trade. Smith argued that freely competitive private enterprise would give all citizens a fair and equal opportunity to do what they did best and would result in greater income for everyone. In early-nineteenth-century Britain this economic liberalism was embraced most enthusiastically by business groups and thus became a doctrine associated with business interests.

In the early nineteenth century liberal political ideals also became more closely associated with narrow class interests. Early-nineteenth-century liberals favored representative government, but they generally wanted property qualifications attached to the right to vote. In practice, this meant limiting the vote to the well-to-do.

As liberalism became increasingly identified with the middle class after 1815, some intellectuals and foes of conservatism felt that liberalism did not go far enough. Inspired by memories of the French Revolution and the example of Jacksonian democracy in America, they called for universal voting rights, at least for males, and for democracy. These democrats and republicans were more radical than the liberals, and they were more willing than most liberals to endorse violent upheaval to achieve goals. All of this meant that liberals and radical democratic republicans could join forces against conservatives only up to a point.

## The Growing Appeal of Nationalism

Nationalism was a second radical idea in the years after 1815—an idea destined to have an enormous influence in the modern world. Nationalism had its immediate origins in the French Revolution and the Napoleonic wars, and there were already hints of its remarkable ability to spread and develop.

Early advocates of the "national idea," or nationalism, were strongly influenced by Johann Gottfried von Herder, an eighteenth-century philosopher and historian who argued that each people had its own genius and its own cultural unity. (See "Listening to the Past: Herder and Mazzini on the Development of Nationalism," page 650.) For nationalists coming after Herder this cultural unity was basically self-evident, manifesting itself especially in a common language, history, and territory. For the most part, in the early nineteenth century such cultural unity was more a dream than a reality. Local dialects abounded. Historical memory divided the inhabitants of the different German or Italian states as much as it unified them. Moreover, a variety of ethnic groups shared the territory of most states.

Despite these basic realities, European nationalists sought to make the territory of each people coincide with well-defined boundaries in an independent nation-state. It was this political goal that made nationalism so explosive in central and eastern Europe after 1815, when there were either too few states (Austria, Russia, and the Ottoman Empire) or too many (the Italian peninsula and the German Confederation), and when different peoples overlapped and intermingled.

**laissez faire** A doctrine of economic liberalism that believes in unrestricted private enterprise and no government interference in the economy.

**nationalism** The idea that each people had its own genius and its own specific unity, which manifested itself especially in a common language and history, and often led to the desire for an independent political state.

| What new ideologies emerged to challenge conservatism? | What were the characteristics of the romantic movement? | How and where was conservatism challenged after 1815? | Why did the revolutions of 1848 fail almost completely? |

**649**

# LISTENING TO THE PAST

## Herder and Mazzini on the Development of Nationalism

*The German historian and philosopher Johann Gottfried von Herder (1744–1803) established the foundations of cultural nationalism. Writing shortly before the French Revolution, Herder's multivolume* Ideas for the Philosophy of History of Humanity *(1784–1791) focused on the long, unconscious evolution of human communities. This process had produced national communities, each of which was joined together by a common language and by popular traditions, such as legends, proverbs, and folk songs. Herder believed that each language and each people was equally valid and equally worthy of respect.*

*A German born in Prussia, Herder hated Prussian militarism and was in no way partial to the Germans in his study. For example, he lauded the peaceful character of the Slavs and often decried the barbaric behavior of the warrior Germans. Stressing the cultural genius of each nationality, Herder advocated the preservation of traditions but not the creation of political entities or nation-states. The following passage is taken from Herder's concluding section on the different peoples of northern Europe.*

### Johann Gottfried von Herder, *Ideas for the Philosophy of History of Humanity*

❝ This is more or less a picture of the peoples of Europe. What a multicolored and composite picture! . . . Sea voyages and long migrations of people finally produced on the small continent of Europe the conditions for a great league of nations. Unwittingly the Romans had prepared it by their conquests. Such a league of nations was unthinkable outside of Europe. Nowhere else have people intermingled so much, nowhere else have they changed so often and so much their habitats and thereby their customs and ways of life. In many European countries it would be difficult today for the inhabitants, especially for single families and individuals, to say, from which people they descend, whether from Goths, Moors, Jews, Carthaginians or Romans, whether from Gauls, Burgundians, Franks, Normans, Saxons, Slavs, Finns or Illyrians, or how in the long line of their ancestors their blood had been mixed. Hundreds of causes have tempered and changed the old tribal composition of the European nations in the course of the centuries; without such an intermingling the common spirit of Europe could hardly have been awakened.

. . . Like the geological layers of our soil, the European peoples have been superimposed on each other and intermingled with each other, and yet can still be discerned in their original character. The scholars who study their customs and languages must hurry and do so while these peoples are still distinguishable: for everything in Europe tends towards the slow extinction of national character. But the historian of mankind should beware lest he exclusively favors one nationality and thereby slights others who were deprived by circumstances of chance and glory. . . .

No European people has become cultured and educated by itself. Each one has tended to keep its old barbarian customs as long as it could, supported therein by the roughness of the climate and the need of primitive warfare. No European people for instance has invented its own alphabet; the whole civilization of northern, eastern and western Europe has grown out of seeds sown by Romans, Greeks and Arabs. It took a long time before this could grow in the hard soil and could produce its own fruit, which at first lacked sweetness and ripeness. A strange vehicle, an alien religion [Christianity], was necessary to accomplish by spiritual means that which the Romans had not been able to do through conquest. Thus we must consider above all this new means of human education, which had no lesser aim than to educate all peoples to become one people, in this world and for a future world, and which was nowhere more effective than in Europe. ❞

*Like Herder, Giuseppe Mazzini (1805–1872) believed that language determined nationality and that each people had its particular genius. But unlike Herder, Mazzini and many other nationalists of the pre-1848 era also believed that each nationality required a politically independent*

Chapter 22
**Ideologies and Upheavals**
**650** 1815–1850

CHAPTER LOCATOR | How was peace restored and maintained after 1815?

*nation-state. Only a Europe of nation-states would provide the proper framework for securing freedom, democracy, social justice, and even international peace.*

*The leading prophet of Italian nationalism and unification before 1848, Mazzini founded a secret society called Young Italy to fight for the unification of the Italian states in a democratic republic. Mazzini's group inspired numerous local insurrections and led Italy's radicals in the unsuccessful revolutions of 1848. Mazzini's best-known work was* The Duties of Man, *a collection of essays. The following selection from this work was written in 1858 and addressed to Italian workingmen.*

## Giuseppe Mazzini, "Duties Towards Your Country"

❝ Your first Duties . . . are to Humanity. . . . But what can each of you, with his isolated powers, do for the moral improvement, for the progress of Humanity? . . .

God gave you the means of multiplying your forces and your powers of action indefinitely when he gave you a Country, when, like a wise overseer of labor, who distributes the different parts of the work according to the capacity of the workmen, he divided Humanity into distinct groups upon the face of our globe, and thus planted the seeds of nations. Evil governments have disfigured the design of God, which you may see clearly marked out, as far, at least, as regards Europe, by the courses of the great rivers, by the lines of the lofty mountains, and by other geographical conditions; they have disfigured it by conquest, by greed, by jealousy of the just sovereignty of others; disfigured it so much that today there is perhaps no nation except England and France whose confines correspond to this design.

[These evil governments] did not, and they do not, recognize any country except their own families and dynasties, the egoism of caste. But the divine design will infallibly be fulfilled. Natural divisions, the innate spontaneous tendencies of the peoples will replace the arbitrary divisions sanctioned by evil governments. The map of Europe will be remade. The Countries of the People will rise, defined by the voice of the free, upon the ruins of the Countries of Kings and privileged castes. Between these Countries there will be harmony and brotherhood. And then the work of Humanity for the general amelioration, for the discovery and application of the real law of life, carried on in association and distributed according to local capacities, will be accomplished by peaceful and progressive development.

Then each of you, strong in the affections and in the aid of many millions of men speaking the same language, endowed with the same tendencies, and educated by the same historic tradition, may hope by your personal effort to benefit the whole of Humanity.

Without Country you have neither name, voice, nor rights, no admission as brothers into the fellowship of the Peoples. You are the bastards of Humanity. Soldiers without a banner, . . . you will find neither faith nor protection. . . . Do not beguile yourselves with the hope of emancipation from unjust social conditions if you do not first conquer a Country for yourselves; where there is no Country there is no common agreement to which you can appeal; the egoism of self-interest rules alone, and he who has the upper hand keeps it, since there is no common safeguard for the interests of all. ❞

**Sources:** Hans Kohn, *Nationalism: Its Idea and History* (Princeton, N.J.: D. Van Nostrand Company Inc., 1955), pp. 108–110; G. Mazzini, *The Duties of Man and Other Essays* (London: J. M. Dent and Sons, 1907), pp. 51–54.

### QUESTIONS FOR ANALYSIS

1. How, according to Herder, did European nationalities evolve to create "the common spirit of Europe"?
2. Why, according to Mazzini, should Italian workers support Italian unification?
3. How are Herder's and Mazzini's views similar? How do they differ?

**Johann Gottfried von Herder, renowned eighteenth-century philosopher and historian (opposite), and Giuseppe Mazzini, Italian patriot in later life after years in exile (left).** (Herder: akg-images; Mazzini: Hulton Archive/Getty Images)

**Building German Nationalism** As popular upheaval in France spread to central Europe in March 1848, Germans from the solid middle classes came together in Frankfurt to draft a constitution for a new united Germany. This woodcut commemorates the solemn procession of delegates entering Saint Paul's Cathedral in Frankfurt, where the delegates would hold their deliberations. Festivals, celebrations, and parades helped create a feeling of belonging to a large unseen community, a nation binding millions of strangers together. (akg-images)

Between 1815 and 1850 most people who believed in nationalism also believed in either liberalism or radical democratic republicanism. A common faith in the creativity and nobility of the people was perhaps the single most important reason for the linking of these two concepts. Liberals and especially democrats saw the people as the ultimate source of all government. Yet liberals and nationalists agreed that the benefits of self-government would be possible only if the people were united by common traditions that transcended local interests and even class differences.

Early nationalists usually believed that every nation, like every citizen, had the right to exist in freedom and to develop its character and spirit. They were confident that a symphony of nations would promote the harmony and ultimate unity of all peoples. As the Italian patriot Giuseppe Mazzini (1805–1872) put it, "in laboring according to the true principles of our country we are laboring for Humanity." (See "Listening to the Past: Herder and Mazzini on the Development of Nationalism," page 650.) Thus the liberty of the individual and the love of a free nation overlapped greatly in the early nineteenth century.

Yet early nationalists also stressed the differences among peoples. Even early nationalism developed a strong sense of "we" and "they." To this "we-they" outlook, it was all too easy for nationalists to add two highly volatile ingredients: a sense of national mission and a sense of national superiority.

## French Utopian Socialism

**socialism** A backlash against the emergence of individualism and the fragmentation of society, and a move toward cooperation and a sense of community; the key ideas were economic planning, greater economic equality, and state regulation of property.

Socialism, the new radical doctrine after 1815, began in France. Early French socialist thinkers were acutely aware that the political revolution in France, the rise of laissez faire, and the emergence of modern industry in Britain were transforming society. They were disturbed because they saw these developments as fomenting selfish individualism and division within communities. There was, they believed, an urgent need for a further reorganization of society to establish cooperation and a new sense of community.

Early French socialists believed in economic planning. Inspired by the emergency measures of 1793 and 1794 in France, they argued that the government should rationally organize the economy. Early socialists also believed that the rich and the poor should be more nearly equal economically. Finally, socialists believed that private property should

Chapter 22
**Ideologies and Upheavals**
652 1815–1850

CHAPTER LOCATOR | How was peace restored and maintained after 1815?

be strictly regulated by the government or that it should be abolished and replaced by state or community ownership.

One of the most influential early socialist thinkers was a nobleman, Count Henri de Saint-Simon (awn-REE duh san-see-MOHN) (1760–1825). Saint-Simon was optimistic about industrial development. In his view, the key to progress was proper social organization that required the "parasites"—the court, the aristocracy, lawyers, and churchmen—to give way, once and for all, to the "doers"—the leading scientists, engineers, and industrialists. The doers would plan the economy and guide it forward by undertaking public works projects and establishing investment banks. Saint-Simon also stressed that every social institution ought to have as its main goal improved conditions for the poor.

After 1830 the socialist critique of capitalism became sharper. Charles Fourier (1772–1837) envisaged a socialist utopia of mathematically precise, self-sufficient communities, each made up of 1,620 people. Fourier was also an early proponent of the total emancipation of women. Fourier called for the abolition of marriage, free unions based only on love, and sexual freedom.

Journalist Louis Blanc (1811–1882) focused on practical improvements. In his *Organization of Work* (1839), he urged workers to agitate for universal voting rights and to take control of the state peacefully. Blanc believed that the state should set up government-backed workshops and factories to guarantee full employment. The right to work had to become as sacred as any other right.

Finally, there was Pierre Joseph Proudhon (1809–1865), a self-educated printer who wrote a pamphlet *What Is Property?* in 1840. His answer was that it was nothing but theft. Property was profit that was stolen from the worker, who was the source of all wealth.

Of great importance, the message of French utopian socialists interacted with the experiences of French urban workers. Workers cherished the memory of the radical phase of the French Revolution, and they became violently opposed to laissez-faire laws that denied workers the right to organize in guilds and unions. Developing a sense of class in the process, workers favored collective action and government intervention in economic life. Thus the aspirations of workers and utopian theorists reinforced each other, and a genuine socialist movement emerged in Paris in the 1830s and 1840s.

## The Birth of Marxian Socialism

In 1848 Karl Marx (1818–1883) and Friedrich Engels (see Chapter 21) published *The Communist Manifesto*, which became the bible of socialism. Marx had studied philosophy at the University of Berlin before turning to journalism and economics. He read widely in French socialist thought, and like Fourier he looked forward to the emancipation of women and the abolition of the family. By the time Marx was twenty-five, he was developing his own socialist ideas.

Early French socialists often appealed to the middle class and the state to help the poor. Marx ridiculed such appeals as naive. He argued that the interests of the middle class and those of the industrial working class were inevitably opposed to each other. Indeed, according to the *Manifesto*, the "history of all previously existing society is the history of class struggles." In Marx's view, one class had always exploited the other, and with the advent of modern industry, society was split more clearly than ever before: between the middle class—the bourgeoisie—and the modern working class—the proletariat (proh-luh-TEHR-ee-uht).

Just as the bourgeoisie had triumphed over the feudal aristocracy, Marx predicted that the proletariat would conquer the bourgeoisie in a violent revolution. While a tiny minority owned the means of production and grew richer, the ever-poorer proletariat was constantly growing in size and in class-consciousness. Marx believed that the critical moment when class conflict would result in revolution was very near.

**bourgeoisie** The middle-class minority who owned the means of production and, according to Marx, exploited the working-class proletariat.

**proletariat** The industrial working class who, according to Marx, were unfairly exploited by the profit-seeking bourgeoisie.

**Mr. and Mrs. Karl Marx** Active in the revolution of 1848, Marx fled from Germany in 1849 and settled in London. There Marx and his young wife lived a respectable middle-class life while he wrote *Capital*, the weighty exposition of his socialist theories. Marx also worked to organize the working class, and he earned a modest income as a journalist and received financial support from his coauthor, Friedrich Engels. (Time Life Pictures/Mansell/Getty Images)

Marx's ideas united sociology, economics, and all human history in a vast and imposing edifice. He synthesized in his socialism not only French utopian schemes but also English classical economics and German philosophy—the major intellectual currents of his day. Following David Ricardo, who had taught that labor was the source of all value, Marx went on to argue Proudhon's case that profits were really wages stolen from the workers.

Marx's theory of historical evolution was built on the philosophy of the German Georg Hegel (HAY-guhl) (1770–1831). Hegel believed that each age is characterized by dominant ideas that produce opposing ideas and eventually a new synthesis. Marx retained Hegel's view of history as a dialectic process of change but made economic relationships between classes the driving force. This dialectic explained the decline of agrarian feudalism and the rise of industrial capitalism.

Marx's next idea, that it was now the bourgeoisie's turn to give way to the socialism of revolutionary workers, appeared to many the irrefutable capstone of a brilliant interpretation of humanity's long development. Thus Marx pulled together powerful ideas and insights to create one of the great secular religions out of the intellectual ferment of the early nineteenth century.

## ▼ What were the characteristics of the romantic movement?

The early nineteenth century was a time of change in literature and the other arts as well as politics. Known as the romantic movement, this artistic change was in part a revolt against the emphasis on rationality, order, and restraint that characterized the Enlightenment and the controlled style of classicism.

Forerunners of the romantic movement appeared from about 1750 on. Of these, Rousseau (see Chapter 17)—the passionate advocate of feeling, freedom, and natural goodness—was the most influential. Romanticism then crystallized fully in the 1790s, primarily in England and Germany. Romanticism gained strength until the 1840s, when it gave gradually way to realism (see Chapter 23).

### Romanticism's Tenets

**romanticism** A movement at its height from about 1790 to the 1840s that was in part a revolt against classicism and the Enlightenment, characterized by a belief in emotional exuberance, unrestrained imagination, and spontaneity in both art and personal life.

Romanticism was characterized by a belief in emotional exuberance, unrestrained imagination, and spontaneity in both art and personal life. Many romantic artists of the early

**Chapter 22**
**Ideologies and Upheavals**
**654** **1815–1850**

CHAPTER LOCATOR │ How was peace restored and maintained after 1815?

nineteenth century lived lives of tremendous emotional intensity. Romantic artists typically led bohemian lives, wearing their hair long and uncombed in preference to powdered wigs, and rejecting the materialism of refined society. Great individualists, the romantics believed the full development of one's unique human potential to be the supreme purpose in life.

Nowhere was the break with classicism more apparent than in romanticism's general conception of nature. Classicism was not particularly interested in nature. The romantics, in contrast, were enchanted by nature. For some it was awesome and tempestuous, while others saw nature as a source of spiritual inspiration.

Most romantics saw the growth of modern industry as an ugly, brutal attack on their beloved nature and on the human personality. They sought escape—in the unspoiled Lake District of northern England, in exotic North Africa, in an imaginary idealized Middle Ages.

The study of history became a romantic passion. History was the key to a universe that was now perceived to be organic and dynamic, not mechanical and static as the Enlightenment thinkers had believed. Nor was it restricted to the biographies of great men or the work of divine providence. Historians such as Jules Michelet, who focused on the development of societies and human institutions, promoted the growth of national aspirations, encouraging entire peoples to seek in the past their special destinies.

## Literature

Romanticism found its distinctive voice in poetry. Its first great poets were British: Wordsworth, Coleridge, and Scott were all active by 1800, to be followed shortly by Byron, Shelley, and Keats.

William Wordsworth (1770–1850) was deeply influenced by Rousseau and the spirit of the early French Revolution. Wordsworth settled in the rural Lake District of England with his sister, Dorothy, and Samuel Taylor Coleridge (1772–1834). In 1798 Wordsworth and Coleridge published their *Lyrical Ballads*, which abandoned flowery classical conventions for the language of ordinary speech and endowed simple subjects with the loftiest majesty.

Classicism remained strong in France under Napoleon and inhibited the growth of romanticism there. In 1813 Germaine de Staël (duh STAHL) (1766–1817), a Franco-Swiss writer living in exile, urged the French to throw away their worn-out classical models. Her study *On Germany* (1810) extolled the spontaneity and enthusiasm of German writers and thinkers, and it had a powerful impact on the post-1815 generation in France. (See "Individuals in Society: Germaine de Staël," page 656.) Between 1820 and 1850, the romantic impulse broke through in the poetry and prose of Lamartine, de Vigny, Hugo, Dumas, and Sand. Of these, Victor Hugo (1802–1885) became the most well known in both poetry and prose.

Son of a Napoleonic general, Hugo achieved an amazing range of rhythm, language, and image in his lyric poetry. His powerful novels exemplified the romantic fascination with fantastic characters, exotic historical settings, and human emotions. Renouncing his early conservatism, Hugo equated freedom in literature with liberty in politics and society. Hugo's political evolution was thus exactly the opposite of Wordsworth's, in whom youthful radicalism gave way to middle-aged caution. As the contrast between the two artists suggests, romanticism was a cultural movement compatible with many political beliefs.

Amandine Aurore Lucie Dupin (1804–1876), generally known by her pen name, George Sand, defied the narrow conventions of her time in an unending search for self-fulfillment. After eight years of unhappy marriage she abandoned her husband and took her two children to Paris to pursue a career as a writer. There Sand soon achieved fame and wealth, eventually writing over eighty novels on a variety of romantic and social themes.

# INDIVIDUALS IN SOCIETY

## Germaine de Staël

**Germaine de Staël, brilliant intellectual and elegant aristocrat.** (Erich Lessing/Art Resource, NY)

**RICH, INTELLECTUAL, PASSIONATE, AND ASSERTIVE,** Germaine Necker de Staël (1766–1817) astonished contemporaries and still fascinates historians. She was strongly influenced by her parents, poor Swiss Protestants who soared to the top of prerevolutionary Parisian society. Her brilliant but rigid mother filled Germaine's head with knowledge, and each week the precocious child listened, wide-eyed and attentive, to illustrious writers and philosophers performing at her mother's salon. At age twelve, she suffered a physical and mental breakdown. Only then was she allowed to have a playmate and romp and run on the family estate. Her adoring father was Jacques Necker, a banker who made an enormous fortune and became France's reform-minded minister of finance before the Revolution. Worshiping her father in adolescence, Germaine also came to love politics.

Accepting at nineteen an arranged marriage with Baron de Staël-Holstein, a womanizing Swedish diplomat bewitched by her dowry, Germaine began her life's work. She opened an intellectual salon and began to write and publish. Her wit and exuberance attracted foreigners and liberal French aristocrats, one of whom became the first of many lovers as her marriage soured and she searched unsuccessfully for the happiness of her parents' union. Fleeing Paris in 1792 and returning after the Thermidorian reaction (see page 604), she subsequently angered Napoleon by criticizing his dictatorial rule. In 1803 he permanently banished her from Paris.

Retiring again to her isolated estate in Switzerland and skillfully managing her inherited wealth, Staël fought insomnia with opium and boredom with parties that attracted luminaries from all over Europe. Always seeking stimulation for her restless mind, she traveled widely in Italy and Germany and drew upon these experiences in her novel *Corinne* (1807) and her study *On Germany* (1810). Both works summed up her romantic faith and enjoyed enormous success.

Staël urged creative individuals to abandon traditional rules and classical models. She encouraged them to embrace experimentation, emotion, and enthusiasm. Enthusiasm, which she had in abundance, was the key, the royal road to creativity, personal fulfillment, and human improvement. Thrilling to music, for example, she felt that only an enthusiastic person could really appreciate this gift of God, this wordless message that "unifies our dual nature and blends senses and spirit in a common rapture."*

Yet a profound sadness runs through her writing. This sadness, so characteristic of the romantic temperament, grew in part out of disappointments in love and prolonged exile. But it also grew out of the insoluble predicament of being an enormously gifted woman in an age of intense male chauvinism. Little wonder that uneasy male competitors and literary critics took delight in ridiculing and defaming her as a neurotic and masculine woman, a mediocre and unnatural talent who had foolishly dared to enter the male world of serious thought and action.

Even her supporters could not accept her for what she was. The admiring poet Lord Byron recognized her genius and called her "the most eminent woman author of this, or perhaps of any century." But he quickly added that "she should have been born a man."†

Buffeted and saddened by scorn and condescension because of her gender, Staël advocated equal rights for women throughout her life. Only with equal rights and duties — in education and careers, in love and marital relations — could an exceptional woman like herself, or indeed any woman, ever hope to realize her intellectual and emotional potential. Practicing what she preached as best she could, Germaine de Staël was a trailblazer in the struggle for women's rights.

## QUESTIONS FOR ANALYSIS

1. In what ways did Germaine de Staël's life and thought reflect basic elements of the romantic movement?
2. Why did male critics often attack Staël? What do these criticisms tell us about gender relations in the early nineteenth century?

*Quoted in G. R. Besser, *Germaine de Staël Revisited* (New York: Twayne Publishers, 1994), p. 106. Enhanced by a feminist perspective, this fine study is highly recommended.
†Quoted ibid., p. 139.

Chapter 22
Ideologies and Upheavals
656     1815–1850

CHAPTER LOCATOR | How was peace restored and maintained after 1815?

**John Constable,** *The Hay Wain* Constable's love of a spiritualized and poetic nature radiates from this masterpiece of romantic art. Exhibited in Paris in 1829, *The Hay Wain* created a sensation and made a profound impression on the young Delacroix. The cottage on the left still stands, open to the public as a small museum devoted to Constable and his paintings. (National Gallery, London, UK/ The Bridgeman Art Library)

In central and eastern Europe, literary romanticism and early nationalism often reinforced each other. Seeking a unique greatness in every people, romantics plumbed their own histories and cultures. Like modern anthropologists, they turned their attention to peasant life and transcribed the folk songs, tales, and proverbs that the Enlightenment had disdained. The brothers Jacob and Wilhelm Grimm were particularly successful at rescuing German fairy tales from oblivion. In the Slavic lands, romantics played a decisive role in converting spoken peasant languages into modern written languages. The most influential of all Russian poets, Aleksander Pushkin (1799–1837), rejecting eighteenth-century attempts to force Russian poetry into a classical straitjacket, used his lyric genius to mold the modern literary language.

## Art and Music

One of the greatest and most moving romantic painters in France was Eugène Delacroix (oo-ZHEHN deh-luh-KWAH) (1798–1863). Delacroix was a master of dramatic, colorful scenes that stirred the emotions. He was fascinated with remote and exotic subjects. Yet he was also a passionate spokesman for freedom.

In England the most notable romantic painters were Joseph M. W. Turner (1775–1851) and John Constable (1776–1837). Both were fascinated by nature, but their interpretations of it contrasted sharply, aptly symbolizing the tremendous emotional range

| What new ideologies emerged to challenge conservatism? | **What were the characteristics of the romantic movement?** | How and where was conservatism challenged after 1815? | Why did the revolutions of 1848 fail almost completely? |

657

of the romantic movement. Turner depicted nature's power and terror; wild storms and sinking ships were favorite subjects. Constable painted gentle landscapes in which human beings were at one with their environment, the comforting countryside of unspoiled rural England.

It was in music that romanticism realized most fully and permanently its goals of free expression and emotional intensity. Abandoning well-defined structures, the great romantic composers used a wide range of forms to create musical landscapes and evoke powerful emotions. Romantic composers also transformed the small classical orchestra, tripling its size by adding wind instruments, percussion, and more brass and strings.

The first great romantic composer is also the most famous today. Ludwig van Beethoven (BAY-toh-vuhn) (1770–1827) used contrasting themes and tones to produce dramatic conflict and inspiring resolutions. As one contemporary admirer wrote, "Beethoven's music sets in motion the lever of fear, of awe, of horror, of suffering, and awakens just that infinite longing which is the essence of Romanticism." Beethoven's range and output were tremendous. At the peak of his fame, he began to lose his hearing. He considered suicide but eventually overcame despair: "I will take fate by the throat; it will not bend me completely to its will."[1] Beethoven continued to pour out immortal music, although his last years were silent, spent in total deafness.

## ▼ How and where was conservatism challenged after 1815?

While the romantic movement was developing, liberal, national, and socialist forces battered against the conservatism of 1815. In some countries, change occurred gradually and peacefully. Elsewhere, pressure built up and eventually caused an explosion in 1848. Three important countries—Greece, Great Britain, and France—experienced variations on this basic theme between 1815 and 1848.

Delacroix, *Massacre at Chios* The Greek struggle for freedom and independence won the enthusiastic support of liberals, nationalists, and romantics. The Ottoman Turks were portrayed as cruel oppressors who were holding back the course of history, as in this moving masterpiece by Delacroix. (Réunion des Musées Nationaux/Art Resource, NY)

## National Liberation in Greece

National, liberal revolution, frustrated in Italy and Spain by conservative statesmen, succeeded first after 1815 in Greece. Since the fifteenth century, the Greeks had been living under the domination of the Ottoman Turks. The general growth of national aspirations and a desire for independence inspired some Greeks in the early nineteenth century. This rising national movement led to the formation of secret societies and then to revolt in 1821, led by Alexander Ypsilanti (ip-suh-LAN-tee), a Greek patriot and a general in the Russian army.

At first, the leaders of the Great Powers, particularly Metternich, refused to back Ypsilanti and supported the Ottoman Empire. Yet for many Europeans, the Greek cause became a holy one. Educated Americans and Europeans were in love with the culture of classical Greece; Russians were stirred by the piety of their Orthodox brethren.

Chapter 22
Ideologies and Upheavals
1815–1850

658

CHAPTER LOCATOR | How was peace restored and maintained after 1815?

**Greek Independence, 1830**

OTTOMAN EMPIRE

Ionian Is. (Gr. Br.)

GREECE · Athens

Navarino Bay 1827

GREECE

Mediterranean Sea

Crete

Writers and artists, moved by the romantic impulse, responded enthusiastically to the Greek national struggle.

In 1827 Great Britain, France, and Russia yielded to popular demands at home and directed Turkey to accept an armistice. When the Turks refused, the navies of these three powers trapped the Turkish fleet at Navarino and destroyed it. Russia then declared another of its periodic wars of expansion against the Turks. This led to the establishment of a Russian protectorate over much of present-day Romania. Great Britain, France, and Russia finally declared Greece independent in 1830 and installed a German prince as king of the new country in 1832.

## Liberal Reform in Great Britain

Eighteenth-century British society had been both flexible and remarkably stable. It was dominated by the landowning aristocracy, but that class was neither closed nor rigidly defined. Basic civil rights for all were balanced by a tradition of deference to one's social superiors. Parliament was manipulated by the king and was thoroughly undemocratic, with only about 8 percent of the population allowed to vote for representatives.

By the 1780s there was growing interest in some kind of political reform, but the French Revolution threw the British aristocracy into a panic for a generation, making it extremely hostile to any attempts to change the status quo. Conflicts between the ruling class and laborers were sparked in 1815 with revision of the Corn Laws. Britain had been unable to import cheap grain from eastern Europe during the war years, leading to high prices and large profits for the landed aristocracy. With the war over, grain could be imported again, allowing the price of wheat and bread to go down and benefiting almost everyone except the aristocracy. The aristocracy, however, rammed far-reaching changes in the Corn Laws through Parliament. The new regulation prohibited the importation of foreign grain unless the price at home rose to improbable levels.

The change in the Corn Laws, coming as it did at a time of widespread unemployment and postwar economic distress, triggered protests and demonstrations by urban laborers. In 1817 the Tory government, which was controlled by the landed aristocracy, responded by temporarily suspending the traditional rights of peaceable assembly and habeas corpus. Two years later, Parliament passed the infamous Six Acts, which, among other things, placed controls on a heavily taxed press and practically eliminated all mass meetings. These acts followed an enormous but orderly protest, at Saint Peter's Fields in Manchester, that had been savagely broken up by armed cavalry. Nicknamed the Battle of Peterloo, this incident demonstrated the government's determination to repress dissenters.

Strengthened by ongoing industrial development, the new manufacturing and commercial groups insisted on a place for their new wealth alongside the landed wealth of the aristocracy in the framework of political power and social prestige. They called for many kinds of liberal reform. In the 1820s, a less frightened Tory government moved in the direction of better urban administration, greater economic liberalism, civil equality for Catholics, and limited imports of foreign grain. These actions encouraged the middle classes to press on for reform of Parliament so they could have a larger say in government.

The Whig Party, though led like the Tories by great aristocrats, had by tradition been more responsive to middle-class commercial and manufacturing interests. In 1830 a Whig ministry introduced "an act to amend the representation of the people of England and Wales." After a series of setbacks, the Whig's Reform Bill of 1832 was propelled into law by a surge of popular support. Significantly, the bill moved British politics in a democratic

**Corn Laws** British laws, revised in 1815, that prohibited the importation of foreign grain unless the price at home rose to improbable levels, thus benefiting the aristocracy but making food prices high for working people.

**Battle of Peterloo** A protest that took place at Saint Peter's Fields in Manchester in reaction to the revision of the Corn Laws; it was broken up by armed cavalry.

**Reform Bill of 1832** A major British political reform that increased the number of male voters by about 50 percent and gave political representation to new industrial areas.

What new ideologies emerged to challenge conservatism?

What were the characteristics of the romantic movement?

How and where was conservatism challenged after 1815?

Why did the revolutions of 1848 fail almost completely?

direction and allowed the House of Commons to emerge as the all-important legislative body. The new industrial areas of the country gained representation in the Commons, and many old "rotten boroughs"—electoral districts that had very few voters and that the landed aristocracy had bought and sold—were eliminated. The number of voters increased by about 50 percent, giving about 12 percent of adult men in Britain and Ireland the right to vote. Thus the pressures building in Great Britain were successfully—though only temporarily—released. A major reform had been achieved peacefully. Continued fundamental reform within the system appeared difficult but not impossible.

The principal radical program for continued reform was embodied in the "People's Charter" of 1838 and the Chartist movement (see Chapter 21). The Chartists' core demand was universal male suffrage. They saw complete political democracy and rule by the common people—the great majority of the population—as the means to a good and just society. Hundreds of thousands of people signed gigantic petitions calling on Parliament to grant all men the right to vote, first and most seriously in 1839, again in 1842, and yet again in 1848. Parliament rejected all three petitions. In the short run, the working poor failed with their Chartist demands, but they learned a valuable lesson in mass politics.

While calling for universal male suffrage, many working-class people joined with middle-class manufacturers in the Anti–Corn Law League, founded in Manchester in 1839. Mass participation made possible a popular crusade led by liberals, who argued that lower food prices and more jobs in industry depended on repeal of the Corn Laws. Much of the working class agreed. When Ireland's potato crop failed in 1845 (see page 661) and famine prices for food seemed likely in England, Tory prime minister Robert Peel joined with the Whigs and a minority of his own party to repeal the Corn Laws in 1846 and allow free imports of grain. England escaped famine.

**The Anti–Corn Law Movement in Action** This contemporary illustration focuses on the Anti–Corn Law League's remarkable ability to mobilize a broad urban coalition that was dedicated to free trade and the end of tariffs on imported grain (or "corn"). Each League supporter was encouraged to join the national organization, attend meetings and lectures, and demonstrate in the streets. (The Granger Collection, NY)

The following year, the Tories passed the Ten Hours Act of 1847, limiting the workday for women and young people in factories to ten hours. Tory aristocrats continued to champion legislation regulating factory conditions. They were competing vigorously with the middle class for the support of the working class. This healthy competition between a still-vigorous aristocracy and a strong middle class was a crucial factor in Great Britain's peaceful evolution. The working classes could make temporary alliances with either competitor to better their own conditions.

## Ireland and the Great Famine

The people of Ireland did not benefit from the political competition in Britain. The great mass of the population (outside of the northern counties of Ulster, which were partly Presbyterian) were Irish Catholics, who rented their land from a tiny minority of Church

*The Discovery of the Potato Blight* Although the leaves usually shriveled and died, they could also look deceptively healthy. In this painting by Daniel McDonald an Irish family has dug up its potato harvest and just discovered to its horror that the blight has rotted the crop. Like thousands of Irish families, the family now faces the starvation and mass epidemics of the Great Famine. (Department of Irish Folklore, University College, Dublin)

of England Protestants. These landlords were content to use their power to grab as much as possible.

The result was that the condition of the Irish peasantry around 1800 was abominable. The typical peasant lived in a wretched cottage and could afford neither shoes nor stockings. A compassionate French traveler wrote that Ireland was "pure misery, naked and hungry. . . . I saw the American Indian in his forests and the black slave in his chains, and I believed that I was seeing the most extreme form of human misery; but that was before I knew the lot of poor Ireland."[2]

Yet in spite of terrible conditions, Ireland's population of 3 million in 1725 grew to 4 million in 1780 and doubled to 8 million by 1840. In addition, between 1780 and 1840, another 1.75 million people left Ireland for Britain and America in search of better living conditions.

Ireland's population explosion, part of Europe's general population growth since the early eighteenth century (see Chapter 18), was caused in part by the extensive cultivation of the potato. A single acre of land spaded and planted with potatoes could feed an Irish family of six for a year, and the potato also could thrive on boggy wastelands. Needing only a big potato patch to survive, Irish men and women married early.

The decision to marry and have large families made sense. Landlords leased land for short periods only. Peasants had no incentive to make permanent improvements because anything beyond what was needed for survival would quickly be taken by higher rent. Rural poverty was inescapable and better shared with a spouse, while a dutiful son or a loving daughter was an old person's best hope of escaping destitution.

As population and potato dependency grew, conditions became more precarious. From 1820 onward deficiencies and diseases in the potato crop became more common. In 1845 and 1846, and again in 1848 and 1851, the potato crop failed in Ireland. The result was

What new ideologies emerged to challenge conservatism? | What were the characteristics of the romantic movement? | **How and where was conservatism challenged after 1815?** | Why did the revolutions of 1848 fail almost completely?

**661**

the Great Famine. Blight attacked the young plants, and the tubers rotted. Widespread starvation and mass fever epidemics followed. Yet the British government, committed to rigid laissez-faire ideology, was slow to act. When it did, its relief efforts were inadequate. Moreover, the government continued to collect taxes, landlords demanded their rents, and tenants who could not pay were evicted and their homes destroyed.

The Great Famine shattered the pattern of Irish population growth. Fully 1 million emigrants fled the famine between 1845 and 1851, and at least 1.5 million died or went unborn because of the disaster. Alone among the countries of Europe, Ireland experienced a declining population in the second half of the nineteenth century, as it became a land of continuous out-migration, late marriage, early death, and widespread celibacy.

The Great Famine also intensified anti-British feeling and promoted Irish nationalism, for the memory of starvation, exile, and British inaction was burned deeply into the popular consciousness. Patriots could call on powerful collective emotions in their campaigns for land reform, home rule, and, eventually, Irish independence.

## The Revolution of 1830 in France

Louis XVIII's Constitutional Charter of 1814 was basically a liberal constitution (see Chapter 20). The economic and social gains made by sections of the middle class and the peasantry in the French Revolution were fully protected, intellectual and artistic freedom was permitted, and a parliament with upper and lower houses was created. Moreover, Louis appointed as his ministers moderate royalists, who sought and obtained the support of a majority of the representatives elected to the lower Chamber of Deputies between 1816 and Louis's death in 1824.

Louis XVIII's charter was anything but democratic. Only about 100,000 of the wealthiest males out of a total population of 30 million had the right to vote for the deputies who, with the king and his ministers, made the laws of the nation. Nonetheless, voters came from diverse backgrounds. There were wealthy businessmen, war profiteers, successful professionals, ex-revolutionaries, large landowners from the old aristocracy and the middle class, Bourbons, and Bonapartists. The old aristocracy was a minority within the voting population. It was this situation that Louis's successor, Charles X (r. 1824–1830), could not abide. A true reactionary, Charles wanted to re-establish the old order in France. Increasingly blocked by the opposition of the deputies, Charles's government turned in 1830 to military adventure in an effort to rally French nationalism and gain popular support. A long-standing economic and diplomatic dispute with Muslim Algeria, a vassal state of the Ottoman Empire, provided the opportunity.

In June 1830, a French force landed to the west of Algiers and took the capital city in three short weeks. Victory seemed complete, but in 1831 tribes in the interior revolted and waged war until 1847, when French armies finally subdued the country. Bringing French, Spanish, and Italian settlers to Algeria and leading to the expropriation of large tracts of Muslim land, the conquest of Algeria marked the rebirth of French colonial expansion.

Emboldened by the good news from Algeria, Charles repudiated the Constitutional Charter in an attempted coup in July 1830. He issued decrees stripping much of the wealthy middle class of its voting rights, and he censored the press. The immediate reaction, encouraged by journalists and lawyers, was an insurrection in the capital by printers, other artisans, and small traders. The government collapsed and Charles fled. Then the upper middle class, which had fomented the revolt, skillfully seated Charles's cousin, Louis Philippe, duke of Orléans, on the throne.

Louis Philippe (r. 1830–1848) accepted the Constitutional Charter of 1814. He adopted the red, white, and blue flag of the French Revolution and admitted that he was merely the "king of the French people." Nonetheless, the situation in France remained fundamentally unchanged. The vote was extended only from 100,000 to 170,000 citizens. For the upper middle class, there had been a change in dynasty in order to protect the status

Chapter 22
**Ideologies and Upheavals**
**662**     1815–1850

CHAPTER LOCATOR    How was peace restored and maintained after 1815?

**The Fall of Algiers** In July 1830 France assembled more than six hundred ships and attacked the Ottoman dependency of Algeria. The ferocious naval bombardment shown in this engraving destroyed the capital's fortifications. After the surrender French soldiers rampaged through the city, and news of this brutal behavior encouraged Muslims in the interior to revolt and fight on until 1847. (Musée de la Ville de Paris, Musée Carnavalet, Paris, France/Lauros/Giraudon/The Bridgeman Art Library)

quo. Republicans, democrats, social reformers, and the poor of Paris were bitterly disappointed. They had made a revolution, but it seemed for naught.

# ▼ Why did the revolutions of 1848 fail almost completely?

The late 1840s in Europe were hard economically and tense politically. Bad harvests jacked up food prices and caused misery, and they caused unemployment in the cities and in the countryside. A profound economic crisis gripped continental Europe. It was caused by a combination of rapid population growth and industrialization efforts that were only beginning to provide more jobs and income.

The political and social response to the economic crisis was unrest and protest. "Prerevolutionary" outbreaks occurred all across Europe. Only the most advanced and the most backward major countries—reforming Great Britain and immobile Russia—escaped untouched. Governments toppled; monarchs and ministers bowed or fled. National independence, liberal democratic constitutions, and social reform: the lofty aspirations of a generation seemed at hand. Yet in the end, the revolutions failed.

## A Democratic Republic in France

By the late 1840s, revolution in Europe was almost universally expected, but it took revolution in Paris to turn expectations into realities. For eighteen years Louis Philippe's "bourgeois monarchy" had been characterized by stubborn inaction and complacency. There

### The Triumph of Democratic Republics

This French illustration offers an opinion of the initial revolutionary breakthrough in 1848. The peoples of Europe, joined together around their respective national banners, are achieving republican freedom, which is symbolized by the Statue of Liberty and the discarded crowns. The woman wearing pants at the base of the statue — very radical attire — represents feminist hopes for liberation. (Museé de la Ville, Paris/Giraudon/The Bridgeman Art Library)

**ANALYZING THE IMAGE**  How many different flags can you count and/or identify? How would you characterize the types of people marching and the mood of the crowd?

**CONNECTIONS**  What do the angels, Statue of Liberty, and discarded crowns suggest about the artist's view of the events of 1848? Do you think this illustration was created before or after the collapse of the revolution in France? Why?

To complete this activity online, go to the Online Study Guide at bedfordstmartins.com/mckaywestunderstanding.

was a glaring lack of social legislation, and politics was dominated by corruption and selfish special interests.

The government's stubborn refusal to consider electoral reform heightened a sense of class injustice among middle-class shopkeepers, skilled artisans, and unskilled working people, and it eventually touched off a popular revolt in Paris. Workers joined by some students began building barricades in the narrow streets of Paris on the night of February 22, 1848. Armed and dug in behind their makeshift fortresses, the workers and students demanded a new government. On February 24, as the National Guard broke ranks and joined the revolutionaries, Louis Philippe abdicated in favor of his grandson. But the common people in arms would tolerate no more monarchy. This refusal led to the proclamation of a provisional republic, headed by a ten-man executive committee.

The revolutionaries immediately set about drafting a constitution for France's Second Republic. The right to vote was given to every adult male. Revolutionary compassion and

Chapter 22
**Ideologies and Upheavals**
**664**   1815–1850

CHAPTER LOCATOR    How was peace restored and maintained after 1815?

**1814** Russia, Prussia, Austria, and Britain form the Quadruple Alliance
Napoleon abdicates
Louis XVIII issues the Constitutional Charter providing for civil liberties and representative government
First Peace of Paris combines leniency with a defensive posture toward France

**1815** Congress of Vienna establishes balance-of-power principle and creates the German Confederation
Napoleon escapes from Elba and marches on Paris
Napoleon defeated at the Battle of Waterloo
Austria, Prussia, and Russia form the Holy Alliance to repress liberal and revolutionary movements
Second Peace of Paris punishes France and establishes the congress system

**1819** Metternich's Carlsbad Decrees impose harsh antiliberal measures throughout the German Confederation

**1820** Revolution in Spain and the kingdom of the Two Sicilies
Congress of Troppau proclaims the principle of intervention to maintain autocratic regimes

**1821** Austria crushes a liberal revolution in Naples and restores the Sicilian autocracy
Greeks revolt against the ruling Ottoman Turks

**1823** French armies restore the Spanish regime

**1830** Charles X repudiates the Constitutional Charter; insurrection and collapse of the government follow
Louis Philippe succeeds to the throne and maintains a narrowly liberal regime
Greece wins independence from the Ottoman Empire

**1832** Reform Bill expands British electorate and encourages the middle class

**1839** Louis Blanc publishes *Organization of Work*

**1840** Pierre Joseph Proudhon publishes *What Is Property?*

**1846** Jules Michelet publishes *The People*

**1848** Karl Marx and Friedrich Engels publish *The Communist Manifesto*

sympathy for freedom were expressed in the freeing of all slaves in French colonies, the abolition of the death penalty, and the establishment of a ten-hour workday for Paris.

Yet there were profound differences within the revolutionary coalition in Paris. On the one hand, there were the moderate liberal republicans of the middle class. They viewed universal male suffrage as the ultimate concession to be made to popular forces, and they strongly opposed any further radical social measures. On the other hand, there were radical republicans and hard-pressed artisans. Influenced by a generation of utopian socialists, and appalled by the poverty and misery of the urban poor, the radical republicans were committed to some kind of socialism. So were many artisans, who hated the unrestrained competition of cutthroat capitalism and advocated a combination of strong craft unions and worker-owned businesses.

Worsening depression and rising unemployment brought these conflicting goals to the fore in 1848. Louis Blanc (see page 653), who along with a worker named Albert represented the republican socialists in the provisional government, pressed for recognition of a socialist right to work. Blanc asserted that permanent government-sponsored cooperative workshops should be established for workers. Such workshops would be an alternative to capitalist employment and a decisive step toward a new, noncompetitive social order.

The moderate republicans wanted no such thing. They were willing to provide only temporary relief. The resulting compromise set up national workshops and established a special commission under Blanc to "study the question." This satisfied no one. The national workshops were, however, better than nothing. An army of desperate poor from the French provinces and even from foreign countries streamed into Paris to sign up.

While the workshops in Paris grew, the French masses went to the election polls in late April. Voting in most cases for the first time, the people of France elected to the new Constituent Assembly about five hundred moderate republicans, three hundred monarchists, and one hundred radicals who professed various brands of socialism. One of the moderate republicans was the author of *Democracy in America*, Alexis de Tocqueville (TOHK-vihl) (1805–1859).

Tocqueville observed that the socialist movement in Paris aroused the fierce hostility of France's peasants as well as the middle and upper classes. The French peasants owned land, and according to Tocqueville, "private property had become with all those who owned it a sort of bond of fraternity."[3] Taking his seat in the new Constituent Assembly, Tocqueville saw that a majority of the members were firmly committed to the republic and strongly opposed to the socialists and their artisan allies, and he shared their sentiments.

This clash of ideologies — of liberal capitalism and socialism — became a clash of classes and arms after the elections. The new government's executive committee dropped Blanc and thereafter included no representative of the Parisian working class. Fearing that their socialist hopes were about to be dashed, artisans and unskilled workers invaded the Constituent Assembly on May 15. But the government was ready and used the middle-class National Guard to squelch this uprising. As the workshops continued to fill and grow more radical, the propertied classes in the Assembly took the offensive. On June 22, the government dissolved the national workshops in Paris, giving the workers the choice of joining the army or going to workshops in the provinces.

The result was a spontaneous and violent uprising. Frustrated in attempts to create a socialist society, masses of desperate people were now losing even their life-sustaining relief. Barricades sprang up again in the narrow streets of Paris, and a terrible class war began. Working people fought with the courage of utter desperation, but this time the government had the army and the support of peasant France. After three terrible "June Days" of street fighting and the death or injury of more than ten thousand people, the republican army under General Louis Cavaignac stood triumphant.

The revolution in France thus ended in spectacular failure. The February coalition of the middle and working classes had in four short months become locked in mortal combat. In place of a generous democratic republic, the Constituent Assembly completed a constitution featuring a strong executive. This allowed Louis Napoleon, nephew of Napoleon Bonaparte, to win a landslide victory in the election of December 1848. The appeal of his great name as well as the desire of the propertied classes for order at any cost had produced a semi-authoritarian regime.

## The Austrian Empire in 1848

Throughout central Europe, the news of the upheaval in France evoked excitement and eventually revolution. Liberals demanded written constitutions, representative government, and greater civil liberties from authoritarian regimes. When governments hesitated, popular revolts followed. Urban workers and students served as the shock troops, but they were allied with middle-class liberals and peasants. In the face of this united front, monarchs collapsed and granted almost everything. The popular revolutionary coalition, having secured great and easy victories, then broke down as it had in France.

The revolution in the Austrian Empire began in Hungary in 1848, where nationalistic Hungarians demanded national autonomy, full civil liberties, and universal suffrage.

**Guarding the Barricades in Vienna** Workers and students took full control of Vienna in May 1848, when they raised the barricades and dug in. In this painting a number of men and women eat, relax, and discuss the situation. Women were active in supportive roles during the revolution. (Wien Museum Karlsplatz, Vienna/The Bridgeman Art Library)

When the monarchy hesitated, Viennese students and workers took to the streets and raised the barricades in defiance of the government, while peasant disorders broke out in parts of the empire. Emperor Ferdinand I (r. 1835–1848) capitulated and promised reforms and a liberal constitution and Metternich fled.

The coalition of revolutionaries was not stable, however. When the monarchy abolished serfdom, the newly free peasants lost interest in the political and social questions agitating the cities. Meanwhile, the coalition of urban revolutionaries also broke down along class lines over the issue of socialist workshops and universal voting rights for men.

The revolutionary coalition was also weakened, and ultimately destroyed, by conflicting national aspirations. In March the Hungarian revolutionary leaders pushed through an extremely liberal, almost democratic, constitution. But the Hungarian revolutionaries also sought to create a unified, centralized, Hungarian nation. To the minority groups that formed half of the population of the kingdom of Hungary—the Croats, Serbs, and Romanians—such unification was completely unacceptable. Each felt entitled to political autonomy and cultural independence. Likewise, Czech nationalists based in Bohemia and the city of Prague came into conflict with German nationalists. Thus conflicting national aspirations within the Austrian Empire enabled the monarchy to play off one ethnic group against the other.

Finally, the conservative aristocratic forces regained their nerve under the rallying call of the archduchess Sophia. Deeply ashamed of the emperor's collapse, she insisted that Ferdinand, who had no heir, abdicate in favor of her son, Francis Joseph.[4] Powerful nobles organized around Sophia in a secret conspiracy to reverse and crush the revolution.

Their first breakthrough came when the army bombarded Prague and crushed a working-class revolt there on June 17. Other Austrian officials and nobles began to lead the minority nationalities of Hungary against the revolutionary government. At the end of October, the regular Austrian army used heavy cannon to attack the student and working-class radicals dug in behind barricades in Vienna and retook the city at the cost of more than four thousand casualties. Thus the determination of the Austrian aristocracy and the loyalty of its army were the final ingredients in the triumph of reaction and the defeat of revolution.

When Francis Joseph (r. 1848–1916) was crowned emperor of Austria immediately after his eighteenth birthday in December 1848, only Hungary had yet to be brought under control. Another determined conservative, Nicholas I of Russia (r. 1825–1855), obligingly lent his iron hand. On June 6, 1849, 130,000 Russian troops poured into Hungary and subdued the country. For a number of years, the Habsburgs ruled Hungary as a conquered territory.

## Prussia and the Frankfurt Assembly

After Austria, Prussia was the largest and most influential German kingdom. Prior to 1848, the goal of middle-class Prussian liberals had been to transform Prussia into a liberal constitutional monarchy, which would lead the German Confederation into the liberal, unified nation desired by liberals throughout the German states. The agitation following the fall of Louis Philippe encouraged Prussian liberals to press their demands. When the artisans and factory workers in Berlin exploded in March 1848 and joined temporarily with the middle-class liberals in the struggle against the monarchy, Frederick William IV (r. 1840–1861) vacillated and finally caved in. On March 21, he promised to grant Prussia a liberal constitution and to merge Prussia into a new national German state that was to be created.

But urban workers wanted much more and the Prussian aristocracy wanted much less than the moderate constitutional liberalism the king conceded. The workers issued a series of democratic and vaguely socialist demands that troubled their middle-class allies, and conservatives gathered around the king to urge counter-revolution.

As an elected Prussian Constituent Assembly met in Berlin to write a constitution for the Prussian state, a self-appointed committee of liberals from various German states began organizing for the creation of a unified German state. Meeting in Frankfurt in May, a National Assembly convened to write a German federal constitution. However, their attention shifted from drafting a constitution to deciding how to respond to Denmark's claims on the provinces of Schleswig (SHLEHS-wihg) and Holstein, which were inhabited primarily by Germans. Debating ponderously, the National Assembly at Frankfurt finally called on the Prussian army to oppose Denmark in the name of the German nation. As the Schleswig-Holstein issue demonstrated, the national ideal was a crucial factor motivating the German middle classes in 1848.

In March 1849, the National Assembly finally completed its drafting of a liberal constitution and elected King Frederick William of Prussia emperor of the new German national state (minus Austria and Schleswig-Holstein). By early 1849, however, reaction had been successful almost everywhere. Frederick William had reasserted his royal authority, disbanded the Prussian Constituent Assembly, and granted his subjects a limited, essentially conservative constitution. Reasserting that he ruled by divine right, Frederick William contemptuously refused to accept the "crown from the gutter." Bogged down

Chapter 22
Ideologies and Upheavals
1815–1850

668

CHAPTER LOCATOR | How was peace restored and maintained after 1815?

by their preoccupation with nationalist issues, the reluctant revolutionaries in Frankfurt had waited too long and acted too timidly.

When Frederick William, who really wanted to be emperor but only on his own authoritarian terms, tried to get the small monarchs of Germany to elect him emperor, Austria balked. Supported by Russia, Austria forced Prussia to renounce all its schemes of unification in late 1850. The German Confederation was re-established. Attempts to unite the Germans—first in a liberal national state and then in a conservative Prussian empire—had failed completely.

← LOOKING BACK **LOOKING AHEAD** →

VIEWED FROM A BROAD HISTORICAL PERSPECTIVE, Europe's economic and social foundations in 1750 remained agricultural and rural. Peasants living in villages tilled the land, while landlords and the ruling classes collected rents and taxes. Political life was dominated by the authoritarian styles associated with absolutism, although the critical thinking of the Enlightenment was beginning to affect the intellectual and cultural elites, who began to challenge and question the status quo. By the 1790s, the British Industrial Revolution and the French Revolution were bringing fundamental changes to economic and political life in parts of Europe. In Great Britain new technologies and factory organization turned the focus away from agriculture and the land and toward industry and cities. In revolutionary France liberal ideals of representative government and legal equality were being realized, if only briefly. After 1815, the dual revolution provided Europe with new visions of political and social life. Liberalism intermingled with nationalism and socialism to challenge the restoration of the conservative order.

Much of world history in the past two centuries can be seen as the progressive unfolding of the dual revolution. In Europe in the nineteenth century, as in Asia and Africa in more recent times, the interrelated economic and political transformation was built on complicated histories, strong traditions, and highly diverse cultures. Although defeated in 1848, the new political ideologies associated with the French Revolution were destined to triumph after 1850. Above all, nationalism, with its commitment to the nation-state and the imagined community of a great national family, would become the dominant political force, responding to national problems and guiding European imperial expansion after 1875. At the same time, industrialization and new relationships between classes would privilege cities and promote a new urban society, as agriculture and rural life gradually declined. Diverse, complicated, and fascinating, this new urban society was emerging by 1850. By 1900, it dominated northwestern Europe and was making steady inroads to the east and south. ■

- **For a list of suggested readings for this chapter, visit** *bedfordstmartins.com/mckaywestunderstanding*.

- **For primary sources from this period, see** *Sources of Western Society*, **Second Edition**.

- **For Web sites, images, and documents related to topics in this chapter, see Make History at** *bedfordstmartins.com/mckaywestunderstanding*.

What new ideologies emerged to challenge conservatism?    What were the characteristics of the romantic movement?    How and where was conservatism challenged after 1815?    Why did the revolutions of 1848 fail almost completely?

669

## Step 1

**GETTING STARTED** Below are basic terms about this period in the history of Western civilization. Can you identify each term below and explain why it matters? To do this exercise online, go to bedfordstmartins.com/mckaywestunderstanding.

| TERMS | WHO (OR WHAT) AND WHEN | WHY IT MATTERS |
|-------|------------------------|----------------|
| Congress of Vienna, p. 644 | | |
| dual revolution, p. 645 | | |
| Holy Alliance, p. 645 | | |
| Carlsbad Decrees, p. 647 | | |
| liberalism, p. 648 | | |
| laissez faire, p. 649 | | |
| nationalism, p. 649 | | |
| socialism, p. 652 | | |
| bourgeoisie, p. 653 | | |
| proletariat, p. 653 | | |
| romanticism, p. 654 | | |
| Corn Laws, p. 659 | | |
| Battle of Peterloo, p. 659 | | |
| Reform Bill of 1832, p. 659 | | |
| Great Famine, p. 662 | | |

## Step 2

**MOVING BEYOND THE BASICS** The exercise below requires a more advanced understanding of the chapter material. Examine the new ideologies that shaped European history in the first half of the nineteenth century by filling in the chart below with the key characteristics and beliefs associated with liberalism, conservatism, nationalism, and socialism. Then assess the impact of the French Revolution on each ideology. When you are finished, consider the following questions: Why did liberals tend to support nationalist movements and conservatives tend to resist them? How did the socialist diagnosis of the problem of nineteenth-century Europe differ from the liberal diagnosis? To do this exercise online, go to bedfordstmartins.com/mckaywestunderstanding.

| IDEOLOGY | KEY CHARACTERISTICS AND BELIEFS | IMPACT OF THE FRENCH REVOLUTION |
|----------|--------------------------------|--------------------------------|
| Liberalism | | |
| Conservatism | | |
| Nationalism | | |
| Socialism | | |

# PUTTING IT ALL TOGETHER
Now that you've reviewed key elements of the chapter, take a step back and try to see the big picture. Remember to use specific examples from the chapter in your answers. To do this exercise online, go to bedfordstmartins.com/mckaywestunderstanding.

## THE AFTERMATH OF THE NAPOLEONIC WARS

• What were the goals of the participants in the Congress of Vienna? How did their experience of the French Revolution and the Napoleonic Wars shape their vision of postwar Europe?

• Why was Metternich so hostile to nationalism and liberalism? Why did he see both as a threat to the Austrian Empire?

## THE SPREAD OF RADICAL IDEAS

• How did liberals tend to see the relationship between the individual and the marketplace? What about between "the people" and the nation? What policies and programs did liberals advance on the basis of these beliefs?

• What influences shaped Marx's vision of European history? What groups were most attracted to Marxian socialism? Why?

## THE ROMANTIC MOVEMENT

• Compare and contrast Romantic and Enlightenment views of nature and religion. What do the differences you note tell us about the essential characteristics of each movement?

• How did romantics see the individual? In their view, what was each person's supreme purpose in life? What examples from Romantic art and literature can you present to support your answer?

## REFORMS AND REVOLUTION

• Compare and contrast Britain and France in 1830. How did Britain avoid the revolutionary upheaval that exploded in France in 1830?

• What explains the near simultaneous eruption of revolution across Europe in 1848? How did revolution in one country help trigger revolution in another? Why did all of the revolutions of 1848 fail?

## ▪ In Your Own Words
Imagine that you must explain Chapter 22 to someone who hasn't read it. What would be the most important points to include and why?

# 23

# Life in the Emerging Urban Society

## 1840–1900

The era of intellectual and political upheaval that culminated in the revolutions of 1848 was also an era of rapid industrialization and urbanization. Industrial growth posed enormous challenges for all elements of Western society, from young factory workers confronting relentless discipline to aristocratic elites maneuvering to retain political power. After 1848, as Western political development veered off in an uncharted direction, the growth of towns and cities rushed forward with undiminished force. Thus Western society was urban and industrial in 1900 as surely as it had been rural and agrarian in 1800. Progress, in the form of new industries and big businesses, better living conditions for the masses, growing secularism, and a budding feminist movement, was the order of the day.

This emerging urban society benefited city dwellers, through improvements in health and the urban environment, but living conditions varied greatly according to one's status. While average people experienced wage increases, poverty was not eliminated and the gap between rich and poor remained as great as ever. The size of the middle classes grew in this period, and as middle-class people reaped the benefits of industrialization and scientific progress, they fragmented into an upper middle class that often mimicked the lives of the aristocracy, a solid middle middle class defined by the professions and business owners, and a lower middle class made up of shopkeepers and office workers. Despite this growing middle class, most urban dwellers continued to belong to the working classes.  ■

**Urban Life in the Nineteenth Century.** The excitement and variety of urban life sparkle in this detail from a depiction of an entertainment gala given for the public by London's Royal Dramatic College. (© Fine Art Photographic Library/Corbis)

# Chapter Preview

▶ How did urban life change in the nineteenth century?

▶ What were the characteristics of urban industrial society?

▶ How did urbanization affect family life?

▶ How and why did intellectual life change in this period?

# ▼ How did urban life change in the nineteenth century?

Since the Middle Ages, European cities had been centers of government, culture, and large-scale commerce. They had also been congested, dirty, and unhealthy. Beginning in the early nineteenth century, the Industrial Revolution took these unfortunate realities of urban life to unprecedented levels. Rapid urban growth worsened long-standing overcrowding and unhealthy living conditions and posed a frightening challenge for society. It would require the full-scale efforts of government leaders, city planners, reformers, scientists, and reform-minded citizens to tame the savagery of the traditional city.

## Industry and the Growth of Cities

The main causes of such a poor quality of urban life—pervasive poverty, lack of medical knowledge, and overcrowding—had existed for centuries. Because the typical city had always been a "walking city" with no public transportation, masses of people needed to live in close proximity to the shops and markets, resulting in dense housing conditions. Packed together, people in cities were always more likely to die from the spread of infectious disease than were their rural counterparts. In the larger towns, more people died each year than were born, on average, and urban populations were able to maintain their numbers only because newcomers were continually arriving from rural areas.

Deplorable urban conditions were made worse by the Industrial Revolution. The steam engine freed industrialists from dependence on the energy of fast-flowing streams and rivers so that by 1800 there was every incentive to build new factories in urban areas. Cities had better shipping facilities than the countryside and thus better supplies of coal and raw materials. There were also many hands wanting work in the cities. And it was a great advantage for a manufacturer to have other factories nearby to supply the business's needs and buy its products. Therefore, as industry grew, there was also a rapid expansion of already overcrowded and unhealthy cities.

The challenge of the urban environment was felt first and most acutely in Great Britain. The number of people living in cities of 20,000 or more in England and Wales jumped from 1.5 million in 1801 to 6.3 million in 1851 and reached 15.6 million in 1891. Such cities accounted for 17 percent of the total English population in 1801, 35 percent as early as 1851, and fully 54 percent in 1891. Other countries duplicated the English pattern as they industrialized (Map 23.1).

Except on the outskirts, early-nineteenth-century cities in Britain were using every scrap of land to the fullest extent. Buildings were erected on the smallest possible lots in order to pack the maximum number of people into a given space. Narrow houses were built wall to wall in long rows. Many people lived in extremely small, often overcrowded cellars or attics. "Six, eight, and even ten occupying one room is anything but uncommon," wrote a Scottish doctor for a government investigation in 1842.

These highly concentrated urban populations lived in extremely unsanitary and unhealthy conditions. Open drains and sewers flowed alongside or down the middle of unpaved streets. In parts of Manchester, as many as two hundred people shared a single outhouse. Such privies filled up rapidly, and since they were infrequently emptied, sewage often overflowed and seeped into cellar dwellings. By the 1840s there was among the better-off classes a growing, shocking "realization that," as one scholar put it, "millions of English men, women, and children were living in shit."[1]

The crucial factors in creating these conditions were the tremendous pressure of more people and the total absence of public transportation. People simply had to jam themselves together if they were to be able to walk to shops and factories. Another factor was that government in Great Britain, both local and national, was slow to provide sanitary facilities and establish adequate building codes.

Most responsible of all was the legacy of rural housing conditions in preindustrial society combined with ignorance. Housing was far down on the newcomer's list of priorities, and many people carried the filth of the mud floor and the dung of the barnyard with them to the city. Moreover, ordinary people generally took dirt for granted. One English miner told an investigator, "I do not think it usual for the lasses [in the coal mines] to wash their bodies; my sisters never wash themselves." As for the men, "their legs and bodies are as black as your hat."[2]

## The Advent of the Public Health Movement

Toward the middle of the nineteenth century, people's acceptance of their overcrowded, unsanitary surroundings began to give way to a growing interest in reform and improvement. The most famous early reformer was Edwin Chadwick, one of the commissioners charged with the administration of relief to paupers under Britain's revised Poor Law of 1834. Chadwick was a follower of philosopher Jeremy Bentham (1748–1832), whose approach to social issues, called utilitarianism, had

**utilitarianism** The idea of Jeremy Bentham that social policies should promote the "greatest good for the greatest number."

## Chapter Chronology

| | |
|---|---|
| ca. 1840s–1890s | Realism dominant in Western literature |
| 1848 | First public health law in Britain |
| ca. 1850–1870 | Modernization of Paris |
| 1850–1914 | Condition of working classes improves |
| 1854 | Pasteur studies fermentation and develops pasteurization |
| 1854–1870 | Development of germ theory |
| 1859 | Darwin, On the Origin of Species by the Means of Natural Selection |
| 1869 | Mendeleev creates periodic table |
| 1880–1913 | Second industrial revolution; birthrate steadily declines in Europe |
| 1890s | Electric streetcars introduced in Europe |

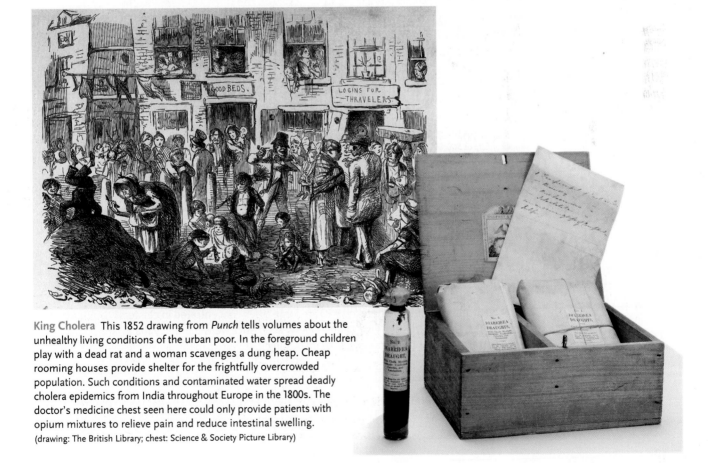

**King Cholera** This 1852 drawing from *Punch* tells volumes about the unhealthy living conditions of the urban poor. In the foreground children play with a dead rat and a woman scavenges a dung heap. Cheap rooming houses provide shelter for the frightfully overcrowded population. Such conditions and contaminated water spread deadly cholera epidemics from India throughout Europe in the 1800s. The doctor's medicine chest seen here could only provide patients with opium mixtures to relieve pain and reduce intestinal swelling. (drawing: The British Library; chest: Science & Society Picture Library)

**CHAPTER LOCATOR** | How did urban life change in the nineteenth century? | What were the characteristics of urban industrial society? | How did urbanization affect family life? | How and why did intellectual life change in this period?

675

taught that public problems ought to be dealt with on a rational, scientific basis and according to the "greatest good for the greatest number." Applying these principles, Chadwick soon became convinced that disease and death actually caused poverty, because a sick worker was an unemployed worker and orphaned children were poor children. Most important, Chadwick believed that disease could be prevented by cleaning up the urban environment.

Chadwick collected detailed reports from local Poor Law officials on the "sanitary conditions of the laboring population" and published his findings in 1842. His evidence proved that disease was related to filthy environmen-

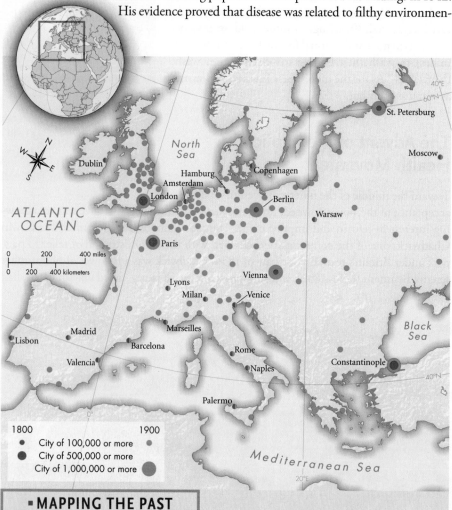

1800                    1900
●   City of 100,000 or more   ●
●   City of 500,000 or more   ●
●   City of 1,000,000 or more   ●

## ▪ MAPPING THE PAST

### Map 23.1 European Cities of 100,000 or More, 1800–1900

There were more large cities in Great Britain in 1900 than in all of Europe in 1800. A comparison of these maps reveals key aspects of nineteenth-century urbanization.

**ANALYZING THE MAP** Compare the spatial distribution of cities in 1800 with the distribution in 1900. Where in 1900 are large cities concentrated in clusters?

**CONNECTIONS** In 1800, what common characteristics were shared by many large European cities? (For example, how many big cities were capitals and/or leading ports?) Were any common characteristics shared by the large cities in 1900? What does this suggest about the reasons behind this dramatic growth?

To complete this activity online, go to the Online Study Guide at bedfordstmartins.com/mckaywestunderstanding.

Chapter 23
**Life in the Emerging Urban**
**676**    **Society • 1840–1900**

tal conditions, which were in turn caused largely by lack of drainage, sewers, and garbage collection.

Chadwick correctly believed that the stinking excrement of communal outhouses could be dependably carried off by water through sewers at less than one-twentieth the cost of removing it by hand. In 1848, with the cause strengthened by the cholera epidemic of 1846, Chadwick's report became the basis of Great Britain's first public health law, which created a national health board and gave cities broad authority to build modern sanitary systems.

The public health movement won supporters in the United States, France, and Germany from the 1840s on. Governments accepted at least limited responsibility for the health of all citizens. By the 1860s and 1870s, European cities were making real progress toward adequate water supplies and sewerage systems, city dwellers were beginning to reap the reward of better health, and death rates began to decline (Figure 23.1).

## The Bacterial Revolution

Although improved sanitation in cities promoted a better quality of life and some improvements in health care, effective control of communicable disease required a leap forward in medical knowledge and biological theory. Early reformers such as Chadwick adhered to the miasmatic theory of disease—the belief that people contract disease when they breathe the bad odors of decay and putrefying excrement. In the 1840s and 1850s doctors and public health officials pinpointed the role of bad drinking water in the transmission of disease and suggested that contagion was spread through filth and not caused by it, thus weakening the miasmatic idea.

The breakthrough was the development of the **germ theory** of disease by French chemist Louis Pasteur (pas-TUHR) (1822–1895), a French chemist who began studying fermentation for brewers in 1854. Pasteur found that fermentation depended on the growth of living organisms and that the activity of these organisms could be suppressed by heating the beverage—by pasteurization. The implication was that specific diseases were caused by specific living organisms—germs—and that those organisms could be controlled in people as well as in beer, wine, and milk.

By 1870 the work of Pasteur and others had demonstrated the general connection between germs and disease. When, in the middle of the 1870s, doctor Robert Koch (kawkh) and his coworkers developed pure cultures of harmful bacteria and described their life cycles, the dam broke. Over the next twenty years, researchers identified the organisms responsible for disease after disease. These discoveries led to the development of a number of effective vaccines.

Acceptance of the germ theory brought about dramatic improvements in hospitals and surgery (see Chapter 19). In 1865, when Pasteur showed that the air was full of bacteria, English surgeon Joseph Lister (1827–1912) immediately grasped the connection between aerial bacteria and the problem of wound infection. He reasoned that a chemical disinfectant applied to a wound dressing would "destroy the life of the floating particles." In the 1880s, German surgeons developed the more sophisticated practice of sterilizing not only the wound but also everything that entered the operating room.

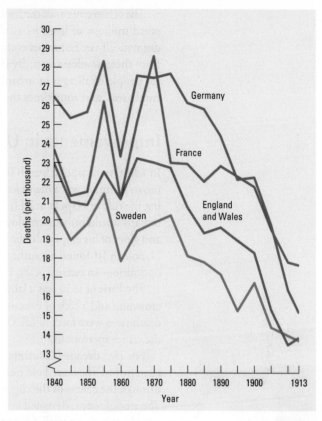

**Figure 23.1 The Decline of Death Rates in England and Wales, Germany, France, and Sweden, 1840–1913** A rising standard of living, improvements in public health, and better medical knowledge all contributed to the dramatic decline of death rates in the nineteenth century.

**germ theory** The idea that disease was caused by the spread of living organisms that could be controlled.

CHAPTER LOCATOR | How did urban life change in the nineteenth century? | What were the characteristics of urban industrial society? | How did urbanization affect family life? | How and why did intellectual life change in this period?

677

The achievements of the bacterial revolution coupled with the public health movement saved millions of lives, particularly after about 1880. Mortality rates began to decline dramatically in European countries (see Figure 23.1). City dwellers benefited especially from these developments. By 1910 a great silent revolution had occurred: the death rates for people of all ages in urban areas were generally no greater than those for people in rural areas, and sometimes they were lower.

## Improvements in Urban Planning

In addition to public health improvements in nineteenth-century cities, more effective urban planning was a major key to a better quality of urban life. France took the lead during the rule of Napoleon III (r. 1848–1870). Napoleon III believed that rebuilding much of Paris would provide employment, improve living conditions, and testify to the power and glory of his empire. In the baron Georges Haussmann (HOWS-muhn) (1809–1884), Napoleon III found an authoritarian planner capable of bulldozing both buildings and opposition. In twenty years, Paris was completely transformed (Map 23.2, p. 680).

The Paris of 1850 was a labyrinth of narrow, dark streets, the results of desperate overcrowding and a lack of effective planning. Terrible slum conditions and extremely high death rates were facts of life. There were few open spaces and only two public parks for the entire metropolis.

For two decades Haussmann and his fellow planners proceeded on many interrelated fronts. They razed old buildings in order to cut broad, straight, tree-lined boulevards through the center of the city as well as in new quarters on the outskirts (see Map 23.2). These boulevards, designed in part to prevent the erection of barricades by revolutionary crowds, permitted traffic to flow freely and afforded impressive vistas. Their creation also demolished some of the worst slums. New streets stimulated the construction of better housing, especially for the middle classes. Small neighborhood parks and open spaces were created throughout the city, and two very large parks were developed — one on the wealthy west side and one on the poor east side of the city. The city also improved its sewers, and a system of aqueducts more than doubled the city's supply of clean, fresh water.

Rebuilding Paris provided a new model for urban planning and stimulated modern urbanism throughout Europe, particularly after 1870. In city after city, public authorities mounted a coordinated attack on many of the interrelated problems of the urban environment. Cities such as Vienna and Cologne followed the Parisian example of tearing down old walled fortifications and replacing them with broad, circular boulevards on which office buildings, town halls, theaters, opera houses, and museums were erected. These ring roads and the new boulevards that radiated outward eased movement and encouraged urban expansion (see Map 23.2).

## Public Transportation

The development of mass public transportation often accompanied urban planning, greatly enhancing urban living conditions toward the end of the nineteenth century. In the 1870s, many European cities authorized private companies to operate horse-drawn streetcars to carry riders along the growing number of major thoroughfares. Then in the 1890s, the real revolution occurred: European countries adopted streetcars that ran on the newly harnessed power of electricity (see page 695). Electric streetcars were cheaper, faster, more dependable, cleaner, and more comfortable than their horse-drawn counterparts. In 1886 the horse-drawn streetcars of Austria-Hungary, France, Germany, and Great Britain were carrying about 900 million riders. By 1910 electric streetcar systems in the four countries were carrying 6.7 billion riders.[3]

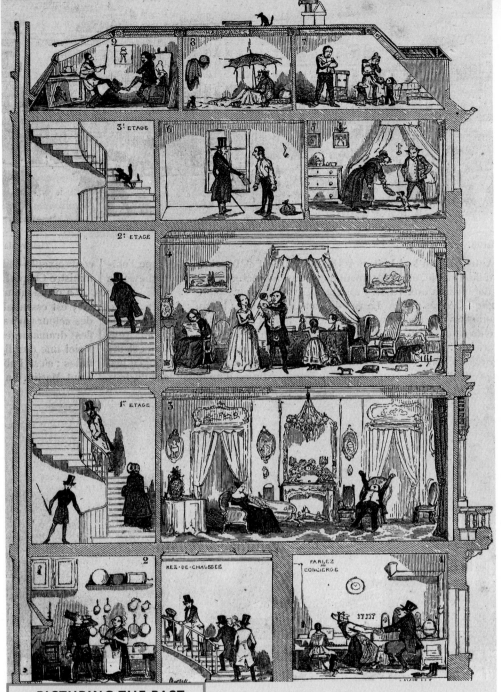

## ▪ PICTURING THE PAST

### Apartment Living in Paris

This drawing shows a typical layout for a European city apartment building in about 1850. (Bibliothèque nationale de France)

**ANALYZING THE IMAGE** Describe the inhabitants of each floor. How does the economic condition of the tenants differ from the 1st étage (American second floor) to the garret apartments on the top floor?

**CONNECTIONS** What does this drawing suggest about urban life in the nineteenth century? How might a sketch of a modern, urban American apartment building differ in terms of the types of people who reside in a single building?

To complete this activity online, go to the Online Study Guide at bedfordstmartins.com/mckaywestunderstanding.

CHAPTER LOCATOR | How did urban life change in the nineteenth century? | What were the characteristics of urban industrial society? | How did urbanization affect family life? | How and why did intellectual life change in this period?

**679**

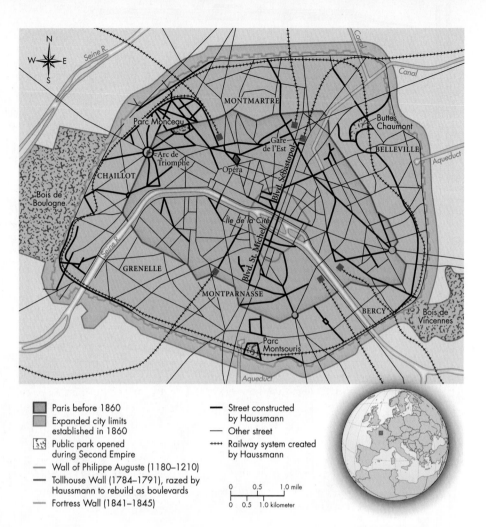

**Map 23.2 The Modernization of Paris, ca. 1850–1870** The addition of broad boulevards, large parks, and grandiose train stations transformed Paris. The cutting of the new north-south axis—known as the Boulevard Saint-Michel—was one of Haussmann's most controversial projects. It razed much of Paris's medieval core and filled the Île de la Cité with massive government buildings.

Paris before 1860
Expanded city limits established in 1860
Public park opened during Second Empire
Wall of Philippe Auguste (1180–1210)
Tollhouse Wall (1784–1791), razed by Haussmann to rebuild as boulevards
Fortress Wall (1841–1845)

Street constructed by Haussmann
Other street
Railway system created by Haussmann

0    0.5    1.0 mile
0    0.5    1.0 kilometer

Good mass transit helped greatly in the struggle for decent housing. The new boulevards and horse-drawn streetcars had facilitated a middle-class move to better and more spacious housing in the 1860s and 1870s; after 1890 electric streetcars meant people of even modest means could access new, improved housing. Though still crowded, the city was able to expand and become less congested. On the continent, many city governments in the early twentieth century were building electric streetcar systems that provided transportation to new public and private housing developments for the working classes beyond the city limits. Suburban commuting was born.

## ▼ What were the characteristics of urban industrial society?

As the quality of urban life was improving across Europe, the class structure was becoming more complex and diverse. Urban society featured many distinct social groups, all of which existed in a state of constant flux and competition. The gap between rich and poor remained enormous, but there were countless gradations between the extremes.

# The Distribution of Income

By 1850 at the latest, working conditions were improving, Moreover, real wages—that is, wages received by workers adjusted for changes in the prices they paid—were rising for the mass of the population, and they continued to do so until 1914. Ordinary people took a major step forward in the centuries-old battle against poverty, reinforcing efforts to improve many aspects of human existence.

Greater economic rewards for the average person did not, however, eliminate hardship and poverty, nor did they make the wealth and income of the rich and the poor significantly more equal. In almost every advanced country around 1900, the richest 5 percent of all households in the population received about a third of all national income, and the richest 20 percent of households received from 50 to 60 percent of all national income. At the other end, the entire bottom 80 percent received only 40 to 50 percent of all income. Moreover, the bottom 30 percent of all households received 10 percent or less of all income.

To understand the full significance of these statistics, one must realize that the middle classes were smaller than they are today. In the nineteenth century, they accounted for less than 20 percent of the population. In short, this meant that the upper and middle classes alone received more than half of all income, while the poorest 80 percent received less altogether than the two richest classes. Thus the gap between rich and poor remained enormous at the beginning of the twentieth century.

The great gap between rich and poor endured, in part, because industrial and urban development made society more diverse and less unified. Economic specialization enabled society to produce more effectively and in the process created more new social groups than it destroyed. There developed an almost unlimited range of jobs, skills, and earnings. Thus the tiny elite of the very rich and the sizable mass of the poor were separated by a range of subclasses, each filled with individuals struggling to rise or at least to hold their own in the social order. In this atmosphere of competition and hierarchy, neither the middle classes nor the working classes acted as a unified force.

# The People and Occupations of the Middle Classes

By the beginning of the twentieth century, the diversity and range within the urban middle class were striking. Indeed, it is more meaningful to think not of a single middle class but of a confederation of middle classes whose members engaged in occupations requiring mental, rather than physical, skill.

At the top of the middle class stood the upper middle class, composed mainly of the most successful business families from banking, industry, and large-scale commerce. As people in the upper middle class gained in income, they were almost irresistibly drawn toward the aristocratic lifestyle. And although the genuine hereditary aristocracy constituted only a tiny minority in every European country, it retained imposing wealth, unrivaled social prestige, and substantial political influence.

The topmost reaches of the upper middle class tended to merge with the old aristocracy to form a new upper class of at most 5 percent of the population. Much of the aristocracy welcomed this development. Having experienced a sharp decline in its relative income in the course of industrialization, the landed aristocracy was often delighted to trade titles, country homes, and snobbish elegance for good hard cash. Correspondingly, wealthy aristocrats tended increasingly to exploit their agricultural and mineral resources as if they were business people.

Below the wealthy upper middle class were much larger, much less wealthy, and increasingly diversified middle-class groups. Here were the moderately successful industrialists and merchants as well as professionals in law and medicine. Below this middle middle class were independent shopkeepers, small traders, and tiny manufacturers—the lower

CHAPTER LOCATOR | How did urban life change in the nineteenth century? | **What were the characteristics of urban industrial society?** | How did urbanization affect family life? | How and why did intellectual life change in this period?

681

middle class. Both of these traditional elements of the middle class grew modestly with economic development.

As industry and technology expanded in the nineteenth century, a growing demand developed for experts with specialized knowledge, and advanced education soared in importance among the middle classes. Architects, chemists, accountants, and surveyors, to name only a few, first achieved professional standing in this period. They established criteria for advanced training and certification, and they banded together in organizations to promote and defend their interests. Management of large public and private institutions also emerged as a kind of profession as governments provided more services and as very large corporations such as railroads came into being.

Industrialization also expanded and diversified the lower middle class. The number of independent, property-owning shopkeepers and small business people grew, and so did the number of white-collar employees—a mixed group of traveling salesmen, bookkeepers, store managers, and clerks who staffed the offices and branch stores of large corporations. White-collar employees often earned no more than the better-paid skilled or semiskilled workers did. Yet white-collar workers were fiercely committed to the middle class and to the ideal of upward mobility. The tie, the suit, and soft, clean hands were no less subtle marks of class distinction than were wages.

Relatively well educated, many white-collar groups aimed at achieving professional standing and the accompanying middle-class status. Elementary school teachers largely succeeded in this effort, riding the wave of mass education to respectable middle-class status and income. Nurses also rose from the lower ranks of unskilled labor to precarious middle-class standing. Dentistry was taken out of the hands of working-class barbers and placed in the hands of highly trained (and middle-class) professionals.

## Middle-Class Culture and Values

In spite of growing occupational diversity and conflicting interests, the middle classes were loosely united by a certain style of life and culture. Food was the largest item in the household budget. The European middle classes consumed meat in abundance, and a well-off family might spend 10 percent of its earnings on meat and fully 25 percent of its income on food and drink. Spending on food was also great because the dinner party was this class's favored social occasion.

The middle-class wife had both servants and money at her disposal. Indeed, the employment of at least one full-time maid to cook and clean was the clearest sign that a family had crossed the cultural divide separating the working classes from the middle classes. The greater a family's income, the greater the number of servants it employed.

The middle classes were also well housed by 1900. Many prosperous families rented, rather than owned, their homes. Apartment living, complete with tiny rooms for servants under the eaves of the top floor, was commonplace. And, just as the aristocracy had long divided the year between country estates and townhouses during "the season," so the upper middle class purchased country places or built beach houses for weekend and summer use.

By 1900 the middle classes were also quite clothes-conscious. The factory, the sewing machine, and the department store had all helped reduce the cost and expand the variety of clothing. Middle-class women were particularly attentive to the dictates of fashion.

Rich businessmen devoted less time to business and more time to "culture" and easy living than was the case in less wealthy or well-established families. The keystones of culture and leisure were books, music, and travel. The long realistic novel, the heroics of composers Wagner and Verdi, the striving of the dutiful daughter at the piano, and the packaged tour to a foreign country were all sources of middle-class pleasure.

In addition to their material tastes, the middle classes generally agreed upon a strict code of behavior and morality. This code laid great stress on hard work, self-discipline,

*A Corner of the Table* With photographic precision, the French artist Paul-Émile Chabas (1869–1937) captures the elegance and intimacy of a sumptuous dinner party. Throughout Europe, members of the upper middle class and aristocracy enjoyed dinners like this with eight or nine separate courses, beginning with appetizers and ending with coffee and liqueurs. (Archives Charmet/The Bridgeman Art Library)

and personal achievement. Men and women who fell into crime or poverty were generally assumed to be responsible for their own circumstances. Drunkenness and gambling were denounced as vices; sexual purity and fidelity were celebrated as virtues. In short, the middle-class person was supposed to know right from wrong and was expected to act accordingly.

## The People and Occupations of the Working Classes

About four out of five people belonged to the working classes at the beginning of the twentieth century. Many members of the working classes were still small landowning peasants and hired farm hands. This was especially true in eastern Europe. In western and central Europe, however, the typical worker had left the land.

The urban working classes were even less unified and homogeneous than the middle classes. In the first place, economic development and increased specialization expanded the traditional range of working-class skills, earnings, and experiences. Meanwhile, the old distinction between highly skilled artisans and unskilled manual workers gradually broke down. Between these extremes there appeared ever more semiskilled groups (Figure 23.2). In the second place, skilled, semiskilled, and unskilled workers developed widely divergent lifestyles and cultural values, and their differences contributed to a keen sense of social status and hierarchy within the working classes. The result was great variety and limited class unity.

Highly skilled workers, who made up about 15 percent of the working classes, became known as the labor aristocracy. These workers earned only about two-thirds of the income of the bottom ranks of the servant-keeping classes, but that was fully twice as much as the earnings of unskilled workers. The labor aristocracy included construction bosses and factory foremen, as well as members of the traditional highly skilled handicraft trades that had not been mechanized or placed in factories, like cabinetmakers, jewelers, and printers.

**labor aristocracy** The highly skilled workers, such as factory foremen and construction bosses, who made up about 15 percent of the working classes from about 1850 to 1914.

CHAPTER LOCATOR | How did urban life change in the nineteenth century? | **What were the characteristics of urban industrial society?** | How did urbanization affect family life? | How and why did intellectual life change in this period?

683

The labor aristocracy as a whole was under constant long-term pressure. Gradually, factory methods were being extended to more crafts, and many skilled artisans were being replaced by lower-paid semiskilled factory workers. At the same time, the labor aristocracy was consistently being enlarged by new kinds of skilled workers such as shipbuilders and railway locomotive engineers. Thus the labor elite remained in a state of flux as individuals and whole crafts moved in and out of it.

To maintain this precarious standing, the upper working class adopted distinctive values and straitlaced, almost puritanical behavior. Like the middle classes, the labor aristocracy was strongly committed to the family and to economic improvement. Despite these similarities, skilled workers viewed themselves not as aspirants to the middle class but as the pacesetters and natural leaders of all the working classes. Well aware of the degradation not so far below them, they practiced self-discipline and stern morality.

Below the labor aristocracy stood an enormously complex sector of the labor world, comprising both semiskilled and unskilled urban workers. Workers in the established crafts—carpenters, bricklayers, pipe fitters—stood near the top of the semiskilled hierarchy. A large number of the semiskilled were factory workers, including substantial numbers of unmarried women, who earned highly variable but relatively good wages and whose relative importance in the labor force was increasing.

Below the semiskilled workers was a larger group of unskilled workers that included day laborers such as longshoremen, wagon-driving teamsters, teenagers, and every kind of

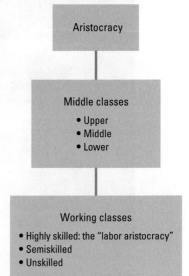

**Figure 23.2**
**The Urban Social Hierarchy**

Aristocracy

Middle classes
- Upper
- Middle
- Lower

Working classes
- Highly skilled: the "labor aristocracy"
- Semiskilled
- Unskilled

**The Labor Aristocracy** This group of British foremen is attending the International Exhibition in Paris in 1862. Their "Sunday best" includes the silk top hats and long morning coats of the propertied classes, but they definitely remain workers, the proud leaders of laboring people. (© The Board of Trustees of the Victoria & Albert Museum)

"helper." Many of these people had real skills and performed valuable services, but they were unorganized and divided, united only by the common fate of meager earnings.

One of the largest components of the unskilled group was domestic servants, whose numbers grew steadily in the nineteenth century. In Great Britain, for example, one out of every seven employed persons in 1911 was a domestic servant. The great majority were women. Throughout Europe and America, a great many female domestics in the cities were recent migrants from rural areas. As in earlier times, domestic service was hard work at low pay with limited personal independence and the danger of sexual exploitation.

Nonetheless, domestic service had real attractions for "rough country girls." Marriage prospects were better, or at least more varied, in the city. And though wages were low, they were higher and more regular than in agricultural work. Finally, young girls and other migrants were drawn to the city by its variety and excitement.

Many young domestics from the countryside made successful transitions to working-class wife and mother. Yet with an unskilled or unemployed husband, a growing family, and limited household income, many working-class wives had to join the broad ranks of working women in the **sweated industries**. These industries flowered after 1850 and resembled the old putting-out and cottage industries of earlier times (see Chapter 18). The women normally worked at home and were paid by the piece, not by the hour. The majority made clothing, especially after the advent of the sewing machine. An army of poor women, usually working at home, accounted for much of the inexpensive ready-made clothes displayed on department store racks and in tiny shops.

**sweated industries** Poorly paid handicraft production, often by married women paid by the piece and working at home.

## Working-Class Leisure and Religion

Despite the difficulties of their lives, the urban working classes still sought fun and recreation. Across the face of Europe, drinking remained the favorite leisure-time activity of working people. Drinking could be a deadly serious business. One English slum dweller recalled that "drunkenness was by far the commonest cause of dispute and misery in working class homes. On account of it one saw many a decent family drift down through poverty into total want."[4]

Generally, however, heavy problem drinking declined in the late nineteenth century as it became less socially acceptable. This decline reflected in part the moral leadership of the upper working class. At the same time, drinking became more publicly acceptable. Cafés and pubs became increasingly bright, friendly places. Working-class political activities were also concentrated in taverns and pubs. Moreover, social drinking in public places by married couples and sweethearts became an accepted and widespread practice for the first time.

The two other leisure-time passions of working-class culture were sports and music halls. Racing and soccer were the most popular sports. Music halls and vaudeville theaters, the working-class counterparts of middle-class opera and classical theater, were enormously popular throughout Europe. Music hall audiences were thoroughly mixed, which may account for the fact that drunkenness, premarital sex, marital difficulties, and mothers-in-law were all favorite themes of broad jokes and bittersweet songs.

In more serious moments, religion continued to provide working people with solace and meaning. The eighteenth-century vitality of popular religion in Catholic countries and the Protestant rejuvenation exemplified by German Pietism and English Methodism (see Chapter 19) carried over into the nineteenth century. By the last few decades of the nineteenth century, however, a considerable decline in both church attendance and church donations was occurring in most European countries. And it seems clear that this decline was greater for the urban working classes than for their rural counterparts or for the middle classes.

Why did working-class church attendance decline? Part of the reason was that the construction of churches failed to keep up with the rapid growth of urban population,

CHAPTER LOCATOR | How did urban life change in the nineteenth century? | **What were the characteristics of urban industrial society?** | How did urbanization affect family life? | How and why did intellectual life change in this period?

685

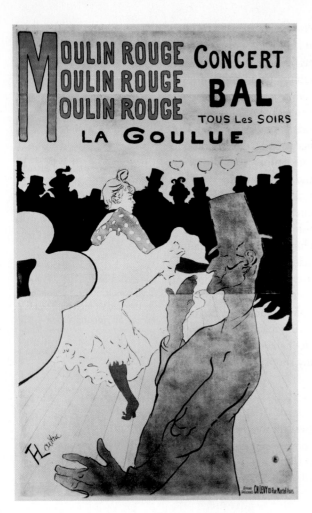

**Big City Nightlife** The most famous dance hall and cabaret in Paris was the Moulin Rouge. There La Goulue ("the Glutton"), who is featured on this poster, performed her provocative version of the cancan and reigned as the queen of Parisian sensuality. This is one of many colorful posters done by Henri de Toulouse-Lautrec (1864–1901), who combined stupendous creativity and dedicated debauchery in his short life. (Bridgeman-Giraudon/Art Resource, NY)

especially in new working-class neighborhoods. Equally important, however, was the fact that throughout the nineteenth century both Catholic and Protestant churches were normally seen as they saw themselves—as conservative institutions defending social order and custom. Therefore, as the European working classes became more politically conscious, they tended to see the established "territorial church" as allied with their political opponents. Especially the men of the urban working classes developed vaguely antichurch attitudes, even though they remained neutral or positive toward religion.

The pattern was different in the United States. There, most churches also preached social conservatism in the nineteenth century. But because church and state had always been separate and because there was always a host of competing denominations and even different religions, working people identified churches much less with the political and social status quo. Instead, individual churches in the United States were often closely identified with an ethnic group rather than with a social class, and churches thrived, in part, as a means of asserting ethnic identity.

## ▼ How did urbanization affect family life?

Urban life wrought many fundamental changes in the family. By the second half of the nineteenth century the family had stabilized considerably after the disruption of the late eighteenth and early nineteenth centuries. The home became more important for both men and women. The role of women and attitudes toward children underwent substantial change, and adolescence emerged as a distinct stage of life.

### Premarital Sex and Marriage

By 1850 the preindustrial pattern of lengthy courtship and marriage for financial gain was pretty well dead among the working classes, replaced by the ideal of romantic love. Couples were ever more likely to come from different, even distant, towns and to be more nearly the same age, further indicating that romantic sentiment was replacing tradition and financial considerations.

Economic considerations in marriage began to decline among the middle classes after 1850, but by no means did they disappear entirely. In France dowries and elaborate legal marriage contracts were common practice among the middle classes in the later nineteenth century, and marriage remained for many families one of life's most crucial financial transactions. A preoccupation with money led many middle-class men in France and elsewhere to marry late, after they had been established economically, and to choose women considerably younger than themselves.

A young woman of the middle class found her romantic life carefully supervised by her well-meaning mother, who schemed for a proper marriage and guarded her daughter's virginity like the family's credit. (See "Listening to the Past: Stephan Zweig on Middle-Class Youth and Sexuality," page 688.) After marriage, middle-class morality sternly demanded fidelity.

Middle-class boys were watched, too, but not as vigilantly. By the time they reached late adolescence, they had usually attained considerable sexual experience with maids or prostitutes. In the early nineteenth century, sexual experimentation before marriage also triumphed for society as a whole, as did illegitimacy. The illegitimacy explosion that had begun in 1750 continued through the 1840s (see Chapter 19). The rising rate of illegitimacy was reversed in the second half of the nineteenth century.

Some observers have argued that this shift reflected the growth of puritanism and a lessening of sexual permissiveness among the unmarried. This explanation, however, is unconvincing because the percentage of working-class brides who were pregnant continued to be high and showed little or no tendency to decline after 1850. Moreover, unmarried people almost certainly used the affordable condoms and diaphragms the industrial age had made available to prevent pregnancy, at least in predominately Protestant countries.

Thus unmarried young people were probably engaging in just as much sexual activity as their parents and grandparents who had created the illegitimacy explosion of 1750 to 1850. But in the later nineteenth century, pregnancy for a young single woman led increasingly to marriage and the establishment of a two-parent household. This important development reflected the growing respectability of the working classes as well as their gradual economic improvement. Skipping out was less acceptable, and marriage was less of an economic challenge. The urban working-class couple of the late nineteenth century thus became more stable, and that stability strengthened the family as an institution.

## Prostitution

Men of all classes visited prostitutes, but the middle and upper classes supplied much of the motivating cash. Thus, though many middle-class men abided by the publicly professed code of stern puritanical morality, others indulged their appetites for prostitutes and sexual promiscuity.

*My Secret Life*, the anonymous eleven-volume autobiography of an English sexual adventurer from the servant-keeping classes, provides a remarkable picture of such a man.[5] Beginning at an early age with a maid, the author becomes progressively obsessed with sex and devotes his life to living his sexual fantasies. In almost every one of his innumerable encounters all across Europe, this man of wealth simply buys his pleasure.

Obviously atypical in its excesses, *My Secret Life* does reveal the dark side of sex and class in urban society. Frequently thinking of their wives largely in terms of money, family, and social position, the men of the comfortable classes often purchased sex and even affection from poor girls both before and after marriage. For many poor young women, prostitution, like domestic service, was a stage of life and not a permanent employment. Having done it for a while in their twenties, they went on to marry (or live with) men of their own class and establish homes and families.

## Kinship Ties

Within working-class homes, ties to relatives after marriage—kinship ties—were generally very strong. Most newlyweds tried to live near their parents, though not in the same house. People turned to their families for help in coping with sickness, unemployment,

CHAPTER LOCATOR | How did urban life change in the nineteenth century? | What were the characteristics of urban industrial society? | How did urbanization affect family life? | How and why did intellectual life change in this period?

687

# LISTENING TO THE PAST

## Stephan Zweig on Middle-Class Youth and Sexuality

*Growing up in Vienna in a prosperous Jewish family, Stephan Zweig (zwighg) (1881–1942) became an influential voice calling for humanitarian values and international culture in early-twentieth-century Europe. Passionately opposed to the First World War, Zweig wrote poetry, plays, and novels. But he was most famous for many outstanding biographies that featured shrewd psychological portraits of intriguing historical figures such as Magellan and Marie Antoinette. After Hitler came to power in Germany in 1933, Zweig lived in exile until his death in 1942.*

*Zweig's last work was* The World of Yesterday *(1943), one of the truly fascinating autobiographies of the twentieth century. In the following passage taken from that work, Zweig recalls and also interprets the romantic experiences and the sexual separation of middle-class youth before the First World War.*

❝ During the eight years of our higher schooling [beyond grade school], something had occurred which was of great importance to each one of us: we ten-year-olds had grown into virile young men of sixteen, seventeen, and eighteen, and Nature began to assert its rights. . . . It did not take us long to discover that those authorities in whom we had previously confided—school, family, and public morals—manifested an astonishing insincerity in this matter of sex. But what is more, they also demanded secrecy and reserve from us in this connection. . . .

This "social morality," which on the one hand privately presupposed the existence of sexuality and its natural course, but on the other would not recognize it openly at any price, was doubly deceitful. While it winked one eye at a young man and even encouraged him with the other "to sow his wild oats," as the kindly language of the home put it, in the case of a woman it studiously shut both eyes and acted as if it were blind. That a man could experience desires, and was permitted to experience them, was silently admitted by custom. But to admit frankly that a woman could be subject to similar desires, or that creation for its eternal purposes also required a female polarity, would have transgressed the conception of the "sanctity of womanhood." In the pre-Freudian era, therefore, the axiom was agreed upon that a female person could have no physical desires as long as they had not been awakened by man, and that,

obviously, was officially permitted only in marriage. But even in those moral times, in Vienna in particular, the air was full of dangerous erotic infection, and a girl of good family had to live in a completely sterilized atmosphere, from the day of her birth until the day when she left the altar on her husband's arm. In order to protect young girls, they were not left alone for a single moment. . . . Every book which they read was inspected, and above all else, young girls were constantly kept busy to divert their attention from any possible dangerous thoughts. They had to practise the piano, learn singing and drawing, foreign languages, and the history of literature and art. They were educated and overeducated. But while the aim was to make them as educated and as socially correct as possible, at the same time society anxiously took great pains that they should remain innocent of all natural things to a degree unthinkable today. A young girl of good family was not allowed to have any idea of how the male body was formed, or to know how children came into the world, for the angel was to enter into matrimony not only physically untouched, but completely "pure" spiritually as well. "Good breeding," for a young girl of that time, was identical with ignorance of life; and this ignorance ofttimes lasted for the rest of their lives. . . .

What possibilities actually existed for a young man of the middle-class world? In all the others, in the so-called lower classes, the problem was no problem at all. . . . In most of our Alpine villages the number of natural children greatly exceeded the legitimate ones. Among the proletariat, the worker, before he could get married, lived with another worker in free love. . . . It was only in our middle-class society that such a remedy as an early marriage was scorned. . . . And so there was an artificial interval of six, eight, or ten years between actual manhood and manhood as society accepted it; and in this interval the young man had to take care of his own "affairs" or adventures.

Those days did not give him too many opportunities. Only a very few particularly rich young men could afford the luxury of keeping a mistress, that is, taking an apartment and paying her expenses. And only a

death, and old age. Although governments typically provided more welfare services by 1900, the average couple and its children inevitably faced crises. Relatives responded hastily to such situations, knowing full well that their own time of need and repayment would undoubtedly come.

Relatives were also valuable at less tragic moments. If a couple was poor, an aged relation often moved in to cook and mind the children so that the wife could work outside the home. Members of a large family group often lived in the same neighborhood, and they frequently shared Sunday dinners, outgrown clothing, and useful information.

An elegant ball for upper-class youth, with debutantes, junior officers, and vigilant chaperons watching in the background. (State Russian Museum, St. Petersburg, Russia/ The Bridgeman Art Library)

clubs, the cabarets, the dance parlours with their dancers and singers, and the bars with their "come-on" girls. At that time female wares were offered for sale at every hour and at every price. . . . And this was the same city, the same society, the same morality, that was indignant when young girls rode bicycles, and declared it a disgrace to the dignity of science when Freud in his calm, clear, and penetrating manner established truths that they did not wish to be true. The same world that so pathetically defended the purity of womanhood allowed this cruel sale of women, organized it, and even profited thereby.

We should not permit ourselves to be misled by sentimental novels or stories of that epoch. It was a bad time for youth. The young girls were hermetically locked up under the control of the family, hindered in their free bodily as well as intellectual development. The young men were forced to secrecy and reticence by a morality which fundamentally no one believed or obeyed. Unhampered, honest relationships — in other words, all that could have made youth happy and joyous according to the laws of Nature — were permitted only to the very few. 🙶

**Source:** Excerpts from pp. 67, 76–78, 81–83, 88 in *The World of Yesterday* by Stephan Zweig, translated by Helmut Ripperger. Copyright © 1943 by the Viking Press, Inc. Used with permission of Viking Penguin, a division of Penguin Group (USA), Inc. © Williams Verlag AG, Zurich (Switzerland). Reprinted by permission.

### QUESTIONS FOR ANALYSIS

1. According to Zweig, how did the sex lives of young middle-class women and young middle-class men differ? What accounted for these differences?
2. What were the differences between the sex lives of the middle class and those of the "so-called lower classes"? What was Zweig's opinion of these differences?
3. Zweig ends this passage with a value judgment: "It was a bad time for youth." Do you agree or disagree? Why?

very few fortunate young men achieved the literary ideal of love of the times — the only one which it was permitted to describe in novels — an affair with a married woman. The others helped themselves for the most part with shopgirls and waitresses, and this offered little inner satisfaction. . . . But, generally speaking, prostitution was still the foundation of the erotic life outside of marriage; in a certain sense it constituted a dark underground vault over which rose the gorgeous structure of middle-class society with its faultless, radiant façade.

The present generation has hardly any idea of the gigantic extent of prostitution in Europe before the [First] World War. Whereas today it is as rare to meet a prostitute on the streets of a big city as it is to meet a wagon in the road, then the sidewalks were so sprinkled with women for sale that it was more difficult to avoid than to find them. To this was added the countless number of "closed houses," the night

## Gender Roles and Early Feminism

Industrialization and the growth of modern cities brought great changes to the lives of European women of all classes. These changes were particularly consequential for married women, and most women did marry in the nineteenth century.

After 1850 the work of most wives became increasingly distinct and separate from that of their husbands. Husbands became wage earners in factories and offices, while wives tended to stay home and manage households and care for children. The preindustrial

CHAPTER LOCATOR | How did urban life change in the nineteenth century? | What were the characteristics of urban industrial society? | **How did urbanization affect family life?** | How and why did intellectual life change in this period?

**689**

**The Well-Managed Home** This painting humanizes the concept of separate spheres and suggests how many homemakers with modest resources made their dwellings happy and appealing with hard work and housekeeping skills. With her clean laundry folded and fresh vegetables carried home beside her market baskets, this woman may soon be thinking of preparing dinner for her returning breadwinner. (V&A Images, London/Art Resource, NY)

pattern among both peasants and cottage workers, in which husbands and wives worked together and divided up household duties and child rearing, declined. Thus many historians have stressed that the societal ideal in nineteenth-century Europe became a strict division of labor by gender and rigidly constructed separate spheres: the wife as mother and homemaker, the husband as wage earner and breadwinner.

This rigid gender division of labor meant that married women faced great obstacles when they needed—or wanted—to work outside the home. Husbands were unsympathetic or hostile. Well-paying jobs were off-limits to women, and a woman's wage was almost always less than a man's, even for the same work.

Moreover, married women were subordinated to their husbands by law and lacked many basic legal rights. In England a wife had no legal identity and hence no right to own property in her own name. Even the wages she might earn belonged to her husband. In France the Napoleonic Code (see Chapter 20) also enshrined the principle of female subordination and gave the wife few legal rights regarding property, divorce, and custody of the children.

With all women facing discrimination in education and employment and with middle-class women suffering especially from a lack of legal rights, there is little wonder that some women rebelled and began the long-continuing fight for equality of the sexes and the rights of women. Their struggle proceeded on two main fronts. First, following in the steps of women such as Mary Wollstonecraft (see Chapter 20), organizations founded by middle-class feminists campaigned for equal legal rights for women as well as access to higher education and professional employment.

In the late nineteenth century, these organizations scored some significant victories, such as the 1882 law giving English married women full property rights. More women gradually found professional and white-collar employment, especially after about 1880. But progress was slow and hard won. Determined pioneers had to fight with tremendous fortitude to break through sexist barriers to advanced education and subsequent professional employment. (See "Individuals in Society: Franziska Tiburtius," page 692.) In the years before 1914, middle-class feminists increasingly focused their attention on political action and fought for the right to vote for women.

Women inspired by utopian and especially Marxian socialism (see Chapter 22) blazed a second path. Often scorning the programs of middle-class feminists, socialist women leaders argued that the liberation of working-class women would come only with the liberation of the entire working class through revolution. In the meantime, they championed the cause of working women and won some practical improvements, especially in Germany, where the socialist movement was most effectively organized. In a general way, these different approaches to women's issues reflected the diversity of classes in urban society.

## The Importance of Homemaking

In recent years some scholars have been rethinking gender roles within the long-term development of consumer behavior and household economies. First, they identified an eighteenth-century "industrious revolution" that saw many wives turning from work for household consumption to working for cash income to buy finished manufactured goods (see Chapter 19). In the industrial era, these scholars have reinterpreted the gender roles associated with separate spheres as rational consumer behavior. They argue that the "breadwinner-homemaker" household developed from about 1850 onward in order to improve the lives of all family members, especially in the working classes.[6] Thus husbands specialized in earning an adequate cash income—the "family wage" that labor unions demanded—and wives specialized in managing the home.

Although the reinterpretation of late nineteenth-century gender roles in terms of a breadwinner-homemaker partnership is a matter of debate, it fits rather well with some key aspects of family life after 1850. As women's horizons narrowed, and as home and children became the typical wife's main concerns, her control and influence there apparently became increasingly strong throughout Europe. In many families, the husband gave all his earnings to his wife to manage, and he received only a small allowance in return. All the major domestic decisions, from the children's schooling and religious instruction to the selection of new furniture or a new apartment, were hers.

Women ruled at home partly because running the urban household was a complicated, demanding, and valuable task. Working yet another job for wages outside the home had limited appeal for most married women unless the earnings were essential for family survival. Still, many married women in the working classes did make a monetary contribution to family income by taking in a boarder or doing piecework at home in the sweated industries (see page 685).

The woman's guidance of the household went hand in hand with the increased pride and emotional importance of home and family. The home she ran was idealized as a warm shelter in a hard and impersonal urban world. According to one historian, "'Home, sweet home,' first heard in the 1870s, had become 'almost a second national anthem.'"[7] By 1900 home and family were what life was all about for millions of people of all classes.

Married couples also developed stronger emotional ties to each other. Even in the comfortable classes, marriages in the late nineteenth century were based more on sentiment and sexual attraction than they had been earlier in the century. Affection and eroticism

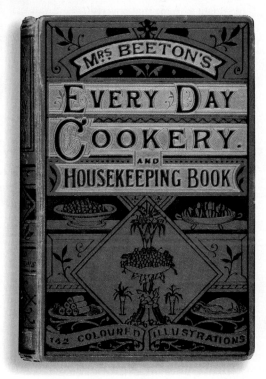

*Mrs. Beeton's Every Day Cookery and Housekeeping Book* The publication of cookbooks and household guides proliferated in the nineteenth century. Mrs. Beeton's bestselling guide offered women housekeeping tips and a wealth of recipes for the homemaker to share with her family. (Graphic Arts Division, Princeton University Library)

CHAPTER LOCATOR | How did urban life change in the nineteenth century? | What were the characteristics of urban industrial society? | How did urbanization affect family life? | How and why did intellectual life change in this period?

691

# INDIVIDUALS IN SOCIETY

## Franziska Tiburtius

**WHY DID A SMALL NUMBER OF WOMEN IN THE** late nineteenth century brave great odds and embark on professional careers? And how did a few of them manage to reach their objectives? The career and personal reflections of Franziska Tiburtius (tigh-bur-TEE-uhs), a pioneer in German medicine, suggest that talent, determination, and economic necessity were critical ingredients.*

Like many women of her time who would study and pursue professional careers, Franziska Tiburtius (1843–1927) was born into a property-owning family of modest means. The youngest of nine children on a small estate in northeastern Germany, the sensitive child wilted under a harsh governess but flowered with a caring teacher and became an excellent student. Graduating at sixteen and needing to support herself, Tiburtius had few opportunities. A young woman from a "proper" background could work as a governess or a teacher without losing her respectability and spoiling her matrimonial prospects, but that was about it. She tried both avenues. Working for six years as a governess in a noble family and no doubt learning that poverty was often one's fate in this genteel profession, she then turned to teaching. Called home from her studies in Britain in 1871 to care for her brother, who had contracted typhus as a field doctor in the Franco-Prussian War, she found her calling. She decided to become a medical doctor.

**Franziska Tiburtius, pioneering woman physician in Berlin.**
(Ullstein Bilderdienst/The Granger Collection, NY)

Supported by her family, Tiburtius's decision was truly audacious. In all Europe, only the University of Zurich in republican Switzerland accepted female students. Moreover, if it became known that she had studied medicine and failed, she would never get a job as a teacher. No parent would entrust a daughter to an "emancipated" radical who had carved up dead bodies! Although the male students at the university sometimes harassed the women with crude pranks, Tiburtius thrived. The revolution of the microscope and the discovery of microorganisms was rocking Zurich, and she was fascinated by her studies. She became close friends with a fellow female medical student from Germany, Emilie Lehmus, with whom she would form a lifelong partnership in medicine. She did her internship with families of cottage workers around Zurich and loved her work.

Graduating at age thirty-three in 1876, Tiburtius went to stay with her brother—the doctor in Berlin. Though well qualified to practice, she ran into pervasive discrimination. She was not even permitted to take the state medical exams and could practice only as an unregulated (and unprofessional) "natural healer." But after persistent fighting with the bureaucrats, she was able to display her diploma and practice as "Franziska Tiburtius, M.D. University of Zurich." She and Lehmus were in business.

Soon the two women realized their dream and opened a clinic, subsidized by a wealthy industrialist, for women factory workers. The clinic filled a great need and was soon treating many patients. A room with beds for extremely sick women was later expanded into a second clinic.

Tiburtius and Lehmus became famous. For fifteen years, they were the only women doctors in all Berlin. An inspiration for a new generation of women, they added the wealthy to their thriving practice. But Tiburtius's clinics always concentrated on the poor, providing them with subsidized and up-to-date treatment. Talented, determined, and working with her partner, Tiburtius experienced fully the joys of personal achievement and useful service. Above all, Tiburtius overcame the tremendous barriers raised up against women seeking higher education and professional careers, and this provided an inspiring model for those who dared to follow.

## QUESTIONS FOR ANALYSIS

1. Analyze Franziska Tiburtius's life. What lessons do you draw from it? How do you account for her bold action and success?
2. In what ways was Tiburtius's career related to improvements in health in urban society and to the expansion of the professions?

*This portrait draws on Conradine Lück, *Frauen: Neun Lebensschicksale* (Reutlingen: Ensslin & Laiblin, n.d.), pp. 153–185.

became more central to the couple after marriage. Gustave Droz (droh), whose bestselling *Mr., Mrs., and Baby* went through 121 editions between 1866 and 1884, saw love within marriage as the key to human happiness.

Many French marriage manuals of the late 1800s stressed that women had legitimate sexual needs, such as the "right to orgasm." Perhaps the French were a bit more enlightened in these matters than other nationalities. But the rise of public socializing by couples in cafés and music halls as well as franker affection within the family suggests a more erotic, pleasurable intimate life for women throughout Western society. This, too, helped make the woman's role as mother and homemaker acceptable and even satisfying.

## Child Rearing

Another striking sign of deepening emotional ties within the family was the growing love and concern that mothers gave their tiny infants. Because so many babies in preindustrial Western society died so early in life, mothers of that era often avoided making strong emotional commitments to newborns in order to shield themselves from recurrent heartbreak. Early emotional bonding and a willingness to make real sacrifices for the welfare of the infant were beginning to spread among the comfortable classes by the end of the eighteenth century, but the ordinary mother of modest means adopted new attitudes only as the nineteenth century progressed.

Mothers increasingly breast-fed their infants, for example, rather than paying wet nurses to do so. Breast-feeding involved sacrifice—a temporary loss of freedom, if nothing else. Yet in an age when there was no good alternative to mother's milk, it saved lives. This surge of maternal feeling also gave rise to a wave of specialized books on child rearing and infant hygiene. Another sign, from France, of increased affection is that fewer illegitimate babies were abandoned as foundlings after about 1850. Moreover, the practice of swaddling disappeared completely. Instead, ordinary mothers allowed their babies freedom of movement and delighted in their spontaneity.

The loving care lavished on infants was matched by greater concern for older children and adolescents. European women began to limit the number of children they bore in order to care adequately for those they had. It was evident by the end of the nineteenth century that the birthrate was declining across Europe (Figure 23.3), and it continued to do so until after World War II. The Englishwoman who married in the 1860s, for example, had an average of about six children; her daughter marrying in the 1890s had only four; and her granddaughter marrying in the 1920s had only two or possibly three.

The most important reason for this revolutionary reduction in family size, in which the comfortable and well-educated classes took the lead, was parents' desires to improve their economic and social position and that of their children. Children were no longer an economic asset in the later nineteenth century. By having fewer youngsters, parents could give those they had a greater share of their resources. A young German skilled worker with only one child spoke for many in his class when he said, "We want to get ahead, and our daughter should have things better than my wife and sisters did."[8]

Thus the growing tendency of couples in the late nineteenth century to use a variety of contraceptive methods certainly reflected increased concern for children. Indeed, many parents,

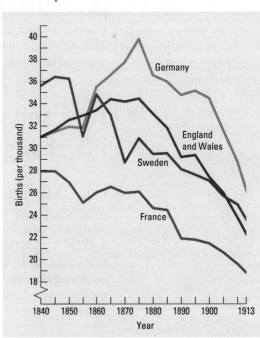

**Figure 23.3 The Decline of Birthrates in England and Wales, France, Germany, and Sweden, 1840–1913** Women had fewer babies for a variety of reasons, including the fact that their children were increasingly less likely to die before reaching adulthood. How does this compare with Figure 23.1 on page 677?

CHAPTER LOCATOR | How did urban life change in the nineteenth century? | What were the characteristics of urban industrial society? | **How did urbanization affect family life?** | How and why did intellectual life change in this period?

693

especially in the middle classes, probably became too concerned about their children, unwittingly subjecting them to an emotional pressure cooker of almost unbearable intensity. The result was that many children, especially adolescents, came to feel trapped and in need of greater independence.

One area of excessive parental concern was the sexual behavior of their children. Masturbation was viewed with horror, for it represented an act of independence and even defiance. Diet, clothing, games, and sleeping were carefully regulated. Girls were discouraged from riding horses and bicycling because rhythmic friction simulated masturbation. Boys were dressed in trousers with shallow and widely separated pockets.

Attempts to repress the child's sexuality were a source of unhealthy tension, often made worse by the rigid division of gender roles within the family. It was widely believed that mother and child loved each other easily but that relations between father and child were necessarily difficult. The father was a stranger; his world of business was far removed from the maternal world of spontaneous affection. Moreover, the father was demanding, often expecting the child to succeed where he himself had failed and making his love conditional on achievement.

Sigmund Freud (1856–1939), the Viennese founder of psychoanalysis, formulated the most striking analysis of the explosive dynamics of the family, particularly the middle-class family in the late nineteenth century. Freud began his career treating mentally ill patients. He noted that the hysteria of his patients appeared to originate in bitter early childhood experiences wherein the child had been obliged to repress strong feelings. When these painful experiences were recalled and reproduced under hypnosis or through the patient's free association of ideas, the patient could be brought to understand the basis of his or her unhappiness and eventually deal with it.

Freud postulated that much of human behavior is motivated by unconscious emotional needs whose nature and origins are kept from conscious awareness by various mental devices he called defense mechanisms. Freud concluded that much unconscious psychological energy is sexual energy, which is repressed and precariously controlled by rational thinking and moral rules. If Freud exaggerated the sexual and familial roots of adult behavior, that exaggeration was itself a reflection of the tremendous emotional intensity of family life in the late nineteenth century.

## ▼ How and why did intellectual life change in this period?

Major changes in Western science and thought accompanied the emergence of urban society. Several aspects of these complex intellectual developments stand out as especially significant. First, scientific knowledge in many areas expanded rapidly. Breakthroughs in chemistry, physics, and electricity profoundly influenced the Western worldview and spurred the creation of new products and whole industries. The natural and social sciences were also established as highly respected fields of study. In addition, between about the 1840s and the 1890s, European literature underwent a shift from romanticism to realism.

### The Triumph of Science in Industry

The intellectual achievements of the scientific revolution (see Chapter 17) had resulted in few practical benefits, and theoretical knowledge had also played a relatively small role in the Industrial Revolution in England (see Chapter 21). But breakthroughs in industrial technology in the late eighteenth century enormously stimulated basic scientific inquiry as researchers sought to explain theoretically how such things as steam engines and blast furnaces actually worked. The result was an explosive growth of fundamental scientific discoveries from the 1830s onward. And in contrast to earlier periods, these theoretical discoveries were increasingly transformed into material improvements for the general population.

A perfect example of the translation of better scientific knowledge into practical human benefits was the work of Louis Pasteur and his followers in biology and the medical sciences (see page 677). Another was the development of the branch of physics known as thermodynamics. Building on Isaac Newton's laws of mechanics and on studies of steam engines, thermodynamics investigated the relationship between heat and mechanical energy. By midcentury, physicists had formulated the fundamental laws of thermodynamics, which were then applied to mechanical engineering, chemical processes, and many other fields.

Chemistry and electricity were two other fields characterized by extremely rapid scientific progress and the practical application of discoveries. Chemists devised ways of measuring the atomic weight of different elements, and in 1869 the Russian chemist Dmitri Mendeleev (men-duh-LAY-uhf) (1834–1907) codified the rules of chemistry in the periodic law and the periodic table. Chemistry was subdivided into many specialized branches, such as organic chemistry—the study of the compounds of carbon. Applying theoretical insights gleaned from this new field, researchers in large German chemical companies discovered ways of transforming the coal tar that accumulated in coke ovens

**thermodynamics** A branch of physics built on Newton's laws of mechanics that investigated the relationship between heat and mechanical energy.

**Madrid in 1900** This wistful painting of a Spanish square on a rainy day, by Enrique Martinez Cubells y Ruiz (1874–1917), includes a revealing commentary on how scientific discoveries transformed urban life. Coachmen wait atop their expensive hackney cabs for a wealthy clientele, while modern electric streetcars that carry the masses converge on the square from all directions. In this way the development of electricity brought improved urban transportation and enabled the city to expand to the suburbs. (Museo Municipal, Madrid/The Bridgeman Art Library)

CHAPTER LOCATOR | How did urban life change in the nineteenth century? | What were the characteristics of urban industrial society? | How did urbanization affect family life? | How and why did intellectual life change in this period?

695

into synthetic dyes. German production of synthetic dyes soared, and by 1900 German chemical companies controlled 90 percent of world production.

Electricity was totally transformed by a century of tremendous technological advancement. It became a commercial form of energy, first used in communications (the telegraph and underwater cables), then in electro-chemistry (refining aluminum, for example), and finally in central power generation (for lighting, transportation, and industrial motors).

The successful application of scientific research in the fast-growing electrical and organic chemical industries between 1880 and 1913 provided a model for other industries. Systematic "R & D"—research and development—was born in the late nineteenth century. Above all, the burst of industrial creativity and technological innovation, which is often called the second industrial revolution, promoted strong economic growth in the later nineteenth century. This ongoing economic development was a leading force driving the urban improvement and the rising standard of living considered in this chapter.

The triumph of science and technology had at least three more significant consequences. First, everyday experience and innumerable articles in newspapers and magazines impressed the importance of science on the popular mind. Second, as science became more prominent in popular thinking, the philosophical implications of science formulated in the Enlightenment spread to broad sections of the population. Natural processes appeared to be determined by rigid laws, leaving little room for either divine intervention or human will. Yet scientific and technical advances had also fed the Enlightenment's optimistic faith in human progress. Third, the methods of science acquired unrivaled prestige after 1850. For many, the union of careful experiment and abstract theory was the only reliable route to truth and objective reality.

**second industrial revolution** The burst of industrial creativity and technological innovation that promoted strong economic growth toward the end of the nineteenth century.

## Darwin and Natural Selection

Scientific research also progressed rapidly outside of the world of industry and technology, sometimes putting forth challenges to traditional beliefs. In geology, for example, Charles Lyell (LIGH-uhl) (1797–1875) discredited the view that the earth's surface had been formed by short-lived cataclysms, such as biblical floods and earthquakes. Instead, according to Lyell's principle of uniformitarianism, the same geological processes that are at work today slowly formed the earth's surface over an immensely long time.

Similarly, the evolutionary view of biological development found its fullest and most profound expression in the work of Charles Darwin (1809–1882). As the official naturalist on a five-year scientific cruise to Latin America and the South Pacific beginning in 1831, Darwin collected specimens of the different animal species he encountered on the voyage. Back in England, convinced by fossil evidence and by his friend Lyell that the earth and life on it were immensely ancient, Darwin came to doubt the general belief in a special divine creation of each species of animal. Instead,

**Satirizing Darwin's Ideas** The heated controversies over Darwin's theory of evolution also spawned innumerable jokes and cartoons. This cartoon depicts a bearded Charles Darwin and the French philosopher and atheistic materialist Emile Littré performing as monkeys in a circus as they supposedly break through ignorance and superstition. (Musée de la Ville de Paris, Musée Carnavalet/Archives Charmet/The Bridgeman Art Library)

he concluded, all life had gradually evolved from a common ancestral origin in an unending "struggle for survival."

Darwin's great originality lay in suggesting precisely how biological evolution might have occurred. His theory is summarized in the title of his work *On the Origin of Species by the Means of Natural Selection* (1859). Darwin argued that chance differences among the members of a given species help some survive while others die. Thus the variations that prove useful in the struggle for survival are selected naturally, and they gradually spread to the entire species through reproduction. Darwin did not explain why such variations occurred in the first place, and not until the early twentieth century did the study of genetics and the concept of mutation provide some answers.

Darwin's theory had a powerful and many-sided influence on European thought and the European middle classes. He was hailed as the great scientist par excellence, the "Newton of biology," and his findings had a significant impact on the young discipline of social science.

## Social Science

From the 1830s onward, many thinkers tried to apply the objective methods of science to the study of society. Using the critical thinking methods of the eighteenth-century philosophes (see Chapter 17), the new "social scientists" studied numerical data that governments had begun to collect on everything from children to crime and from population to prostitution. Social scientists developed new statistical methods to analyze these facts "scientifically" and supposedly to test their theories. As a result, the systems of the leading nineteenth-century social scientists were typically more unified, all-encompassing, and dogmatic than those of the philosophes. Karl Marx was a prime example (see Chapter 22).

Another extremely influential system builder was French philosopher Auguste Comte (kont) (1798–1857). In his six-volume *System of Positive Philosophy* (1830–1842), Comte postulated that all intellectual activity progresses through predictable stages:

> *The great fundamental law . . . is this: — that each of our leading conceptions — each branch of our knowledge — passes successively through three different theoretical conditions: the Theological, or fictitious; the Metaphysical, or abstract; and the Scientific, or positive. . . . The first is the necessary point of departure of human understanding, and the third is the fixed and definitive state. The second is merely a transition.*[9]

By way of example, Comte noted that the prevailing explanation of cosmic patterns had shifted, as knowledge of astronomy developed, from the will of God (the theological) to the will of an orderly nature (the metaphysical) to the rule of unchanging laws (the scientific). Comte believed that by applying the scientific method, also called the positivist method, his new discipline of sociology would soon discover the eternal laws of human relations. This achievement would in turn enable expert social scientists to impose a disciplined harmony and well-being on less enlightened citizens.

Comte's stages of knowledge exemplify the nineteenth-century fascination with the idea of evolution and dynamic development so prominent in Darwin's theory of natural selection. Thinkers in many fields, such as the romantic historians and "scientific" Marxists, shared and applied this basic concept. Reinforced by Darwin's findings, the teachings of secularists such as Comte and Marx scornfully dismissed religious belief in favor of agnostic or atheistic materialism.

Many thinkers went a step further and applied Darwin's theory of biological evolution to human affairs. English philosopher Herbert Spencer (1820–1903) saw the human race as driven forward to ever-greater specialization and progress by an economic struggle that determined the "survival of the fittest." The poor were the ill-fated weak; the prosperous

**evolution** The idea, applied by thinkers in many fields, that stresses gradual change and continuous adjustment.

CHAPTER LOCATOR | How did urban life change in the nineteenth century? | What were the characteristics of urban industrial society? | How did urbanization affect family life? | **How and why did intellectual life change in this period?**

697

**Social Darwinists** A group of thinkers who applied the theory of biological evolution to human affairs and saw the human race as driven by an unending economic struggle that would determine the survival of the fittest.

**realism** A literary movement that stressed the depiction of life as it actually was.

were the chosen strong. Not surprisingly, Spencer and other Social Darwinists were especially popular with the upper middle class.

## Realism in Literature

In literature, the key themes of realism emerged in the 1840s and continued to dominate Western culture and style until the 1890s. Realist writers believed that literature should depict life exactly as it was. Forsaking poetry for prose and the personal, emotional viewpoint of the romantics for strict, scientific objectivity, the realists simply observed and recorded.

The major realist writers focused on creating fiction based on contemporary everyday life. Emphatically rejecting the romantic search for the exotic and the sublime, they energetically pursued the typical and the commonplace. The realists put a microscope to many unexplored and taboo subjects—sex, strikes, violence, alcoholism—and hastened to report that slums and factories teemed with savage behavior. Many shocked middle-class critics denounced realism as ugly sensationalism wrapped provocatively in pseudoscientific declarations and crude language.

Unlike the romantics, who had gloried in individual freedom and an unlimited universe, realists were strict determinists. Human beings, like atoms, were components of the physical world, and all human actions were caused by unalterable natural laws. Heredity and environment determined human behavior; good and evil were merely social conventions.

The realist movement began in France, where romanticism had never been completely dominant, and three of its greatest practitioners—Balzac, Flaubert, and Zola—were French. Honoré de Balzac (1799–1850) created a vastly ambitious panorama of postrevolutionary French life. Known collectively as *The Human Comedy*, this series of nearly one hundred books vividly portrays more than two thousand characters from virtually all sectors of French society.

*Madame Bovary* (1857), the masterpiece of Gustave Flaubert (floh-BEHR) (1821–1880), is far narrower in scope than Balzac's work, but unparalleled in its depth and accuracy of psychological insight. Flaubert's novel tells the ordinary, even banal, story of a frustrated middle-class housewife who has an adulterous love affair and is betrayed by her lover. Without moralizing, Flaubert portrays the provincial middle class as petty, smug, and hypocritical.

Émile Zola (1840–1902) was most famous for his seamy, animalistic view of working-class life. But he also wrote gripping, carefully researched stories featuring the stock exchange, the big department store, and the army, as well as urban slums and bloody coal strikes. Like many later realists, Zola sympathized with socialism, a sympathy evident in his novel *Germinal* (1885).

Realism quickly spread beyond France. In England, Mary Ann Evans (1819–1880), who wrote under the pen name George Eliot, achieved a more deeply felt, less sensational kind of realism. Her great novel *Middlemarch: A Study of Provincial Life* (1871–1872) examines the ways in which people are shaped by their social medium as well as their own inner strivings, conflicts, and moral choices. Thomas Hardy (1840–1928) was more in the Zola tradition. His novels, such as *Tess of the D'Urbervilles*

**Edouard Manet, *Emile Zola*** The young novelist's sensitivity and strength of character permeate this famous portrait by the great French painter Edouard Manet. Focusing on nuances and subtle variations, Manet was at first denounced by the critics, and after Zola lost a newspaper job defending Manet, they became close friends. Manet was strongly influenced by Japanese prints, seen in the background. (Erich Lessing/Art Resource, NY)

(1891) and *The Return of the Native* (1878), depict men and women frustrated and crushed by fate and bad luck.

The greatest Russian realist Count Leo Tolstoy (1828–1910) combined realism in description and character development with an atypical moralizing, which came to dominate his later work. Tolstoy's greatest work is *War and Peace* (1864–1869), a monumental novel set against the historical background of Napoleon's invasion of Russia in 1812. Tolstoy went to great pains to develop his fatalistic theory of history, which regards free will as an illusion and the achievements of even the greatest leaders as only the channeling of historical necessity. Yet Tolstoy's central message is one that most of the people discussed in this chapter would have readily accepted: human love, trust, and everyday family ties are life's enduring values.

Thoroughgoing realism (or "naturalism," as it was often called) arrived late in the United States, most arrestingly in the work of Theodore Dreiser (1871–1945). His first novel, *Sister Carrie* (1900), a story of an ordinary farm girl who does well by going wrong in Chicago, so outraged conventional morality that the publisher withdrew the book. The United States subsequently became a bastion of literary realism in the twentieth century after the movement had faded away in Europe.

## ←LOOKING BACK **LOOKING AHEAD** →

WHEN EUROPEANS IN NORTHWESTERN EUROPE looked back at the economic and social landscape in the early twentieth century, they had good reason to feel that the promise of the Industrial Revolution was being realized. The dark days of urban squalor and brutal working hours had given way after 1850 to a gradual rise in the standard of living for all classes. Scientific discoveries were combining with the applied technology of public health and industrial production to save lives and drive continued economic growth.

Moreover, social and economic advance seemed to be matched by progress in the political sphere. The years following the dramatic failure of the revolutions of 1848 saw the creation of unified nation-states in Italy and Germany, and after 1870 nationalism and the nation-state reigned in Europe. Although the rise of nationalism created tensions among the European countries, these tensions would not explode until 1914 and the outbreak of the First World War. Instead, the most aggressive and destructive aspects of European nationalism found their initial outlet in the final and most powerful surge of Western overseas expansion. Thus Europe, transformed by industrialization and nationalism, rushed after 1875 to seize territory and build new or greatly expanded authoritarian empires in Asia and Africa. ▪

- **For a list of suggested readings for this chapter, visit** *bedfordstmartins.com/mckaywestunderstanding*.

- **For primary sources from this period, see** *Sources of Western Society*, Second Edition.

- **For Web sites, images, and documents related to topics in this chapter, see Make History at** *bedfordstmartins.com/mckaywestunderstanding*.

CHAPTER LOCATOR | How did urban life change in the nineteenth century? | What were the characteristics of urban industrial society? | How did urbanization affect family life? | How and why did intellectual life change in this period?

699

# Chapter 23 Study Guide

Online Study Guide
bedfordstmartins.com/mckaywestunderstanding

## Step 1

**GETTING STARTED** Below are basic terms about this period in the history of Western civilization. Can you identify each term below and explain why it matters? To do this exercise online, go to bedfordstmartins.com/mckaywestunderstanding.

| TERMS | WHO (OR WHAT) AND WHEN | WHY IT MATTERS |
|---|---|---|
| utilitarianism, p. 675 | | |
| germ theory, p. 677 | | |
| labor aristocracy, p. 683 | | |
| sweated industries, p. 685 | | |
| thermodynamics, p. 695 | | |
| second industrial revolution, p. 696 | | |
| evolution, p. 697 | | |
| Social Darwinists, p. 698 | | |
| realism, p. 698 | | |

## Step 2

**MOVING BEYOND THE BASICS** The exercise below requires a more advanced understanding of the chapter material. Examine the increasingly diverse working and middle classes of the second half of the nineteenth century by filling in the chart below with the members and values of the principle groups within the working and middle classes. When you are finished, consider the following questions: What values of the middle class and the labor aristocracy did they have in common? What were the primary areas of conflict between middle-class and working-class culture in the second half of the nineteenth century? To do this exercise online, go to bedfordstmartins.com/mckaywestunderstanding.

| GROUP | MEMBERS | CORE VALUES |
|---|---|---|
| Upper Middle Class | | |
| Middle Middle Class | | |
| Lower Middle Class | | |
| Labor Aristocracy | | |
| Semiskilled Workers | | |
| Unskilled Workers | | |

## THE CITY

- Compare and contrast the eighteenth- and nineteenth-century cities. What role did industrialization play in producing the differences you note?

- How did government officials try to overcome the challenges of the nineteenth-century city? What role did advances in medicine and transportation play in alleviating the problems of the nineteenth-century city? What about new approaches to city planning?

A COURT FOR KING CHOLERA.

## URBAN SOCIETY

- What groups made up the middle class? What values helped define this economically diverse strata of society?

- What explains the increasing diversity of the working classes in nineteenth-century Europe? What were the economic and political implications of this diversity?

## THE FAMILY

- How did the ideal model of family relationships change over the course of the nineteenth century? How would you explain the transformation you describe?

- Compare and contrast the gender division of labor in the eighteenth and nineteenth centuries. Why was the world of work increasingly seen as a "man's world" in the nineteenth century?

## SCIENCE AND THOUGHT

- In what ways did the scientific revolution of the nineteenth century differ from the scientific revolution of the sixteenth and seventeenth centuries? What was the relationship between science and industry in the second half of the nineteenth century?

- How did science influence late-nineteenth-century trends in literature and art? Is it fair to describe science as the dominant intellectual influence in the second half of the nineteenth century?

■ **In Your Own Words** Imagine that you must explain Chapter 23 to someone who hasn't read it. What would be the most important points to include and why?

# 24

# The Age of Nationalism

## 1850–1914

The revolutions of 1848 closed one era and opened another. Urban industrial society began to take a strong hold on the continent and in the young United States, as it already had in Great Britain. Internationally, the repressive peace and diplomatic stability of Metternich's time were replaced by a period of war and rapid change. In thought and culture, exuberant romanticism gave way to hard-headed realism. In the Atlantic economy, the hard years of the 1840s were followed by good times and prosperity throughout most of the 1850s and 1860s. Perhaps most important of all, Western society progressively developed, for better or worse, a new and effective organizing principle capable of coping with the many-sided challenge of the dual revolution and the emerging urban civilization. That principle was nationalism—dedication to an identification with the nation-state.

The triumph of nationalism is an enormously significant historical development that was by no means completely predictable. After all, nationalism had been a powerful force since at least 1789, but it had repeatedly failed to realize its goals, most spectacularly in 1848. Yet by 1914 nationalism had become in one way or another an almost universal faith in Europe and in the United States, a faith that had evolved to appeal not only to predominately middle-class liberals but also to the broad masses of society. ∎

**Life in the Age of Nationalism.** Committed to Italian unity, the people of Venice cheer their uplifted nationalist leader, Daniel Manin, during the unsuccessful revolution of 1848. Scenes like this would be validated in the decades to come as nationalism came to predominate in all levels of society across Europe. (Cameraphoto Arte, Venice/Art Resource, NY)

# Chapter Preview

▶ What kind of state did Napoleon III build in France?

▶ How were Italy and Germany able to unify?

▶ How did the American Civil War change the United States?

▶ Why did Russia and the Ottoman Empire try to modernize?

▶ What general domestic political trends emerged after 1871?

▶ What explains the rise of socialism?

# ▼ What kind of state did Napoleon III build in France?

Early nationalism was generally liberal and idealistic though it was often democratic and radical as well. Yet nationalism can also flourish in dictatorial states, which may be conservative, fascist, or communist, and which may impose social and economic changes from above. Napoleon I's France had already combined national feeling with authoritarian rule. Significantly, it was Napoleon's nephew, Louis Napoleon, who revived and extended this merger.

## France's Second Republic

Although Louis Napoleon Bonaparte had played no part in French politics before 1848, universal male suffrage and widespread popular support gave him three times as many votes as the four other presidential candidates combined in the French presidential election of December 1848. This outcome occurred for several reasons. First, Louis Napoleon had the great name of his uncle. Second, middle-class and peasant property owners feared the socialist challenge of urban workers, and they wanted a tough ruler to provide protection. Third, Louis Napoleon had a positive "program" for France, which had been elaborated in widely circulated pamphlets before the election and which guided him through his long reign.

**Paris in the Second Empire** The flash and glitter of unprecedented prosperity in the Second Empire come alive in this vibrant contemporary painting. Writers and intellectuals chat with elegant women and trade witticisms with financiers and government officials at the Café Tortoni, a favorite rendezvous for fashionable society. Horse-drawn omnibuses with open top decks mingle with cabs and private carriages on the broad new boulevard. (Lauros/Giraudon/The Bridgeman Art Library)

Chapter 24
**The Age of Nationalism**
704    1850–1914

CHAPTER LOCATOR    What kind of state did Napoleon III build in France?

Above all, Louis Napoleon believed that the government should represent the people and that it should try hard to help them economically. But how were these tasks to be done? Parliaments and political parties were not the answer, according to Louis Napoleon. French politicians represented special-interest groups, particularly middle-class ones. The answer was a strong, even authoritarian, national leader, a reformer who would serve all the people, rich and poor. This leader would be linked to each citizen by direct democracy, his sovereignty uncorrupted by politicians and legislative bodies. To the many common people who voted for him, he appeared to be a forward-looking champion of their interests.

Elected to a four-year term, President Louis Napoleon had to share power with a conservative National Assembly, according to the constitution. With some misgivings, he signed a bill to increase the role of the Catholic Church in primary and secondary education, and he approved a law depriving many poor people of the right to vote. He took these conservative measures for two main reasons: he wanted the assembly to vote funds to pay his personal debts, and he wanted to change the constitution so he could run for a second term.

But in 1851, after the Assembly failed to cooperate, Louis Napoleon began to conspire with key army officers. On December 2, 1851, he illegally dismissed the Assembly and seized power in a coup d'état, using the army to crush protests. After restoring universal male suffrage, Louis Napoleon called on the French people, as the first Napoleon had done, to legalize his actions. They did: 92 percent voted to make him president for ten years. A year later, 97 percent in a plebiscite made him hereditary emperor.

## Napoleon III's Second Empire

Louis Napoleon — now proclaimed Emperor Napoleon III — experienced both success and failure between 1852 and 1870. His greatest success was with the economy, particularly in the 1850s. His government encouraged the new investment banks and railroad construction that were at the heart of the Industrial Revolution on the continent (see Chapter 21). The government also fostered general economic expansion through an ambitious program of public works, which included rebuilding Paris (see Chapter 23).

Louis Napoleon hoped that economic progress would reduce social and political tensions. This hope was at least partially realized. Until the mid-1860s there was considerable support from France's most dissatisfied group, the urban workers. Napoleon III's regulation of pawnshops and his support of credit unions and better housing for the working classes were evidence of helpful reform and positive concern in the 1850s. In the 1860s, he granted workers the right to form unions and the right to strike.

At first, political power remained in the hands of the emperor. At the same time, Napoleon III restricted but did not abolish the Assembly. Members were elected by universal male suffrage every six years, and Louis Napoleon and his government took the parliamentary elections very seriously. They tried to entice notable people, even those who had opposed the regime, to stand as government candidates in order to expand the base

## Chapter Chronology

| | |
|---|---|
| 1839–1876 | Western-style reforms in Ottoman Empire |
| 1852–1870 | Reign of Napoleon III in France |
| 1859–1870 | Unification of Italy |
| 1861 | Freeing of Russian serfs |
| 1861–1865 | U.S. Civil War |
| 1866 | Austro-Prussian War |
| 1870–1871 | Franco-Prussian War |
| 1870–1878 | Kulturkampf, Bismarck's attack on the Catholic Church |
| 1873 | Stock market crash spurs renewed anti-Semitism in central and eastern Europe |
| 1880s | Educational reforms in France create more secular public schools |
| 1880s–1890s | Widespread return to protectionism among European states |
| 1883 | First social security laws to help workers in Germany |
| 1890–1900 | Massive industrialization surge in Russia |
| 1905 | Revolution in Russia |
| 1906–1914 | Social reform in Great Britain |
| 1908 | Young Turks in power in Ottoman Empire |

How were Italy and Germany able to unify?

How did the American Civil War change the United States?

Why did Russia and the Ottoman Empire try to modernize?

What general domestic political trends emerged after 1871?

What explains the rise of socialism?

705

of support. Moreover, the government used its officials and appointed mayors to spread the word that the election of the government's candidates was the key to roads, tax rebates, and a thousand other local concerns.

In the 1860s Napoleon III's electoral system gradually disintegrated. Problems in Italy and the rising power of Prussia led to increasing criticism at home from his Catholic and nationalist supporters. With increasing effectiveness, the middle-class liberals who had always wanted a less authoritarian regime continued to denounce his rule.

Louis Napoleon was always sensitive to the public mood. Thus in the 1860s, he responded to critics by progressively liberalizing his empire. He gave the Assembly greater powers and the opposition candidates greater freedom, which they used to good advantage. In 1869 the opposition, consisting of republicans, monarchists, and liberals, polled almost 45 percent of the vote.

The next year, Louis Napoleon again granted France a new constitution, which combined a basically parliamentary regime with a hereditary emperor as chief of state. In a final great plebiscite on the eve of the disastrous war with Prussia, 7.5 million Frenchmen voted in favor of the new constitution, and only 1.5 million opposed it. Napoleon III's attempt to reconcile a strong national state with universal male suffrage was still evolving and was doing so in a democratic direction.

# ▼ How were Italy and Germany able to unify?

Louis Napoleon's authoritarian rule provided the old ruling classes of Europe with a new model in politics. To what extent might the urban middle classes and even portions of the working classes rally to a strong and essentially conservative national state that also promised change? This was one of the great political questions in the 1850s and 1860s. In central Europe, a resounding answer came with the unification of Italy and Germany.

## Italy to 1850

Italy had never been united prior to 1850. A battleground for the Great Powers after 1494, Italy was reorganized in 1815 at the Congress of Vienna. The rich northern provinces of Lombardy and Venetia were taken by Metternich's Austria. Sardinia and Piedmont were under the rule of an Italian monarch, and Tuscany shared north-central Italy with several smaller states. Central Italy and Rome were ruled by the papacy. Naples and Sicily were ruled by a branch of the Bourbons (Map 24.1).

Between 1815 and 1848, the goal of a unified Italian nation captured the imaginations of many Italians. There were three basic approaches. The first was the radical program of Giuseppe Mazzini, who preached a centralized democratic republic based on universal male suffrage and the will of the people. (See "Listening to the Past: Herder and Mazzini on the Development of Nationalism," page 650.) The second was that of Vincenzo Gioberti, a Catholic priest who called for a federation of existing states under the presidency of a progressive pope. The third was the program of those who looked for leadership to the autocratic kingdom of Sardinia-Piedmont, much as many Germans looked to Prussia.

The third alternative was strengthened by the failures of 1848, when Austria smashed Mazzini's republicanism. Sardinia's new monarch, Victor Emmanuel, retained the liberal constitution granted by his father under duress in March 1848. To some of the Italian middle classes, Sardinia appeared to be a liberal, progressive state ideally suited to drive Austria out of northern Italy and lead a free Italy of independent states.

Chapter 24
The Age of Nationalism
706    1850–1914

CHAPTER LOCATOR    What kind of state did Napoleon III build in France?

Map 24.1 **The Unification of Italy, 1859–1870** The leadership of Sardinia-Piedmont, nationalist fervor, and Garibaldi's attack on the kingdom of the Two Sicilies were decisive factors in the unification of Italy.

As for the papacy, the initial cautious support for unification by Pius IX (pontificate 1846–1878) had given way to fear and hostility after he was temporarily driven from Rome during the upheavals of 1848. For a long generation, the papacy would stand resolutely opposed not only to national unification but also to most modern trends.

## Cavour and Garibaldi in Italy

Sardinia had the good fortune of being led by Count Camillo Benso di Cavour (kuh-VOOR), the dominant figure in the Sardinian government from 1850 until his death in 1861. Cavour came from a noble family, and he made a substantial fortune in business before entering politics. Cavour's national goals were limited and realistic. Until 1859 he sought unity only for the states of northern and perhaps central Italy in a greatly expanded kingdom of Sardinia.

In the 1850s, Cavour worked to consolidate Sardinia as a liberal constitutional state capable of leading northern Italy. His program of highways and railroads, of civil liberties and opposition to clerical privilege, increased support for Sardinia throughout northern Italy. Yet Cavour realized that Sardinia could not drive Austria out of northern Italy without the help of a powerful ally. Accordingly, he worked for a secret diplomatic alliance with Napoleon III.

Finally, in July 1858 Cavour succeeded and goaded Austria into attacking Sardinia in 1859. Napoleon III came to Sardinia's defense. Then after the victory of the combined

How were Italy and Germany able to unify?

How did the American Civil War change the United States?

Why did Russia and the Ottoman Empire try to modernize?

What general domestic political trends emerged after 1871?

What explains the rise of socialism?

707

Franco-Sardinian forces, Napoleon III did a sudden about-face. Worried by criticism from French Catholics for supporting the pope's declared enemy, he made a compromise peace with the Austrians at Villafranca in July 1859. Sardinia would receive only Lombardy, the area around Milan, from Austria. Cavour resigned in a rage.

Yet Cavour's plans were salvaged by the skillful maneuvers of his allies in the moderate nationalist movement. While the war against Austria had raged in the north, pro-Sardinian nationalists in Tuscany and the other small states of central Italy had fanned popular revolts and easily toppled their ruling princes. The middle-class nationalist leaders in central Italy then called for fusion with Sardinia. Cavour returned to power in early 1860 and gained Napoleon III's support by ceding Savoy and Nice to France. The people of central Italy then voted overwhelmingly to join a greatly enlarged kingdom of Sardinia under Victor Emmanuel (see Map 24.1).

For superpatriots such as Giuseppe Garibaldi (1807–1882), the job of unification was still only half done. The son of a poor sailor, Garibaldi personified the romantic, revolutionary nationalism and republicanism of Mazzini and 1848. Leading a corps of volunteers against Austria in 1859, Garibaldi emerged in 1860 as an independent force in Italian politics.

Partly to use him and partly to get rid of him, Cavour secretly supported Garibaldi's plan to "liberate" the kingdom of the Two Sicilies. Landing on the shores of Sicily in May 1860, Garibaldi's guerrilla band of a thousand Red Shirts captured the imagination of the Sicilian peasantry, which rose in bloody rebellion. Outwitting the royal army, Garibaldi captured Palermo. Then Garibaldi and his men crossed to the mainland, marched triumphantly toward Naples, and prepared to attack Rome. But Cavour quickly sent Sardinian forces to occupy most of the Papal States (but not Rome) and to intercept Garibaldi.

**Red Shirts** The guerrilla army of Giuseppe Garibaldi, who invaded Sicily in 1860 in an attempt to liberate it, winning the hearts of the Sicilian peasantry.

**Garibaldi and Victor Emmanuel** The historic meeting in Naples between the leader of Italy's revolutionary nationalists and the king of Sardinia sealed the unification of northern and southern Italy. With the sleeve of his red shirt showing, Garibaldi offers his hand—and his conquests—to the uniformed king and his moderate monarchical government. (Scala/Art Resource, NY)

Chapter 24
**The Age of Nationalism**
1850–1914

708

CHAPTER LOCATOR    What kind of state did Napoleon III build in France?

Cavour realized that an attack on Rome would bring about war with France, and he also feared Garibaldi's radicalism and popular appeal. Thus he immediately organized a plebiscite in the conquered territories. The people of the south voted to join the kingdom of Sardinia, creating a united Italy in the process.

Cavour had succeeded. He had controlled Garibaldi and had turned popular nationalism in a conservative direction. The new kingdom of Italy, which expanded to include Venice in 1866 and Rome in 1870, was a parliamentary monarchy under Victor Emmanuel, neither radical nor democratic. It was politically unified, but only a half million out of 22 million Italians had the right to vote. The propertied classes and the common people remained divided. A great and growing social and cultural gap also separated the progressive, industrializing north from the stagnant, agrarian south. The new Italy was united on paper, but profound divisions remained.

## The Growing Austro-Prussian Rivalry

In the aftermath of 1848, the German states were locked in a political stalemate. After Austria and Russia blocked Frederick William's attempt in 1850 to unify Germany, tension grew between Austria and Prussia as each power sought to block the other within the German Confederation (see Chapter 22).

At the same time, powerful economic forces were contributing to the Austro-Prussian rivalry. Austria had not been included initially in the German customs union, or Zollverein, which had been founded in 1834 to stimulate trade and increase the revenue of member states. By the end of 1853 Austria was the only state in the German Confederation that had not joined. Prussia's leading role within the Zollverein gave it a valuable advantage in its struggle against Austria's supremacy in German political affairs.

Prussia had emerged from the upheavals of 1848 with a parliament of sorts, which was in the hands of the wealthy liberal middle class by 1859. Patriotic and longing for national unification, these middle-class representatives also wanted to establish that the parliament, not the king, had the ultimate political power and that the army was responsible to Prussia's elected representatives. The national uprising in Italy in 1859, however, made a profound impression on Prussia's William I (r. 1861–1888). Convinced that great political change and war—perhaps with Austria, perhaps with France—were quite possible, William I pushed to raise taxes and increase the defense budget in order to double the size of the army. The Prussian parliament rejected the military budget in 1862, and the liberals triumphed completely in new elections. King William then called on Count Otto von Bismarck to head a new ministry and defy the parliament.

## Bismarck and the Austro-Prussian War

Otto von Bismarck (1815–1898) was above all a master of politics. Born into the Prussian landowning aristocracy, Bismarck had a strong personality and an unbounded desire for power. Yet in his drive to secure power for himself and for Prussia, Bismarck was extraordinarily flexible and pragmatic. He kept his options open, pursuing one policy and then another as he moved with skill and cunning toward his goal.

When Bismarck took office as chief minister in 1862, he made a strong but unfavorable impression. Declaring that the government would rule without parliamentary consent, Bismarck lashed out at the middle-class opposition: "The great questions of the day will not be decided by speeches and resolutions—that was the blunder of 1848 and 1849—but by blood and iron."

Bismarck had the Prussian bureaucracy go right on collecting taxes, even though the parliament refused to approve the budget. Bismarck reorganized the army. And for four years, from 1862 to 1866, the voters of Prussia continued to express their opposition by sending large liberal majorities to the parliament.

How were Italy and Germany able to unify?    How did the American Civil War change the United States?    Why did Russia and the Ottoman Empire try to modernize?    What general domestic political trends emerged after 1871?    What explains the rise of socialism?

709

**■ MAPPING THE PAST**

## Map 24.2 The Unification of Germany, 1866–1871

This map shows how Prussia expanded and a new German Empire was created through two wars, the Austro-Prussian War of 1866 and the Franco-Prussian War of 1870–1871.

- **ANALYZING THE MAP** What losses did Austria experience in 1866? What territories did France lose as a result of the Franco-Prussian War? Which of the predominately Catholic states of southern Germany joined with Prussia to form the German Empire in 1871?

**CONNECTIONS** How was central Europe remade and the power of Prussia-Germany greatly increased as a result of the Austro-Prussian War and the Franco-Prussian War?

To complete this activity online, go to the Online Study Guide at **bedfordstmartins.com/mckaywestunderstanding**.

---

Opposition at home spurred the search for success abroad. The extremely complicated question of Schleswig-Holstein—two provinces that belonged to Denmark but were members of the German Confederation (Map 24.2)—provided an opportunity. In 1864, when the Danish king tried to bring these two provinces into a more centralized Danish

Chapter 24
**The Age of Nationalism**
710     1850–1914

CHAPTER LOCATOR     What kind of state did Napoleon III build in France?

state against the will of the German Confederation, Prussia joined Austria in a short and successful war against Denmark. However, Bismarck was convinced that Prussia had to control completely the northern, predominately Protestant part of the German Confederation, which meant expelling Austria from German affairs. Bismarck knew that a war with Austria would have to be a localized one that would not provoke a mighty alliance against Prussia. By skillfully neutralizing Russia and France, he was in a position to engage in a war of his own making.

The Austro-Prussian War of 1866 lasted only seven weeks. Utilizing railroads to mass troops and the new breech-loading needle gun to maximize firepower, the reorganized Prussian army overran northern Germany and defeated Austria decisively at the Battle of Sadowa (SAH-daw-vah) in Bohemia. Anticipating Prussia's future needs, Bismarck offered Austria easy peace terms. Austria paid no reparations and lost no territory to Prussia. But the existing German Confederation was dissolved, and Austria agreed to withdraw from German affairs. Prussia also conquered and annexed several small states north of the Main River. It completely dominated the remaining principalities in the newly formed North German Confederation. The mainly Catholic states of the south remained independent while forming alliances with Prussia. Bismarck's fundamental goal of Prussian expansion was being realized (see Map 24.2).

## The Taming of the Parliament

Bismarck had long been convinced that the old order he represented should make peace with the liberal middle class and the nationalist movement. He realized that nationalism was not necessarily hostile to conservative, authoritarian government. Moreover, Bismarck believed that the German middle class could be led to prefer a national unity under conservative leadership rather than a long, uncertain battle for truly liberal institutions.

In the aftermath of victory, Bismarck fashioned a federal constitution for the new North German Confederation. Each state retained its own local government, but the king of Prussia became president of the confederation, and the chancellor — Bismarck — was responsible only to the president. There was also a legislature with members of the lower house elected by universal, single-class male suffrage. Thus, Bismarck opened the door to popular participation and the possibility of going over the head of the middle class directly to the people. All the while, however, ultimate power rested in the hands of the dominant state of Prussia and its king and army.

In Prussia itself, Bismarck held out an olive branch to the parliamentary opposition. He asked the parliament to pass a special indemnity bill to approve after the fact all the government's spending between 1862 and 1866. With German unity in sight, most of the liberals jumped at the chance to cooperate. The constitutional struggle in Prussia was over, and the German middle class respectfully accepted the monarchical authority and the aristocratic superiority that Bismarck represented.

## The Franco-Prussian War

The final act in the drama of German unification followed quickly. Bismarck realized that a patriotic war with France would drive the south German states into his arms. The French obligingly played their part. By 1870 the French leaders of the Second Empire, goaded by Bismarck and alarmed by their powerful new neighbor on the Rhine, had decided on a war to teach Prussia a lesson.

As soon as war against France began in 1870, Bismarck had the wholehearted support of the south German states. German forces under Prussian leadership defeated the main French army at Sedan on September 1, 1870. Louis Napoleon himself was captured. Three days later, French patriots in Paris proclaimed yet another French republic and vowed to continue fighting. But after five months, in January 1871, a starving Paris surrendered,

How were Italy and Germany able to unify? · How did the American Civil War change the United States? · Why did Russia and the Ottoman Empire try to modernize? · What general domestic political trends emerged after 1871? · What explains the rise of socialism?

711

**Proclaiming the German Empire, January 1871** This commemorative painting by Anton von Werner testifies to the nationalistic intoxication in Germany after the victory over France. William I of Prussia stands on a platform surrounded by princes and generals in the famous Hall of Mirrors in the palace of Versailles, while officers from all the units around a besieged Paris cheer and salute him with uplifted swords as emperor of a unified Germany. Bismarck, in white (center), stands between king and army. (akg-images)

and France went on to accept Bismarck's harsh peace terms. By this time, the south German states had agreed to join a new German Empire. William I was proclaimed emperor of Germany in the Hall of Mirrors in the palace of Versailles. As in the 1866 constitution, the king of Prussia and his ministers had ultimate power in the new German Empire, and the lower house of the legislature was elected by universal male suffrage.

Under the peace terms, France was forced to pay a colossal indemnity of 5 billion francs and to cede the rich eastern province of Alsace and part of Lorraine to Germany. French men and women of all classes viewed the seizure of Alsace and Lorraine as a terrible crime, and thus relations between France and Germany after 1871 were tragically poisoned.

The weakest of the Great Powers in 1862 (after Austria, Britain, France, and Russia), Prussia had become, with fortification by the other German states, the most powerful state in Europe in less than a decade. Most Germans were enormously proud, imagining themselves, in Darwinian terms, as the fittest and best of the European species. Semi-authoritarian nationalism and a "new conservatism," which was based on an alliance of the propertied classes and sought the active support of the working classes, had triumphed in Germany.

## ▼ How did the American Civil War change the United States?

Closely linked to European developments in the nineteenth century, the United States also experienced the full drama of nation building. Economic development in the "United" States carried free and slaveholding states in very different directions. Northerners extended family farms westward and began building factories in the northeast. By 1850 an industrializing, urbanizing North was also building a system of canals and railroads and attracting most of the European immigrants.

In sharp contrast, industry and cities did not develop in the South. European immigrants largely avoided the region. Plantation owners dominated the economy and society. These profit-minded slave owners used black slaves to claim a vast new cotton kingdom across the Deep South (Map 24.3). By 1850, this kingdom produced 5 million bales a year, supplying textile mills in Europe and New England.

Chapter 24
**The Age of Nationalism**
712        1850–1914

CHAPTER LOCATOR        What kind of state did Napoleon III build in France?

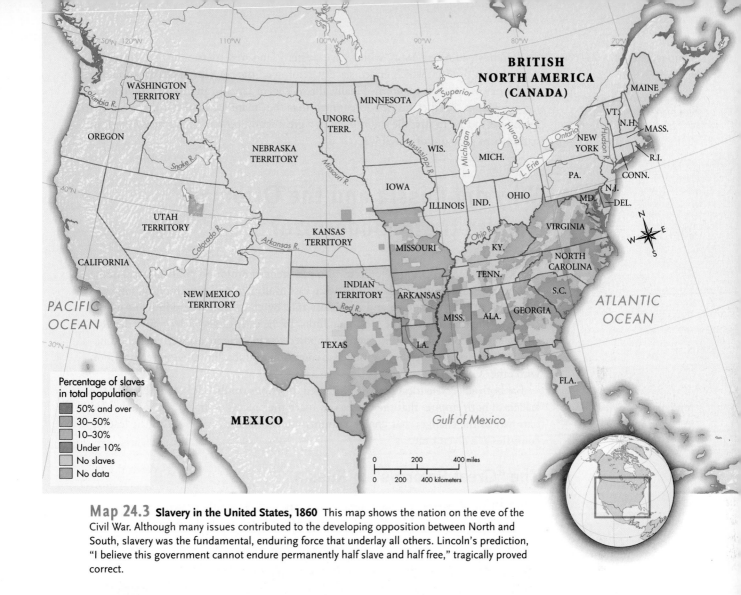

**Map 24.3 Slavery in the United States, 1860** This map shows the nation on the eve of the Civil War. Although many issues contributed to the developing opposition between North and South, slavery was the fundamental, enduring force that underlay all others. Lincoln's prediction, "I believe this government cannot endure permanently half slave and half free," tragically proved correct.

**Percentage of slaves in total population**
- 50% and over
- 30–50%
- 10–30%
- Under 10%
- No slaves
- No data

The rise of the cotton empire greatly expanded slave-based agriculture in the South, spurred exports, and played a key role in igniting rapid U.S. economic growth. The large profits flowing from cotton also led influential Southerners to defend slavery. Northern whites viewed their free-labor system as being just, economical, and morally superior to slavery. Thus regional antagonisms intensified.

These antagonisms came to a climax after 1848 when a defeated Mexico ceded to the United States a vast area stretching from west Texas to the Pacific Ocean. Debate over the extension of slavery in this new territory caused attitudes to harden on both sides. In Abraham Lincoln's election as president in 1860 gave Southern secessionists the chance they had been waiting for. Eventually eleven states left the Union and formed the Confederate States of America. When Southern troops fired on a Union fort in South Carolina's Charleston harbor, war began.

The Civil War (1861–1865) was the bloodiest conflict in all of American history, but in the end the South was defeated. In the aftermath of the war, certain dominant characteristics of American life and national culture took shape. Powerful business corporations emerged, steadfastly supported by the Republican Party during and after the war.

**U.S. Secession, 1860–1861**

How were Italy and Germany able to unify?

How did the American Civil War change the United States?

Why did Russia and the Ottoman Empire try to modernize?

What general domestic political trends emerged after 1871?

What explains the rise of socialism?

**Homestead Act** A result of the American Civil War that gave western land to settlers, reinforcing the concept of free labor in a market economy.

The Homestead Act of 1862, which gave western land to settlers, and the Thirteenth Amendment of 1865, which ended slavery, reinforced the concept of free labor taking its chances in a market economy. Finally, the success of Lincoln and the North in holding the Union together seemed to confirm that the "manifest destiny" of the United States was indeed to straddle a continent as a great world power. Thus a new American nationalism grew out of a civil war.

# ▼ Why did Russia and the Ottoman Empire try to modernize?

The Russian and the Ottoman empires also experienced profound political crises in the mid-nineteenth century. Both empires were vast multinational states built on long traditions of military conquest and absolutist rule by elites from the dominant ethnic groups—the Russians and the Ottoman Turks. In the early nineteenth century the governing elites in both states were strongly opposed to representative government and national self-determination. They continued to concentrate on absolutist rule and competition with other Great Powers.

For both states relentless power politics led to serious trouble. It became clear to the leaders of both empires that they had to embrace the process of modernization, defined narrowly as the changes that enable a country to compete effectively with the leading countries at a given time.

**modernization** The changes that enable a country to compete effectively with the leading countries at a given time.

## The "Great Reforms" in Russia

In the 1850s, Russia was a poor agrarian society with a rapidly growing population. Bound to the lord on a hereditary basis, the peasant serf was little more than a slave, and serfdom had become the great moral and political issue for the government by the 1840s. Then the Crimean War of 1853 to 1856, arising out of a dispute with France over who should protect certain Christian shrines in the Ottoman Empire, brought crisis. Because the fighting was concentrated in the Crimean peninsula on the Black Sea, Russia's weak transportation network of rivers and wagons failed to supply the distant Russian armies adequately.

France and Great Britain, aided by Sardinia and the Ottoman Empire, inflicted a humiliating defeat on Russia. This military defeat demonstrated that Russia had fallen behind the nations of western Europe in many areas. Russia needed railroads, better armaments, and reorganization of the army if it was to maintain its international position. Moreover, the disastrous war had caused hardship and raised the specter of peasant rebellion. Reform of serfdom was imperative. Military disaster thus forced Tsar Alexander II (r. 1855–1881) and his ministers along the path of rapid social change and general modernization.

The first and greatest of the reforms was the freeing of the serfs in 1861. The emancipated peasants received, on average, about half of the land. Yet they had to pay fairly high prices for their land and the land was owned collectively by peasant villages. Collective ownership and responsibility made it very difficult for individual peasants to improve agricultural methods or leave their villages. Thus old patterns of behavior predominated, and the effects of reform were limited.

**The Crimean War, 1853–1856**

Chapter 24
**The Age of Nationalism**
**714** 1850–1914

CHAPTER LOCATOR | What kind of state did Napoleon III build in France?

Most of the later reforms were also halfway measures. In 1864 the government established a new institution of local government, the zemstvo. Members of this local assembly were elected by a three-class system of towns, peasant villages, and noble landowners. A zemstvo executive council dealt with local problems. However, the local zemstvo remained subordinate to the traditional bureaucracy and the local nobility. More successful was reform of the legal system, which established independent courts and equality before the law.

Until the twentieth century, Russia's greatest strides toward modernization were economic rather than political. Transportation and industry were transformed in two industrial surges. The first of these came after 1860, when the government encouraged and subsidized private railway companies. The railroads enabled agricultural Russia to export grain and thus earn money for further economic development. A class of modern factory workers began to take shape. Strengthened by industrial development, Russia's military forces began seizing territory to the south and east, exciting many Russian nationalists, who became some of the government's most enthusiastic supporters. Industrial development and the growing proletariat class also contributed to the spread of Marxian thought and the transformation of the Russian revolutionary movement after 1890.

In 1881 Alexander II was assassinated by a small group of anarchist terrorists. The new tsar, Alexander III (r. 1881–1894), was a determined reactionary. Nevertheless, economic modernization sped forward for the second time, as Russia achieved a massive industrialization surge from 1890 to 1900. The key leader was Sergei Witte (suhr-GAY VIH-tuh), the minister of finance from 1892 to 1903. Under Witte's leadership, the government doubled Russia's railroad network to thirty-five thousand miles by the end of the century. Witte established protective tariffs to build Russian industry, and he put the country on the gold standard in order to strengthen Russian finances.

Witte's greatest innovation was to use Westerners to catch up with the West. He encouraged foreigners to build factories in Russia, efforts that were especially successful in southern Russia. There, in eastern Ukraine, foreign capitalists and their engineers built an enormous and very modern steel and coal industry. In 1900 peasants still constituted the great majority of the population, but Russia was industrializing and catching up with the advanced nations of the West.

## The Russian Revolution of 1905

Catching up partly meant vigorous territorial expansion, for this was the age of Western imperialism. By 1903 Russia had established a sphere of influence in Chinese Manchuria and was eyeing northern Korea. When the protests of equally imperialistic Japan were ignored, the Japanese launched a surprise attack in February 1904. After Japan scored repeated victories, Russia was forced in September 1905 to accept defeat.

Military disaster abroad brought political upheaval at home. The business and professional classes had long wanted a liberal, representative government. Urban factory workers were organized in a radical and still illegal labor movement. Peasants had gained little from the era of reforms. They were suffering from poverty and overpopulation as well. At the same time, nationalist sentiment was emerging among the empire's minorities and subject nationalities. All these currents of discontent converged in the revolution of 1905.

On a Sunday in January 1905, a massive crowd of workers and their families converged peacefully on the Winter Palace in St. Petersburg to present a petition to the tsar. Suddenly troops opened fire, killing and wounding hundreds. The Bloody Sunday massacre turned ordinary workers against the tsar and produced a wave of general indignation.

By the summer of 1905 strikes, peasant uprisings, revolts among minority nationalities, and troop mutinies were sweeping the country. The revolutionary surge culminated in October 1905 in a general strike that forced the government to capitulate. The tsar

**Bloody Sunday** A massacre of peaceful protesters at the Winter Palace in St. Petersburg in 1905 that triggered a revolution that overturned absolute tsarist rule and made Russia into a conservative constitutional monarchy.

How were Italy and Germany able to unify?

How did the American Civil War change the United States?

Why did Russia and the Ottoman Empire try to modernize?

What general domestic political trends emerged after 1871?

What explains the rise of socialism?

715

**October Manifesto** The result of a great general strike in October 1905, it granted full civil rights and promised a popularly elected Duma (parliament) with real legislative power.

**Duma** The Russian parliament that opened in 1906, elected indirectly by universal male suffrage but controlled after 1907 by the tsar and the conservative classes.

issued the October Manifesto, which granted full civil rights and promised a popularly elected Duma (DOO-muh; parliament) with real legislative power. The manifesto split the opposition. Frightened middle-class leaders helped the government repress the uprising and survive as a constitutional monarchy.

On the eve of the opening of the first Duma in May 1906, the government issued the new constitution, the Fundamental Laws. The Duma, elected indirectly by universal male suffrage, and a largely appointive upper house could debate and pass laws, but the tsar had an absolute veto. As in Bismarck's Germany, the tsar appointed his ministers, who did not need to command a majority in the Duma.

The disappointed, predominately middle-class liberals, the largest group in the newly elected Duma, saw the Fundamental Laws as a step backward. Efforts to cooperate with the tsar's ministers soon broke down, the tsar dismissed the Duma. Thereupon he and his advisers rewrote the electoral law so as to increase greatly the weight of the propertied classes. When elections were held, the tsar could count on a loyal majority in the Duma.

☐ Area of peasant unrest
● Major strikes and mutinies

**The Russian Revolution of 1905**

**The October Manifesto of 1905** This painting by the famous realist Ilya Repin captures the riotous joy that seized most moderate, well-educated Russians after Tsar Nicholas II issued the October Manifesto. At long last, they thought, Russia would become a liberal constitutional state, with guaranteed liberties and representative assemblies. (akg-images)

Chapter 24
**The Age of Nationalism**
716    1850–1914

CHAPTER LOCATOR    What kind of state did Napoleon III build in France?

In 1914, Russia was partially modernized, a conservative constitutional monarchy with a peasant-based but industrializing economy.

## Decline and Reform in the Ottoman Empire

The Ottoman Empire had reached its high point of development under Suleiman the Magnificent in the sixteenth century. By the eighteenth century it was falling rapidly behind western Europe in science, industrial skill, and military technology. Also during the eighteenth century, Russia's powerful westernized army was able to occupy Ottoman provinces on the Danube River. The danger that the Great Powers of Europe would gradually conquer the Ottoman Empire and divide up its territories was real.

**Pasha Hilim Receiving Archduke Maximillian of Austria** As this painting suggests, Ottoman leaders became well versed in European languages and culture. They also mastered the game of power politics, playing one European state off against another and securing the Ottoman Empire's survival. The black servants on the right may be slaves from Sudan. (Miramare Palace Trieste/Dagli Orti/The Art Archive)

How were Italy and Germany able to unify?   How did the American Civil War change the United States?   Why did Russia and the Ottoman Empire try to modernize?   What general domestic political trends emerged after 1871?   What explains the rise of socialism?

717

Caught up in the Napoleonic wars and losing more territory to Russia, the Ottomans were forced in 1816 to grant Serbia local autonomy. In 1830, the Greeks won their national independence, while French armies began conquest of the province of Algeria. Another threat to the empire came from within: the rise of Muhammad Ali, the Ottoman governor in Egypt. In 1831, and again in 1839, his French-trained forces occupied the Ottoman provinces of Syria and then Iraq, and they appeared ready to depose the Ottoman sultan (emperor) Mahmud II (r. 1808–1839). The sultan survived, but only because the European powers forced Muhammad Ali to withdraw. The European powers, minus France, preferred a weak and dependent Ottoman state.

**Tanzimat** A set of reforms designed to remake the Ottoman Empire on a western European model.

Realizing their precarious position, liberal Ottoman statesmen launched in 1839 an era of radical reforms, which lasted until 1876 and culminated in a constitution and a short-lived parliament. Known as the Tanzimat (TAHN-zee-MAT; literally, regulations or orders), these reforms were designed to remake the empire on a western European model. The high point of reform came with Sultan Abdul Mejid's Imperial Rescript of 1857. Articles in the decree called for equality before the law, a modernized administration and military, and religious freedom for Muslims, Christians, and Jews.

As part of its new policy of tolerance, new commercial laws allowed free importation of foreign goods and permitted foreign merchants to operate freely throughout the empire. Of great importance for later developments, growing numbers among the elite and the upwardly mobile embraced Western education. To some extent they accepted secular values.

Intended to bring revolutionary modernization, the Tanzimat permitted partial recovery but fell short of its goals for several reasons. First, the liberal reforms failed to halt the growth of nationalism among Christian subjects in the Balkans, which resulted in crises and defeats that undermined all reform efforts. Second, the Ottoman initiatives did not curtail Western imperialism, which secured a stranglehold on the Ottoman economy.

Finally, equality before the law for all citizens and religious communities actually increased religious disputes, which were in turn exacerbated by the relentless interference of the European powers. This development embittered relations between the religious communities, distracted the government from its reform mission, and split Muslims into secularists and religious conservatives. Islamic conservatives became the most dependable support of Sultan Abdülhamid (ahb-dool-hah-MEED) (r. 1876–1909), who abandoned the model of European liberalism in his long and repressive reign.

**Young Turks** Fervent patriots who seized power in the revolution of 1908 in the Ottoman Empire, forcing the conservative sultan to implement reforms.

The combination of declining international power and conservative tyranny eventually led to a resurgence of the modernizing impulse among idealistic Turkish exiles in Europe and young army officers in Istanbul. These so-called Young Turks seized power in the revolution of 1908 and forced the sultan to implement reforms. Although they failed to stop the rising tide of anti-Ottoman nationalism in the Balkans, the Young Turks helped prepare the way for the birth of modern secular Turkey after the defeat and collapse of the Ottoman Empire in World War I.

## ▼ What general domestic political trends emerged after 1871?

For central and western Europe, the unification of Italy and of Germany marked the end of a dramatic period of nation building. Only on the borders of Europe—in Ireland and Russia, in Austria-Hungary and the Ottoman Empire—did subject peoples still strive for national unity and political independence.

Chapter 24
**The Age of Nationalism**
1850–1914

718

CHAPTER LOCATOR | What kind of state did Napoleon III build in France?

## General Trends

Despite some major differences between countries, European domestic politics after 1871 had a common framework, the firmly established national state. The common themes within that framework were the emergence of mass politics and growing loyalty toward the national state.

For good reason, ordinary people felt increasing loyalty to their governments. More people could vote. By 1914 universal male suffrage had become the rule rather than the exception. This development had as much psychological as political significance. Ordinary men felt that they counted; they could influence the government to some extent. They were becoming "part of the system." The women's suffrage movement also made some gains. By 1913 women could vote in twelve of the western United States. Europe, too, moved slowly in this direction.

As the right to vote spread, politicians and parties in national parliaments represented the people more responsively. The multiparty system prevailing in most countries meant that parliamentary majorities were built on shifting coalitions of different parties, and this gave individual parties leverage to obtain benefits for their supporters. Governments also passed laws to alleviate general problems, thereby acquiring greater legitimacy.

There was a less positive side to building popular support for strong nation-states after 1871. Governments found that they could manipulate national feeling to create a sense of unity and to divert attention away from underlying class conflicts. Conservative and moderate leaders found that workers who voted socialist would rally around the

**"Votes for Women!"** The long-simmering campaign for women's suffrage in England came to a boil after 1903, as militants took to the streets, disrupted political meetings, and tried to storm Parliament. This 1908 illustration shows demonstrators giving a hero's welcome to Mary Leigh, the first suffragette imprisoned for property damage after she threw rocks through the windows of the prime minister's house. (The Art Archive)

How were Italy and Germany able to unify?

How did the American Civil War change the United States?

Why did Russia and the Ottoman Empire try to modernize?

**What general domestic political trends emerged after 1871?**

What explains the rise of socialism?

719

flag in a diplomatic crisis or cheer when territory was seized in Africa or Asia. Therefore, after 1871 governing elites frequently used antiliberal and militaristic policies to help manage domestic conflicts, but at the expense of increasing international tensions.

In these same years some fanatics and demagogic political leaders also sought to build nationalist movements by whipping up popular animosity toward imaginary enemies, especially the Jews. The growth of modern anti-Semitism after 1880 epitomized the most negative aspects of European nationalism before the First World War.

## The German Empire

Politics in Germany after 1871 reflected many of the general European developments. The new German Empire was a federal union of Prussia and twenty-four smaller states. Much of the everyday business of government was conducted by the separate states, but there was a strong national government with a chancellor—until 1890, Bismarck—and a popularly elected lower house called the Reichstag (RIGHKHS-tahg). Although Bismarck refused to be bound by a parliamentary majority, he tried nonetheless to maintain one. Until 1878 Bismarck relied mainly on the National Liberals, who had rallied to him after 1866. They supported legislation useful for further economic and legal unification of the country.

Less wisely, they backed Bismarck's attack on the Catholic Church, the so-called Kulturkampf (kool-TOOR-kahmpf). Like Bismarck, the middle-class National Liberals were particularly alarmed by Pius IX's declaration of papal infallibility in 1870. That dogma seemed to ask German Catholics to put loyalty to their church, a foreign power, above loyalty to their nation. Kulturkampf initiatives generally aimed at making the Catholic Church subject to government control. However, only in Protestant Prussia did the Kulturkampf have even limited success, because Catholics throughout the country generally voted for the Center Party, which blocked passage of national laws hostile to the church.

In 1878 Bismarck abandoned his attack on the church and instead courted the Catholic Center Party, whose supporters included many small farmers in western and southern Germany. By enacting high tariffs on cheap foreign grain, he won over both the Catholic Center and the Protestant Junkers, who had large landholdings in the east.

Many other governments followed Bismarck's lead, and the 1880s and 1890s saw a widespread return to protectionism in Europe. France, in particular, established very high tariffs to protect agriculture and industry, peasants and manufacturers, from foreign competition.

Bismarck also tried to stop the growth of socialism in Germany. In 1878, after two attempts on the life of William I by radicals (though not socialists), Bismarck used a carefully orchestrated national outcry to pass a law that strictly controlled socialist meetings and publications and that outlawed the Social Democratic Party. German socialists, however, continued to hold influence, and Bismarck decided to try another tack.

In an attempt to win the support of working-class people, Bismarck urged the Reichstag to take bold action and enact a variety of state-supported social measures. Big business and some conservatives accused Bismarck of creating "state socialism," but Bismarck and his supporters carried the day. His essentially conservative nation-state pioneered in the provision of social welfare programs. In 1883 he pushed through the Reichstag the first of several modern social security laws to help wage earners. The laws of 1883 and 1884 established national sickness and accident insurance; the law of 1889 established old-age pensions and retirement benefits. This national social security system, paid for through compulsory contributions by wage earners and employers as well as grants from the state, was the first of its kind anywhere. Bismarck's social security system did not wean workers from voting socialist, but it did give them a small stake in the system and protect them from some of the uncertainties of the complex urban industrial world.

---

**Reichstag** The popularly elected lower house of government of the new German Empire after 1871.

**Kulturkampf** Bismarck's attack on the Catholic Church within Germany from 1870 to 1878, resulting from Pius IX's declaration of papal infallibility.

CHAPTER LOCATOR | What kind of state did Napoleon III build in France?

Increasingly, the great issues in German domestic politics were socialism and the Marxian Social Democratic Party. In 1890 the new emperor, William II (r. 1888–1918), opposed Bismarck's attempt to renew the law outlawing the Social Democratic Party. Eager to rule in his own right and to earn the support of the workers, William II forced Bismarck to resign. After the "dropping of the pilot," German foreign policy changed profoundly and mostly for the worse, but the government did pass new laws to aid workers and to legalize socialist political activity.

Yet William II was no more successful than Bismarck in getting workers to renounce socialism. Indeed, Social Democrats won more and more seats in the Reichstag, becoming Germany's largest single party in 1912. Yet the "revolutionary" socialists were actually becoming less radical in Germany. In the years before World War I, the German Social Democratic party broadened its base by adopting a more patriotic tone, allowing for greater military spending and imperialist expansion. German socialists concentrated instead on gradual social and political reform.

## Republican France

Although Napoleon III's reign made some progress in reducing antagonisms between classes, the war with Prussia undid these efforts, and in 1871 France seemed hopelessly divided once again. The republicans who proclaimed the Third Republic in Paris refused to admit defeat. They defended Paris with great heroism for weeks, until they were starved into submission by German armies in January 1871. When national elections then sent a large majority of conservatives and monarchists to the National Assembly and France's new leaders decided they had no choice but to surrender Alsace (al-SAS) and Lorraine to Germany, the Parisians proclaimed the Paris Commune in March 1871. Vaguely radical, the leaders of the Commune wanted to govern Paris without interference from the conservative French countryside. The National Assembly, led by aging politician Adolphe Thiers (TEE-ehr), ordered the French army into Paris and brutally crushed the Commune. Twenty thousand people died in the fighting.

Out of this tragedy, France slowly formed a new national unity, achieving considerable stability before 1914. Until 1875 the monarchists in the "republican" National Assembly had a majority, but they could not agree who should be king. In the meantime, Thiers's destruction of the radical Commune and his other firm measures showed the fearful provinces and the middle class that the Third Republic might be moderate and socially conservative. France therefore retained the republic, though reluctantly.

Another stabilizing factor was the skill and determination of the moderate republican leaders in the early years. By 1879 the great majority of members of both the upper and the lower houses of the National Assembly were republicans, and the Third Republic had firm foundations after almost a decade.

The moderate republicans sought to preserve their creation by winning the loyalty of the next generation. Trade unions were fully legalized, and France acquired a colonial empire. More important, a series of laws between 1879 and 1886 established free compulsory elementary education for both girls and boys. At the same time, they greatly expanded the state system of public tax-supported schools. In France and throughout the Western world, the general expansion of public education served as a critical nation-building tool in the late nineteenth century. In France most elementary and much secondary education had been in the parochial schools of the Catholic Church, which had long been hostile to republics and to much of secular life. Free compulsory elementary education in France became secular republican education.

Although the educational reforms of the 1880s disturbed French Catholics, many of them rallied to the republic in the 1890s. The limited acceptance of the modern world by the more liberal Pope Leo XIII (pontificate 1878–1903) eased tensions between church and state. Unfortunately, the **Dreyfus affair** changed all that.

**Dreyfus affair** A divisive case in which Alfred Dreyfus, a Jewish captain in the French army, was falsely accused and convicted of treason. The Catholic Church sided with the anti-Semites against Dreyfus; after Dreyfus was declared innocent, the French government severed all ties between the state and the church.

How were Italy and Germany able to unify?　　How did the American Civil War change the United States?　　Why did Russia and the Ottoman Empire try to modernize?　　**What general domestic political trends emerged after 1871?**　　What explains the rise of socialism?

721

In 1894 Alfred Dreyfus, a Jewish captain in the French army, was falsely accused and convicted of treason. In 1898 and 1899, the case split France apart. On one side was the army, which had manufactured evidence against Dreyfus, joined by anti-Semites and most of the Catholic establishment. On the other side stood the civil libertarians and most of the more radical republicans.

This battle, which eventually led to Dreyfus's being declared innocent, revived republican feeling against the church. Between 1901 and 1905, the government severed all ties between the state and the Catholic Church after centuries of close relations. In France only the growing socialist movement, with its very different and thoroughly secular ideology, stood in opposition to patriotic, republican nationalism.

**Captain Alfred Dreyfus** Leaving an 1899 reconsideration of his original court martial, Dreyfus receives an insulting "guard of dishonor" from soldiers whose backs are turned. (Roger-Viollet/Getty Images)

## Great Britain and Ireland

In Britain, after the right to vote was granted to males of the solid middle class in 1832, opinion leaders and politicians wrestled with the uncertainties of a further expansion of the franchise. In 1867 the Second Reform Bill of Benjamin Disraeli and the Conservatives extended the vote to all middle-class males and the best-paid workers in order to broaden the Conservative Party's base. The Third Reform Bill of 1884 gave the vote to almost every adult male.

While the House of Commons was drifting toward democracy, the House of Lords was content to slumber nobly. Between 1901 and 1910, however, it tried to reassert itself. Acting as supreme court of the land, it ruled against labor unions in two important decisions. And after the Liberal Party came to power in 1906, the Lords vetoed several measures passed by the Commons, including the so-called **People's Budget**, which was designed to increase spending on social welfare services. The Lords finally capitulated, as they had with the Reform Bill of 1832 (see Chapter 22), when the king threatened to create enough new peers to pass the bill, and aristocratic conservatism yielded to popular democracy once and for all.

**People's Budget** A bill proposed after the Liberal Party came to power in England in 1906, it was designed to increase spending on social welfare services, but was initially vetoed in the House of Lords.

The result was that extensive social welfare measures were passed in a spectacular rush between 1906 and 1914. During those years, the Liberal Party, inspired by David Lloyd George (1863–1945), substantially raised taxes on the rich as part of the People's Budget. This income helped the government pay for national health insurance, unemployment benefits, old-age pensions, and a host of other social measures.

On the eve of World War I, however, the unanswered question of Ireland brought Great Britain to the brink of civil war. The terrible Irish famine fueled an Irish revolutionary movement. Thereafter, the English slowly granted concessions, such as the abolition of the privileges of the Anglican Church and rights for Irish peasants. Liberal prime minister William Gladstone (1809–1898) introduced bills to give Ireland self-government in 1886 and in 1893. They failed to pass, but in 1913 Irish nationalists in the British Parliament finally gained a home-rule bill for Ireland.

Thus Ireland was on the brink of achieving self-government. Yet as much as the Irish Catholic majority in the southern counties wanted home rule, precisely that much did the Irish Protestants of the northern counties of Ulster come to oppose it. Motivated by

Chapter 24
**The Age of Nationalism**
1850–1914

722

CHAPTER LOCATOR | What kind of state did Napoleon III build in France?

the accumulated fears and hostilities of generations, the Protestants of Ulster refused to submerge themselves in a Catholic Ireland, just as Irish Catholics had refused to submit to a Protestant Britain.

The Ulsterites vowed to resist home rule in northern Ireland. They were supported by much of English public opinion. Thus in 1914 the Liberals in the House of Lords introduced a compromise home-rule bill that did not apply to the northern counties. This bill, which openly betrayed promises made to Irish nationalists, was rejected, and in September the original home-rule bill was passed but simultaneously suspended for the duration of World War I.

Irish developments illustrated once again the power of national feeling and national movements in the nineteenth century. Though Great Britain had much going for it—power, Parliament, prosperity—none of these availed in the face of the conflicting nationalisms created by Catholics and Protestants in northern Ireland. Similarly, progressive Sweden was powerless to stop the growth of the Norwegian national movement, which culminated in Norway's breaking away from Sweden and becoming a fully independent nation in 1905. In this light, one can also see how hopeless was the case of the Ottoman Empire in Europe in the later nineteenth century. It was only a matter of time before the Serbs, Bulgarians, and Romanians would break away.

## The Austro-Hungarian Empire

Conflicting nationalisms had created a desperate situation in the Austro-Hungarian Empire by the early twentieth century. In 1849 Magyar nationalism had driven Hungarian patriots to declare an independent Hungarian republic, which was savagely crushed by Russian and Austrian armies (see Chapter 22).

Then in the wake of defeat by Prussia in 1866, a weakened Austria was forced to strike a compromise and establish the so-called dual monarchy. The empire was divided in two, and the nationalistic Magyars gained virtual independence for Hungary. Henceforth, each half of the empire agreed to deal with its own ethnic minorities. The two states were joined only by a shared monarch and common ministries for finance, defense, and foreign affairs.

In Austria ethnic Germans were only one-third of the population, and in 1895 many Germans saw their traditional dominance threatened by Czechs, Poles, and other Slavs. From 1900 to 1914 the parliament was so divided that ministries generally could not obtain a majority and ruled instead by decree. Efforts by both conservatives and socialists to defuse national antagonisms by stressing economic issues that cut across ethnic lines were largely unsuccessful.

"No Home Rule" Posters like this one helped to incite pro-British, anti-Catholic sentiment in the northern Irish counties of Ulster before the First World War. The rifle raised defiantly and the accompanying rhyme are a thinly veiled threat of armed rebellion and civil war. (Reproduced with the kind permission of the Trustees of the National Museums & Galleries of Northern Ireland. Photograph © Ulster Museum, Belfast)

How were Italy and Germany able to unify?   How did the American Civil War change the United States?   Why did Russia and the Ottoman Empire try to modernize?   **What general domestic political trends emerged after 1871?**   What explains the rise of socialism?

723

# INDIVIDUALS IN SOCIETY

## Theodor Herzl

**IN SEPTEMBER 1897, ONLY DAYS AFTER HIS VISION** and energy had called into being the First Zionist Congress in Basel, Switzerland, Theodor Herzl (1860–1904) assessed the results in his diary: "If I were to sum up the Congress in a word — which I shall take care not to publish — it would be this: At Basel I founded the Jewish state. If I said this out loud today I would be greeted by universal laughter. In five years perhaps, and certainly in fifty years, everyone will perceive it."*

Herzl's buoyant optimism, which so often carried him forward, was prophetic. Leading the Zionist movement until his death at age forty-four in 1904, Herzl guided the first historic steps toward modern Jewish political nationhood and the creation of Israel in 1948. Theodor Herzl was born in Budapest, Hungary, into an upper-middle-class, German-speaking Jewish family. When Herzl was eighteen, his family moved to Vienna, where he studied law. As a university student, he soaked up the liberal beliefs of most well-to-do Viennese Jews, who also championed the assimilation of German culture. Wrestling with his nonreligious Jewishness and his strong pro-German feeling, Herzl embraced German nationalism and joined a German dueling fraternity.

There he discovered that full acceptance required openly anti-Semitic attitudes and a repudiation of all things Jewish. This Herzl could not tolerate, and

**Theodor Herzl** (Library of Congress)

he resigned. After receiving his law degree, he embarked on a literary career. In 1889 Herzl married into a wealthy Viennese Jewish family, but he and his socialite wife were mismatched and never happy together.

Herzl achieved considerable success as both a journalist and a playwright. His witty comedies focused on the bourgeoisie, including Jewish millionaires trying to live like aristocrats. Accepting many German stereotypes, Herzl sometimes depicted eastern Jews as uneducated and grasping. But as a dedicated, highly educated liberal, he mainly believed that the Jewish shortcomings he perceived were the results of age-old persecution and would disappear through education and assimilation. Herzl also took a growing pride in Jewish steadfastness in the face of victimization and suffering. He savored memories of his early Jewish education and going with his father to the synagogue.

The emergence of modern anti-Semitism (see page 725) shocked Herzl, as it did many acculturated Jewish Germans. Moving to Paris in 1891 as the correspondent for Vienna's leading liberal newspaper, Herzl studied politics and pondered recent historical developments. He then came to a bold conclusion, published in 1896 as *The Jewish State: An Attempt at a Modern Solution to the Jewish Question.* According to Herzl, Jewish assimilation had failed, and attempts to combat anti-Semitism would never succeed. Only by building an independent Jewish state could the Jewish people achieve dignity and renewal.

Herzl developed his political nationalism, or Zionism, before the anti-Jewish agitation accompanying the Dreyfus affair, which only served to strengthen his faith in his analysis. Generally rebuffed by skeptical Jewish elites in western and central Europe, Herzl turned for support to youthful idealists and the poor Jewish masses. He became an inspiring man of action, rallying the delegates to the annual Zionist congresses, directing the growth of the worldwide Zionist organization, and working himself to death. Herzl also understood that national consciousness required powerful emotions and symbols, such as a Jewish flag. Flags build nations, he said, because people "live and die for a flag."

Putting the Zionist vision before non-Jews and world public opinion, Herzl believed in international diplomacy and political agreements. He traveled constantly to negotiate with European rulers and top officials, seeking their support in securing territory for a Jewish state, usually in the Ottoman Empire. Aptly described by an admiring contemporary as "the first Jewish statesman since the destruction of Jerusalem," Herzl proved most successful in Britain. He paved the way for the 1917 Balfour Declaration, which solemnly pledged British support for a "Jewish homeland" in Palestine.

## QUESTIONS FOR ANALYSIS

1. Describe Theodor Herzl's background and early beliefs. Do you see a link between Herzl's early German nationalism and his later Zionism?
2. Why did Herzl believe an independent Jewish state with its own national flag was necessary?
3. How did Herzl work as a leader to turn his Zionist vision into a reality?

*Quotes are from Theodor Herzl, *The Diaries of Theodor Herzl*, trans. and ed. with an introduction by Marvin Lowenthal (New York: Grosset & Dunlap, 1962), pp. 224, 22, xxi.

Chapter 24
**The Age of Nationalism**
724    1850–1914

CHAPTER LOCATOR | What kind of state did Napoleon III build in France?

In Hungary the Magyar nobility in 1867 restored the constitution of 1848 and used it to dominate both the Magyar peasantry and the minority populations until 1914. Only the wealthiest one-fourth of adult males had the right to vote, making the parliament the creature of the Magyar elite. While Magyar extremists campaigned for total separation from Austria, the leaders of the subject nationalities dreamed in turn of independence from Hungary. Unlike most major countries, which harnessed nationalism to strengthen the state after 1871, the Austro-Hungarian Empire was progressively weakened and destroyed by it.

## Jewish Emancipation and Modern Anti-Semitism

Revolutionary changes in political principles and the triumph of the nation-state brought equally revolutionary changes in Jewish life in western and central Europe. The decisive turning point came in 1848, when Jews formed part of the revolutionary vanguard in Vienna and Berlin and the Frankfurt Assembly endorsed full rights for German Jews. In 1871 the constitution of the new German Empire consolidated the process of Jewish emancipation in central Europe. It abolished all restrictions on Jewish marriage, choice of occupation, place of residence, and property ownership. The process of emancipation presented Jews with challenges and opportunities. Traditional Jewish occupations, such as court financial agent, village moneylender, and peddler, were undermined by free-market reforms, but careers in business, the professions, and the arts were opening to Jewish talent. By 1871 a majority of Jewish people in western and central Europe had improved their economic situation and entered the middle classes. Most Jewish people also identified strongly with their respective nation-states and saw themselves as patriotic citizens.

Vicious anti-Semitism reappeared after the stock market crash of 1873, beginning in central Europe. Drawing on long traditions of religious intolerance, ghetto exclusion, and periodic anti-Jewish riots and expulsions, this anti-Semitism was also a modern development, building on the general reaction against liberalism. Modern anti-Semitism whipped up resentment against Jewish achievement and Jewish "financial control," while fanatics claimed that the Jewish race (rather than the Jewish religion) posed a biological threat to the German people. Anti-Semitic beliefs were particularly popular among conservatives, extremist nationalists, and people who felt threatened by Jewish competition, such as small shopkeepers, office workers, and professionals.

Anti-Semites also created modern political parties. In Austrian Vienna in the early 1890s, Karl Lueger (LOO-guhr) and his "Christian socialists" won striking electoral victories, spurring Theodor Herzl to turn from German nationalism and advocate political Zionism and the creation of a Jewish state. (See "Individuals in Society: Theodor Herzl," opposite page.) Lueger, mayor of Vienna from 1897 to 1910, combined fierce anti-Semitic rhetoric with municipal ownership of basic services, and he appealed especially to the German-speaking lower middle class—and an unsuccessful young artist named Adolf Hitler.

**Zionism** A movement toward Jewish political nationhood started by Theodor Herzl.

Before 1914 anti-Semitism was most oppressive in eastern Europe, where Jews also suffered from terrible poverty. In the Russian empire, where there was no Jewish emancipation and 4 million of Europe's 7 million Jewish people lived in 1880, officials used anti-Semitism to channel popular discontent away from the government. Russian Jews were denounced as foreign exploiters who corrupted national traditions, and in 1881–1882 a wave of violent pogroms commenced in southern Russia. The police and the army stood aside for days while peasants looted and destroyed Jewish property. Official harassment continued in the following decades, and some Russian Jews turned toward self-emancipation and the vision of a Zionist settlement in Palestine. Large numbers also emigrated to western Europe and the United States.

How were Italy and Germany able to unify?

How did the American Civil War change the United States?

Why did Russia and the Ottoman Empire try to modernize?

What general domestic political trends emerged after 1871?

What explains the rise of socialism?

725

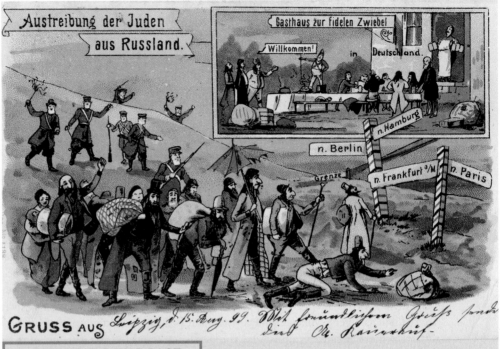

### PICTURING THE PAST

### "The Expulsion of the Jews from Russia"

So reads this postcard, correctly suggesting that Russian government officials often encouraged popular anti-Semitism and helped drive many Jews out of Russia in the late nineteenth century. The road signs indicate that these poor Jews are crossing into Germany, where they will find a grudging welcome and a meager meal at the Jolly Onion Inn. Other Jews from eastern Europe settled in France and Britain, thereby creating small but significant Jewish populations in both of these countries for the first time since they had expelled most of their Jews in the Middle Ages. (Alliance Israelite Universelle, Paris/Archives Charmet/The Bridgeman Art Library)

**ANALYZING THE IMAGE** The inset image in the upper-right shows an armed German soldier at the table, carefully watching the Jewish refugees. What similarity do you see between this and the larger image on the postcard to suggest how Jewish refugees were treated in Germany as compared to Russia? The postcard was sent on August 15, 1899, from Leipzig, Germany, and the message is in German. To whom might this card have been sent and what message might the postcard convey to the recipient?

**CONNECTIONS** What famous event marked the rise of vicious anti-Semitism in the late nineteenth century, and what characterized the modern anti-Semitism of this period? Did the Jews like the ones shown on this postcard find an acceptable haven in Germany in the period before World War I?

To complete this activity online, go to the Online Study Guide at bedfordstmartins.com/mckaywestunderstanding.

## ▼ What explains the rise of socialism?

Nationalism served, for better or worse, as a new unifying principle. But what about socialism? Socialist parties, which were generally Marxian parties dedicated to an international proletarian revolution, grew rapidly in these years. Did this mean that national states had failed to gain the support of workers?

Chapter 24
**The Age of Nationalism**
**726**    1850–1914

CHAPTER LOCATOR | What kind of state did Napoleon III build in France?

## The Socialist International

The growth of socialist parties after 1871 was phenomenal, particularly that of the German Social Democratic Party, which espoused the Marxian ideology. (See "Listening to the Past: Adelheid Popp, the Making of a Socialist," page 728.) By 1912 it had millions of followers—mostly people from the working classes—and was the largest party in the Reichstag. Socialist parties also grew in other countries, though nowhere else with such success.

Marxian socialist parties were eventually linked together in an international organization. Marx himself played an important role in founding the First International of socialists—the International Working Men's Association. In the following years, he battled successfully to control the organization and used its annual meetings as a means of spreading his doctrines of inevitable socialist revolution. Then Marx enthusiastically embraced the radical patriotism of the Paris Commune and its conflict with the French National Assembly as a step toward socialist revolution. This frightened many of his early supporters, especially the more moderate British labor leaders. The First International collapsed.

Yet international proletarian solidarity remained an important objective for Marxists. In 1889, as the individual parties in different countries grew stronger, socialist leaders came together to form the Second International, which lasted until 1914. Every three years, delegates from the different parties met to interpret Marxian doctrines and plan coordinated action. May 1 (May Day) was declared an annual international one-day strike, a day of marches and demonstrations. A permanent executive for the International was

"Greetings from the May Day Festival" Workers participated enthusiastically in the annual one-day strike on May 1 in Stuttgart, Germany, to honor internationalist socialist solidarity, as this postcard suggests. Speeches, picnics, and parades were the order of the day, and workers celebrated their respectability and independent culture. Picture postcards like this one and the one on page 726 developed with railroads, mass travel, and high-speed printing. (akg-images)

How were Italy and Germany able to unify?

How did the American Civil War change the United States?

Why did Russia and the Ottoman Empire try to modernize?

What general domestic political trends emerged after 1871?

What explains the rise of socialism?

727

# LISTENING TO THE PAST

## Adelheid Popp, the Making of a Socialist

*Nationalism and socialism appeared locked in bitter competition in Europe before 1914, but they actually complemented each other in many ways. Both faiths were secular as opposed to religious, and both fostered political awareness. A working person who became interested in politics and developed nationalist beliefs might well convert to socialism at a later date.*

*This was the case for Adelheid Popp (1869–1939), a self-taught working-woman who became an influential socialist leader. Born into a desperately poor working-class family in Vienna and remembering only a "hard and gloomy childhood," she was forced by her parents to quit school at age ten to begin full-time work. She struggled with low-paying piecework for years before she landed a solid factory job, as she recounts in the following selection from her widely read autobiography. Always an avid reader, Popp became the editor of a major socialist newspaper for German working-women. She then told her life story so that all workingwomen might share her truth: "Socialism could change and strengthen others, as it did me."*

**❝** [Finally] I found work again; I took everything that was offered me in order to show my willingness to work, and I passed through much. But at last things became better. [At age fifteen] I was recommended to a great factory which stood in the best repute. Three hundred girls and about fifty men were employed. I was put in a big room where sixty women and girls were at work.

Against the windows stood twelve tables, and at each sat four girls. We had to sort the goods which had been manufactured, others had to count them, and a third set had to brand on them the mark of the firm. We worked from 7 A.M. to 7 P.M. We had an hour's rest at noon, half-an-hour in the afternoon. . . . I had never yet been paid so much. . . .

I seemed to myself to be almost rich. . . . [Yet] from the women of this factory one can judge how sad and full of deprivation is the lot of a factory worker. In none of the neighbouring factories were the wages so high; we were envied everywhere. Parents considered themselves fortunate if they could get their daughters of fourteen in there on leaving school. . . . And even here, in this paradise, all were badly nourished. Those who stayed at the factory for the dinner hour would buy themselves for a few pennies a sausage or the leavings of a cheese shop. . . . In spite of all the diligence and economy, every one was poor, and trembled at the thought of losing her work. All humbled themselves, and suffered the worst injustice from the foremen, not to risk losing this good work, not to be without food. . . .

I did not only read novels and tales; I had begun . . . to read the classics and other good books. I also began to take an interest in public events. . . . I was not democratically inclined. I was full of enthusiasm then for emperors, and kings and highly placed personages played no small part in my fancies. . . . I bought myself a strict Catholic paper, that criticised very adversely the workers' movement, which was attracting notice. Its aim was to educate in a patriotic and religious direction. . . . I took the warmest interest in the events that occurred in the royal families, and I took the death of the Crown Prince of Austria so much to heart that I wept a whole day. . . . Political events [also] held me in suspense. The possibility of a war with Russia roused my patriotic enthusiasm. I saw my brother already returning from the battlefield covered with glory. . . .

When a particularly strong anti-Semitic feeling was noticeable in political life, I sympathised with it for a time. A broad sheet, "How Israel Attained Power and Sovereignty over all the Nations of the Earth," fascinated me. . . .

About this time an Anarchist group was active. Some mysterious murders which had taken place were ascribed to the Anarchists, and the police made use of them to oppress the rising workmen's movement. . . . I followed the trial of the Anarchists with passionate sympathy. I read all the speeches, and because, as always happens, Social Democrats, whom the authorities really wanted to attack, were among the accused, I learned their views. I became full of enthusiasm. Every single Social Democrat . . . seemed to me a hero. . . . There was unrest among the workers . . . and demonstrations of protest followed. When these were repeated the military entered the "threatened" streets. . . . In the evenings I rushed in the greatest excitement from the factory to the scene of the disturbance. The military did not frighten me; I only left the place when it was "cleared."

Later on my mother and I lived with one of my brothers who had married. Friends came to him, among

established. Many feared and many others rejoiced in the growing power of socialism and the Second International.

## Unions and Revisionism

Was socialism really radical and revolutionary in these years? On the whole, it was not. As socialist parties grew and attracted large numbers of members, they looked more and

Chapter 24
**The Age of Nationalism**
728    1850–1914

CHAPTER LOCATOR    What kind of state did Napoleon III build in France?

**1890 engraving of a meeting of workers in Berlin.** (Bildarchiv Preussischer Kulturbesitz/Art Resource, NY)

them some intelligent workmen. One of these work-men was particularly intelligent, and . . . could talk on many subjects. He was the first Social Democrat I knew. He brought me many books, and explained to me the difference between Anarchism and Socialism. I heard from him, also for the first time, what a republic was, and in spite of my former enthusiasm for royal dynas-ties, I also declared myself in favour of a republican form of government. I saw everything so near and so clearly, that I actually counted the weeks which must still elapse before the revolution of state and society would take place. From this workman I received the first Social Democratic party organ. . . . I first learned from it to understand and judge of my own lot. I learned to see that all I had suffered was the result not of a divine ordinance, but of an unjust organization of society. . . .

In the factory I became another woman. . . . I told my [female] comrades all that I had read of the workers' movement. Formerly I had often told stories when they

had begged me for them. But instead of narrating . . . the fate of some queen, I now held forth on oppression and exploitation. I told of ac-cumulated wealth in the hands of a few, and introduced as a contrast the shoemakers who had no shoes and the tailors who had no clothes. On breaks I read aloud the articles in the Social Democratic paper and explained what Socialism was as far as I understood it. . . . [While I was reading] it often happened that one of the clerks passing by shook his head and said to another clerk: "The girl speaks like a man." 〞

**Source:** Slightly adapted from A. Popp, *The Autobiography of a Working Woman*, trans. E. C. Harvey (Chicago: F. G. Browne, 1913), pp. 29, 34–35, 39, 66–69, 71, 74, 82–90.

### QUESTIONS FOR ANALYSIS

1. How did Popp describe and interpret work in the factory?
2. According to her autobiography, what accounts for Popp's nation-alist sentiments early on? How and why did she become a Social Democrat?
3. Was Popp likely to lead other workingwomen to socialism by read-ing them articles from socialist newspapers? Why or why not?

more toward gradual change and steady improvement for the working class and less and less toward revolution. The mainstream of European socialism increasingly combined radical rhetoric with sober action.

Workers themselves were progressively less inclined to follow radical programs. There were several reasons for this. As workers gained the right to vote and to participate politi-cally in the nation-state, they focused their attention more on elections than on revolu-tions. And as workers won real, tangible benefits, this furthered the process. Workers were

How were Italy and Germany able to unify?

How did the American Civil War change the United States?

Why did Russia and the Ottoman Empire try to modernize?

What general domestic political trends emerged after 1871?

**What explains the rise of socialism?**

also not immune to patriotic education and indoctrination during military service. Nor were workers a unified social group.

Perhaps most important of all, workers' standard of living rose gradually but substantially after 1850. In Great Britain, for example, workers could buy almost twice as much with their wages in 1906 as in 1850, and most of the increase came after 1870. Workers experienced similar gradual increases in most continental countries after 1850. The quality of life in urban areas improved dramatically as well. For all these reasons, workers tended more and more to become militantly moderate: they demanded gains, but they were less likely to take to the barricades in pursuit of them.

The growth of labor unions reinforced this trend toward moderation. In the early stages of industrialization, modern unions were generally prohibited by law. In Great Britain, attempts by workers to unite were considered criminal conspiracies after 1799. Other countries had similar laws. Unions were considered subversive bodies to be hounded and crushed.

Workers struggled to escape from this sad position. Great Britain led the way in 1824 and 1825 when unions won the right to exist but (generally) not the right to strike. After the collapse of Robert Owen's attempt to form one big union in the 1830s (see Chapter 21), new and more practical kinds of unions appeared. Limited primarily to highly skilled workers such as machinists and carpenters, these "new model unions" concentrated on winning better wages and hours through collective bargaining and compromise. This approach helped pave the way to full acceptance in Britain in the 1870s, and after 1890 unions for unskilled workers developed.

Developments in Germany—the most industrialized, socialized, and unionized continental country by 1914—were particularly instructive. German unions were not granted important rights until 1869, and until the antisocialist law was repealed in 1890, they were frequently harassed by the government. The result was that as late as 1895, there were only about 270,000 union members in a male industrial workforce of nearly 8 million. Then, with German industrialization still storming ahead and almost all legal harassment eliminated, union membership skyrocketed, reaching roughly 3 million in 1912.

This great expansion both reflected and influenced the changing character of German unions. Increasingly, unions in Germany focused on wages, hours, working conditions, rather than on the dissemination of pure socialist doctrine. Genuine collective bargaining, long opposed by socialist intellectuals as a "sellout," was officially recognized as desirable by the German Trade Union Congress in 1899. In 1913 alone, over ten thousand collective bargaining agreements benefiting 1.25 million workers were signed.

**revisionism** An effort by moderate socialists to update Marxian doctrines to reflect the realities of the time.

The German trade unions and their leaders were thoroughgoing revisionists. Revisionism was an effort by various socialists to update Marxian doctrines to reflect the realities of the time. Thus the socialist Eduard Bernstein (BEHRN-shtighn) (1850–1932) argued in 1899 in his *Evolutionary Socialism* that many of Marx's predictions had been proved false. Therefore, Bernstein argued, socialists should reform their doctrines and tactics. They should combine with other progressive forces to win continued evolutionary gains for workers through legislation, unions, and further economic development. These views were denounced by the German Social Democratic Party and later by the entire Second International. Yet the revisionist, gradualist approach continued to gain the tacit acceptance of many German socialists, particularly in the trade unions.

Moderation found followers elsewhere. In France the great socialist leader Jean Jaurès (1859–1914) formally repudiated revisionist doctrines in order to establish a unified socialist party, but he remained at heart a gradualist and optimistic secular humanist. Questions of revolution also split Russian Marxists.

Socialist parties before 1914 had clear-cut national characteristics. Russians and socialists in the Austro-Hungarian Empire tended to be the most radical. The German party talked revolution and practiced reformism, greatly influenced by its enormous trade-union movement. The French party talked revolution and tried to practice it, unrestrained

CHAPTER LOCATOR    What kind of state did Napoleon III build in France?

by a trade-union movement that was both very weak and very radical. In England the socialist but non-Marxian Labour Party, reflecting the well-established union movement, was formally committed to gradual reform. In Spain and Italy, Marxian socialism was very weak. There anarchism, seeking to smash the state rather than the bourgeoisie, dominated radical thought and action.

In short, socialist policies and doctrines varied from country to country. Socialism itself was to a large extent "nationalized." This helps explain why when war came in 1914, almost all socialist leaders and most workers supported their governments.

## ←LOOKING BACK LOOKING AHEAD→

IN 1900, THE TRIUMPH OF NATIONALISM in Europe seemed almost complete. Only in eastern Europe, in the three aging multinational empires of Austria-Hungary, Russia, and the Ottomans, did several nationalities still struggle to form their own states. Elsewhere the ethnically unified nation-state, resting solidly upon the continent's ongoing industrialization and its emerging urban society, governed with the consent and even the devotion of its citizens. Responsive and capable of tackling many practical problems, the European nation-state of 1900 was in part the realization of ideologues and patriots like Mazzini and the middle-class liberals active in the unsuccessful revolutions of 1848. Yet whereas early nationalists had envisioned a Europe of free peoples and international peace, the nationalists of 1900 had been nurtured in the traditional competition between European states and the wars of unification in the 1850s and 1860s. This generation of nationalists reveled in the strength of their unity, and the nation-state became a system of power.

Thus after 1870, at the same time the responsive nation-state improved city life and brought social benefits to ordinary people, Europe's leading countries also projected raw power throughout the world. In the expanding colonies of Asia and Africa, the nations of Britain, France, Germany, and Russia seized territory, fought brutal colonial wars, and built authoritarian empires. Moreover, in Europe itself the universal faith in nationalism, which usually reduced social tensions within states, promoted a bitter, almost Darwinian, competition between states. Thus European nationalism threatened the very progress and unity it had helped to build. In 1914, the power of unified nation-states would turn on itself, unleashing the First World War and doling out self-inflicted wounds of enormous proportions to all of Europe's peoples. ■

- **For a list of suggested readings for this chapter, visit** *bedfordstmartins.com/mckaywestunderstanding*.

- **For primary sources from this period, see** *Sources of Western Society*, Second Edition.

- **For Web sites, images, and documents related to topics in this chapter, see Make History at** *bedfordstmartins.com/mckaywestunderstanding*.

How were Italy and Germany able to unify?

How did the American Civil War change the United States?

Why did Russia and the Ottoman Empire try to modernize?

What general domestic political trends emerged after 1871?

What explains the rise of socialism?

## Step 1

**GETTING STARTED** Below are basic terms about this period in the history of Western civilization. Can you identify each term below and explain why it matters? To do this exercise online, go to bedfordstmartins.com/mckaywestunderstanding.

| TERMS | WHO (OR WHAT) AND WHEN | WHY IT MATTERS |
|---|---|---|
| Red Shirts, p. 708 | | |
| Homestead Act, p. 714 | | |
| modernization, p. 714 | | |
| Bloody Sunday, p. 715 | | |
| October Manifesto, p. 716 | | |
| Duma, p. 716 | | |
| Tanzimat, p. 718 | | |
| Young Turks, p. 718 | | |
| Reichstag, p. 720 | | |
| Kulturkampf, p. 720 | | |
| Dreyfus affair, p. 721 | | |
| People's Budget, p. 722 | | |
| Zionism, p. 725 | | |
| revisionism, p. 730 | | |

## Step 2

**MOVING BEYOND THE BASICS** The exercise below requires a more advanced understanding of the chapter material. Examine the forces behind Italian and German unification by describing the key participants, the key events, and the role of ideology in unification of the two countries. When you are finished, consider the following questions: How did the key participants in German and Italian unification work to gain public support for unification? How did ideology shape the kinds of governments that emerged to lead these two newly created countries? To do this exercise online, go to bedfordstmartins.com/mckaywestunderstanding.

| COUNTRY | KEY PARTICIPANTS | KEY EVENTS | ROLE OF IDEOLOGY |
|---|---|---|---|
| Italy | | | |
| Germany | | | |

**PUTTING IT ALL TOGETHER** Now that you've reviewed key elements of the chapter, take a step back and try to see the big picture. Remember to use specific examples from the chapter in your answers. To do this exercise online, go to bedfordstmartins.com/mckaywestunderstanding.

## NATION BUILDING

- How did Napoleon III use the memory of the French Revolution to promote national unity and legitimize his own authority? How did he see the relationship between his government and the French people?

- Compare and contrast the role that liberalism played in the unification of Italy and of Germany.

- How did Bismarck use war to promote German unification under Prussian leadership? How did he use war to tame his domestic opponents?

## THE MODERNIZATION OF RUSSIA AND THE OTTOMAN EMPIRE

- Compare and contrast the Russian and Ottoman empires. What did the two empires have in common? What challenges did both face in the second half of the nineteenth century?

- What did Russian and Ottoman leaders mean by "modernization"? What advantages did they believe modernization would produce? How successful were their modernization efforts?

## THE RESPONSIVE NATIONAL STATE, 1871–1914

- Compare and contrast the relationship between the people and the government in France and Britain in the late nineteenth century. How did each government work to cement the loyalty of its citizens? How effective were their efforts?

- Compare and contrast the domestic politics of Germany and Austria-Hungary in the late nineteenth century. How would you explain the differences you note?

## MARXISM AND THE SOCIALIST MOVEMENT

- What was the relationship between nationalism and socialism in the late nineteenth century? How did European governments respond to the challenge of international socialism?

- Why did most workers reject radical socialism? What does this tell us about working class values and ambitions in the late nineteenth century?

■ **In Your Own Words** Imagine that you must explain Chapter 24 to someone who hasn't read it. What would be the most important points to include and why?

# 25

# The West and the World

## 1815–1914

While industrialization and nationalism were transforming urban and agricultural life throughout Europe, Western society itself was reshaping the world. At the peak of its power and pride, the West entered the third and most dynamic phase of the aggressive expansion that had begun with the Crusades and continued with the great discoveries and the rise of seaborne colonial empires. An ever-growing stream of products and ideas flowed out of Europe in the nineteenth century. Hardly any corner of the globe was left untouched. At the same time millions of Europeans picked up stakes and emigrated abroad, primarily to North and South America but also to Australia, North and South Africa, and Asiatic Russia.

The most spectacular manifestations of Western expansion came in the late nineteenth century when the leading European nations established or enlarged their far-flung political empires. This political annexation of territory in the 1880s—the "new imperialism," as it is often called by historians—was the capstone of Europe's underlying economic and technological transformation. More directly, Europe's new imperialism rested on a formidable combination of superior military might and strong authoritarian rule, and it posed a brutal challenge to African and Asian peoples. Different societies met this Western challenge in different ways and with changing tactics, as we shall see. Nevertheless, by 1914 non-Western elites in many lands were rallying their peoples and leading an anti-imperialist struggle for dignity and genuine independence that would eventually triumph after 1945. ■

**Living in the Age of New Imperialism.** The late nineteenth century witnessed the spread of European empires abroad and the intertwining of the lives of Europeans and native populations. Here European tourists look on at the well-tended trees and handsome buildings of Cairo's new quarter, a result of European involvement in modernizing the city. (North Wind Picture Archives/Alamy)

# Chapter Preview

▶ How did Western industrialization change the world economy?

▶ What explains global migration patterns in this period?

▶ What characterized Western imperialism after 1880?

▶ How did non-Westerners respond to Western imperialism?

# ▼ How did Western industrialization change the world economy?

The Industrial Revolution created, first in Great Britain and then in continental Europe and North America, a tremendously dynamic economic system. In the course of the nineteenth century, that system was extended across the face of the earth. Some of this extension into non-Western areas was peaceful and beneficial for all concerned, for the West had many products and techniques the rest of the world desired. If peaceful methods failed, however, Europeans used their superior military power to force non-Western nations to open their doors to Western economic interests. In general, Westerners fashioned the global economic system so that the largest share of the ever-increasing gains from trade, technology, and migration flowed to the West and its propertied classes.

## The Rise of Global Inequality

**Third World** A term that refers to the nonindustrialized nations of Africa, Asia, and Latin America as a single unit.

The Industrial Revolution in Europe marked a momentous turning point in human history. Those regions of the world that industrialized in the nineteenth century (mainly Europe and North America) increased their wealth and power enormously in comparison to those that did not. A gap between the industrializing regions and the nonindustrializing or Third World regions (mainly Africa, Asia, and Latin America) opened up and grew steadily throughout the nineteenth century. Moreover, this pattern of uneven global development became institutionalized, or built into the structure of the world economy.

In recent years historical economists have been charting the long-term evolution of this gap, and Figure 25.1 summarizes the findings of one important study. Three main points stand out. First, in 1750 the average standard of living was no higher in Europe as a whole than in the rest of the world. Second, it was industrialization that opened the gaps in average wealth and well-being among countries and regions. Third, income per person stagnated in the Third World before 1913, in striking contrast to the industrializing regions.

The rise of these enormous income disparities has generated a great deal of debate. One school of interpretation stresses that the West used science, technology, capitalist organization, and even its critical worldview to create its wealth and

**British Ships and Shipbuilders** The British continued to dominate international trade before the First World War. This handsome membership certificate of the British shipbuilders union features the vessels that tied the world together economically. Britain's thriving shipbuilding industry was concentrated in southern Scotland. (Trade Union Congress, London/The Bridgeman Art Library)

greater physical well-being. Another school argues that the West used its political and economic power to steal much of its riches, continuing in the nineteenth and twentieth centuries the rapacious colonialism born of the era of expansion. Because these issues are complex and there are few simple answers, it is helpful to consider them in the context of world trade in the nineteenth century.

## The World Market

Commerce between nations has always stimulated economic development. In the nineteenth century, Europe directed an enormous increase in international commerce. Great Britain took the lead in cultivating export markets for its booming industrial output, as British manufacturers looked first to Europe and then around the world.

In addition to its dominance in the export market, Britain was also the world's largest importer of goods. From the repeal of the Corn Laws in 1846 (see Chapter 22) to the outbreak of World War I in 1914, Britain remained the world's emporium, where not only agricultural products and raw materials but also manufactured goods entered freely. Free access to Britain's market stimulated the development of mines and plantations in many non-Western areas.

International trade also grew as transportation systems improved. Wherever railroads were built, they drastically reduced transportation costs and opened new economic opportunities. Much of the railroad construction undertaken in Latin America, Asia, and Africa connected seaports with inland cities and regions, as opposed to linking and developing cities and regions within a given country. Thus railroads dovetailed with Western economic interests, facilitating the inflow and sale of Western manufactured goods as well as the export and the development of local raw materials.

The power of steam revolutionized transportation by sea as well as by land. Steam power began to supplant sails on the oceans of the world in the late 1860s. Passenger and freight rates tumbled as ship design became more sophisticated, and the intercontinental shipment of low-priced raw materials became feasible. The opening of the Suez Canal and the Panama Canal (in 1914) shortened global transport time considerably.

The revolution in land and sea transportation encouraged European entrepreneurs to open up vast new territories around the world. They developed agricultural products and raw materials there for sale in Europe. Improved transportation enabled Asia, Africa, and Latin America to ship not only the traditional tropical products—spices, tea, sugar, coffee—but also new raw materials for industry, such as jute, rubber, cotton, and coconut oil.

New communications systems directed the flow of goods across global networks. Transoceanic telegraph cables inaugurated rapid communications among the financial centers

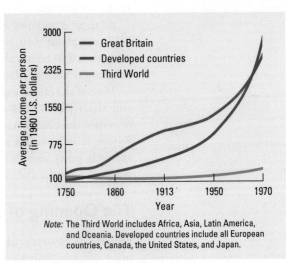

*Note:* The Third World includes Africa, Asia, Latin America, and Oceania. Developed countries include all European countries, Canada, the United States, and Japan.

**Figure 25.1** **The Growth of Average Income per Person in the Third World, Developed Countries, and Great Britain, 1750–1970** Growth is given in 1960 U.S. dollars and prices.

CHAPTER LOCATOR | How did Western industrialization change the world economy? | What explains global migration patterns in this period? | What characterized Western imperialism after 1880? | How did non-Westerners respond to Western imperialism?

737

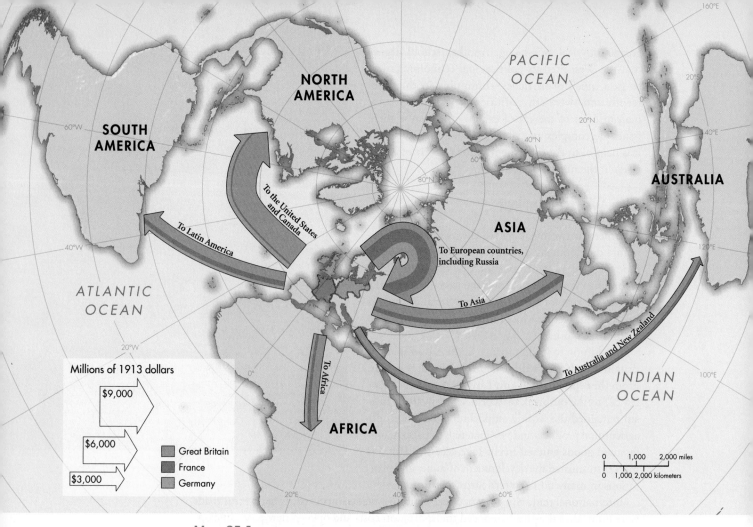

**Map 25.1 European Investment to 1914** Foreign investment grew rapidly after 1850. Britain, France, and Germany were the major investing nations. As this map suggests, most European investment was not directed to the African and Asian areas seized by the new imperialism after 1880.

of the world. While a British tramp freighter steamed from Calcutta to New York, a broker in London was arranging by telegram for it to carry an American cargo to Australia.

As their economies grew, Europeans began to make massive foreign investments beginning about 1840. By the outbreak of World War I in 1914, Europeans had invested more than $40 billion abroad. Great Britain, France, and Germany were the principal investing countries (Map 25.1).

Most of the capital exported did not go to European colonies or protectorates in Asia and Africa. About three-quarters of total European investment went to other European countries, the United States and Canada, Australia and New Zealand, and Latin America. Europe found its most profitable opportunities for investment in construction of the railroads, ports, and utilities that were necessary to settle and develop the lands in such places as Australia and the Americas.

## The Opening of China

Europe's development of offshoots in sparsely populated North America, Australia, and much of Latin America absorbed huge quantities of goods, investments, and migrants. Yet Europe's economic and cultural penetration of old, densely populated civilizations was also profoundly significant. With such civilizations Europeans also increased their trade and profit, and they were prepared to use force, if necessary, to attain their desires.

**Britain and China at War** Britain capitalized on its overwhelming naval superiority in its war against China, as shown in this British painting celebrating a dramatic moment in a crucial 1841 battle near Guangzhou. Having received a direct hit from a steam-powered British ironclad, a Chinese sailing ship explodes into a wall of flame. The Chinese lost eleven ships and five hundred men in the two-hour engagement; the British suffered only minor damage. (National Maritime Museum, London)

This was what happened in China, a striking example of the pattern of intrusion into non-Western lands.

For centuries China had sent more goods and inventions to Europe than it had received, and this was still the case in the early nineteenth century. Trade with Europe was carefully regulated by the Chinese imperial government—the Qing (ching), or Manchu (MAN-choo), Dynasty. It required all foreign merchants to live in the southern port of Guangzhou (Canton) and to buy and sell only to licensed Chinese merchants. Practices considered harmful to Chinese interests were strictly forbidden.

By the 1820s, however, the dominant group of foreign merchants in Canton, the British, were flexing their muscles. Moreover, in the smoking of opium, British merchants had found something that the Chinese really wanted. Grown legally in British-occupied India, opium was smuggled into China, where its use and sale were illegal. Huge profits and growing addiction led to a rapid increase in sales. By 1836 the aggressive goal of the British merchants in Canton was an independent British colony in China and "safe and unrestricted liberty" in their Chinese trade. Spurred on by economic motives, they pressured the British government to take decisive action.

At the same time, the Qing government decided that the **opium trade** had to be stamped out. The government began to prosecute Chinese drug dealers vigorously. In 1839 it sent special envoy Lin Zexu to Canton to deal with the crisis. Lin Zexu dealt harshly with Chinese who purchased opium, and he seized the opium stores of the British merchants, who then withdrew to the island of Hong Kong. He sent a famous letter justifying his policy to Queen Victoria in London. (See "Listening to the Past: Lin Zexu and Yamagata Aritomo, Confronting Western Imperialism," page 758.)

The wealthy, well-connected British merchants appealed to their allies in London for support, and the British government responded. It also wanted free, unregulated trade with China, as well as the establishment of diplomatic relations on the European model. Using troops from India and being in control of the seas, Britain occupied several coastal cities and forced China to give in to British demands. In the Treaty of Nanking in 1842, the imperial government was required to cede the island of Hong Kong to Britain

**opium trade** The sale of opium—grown legally in British-occupied India—by British merchants in China, where the drug was illegal; it became a destructive and ensnaring vice of the Chinese.

CHAPTER LOCATOR | How did Western industrialization change the world economy? | What explains global migration patterns in this period? | What characterized Western imperialism after 1880? | How did non-Westerners respond to Western imperialism?

739

forever, pay an indemnity of $100 million, and open up four large cities to unlimited foreign trade with low tariffs.

With Britain's new power over Chinese commerce, the opium trade flourished, and Hong Kong developed rapidly as an Anglo-Chinese enclave. China continued to accept foreign diplomats in Beijing (Peking), the imperial capital. But disputes over trade between China and the Western powers continued. Finally, there was a second round of foreign attack between 1856 and 1860, culminating in the occupation of Beijing by British and French troops. Another round of harsh treaties gave European merchants and missionaries greater privileges and protection. They also forced the Chinese to accept trade and investment on unfavorable terms for several more cities. Thus did Europeans use military aggression to end Chinese seclusion and open the country to foreign trade and foreign ideas.

## Japan and the United States

European traders and missionaries first arrived in Japan in the sixteenth century. By 1640 Japan had reacted quite negatively to their presence. The government decided to seal off the country from all European influences in order to preserve traditional Japanese culture and society. When American and British whaling ships began to appear off Japanese coasts almost two hundred years later, the policy of exclusion was still in effect.

Japan's unbending isolation seemed hostile and barbaric to the West, particularly to the United States. Americans shared the self-confidence and dynamism of expanding Western society, and they felt destined to play a great economic role in the Pacific. To Americans it seemed the duty of the United States to force the Japanese to share their ports and behave as a "civilized" nation.

After several unsuccessful American attempts to establish commercial relations with Japan, Commodore Matthew Perry steamed into Edo (now Tokyo) Bay in 1853. Relying on gunboat diplomacy and threatening to attack, Perry demanded diplomatic negotiations with the emperor. Realizing how defenseless their cities were against naval bombardment, Japanese leaders reluctantly signed a treaty with the United States that opened two ports and permitted trade. Over the next five years, more treaties spelled out the rights and privileges of the Western nations and their merchants in Japan. Japan was "opened." What the British had done in China with war, the Americans had done in Japan with the threat of war.

**gunboat diplomacy** The use or threat of military force to coerce a government into economic or political agreements.

## Western Penetration of Egypt

Egypt's experience illustrates not only the power of the expanding European economy and society but also their seductive appeal. European involvement in Egypt also led to a new model of formal political control, which European powers applied widely in Africa and Asia after 1882.

Since 525 B.C.E., Egypt had been ruled by a succession of foreigners, most recently by the Ottoman Turks. In 1798 French armies under Napoleon Bonaparte invaded the Egyptian part of the Ottoman Empire and occupied the territory for three years. Into the power vacuum left by the French withdrawal stepped an extraordinary Turkish general, Muhammad Ali (1769–1849).

First appointed governor of Egypt in 1805 by the Turkish sultan, Muhammad Ali set out to build his own state on the strength of a large, powerful army organized along European lines. He drafted for the first time Egypt's peasants. Then he hired French and Italian army officers to train these raw recruits and their Turkish officers. The government was also reformed, new lands were cultivated, and communications were improved. By the end of his reign in 1848, Muhammad Ali had established a strong and virtually independent Egyptian state, to be ruled by his family on a hereditary basis within the Turkish empire.

Muhammad Ali's policies of modernization attracted large numbers of Europeans. The port city of Alexandria had more than fifty thousand Europeans by 1864. Europeans served not only as army officers but also as engineers, doctors, government officials, and police officers. Others turned to trade, finance, and shipping.

To pay for his ambitious plans, Muhammad Ali encouraged the development of commercial agriculture. This development had profound implications. Egyptian peasants grew food for their own consumption on state-owned lands allotted to them by tradition. Faced with the possibility of export agriculture, high-ranking officials and members of Muhammad Ali's family began carving large private landholdings out of the state domain. The new landlords made the peasants their tenants and forced them to grow cash crops such as cotton and rice geared to European markets. Thus Egyptian landowners "modernized" agriculture, but to the detriment of peasant well-being.

These trends continued under Muhammad Ali's grandson Ismail (ihs-MAH-eel), who in 1863 began his sixteen-year rule as Egypt's khedive (kuh-DEEV), or prince. Educated in France, Ismail was a westernizing autocrat. The large irrigation networks he promoted caused cotton production and exports to Europe to boom. With his support the Suez Canal was completed by a French company in 1869. Young Egyptians educated in Europe spread new skills, and Cairo acquired modern boulevards and Western hotels. As Ismail proudly declared, "My country is no longer in Africa, we now form part of Europe."[1]

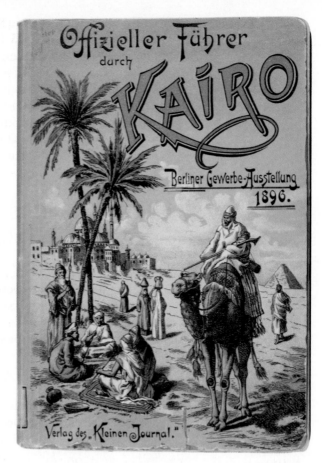

**Egyptian Travel Guide** Ismail's efforts to transform Cairo were fairly successful. As a result European tourists could more easily visit the country that their governments dominated. Ordinary Europeans were lured to exotic lands by travel books like this colorful "Official Guide" to an exhibition on Cairo held in Berlin. (Private Collection/Archives Charmet/The Bridgeman Art Library)

**The Suez Canal, 1869**

Mediterranean Sea

Cairo
Bitter Lakes
Suez Canal
SINAI
EGYPT
Gulf of Suez
Nile R.
OTTOMAN EMPIRE
Red Sea

Yet Ismail was too impatient and reckless. His projects were enormously expensive, and by 1876 Egypt was hopelessly in debt. France and Great Britain intervened and forced Ismail to appoint French and British commissioners to oversee Egyptian finances so that the Egyptian debt would be paid in full. In essence, Europeans were now going to determine the state budget and effectively rule Egypt.

Foreign financial control evoked a violent nationalistic reaction among Egyptian religious leaders, young intellectuals, and army officers. In 1879, under the leadership of Colonel Ahmed Arabi, they formed the Egyptian Nationalist Party. Continuing diplomatic pressure, which forced Ismail to abdicate in favor of his weak son, Tewfiq (r. 1879–1892), resulted in bloody anti-European riots in Alexandria in 1882. A number of Europeans were killed, and Tewfiq and his court had to flee to British ships for safety. When the British fleet bombarded Alexandria, more riots swept the country, and Colonel Arabi led a revolt. But a British expeditionary force put down the rebellion and occupied all of Egypt.

CHAPTER LOCATOR | How did Western industrialization change the world economy? | What explains global migration patterns in this period? | What characterized Western imperialism after 1880? | How did non-Westerners respond to Western imperialism?

741

The British said their occupation was temporary, but British armies remained in Egypt until 1956. They maintained the façade of the khedive's government as an autonomous province of the Ottoman Empire, but the khedive was a mere puppet. British rule did result in tax reforms and somewhat better conditions for peasants.

British rule in Egypt also provided a new model for European expansion in densely populated lands. Such expansion was based on military force, political domination, and a self-justifying ideology of beneficial reform. This model was to predominate until 1914. Thus did Europe's Industrial Revolution lead to tremendous political as well as economic expansion throughout the world after 1880.

## ▼ What explains global migration patterns in this period?

A human drama was interwoven with economic expansion: millions of people pulled up stakes and left their ancestral lands in the course of history's greatest migration. It was, in part, because of this great migration that the West's impact on the world in the nineteenth century was so powerful and many-sided.

**great migration** The mass movement of people from Europe in the nineteenth century; one reason why the West's impact on the world was so powerful and many-sided.

### The Pressure of Population

In the early eighteenth century, the growth of European population entered its third and decisive stage, which continued unabated until the early twentieth century (Figure 25.2). Birthrates eventually declined in the nineteenth century, but so did death rates, mainly because of the rising standard of living and secondarily because of the revolution in medicine (see Chapter 23). Thus the population of Europe (including Asiatic Russia) more than doubled, from approximately 188 million in 1800 to roughly 432 million in 1900.

These figures actually understate Europe's population explosion, for between 1815 and 1932 more than 60 million people left Europe. Since population grew more slowly in Africa and Asia than in Europe and the Americas, as Figure 25.2 shows, Europeans and people of predominately European origin jumped from about 24 percent of the world's total in 1800 to about 38 percent on the eve of World War I.

The growing number of Europeans provided further impetus for Western expansion, and it was a driving force behind emigration. As in the eighteenth century, the rapid increase in numbers put pressure on the land. This led to land hunger and relative overpopulation in area after area. As a result, millions of country folk went abroad as well as to nearby cities in search of work and economic opportunity.

Before looking at the people who migrated, let us consider three facts. First, the number of men and women who left Europe increased rapidly at the end of the nineteenth century and leading up to World War I. As Figure 25.3 shows, more than 11 million left in the first decade of the twentieth century, over five times the number departing in the 1850s.

Second, different countries had very different patterns of movement. As Figure 25.3 also shows, people left Britain and

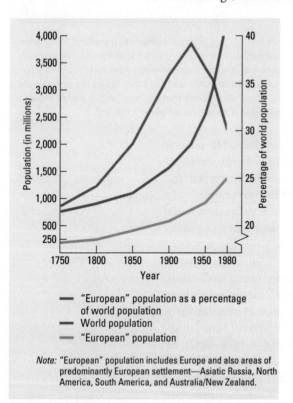

**Figure 25.2** **The Increase of European and World Populations, 1750–1980** Europeans and peoples of predominantly European origin became a growing percentage of total world population between roughly 1750 and 1914.

Ireland (which are not distinguished in the British figures) in large numbers from the 1840s on. This emigration reflected not only rural poverty but also the movement of skilled industrial technicians and the preferences shown to British migrants in the British Empire. German migration was quite different. It grew irregularly after about 1830, reaching a first peak in the early 1850s and another in the early 1880s. Thereafter it declined rapidly, for Germany's rapid industrialization was providing adequate jobs at home. This pattern contrasted sharply with that of Italy. More and more Italians left the country right up to 1914, reflecting severe problems in Italian villages and relatively slow industrial growth. Thus migration patterns mirrored social and economic conditions in the various European countries and provinces.

Third, although the United States did absorb the largest overall number of European migrants, fewer than half

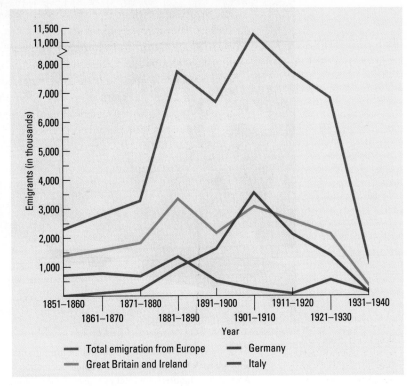

**Figure 25.3** **Emigration from Europe by Decades, 1851–1940** Emigration from Europe grew greatly until the outbreak of World War I in 1914, and it declined rapidly thereafter.

of all migrants went to the United States (Figure 25.4). Moreover, migrants accounted for a larger proportion of the total population in Argentina, Brazil, and Canada than it did in the United States. The common American assumption that European migration meant migration to the United States is quite inaccurate.

## European Migrants

What kind of people left Europe, and what were their reasons for doing so? The European migrant was generally an energetic small farmer or skilled artisan trying hard to stay ahead of poverty, not a desperately impoverished landless peasant or urban proletarian.

**Figure 25.4** **Origins and Destinations of European Emigrants, 1851–1960** European emigrants came from many countries; almost half of them went to the United States.

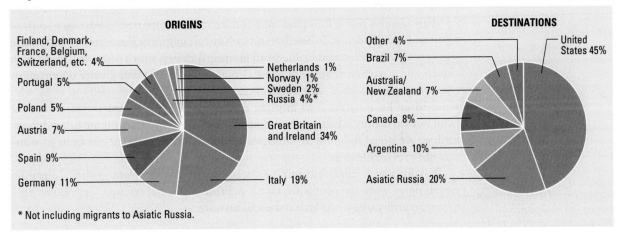

CHAPTER LOCATOR | How did Western industrialization change the world economy? | What explains global migration patterns in this period? | What characterized Western imperialism after 1880? | How did non-Westerners respond to Western imperialism?

**743**

**An Italian Custom in Argentina** Italian immigrants introduced the game of bocce to Argentina, where it took hold and became a popular recreation for men. Dressed up in their Sunday best, these Argentinean laborers are totally focused on the game, which is somewhat like horseshoes or shuffleboard. (Hulton Archive/Getty Images)

These small peasant landowners and village craftsmen typically left Europe because their traditional way of life was threatened by too little land, estate agriculture, and cheap factory-made goods.

Many Europeans moved but remained within Europe, settling temporarily or permanently in another European country. Jews from eastern Europe and peasants from Ireland migrated to Great Britain, Russians and Poles sought work in Germany, and Latin peoples from Spain, Portugal, and Italy entered France. Many Europeans were truly migrants as opposed to immigrants—that is, they returned home after some time abroad. One in two migrants to Argentina and probably one in three to the United States eventually returned to their native land.

Ties of family and friendship played a crucial role in the movement of peoples. Many people from a given province or village settled together in rural enclaves or tightly knit urban neighborhoods. Very often a strong individual—a businessman, a religious leader—would blaze the way, and others would follow, forming a "migration chain."

Many landless young European men and women were spurred to leave by a spirit of revolt and independence. In Sweden and in Norway, in Jewish Russia and in Italy, these young people felt frustrated by the small privileged classes, which often controlled both church and government while resisting demands for change and greater opportunity. Many young Jews agreed with a spokesman of Kiev's Jewish community in 1882, who summed up his congregation's growing defiance in the face of brutal discrimination: "Our human dignity is being trampled upon, our wives and daughters are being dishonored, we are looted and pillaged; either we get decent human rights or else let us go wherever our eyes may lead us."[2]

Thus for many, migration was a radical way to "get out from under." Migration slowed down when the people won basic political and social reforms, such as the right to vote, equality before the law, and social security.

## Asian Migrants

Not all migration was from Europe. A substantial number of Chinese, Japanese, Indians, and Filipinos—to name only four key groups—responded to rural hardship with temporary or permanent migration. At least 3 million Asians moved abroad before 1920. Most went as indentured laborers to work on the plantations or in the gold mines of Latin America, southern Asia, Africa, California, Hawaii, and Australia. White estate owners very often used Asians to replace or supplement blacks after the suppression of the slave trade.

Such migration from Asia would undoubtedly have grown to much greater proportions if planters and mine owners in search of cheap labor had been able to hire as many Asian workers as they wished. But they could not. Asians fled the plantations and gold mines as soon as possible, seeking greater opportunities in trade and towns. There they came into conflict with local populations, whether in Malaya, East Africa, or areas settled by Europeans. These European settlers demanded a halt to Asian migration. By the 1880s, Americans and Australians were building **great white walls**—discriminatory laws designed to keep Asians out.

A crucial factor in the migrations before 1914 was, therefore, the general policy of "whites only" in the open lands of possible permanent settlement. This, too, was part of the West's growing dominance. Largely successful in monopolizing the best overseas opportunities, Europeans and people of European ancestry reaped the main benefits from the great migration. By 1913 people in Australia, Canada, and the United States all had higher average incomes than people in Great Britain, still Europe's wealthiest nation.

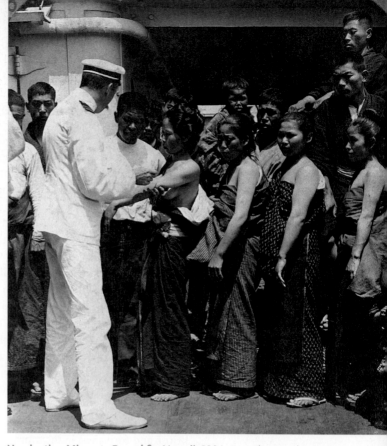

**Vaccinating Migrants Bound for Hawaii, 1904** First Chinese, then Japanese, and finally Koreans and Filipinos went across the Pacific in large numbers to labor in Hawaii on American-owned sugar plantations in the late nineteenth century. The native Hawaiians had been decimated by disease, creating a severe labor shortage for Hawaii's plantation economy. (Corbis)

**great white walls** Laws designed by Americans and Australians to keep Asians from settling in their countries.

# ▼ What characterized Western imperialism after 1880?

The expansion of Western society reached its apex between about 1880 and 1914, with Western powers rushing to create or enlarge vast political empires abroad. This political empire building contrasted sharply with the economic penetration of non-Western territories between 1816 and 1880, which had left a China or a Japan "opened" but politically independent. By contrast, the empires of the late nineteenth century recalled the old European colonial empires of the seventeenth and eighteenth centuries and led contemporaries to speak of the **new imperialism**.

Characterized by a frantic rush to conquer as many people and as much territory as possible, the new imperialism had momentous consequences. It resulted in new tensions among competing European states, and it led to wars and threats of war with

**new imperialism** The late-nineteenth-century drive by European countries to create vast political empires abroad.

**CHAPTER LOCATOR** | How did Western industrialization change the world economy? | What explains global migration patterns in this period? | **What characterized Western imperialism after 1880?** | How did non-Westerners respond to Western imperialism?

745

non-European powers. The new imperialism was aimed primarily at Africa and Asia. It put millions of black, brown, and yellow peoples directly under the rule of whites.

## The European Presence in Africa Before 1880

Prior to 1880, European nations controlled only 10 percent of the African continent, and their possessions were hardly increasing. The French had begun conquering Algeria in 1830, and by 1880 substantial numbers of French, Italian, and Spanish colonists had settled among the overwhelming Arab majority there. Yet the overall effect on Africa was minor.

At the southern tip of the continent, Britain had taken possession of the Dutch settlements at Cape Town during the Napoleonic wars. This British takeover of the Cape Colony had led disgruntled Dutch cattle ranchers and farmers in 1835 to make their so-called Great Trek into the interior, where they fought the Zulu and Xhosa peoples for land. After 1853 the Boers or **Afrikaners** (a-frih-KAH-nuhrz), as the descendants of the Dutch in the Cape Colony were beginning to call themselves, proclaimed their political independence and defended it against British armies. By 1880 Afrikaner and British settlers had wrested control of much of South Africa from the Zulu, Xhosa, and other African peoples.

Other than the French presence in the north and the British and Afrikaners in the south, Africa was largely free of Westerners. After 1880, the situation changed drastically. In a spectacular manifestation of the new imperialism, European countries jockeyed for territory in Africa, breaking sharply with previous patterns of colonization and diplomacy.

**Afrikaners** Descendants of the Dutch settlers in the Cape Colony in southern Africa.

**The Struggle for South Africa, 1878**

## The Scramble for Africa After 1880

Between 1880 and 1900, Britain, France, Germany, and Italy scrambled for African possessions (Map 25.2). By 1900 nearly the whole continent had been carved up and placed under European rule: only Ethiopia in northeast Africa, which was able to fight off Italian invaders, and Liberia on the West African coast, which had been settled by freed slaves from the United States, remained independent. In all other African territories, the European powers tightened their control and established colonial governments in the years before 1914.

The Dutch settler republics also succumbed to imperialism, but the final outcome was different. The British, led by Cecil Rhodes (1853–1902) in the Cape Colony, leapfrogged over the two Afrikaner states—Orange Free State and the Transvaal—in the early 1890s and established protectorates over Bechuanaland (bech-WAH-nuh-land) (now Botswana) and Rhodesia (now Zimbabwe and Zambia). Although unable to undermine the Afrikaners in the Transvaal, English-speaking capitalists like Rhodes developed gold mines there, and the British eventually conquered their white rivals in the South African War (1899–1902). In 1910 the old Afrikaner territories were united with the old Cape Colony and the eastern province of Natal in a new Union of South Africa, established as a largely "self-governing" colony. This enabled the defeated Afrikaners to use their numerical superiority over the British settlers to gradually take political power, as even the most educated nonwhites lost the right to vote outside the Cape Colony. (See "Individuals in Society: Cecil Rhodes," page 748.)

In the complexity of the European seizure of Africa, certain events and individuals stand out. Of enormous importance was the British occupation of Egypt in 1882, which

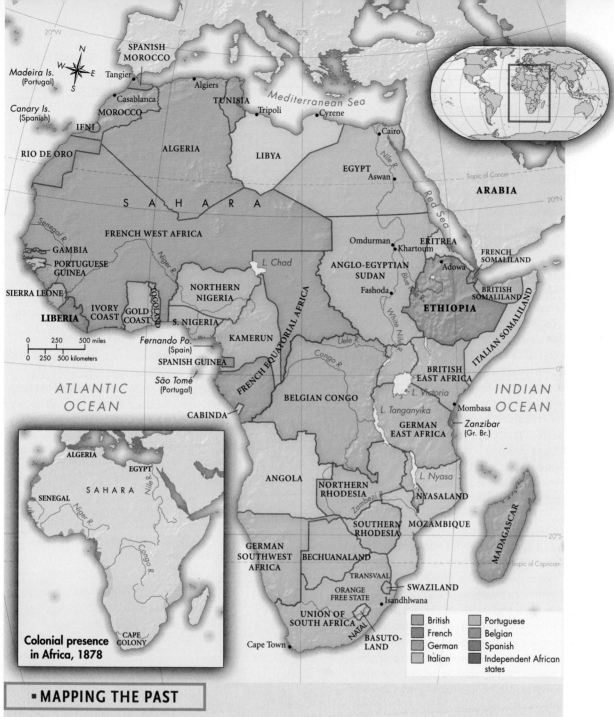

Colonial presence
in Africa, 1878

| British | Portuguese |
| French | Belgian |
| German | Spanish |
| Italian | Independent African states |

## ▪ MAPPING THE PAST

### Map 25.2 The Partition of Africa

The European powers carved up Africa after 1880 and built vast political empires. European states also seized territory in Asia in the nineteenth century, although some Asian states and peoples managed to maintain their political independence (see Map 25.3, page 751). Compare the patterns of European imperialism in Africa and Asia, using this map and Map 25.3.

**ANALYZING THE MAP** What European countries were leading imperialist states in both Africa and Asia, and what lands did they hold? What countries in Africa and Asia maintained their political independence? What did the United States and Japan have in common in Africa and Asia?

**CONNECTIONS** The late nineteenth century was the high point of European imperialism. What were the motives behind the rush for land and empire in Africa and Asia?

To complete this activity online, go to the Online Study Guide at bedfordstmartins.com/mckaywestunderstanding.

CHAPTER LOCATOR | How did Western industrialization change the world economy? | What explains global migration patterns in this period? | What characterized Western imperialism after 1880? | How did non-Westerners respond to Western imperialism?

747

# INDIVIDUALS IN SOCIETY

## Cecil Rhodes

**CECIL RHODES (1853-1902) EPITOMIZED THE**
dynamism and the ruthlessness of the new imperialism. He built a corporate monopoly, claimed vast tracts in Africa, and established the famous Rhodes scholarships to develop colonial (and American) leaders who would love and strengthen the British Empire. But to Africans, he left a bitter legacy.

Rhodes came from a large middle-class family and at seventeen went to southern Africa to seek his fortune. He soon turned to diamonds, newly discovered at Kimberley, picked good partners, and was wealthy by 1876. But Rhodes, often called a dreamer, wanted more. He entered Oxford University, while returning periodically to Africa, and his musings crystallized in a belief in progress through racial competition and territorial expansion. "I contend," he wrote, "that we [English] are the finest race in the world and the more of the world we inhabit the better it is for the human race."*

Rhodes's belief in British expansion never wavered. In 1880 he formed the De Beers Mining Company, and by 1888 his firm monopolized southern Africa's diamond production and earned fabulous profits. Rhodes also entered the Cape Colony's legislature and became the all-powerful prime minister from 1890 to 1896.

His main objective was to dominate the Afrikaner republics and to impose British rule on as much land as possible beyond their northern borders. Working through a state-approved private company financed in part by De Beers, Rhodes's agents forced and cajoled African kings to accept British "protection," then put down rebellions with Maxim machine guns. Britain thus obtained a great swath of empire on the cheap.

But Rhodes, like many high achievers obsessed with power and personal aggrandizement, went too far. He backed, and then in 1896 declined to call back, a failed invasion of the Transvaal, which was designed to topple the Dutch-speaking republic. Repudiated by top British leaders who had encouraged his plan, Rhodes had to resign as prime minister. In declining health, he continued to agitate against the Afrikaner republics. He died at age forty-nine as the South African War (1899–1902) ended.

In accounting for Rhodes's remarkable but flawed achievements, both sympathetic and critical biographers stress his imposing size, enormous energy, and powerful personality. His ideas were commonplace, but he believed in them passionately, and he could persuade and inspire others to follow his lead. Rhodes the idealist was nonetheless a born negotiator, a crafty deal maker who believed that everyone could be had for a price. According to his most insightful biographer, Rhodes's homosexuality — discreet, partially repressed, and undeniable — was also "a major component of his magnetism and his success."† Never comfortable with women, he loved male companionship. He drew together a "band of brothers," both gay and straight, to share in the pursuit of power.

Rhodes cared nothing for the rights of blacks. Ever a combination of visionary and opportunist, he looked forward to an eventual reconciliation of Afrikaners and British in a united white front. Therefore, as prime minister of the Cape Colony, he broke with the colony's liberal tradition and supported Afrikaner demands to reduce drastically the number of black voters and limit black freedoms. This helped lay the foundation for the Union of South Africa's brutal policy of racial segregation known as *apartheid* after 1948.

## QUESTIONS FOR ANALYSIS

1. In what ways does Rhodes's career epitomize the new imperialism in Africa?
2. How did Rhodes relate to Afrikaners and to black Africans? How do you account for the differences and the similarities?

*Robert Rotberg, *The Founder: Cecil Rhodes and the Pursuit of Power* (New York: Oxford University Press, 1988), p. 150.
†Ibid., p. 408.

**Cecil Rhodes, after crushing the last African revolt in Rhodesia in 1896.** (Brown Brothers)

established the new model of formal political control (see pages 740–742). There was also the role of Leopold II of Belgium (r. 1865–1909). As early as 1861, he had laid out his vision of expansion: "The sea bathes our coast, the world lies before us. Steam and electricity have annihilated distance, and all the nonappropriated lands on the surface of the globe can become the field of our operations and of our success."[3]

By 1876 Leopold was focusing on central Africa. Subsequently, he formed a financial syndicate under his personal control to send Henry M. Stanley, a journalist and part-time explorer, to the Congo basin. Stanley was able to establish trading stations, sign "treaties" with African chiefs, and plant Leopold's flag. Leopold's actions alarmed the French, who quickly sent out an expedition under Pierre de Brazza. In 1880 de Brazza signed a treaty of protection with the chief of the large Teke tribe and began to establish a French protectorate on the north bank of the Congo River.

Leopold's intrusion into the Congo area raised the question of the political fate of Africa. By 1882 Europe had caught "African fever" and the race for territory was on. To lay down some basic rules for this new and dangerous game of imperialist competition in sub-Saharan Africa, Jules Ferry of France and Otto von Bismarck (see Chapter 24) of Germany arranged an international conference on Africa in Berlin in 1884 and 1885. The Berlin conference established the principle that European claims to African territory had to rest on "effective occupation" in order to be recognized by other states. This meant that Europeans would push relentlessly into interior regions from all sides and that no single European power would be able to claim the entire continent. The conference recognized Leopold's personal rule over a neutral Congo free state and agreed to work to stop slavery and the slave trade in Africa.

The Berlin conference coincided with Germany's sudden emergence as an imperial power. Prior to about 1880, Bismarck had seen little value in colonies. Then in 1884 and 1885, as political agitation for expansion increased, Bismarck did an abrupt about-face, and Germany established protectorates over a number of small African kingdoms and tribes in Togo, the Cameroons region, southwest Africa, and, later, East Africa. In acquiring colonies, Bismarck cooperated against the British with France's Jules Ferry, an ardent republican who also embraced imperialism. With Bismarck's tacit approval, the French pressed southward from Algeria, eastward from their old forts on the Senegal coast, and northward from their protectorate on the Congo River.

Meanwhile, the British began enlarging their West African enclaves and pushed northward from the Cape Colony and westward from Zanzibar. Their thrust southward from Egypt was blocked in Sudan by fiercely independent Muslims who massacred a British force at Khartoum in 1885.

A decade later, another British force, under General Horatio H. Kitchener, moved up the Nile River, building a railroad to supply arms and reinforcements as it went. Finally, in 1898 these British troops met their foe at Omdurman (ahm-duhr-MAHN) (see Map 25.2), where Muslim tribesmen armed with spears were cut down by the recently invented Maxim machine gun. In the end, eleven thousand Muslim tribesmen lay dead, while only twenty-eight Britons had been killed.

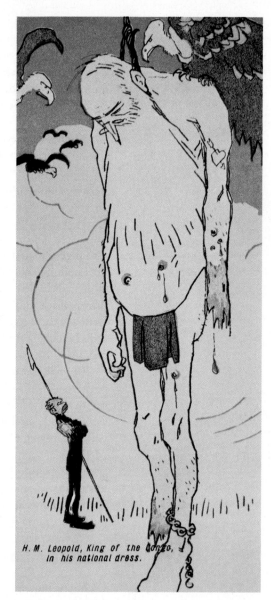

H. M. Leopold, King of the Congo, in his national dress.

**European Imperialism at Its Worst** This 1908 English cartoon, "Leopold, King of the Congo, in his national dress," focuses on the barbaric practice of cutting off the hands and feet of Africans who refused to gather as much rubber as Leopold's company demanded. In 1908 an international human rights campaign forced the Belgian king to cede his personal fief to the Belgian state. (The Granger Collection, NY)

**Berlin conference** A meeting of European leaders held in 1884 and 1885 in order to lay down some basic rules for imperialist competition in sub-Saharan Africa.

CHAPTER LOCATOR | How did Western industrialization change the world economy? | What explains global migration patterns in this period? | What characterized Western imperialism after 1880? | How did non-Westerners respond to Western imperialism?

749

Continuing up the Nile after the Battle of Omdurman, Kitchener's armies found that a small French force had already occupied the village of Fashoda (fuh-SHOH-duh). The result was a serious diplomatic crisis and the threat of war. Eventually, wracked by the Dreyfus affair (see Chapter 24) and unwilling to fight, France backed down and withdrew its forces, allowing the British to take over.

The British conquest of Sudan exemplifies the general process of empire building in Africa. The fate of the Muslim force at Omdurman was eventually inflicted on all native peoples who resisted European rule: destruction by a vastly superior military force. But however much the European powers squabbled for territory and privilege around the world, they always had the sense to stop short of actually fighting each other. Imperial ambitions were not worth a great European war.

## Imperialism in Asia

Although the sudden division of Africa was more spectacular, Europeans also extended their political control in Asia. In 1815 the Dutch ruled little more than the island of Java in the East Indies. Thereafter they gradually brought almost all of the archipelago under their political authority, though they had to share some of the spoils with Britain and Germany. In the critical decade of the 1880s, the French under the leadership of Ferry took Indochina. India, Japan, and China also experienced a profound imperialist impact (Map 25.3).

Two other great imperialist powers, Russia and the United States, also acquired rich territories in Asia. Russia moved steadily forward on two fronts throughout the nineteenth century. Russians conquered Muslim areas to the south in the Caucasus and in Central Asia, reaching the border of Afghanistan in 1885. Russia also encroached on China's outlying provinces in the Far East, especially in the 1890s.

The great conquest by the United States was the Philippines, taken from Spain in 1898 after the Spanish-American War. When it quickly became clear that the United States had no intention of granting independence, Philippine patriots rose in revolt and were suppressed only after long, bitter fighting. Thus another great Western power joined the imperialist ranks in Asia.

## Causes of the New Imperialism

Economic motives played an important role in the extension of political empires, especially in the British Empire. By the late 1870s, France, Germany, and the United States were industrializing rapidly behind rising tariff barriers. Great Britain was losing its early lead and facing increasingly tough competition in foreign markets. In this new economic climate, Britain came to value old possessions, especially India, which it had exploited most profitably for more than a century. When continental powers began to grab Asian and African territory in the 1880s, the British followed suit immediately. They feared that France and Germany would seal off their empires with high tariffs and that future economic opportunities would be lost forever.

Actually, the overall economic gains of the new imperialism proved quite limited before 1914. The new colonies were simply too poor to buy much, and they offered few immediately profitable investments. Nonetheless, even the poorest colony was jealously prized, and no territory was ever abandoned. This was because colonies became important for political and diplomatic reasons. Each leading country saw colonies as crucial to national security and military power. For instance, safeguarding the Suez Canal played a key role in the British occupation of Egypt, and protecting Egypt in turn led to the bloody conquest of Sudan.

Many people were convinced that colonies were essential to great nations. The famous and influential nationalist historian of Germany, Heinrich von Treitschke (HAHYN-

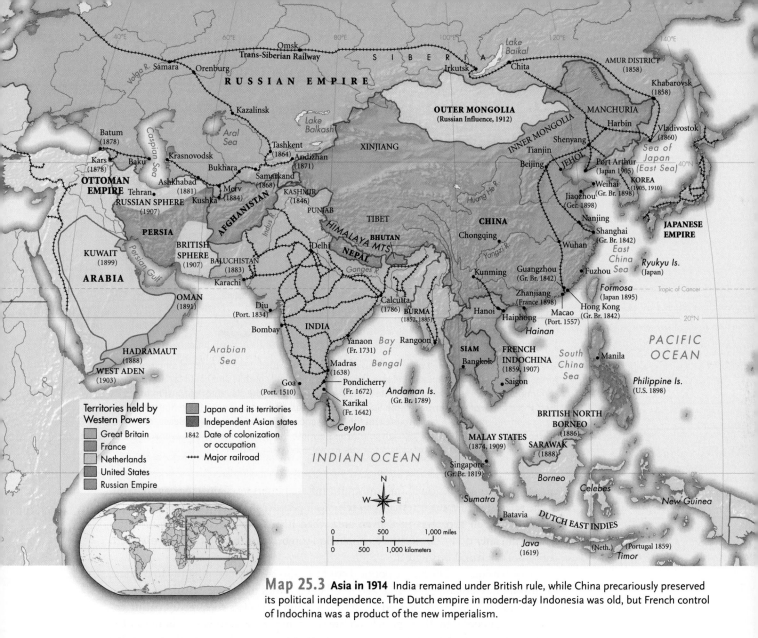

**Map 25.3 Asia in 1914** India remained under British rule, while China precariously preserved its political independence. The Dutch empire in modern-day Indonesia was old, but French control of Indochina was a product of the new imperialism.

rihkh fuhn TRIGHCH-kuh), spoke for many when he wrote: "Every virile people has established colonial power. . . . All great nations in the fullness of their strength have desired to set their mark upon barbarian lands and those who fail to participate in this great rivalry will play a pitiable role in time to come."[4]

Treitschke's statement reflects not only the increasing aggressiveness of European nationalism after Bismarck's wars of German unification, but also Social Darwinian theories of competition among races. European nations, which were seen as racially distinct parts of the dominant white race, had to seize colonies to show they were strong and virile. Moreover, since racial struggle was nature's inescapable law, the conquest of "inferior" peoples was just. "The path of progress is strewn with the wreck . . . of inferior races," wrote one professor in 1900. Social Darwinism and harsh racial doctrines fostered imperialist expansion.

So did the industrial world's unprecedented technological and military superiority. Three aspects were particularly important. First, the rapidly firing Maxim machine gun, so lethal at Omdurman in Sudan, was an ultimate weapon in many another unequal battle. Second, newly discovered quinine proved no less effective in controlling attacks of malaria, which had previously decimated whites in the tropics whenever they left their

**CHAPTER LOCATOR**

How did Western industrialization change the world economy?

What explains global migration patterns in this period?

What characterized Western imperialism after 1880?

How did non-Westerners respond to Western imperialism?

**751**

**Tools for Empire Building** Western technological advances aided Western political ambitions in Africa and Asia. The Maxim machine gun shown here was highly mobile and could lay down a continuous barrage that would decimate charging enemies, as in the slaughter of Muslim tribesmen at the battle of Omdurman in the Sudan. Quinine was also very important to empire building. First taken around 1850 in order to prevent the contraction of the deadly malaria disease, quinine enabled European soldiers and officials to move safely into the African interior and overwhelm native peoples. (gun: Lordprice Collection/Alamy; quinine: Wellcome Library, London)

coastal enclaves and ventured into mosquito-infested interiors. Third, the combination of the steamship and the international telegraph permitted Western powers to quickly concentrate their firepower in a given area when it was needed. Never before — and never again after 1914 — would the technological gap between the West and non-Western regions of the world be so great.

Social tensions and domestic political conflicts also contributed mightily to overseas expansion. In Germany, in Russia, and in other countries to a lesser extent, contemporary critics of imperialism charged conservative political leaders with manipulating colonial issues in order to divert popular attention from the class struggle at home and to create a false sense of national unity. Thus imperial propagandists relentlessly stressed that colonies benefited workers as well as capitalists, providing jobs and cheap raw materials that raised workers' standard of living. Government leaders encouraged the masses to savor foreign triumphs and glory in the supposed increase in national prestige. In short, conservative leaders defined imperialist development as a national necessity, which they used to justify the status quo and their hold on power.

Finally, certain special-interest groups in each country were powerful agents of expansion. Shipping companies wanted lucrative subsidies. White settlers demanded more land and greater protection. Missionaries and humanitarians wanted to spread religion and stop the slave trade within Africa. Military men and colonial officials, whose role has often been overlooked, foresaw rapid advancement and highly paid positions in growing empires. The actions of such groups pushed the course of empire forward.

## A "Civilizing Mission"

Western society did not rest the case for empire solely on a Darwinian racial struggle or on power politics. Imperialists developed additional arguments in order to satisfy their consciences and answer their critics.

A favorite idea was that Europeans could and should "civilize" more primitive non-white peoples. According to this view, nonwhites would eventually receive the benefits of modern economies, cities, advanced medicine, and higher standards of living. In time, they might be ready for self-government and Western democracy. Thus the French spoke of their sacred "civilizing mission." In 1899 Rudyard Kipling (1865–1936) exhorted Europeans (and Americans in the United States) to unselfish service in distant lands in his poem "The White Man's Burden":

> *Take up the White Man's Burden—*
> *Send forth the best ye breed—*
> *Go bind your sons to exile*
> *To serve your captives' need,*
> *To wait in heavy harness,*
> *On fluttered folk and wild—*
> *Your new-caught, sullen peoples*
> *Half-devil and half-child.*[5]

Many Americans accepted the ideology of the white man's burden. It was an important factor in the decision to rule, rather than liberate, the Philippines after the Spanish-American War. Like their European counterparts, these Americans believed that their civilization had reached unprecedented heights and that they had unique benefits to bestow on all "less advanced" peoples.

Peace and stability under European control also facilitated the spread of Christianity. In Africa Catholic and Protestant missionaries competed with Islam south of the Sahara, seeking converts and building schools to spread the Gospel. Some peoples, such as the Ibo in Nigeria, became highly Christianized.

Such occasional successes in black Africa contrasted with the general failure of missionary efforts in India, China, and the Islamic world. Yet the number of Christian believers around the world did increase substantially in the nineteenth century, and missionary groups kept trying.

## Critics of Imperialism

The expansion of empire aroused sharp, even bitter, critics. A forceful attack was delivered in 1902, after the unpopular South African War, by radical English economist J. A. Hobson (1858–1940) in his *Imperialism*, a work that influenced Lenin and others. Hobson contended that the rush to acquire colonies was due to the economic needs of unregulated capitalism, particularly the need of the rich to find outlets for their surplus capital. Yet, Hobson argued, imperial possessions did not pay off economically for the country as a whole. Only unscrupulous special-interest groups profited from them, at the expense of both the European taxpayer and the natives. Moreover, Hobson argued that the quest for empire diverted popular attention away from domestic reform and the need to reduce the great gap between rich and poor.

Hobson and many other critics rebelled against crude Social Darwinian thought. "O Evolution, what crimes are committed in thy name!" cried one foe. Another sardonically coined a new beatitude: "Blessed are the strong, for they shall prey on the weak."[6] In 1902 in *Heart of Darkness* Polish-born novelist Joseph Conrad (1857–1924) castigated the "pure selfishness" of Europeans in "civilizing" Africa; the main character, once a liberal scholar, turns into a savage brute.

Critics charged Europeans with applying a degrading double standard and failing to live up to their own noble ideals. At home Europeans had won or were winning representative government, individual liberties, and a certain equality of opportunity. In their empires, Europeans imposed military dictatorships on Africans and Asians; forced

**white man's burden** The idea that Europeans could and should civilize more primitive nonwhite peoples and that imperialism would eventually provide nonwhites with modern achievements and higher standards of living.

CHAPTER LOCATOR | How did Western industrialization change the world economy? | What explains global migration patterns in this period? | **What characterized Western imperialism after 1880?** | How did non-Westerners respond to Western imperialism?

753

them to work involuntarily, almost like slaves; and discriminated against them shamelessly. Only by renouncing imperialism, its critics insisted, and giving captive peoples the freedoms Western society had struggled for since the French Revolution would Europeans be worthy of their traditions. Europeans who denounced the imperialist tide provided colonial peoples with a Western ideology of liberation.

# ▼ How did non-Westerners respond to Western imperialism?

To peoples in Africa and Asia, Western expansion represented a profoundly disruptive assault. Everywhere it threatened traditional ruling classes, local economies, and existing ways of life. Christian missionaries and European secular ideologies challenged established beliefs and values. Non-Western peoples experienced a crisis of identity, one made all the more painful by the power and arrogance of the white intruders.

## The Pattern of Response

Generally, the initial response of African and Asian rulers to aggressive Western expansion was to try to drive the unwelcome foreigners away. However, the superior military technology of the industrialized West almost invariably prevailed. Beaten in battle, many Africans and Asians concentrated on preserving their cultural traditions at all costs. Others found themselves forced to reconsider their initial hostility. Some (such as Ismail of Egypt) concluded that the West was indeed superior in some ways and that it was therefore necessary to reform their societies and copy some European achievements. Thus it is possible to think of responses to the Western impact as a spectrum, with "traditionalists" at one end, "westernizers" or "modernizers" at the other, and many shades of opinion in between. Both before and after European domination, the struggle among these groups was often intense. With time, however, the modernizers tended to gain the upper hand.

When the power of both the traditionalists and the modernizers was thoroughly shattered by superior force, the great majority of Asians and Africans accepted imperial rule. In these circumstances Europeans governed smoothly and effectively, receiving considerable support from both traditionalists (local chiefs, landowners, religious leaders) and modernizers (Western-educated professional classes and civil servants).

Nevertheless, imperial rule was in many ways an imposing edifice built on sand. Support for European rule among the conquered masses was shallow and weak. Thus the native people followed with greater or lesser enthusiasm a few determined personalities who came to oppose the Europeans. Such leaders always arose, both when Europeans ruled directly and when they manipulated native governments, for at least two basic reasons.

First, the nonconformists—the eventual anti-imperialist leaders—came to feel that human dignity was incompatible with foreign rule. Second, and somewhat ironically, potential leaders found in the Western world the ideologies and justification for their protest. They discovered liberalism, with its credo of civil liberty and political self-determination. They echoed the demands of anti-imperialists in Europe and America that the West live up to its own ideals. Above all, they found themselves attracted to modern nationalism, which asserted that every people had the right to control its own destiny. After 1917 anti-imperialist revolt would find another weapon in Lenin's version of Marxian socialism. Thus the anti-imperialist search for dignity drew strength from

Western thought and culture, as is particularly apparent in the development of three major Asian countries—India, Japan, and China.

## Empire in India

No colonial area experienced a more profound British impact than India. Unlike Japan and China, which maintained a real or precarious independence, and unlike African territories, which were annexed by Europeans only at the end of the nineteenth century, India was ruled more or less absolutely by Britain for a very long time.

Arriving in India in the seventeenth century, the British East India Company had conquered the last independent native state by 1848. The last "traditional" response to European rule—the attempt by the established ruling classes to drive the British out by military force—was broken in India in 1857 and 1858. Those were the years of the Great Rebellion (which the British called a "mutiny"), when an insurrection by Muslim and Hindu mercenaries in the British army spread throughout northern and central India before it was finally crushed, primarily by loyal native troops from southern India. Britain then ruled India directly until Indian independence was gained in 1947.

After 1858 India was ruled by the British Parliament in London and administered by a tiny, all-white civil service in India. The British white elite, backed by white officers and native troops, was competent and generally well-disposed toward the welfare of the Indian peasant masses. Yet it practiced strict job discrimination and social segregation, as most of its members quite frankly considered Indian peoples to be racially inferior. As Lord Kitchener, a top military commander in India, stated:

**The Great Rebellion, 1857–1858**

Under British control
Area of rebellion

**Great Rebellion** The 1857 and 1858 insurrection by Muslim and Hindu mercenaries in the British army that spread throughout northern and central India before finally being crushed.

*It is this consciousness of the inherent superiority of the European which has won for us India. However well educated and clever a native may be, and however brave he may prove himself, I believe that no rank we can bestow on him would cause him to be considered an equal of the British officer.*[7]

British women played an important part in the imperial enterprise, especially after the opening of the Suez Canal in 1869 made it much easier for British men to bring their wives and children with them to India. These British families tended to live in their own separate communities, where they occupied large houses with a multitude of servants. It was the wife's responsibility to manage this complex household.

A small minority of British women—many of them feminists, social reformers, or missionaries, both married and single—sought to go further and shoulder the "white women's burden" in India, as one historian has described it.[8] These women tried especially to improve the lives of Indian women, both Hindu and Muslim, and to move them closer through education and legislation to the better conditions that they believed Western women had attained. Their greatest success was educating some elite Hindu women who took up the cause of reform.

With British men and women sharing a sense of mission as well as strong feelings of racial and cultural superiority, the British acted energetically and introduced many desirable changes to India. Realizing that they needed well-educated Indians to serve as skilled subordinates in the government and army, the British established a modern system of progressive secondary education in which all instruction was in English. Thus

CHAPTER LOCATOR | How did Western industrialization change the world economy? | What explains global migration patterns in this period? | What characterized Western imperialism after 1880? | How did non-Westerners respond to Western imperialism?

755

**Imperial Complexities in India** Britain permitted many native princes to continue their rule, if they accepted British domination. This photo shows a road-building project designed to facilitate famine relief in a southern native state. Officials of the local Muslim prince and their British "advisers" watch over workers drawn from the Hindu majority. (Nizam's Good Works Project—Famine Relief: Road Building, Aurangabad 1895–1902, from Judith Mara Gutman, *Through Indian Eyes*. Courtesy, Private Collection)

through education and government service, the British offered some Indians opportunities for both economic and social advancement. High-caste Hindus emerged as skillful intermediaries between the British rulers and the Indian people, and soon they formed a new elite profoundly influenced by Western thought and culture.

This new bureaucratic elite played a crucial role in modern economic development, which was a second result of British rule. Irrigation projects for agriculture, the world's third-largest railroad network for good communications, as well as large tea and jute plantations geared to the world economy were all developed.

Finally, with a well-educated, English-speaking Indian bureaucracy and modern communications, the British created a unified, powerful state. They placed under the same general system of law and administration the different Hindu and Muslim peoples as well as the vanquished kingdoms of the entire subcontinent—groups that had fought each other for centuries and had been repeatedly conquered by Muslim and Mongol invaders.

In spite of these achievements, the decisive reaction to European rule was the rise of nationalism among the Indian elite. No matter how anglicized and necessary a member of the educated classes became, he or she could never become the white ruler's equal. The top jobs, the best clubs, the modern hotels, and even certain railroad compartments were sealed off to brown-skinned Indians. The peasant masses might accept such inequality as the latest version of age-old oppression, but the well-educated, English-speaking elite eventually could not. For the elite, racial discrimination flagrantly contradicted the cherished Western concepts of human rights and equality. Moreover, it was based on dictatorship, no matter how benign.

By 1885, when educated Indians came together to found the predominately Hindu Indian National Congress, demands were increasing for the equality and self-government that Britain had already granted white-settler colonies, such as Canada and Australia. By 1907, emboldened in part by Japan's success (see the next section), the radicals in the Indian National Congress were calling for complete independence. Although there were sharp divisions between Hindus and Muslims, Indians were finding an answer to the foreign challenge. The common heritage of British rule and Western ideals, along with the reform and revitalization of the Hindu religion, had created a genuine movement for national independence.

## The Example of Japan

When Commodore Matthew Perry arrived in Japan in 1853, Japan was a complex feudal society. At the top stood a figurehead emperor, but real power was in the hands of a hereditary military governor, the shogun. With the help of a warrior nobility known as samurai, the shogun governed a country of peasants and city dwellers. The intensely proud samurai were humiliated by the sudden American intrusion and the unequal treaties with Western countries.

When foreign diplomats and merchants began to settle in Yokohama, radical samurai reacted with a wave of antiforeign terrorism and antigovernment assassinations between 1858 and 1863. In, response an allied fleet of American, British, Dutch, and French warships demolished key forts, further weakening the power and prestige of the shogun's government. Then in 1867, a coalition of samurai seized control of the government and restored the political power of the emperor. This was the **Meiji Restoration**, a great turning point in Japanese development.

The immediate, all-important goal of the new government was to meet the foreign threat. The battle cry of the Meiji (MAY-jee) reformers was "Enrich the state and strengthen the armed forces." Yet how were these tasks to be done? In an about-face, the leaders of Meiji Japan dropped their antiforeign attacks. Convinced that Western civilization was indeed superior in its military and industrial aspects, they initiated from above a series of measures to reform Japan along modern lines. In the broadest sense, the Meiji leaders tried to harness the power inherent in Europe's dual revolution in order to protect their country and catch up with the West.

In 1871 the new leaders abolished the old feudal structure of aristocratic, decentralized government and formed a strong unified state. Following the example of the French Revolution, they dismantled the four-class legal system and declared social equality. They created a free, competitive, government-stimulated economy. Japan began to build railroads and modern factories. Thus the new generation adopted many principles of a free, liberal society, and, as in Europe, such freedom resulted in a tremendously creative release of human energy.

Yet the overriding concern of Japan's political leadership was always a powerful state and a strong military. (See "Listening to the Past: Lin Zexu and Yamagata Aritomo, Confronting Western Imperialism," page 758.) A powerful modern navy was created, and the army was completely reorganized along European lines, with three-year military service required for all males and a professional officer corps. Japan also borrowed rapidly and adapted skillfully the West's science and modern technology, particularly in industry,

**Meiji Restoration** The restoration of the Japanese emperor to power in 1867, leading to the subsequent modernization of Japan.

CHAPTER LOCATOR | How did Western industrialization change the world economy? | What explains global migration patterns in this period? | What characterized Western imperialism after 1880? | **How did non-Westerners respond to Western imperialism?**

757

# LISTENING TO THE PAST

## Lin Zexu and Yamagata Aritomo, Confronting Western Imperialism

*For centuries China was the world's largest and most self-sufficient state, and in 1800 the Qing (Manchu) Dynasty was still upholding China's traditional sovereignty and majesty. Foreign merchants could trade only with licensed Chinese merchants through the port of Guangzhou (Canton) on the south China coast. By 1830, however, British merchants were also smuggling highly addictive opium into China and earning colossal illegal profits.*

*In 1838 the Chinese government moved aggressively to deal with the crisis. It dispatched Lin Zexu, an energetic top official, to Guangzhou to stamp out the opium trade. Lin dealt harshly with Chinese buyers and then confiscated the opium stores of the British merchants. He also wrote a famous letter to Queen Victoria, calling on her to help end the drug trade and explaining why the Chinese government had acted. Neither Lin's action nor his eloquent letter, a portion of which follows, were successful. British armies attacked, China was "opened," and the opium trade continued.*

### Lin Zexu, Letter to Queen Victoria

❝ His Majesty the Emperor comforts and cherishes foreigners as well as Chinese: he loves all the people of the world without discrimination. Whenever profit is found, he wishes to share it with all men; whenever harm appears, he likewise will eliminate it on behalf of all mankind. His heart is in fact the heart of the universe.

Generally speaking, the succeeding rulers of your honorable country have been respectful and obedient. Time and again they have sent petitions to China, saying: "We are grateful to His Majesty the Emperor for the impartial and favorable treatment he has granted to the citizens of my country who have come to China to trade. . . ."

As this trade has lasted for a long time, there are bound to be unscrupulous as well as honest traders. Among the unscrupulous are those who bring opium to China to harm the Chinese; they succeed so well that this poison has spread far and wide in all the provinces. You, I hope, will certainly agree that people who pursue material gains to the great detriment of the welfare of others can be neither tolerated by Heaven nor endured by men. . . .

I have heard that the areas under your direct jurisdiction such as London, Scotland, and Ireland do not produce opium; it is produced instead in your Indian possessions. . . . In these possessions the English people . . . also open factories to manufacture this terrible drug. As months accumulate and years pass by, the poison they have produced increases in its wicked intensity, and its repugnant odor reaches as high as the sky. Heaven is furious with anger, and all the gods are moaning with pain. It is hereby suggested that you destroy and plow under all of these opium plants and grow food crops instead,

while issuing an order to punish severely anyone who dares to plant opium poppies again. . . .

Since a foreigner who goes to England to trade has to obey the English law, how can an Englishman not obey the Chinese law when he is physically within China? The present law calls for the imposition of the death sentence on any Chinese who has peddled or smoked opium. Since a Chinese could not peddle or smoke opium if foreigners had not brought it to China, it is clear that the true culprits are the opium traders from foreign countries. Being the cause of other people's death, why should they be spared from capital punishment? A murderer of one person is subject to the death sentence; just imagine how many people opium has killed! This is the rationale behind the new law which says that any foreigner who brings opium to China will be sentenced to death by hanging or beheading. Our purpose is to eliminate this poison once and for all and to the benefit of all mankind. ❞

*European traders and missionaries arrived in Japan in the sixteenth century, but in 1640 the government expelled the Europeans in order to preserve the existing Japanese culture and society. Three centuries later, Japan met the challenge of the West by adopting many of the methods and technologies of the West. Yamagata Aritomo (1838–1922) contributed significantly to this effort and its success.*

*Born into the military nobility known as the samurai, Yamagata Aritomo joined in the Meiji Restoration (see page 757), and to him fell the task of strengthening the armed forces, which the Meiji reformers had separated from the civilian officials. Traveling to Europe and carefully studying European armies and navies, he returned home in 1872 and wrote the memorandum reprinted here, "Opinion on Military Affairs and Conscription." The next year, he helped reorganize Japanese society by writing a new law calling for a Japanese army drafted from the whole male population, on the Western pattern. No longer would fighting be the province of samurai alone.*

### Yamagata Aritomo, "Opinion on Military Affairs and Conscription"

❝ A military force is required to defend the country and protect its people. Previous laws of this country inculcated in the minds of the samurai those basic functions, and there was no separation between the civilian and military affairs. Nowadays civilian officials and military officials have separate functions, and the

The new Japanese army in about 1870, wearing Western uniforms and marching in formation. (Laurie Platt Winfrey, Inc./The Granger Collection, NY)

It is recommended that our country adopt a system under which any able-bodied man twenty years of age be drafted into military service, . . . and after completion of a period of service, they shall be returned to their homes. In this way every man will become a soldier, and not a single region in the country will be without defense. Thus our defense will become complete.

The second concern of the Ministry is coastal defense. This includes building of warships and constructing coastal batteries. Actually, battleships are moveable batteries. Our country has thousands of miles of coastline, and any remote corner of our country can become the advance post of our enemy. . . .

At a time like this it is very clear where the priority of this country must lie. We must now have a well-trained standing army supplemented by a large number of reservists. We must build warships and construct batteries. We must train officers and soldiers. We must manufacture and store weapons and ammunitions. The nation may consider that it cannot bear the expenses. . . . [but] we cannot do without our defense for a single day. **》**

practice of having the samurai serve both functions has been abandoned. It is now necessary to select and train those who can serve the military functions, and herein lies the change in our military system. . . .

The creation of a standing army for our country is a task which cannot be delayed. . . .

The so-called reservists do not normally remain within military barracks. During peacetime they remain in their homes, and in an emergency they are called to service. All of the countries in Europe have reservists, and amongst them Prussia has most of them. There is not a single able-bodied man in Prussia who is not trained in military affairs. Recently Prussia and France fought each other and the former won handily. . . .

**Sources:** Lin Zexu, "Letter to Queen Victoria, 1839," from *China in Transition, 1517–1911,* ed. Zen Kuofan and Dun J. Li (Van Nostrand, 1969), pp. 64–67; "Opinion on Military Affairs and Conscription" from *Japan: A Documentary History,* ed. David J. Lu. (Armonk, N.Y.: M. E. Sharpe, 1997), pp. 315–318. Translation © 1997 by David J. Lu. Reprinted by permission of M. E. Sharpe, Inc. All rights reserved. Not for reproduction.

## QUESTIONS FOR ANALYSIS

1. According to Lin, why did China move against the drug trade, and why should Queen Victoria help?
2. What measures does Yamagata advocate? Why? What lessons does he draw from Europe?
3. What similarities and differences do you see in the situations and the thinking of Lin and Yamagata?

**CHAPTER LOCATOR** | How did Western industrialization change the world economy? | What explains global migration patterns in this period? | What characterized Western imperialism after 1880? | How did non-Westerners respond to Western imperialism?

**759**

medicine, and education. Many Japanese were encouraged to study abroad, and the government paid large salaries to attract foreign experts. These experts were replaced by trained Japanese as soon as possible.

By 1890, when the new state was firmly established, the wholesale borrowing of the early restoration had given way to more selective emphasis on those things foreign that were in keeping with Japanese tradition. Following the model of the German Empire, Japan established an authoritarian constitution and rejected democracy.

Japan successfully copied the imperialism of Western society. Expansion not only proved that Japan was strong but it also cemented the nation together in a great mission. Having "opened" Korea with the gunboat diplomacy of imperialism in 1876, Japan decisively defeated China in a war over Korea in 1894 and 1895 and took Formosa (modern-day Taiwan). In the next years, Japan competed aggressively with the leading European powers for influence and territory in China, particularly in Manchuria. There Japanese and Russian imperialism met and collided. In 1904 Japan attacked Russia. After a bloody war, Japan emerged with a valuable foothold in China, Russia's former protectorate over Port Arthur (see Map 25.3). By 1910, with the annexation of Korea, Japan had become a major imperialist power.

Japan became the first non-Western country to use love of country to transform itself and thereby meet the challenge of Western expansion. Moreover, Japan demonstrated convincingly that a modern Asian nation could defeat and humble a great Western power. Japan provided patriots throughout Asia and Africa with an inspiring example of national recovery and liberation.

## Toward Revolution in China

In 1860 the two-hundred-year-old Qing Dynasty in China appeared on the verge of collapse. Efforts to repel foreigners had failed. Rebellion and chaos wracked the country. Yet the government drew on its traditional strengths and made a surprising comeback that lasted more than thirty years.

Two factors were crucial in this reversal. First, the traditional ruling groups temporarily produced new and effective leadership. Loyal scholar-statesmen and generals quelled disturbances such as the great Tai Ping (tigh-PIHNG) rebellion. The remarkable empress dowager Tzu Hsi (tsoo shee) governed in the name of her young son, combining shrewd insight with vigorous action to revitalize the bureaucracy.

Second, destructive foreign aggression lessened, for the Europeans had obtained their primary goal of commercial and diplomatic relations. Indeed, some Europeans contributed to the dynasty's recovery. An Irishman effectively reorganized China's customs office, increasing government tax receipts, and a sympathetic American diplomat represented China in foreign lands, helping to strengthen the central government. Such efforts dovetailed with the dynasty's efforts to adopt some aspects of Western government and technology while maintaining traditional Chinese values and beliefs.

The parallel movement toward domestic reform and limited cooperation with the West collapsed under the blows of Japanese imperialism. The Sino-Japanese War of 1894 to 1895 and the subsequent harsh peace treaty revealed China's helplessness in the face of aggression, triggering a rush for foreign concessions and protectorates in China. At the high point of this rush in 1898, it appeared that the European powers might actually divide China among themselves. Probably only the jealousy each nation felt toward its imperialist competitors saved China from partition. In any event, the tempo of foreign encroachment greatly accelerated after 1894.

China's precarious position after the war with Japan led to a renewed drive for fundamental reforms. Like the leaders of the Meiji Restoration, some modernizers saw salvation in Western institutions. In 1898 they convinced the young emperor to launch a

# Le Petit Parisien

**SUPPLÉMENT LITTÉRAIRE ILLUSTRÉ**

TOUS LES JOURS
Le Petit Parisien
5 CENTIMES.

DIRECTION: 18, rue d'Enghien, PARIS

TOUS LES JEUDIS
SUPPLÉMENT LITTÉRAIRE
5 CENTIMES.

## ▪ PICTURING THE PAST

### Demonizing the Boxer Rebellion

For months this Sunday supplement to a very popular French newspaper ran gruesome front page pictures of ferocious Boxers burning buildings, murdering priests, and slaughtering Chinese Christians. Whipping up European outrage about native atrocities was a prelude to harsh reprisals by the Western powers. (Mary Evans Picture Library/The Image Works)

**ANALYZING THE IMAGE**  What is happening in this picture? How would you characterize the mood of the crowd?

**CONNECTIONS**  The images of Cairo's new quarter (page 735), the Egyptian travel guide (page 741), and the Chinese shown here were all drawn by European artists for Europeans. What, if any, similarities do these images share? What do they suggest to Europeans at home about colonial empires abroad and the native peoples who lived there? How does the perspective in the print by a Japanese artist for a Japanese audience (page 759) differ?

To complete this activity online, go to the Online Study Guide at **bedfordstmartins.com/ mckaywestunderstanding**.

**hundred days of reform**
A series of Western-style reforms
launched in 1898 by the Chinese
government in an attempt to
meet the foreign challenge.

hundred days of reform in an attempt to meet the foreign challenge. More radical reformers, such as the revolutionary Sun Yatsen (soun yaht-SEN) (1866–1925) sought to overthrow the dynasty altogether and establish a republic.

The efforts at radical reform by the young emperor and his allies threatened the Manchu establishment and the empress dowager Tzu Hsi, who had dominated the court for the past quarter of a century. Pulling a palace coup, she and her supporters imprisoned the emperor, rejected the reform movement, and put reactionary officials in charge. Hope for reform from above was crushed.

A violent reaction swept the country, encouraged by the Manchu court and led by a secret society that foreigners called the Boxers. These Boxers blamed China's ills on foreigners. Above all, the conservative, patriotic, antiforeign Boxers charged foreign missionaries with undermining the Chinese reverence for their ancestors thereby threatening the Chinese family and the entire society. The Boxers and other secret societies struck out at their enemies. In northeastern China, more than two hundred foreign missionaries and several thousand Chinese Christians were killed, prompting threats and demands from Western governments. The empress dowager answered by declaring war, hoping that the Boxers might relieve the foreign pressure on the Manchu dynasty.

The imperialist response was swift and harsh. After the Boxers besieged the embassy quarter in Beijing, foreign governments organized an international force of twenty thousand soldiers to rescue their diplomats and punish China. Beijing was occupied and plundered by Western armies. In 1901 China was forced to accept a long list of penalties, including a heavy financial indemnity.

The years after this heavy defeat were ever more troubled. Anarchy and foreign influence spread as the power and prestige of the Qing Dynasty declined still further. Finally in 1912, a spontaneous uprising toppled the Qing Dynasty. After thousands of years of emperors and empires, a loose coalition of revolutionaries proclaimed a Western-style republic and called for an elected parliament. The transformation of China under the impact of expanding Western society entered a new phase, and the end was not in sight.

# ← LOOKING BACK LOOKING AHEAD →

IN THE EARLY TWENTIETH CENTURY, educated Europeans had good reason to believe that they were living in an age of progress. The ongoing triumphs of industry and science and the steady improvements in the standard of living from about 1850 were undeniable, and it was generally assumed that that these favorable trends would continue. There had also been progress in the political realm. The bitter class conflicts that culminated in the bloody civil strife of 1848 had given way in most European countries to stable nation-states with elected legislative bodies that reflected the general population, responded to real problems, and enjoyed popular support. Moreover, there had been no general European war since Napoleon I had been defeated in 1815. Only the brief, limited wars connected with German and Italian unification at mid-century had broken the peace in the European heartland.

In the global arena, peace was much more elusive. In the name of imperialism, Europeans (and North Americans) used war and the threat of war to open markets and punish foreign governments around the world. Although criticized by some intellectuals and leftists such as J. A. Hobson, these foreign campaigns in the late-nineteenth century resonated with European citizens and stimulated popular nationalism. Like fans in a sports bar, the peoples of Europe followed their teams and cheered them on to victories that were almost certain. Thus imperialism and nationalism reinforced and strengthened each other in Europe, especially after 1875.

This was a dangerous development. Easy imperialist victories over weak states and poorly armed non-Western peoples encouraged excessive pride and led Europeans to underestimate the fragility of their accomplishments. Imperialism also made nationalism more aggressive and militaristic. And as European imperialism was dividing the world after 1875, the leading European states were also dividing themselves into two opposing military alliances. Thus when the two armed camps stumbled into war in 1914, there would be a superabundance of nationalistic fervor, patriotic sacrifice, and military destruction. ■

- **For a list of suggested readings for this chapter, visit** *bedfordstmartins.com/mckaywestunderstanding.*

- **For primary sources from this period, see** *Sources of Western Society,* Second Edition.

- **For Web sites, images, and documents related to topics in this chapter, see Make History at** *bedfordstmartins.com/mckaywestunderstanding.*

CHAPTER LOCATOR | How did Western industrialization change the world economy? | What explains global migration patterns in this period? | What characterized Western imperialism after 1880? | How did non-Westerners respond to Western imperialism?

763

# Chapter 25 Study Guide

Online Study Guide
bedfordstmartins.com/mckaywestunderstanding

## Step 1

**GETTING STARTED** Below are basic terms about this period in the history of Western civilization. Can you identify each term below and explain why it matters? To do this exercise online, go to bedfordstmartins.com/mckaywestunderstanding.

| TERMS | WHO (OR WHAT) AND WHEN | WHY IT MATTERS |
|---|---|---|
| Third World, p. 736 | | |
| opium trade, p. 739 | | |
| gunboat diplomacy, p. 740 | | |
| great migration, p. 742 | | |
| great white walls, p. 745 | | |
| new imperialism, p. 745 | | |
| Afrikaners, p. 746 | | |
| Berlin conference, p. 749 | | |
| white man's burden, p. 753 | | |
| Great Rebellion, p. 755 | | |
| Meiji Restoration, p. 757 | | |
| hundred days of reform, p. 762 | | |

## Step 2

**MOVING BEYOND THE BASICS** The exercise below requires a more advanced understanding of the chapter material. Examine the "new imperialism" of the late nineteenth century by filling in the chart below with descriptions of the causes, motives, and characteristics of Western expansion before and after 1880. When you are finished, consider the following questions: How did the nature of Western domination change after 1880? How would you explain this change? To do this exercise online, go to bedfordstmartins.com/mckaywestunderstanding.

| | CAUSES AND MOTIVES | KEY CHARACTERISTICS |
|---|---|---|
| Western Expansion Before 1880 | | |
| Western Expansion After 1880 | | |

**PUTTING IT ALL TOGETHER** Now that you've reviewed key elements of the chapter, take a step back and try to see the big picture. Remember to use specific examples from the chapter in your answers. To do this exercise online, go to bedfordstmartins.com/mckaywestunderstanding.

### INDUSTRIALIZATION AND THE WORLD ECONOMY

- How did the West come to dominate the world economy? What role did industrialization and its products play in this process?

- Compare and contrast Western penetration and domination of China, Japan, and Egypt. What common patterns do you note? How would you explain them?

### THE GREAT MIGRATION

- How did population pressure contribute to European migration in the nineteenth century? What other factors spurred Europeans to leave their homelands?

- Compare and contrast European and Asian migration during the nineteenth century. What important differences do you note? What common factors help explain the movements of both groups of migrants?

### WESTERN IMPERIALISM, 1880–1914

- What role did Western domestic politics play in Western imperialism after 1880? How did European governments use the acquisition of colonies to their political advantage?

- How did Westerners justify imperialism? How did Western critics of imperialism challenge such justifications?

### RESPONDING TO WESTERN IMPERIALISM

- Compare and contrast the positions of "traditionalists" and "modernizers." Which group tended to gain the upper hand in colonized societies? Why?

- How did non-Westerners use Western ideas and culture to resist imperialism?

■ **In Your Own Words** Imagine that you must explain Chapter 25 to someone who hasn't read it. What would be the most important points to include and why?

# 26

# War and Revolution

## 1914–1919

In the summer of 1914, the nations of Europe went willingly to war. Both peoples and governments confidently expected a short war leading to a decisive victory and thought that European society would be able to go on as before. These expectations were almost totally mistaken. The First World War was long, indecisive, and tremendously destructive. To the shell-shocked generation of survivors, it was known simply as the Great War because of its unprecedented scope and intensity.

From today's perspective, it is clear that the First World War was closely connected to the ideals and developments of the previous century. Industrialization, which promised a rising standard of living for the people, now produced horrendous weapons that killed and maimed millions. Imperialism, which promised to "civilize" those the Europeans considered savages, now led to intractable international conflicts. Nationalism, which promised to bring compatriots together in a harmonious nation state, now encouraged hateful prejudice and chauvinism.

The war would also have an enormous impact on the century that followed. The need to provide extensive supplies and countless soldiers for the war effort created mass suffering, encouraged the rise of the bureaucratic state, and brought women in increasing numbers into the workplace. Millions were killed or wounded at the front and millions more grieved these losses. Grand states collapsed: the Russian, Austro-Hungarian, and Ottoman empires passed into history. The trauma of war contributed to the rise of extremist politics: in the Russian Revolution of 1917 the Bolsheviks established a radical communist regime, and totalitarian fascist movements gained popularity across Europe in the postwar decades. Explaining the war's causes and consequences remains one of the great challenges for historians of modern Europe. ■

**Life in World War I.** This painting by British artist Paul Nash portrays a supply road on the western front. Nash's somber palate, tiny figures, and cubist-influenced landscape capture the devastation and anonymous violence of total war. (© Imperial War Museum, London, UK/The Bridgeman Art Library)

# Chapter Preview

▶ What caused the outbreak of the First World War?

▶ How did the First World War differ from previous wars?

▶ In what ways did the war transform life on the home front?

▶ Why did world war lead to revolution in Russia?

▶ In what ways was the Allied peace settlement flawed?

# ▼ What caused the outbreak of the First World War?

The war had no single most important cause. Growing competition over colonies and world markets, a belligerent arms race, and a series of diplomatic crises sharpened international tensions. On the home front, new forms of populist nationalism strengthened people's unquestioning belief in their country. At the same time, ongoing domestic conflicts encouraged governments to pursue aggressive foreign policies in attempts to bolster national unity. All helped pave the road to war.

## Growing International Conflict

The First World War began, in part, because European statesmen failed to resolve the diplomatic problems created by Germany's rise to Great Power status. The Franco-Prussian War and the unification of Germany opened a new era in international relations. By war's end in 1871, France was defeated, and Bismarck had made Prussia-Germany the most powerful nation in Europe (see Chapter 24). After 1871, Bismarck declared Germany to be a "satisfied" power. Within Europe, he claimed, Germany had no territorial ambitions and wanted only peace.

But how was peace to be preserved? Bismarck's first concern was to keep France diplomatically isolated and without military allies. His second concern was the threat to peace posed by the conflicting interests of Austria-Hungary and Russia, particularly in southeastern Europe, where the decline of the Ottoman Empire had created a power vacuum in the disputed border territories of the Balkans.

Bismarck's accomplishments in foreign policy were great, but only temporary. From 1871 to the late 1880s, he maintained German leadership in international affairs, and he signed a series of defensive alliances with Austria-Hungary and Russia designed to isolate a hostile France. Yet in 1890 the new emperor William II dismissed Bismarck, in part because he disagreed with the chancellor's friendly policy toward Russia. Under William II, Bismarck's carefully planned alliance system began to unravel. Germany refused to renew a nonaggression pact with Russia, the centerpiece of Bismarck's system, in spite of Russian willingness to do so. This prompted France to court Russia, offering loans, arms, and support. In early 1894 France and Russia became military allies. As a result, continental Europe was divided into two rival blocs. The **Triple Alliance** of Austria, Germany, and Italy faced an increasingly hostile Dual Alliance of Russia and France.

As rivalries deepened on the continent, Great Britain's foreign policy became increasingly crucial. After 1891, Britain was the only uncommitted Great Power. Many Germans and some Britons felt that the racially related Germanic and Anglo-Saxon peoples were natural allies. However, the good relations that had prevailed between Prussia and Great Britain since the mid-eighteenth century gave way to a bitter Anglo-German rivalry.

There were several reasons for this development. Commercial rivalry in world markets between Germany and Great Britain increased sharply in the 1890s, as Germany became a great industrial power. Germany's ambitious pursuit of colonies further threatened British interests. Above all, Germany's decision in 1900 to expand greatly its battle fleet posed a challenge to Britain's long-standing naval supremacy.

Increased Anglo-German tensions coincided with the Boer War between the British and the Dutch in South Africa, which encouraged worldwide opposition to British imperialism. Thus British leaders prudently set about shoring up their exposed position with alliances and agreements. Britain improved its relations with the United States, concluded an alliance with Japan in 1902, and allied with France in the Anglo-French Entente of 1904.

**Triple Alliance** The alliance of Austria, Germany, and Italy. Italy left the alliance when war broke out in 1914 on the grounds that Austria had launched a war of aggression.

Chapter 26
**War and Revolution**
768          1914–1919

CHAPTER LOCATOR | What caused the outbreak of the First World War?

Alarmed by Britain's ever-closer ties to France, Germany's leaders decided to test the strength of their alliance. In 1905 William II declared that Morocco was an independent, sovereign state and demanded that Germany receive the same trading rights as France. This saber rattling, termed the First Moroccan Crisis, clearly violated long-standing French colonial interests in the region. William II insisted on an international conference in hopes of settling the Moroccan question to Germany's benefit. But William II's bullying only brought France and Britain closer together, and Germany left the conference empty-handed.

The result of the First Moroccan Crisis was something of a diplomatic revolution. Britain, France, Russia, and even the United States began to see Germany as a potential threat. At the same time, German leaders began to see sinister plots to encircle Germany and block its development as a world power. In 1907 Russia, battered by its disastrous war with Japan and the revolution of 1905, agreed to settle its quarrels with Great Britain and signed the Anglo-Russian Agreement. This agreement laid the foundation of the Triple Entente (ahn-TAHNT), an alliance between Britain, Russia, and France.

Germany's decision to add a large, enormously expensive fleet of big-gun battleships to its already expanding navy also heightened tensions. German patriots saw a large navy as the legitimate right of a great world power and as a source of national pride. But British leaders saw the German buildup as a military challenge that forced them to spend the "People's Budget" (see Chapter 24) on battleships rather than on social welfare. By 1909, Britain had sided psychologically, if not officially, with France and Russia.

The leading nations of Europe were divided into two hostile camps, both ill-prepared to deal with the worsening situation in the Balkans. Britain, France, and Russia—the members of the Triple Entente—were allied in direct opposition to the German-led Triple Alliance (Map 26.1). By 1914, many believed that war was inevitable.

## The Mood of 1914

Diplomatic rivalries and international crises played key roles in the rush to war, but a complete understanding of the war's origins requires an account of the "mood of 1914"—the attitudes and convictions of Europeans around 1914.[1] Widespread militarism (the popular approval of military institutions and their values) and nationalism encouraged leaders and citizens alike to see international relations as an arena for the testing of national power, with war if necessary.

Military institutions played a prominent role in affairs of state and in the lives of ordinary people across Europe. In a period marked by diplomatic tensions, politicians relied on generals and military experts to help shape public policy. All the Great Powers

# Chapter Chronology

| | |
|---|---|
| **1914–1918** | World War I |
| **June 28, 1914** | Serbian nationalist assassinates Archduke Francis Ferdinand |
| **August 1914** | War begins; Ottoman Empire joins the Central Powers |
| **September 1914** | Battle of the Marne; German victories on the eastern front |
| **1915** | Italy joins the Triple Entente; German submarine sinks the *Lusitania*; Germany halts unrestricted submarine warfare |
| **1915–1918** | Armenian genocide; German armies occupy large parts of east-central Europe |
| **1916** | Battles of Verdun and the Somme |
| **1916–1918** | Antiwar movement spreads throughout Europe; Arab rebellion against Ottoman Empire |
| **1917** | Germany resumes unrestricted submarine warfare |
| **March 1917** | February Revolution in Russia |
| **April 1917** | United States enters the war |
| **October– November 1917** | Battle of Caporetto |
| **November 1917** | Bolshevik Revolution in Russia; Balfour Declaration on Jewish Homeland in Palestine |
| **1918** | Treaty of Brest-Litovsk; revolution in Germany |
| **1918–1920** | Civil war in Russia |
| **1919** | Treaty of Versailles; Allies invade Turkey |
| **1923** | Treaty of Lausanne recognizes Turkish independence |

**Triple Entente** The alliance of Great Britain, France, and Russia in the First World War.

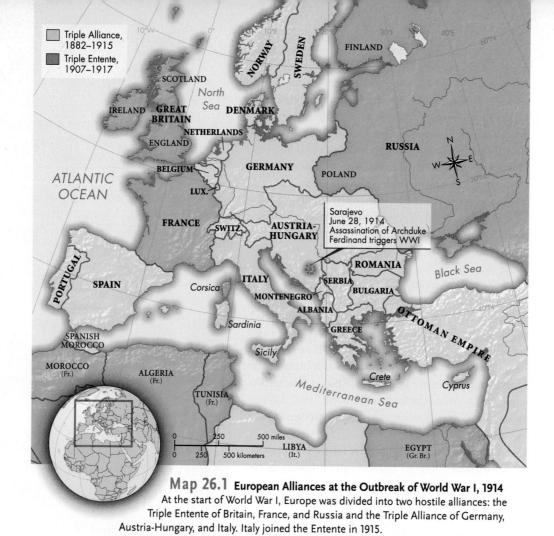

**Map 26.1** European Alliances at the Outbreak of World War I, 1914
At the start of World War I, Europe was divided into two hostile alliances: the Triple Entente of Britain, France, and Russia and the Triple Alliance of Germany, Austria-Hungary, and Italy. Italy joined the Entente in 1915.

*Map legend:*
Triple Alliance, 1882–1915
Triple Entente, 1907–1917

*Map callout:*
Sarajevo June 28, 1914 Assassination of Archduke Ferdinand triggers WWI

built up their armed forces and designed mobilization plans to rush men and weapons to the field of battle. Universal conscription in Germany, France, Italy, Austria-Hungary, and Russia—only Britain still relied on a volunteer army—exposed young men to military culture and discipline.

The continent had not experienced a major conflict since the Franco-Prussian War (1870–1871), and Europeans vastly underestimated the destructive potential of modern weapons. Encouraged by the patriotic national press, many believed that war was glorious, manly, and heroic. As one German volunteer wrote in his diary as he left for the front in 1914, "I believe that this war is a challenge for our time and for each individual, a test by fire, that we may ripen into manhood, become men able to cope with the coming stupendous years and events."[2]

Support for military values was closely linked to a growing sense of popular nationalism. Since the 1850s, the spread of the idea that members of an ethnic group should live together in a homogeneous, united national state had provoked all kinds of international conflicts over borders and citizenship rights. Nationalism also drove the arms race and the struggle over colonies. Broad popular commitment to national interests above all else weakened groups that thought in terms of international communities and consequences. Expressions of antiwar sentiment by socialists or women's groups were seen as a betrayal of country in time of need. Inspired by nationalist beliefs, much of the population was ready for war.

Chapter 26
**War and Revolution**
**770** 1914–1919

CHAPTER LOCATOR | What caused the outbreak of the First World War?

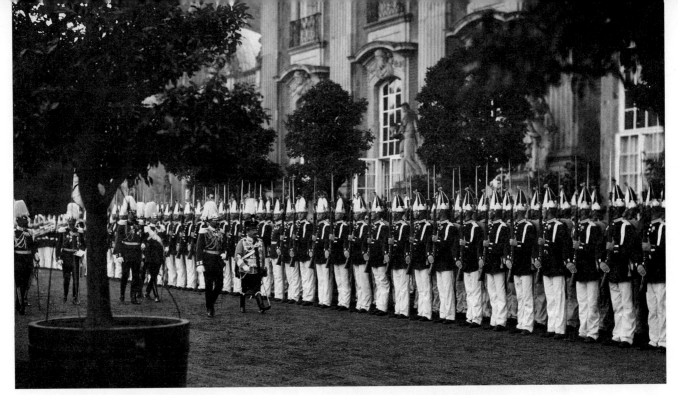

**German Militarism** The German emperor William II (left) reviews his troops with the Italian king Victor Emmanuel in front of the royal palace in Potsdam in 1902. Aggressive militarism and popular nationalism helped pave the road to war. (© Scherl/SV-Bilderdienst/The Image Works)

## The Outbreak of War

On June 28, 1914, Archduke Francis Ferdinand, heir to the Austro-Hungarian throne, was assassinated by Serbian revolutionaries during a state visit to the Bosnian capital of Sarajevo (sar-uh-YAY-voh). Gavrilo Princip, a member of the radical group Young Bosnia, shot the archduke and his wife Sophie as they passed by in their automobile.

Princip's deed, in the crisis-ridden territories of the Balkans on the border between the weakened Ottoman and Austro-Hungarian Empires, led Europe into world war. In the early years of the twentieth century, war in the Balkans seemed inevitable. Between 1900 and 1914, the Western powers had successfully forced the Ottoman rulers to give up their European territories (Map 26.2). The ethnic nationalism inspired by these changing state boundaries was destroying the Ottoman Empire and threatening Austria-Hungary. The only questions were what kinds of wars would result and where they would lead.

By the early twentieth century, nationalism in southeastern Europe was on the rise. Independent Serbia in particular was eager to build a state that would include all ethnic Serbs. Serbia was thus openly hostile to Austria-Hungary and the Ottoman Empire, since both states included substantial Serbian minorities within their borders. To block Serbian expansion, Austria in 1908 formally annexed the territories of Bosnia and Herzegovina (hert-suh-goh-VEE-nuh). The southern part of the Austro-Hungarian Empire now included an even larger Serbian population. Serbians expressed rage but could do nothing without support from Russia, their traditional ally.

The tensions in the Balkans soon erupted into a regional war. In the First Balkan War (1912), Serbia joined Greece and Bulgaria to attack the Ottoman Empire and then quarreled with Bulgaria over the spoils of victory. In the Second Balkan War (1913), Bulgaria attacked its former allies. Austria intervened and forced Serbia to give up Albania.

How did the First World War differ from previous wars?

In what ways did the war transform life on the home front?

Why did world war lead to revolution in Russia?

In what ways was the Allied peace settlement flawed?

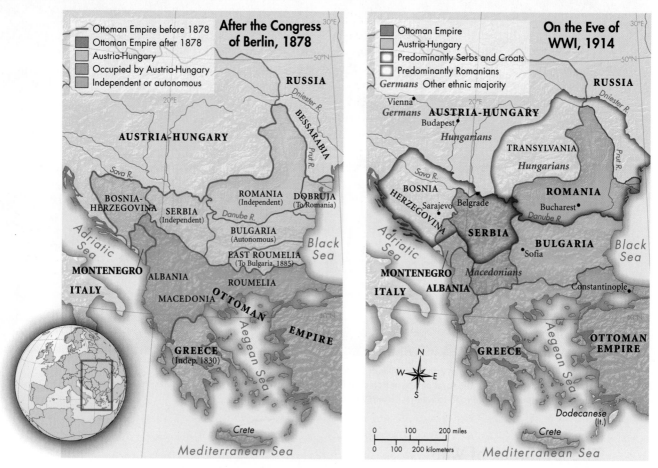

**Map 26.2** **The Balkans, 1878–1914** After the Congress of Berlin in 1878, the Ottoman Empire suffered large territorial losses but remained a power in the Balkans. By 1914 Ottoman control had given way to ethnic boundaries that did not follow political boundaries, and Serbian national aspirations threatened Austria-Hungary.

Encouraged by their success against the Ottoman Empire, Balkan nationalists increased their demands for freedom from Austrian control, dismaying the leaders of the multinational Austro-Hungarian Empire. The former hoped and the latter feared that Austria might next be broken apart.

Within this complex context, the assassination of Archduke Ferdinand instigated a five-week period of intense diplomatic activity that culminated in world war. The leaders of Austria-Hungary concluded that Serbia was implicated in the assassination and deserved severe punishment. On July 23 Austria-Hungary presented Serbia with an unconditional ultimatum, including demands that would violate Serbian sovereignty. When Serbia replied moderately but evasively, Austria mobilized its armies and declared war on Serbia on July 28.

From the beginning of the crisis, Germany pushed Austria-Hungary to confront Serbia and thus bore much responsibility for escalating the conflict. Emperor William II and his chancellor Theobald von Bethmann-Hollweg realized that war between Austria and Russia was likely, for Russia would not stand by and watch the Austrians crush the Serbs. Yet Bethmann-Hollweg hoped that, although Russia (and its ally France) would go to war, Great Britain would remain neutral. To take advantage of these conditions, the German chancellor sent a telegram to Austria-Hungary that promised Germany's unconditional support in case of war. Germany's actions encouraged the Austrians to take a

Chapter 26
**War and Revolution**
772    1914–1919

CHAPTER LOCATOR    What caused the outbreak of the First World War?

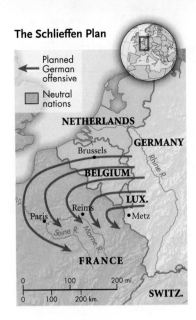

**The Schlieffen Plan**

Planned German offensive

Neutral nations

NETHERLANDS

GERMANY

Brussels

BELGIUM

Rhine R.

LUX.

Paris • Reims • Metz

Seine R. Marne R.

FRANCE

0   100   200 mi.
0   100   200 km.

SWITZ.

hard line against the Serbs at a time when moderation might still have limited the crisis.

In fact, the diplomatic situation quickly spiraled out of control as military plans and timetables began to dictate policy. Russia required much more time to mobilize its armies than did Germany and Austria-Hungary. And since the complicated mobilization plans of the Russian general staff assumed a two-front war with both Austria and Germany, Russia could not mobilize against one without mobilizing against the other. Therefore, on July 29 Tsar Nicholas II ordered full mobilization and in effect declared war. The German general staff also thought in terms of a two-front war. Their misguided **Schlieffen Plan** called for a quick victory over France after a lightning attack through neutral Belgium before turning on Russia. On August 3 German armies invaded Belgium. Great Britain declared war on Germany the following day.

**Schlieffen Plan** Failed German plan calling for a lightning attack through neutral Belgium and a quick defeat of France before turning on Russia.

# ▼ How did the First World War differ from previous wars?

When the Germans invaded Belgium in August 1914, they and everyone else thought, incorrectly, that the war would be short and relatively painless. Instead, on the western front in France and the eastern front in Russia, the belligerent armies bogged down in a new kind of war, termed total war by German general Erich Ludendorff. Total war meant new roles for soldiers and civilians alike. At the front, total war meant lengthy, violent, and deadly battles fought with all the weapons industrialized society could produce. At home, national economies were geared toward the war effort. Governments revoked civil liberties, and many civilians lost lives or livelihoods as occupying armies moved through their towns and cities. The struggle expanded beyond Europe, and the Middle East, Africa, East Asia, and the United States were all brought into the maelstrom of total war.

**total war** A war in which distinctions between the soldiers on the battlefield and civilians at home are blurred, and where the government plans and controls economic and social life in order to supply the armies at the front with supplies and weapons.

## Stalemate and Slaughter on the Western Front

In the face of the German invasion, the Belgian army defended its homeland and fell back in good order to join a rapidly landed British army corps near the Franco-Belgian border. With the outbreak of the war, Russian armies immediately attacked eastern Germany, forcing the Germans to transfer much-needed troops to the east. Instead of quickly capturing Paris per the Schlieffen Plan, by the end of August German soldiers were advancing slowly along an enormous front.

On September 6 the French attacked a gap in the German line at the Battle of the Marne. For three days, France threw everything into the attack. At one point, the French government desperately requisitioned all the taxis of Paris to rush reserves to the troops at the front. Finally, the Germans fell back. France had been miraculously saved (Map 26.3).

By November 1914, an unbroken line of four hundred miles of defensive trenches extended from the Belgian coast through northern France and on to the Swiss frontier. Armies on both sides dug in behind rows of trenches, mines, and barbed wire defenses. The cost in lives of trench warfare was staggering. Recently invented weapons made battle impersonal, traumatic, and extremely deadly. The machine gun, hand grenades, poison

**trench warfare** A type of fighting behind rows of trenches, mines, and barbed wire; the cost in lives was staggering and the gains in territory minimal.

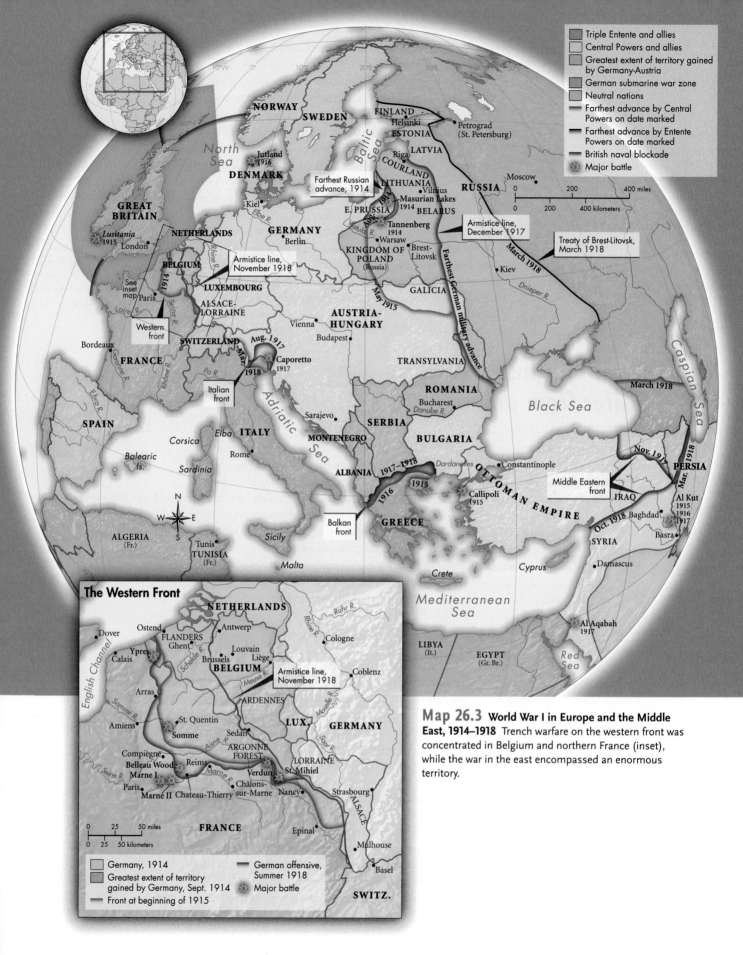

### The Western Front

**Map 26.3 World War I in Europe and the Middle East, 1914–1918** Trench warfare on the western front was concentrated in Belgium and northern France (inset), while the war in the east encompassed an enormous territory.

Triple Entente and allies
Central Powers and allies
Greatest extent of territory gained by Germany-Austria
German submarine war zone
Neutral nations
Farthest advance by Central Powers on date marked
Farthest advance by Entente Powers on date marked
British naval blockade
Major battle

Germany, 1914
Greatest extent of territory gained by Germany, Sept. 1914
Front at beginning of 1915
German offensive, Summer 1918
Major battle

Chapter 26
War and Revolution
1914–1919

774

CHAPTER LOCATOR

What caused the outbreak of the First World War?

gas, flamethrowers, long-range artillery, the airplane, and the tank were all used to maximum effect, some for the first time. All these favored the defense, increased casualty rates, and revolutionized the practice of war.

The high commands of the combatant nations, who had learned military tactics and strategy in the nineteenth century, hardly understood trench warfare. For four years the generals repeated the same mistakes, mounting massive offensives designed to achieve decisive breakthroughs. Brutal frontal assaults against highly fortified trenches might overrun the enemy's front line, but attacking soldiers rarely captured any substantial territory. In hard-fought battles on all fronts, millions of young men were wounded or lost their lives for no real gain.

The Battle of the Somme, a great British offensive undertaken in the summer of 1916 in northern France, exemplified the horrors of trench warfare. The battle began with a week-long heavy artillery bombardment on the German line, intended to cut the barbed wire fortifications, decimate the enemy trenches, and prevent the Germans from making an effective defense. On July 1 British troops climbed out of the trenches and moved into no-man's land in the direction of the German lines.

At the beginning of the bombardment, the Germans had fled into their dugouts—underground shelters dug deep into the trenches—where they waited out the artillery attack. As the British soldiers neared the German lines and the shelling stopped, the Germans emerged from their bunkers, set up their machine guns, and mowed down the approaching troops. In many places, the wire had not been cut by the bombardment, so the struggling attackers made especially easy targets. About 20,000 British men were killed and 40,000 wounded on the first day of the attack. The battle dragged on until November, and in the end the British did push the Germans back—a whole seven miles. Some 420,000 British, 200,000 French, and 600,000 Germans were killed or wounded defending an insignificant piece of land.

**The Battle of the Somme, 1916**

As of July 1, 1916
- British- and French-held territory
- German-held territory
- Woods
- Road
- Front lines July–Nov. 1916

## The Widening War

On the eastern front, the slaughter did not immediately degenerate into trench warfare, and the fighting was dominated by Germany. Repulsing the initial Russian attacks, the Germans won major victories at the Battles of Tannenberg and the Masurian Lakes in August and September 1914. By 1915 the eastern front had stabilized in Germany's favor. A staggering 2.5 million Russian soldiers had been killed, wounded, or captured. German armies occupied huge swaths of the Russian empire in central Europe, including ethnic Polish, Belarusian, and Baltic territories. Yet Russia was not knocked out of the war, marking another failure of the Schlieffen Plan.

To govern the occupied territories in central Europe, the Germans installed a vast military bureaucracy. Anti-Slavic prejudice dominated the mind-set of the occupiers. The local Slavs were seen as savages and ethnic "mongrels." The military administration used prisoners of war and refugees as forced labor. About one-third of the civilian population was killed or became refugees under this brutal occupation. In the long run, the German state hoped to turn these territories into German possessions, a forerunner of Nazi policies in World War II.[3]

The changing tides of victory and hopes for territorial gains brought neutral countries into the war (see Map 26.3). Italy, a member of the Triple Alliance since 1882, had

| How did the First World War differ from previous wars? | In what ways did the war transform life on the home front? | Why did world war lead to revolution in Russia? | In what ways was the Allied peace settlement flawed? |

775

**Writing Home from the Front** Cramped within the tight network of trenches on the western front, a British soldier writes a letter home while his compatriots rest before the next engagement. The post was typically the only connection between soldiers and their relatives, and over 28 billion pieces of mail passed between home and front on all sides during the war. Mass-produced postcards such as this one often displayed fantasies about loved ones at home. (photo: Courtesy of the Trustees of the Imperial War Museum; postcard: Imperial War Museum/The Art Archive)

declared its neutrality in 1914 on the grounds that Austria had launched a war of aggression. Then in May 1915 Italy joined the Triple Entente of Great Britain, France, and Russia in return for promises of Austrian territory.

In October 1914 the Ottoman Empire entered the war on the side of Austria and Germany, by then known as the Central Powers. The following September Bulgaria decided to follow the Ottoman Empire's lead in order to settle old scores with Serbia. The Balkans, with the exception of Greece, were occupied by the Central Powers.

The entry of the Ottoman Turks carried the war into the Middle East. Heavy fighting between the Ottomans and the Russians enveloped the Armenians, who lived on both sides of the border and had experienced brutal repression by the Turks in 1909. When in 1915 some Armenians welcomed Russian armies as liberators, the Ottoman government, with German support, ordered a mass deportation of its

**The Armenian Genocide, 1915–1918**

Black Sea

RUSSIAN EMPIRE

Caspian Sea

Constantinople

GREECE

OTTOMAN EMPIRE

PERSIA (IRAN)

☐ Armenian ethnic area
● Massacre and deportation site (size indicates relative death toll)
☐ Modern Armenia

Chapter 26
War and Revolution
1914–1919

776

CHAPTER LOCATOR | What caused the outbreak of the First World War?

**Armenian Deportation** In 1915 when some Armenians welcomed Russian armies as liberators after years of persecution, the Ottoman government ordered a genocidal mass deportation of its Armenian citizens from their homeland in the empire's eastern provinces. This photo, taken from a hotel window in Kharpert by a German businessman in 1915, shows Turkish guards marching Armenian men off to prison, where they were tortured to death. A million Armenians died from murder, starvation, and disease during World War I. (Courtesy of the Armenian Library, Watertown, Mass.)

Armenian citizens from their homeland. In this example of modern ethnic cleansing, now termed the Armenian genocide, a million innocent civilians died from murder, starvation, and disease.

In 1915, at the Battle of Gallipoli, British forces tried and failed to take the Dardanelles and Constantinople from the Ottoman Turks. The invasion force was pinned down on the beaches, and the ten-month-long battle cost the Turks 300,000 and the British 265,000 men killed, wounded, or missing.

The British were more successful at inciting the Arabs to revolt against their Turkish rulers. They bargained with the foremost Arab leader, Hussein ibn-Ali (1856–1931). Controlling much of the Ottoman Empire's territory along the Red Sea, an area known as the Hejaz (see Map 26.5, on page 795), Hussein managed in 1915 to win vague British commitments for an independent Arab kingdom. Thus in 1916 Hussein revolted against the Turks, proclaiming himself king of the Arabs. He joined forces with the British under T. E. Lawrence, who in 1917 helped lead Arab soldiers in a successful guerrilla war against the Turks on the Arabian peninsula.

Similar victories were eventually scored in the Ottoman province of Iraq. Britain occupied the southern Iraqi city of Basra in 1914 and captured Baghdad in 1917. The British armies and their Arab allies also invaded Palestine and in September 1918 rolled into Syria. Arab patriots in Syria and Iraq now expected a large, unified Arab nation-state to rise from the dust of the Ottoman collapse — though in the event the Western Powers

How did the First World War differ from previous wars?    In what ways did the war transform life on the home front?    Why did world war lead to revolution in Russia?    In what ways was the Allied peace settlement flawed?

777

refused to allow Arab independence as promised, and instead established a mandate system that replaced Ottoman rule with British and French control (see page 793).

The war spread to colonial Africa and East Asia as well. Instead of revolting as the Germans hoped, the colonial subjects of the British and French generally supported the allied powers. Colonized peoples helped local British and French commanders seize Germany's colonies around the globe. More than a million Africans and Asians served in the various armies of the warring powers.

In April 1917 the United States declared war on Germany, another crucial development in the expanding conflict. American intervention grew out of the war at sea and general sympathy for the Triple Entente. At the beginning of the war, Britain and France established a naval blockade to strangle the Central Powers. No neutral cargo ship was permitted to sail to Germany. In early 1915 Germany retaliated with submarine warfare.

In May 1915 a German submarine sank the British passenger liner *Lusitania*, claiming more than 1,000 lives, among them 139 U.S. citizens. President Woodrow Wilson protested vigorously, using the tragedy to incite American public opinion against the Germans. As a result, Germany halted its submarine warfare for almost two years; the alternative was almost certain war with the United States.

Early in 1917 the German military command—confident that improved submarines could starve Britain into submission before the United States could come to its rescue—resumed unrestricted submarine warfare. This was a reckless gamble, and the United States declared war on Germany. Eventually the United States tipped the balance in favor of the Triple Entente and its allies.

## ▼ In what ways did the war transform life on the home front?

The war's impact on civilians was no less massive than it was on the men in the trenches. Total war encouraged the growth of state bureaucracies, changed the lives of ordinary women and men, and by the end inspired mass antiwar protest movements.

### Mobilizing for Total War

In August 1914 many people greeted the outbreak of hostilities enthusiastically. In every country, ordinary folk believed that their nation was right to defend itself from foreign aggression. Yet by mid-October generals and politicians had begun to realize that victory would require more than patriotism. Each combatant country experienced a desperate need for men and weapons. To keep the war machine moving, national leaders aggressively intervened in society and the economy.

By the late nineteenth century the responsive national state had already shown an eagerness to manage the welfare of its citizens (see Chapter 24). Now the state intruded even further into people's daily lives. Each combatant state established new government ministries to mobilize soldiers and armaments and to provide care for war widows and wounded veterans. Censorship offices controlled news about the course of the war. Government planning boards set mandatory production goals, established rationing programs, and set limits on wages and prices.

Germany went furthest in developing a planned economy to wage total war. As soon as war began, the Jewish industrialist Walter Rathenau convinced the government to set up the War Raw Materials Board to ration and distribute raw materials. Under Rathenau's direction, every useful material from foreign oil to barnyard manure was inventoried and rationed. Moreover, the board launched successful attempts to produce substitutes,

Chapter 26
**War and Revolution**
**778    1914–1919**

CHAPTER LOCATOR    What caused the outbreak of the First World War?

**German Ration Card** The burdens of total war forced governments to control the distribution of the most basic goods, including food. This German ration card from 1915 has tear-away coupons for weekly allotments of potatoes. (Private Collection Newbury/The Art Archive)

such as synthetic rubber and synthetic nitrates, for scarce war supplies. Food was also rationed in accordance with physical need.

Following the terrible Battles of Verdun and the Somme in 1916, German military leaders forced the Reichstag to accept the Auxiliary Service Law, which required all males between seventeen and sixty to work only at jobs considered critical to the war effort. Women also worked in war factories, mines, and steel mills, where they labored at heavy and dangerous jobs. With the passage of the law, many more women followed. People lived on little more than one thousand calories a day. War production increased while some Germans starved to death.

After 1917 Germany's leaders ruled by dictatorial decree. Generals Hindenburg and Ludendorff drove Chancellor Bethmann-Hollweg from office. With the support of the newly formed ultra-conservative Fatherland Party, the generals established a military dictatorship. Hindenburg called for the ultimate mobilization for total war. Germany could win, he said, only "if all the treasures of our soil that agriculture and industry can produce are used exclusively for the conduct of War. . . . All other considerations must come second."[4] Thus in Germany total war led to the establishment of history's first "totalitarian" society.

Only Germany was directly ruled by a military government, yet leaders in all the belligerent nations took power from parliaments, suspended civil liberties, and ignored democratic procedures. The war may have been deadly for citizen armies, but it was certainly good for the growth of the bureaucratic nation-state.

## The Social Impact

The social impact of total war was no less profound than the economic impact, though again there were important national variations. National conscription sent millions of men to the front, exposing many to foreign lands for the first time in their lives. The insatiable needs of the military created a tremendous demand for workers, and jobs were readily available. This situation—seldom, if ever, seen before 1914—brought momentous changes.

The need for workers meant greater power and prestige for labor unions. Unions now cooperated with war governments in return for real participation in important decisions. The entry of labor leaders and unions into policymaking councils paralleled the entry of socialist leaders into the war governments. Both reflected a new government openness to the needs of those at the bottom of society.

The role of women also changed dramatically. In every country, large numbers of women left home and domestic service to work in industry, transportation, and offices. The production of vast amounts of arms and ammunition required huge numbers of laborers, and women moved into skilled industrial jobs long considered men's work only. Moreover, women became highly visible in public—not only as munitions workers but also as bank tellers and mail carriers, and even as police officers, firefighters, and farm laborers. Women also served as auxiliaries and nurses at the front. (See "Individuals in Society: Vera Brittain," page 780.)

# INDIVIDUALS IN SOCIETY

## Vera Brittain

**ALTHOUGH THE GREAT WAR UPENDED MILLIONS** of lives, it struck Europe's young people with the greatest force. For Vera Brittain (1893–1970), as for so many in her generation, the war became life's defining experience, which she captured forever in her famous autobiography, *Testament of Youth* (1933).

Brittain grew up in a wealthy business family in northern England, bristling at small-town conventions and discrimination against women. Very close to her brother Edward, two years her junior, Brittain read voraciously and dreamed of being a successful writer. Finishing boarding school and beating down her father's objections, she prepared for Oxford's rigorous entry exams and won a scholarship to its women's college. Brittain also fell in love with Roland Leighton, an equally brilliant student from a literary family and her brother's best friend. All three, along with two more close friends, Victor Richardson and Geoffrey Thurlow, confidently prepared to enter Oxford in late 1914.

When war suddenly loomed in July 1914, Brittain shared with millions of Europeans a thrilling surge of patriotic support for her government, a prowar enthusiasm she later played down in her published writings. She wrote in her diary that her "great fear" was that England would declare its neutrality and commit the "grossest treachery" toward France.* She supported Roland's decision to enlist, agreeing with his glamorous view of war as "very ennobling and very beautiful." Later, exchanging anxious letters with Roland in France in 1915, Brittain began to see the conflict in personal, human terms. She wondered if any victory or defeat could be worth Roland's life.

Struggling to quell her doubts, Brittain redoubled her commitment to England's cause and volunteered as an army nurse. For the next three years she served with distinction in military hospitals in London,

**Vera Brittain was marked forever by her wartime experiences.** (Vera Brittain Archive, William Ready Division of Archives and Research Collections, McMaster University Library)

Malta, and northern France, repeatedly torn between the vision of noble sacrifice and the reality of human tragedy. She lost her sexual inhibitions caring for mangled male bodies, and she longed to consummate her love with Roland. Awaiting his return on leave on Christmas Day in 1915, she was greeted instead with a telegram: Roland had been killed two days before.

Roland's death was the first of the devastating blows that eventually overwhelmed Brittain's idealistic patriotism. In 1917 first Geoffrey and then Victor died from gruesome wounds. In early 1918, as the last great German offensive covered the floors of her war-zone hospital with maimed and dying German prisoners, the bone-weary Vera felt a common humanity and saw only more victims. A few weeks later brother Edward — her last hope — died in action. When the war ended, she was, she said, a "complete automaton," with "my deepest emotions paralyzed if not dead."

Returning to Oxford and finishing her studies, Brittain gradually recovered. She formed a deep, restorative friendship with another talented woman writer, Winifred Holtby, published novels and articles, and became a leader in the feminist campaign for gender equality. She also married and had children. But her wartime memories were always with her. Finally, Brittain succeeded in coming to grips with them in *Testament of Youth*, her powerful antiwar autobiography. The unflinching narrative spoke to the experiences of an entire generation and became a runaway bestseller. Above all, Brittain captured the ambivalent, contradictory character of the war, when millions of young people found excitement, courage, and common purpose but succeeded only in destroying their lives with their superhuman efforts and futile sacrifices. Becoming ever more committed to pacifism, Brittain opposed England's entry into World War II.

### QUESTIONS FOR ANALYSIS

1. What were Brittain's initial feelings toward the war? How and why did they change as the conflict continued?
2. Why did Brittain volunteer as a nurse, as many women did? How might wartime nursing have influenced women of her generation?
3. In portraying the ambivalent, contradictory character of World War I for Europe's youth, was Brittain describing the character of all modern warfare?

*Quoted in the excellent study by P. Berry and M. Bostridge, *Vera Brittain: A Life* (London: Virago Press, 2001), p. 59; additional quotations are from pp. 80 and 136.

Chapter 26
**War and Revolution**
780     1914–1919

CHAPTER LOCATOR | What caused the outbreak of the First World War?

**Women Factory Workers Building a Truck, London, 1917** Millions of men on all sides were drafted to fight in the war, creating a serious labor shortage. When women left home to fill jobs formerly reserved for men, they challenged traditional gender roles. (© Hulton-Deutsch Collection/Corbis)

The war expanded the range of women's activities and helped change attitudes about gender, but the long-term results were mixed. Women across Europe gained experience in jobs previously reserved for men, and as a result of women's many-sided war efforts, the United States, Britain, Germany, Poland, and other countries granted women the right to vote immediately after the war. At the war's end, however, millions of demobilized soldiers demanded their jobs back, and governments forced women out of the workplace. Women's rights movements faded in the 1920s and 1930s, in large part because feminist leaders found it difficult to regain momentum after the crisis of war.

To some extent, the war promoted greater social equality, blurring class distinctions and lessening the gap between rich and poor. This blurring was most apparent in Great Britain, where the bottom third of the population generally lived better than they ever had, for the poorest gained most from the severe shortage of labor. Elsewhere, greater equality was reflected in full employment, rationing according to physical needs, and a sharing of hardships. In general, European society became more uniform and egalitarian, in spite of some war profiteering.

## Growing Political Tensions

During the first two years of war, many soldiers and civilians supported their governments. Belief in a just cause and patriotic nationalism united peoples behind their national leaders. Each government used rigorous censorship and crude propaganda to bolster popular support.

How did the First World War differ from previous wars? | **In what ways did the war transform life on the home front?** | Why did world war lead to revolution in Russia? | In what ways was the Allied peace settlement flawed?

781

### Wartime Propaganda Posters

This famous French propaganda poster from 1918 (left) proclaims "They shall not pass" and expresses the French determination to hold back the German invaders at any cost. The American recruitment poster from 1917 (right) encourages "fighting men" to "join the Navy." (French poster: Archives Municipales Versailles/Gianni Dagli Orti/The Art Archive; American poster: Museum of the City of New York/ The Art Archive)

**ANALYZING THE IMAGE** How would you describe the soldier and sailor pictured on these posters? What messages about the war do the posters convey?

**CONNECTIONS** The "They shall not pass" poster was created after France had been at war for four years, while the naval recruitment poster came out before American troops were actively engaged overseas. How might the country of origin and the date of publication have affected the messages conveyed?

To complete this activity online, go to the Online Study Guide at bedfordstmartins.com/ mckaywestunderstanding.

Despite such efforts, by the spring of 1916 people were beginning to crack under the strain of total war. On May 1 that year, several thousand demonstrators in Berlin heard the radical socialist leader Karl Liebknecht (1871–1919) attack the costs of the war effort. Strikes and protest marches over inadequate food flared up on every home front.

On all sides, soldiers' morale began to decline. Numerous French units refused to fight after the disastrous French offensive of May 1917. Facing defeat, wretched conditions at the front, and growing hopelessness, Russian soldiers deserted in droves, providing fuel for the Russian Revolution of 1917. After the Battle of Caporetto in northern Italy in the autumn of 1917, the Italian army collapsed in despair. In the massive battles of 1916 and 1917, the British armies had been "bled dry." Only the promised arrival of fresh troops from the United States stiffened the resolve of the allies.

Chapter 26
**War and Revolution**
**782** 1914–1919

CHAPTER LOCATOR | What caused the outbreak of the First World War?

The strains were even worse for the Central Powers. In October 1916, a young socialist assassinated the chief minister of Austria. In spite of absolute censorship, political dissatisfaction and conflicts among nationalities grew. Both Czech and Yugoslav leaders demanded independent states for their peoples. In April 1917 Austria's chief minister summed up the situation in the gloomiest possible terms. The country and army were exhausted. Another winter of war would bring revolution and disintegration.

Germans on the home front likewise suffered immensely from the burdens of total war. The British naval blockade greatly limited food imports, and scarcity and poorly implemented rationing plans had horrific results: some 750,000 German civilians starved to death. The national political unity of the first year of the war collapsed as the social conflicts of prewar Germany re-emerged. A growing minority of moderate socialists in the Reichstag called for a compromise "peace without annexations or reparations."

Such a peace was unthinkable for the conservatives and military leaders in the Fatherland Party. So also was the surge in revolutionary agitation and strikes by war-weary workers that occurred in early 1917. When the bread ration was further reduced in April, more than 200,000 workers and women struck and demonstrated for a week in Berlin. That same month, radicals left the Social Democratic Party to form the Independent Social Democratic Party; in 1918 they would found the German Communist Party. Thus Germany, like its ally Austria-Hungary (and its enemy France), was beginning to crack in 1917. Yet it was Russia that collapsed first and saved the Central Powers — for a time.

# ▼ Why did world war lead to revolution in Russia?

Directly related to the growing tensions of World War I, the Russian Revolution of 1917 was one of modern history's most momentous events. For some, the revolution was Marx's socialist vision come true; for others, it was the triumph of dictatorship. To all, it presented a radically new prototype of state and society.

## The Fall of Imperial Russia

Like its allies and its enemies, Russia had embraced war with patriotic enthusiasm in 1914. At the Winter Palace, while throngs of people knelt and sang "God save the tsar," Tsar Nicholas II (r. 1894–1917) repeated the oath Alexander I had sworn in 1812 during Napoleon's invasion of Russia (see Chapter 20), vowing never to make peace as long as the enemy stood on Russian soil. For a moment, Russia was united.

Enthusiasm for the war soon waned as better-equipped German armies inflicted terrible losses. By 1915 substantial numbers of Russian soldiers were sent to the front without rifles. Russia's peasant army nonetheless continued to fight, and Russia moved toward full mobilization on the home front. The Duma, Russia's lower house of parliament, and organs of local government set up special committees to coordinate defense, industry, transportation, and agriculture. These efforts improved the military situation, but overall Russia mobilized less effectively than the other combatants.

One problem was weak leadership. Under the constitution resulting from the revolution of 1905 (see Chapter 24), the tsar had retained complete control over the bureaucracy and the army. A kindly but narrow-minded aristocrat, Nicholas II distrusted the publicly elected Duma and resisted popular involvement in government, relying instead on the old bureaucratic apparatus. As a result, the Duma, the educated middle classes, and the masses became increasingly critical of the tsar's leadership. In September 1915 parties ranging from conservative to moderate socialist formed the Progressive bloc, which

## ▪ Key Events of the Russian Revolution

| | |
|---|---|
| **August 1914** | Russia enters the war |
| **1916–1917** | Tsarist government in crisis |
| **March 1917** | February Revolution; establishment of provisional government; tsar abdicates |
| **April 1917** | Lenin returns from exile |
| **July 1917** | Bolshevik attempt to seize power fails |
| **October 1917** | Bolsheviks gain a majority in the Petrograd Soviet |
| **November 7, 1917** | Bolsheviks seize power; Lenin named head of new communist government |
| **March 1918** | Treaty of Brest-Litovsk; Trotsky becomes head of the Red Army |
| **1918–1920** | Civil war |
| **1920** | Civil war ends; Lenin and Bolshevik-Communists take control of Russia |

called for a completely new government responsible to the Duma instead of the tsar. In answer, Nicholas temporarily adjourned the Duma. The tsar then announced that he was traveling to the front in order to lead and rally Russia's armies, leaving the government in the hands of his wife, Tsarina Alexandra.

His departure was a fatal turning point. In his absence, Tsarina Alexandra dismissed loyal political advisers and turned to her court favorite, Rasputin. Rasputin was an uneducated Siberian preacher whose influence with the tsarina rested on his purported healing powers. Alexis, who was Alexandra's only son and heir to the throne, suffered from the rare blood disease hemophilia. Rasputin claimed that only he could stop the bleeding, using his miraculous powers. In a desperate attempt to right the situation and end unfounded rumors that Rasputin was the empress's lover, three members of the high aristocracy murdered Rasputin in December 1916. The ensuing scandal further undermined support for the tsarist government.

Imperial Russia had entered a terminal crisis. Tens of thousands of soldiers deserted, swelling the number of the disaffected at home. By early winter 1917, the cities were wracked by food shortages, heating fuel was in short supply, and the economy was breaking down. In late March violent street demonstrations broke out in Petrograd (formerly St. Petersburg), spread to the factories, and then engulfed the city. The tsar ordered the army to open fire on the protesters, but the soldiers refused and joined the revolutionary crowd. The Duma declared a provisional government on March 12, 1917. Three days later, Nicholas abdicated.

## The Provisional Government

**February Revolution**
Unplanned uprisings accompanied by violent street demonstrations begun in March 1917 (old-calendar February) in Petrograd, Russia, and that led to the abdication of the tsar and the establishment of a provisional government.

This **February Revolution** that led to the establishment of the provisional government and the abdication of the tsar was the result of an unplanned uprising in the capital, but it was eagerly accepted throughout the country. (The name of the revolution matches the Russian calendar, which used to use a different dating system.)

The upper and middle classes embraced the prospect of a more determined war effort, while workers anticipated better wages and more food. After generations of autocracy, the provisional government established equality before the law; freedom of religion, speech, and assembly; and the right of unions to organize and strike.

Yet both liberal and moderate socialist leaders of the provisional government rejected these broad political reforms. Though the Russian people were sick of fighting, the new leaders also refused to take Russia out of the war. A new government formed in May 1917 included the socialist Alexander Kerensky, who became prime minister in July. He refused to confiscate large landholdings and give them to peasants, fearing that such drastic action would only complete the disintegration of Russia's peasant army. For the patriotic Kerensky, as for other moderate socialists, the continuation of war was still a national duty.

From its first day, the provisional government had to share power with a formidable rival — the **Petrograd Soviet** (or council) of Workers' and Soldiers' Deputies. Modeled on the revolutionary soviets of 1905, the Petrograd Soviet comprised two to three thousand workers, soldiers, and socialist intellectuals. Seeing itself as a grassroots product of revolutionary democracy, the Soviet acted as a parallel government. It issued its own radical orders, weakening the authority of the provisional government.

The most famous edict of the Petrograd Soviet was Army Order No. 1, issued in May 1917, which stripped officers of their authority and placed power in the hands of elected committees of common soldiers. The order led to a collapse of army discipline.

In July 1917 the provisional government ordered a summer offensive against the Germans. The campaign was a miserable failure, and peasant soldiers began deserting

**Petrograd Soviet** A huge, fluctuating mass meeting of two to three thousand workers, soldiers, and socialist intellectuals modeled on the revolutionary soviets of 1905.

**The Radicalization of the Russian Army** Russian soldiers inspired by the Bolshevik cause carry banners with Marxist slogans calling for revolution and democracy, around July 1917. One reads "All Power to the Proletariat," a telling response to the provisional government's failure to pull Russia out of the war. Sick of defeat and wretched conditions at the front, the tzar's troops welcomed Lenin's promises of "Bread, Land, and Peace" and were enthusiastic participants in the Russian Revolution. (Hulton/Getty Images)

How did the First World War differ from previous wars?

In what ways did the war transform life on the home front?

**Why did world war lead to revolution in Russia?**

In what ways was the Allied peace settlement flawed?

in droves, returning to their villages to help their families get a share of the land, which peasants were seizing as they settled old scores in a great agrarian upheaval. Russia was descending into anarchy in the summer of 1917. It was an unparalleled opportunity for the radical revolutionary leader Vladimir Ilyich Lenin (VLA-duh-mihr IL-ihch LEHN-uhn) (1870–1924).

## Lenin and the Bolshevik Revolution

Born into the middle class, Lenin became an enemy of imperial Russia when his older brother was executed for plotting to kill the tsar in 1887. As a law student, Lenin eagerly studied Marxian socialism. A pragmatic and flexible thinker, Lenin updated Marx's revolutionary philosophy to address existing conditions in Russia.

Three interrelated concepts were central for Lenin. First, he stressed that only violent revolution could destroy capitalism. Second, Lenin argued that a socialist revolution was possible even in a nonindustrialized agrarian country like Russia. The Russian industrial working class was tiny, but peasants, like workers, were numerous, poor, and exploited. They could thus take the place of Marx's traditional working class in the coming conflict.

Third, Lenin believed that the possibility of revolution was determined more by human leadership than by vast historical laws. He called for a highly disciplined workers' party strictly controlled by a small, dedicated elite of intellectuals and professional revolutionaries. Lenin's version of Marxism had a major impact on events in Russia and ultimately changed the way future revolutionaries undertook radical revolt around the world.

Lenin's ideas did not go unchallenged by other Russian Marxists. At meetings of the Russian Social Democratic Labor Party in London in 1903, matters came to a head. Lenin demanded a small, disciplined, elitist party, while his opponents wanted a more democratic party with mass membership. The Russian Marxists split into two rival factions. Lenin called his camp the Bolsheviks (BOHL-shuh-viks), or "majority group"; his opponents were Mensheviks, or "minority group."

Unlike most other socialists, Lenin had not rallied round the national flag in 1914. Observing events from Switzerland, where he lived in exile, Lenin viewed the war as a product of imperialist rivalries and an opportunity for socialist revolution. After the February Revolution of 1917, the German government provided Lenin safe passage across Germany and back into Russia, hoping he would undermine the provisional government. They were not disappointed. Arriving in Petrograd on April 3, Lenin attacked at once. To the astonishment of the local Bolsheviks, he rejected all cooperation with what he called the "bourgeois" provisional government. Lenin's promises of "Bread, Land, and Peace" spoke to the expectations of suffering workers, peasants, and soldiers alike, and earned the Bolsheviks substantial popular support. The moment for revolution was at hand.

Yet Lenin and the Bolsheviks almost lost the struggle for Russia. An attempt to seize power in July collapsed, and Lenin went into hiding. This temporary setback made little difference in the long run. Intrigue between Kerensky, who became prime minister in July, and his commander in chief, General Lavr Kornilov, resulted in Kornilov's leading a coup against the provisional government in September. In the face of this rightist counter-revolutionary threat, the Bolsheviks were rearmed and redeemed. Kornilov's forces disintegrated, but Kerensky lost all credit with the army, the only force that might have saved democratic government in Russia.

## Trotsky and the Seizure of Power

Throughout the summer, the Bolsheviks greatly increased their popular support. Party membership soared from 50,000 to 240,000, and in October the Bolsheviks gained a fragile majority in the Petrograd Soviet. Now Lenin's supporter Leon Trotsky (1879–1940) brilliantly executed the Bolshevik seizure of power.

**Bolsheviks** Lenin's radical, revolutionary arm of the Russian party of Marxian socialism, which successfully installed a dictatorial socialist regime in Russia.

**Lenin Rallies Soldiers** Lenin, known for his fiery speeches, addresses Red Army soldiers in Moscow in the midst of the Russian civil war, May 1920. Leon Trotsky, the leader of the Red Army, stands on the podium stairs to the right. (Mansell/Time Life Images/Getty Images)

Painting a vivid but untruthful picture of German and counter-revolutionary plots, Trotsky convinced the Petrograd Soviet to form a special military-revolutionary committee in October and make him its leader. Thus military power in the capital passed into Bolshevik hands. On the night of November 6, militants from Trotsky's committee joined with trusted Bolshevik soldiers to seize government buildings and pounce on members of the provisional government. Then they went on to the Congress of Soviets where a Bolshevik majority declared that all power had passed to the soviets and named Lenin head of the new government.

The Bolsheviks came to power for three key reasons. First, by late 1917 democracy had given way to anarchy. Second, in Lenin and Trotsky the Bolsheviks had an utterly determined and superior leadership, which both the tsarist and the provisional governments lacked. Third, the Bolsheviks appealed to soldiers and urban workers who were exhausted by war, weary of tsarist autocracy, and ready for radical changes.

## Dictatorship and Civil War

The true accomplishment of the Bolsheviks was not taking power, but keeping it. Over the next four years, the Bolsheviks conquered the chaos they had helped create and began to build a communist society. How was this done?

Lenin took advantage of developments over which he and the Bolsheviks had little control. Since summer, a peasant revolution had swept across Russia, as impoverished peasants divided among themselves the estates of the landlords and the church. Thus when Lenin mandated land reform from above, he merely approved what peasants were already doing. Popular unrest had also spread to the cities. Urban workers established their own local soviets or committees and demanded direct control of individual factories. This, too, Lenin ratified with a decree in November 1917.

The Bolsheviks proclaimed their regime a "provisional workers' and peasants' government," promising that a freely elected Constituent Assembly would draw up a new constitution. But in free elections in November, the Bolsheviks won only 23 percent of the elected delegates. The Constituent Assembly met for only one day, on January 18, 1918. It was then permanently disbanded by Bolshevik soldiers acting under Lenin's orders. Thus just two months after the Bolshevik victory, Lenin began to form a one-party state.

Lenin acknowledged that Russia had effectively lost the war with Germany and that the only realistic goal was peace at any price. That price was very high. Germany demanded that the Soviet government give up all its western territories, and a third of old Russia's population was sliced away by the **Treaty of Brest-Litovsk** (BREHST lih-TAWFSK), signed with Germany in March 1918. With peace, Lenin escaped the disaster of continued war and could pursue his goal of absolute political power for the Bolsheviks—now also called Communists—within Russia.

The war's end and the destruction of the democratically elected Constituent Assembly inspired armed opposition to the Bolshevik regime. The officers of the old army rejected the peace treaty and organized the so-called White opposition to the Bolsheviks in southern Russia, Ukraine, and Siberia and west of Petrograd. The Whites came from many social groups and were united only by their hatred of communism and the Bolsheviks—the Reds.

By the summer of 1918, Russia was in a full-fledged civil war. Fully eighteen self-proclaimed regional governments—several of which represented minority nationalities—were challenging Lenin's government in Moscow. By the end of the year, White armies were on the attack. In October 1919 they closed in on central Russia from three sides, and it appeared they might triumph. They did not.

Lenin and the Red Army beat back the counter-revolutionary White armies for several reasons. Most important, the Bolsheviks had quickly developed a better army. In March 1918, Trotsky became war commissar of the newly formed Red Army. He re-established strict discipline and the draft. Moreover, Trotsky made effective use of former tsarist army officers, who were actively recruited and given unprecedented powers over their troops. In short, Trotsky formed a disciplined and effective fighting force, which repeatedly defeated the Whites in the field.

Other conditions favored the Bolsheviks. Strategically, the Reds controlled central Russia and the crucial cities of Moscow and Petrograd. The Whites attacked from the fringes and lacked coordination. Moreover, the political program of the Whites was a mishmash of liberal republicanism and monarchism, and it never united the Bolsheviks' enemies under a progressive democratic banner. While the Bolsheviks promised the ethnic minorities in Russian-controlled territories substantial autonomy, the nationalist Whites wished to preserve the tsarist empire.

The Bolsheviks mobilized the home front for the war effort by establishing a system of centralized controls called **war communism**. All banks and industries were nationalized, and private enterprise was outlawed. Bolshevik commissars introduced rationing, seized grain from peasants to feed the cities, and maintained strict workplace discipline. Although these measures contributed to a breakdown of normal eco-

**Treaty of Brest-Litovsk**
Peace treaty signed in March 1918 between the Central Powers and Russia that ceded Russian territories containing a third of the Russian empire's population to the Central Powers.

**war communism** The application of centralized state control during the Russian civil war, in which the Bolsheviks seized grain from peasants, introduced rationing, nationalized all banks and industry, and required everyone to work.

◾ Ceded after Treaty of Brest-Litovsk, 1918
◾ Bolshevik territory, 1919
◾ Occupied by Allies, 1919
➜ White Army forces
— Boundary of U.S.S.R., 1921

**The Russian Civil War, 1917–1922**

Chapter 26
**War and Revolution**
788 1914–1919

CHAPTER LOCATOR | What caused the outbreak of the First World War?

nomic activity, they maintained labor discipline and kept the Red Army supplied with men and materiel.

Revolutionary terror also contributed to the Communist victory. Lenin and the Bolsheviks set up a secret police known as the Cheka. During the civil war, the Cheka imprisoned and executed without trial tens of thousands of supposed class enemies, including the tsar and his family, who were executed in July 1918. The "Red Terror" of 1918–1920 helped establish the secret police as a central tool of the new communist government.

Foreign military intervention to support the White armies in the civil war also ironically helped the Bolsheviks. For a variety of reasons, but primarily to stop the spread of communism, the Western Allies sent troops to support the Whites. Yet their efforts were limited and halfhearted. Thus Allied intervention did not aid the Whites effectively, though it did permit the Bolsheviks to appeal to the patriotic nationalism of ethnic Russians.

By the spring of 1920, the White armies were almost completely defeated, and the Bolsheviks had retaken much of the territory ceded to Germany under the Treaty of Brest-Litovsk. The Red Army reconquered Belarus and Ukraine, both of which had gained a brief moment of independence at the end of World War I. Building on this success, the Bolsheviks moved westward into Polish territory, but they were halted on the outskirts of Warsaw in August 1920. The defeat ended Bolshevik attempts to spread communism into western Europe, though in 1921 the Red Army overran the independent nationalist governments of the Caucasus. The Russian civil war was over. Despite losses to Poland, the Bolsheviks had won an impressive victory.

# ▼ In what ways was the Allied peace settlement flawed?

Even as civil war spread in Russia and chaos engulfed much of eastern Europe, the war in the west was coming to an end. In the spring of 1918, the German high command launched a desperate attack against France. This offensive failed and Germany was defeated. The victorious Western Allies came together in Paris to establish a lasting peace.

The Allies soon worked out terms for peace with Germany and for the creation of the peacekeeping League of Nations. Nevertheless, the peace settlement of 1919 turned out to be a failure. Rather than lasting peace, the immediate postwar years brought economic crisis and violent political conflict.

## The End of the War

In early 1918 the German leadership decided that the time was ripe for a last ditch, all-out attack on France. The great spring offensive of 1918 brought German armies within thirty-five miles of Paris, but the exhausted, overextended forces never broke through. They were stopped in July at the second Battle of the Marne, where 140,000 American soldiers saw action. The late but massive American intervention tipped the scales in favor of Allied victory.

By September British, French, and American armies were advancing steadily on all fronts, and General Ludendorff realized that Germany had lost the war. Not wanting to shoulder the blame, he insisted that moderate politicians should take responsibility for the defeat. On October 4 the German emperor formed a new, more liberal civilian government to sue for peace.

As negotiations over an armistice dragged on, the frustrated German people rose up in revolt. On November 3 sailors in Kiel (keel) mutinied, and throughout northern Germany soldiers and workers began to establish revolutionary councils on the Russian soviet model. The same day, Austria-Hungary surrendered to the Allies and began breaking apart. Revolution broke out in Germany. With army discipline collapsing, Emperor William II abdicated and fled to Holland. Socialist leaders in Berlin proclaimed a German republic on November 9 and agreed to tough Allied terms of surrender. The armistice went into effect on November 11, 1918.

## Revolution in Austria-Hungary and Germany

Military defeat brought turmoil and revolution to Austria-Hungary and Germany, as it had to Russia. The independent states of Austria, Hungary, and Czechoslovakia, and a larger Romania, were carved out of the Austro-Hungarian Empire (Map 26.4). A greatly expanded Serbian monarchy gained control of the western Balkans and took the name Yugoslavia. Austria-Hungary no longer existed.

In late 1918 Germany likewise experienced a dramatic revolution that resembled the Russian Revolution of March 1917. In both cases, a genuine popular uprising welled up from below, toppled an authoritarian monarchy, and created a liberal provisional republic. In both countries, liberals and moderate socialist politicians struggled with more radical workers' and soldiers' councils (or soviets) for political dominance. In Germany, however, moderates from the Social Democratic Party and their liberal allies held on to power and established the Weimar Republic—a democratic government that would lead Germany for the next fifteen years.

There were several reasons for the German outcome. The great majority of the Marxist politicians in the Social Democratic Party were really moderates. They wanted political democracy and civil liberties, and they favored the gradual elimination of capitalism. They were also German nationalists, appalled by the prospect of civil war and revolutionary terror. Of crucial importance was the fact that the moderate Social Democrats quickly came to terms with the army and big business, which helped prevent Germany from reaching total collapse.

Yet the triumph of the German Social Democrats brought violent chaos to Germany in 1918–1919. The new republic was attacked from both sides of the political spectrum. Radical communists led by Karl Liebknecht and Rosa Luxemburg tried to seize control of the government in the Spartacist Uprising in Berlin in January 1919. The moderate Social Democrats called in nationalist Free Corps militias, bands of demobilized soldiers who had kept their weapons, to crush the uprising. Liebknecht and Luxemburg were murdered by Free Corps soldiers. In Bavaria, a short-lived Soviet-style republic was violently overthrown on government orders by the Free Corps. Nationwide strikes by leftist workers and a short-lived military takeover—the Kapp Putsch—were also repressed by the central government.

By the summer of 1920, the situation had calmed down, but the new republican government faced deep discontent. Communists and radical socialists blamed the Social Democrats for the murders of Liebknecht and Luxemburg and the repression of the Bavarian Soviet. Right-wing nationalists, including the new Nazi Party, spread the myth that the German army had never actually lost the war—instead, the nation was "stabbed in the back" by socialists and pacifists at home. In Germany, the end of the war brought only a fragile sense of political stability.

## The Treaty of Versailles

**Treaty of Versailles** The 1919 peace settlement that ended war between Germany and the Allied powers.

In January 1919 over seventy delegates from twenty-seven nations met in Paris to craft a peace accord. The conference produced the Treaty of Versailles, which laid out the terms

## ■ MAPPING THE PAST

## Map 26.4 Territorial Changes After World War I

World War I brought tremendous changes to eastern Europe. New nations and new boundaries were established, and a dangerous power vacuum was created by the relatively weak states established between Germany and Soviet Russia.

**ANALYZING THE MAP** What territory did Germany lose, and to whom? Why was Austria referred to as a head without a body in the 1920s? What new independent states were formed from the old Russian empire?

**CONNECTIONS** How were the principles of national self-determination applied to the redrawing of Europe after the war, and why didn't this theory work in practice?

To complete this activity online, go to the Online Study Guide at bedfordstmartins.com/mckaywestunderstanding.

---

of the postwar settlement and was signed by the victorious Allies and the defeated Germany. The peace negotiations inspired great expectations. A British diplomat later wrote that the victors "were journeying to Paris . . . to found a new order in Europe. We were preparing not Peace only, but Eternal Peace."[5]

This idealism was greatly strengthened by U.S. President Wilson's January 1918 peace proposal, the **Fourteen Points**. The proposal called for open diplomacy, a reduction in

**Fourteen Points** Wilson's 1918 peace proposal calling for open diplomacy, a reduction in armaments, freedom of commerce and trade, the establishment of the League of Nations, and national self-determination.

How did the First World War differ from previous wars?

In what ways did the war transform life on the home front?

Why did world war lead to revolution in Russia?

In what ways was the Allied peace settlement flawed?

**League of Nations** A permanent international organization, established during the 1919 Paris peace conference, designed to protect member states from aggression and avert future wars.

**national self-determination** The notion that people should be able to live free from outside interference in nations with clearly defined borders, and that they should be able to choose their own national governments through democratic majority-rule elections.

armaments, freedom of commerce and trade, and the establishment of a League of Nations, an international body designed to provide a place for peaceful resolution of world problems. Perhaps most important, Wilson demanded that the peace be based on the notion of national self-determination, meaning that peoples should be able to choose their own national governments through democratic majority-rule elections and live free from outside interference in territories with clearly defined permanent borders. Despite the general optimism inspired by these ideas, the conference and the treaty itself quickly generated disagreement.

The controlling powers at the conference were termed the "Big Three": the United States, Great Britain, and France. Germany, Austria-Hungary, and Russia were excluded from the conference. Italy was included, but its role was quite limited. The conference included representatives of smaller nations as well, from the Middle East, Africa, and East Asia, but their concerns, for the most part, were simply ignored.

Almost immediately upon their arrival in Paris, the Big Three began to quarrel. President Wilson was almost obsessed with creating the League of Nations. Wilson insisted that this question come first, for he believed that only a permanent international organization could avert future wars. Wilson had his way, although prime ministers Lloyd George of Great Britain and especially Georges Clemenceau of France were unenthusiastic. They were primarily concerned with punishing Germany.

The question of what to do with Germany in fact dominated discussions among the Big Three. Clemenceau wanted Germany to pay for its aggression, and he sought revenge, economic retribution, and lasting security for France. This, he believed, required the creation of a buffer state between France and Germany, the permanent demilitarization of Germany, and vast German reparations. Lloyd George supported Clemenceau, but he was less harsh. Wilson disagreed, and by April the countries attending the conference were deadlocked on the German question.

In the end, Clemenceau agreed to a compromise. He gave up the French demand for a Rhineland buffer state in return for a formal defensive alliance with the United States and Great Britain. Under the terms of this alliance, both Wilson and Lloyd George promised that their countries would come to France's aid in the event of a German attack. The Allies moved quickly to finish the settlement, believing that further adjustments would be possible within the dual framework of a strong Western alliance and the League of Nations.

The Treaty of Versailles was the key to the settlement. Its terms redrew the map of Europe (see Map 26.4, page 791), dismantled the Ottoman Empire, and placed Germany's overseas colonies under French, British, and Japanese control. Poland was granted national independence. In addition, Germany had to limit its army to one hundred thousand men and agree to build no military fortifications in the Rhineland.

**war guilt clause** An article in the Treaty of Versailles that declared that Germany (with Austria) was solely responsible for the war and had to pay reparations equal to all civilian damages caused by the fighting.

More harshly, in Article 231, the war guilt clause, the Allies declared that Germany (with Austria) was solely responsible for the war. Germany therefore had to pay reparations to cover damages caused by the fighting. For the Germans, reparations were a crippling financial burden. Moreover, the war guilt clause was an insult to German national pride. Many Germans believed wartime propaganda that had repeatedly claimed that Germany was an innocent victim, forced into war by its enemies.

When presented with the treaty, the new German government protested vigorously to no avail. On June 28, 1919, German representatives of the ruling moderate Social Democrats and the Catholic Party signed the treaty.

The Versailles treaty was far from perfect, but within the context of war-shattered Europe it was a beginning. Germany had been punished, but not dismembered. A new world organization complemented a traditional defensive alliance of satisfied powers: Britain, France, and the United States. Yet the great hopes of early 1919 had turned to ashes by the end of the year. The Western alliance had collapsed, and plans for permanent peace had given way to a fragile European truce. There were several reasons for this turn of events. First, the U.S. Senate rejected the treaty. Republican senators led by Henry Cabot Lodge believed that the treaty gave away Congress's constitutional right to declare war and demanded changes in the articles. In failing health, Wilson rejected all attempts at compromise. In doing so, he ensured that the treaty would never be ratified by the United States in any form and that the United States would never join the League of Nations. Moreover, the Senate refused to ratify Wilson's treaties forming a defensive alliance with France and Great Britain. America in effect had turned its back on Europe. Using U.S. actions as an excuse, Great Britain too refused to ratify its defensive alliance with France. Betrayed by its allies, France stood alone.

The principle of national self-determination, which had engendered such enthusiasm after the war, was good in theory but flawed in practice. Even in Europe, the borders of new states such as Poland, Czechoslovakia, and Yugoslavia cut through a jumble of ethnic and religious groups who often despised each other. The new central European nations would prove to be economically weak and politically unstable, the focus of conflict in the interwar years. In the colonies, desires for self-determination were simply ignored. The Great Powers happily received Germany's colonies but were hardly ready to give up their own. The problems with self-determination were particularly evident in the fate of the territories of the former Ottoman Empire, where the victorious allies paid little attention to the desires of the native peoples of the Middle East.

## The Peace Settlement in the Middle East

Although Allied leaders at Versailles focused mainly on European questions, they also imposed a political settlement on what had been the Ottoman Empire, which was broken up. Britain and France expanded their power and influence in the Middle East, and Arab nationalists felt cheated and betrayed

The British government had encouraged the wartime Arab revolt against the Ottoman Turks (see page 777) and had even made vague promises of an independent Arab kingdom. However, when the fighting stopped, the British and the French chose instead to honor secret wartime agreements to divide and rule the Ottoman lands. In the Sykes-Picot Agreement of 1916, Britain and France basically agreed that France would receive modern-day Lebanon and Syria and much of southern Turkey, and that Britain would receive Palestine, Transjordan, and Iraq. When Britain and France set about implementing their secret plans after the armistice, Arab nationalists reacted with surprise and resentment.

British plans for the Ottoman province of Palestine also angered Arab nationalists. The Balfour Declaration of November 1917 declared that Britain favored a "National Home for the Jewish People" in Palestine, but without prejudicing the civil and religious rights of the non-Jewish communities already living in Palestine. Some members of the British cabinet believed that the declaration would appeal to German, Austrian, and American Jews and thus help the British war effort. Others supported the Zionist vision of a Jewish homeland (see Chapter 24), which they hoped would also help Britain maintain control of the Suez Canal. In any event, Palestinian Arabs were dismayed.

In 1914 Jews accounted for about 11 percent of the population in the three Ottoman districts that would subsequently be combined by the British to form Palestine; the rest of the population was predominantly Arab. Yet both groups understood that the National Home for the Jewish People mentioned in the Balfour Declaration implied the establishment of some kind of Jewish state that would violate majority rule. Moreover, a state founded on religious and ethnic exclusivity was out of keeping with both Islamic and Ottoman tradition.

**Balfour Declaration** A 1917 British statement that declared British support of a National Home for the Jewish People in Palestine.

**Prince Faisal at the Versailles Peace Conference, 1919** Standing in front, Faisal is supported by his allies and black slave. Nur-as-Said, an officer in the Ottoman army who joined the Arab revolt, is second from the left, and the British officer T. E. Lawrence—popularly known as Lawrence of Arabia—is fourth from the left in back. Faisal failed to win political independence for the Arabs, as the British backed away from the vague promises they had made during the war. (Courtesy of the Trustees of the Imperial War Museum)

Though Arab leaders attended the Versailles Peace Conference, efforts to secure autonomy in the Middle East came to nothing. Only the kingdom of Hejaz—today part of Saudi Arabia—was granted independence (Map 26.5). In response, Arab nationalists came together in Damascus as the General Syrian Congress in 1919 and unsuccessfully called again for political independence. (See "Listening to the Past: Resolution of the General Syrian Congress at Damascus," page 796.) The Congress proclaimed Syria an independent kingdom, and a similar congress declared Iraqi independence.

The Western reaction was swift and decisive. A French army stationed in Lebanon attacked Syria, taking Damascus in July 1920. The Arab government fled, and the French took over. Meanwhile, the British put down an uprising in Iraq and established effective control there. Under the so-called mandate system, Western imperialism appeared to have replaced Ottoman rule in the Arab Middle East.

The Allies sought to impose even harsher terms on the defeated Turks than on the "liberated" Arabs. A treaty forced on the Ottoman sultan dismembered the Turkish heartland. Great Britain and France occupied parts of modern-day Turkey, and Italy and Greece also claimed shares. In 1919 Greek armies carried by British ships landed on the Turkish

Chapter 26
**War and Revolution**

794   1914–1919

CHAPTER LOCATOR   What caused the outbreak of the First World War?

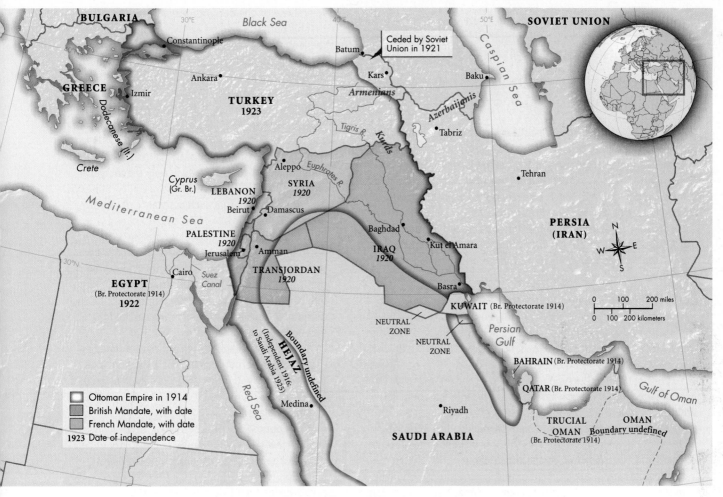

**Map 26.5 The Partition of the Ottoman Empire, 1914–1923** By 1914 the Ottoman Turks had been pushed out of the Balkans, and their Arab provinces were on the edge of revolt. That revolt, in alliance with the British, erupted during the First World War and contributed greatly to the Ottoman defeat. Refusing to grant independence to the Arabs, the Allies established League of Nations mandates and replaced Ottoman rulers in Syria, Iraq, Transjordan, and Palestine.

coast at Smyrna (SMUHR-nuh) and advanced unopposed into the interior, while French troops moved in from the south. Turkey seemed finished.

Yet Turkey survived the postwar invasions. Led by Mustafa Kemal (1881–1938), the Turks refused to acknowledge the Allied dismemberment of their country and gradually mounted a forceful resistance. Despite staggering losses, the newly established Turkish army repulsed the invaders. The Greeks and their British allies sued for peace. In 1923, after long negotiations, the Treaty of Lausanne (loh-ZAN) recognized the territorial integrity of a truly independent Turkey.

Kemal believed that Turkey should modernize and secularize along Western lines. He established a republic, had himself elected president, and created a one-party system to transform his country. The most radical reforms pertained to religion and culture. Profoundly influenced by the example of western Europe, Kemal set out to limit the place of religion and religious leaders in daily affairs. He decreed a revolutionary separation of church and state, promulgated law codes inspired by European models, and established a secular public school system. Women received rights that they never had before. By the time of his death in 1938, Kemal had moved Turkey much closer to Europe.

# LISTENING TO THE PAST

## Resolution of the General Syrian Congress at Damascus

*President Wilson insisted at Versailles that the right of self-determination should be applied to the conquered Ottoman territories, and he sent an American commission of inquiry to Syria, even though the British and French refused to participate. The commission canvassed political views throughout greater Syria, and its long report with many documents reflected public opinion in the region in 1919.*

*To present their view to the Americans, Arab nationalists from present-day Syria, Lebanon, Israel, and Jordan came together in Damascus as the General Syrian Congress and passed the following resolution on July 2, 1919.*

❝ We the undersigned members of the General Syrian Congress, meeting in Damascus on Wednesday, July 2nd, 1919, . . . provided with credentials and authorizations by the inhabitants of our various districts, Moslems, Christians, and Jews, have agreed upon the following statement of the desires of the people of the country who have elected us to present them to the American Section of the International Commission; the fifth article was passed by a very large majority; all the other articles were accepted unanimously.

1. We ask absolutely complete political independence for Syria within these boundaries. [Describes the area including the present-day states of Syria, Lebanon, Israel, and Jordan.]

2. We ask that the Government of this Syrian country should be a democratic civil constitutional Monarchy on broad decentralization principles, safeguarding the rights of minorities, and that the King be the Emir Faisal, who carried on a glorious struggle in the cause of our liberation and merited our full confidence and entire reliance.

3. Considering the fact that the Arabs inhabiting the Syrian area are not naturally less gifted than other more advanced races and that they are by no means less developed than the Bulgarians, Serbians, Greeks, and Roumanians at the beginning of their independence, we protest against Article 22 of the Covenant of the League of Nations, placing us among the nations in their middle stage of development which stand in need of a mandatory power.

4. In the event of the rejection by the Peace Conference of this just protest for certain considerations that we may not understand, we, relying on the declarations of President Wilson that his object in waging war was to put an end to the ambition of conquest and colonization, can only regard the mandate mentioned in the Covenant of the League of Nations as equivalent to the rendering of economical and technical assistance that does not prejudice our complete independence. And desiring that our country should not fall a prey to colonization and believing that the American Nation is farthest from any thought of colonization and has no political ambition in our country, we will seek the technical and economical assistance from the United States of America, provided that such assistance does not exceed 20 years.

5. In the event of America not finding herself in a position to accept our desire for assistance, we will seek this assistance from Great Britain, also provided that such assistance does not infringe the complete independence and unity of our country and that the duration of such assistance does not exceed that mentioned in the previous article.

6. We do not acknowledge any right claimed by the French Government in any part whatever of our Syrian country and refuse that she should assist us or have a hand in our country under any circumstances and in any place.

7. We oppose the pretensions of the Zionists to create a Jewish commonwealth in the southern part of Syria, known as Palestine, and oppose Zionist migration to any part of our country; for we do not acknowledge their title but consider them a grave peril to our people from the national, economical, and political points of view. Our Jewish compatriots shall enjoy our common rights and assume the common responsibilities.

8. We ask that there should be no separation of the southern part of Syria, known as Palestine, nor of the littoral western zone, which includes Lebanon, from the Syrian country. We desire that the unity of the country should be guaranteed against partition under whatever circumstances.

9. We ask complete independence for emancipated Mesopotamia [today's Iraq] and that there

## The Human Costs

World War I broke empires, inspired revolutions, and changed national borders on a world scale. It also had immense human costs, and ordinary people in the combatant nations struggled to deal with its legacy in the years that followed. The raw numbers are astonishing: estimates vary, but total deaths on the battlefield numbered between 10 and 13 million soldiers (Figure 26.1). Between 7 and 10 million civilians died because of the

**Palestinian Arabs protest against large-scale Jewish migration into Palestine.** (Roger-Viollet/Getty Images)

should be no economical barriers between the two countries. . . .

The noble principles enunciated by President Wilson strengthen our confidence that our desires emanating from the depths of our hearts, shall be the decisive factor in determining our future; and that President Wilson and the free American people will be our supporters for the realization of our hopes, thereby proving their sincerity and noble sympathy with the aspiration of the weaker nations in general and our Arab people in particular.

We also have the fullest confidence that the Peace Conference will realize that we would not have risen against the Turks, with whom we had participated in all civil, political, and representative privileges, but for their violation of our national rights, and so will grant us our desires in full in order that our politi-

cal rights may not be less after the war than they were before, since we have shed so much blood in the cause of our liberty and independence.

We request to be allowed to send a delegation to represent us at the Peace Conference to defend our rights and secure the realization of our aspirations. **»**

**Source:** "Resolution of the General Syrian Congress at Damascus, 2 July 1919," from the King-Crane Commission Report, in *Foreign Relations of the United States: Paris Peace Conference*, 1919, 12: 780–781.

### QUESTIONS FOR ANALYSIS

1. What kind of state did the delegates want?
2. Did the delegates view their "Jewish compatriots" and the Zionists in different ways? Why?
3. How did the delegates appeal to American sympathies?

war and war-related hardships, and another 20 million people died in the worldwide influenza epidemic that followed the war in 1918.

The victims of the First World War included millions of widows and orphans and huge numbers of disabled and emotionally scarred veterans. Some 10 million soldiers came home disfigured or mutilated. Governments tried to take care of the disabled and the survivor families, but there was never enough money to adequately fund pensions and

How did the First World War differ from previous wars?

In what ways did the war transform life on the home front?

Why did world war lead to revolution in Russia?

In what ways was the Allied peace settlement flawed?

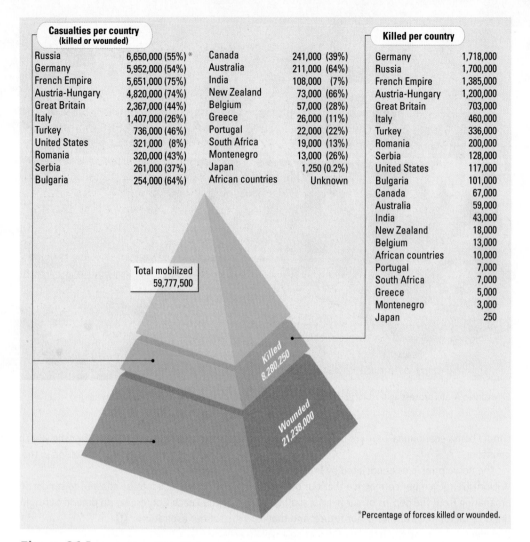

**Casualties per country**
**(killed or wounded)**

| Country | Casualties | Country | Casualties |
|---|---|---|---|
| Russia | 6,650,000 (55%) * | Canada | 241,000 (39%) |
| Germany | 5,952,000 (54%) | Australia | 211,000 (64%) |
| French Empire | 5,651,000 (75%) | India | 108,000 (7%) |
| Austria-Hungary | 4,820,000 (74%) | New Zealand | 73,000 (66%) |
| Great Britain | 2,367,000 (44%) | Belgium | 57,000 (28%) |
| Italy | 1,407,000 (26%) | Greece | 26,000 (11%) |
| Turkey | 736,000 (46%) | Portugal | 22,000 (22%) |
| United States | 321,000 (8%) | South Africa | 19,000 (13%) |
| Romania | 320,000 (43%) | Montenegro | 13,000 (26%) |
| Serbia | 261,000 (37%) | Japan | 1,250 (0.2%) |
| Bulgaria | 254,000 (64%) | African countries | Unknown |

**Killed per country**

|  |  |
|---|---|
| Germany | 1,718,000 |
| Russia | 1,700,000 |
| French Empire | 1,385,000 |
| Austria-Hungary | 1,200,000 |
| Great Britain | 703,000 |
| Italy | 460,000 |
| Turkey | 336,000 |
| Romania | 200,000 |
| Serbia | 128,000 |
| United States | 117,000 |
| Bulgaria | 101,000 |
| Canada | 67,000 |
| Australia | 59,000 |
| India | 43,000 |
| New Zealand | 18,000 |
| Belgium | 13,000 |
| African countries | 10,000 |
| Portugal | 7,000 |
| South Africa | 7,000 |
| Greece | 5,000 |
| Montenegro | 3,000 |
| Japan | 250 |

Total mobilized
59,777,500

Killed
8,280,250

Wounded
21,238,000

*Percentage of forces killed or wounded.

**Figure 26.1** **Casualties of World War I** The losses of World War I were the highest ever for a war in Europe. These numbers are approximate because of problems with record keeping caused by the destructive nature of total war.

job-training programs. Crippled veterans were often forced to beg on the streets, a common sight for the next decade.

The German case is instructive. Nearly 10 percent of German civilians were direct victims of the war, and taking care of them was one of the most difficult problems faced by the new German government. Veterans groups organized to lobby for state support, and fully one-third of the federal budget of the Weimar Republic was tied up in war-related pensions and benefits. With the onset of the Great Depression in 1929, benefits were cut, leaving bitter veterans vulnerable to Nazi propagandists. The human cost of the war thus had another steep price: across Europe, newly formed radical right-wing parties, including the German National Socialists and the Italian Fascists, successfully manipulated popular feelings of loss and resentment to undermine fragile parliamentary governments.

Chapter 26
**War and Revolution**
**1914–1919**

CHAPTER LOCATOR | What caused the outbreak of the First World War?

# ← LOOKING BACK **LOOKING AHEAD** →

WHEN CHIEF OF THE GERMAN GENERAL STAFF Count Helmuth von Moltke imagined the war of the future in a letter to his wife in 1905, his comments were surprisingly accurate. "It will become a war between peoples which will not be concluded with a single battle," the general wrote, "but which will be a long, weary struggle with a country that will not acknowledge defeat until the whole strength of its people is broken."[6] As von Moltke foresaw, World War I broke peoples and nations. The trials of total war increased the power of the centralized state and in the end brought down the Austro-Hungarian, Ottoman, and Russian empires. The brutal violence shocked and horrified observers across the world; ordinary citizens were left to mourn their losses.

Despite high hopes for Wilson's Fourteen Points, the Treaty of Versailles hardly brought a lasting peace. The war's disruptions encouraged the radical political struggles of the 1920s and 1930s as well as the rise of totalitarian regimes across Europe, which led to the even more extreme violence of the Second World War. Indeed, some historians believe that the interwar years of 1914 to 1945 might mostly accurately be labeled a modern European Thirty Years' War, since the problems unleashed in August 1914 were only really resolved in the 1950s. This strong assertion contains a great amount of truth. For all of Europe, World War I was a revolutionary conflict of gigantic proportions with lasting traumatic effects. ■

- ▪ For a list of suggested readings for this chapter, visit *bedfordstmartins.com/mckaywestunderstanding*.

- ▪ For primary sources from this period, see *Sources of Western Society*, Second Edition.

- ▪ For Web sites, images, and documents related to topics in this chapter, see Make History at *bedfordstmartins.com/mckaywestunderstanding*.

| How did the First World War differ from previous wars? | In what ways did the war transform life on the home front? | Why did world war lead to revolution in Russia? | In what ways was the Allied peace settlement flawed? |
|---|---|---|---|

# Chapter 26 Study Guide

Online Study Guide
bedfordstmartins.com/mckaywestunderstanding

## Step 1

**GETTING STARTED** Below are basic terms about this period in the history of Western civilization. Can you identify each term below and explain why it matters? To do this exercise online, go to bedfordstmartins.com/mckaywestunderstanding.

| TERMS | WHO (OR WHAT) AND WHEN | WHY IT MATTERS |
|---|---|---|
| Triple Alliance, p. 768 | | |
| Triple Entente, p. 769 | | |
| Schlieffen Plan, p. 773 | | |
| total war, p. 773 | | |
| trench warfare, p. 773 | | |
| February Revolution, p. 784 | | |
| Petrograd Soviet, p. 785 | | |
| Bolsheviks, p. 786 | | |
| Treaty of Brest-Litovsk, p. 788 | | |
| war communism, p. 788 | | |
| Treaty of Versailles, p. 790 | | |
| Fourteen Points, p. 791 | | |
| League of Nations, p. 792 | | |
| national self-determination, p. 792 | | |
| war guilt clause, p. 792 | | |
| Balfour Declaration, p. 793 | | |

## Step 2

**MOVING BEYOND THE BASICS** The exercise below requires a more advanced understanding of the chapter material. Examine the nature and consequences of "total war" by filling in the chart below with descriptions of the military, political, social, and economic impact of total war. When you are finished, consider the following questions: In what ways was the First World War a conflict between nations, as opposed to armies? In what ways did World War I differ from earlier conflicts? To do this exercise online, go to bedfordstmartins.com/mckaywestunderstanding.

| | MILITARY | POLITICAL | SOCIAL | ECONOMIC |
|---|---|---|---|---|
| Impact of Total War | | | | |

**PUTTING IT ALL TOGETHER** Now that you've reviewed key elements of the chapter, take a step back and try to see the big picture. Remember to use specific examples from the chapter in your answers. To do this exercise online, go to bedfordstmartins.com/mckaywestunderstanding.

**THE ROAD TO WAR**

- What factors contributed to the division of Europe into two hostile blocs? Why did European leaders fail to resolve the tensions and conflicts that led to this situation?

- How did the "mood of 1914" contribute to the outbreak of war? How would you explain the enthusiasm many Europeans had for war on the eve of the conflict?

**TOTAL WAR ON THE BATTLEFIELD AND THE HOME FRONT**

- How did industrialization change the nature of warfare? Is it accurate to describe World War I as the first fully industrialized war?

- How did political leaders channel their nation's resources into the war effort? How did their policies affect European society and government?

**THE RUSSIAN REVOLUTION**

- How did the war undermine the tsarist regime in Russia? How did the tsar himself contribute to the collapse of his government?

- Compare and contrast the wartime revolutionary movements in Russia and Germany. Why were the radicals able to take power in Russia, but not in Germany?

**THE PEACE SETTLEMENT**

- Compare and contrast the peace settlements that followed the Napoleonic wars and World War I. Which was more successful? Why?

- Who was excluded from the negotiations that led to the Treaty of Versailles? What were the long-term consequences of these exclusions?

■ **In Your Own Words** Imagine that you must explain Chapter 26 to someone who hasn't read it. What would be the most important points to include and why?

# 27

# The Age of Anxiety

## ca. 1900–1940

---

When Allied diplomats met in Paris in early 1919 with their optimistic plans for building a lasting peace, most people looked forward to happier times. After the terrible trauma of total war, they hoped that life would return to normal and would make sense in the familiar prewar terms of peace, prosperity, and progress. Their hopes were in vain. The First World War and the Russian Revolution had mangled too many things beyond repair. Life would no longer fit neatly into the old molds.

Instead, great numbers of men and women felt themselves increasingly adrift in a strange, uncertain, and uncontrollable world. They saw themselves living in an age of anxiety and continual crisis. Radical developments in the arts and sciences challenged received wisdom of all kinds. Political stability remained elusive, and the Great Depression in 1929 shocked the status quo. Democratic liberalism was besieged by the rise of authoritarian and fascist governments, and another world conflict seemed imminent. In the early 1920s the French poet and critic Paul Valéry (va-lay-REE) (1871–1945) described the widespread "impression of darkness" in this age of anxiety, where "almost all the affairs of men remain in a terrible uncertainty. We think of what has disappeared, and we are almost destroyed by what has been destroyed; we do not know what will be born, and we fear the future, not without reason."[1] Valéry's words captured the sense of gloom and foreboding that dominated the decades between the world wars. ∎

**Life in the Age of Anxiety.** Dadaist George Grosz's *Inside and Outside* is a disturbing image of the class conflict wrought by the economic crises of the 1920s. Wealthy and bestial elites celebrate a luxurious New Year's Eve "inside," while "outside" a disabled veteran begs in vain for money from uncaring passersby. (akg-images. Estate of George Grosz/Licensed by VAGA, New York, NY)

# Chapter Preview

▶  How did intellectual developments reflect postwar anxieties?

▶  How did modernism revolutionize European culture?

▶  How did consumer culture change the lives of Europeans?

▶  What obstacles to lasting peace did European leaders face?

▶  What were the causes and consequences of the Great Depression?

# ▼ How did intellectual developments reflect postwar anxieties?

The decades surrounding the First World War—from the 1880s to the 1930s—brought intense cultural and intellectual experimentation. Dramatic changes shook the fields of philosophy, science, and literature. Western society began to question and even abandon many of the cherished values and beliefs that had guided it since the eighteenth-century Enlightenment. Ordinary people found many of these revolutionary ideas unsettling. In response, many turned to Christianity, which experienced a remarkable revival in this period.

## Modern Philosophy

Before 1914 most people still believed in Enlightenment philosophies of progress, reason, and individual rights. At the turn of the century, supporters of these philosophies had some cause for optimism. Political rights were gradually spreading to women and workers, and the rising standard of living, the taming of the city, and the growth of state-supported social programs suggested that things were indeed improving. Just as there were laws of science, many thinkers felt that there were laws of society that rational human beings could discover and then wisely act on.

Nevertheless, as the nineteenth century drew to a close, a small group of serious thinkers and creative writers mounted a determined attack on such ideas. These critics rejected the general faith in progress and the rational human mind. The German philosopher Friedrich Nietzsche (NEE-chuh) (1844–1900) was particularly influential. In the first of his *Untimely Meditations* (1873), he argued that ever since classical Athens, the West had overemphasized rationality and stifled the authentic passions and animal instincts that drive human activity and true creativity.

**"Existence Precedes Essence"** Slogans such as this one captured the basic meaning of the philosophy of existentialism by underscoring the meaninglessness of human life and helped turn French intellectual Jean-Paul Sartre into a public celebrity. Here Sartre gives a radio interview in 1948 as his intellectual partner Simone de Beauvoir looks on. (Bettmann/Corbis)

Nietzsche went on to question the conventional values of Western society. He believed that reason, democracy, progress, and respectability were outworn social and psychological constructs whose influence was suffocating self-realization and excellence. Rejecting religion, Nietzsche claimed that Christianity embodied a "slave morality" that glorified weakness, envy, and mediocrity. Nietzsche painted a dark world. The West was in decline; false values had triumphed. According to Nietzsche, the only hope for the individual was to accept the meaninglessness of human existence and then make that very meaninglessness a source of self-defined personal integrity and hence liberation. In this way, at least a few superior individuals could free themselves from the humdrum thinking of the masses and become true heroes. Little read during his active years, Nietzsche's works attracted growing attention in the early twentieth century. Artists and writers experimented with his ideas, which were fundamental to the rise of the philosophy of existentialism in the 1920s.

The growing dissatisfaction with established ideas before 1914 was apparent in other important thinkers. In the 1890s French philosophy professor Henri Bergson (1859–1941) argued that immediate experience and intuition were as important as rational and scientific thinking for understanding reality. According to Bergson, a religious experience or a mystical poem was often more accessible to human comprehension than was a scientific law or a mathematical equation.

Another thinker who challenged the certainties of rational thinking was French socialist Georges Sorel (1847–1922). Sorel concluded that Marxian socialism was an inspiring but unprovable religion, rather than a scientific truth as Marx himself had argued. Socialism would shatter capitalist society, Sorel believed, through a great general strike of all working people inspired by a myth of revolution. Sorel rejected democracy and believed that the masses of the new society would have to be controlled by a small revolutionary elite.

The First World War accelerated the revolt against established certainties in philosophy, but that revolt went in two very different directions. In English-speaking countries, the main development was the acceptance of logical positivism. In the continental countries, the primary development in philosophy was existentialism.

Logical positivism was truly revolutionary. Adherents of this worldview argued that what we know about human life must be based on rational facts and direct observation. They concluded that theology and most of traditional philosophy was meaningless because their propositions were impossible to prove using logic. This outlook is often associated with the Austrian philosopher Ludwig Wittgenstein (VIT-guhn-shtighn) (1889–1951), who later immigrated to England, where he trained numerous disciples. Wittgenstein argued that philosophy is only the logical clarification of thoughts, and that therefore it should concentrate on the study of language, which expresses thoughts. In his view, the great philosophical issues of the ages — God, freedom, morality, and so on — were a great waste of time, for neither scientific experiments nor the logic of mathematics could demonstrate their validity. Logical positivism, which has remained dominant in England and the United States to this day, drastically reduced the scope of philosophical inquiry.

## Chapter Chronology

| | |
|---|---|
| **1919** | Treaty of Versailles; Freudian psychology gains popularity; Rutherford splits the atom; Bauhaus school founded |
| **1920s** | Existentialism, Dadaism, and surrealism gain prominence |
| **1922** | Eliot, *The Waste Land*; Joyce, *Ulysses*; Woolf, *Jacob's Room*; Wittgenstein writes on logical positivism |
| **1923** | French and Belgian armies occupy the Ruhr |
| **1924** | Dawes Plan |
| **1925** | Berg's opera *Wozzeck* first performed; Kafka, *The Trial* |
| **1926** | Germany joins the League of Nations |
| **1928** | Kellogg-Briand Pact |
| **1929** | Faulkner, *The Sound and the Fury* |
| **1929–1939** | Great Depression |
| **1933** | Hitler and the Nazi Party take power in Germany |
| **1935** | Riefenstahl's documentary film *The Triumph of the Will* |
| **1936** | Formation of Popular Front in France |

**logical positivism** A philosophy that sees meaning in only those beliefs that can be empirically proven, and that therefore rejects most of the concerns of traditional philosophy as nonsense—from the existence of God to the meaning of happiness.

How did modernism revolutionize European culture?

How did consumer culture change the lives of Europeans?

What obstacles to lasting peace did European leaders face?

What were the causes and consequences of the Great Depression?

**805**

On the continent, others looked for answers in existentialism. This new philosophy loosely united highly diverse and even contradictory thinkers in a search for usable moral values in a world of anxiety and uncertainty. Most existential thinkers in the twentieth century were atheists. Often inspired by Nietzsche, they did not believe that a supreme being had established humanity's fundamental nature and given life its meaning. In the words of the famous French existentialist Jean-Paul Sartre (ZHAWN-pawl SAHRT) (1905–1980), "existence precedes essence." By that, Sartre meant that there are no God-given, timeless truths outside or independent of individual existence. Only after they are born do people struggle to define their essence, entirely on their own. The crisis of the existential thinker epitomized the modern intellectual crisis—the shattering of beliefs in God, reason, and progress.

Existentialists did recognize that human beings must act in the world. Indeed, in the words of Sartre, "man is condemned to be free." Because life is meaningless, existentialists believe that individuals are forced to create their own meaning and define themselves through their actions. Such radical freedom is frightening, and Sartre concluded that most people try to escape their unwanted freedom by structuring their lives around conventional social norms. According to Sartre, to escape is to live in "bad faith," to hide from the hard truths of existence. To live authentically, individuals must become "engaged" and choose their own actions in full awareness of their inescapable responsibility for their own behavior. Existentialism thus had a powerful ethical component.

## The Revival of Christianity

Though philosophers such as Nietzsche, Wittgenstein, and Sartre all argued that religion had little to teach people in a modern age, the decades after the First World War witnessed a revival of Christian thought. Christianity and religion in general had been on the defensive in intellectual circles since the Enlightenment. In the years before 1914, some theologians, especially Protestant ones, had felt the need to interpret Christian doctrine and the Bible so that they did not seem to contradict science, evolution, and common sense. Indeed, some modern theologians were embarrassed by the miraculous, unscientific aspects of Christianity and turned away from them.

Especially after World War I, a number of thinkers and theologians began to revitalize the fundamentals of Christianity. Sometimes described as Christian existentialists because they shared the loneliness and despair of atheistic existentialists, they stressed human beings' sinful nature, the need for faith, and the mystery of God's forgiveness. The revival of fundamental Christian belief after World War I was fed by the rediscovery of the work of the nineteenth-century Danish theologian Søren Kierkegaard (1813–1855). Kierkegaard (KIHR-kuh-gahrd) believed it was impossible for ordinary individuals to prove the existence of God, but he rejected the notion that Christianity was an empty practice. Kierkegaard felt that people must take a "leap of faith" and accept the existence of an objectively unknowable but nonetheless awesome and majestic God.

In the 1920s the Swiss Protestant theologian Karl Barth (1886–1968) propounded similar ideas. Barth argued that human beings were imperfect, sinful creatures whose reason and will are hopelessly flawed. Religious truth is therefore made known to human beings only through God's grace, not through reason. People have to accept God's word and the supernatural revelation of Jesus Christ with awe, trust, and obedience, not reason or logic.

Among Catholics, the leading existential Christian was Gabriel Marcel (1887–1973). Born into a cultivated French family, Marcel found in the Catholic Church an answer to what he called the postwar "broken world." Catholicism and religious belief provided the hope, humanity, honesty, and piety for which he hungered. Flexible and gentle, Marcel and his countryman Jacques Maritain (1882–1973) denounced anti-Semitism and supported closer ties with non-Catholics.

After 1914 religion became much more relevant and meaningful to thinking people than it had been before the war. Many intellectuals turned to religion between about 1920 and 1950. Poets T. S. Eliot and W. H. Auden, novelists Evelyn Waugh and Aldous Huxley, historian Arnold Toynbee, writer C. S. Lewis, psychoanalyst Karl Stern, physicist Max Planck, and philosopher Cyril Joad were all either converted to religion or attracted to it for the first time. Religion, often of a despairing, existential variety, was one meaningful answer to uncertainty and anxiety.

## The New Physics

By the late nineteenth century, science was one of the main pillars supporting Western society's optimistic and rationalistic worldview. Unchanging natural laws seemed to determine physical processes and permit useful solutions to more and more problems. All this was comforting, especially to people who were no longer committed to traditional religious beliefs. And all this was challenged by the new physics.

A series of discoveries at the end of the nineteenth century challenged the old view of atoms as the stable basic building blocks of nature, with a different kind of unbreakable atom for each of the ninety-two chemical elements. Polish-born physicist Marie Curie (1867–1934) and her French husband, Pierre, discovered that radium constantly emits subatomic particles and thus does not have a constant atomic weight. Building on this and other work in radiation, German physicist Max Planck (1858–1947) showed in 1900 that subatomic energy is emitted in uneven little spurts, which Planck called "quanta," and not in a steady stream, as previously believed. Planck's discovery called into question the old sharp distinction between matter and energy: the implication was that matter and energy might be different forms of the same thing.

**theory of special relativity** Albert Einstein's theory that time and space are relative to the observer, and that only the speed of light remains constant.

In 1905 the German-Jewish genius Albert Einstein (1879–1955) went further than the Curies and Planck in undermining Newtonian physics. His famous **theory of special relativity** postulated that time and space are relative to the viewpoint of the observer and that only the speed of light is constant for all frames of reference in the universe. In addition, Einstein's theory stated clearly that matter and energy are interchangeable and that even a particle of matter contains enormous levels of potential energy. Einstein's ideas unified an apparently infinite universe with the incredibly small, fast-moving subatomic world.

**Unlocking the Power of the Atom** Many of the fanciful visions of science fiction came true in the twentieth century, although not exactly as first imagined. This 1927 cartoon satirizes a professor who has split the atom and unwittingly destroyed his building and neighborhood in the process. In the Second World War professors harnessed the atom to bombs and decimated faraway cities and foreign civilians. (Mary Evans Picture Library/The Image Works)

How did modernism revolutionize European culture?

How did consumer culture change the lives of Europeans?

What obstacles to lasting peace did European leaders face?

What were the causes and consequences of the Great Depression?

807

The 1920s opened the "heroic age of physics," in the apt words of Ernest Rutherford (1871–1937), one of its leading pioneers. Breakthrough followed breakthrough. In 1919 Rutherford showed that the atom could be split. By 1944 seven subatomic particles had been identified, the most important of which was the neutron. The neutron's capacity to pass through other atoms allowed for an even more intense bombardment of matter, leading to chain reactions of unbelievable force. This discovery was fundamental to the subsequent construction of the atomic bomb.

Although few nonscientists understood this revolution in physics, the implications of the new theories and discoveries, as presented by newspapers and popular writers, were disturbing to millions of men and women in the 1920s and 1930s. Instead of Newton's dependable, rational laws, there seemed to be only tendencies and probabilities in an extraordinarily complex and uncertain universe. Like modern philosophy, physics no longer provided comforting truths about natural laws or optimistic answers about humanity's place in an understandable world.

## Freudian Psychology

With physics presenting an uncertain universe so unrelated to ordinary human experience, questions regarding the power and potential of the human mind assumed special significance. The findings and speculations of psychologist Sigmund Freud (Chapter 23) were particularly influential, yet also deeply disturbing.

Before Freud, most professional scientific psychologists assumed that the conscious mind processed sense experiences in a rational and logical way. Human behavior in turn was the result of rational calculation—of "thinking." Freud developed a very different view of the human psyche beginning in the late 1880s. Basing his insights on the analysis of dreams and of hysteria, Freud concluded that human behavior was basically irrational, governed by the unconscious, a sort of mental reservoir that contained vital instinctual drives and powerful memories. The unconscious was unknowable to the conscious mind but, nonetheless, it deeply influenced people's behavior.

**id, ego, and superego**
Freudian terms to describe the three parts of the self and the basis of human behavior, which Freud saw as basically irrational.

Elaborating on these ideas, Freud described three structures of the self—the id, the superego, and the ego—that were basically at war with one another. The primitive, irrational id was entirely unconscious. The source of sexual, aggressive, and pleasure-seeking instincts, the id sought immediate fulfillment of all desires and was totally amoral. The id was kept in check by the superego, the conscience or internalized voice of parental or social control. For Freud, the superego was also irrational and was in constant in conflict with the pleasure-seeking id. The third component of human psychology was the ego, the rational self that was mostly conscious and worked to negotiate between the demands of the id and the superego.

For Freud, the healthy individual possessed a strong ego that effectively balanced the id and superego. Neurosis, or mental illness, resulted when the three structures were somehow out of balance. Since the id's instinctual drives were extremely powerful, the ever-present danger for individuals and whole societies was that unacknowledged drives might overwhelm the control mechanisms of the ego. Freud's famous "talking cure"—in which neurotic patients lay back on a couch and shared their innermost thoughts with the psychoanalyst—was an attempt to resolve such unconscious tensions and restore the rational ego to its predominant role.

Freudian psychology and clinical psychiatry had become an international movement by 1910, but only after 1919 did they receive popular attention, especially in northern Europe and the United States. Many opponents and even some enthusiasts interpreted Freud as saying that the first requirement for mental health was an uninhibited sex life. Thus after the First World War, the popular interpretation of Freud reflected and encouraged growing sexual experimentation. For more serious students, the psychology of Freud and his followers drastically undermined the old easy optimism about the rational and progressive nature of the human mind.

## Twentieth-Century Literature

Western literature was deeply influenced by the general intellectual climate of pessimism, relativism, and alienation. Nineteenth-century novelists had typically written as all-knowing narrators, describing realistic characters and their relationships to an understandable, if sometimes harsh, society. Writers now developed new techniques to express new realities. In the twentieth century, many authors adopted the limited, often confused viewpoint of a single individual. Like Freud, these novelists focused their attention on the complexity and irrationality of the human mind, where feelings, memories, and desires are forever scrambled.

Serious novelists also used the **stream-of-consciousness technique** with its reliance on internal monologues to explore the psyche. In *Jacob's Room* (1922), Virginia Woolf (1882–1941) created a novel made up of a series of internal monologues in which she tried to capture the inner voice in prose. The American novelist William Faulkner (1897–1962) used the same technique in *The Sound and the Fury* (1929), much of whose intense drama is confusedly seen through the eyes of a man who is mentally disabled.

The most famous stream-of-consciousness novel is *Ulysses* (1922) by Irish novelist James Joyce (1882–1941). Into an account of a single day in the life of an ordinary man, Joyce weaves an extended ironic parallel between his hero's aimless wanderings through the streets and pubs of Dublin and the adventures of Homer's hero Ulysses on his way home from Troy. Abandoning any sense of a conventional plot, breaking formal rules of grammar, and blending foreign words, puns, bits of knowledge, and scraps of memory together in bewildering confusion, the language of *Ulysses* is intended to mirror modern life itself.

As creative writers turned their attention from society to the individual and from realism to psychological relativity, they rejected the idea of progress. Some described "anti-utopias," nightmare visions of things to come. In 1918 an obscure German high school teacher named Oswald Spengler (1880–1936) published *The Decline of the West*, which quickly became an international sensation. Western civilization, in Spengler's opinion, was in its old age and would soon be overtaken by the rise of East Asia. T. S. Eliot (1888–1965), in his famous poem *The Waste Land* (1922), likewise depicted a world of growing desolation:

> *April is the cruelest month, breeding*
> *Lilacs out of the dead land, mixing*
> *Memory and desire, stirring*
> *Dull roots with spring rain. . . .*
> *What are the roots that clutch, what branches grow*
> *Out of this stony rubbish? Son of man,*
> *You cannot say, or guess, for you know only*
> *A heap of broken images, where the sun beats,*
> *And the dead tree gives no shelter, the cricket no relief,*
> *And the dry stone no sound of water.*[2]

Eliot's poem expressed the widespread despair that followed the First World War. Writer Franz Kafka (1883–1924) also portrayed an incomprehensible, alienated world. Kafka's novels *The Trial* (1925) and *The Castle* (1926), as well as his famous novella *The Metamorphosis* (1915), portray helpless individuals crushed by inexplicably hostile forces. In these and many other works, authors between the wars used new literary techniques and dark imagery to portray the widespread unease of the age of anxiety.

**stream-of-consciousness technique** A literary technique, found in works by Virginia Woolf, James Joyce, and others, that uses interior monologue—a character's thoughts and feelings as they occur—to explore the human psyche.

How did modernism revolutionize European culture?

How did consumer culture change the lives of Europeans?

What obstacles to lasting peace did European leaders face?

What were the causes and consequences of the Great Depression?

**809**

## ▼ How did modernism revolutionize European culture?

**modernism** A label given to Western artistic and cultural movements of the late nineteenth and early twentieth centuries, which were typified by radical experimentation that challenged traditional forms of artistic expression.

Like the scientists and intellectuals who were part of the same modern culture, creative artists rejected old forms and old values. Modernism in architecture, art, and music meant constant experimentation and a search for new kinds of expression. Even today the modernism of the immediate prewar years and the 1920s seems strikingly fresh and original. And though many people find the varied modern visions of the arts strange and disturbing, the first half of the twentieth century, so dismal in many respects, stands as one of Western civilization's great artistic eras.

### Architecture and Design

Already in the late nineteenth century, architects inspired by modernism had begun to transform the physical framework of urban society. The United States pioneered in the new architecture. In the 1890s the Chicago school of architects, led by Louis H. Sullivan (1856–1924), used cheap steel, reinforced concrete, and electric elevators to build skyscrapers and office buildings lacking almost any exterior ornamentation. In the first decade of the twentieth century, Sullivan's student Frank Lloyd Wright (1869–1959) built a series of radically modern houses featuring low lines, open interiors, and mass-produced building materials. Europeans were inspired by these and other American examples of functional construction.

**functionalism** The principle that buildings, like industrial products, should serve as well as possible the purpose for which they were made.

Promoters of modern architecture argued that buildings and living spaces in general should be ordered according to a new principle: functionalism. Buildings, like industrial products, should be useful and "functional" — that is, they should serve, as well as possible, the purpose for which they were made. According to the Franco-Swiss architect Le Corbusier (luh cor-booz-YAY) (1887–1965), "a house is a machine for living in."[3]

Corbusier's *Towards a New Architecture*, published in 1923, laid out a series of guidelines meant to revolutionize building design. Corbusier argued that architects should adopt the latest technologies in their construction practices. Rejecting fancy ornamentation, they should find beauty in the clean straight lines of practical construction and efficient machinery. The resulting buildings, fashioned according to what was soon called the "international style," were typically symmetrical rectangles made of concrete, glass, and steel.

**Bauhaus** A German interdisciplinary school of fine and applied arts that brought together many leading modern architects, designers, and theatrical innovators.

In Europe architectural leadership centered in German-speaking countries until Hitler took power in 1933. In 1919 Walter Gropius (1883–1969) merged the schools of fine and applied arts at Weimar into a single interdisciplinary school, the Bauhaus. The Bauhaus brought together many leading modern architects, designers, and theatrical innovators. Working as a team, they combined the study of fine art, including painting and sculpture, with the study of applied art in the crafts of printing, weaving, and furniture making. Throughout the 1920s the Bauhaus, with its stress on functionalism and good design for everyday life, attracted enthusiastic students from all over the world.

### New Artistic Movements

In the decades surrounding the First World War, the visual arts, like other realms of culture, experienced radical change and experimentation. For the last several centuries, artists had tried to portray accurate representations of reality. Now a new artistic avant-garde emerged to challenge the assumptions of their elders. Artists turned their backs on figurative representation and began to break down form into its constituent parts: lines, shapes, and colors.

One of the earliest and best-known modernist movements was Impressionism, which blossomed in Paris in the 1870s. French artists such as Claude Monet (1840–1926) and Edgar Degas (1834–1917) and the American Mary Cassatt (1844–1926), who settled in Paris in 1875, tried to portray their sensory "impressions" in their work. Impressionists looked to the world around them for subject matter, rejecting traditional themes such as battles, religious scenes, and wealthy elites. They also moved toward abstraction. Capturing a fleeting moment of color and light, in often blurry and quickly painted images, was far more important than portraying a heavily detailed and precise rendering of an actual object.

By the 1890s new artistic movements had emerged alongside of Impressionism. Post-impressionists and Expressionists, such as Vincent van Gogh (1853–1890), built on Impressionist motifs of color and light but added a deep psychological element to their pictures, reflecting the attempt to search within the self and reveal (or express) deep inner feelings on the canvas.

In Paris in 1907 the famous painter Pablo Picasso, along with other artists, established Cubism—a highly analytical approach to art concentrated on a complex geometry of zigzagging lines and sharply angled overlapping planes. About three years later came the ultimate stage in the development of abstract, nonrepresentational art. Artists such as the Russian-born Wassily Kandinsky (VAS-uh-lee kan-DIHN-skee) (1866–1944) turned away from nature completely. "The observer," said Kandinsky, "must learn to look at [my] pictures . . . as form and color combinations . . . as a representation of mood and not as a representation of *objects*."[4]

**Dadaism** An artistic movement of the 1920s and 1930s that attacked all accepted standards of art and behavior and delighted in outrageous conduct.

The shock of World War I encouraged further radicalization. In 1916 a group of artists and intellectuals in exile in Zurich, Switzerland, championed a new movement they called Dadaism, which attacked all the familiar standards of art and delighted in outrageous behavior. The war had shown once and for all that life was meaningless, the Dadaists argued, so Dadaists tried to shock their audiences with what they called "anti-art," works and public performances that were entirely nonsensical. After the war, Dadaism became an international movement, spreading to Paris, New York, and particularly Berlin in the early 1920s.

After 1924 many Dadaists were attracted to surrealism. Surrealists such as Salvador Dali (1904–1989) were deeply influenced by Freudian psychology and portrayed images of the unconscious in their art. They painted fantastic worlds of wild dreams and uncomfortable symbols.

Many modern artists sincerely believed that art had a radical mission. By calling attention to the supposed bankruptcy of mainstream society, art had the power to produce radical social change.

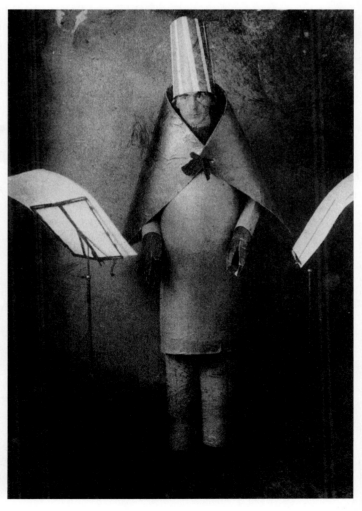

**The Shock of the Avant-Garde** Dadaist Hugo Ball recites his nonsense poem "Karawane" at the notorious Cabaret Voltaire in Zurich, Switzerland, in 1916. Avant-garde artists such as Ball consciously used their work to overturn familiar artistic conventions and challenge the assumptions of the European middle classes. (Apic/Getty Images)

How did modernism revolutionize European culture?

How did consumer culture change the lives of Europeans?

What obstacles to lasting peace did European leaders face?

What were the causes and consequences of the Great Depression?

811

Dadaist Richard Huelsenbeck's *Collective Dada Manifesto* of 1920 captured the playfulness of Dada but also the movement's serious critical edge:

> *Art in its execution and direction is dependent on the time in which it lives, and artists are creatures of their epoch. The highest art will be that which in its conscious content presents the thousandfold problems of the day, the art which has been visibly shattered by the explosions of last week, which is forever trying to collect its limbs after yesterday's crash. . . . Dada is the international expression of our times, the great rebellion of artistic movements, the artistic reflex of all these offensives, peace congresses, riots in the vegetable market. . . . Blast the bloodless abstraction of expressionism! Blast the literary hollowheads and their theories for improving the world! . . . To be against this manifesto is to be a Dadaist![5]*

## Modern Music

Developments in modern music were strikingly parallel to those in painting. Composers, too, attempted to express emotional intensity in radically experimental forms. The ballet *The Rite of Spring* by composer Igor Stravinsky (1882–1971) practically caused a riot when it was first performed in Paris in 1913. The combination of pulsating, dissonant rhythms from the orchestra pit and the earthy representation of lovemaking by the strangely dressed dancers on the stage was a shocking enactment of a primitive fertility rite.

After the First World War, when irrationality and violence had seemed to pervade human experience, modernism flourished in opera and ballet. The opera *Wozzeck*, by Alban Berg (1885–1935), blended a half-sung, half-spoken kind of dialogue with harsh, atonal

**Musical Modernism** Dancers in Russian composer Igor Stravinsky's avant-garde ballet *The Rite of Spring* perform at the Paris premiere. The dissonant music, wild sets and costumes, and unpredictable dance movements shocked and insulted the audience, which rioted on the opening night in May 1913. (Lebrecht/The Image Works)

music. *Wozzeck* is a gruesome tale of a soldier driven by Kafka-like inner terrors and vague suspicions of unfaithfulness to murder his mistress.

Some composers turned their backs on long-established musical conventions, arranging sounds without creating recognizable harmonies. Led by Viennese composer Arnold Schönberg (SHUHN-buhrg) (1874–1951), they abandoned traditional harmony and tonality. The musical notes in a given piece were no longer united and organized by a key; instead they were independent and unrelated. Accustomed to the harmonies of classical and romantic music, audiences generally resisted modern atonal music. Only after the Second World War did it begin to win acceptance.

# ▼ How did consumer culture change the lives of Europeans?

After the First World War, European society experienced fundamental changes in the basic consumption of goods and services. Modern business forms of credit, retail, and advertising helped sell increasing numbers of mass-produced goods—the products of a highly industrialized factory system—to ever-larger numbers of people. With the arrival of cinema and radio, the leisure time of ordinary people was increasingly dominated by commercial entertainment. In the years between the end of World War I in 1918 and the start of World War II in 1939 the outlines of a modern consumer society emerged with startling clarity.

## Mass Culture

The emerging consumer society of the 1920s is a good example of the way technological developments can lead to widespread social change. The arrival of a highly industrialized manufacturing system dedicated to mass producing inexpensive goods, the establishment of efficient transportation systems that could bring these goods to national markets, and the rise of professional advertising experts and agencies to sell them were all part of a revolution in the way consumer goods were made, marketed, and used by ordinary people. Some people embraced the new ways, while others worried that the changes wrought by an increasingly unavoidable consumer culture threatened familiar values and precious traditions.

Critics had good reason to worry. Mass-produced goods indeed had a profound impact on the lives of ordinary people. Housework and private life were increasingly organized around an array of modern appliances. The aggressive marketing of fashionable clothing and personal care products encouraged a cult of youthful "sex appeal." The mass production and marketing of automobiles and the rise of established tourist agencies opened roads to increased mobility and travel.

Commercialized mass entertainment likewise prospered and began to dominate the way people spent their leisure time. Movies and radio thrilled millions (see pages 815–816). Professional sporting events drew throngs of fans. Thriving print media brought readers an astounding variety of newspapers, inexpensive books, and glossy illustrated magazines; and flashy restaurants, theatrical revues, and nightclubs competed for evening customers.

The emergence of modern consumer culture both undermined and reinforced existing social differences. On the one hand, consumerism helped democratize Western society. Since everyone could purchase any good, if he or she had the means, mass culture helped break down old social barriers between class, region, and religion. Yet it also reinforced social differences. Manufacturers soon realized they could profit by marketing goods to

How did modernism revolutionize European culture?

**How did consumer culture change the lives of Europeans?**

What obstacles to lasting peace did European leaders face?

What were the causes and consequences of the Great Depression?

813

specific groups. Catholics, for example, could purchase their own popular literature, and young people bought the latest fashions marketed directly to them. The expense of many items meant that only the wealthy could purchase them. Automobiles and, in the 1920s, even vacuum cleaners cost so much that ownership became a sign of status.

The changes in women's lives were particularly striking. The new household items transformed the way women performed housework. Advice literature of all kinds encouraged housewives to buy the latest appliances so they could "modernize" their domes-

### ▪ PICTURING THE PAST

### The New Woman: Image or Reality?

A young woman enjoys a drink at the Romanesque Café in Berlin in 1924. The independence of this "new woman" wearing fashionable clothes with a revealing hemline, and lacking an escort, transgressed familiar gender roles and shocked and fascinated contemporaries. Images of the new woman appeared in movies, illustrated magazines, and advertisements, such as this German poster selling "the perfume for this winter."
(café: Bildarchiv Preussischer Kulturbesitz/Art Resource, NY; advertisement: Lordprice Collection/Alamy)

**ANALYZING THE IMAGE** How do these portrayals of the new woman challenge conventional gender roles? Do you think the woman in the Berlin café was influenced by advertisements for consumer products such as perfume and clothing?

**CONNECTIONS** What role did the emergence of a modern consumer culture play in the way contemporaries understood the new woman? Did consumer goods marketed to women open doors for liberating behavior, or did they set new standards that limited women's options?

To complete this activity online, go to the Online Study Guide at bedfordstmartins.com/mckaywestunderstanding.

tic labor. In public, consumer culture brought growing visibility to women, especially the young. Girls and young women worked behind the counters and shopped in the aisles of department stores, and they went out on the street alone in ways unthinkable in the nineteenth century. Contemporaries spoke about the arrival of the "new woman," a surprisingly independent female who voted and held a job, spent her salary on the latest fashions, applied makeup and smoked cigarettes, and used her sex appeal to charm any number of young men. The new woman was in some ways a stereotype, a product of marketing campaigns dedicated to selling consumer goods to the masses. Few young women could afford to live up to the image promoted in the mass press, even if they had jobs. Yet the changes associated with the First World War (see Chapter 26) and the emergence of consumer society did loosen traditional limits on women's behavior.

"new woman" Somewhat stereotypical image of the modern and independent working woman popular in the 1920s.

The emerging consumer culture generated a chorus of complaints from cultural critics. On the left, socialist writers worried that the appeal of mass culture was undermining working-class radicalism. On the right, conservatives complained that money spent on poor-quality mass-produced goods sapped the livelihood of industrious artisans and undermined national traditions. Religious leaders believed that modern consumerism encouraged rampant individualism and that greedy materialism was replacing spirituality. Many others bemoaned the loose morals of the new woman and the decline of traditional family values. Despite such criticism, ordinary people enjoyed the pleasures of mass consumption, and individual identities were tied ever more closely to modern mass-produced goods.

## The Appeal of Cinema

Nowhere was the influence of mass culture more evident than in the rapid growth of standardized commercial entertainment, especially cinema and radio. Both became major industries in the interwar years, and an eager public enthusiastically embraced the new media. The arrival of the modern mass media overshadowed and began to replace the traditional arts and amusements of people in villages and small towns, changing familiar ways of life.

Cinema first emerged in the United States around 1880, driven in part by the inventions of Thomas Edison. By 1910 American directors and business people had set up "movie factories," at first in the New York area and then in Los Angeles. Europeans were quick to follow. World War I quickened the pace. National leaders realized that movies offered distraction to troops and citizens. They were an effective means of spreading propaganda as well.

Cinema became a true mass medium in the 1920s, the golden age of silent film, and motion pictures would remain the central entertainment of the masses until after the Second World War. Growing numbers of ordinary people flocked to the gigantic movie palaces built across Europe in the mid-1920s, splendid theaters that could seat thousands. There they viewed the latest features, which were reviewed by critics in newspapers and illustrated magazines. Cinema audiences grew rapidly in the 1930s. In Great Britain in the late 1930s, one in every four adults went to the movies twice a week, and two in five went at least once a week. Other countries had similar figures.

As these numbers suggest, motion pictures could be powerful tools of indoctrination, especially in countries with dictatorial regimes. Lenin encouraged the development of Soviet film making, believing that the new medium was essential to the social and ideological transformation of the country. Beginning in the mid-1920s, a series of epic films, the most famous of which were directed by Sergei Eisenstein (1898–1948), dramatized the communist view of Russian history. In Nazi Germany, Leni Riefenstahl (1902–2003) directed a masterpiece of documentary propaganda, *The Triumph of the Will*, based on the 1934 Nazi Party rally at Nuremberg. Her film, released in 1935, was a brilliant and all-too-powerful documentary of Germany's Nazi rebirth.

How did modernism revolutionize European culture?

How did consumer culture change the lives of Europeans?

What obstacles to lasting peace did European leaders face?

What were the causes and consequences of the Great Depression?

815

## The Arrival of Radio

Like film, radio became a full-blown mass medium in the 1920s. Experimental sets were available in the 1880s; the work of Italian inventor Guglielmo Marconi (1874–1937) around 1900 and the development of the vacuum tube in 1904 made possible primitive transmissions of speech and music. But the first major public broadcasts in Great Britain and the United States did not occur until 1920.

Every major country quickly established national broadcasting networks. In the United States such networks were privately owned and were financed by advertising, but in Europe the typical pattern was direct control by the government. Whatever the institutional framework, radio became popular and influential. By the late 1930s more than three out of every four households in both democratic Great Britain and dictatorial Germany had at least one cheap mass-produced radio.

Like the movies, radio was well suited for political propaganda. Dictators such as Mussolini and Hitler controlled the airwaves and could reach enormous national audiences with their speeches. In

"The Greatest Cinema in the World"  With 3,400 seats, the Gaumont Palace in Paris was the largest cinema in the world in its heyday. Crowds lined up to see films such as this 1931 family drama by the noted French writer and film director Marcel Pagnol. (photo: Maurice Branger/Roger-Viollet/The Image Works; poster: Paramount Pictures/Photofest © Paramount Pictures)

democratic countries, politicians such as American president Franklin Roosevelt and British prime minister Stanley Baldwin effectively used informal "fireside chats" to bolster their support. The new media of mass culture offered audiences pleasant distractions but were at the same time potentially dangerous instruments of political manipulation.

# ▼ What obstacles to lasting peace did European leaders face?

As established patterns of thought and culture were challenged by World War I, so too was the political fabric stretched and torn. The Versailles settlement had established a shaky truce, not a solid peace. Thus national leaders faced a gigantic task as they sought to create a stable international order within the general context of intellectual crisis and revolutionary artistic experimentation.

The pursuit of real and lasting peace proved difficult for many reasons. Germany hated the Treaty of Versailles. France was fearful and isolated. Britain was undependable, and the United States had turned its back on European problems. Eastern Europe was in ferment, and no one could predict the future of communist Russia. Moreover, the international economic situation was poor and greatly complicated by war debts and disrupted patterns of trade. Yet from 1925 to late 1929, it appeared that peace and stability were within reach.

## Germany and the Western Powers

Germany was the key to lasting peace. Yet to Germans of all political parties, the Treaty of Versailles represented a harsh dictated peace, to be revised or repudiated as soon as possible. Germany still had the potential to become the strongest country in Europe and remained a source of instability. Moreover, with ominous implications for the future, France and Great Britain did not see eye to eye on Germany. By the end of 1919, France wanted to stress the harsh elements in the Treaty of Versailles. Most of the war in the west had been fought on French soil, and the expected costs of reconstruction, as well as of repaying war debts to the United States, were staggering. Thus the French believed reparations from Germany were an economic necessity. And after having compromised with President Wilson only to be betrayed by America's failure to ratify the treaty, many French leaders saw strict implementation of all provisions of the Treaty of Versailles as France's last best hope. Large reparation payments could hold Germany down indefinitely, and France would realize its goal of security.

The British soon felt differently. Prewar Germany had been Great Britain's second-best market, and after the war a healthy, prosperous Germany appeared to be essential to the British economy. The British were also suspicious of France's army — the largest in Europe, and authorized at Versailles to occupy the German Rhineland until 1935 — and of France's foreign policy. Ever since 1890 France had looked to Russia as a powerful ally against Germany. But with Russia hostile and communist, and with Britain and the United States unwilling to make any firm commitments, France turned to the newly formed states of eastern Europe for diplomatic support. In 1921 France signed a mutual defense pact with Poland and associated itself closely with the so-called Little Entente, an alliance that joined Czechoslovakia, Romania, and Yugoslavia against defeated and bitter Hungary.

While French and British leaders drifted in different directions, the Allied reparations commission completed its work. In April 1921 it announced that Germany had to pay the enormous sum of 132 billion gold marks ($33 billion) in annual installments of

How did modernism revolutionize European culture?   How did consumer culture change the lives of Europeans?   **What obstacles to lasting peace did European leaders face?**   What were the causes and consequences of the Great Depression?

817

2.5 billion gold marks. The young German republic—generally known as the Weimar Republic—made its first payment in 1921. Then in 1922, wracked by rapid inflation and political assassinations and motivated by hostility and arrogance as well, the Weimar Republic announced its inability to pay more. It proposed a moratorium on reparations for three years, with the clear implication that thereafter reparations would be either drastically reduced or eliminated entirely.

The British were willing to accept a moratorium on reparations, but the French were not. Led by their prime minister, Raymond Poincaré (pwan-kah-RAY) (1860–1934), they decided they had to either call Germany's bluff or see the entire peace settlement dissolve to France's great disadvantage. So, in early January 1923 armies of France and its ally Belgium moved out of the Rhineland and began to occupy the Ruhr district, the heartland of industrial Germany, creating the most serious international crisis of the 1920s. If forcible collection proved impossible, France would use occupation to paralyze Germany and force it to accept the Treaty of Versailles.

Strengthened by a wave of patriotism, the German government ordered the people of the Ruhr to stop working and passively resist the French occupation. The French answer to passive resistance was to seal off the Ruhr and the entire Rhineland from the rest of Germany, letting in only enough food to prevent starvation.

**French Occupation of the Ruhr, 1923–1925**

By the summer of 1923, France and Germany were engaged in a great test of wills. French armies could not collect reparations from striking workers at gunpoint. But French occupation was paralyzing Germany and its economy. Faced with the need to support the striking Ruhr workers and their employers, the German government began to print money to pay its bills, causing runaway inflation. Prices soared as German money rapidly lost all value. The accumulated savings of many retired and middle-class people were wiped out. Catastrophic inflation cruelly mocked the old middle-class virtues of thrift, caution, and self-reliance. Many Germans felt betrayed. They hated and blamed the Western governments, their own government, big business, the Jews, the workers, and the communists for their misfortune. Right-wing nationalists including Adolf Hitler and the newly established Nazi Party eagerly capitalized on the widespread feelings of discontent.

In August 1923, as the mark lost value and political unrest grew throughout Germany, Gustav Stresemann (GOOS-tahf SHTRAY-zuh-mahn) (1878–1929) assumed leadership of the government. Stresemann

**"German Women Protest the Colored Occupation on the Rhine"** In 1923 the French army occupied the industrial district of the Ruhr in Germany in an effort to force reparations payments. The occupying forces included colonial troops from West Africa, and Germans responded with a racist propaganda campaign that cast the West African troops as uncivilized savages. (Stiftung Deutsches Historiches Museum, Berlin, P62/1483.2)

CHAPTER LOCATOR     How did intellectual developments reflect postwar anxieties?

adopted an attitude of compromise. He called off passive resistance in the Ruhr and in October agreed in principle to pay reparations, but he asked for a re-examination of Germany's ability to pay. Poincaré accepted. His hard line was becoming increasingly unpopular with French citizens, and it was hated in Britain and the United States. (See "Individuals in Society: Gustav Stresemann," page 820.)

More generally, in both Germany and France, power was finally passing to more moderate leaders who realized that continued confrontation was a destructive, no-win situation. Thus, after five long years of hostility and tension, culminating in a kind of undeclared war in the Ruhr in 1923, Germany and France decided to give compromise and cooperation a try. The British, and even the Americans, were willing to help. The first step was a reasonable agreement on the reparations question.

## Hope in Foreign Affairs

In 1924 an international committee of financial experts headed by American banker Charles G. Dawes met to re-examine reparations from a broad perspective. The resulting Dawes Plan (1924) was accepted by France, Germany, and Britain. Germany's yearly reparations were reduced and linked to the level of German economic prosperity. Germany would also receive large loans from the United States to promote economic recovery. In short, Germany would get private loans from the United States in order to pay reparations to France and Britain, thus enabling those countries to repay the large war debts they owed the United States.

**Dawes Plan** War reparations agreement that reduced Germany's yearly payments, made payment dependent on economic prosperity, and granted large U.S. loans to promote recovery.

This circular flow of international payments was complicated and risky, but for a while it worked. The German republic experienced a shaky economic recovery. With continual inflows of American capital, Germany paid about $1.3 billion in reparations in 1927 and 1928, enabling France and Britain to repay the United States. In this way the Americans belatedly played a part in the general economic settlement that facilitated the worldwide recovery of the late 1920s.

This economic settlement was matched by a political settlement. In 1925 the leaders of Europe signed a number of agreements at Locarno, Switzerland. Germany and France solemnly pledged to accept their common border, and both Britain and Italy agreed to fight either France or Germany if one invaded the other. Stresemann reluctantly agreed to settle boundary disputes with Poland and Czechoslovakia by peaceful means, but he did not agree to permanent borders to Germany's east. In response, France promised those countries military aid if Germany attacked them. The refusal to settle Germany's eastern borders angered the Poles, and though the "spirit of Locarno" lent some hope to those seeking security and stability in international affairs, political tensions deepened in eastern Europe.

Other developments strengthened hopes for international peace. In 1926 Germany joined the League of Nations, and in 1928 fifteen countries signed the Kellogg-Briand Pact, initiated by French prime minister Aristide Briand and U.S. secretary of state Frank B. Kellogg. The signing states agreed to "renounce [war] as an instrument of international policy" and settle international disputes peacefully. The pact made no provisions for action in case war actually occurred, but it nonetheless fostered a cautious optimism in the late 1920s and encouraged the hope that the United States would accept its responsibilities as a great world power by contributing to European stability.

## Hope in Democratic Government

Domestic politics also offered reason to hope. During the occupation of the Ruhr and the great inflation, republican government in Germany had appeared on the verge of collapse. In 1923 communists momentarily entered provincial governments, and in November

How did modernism revolutionize European culture?    How did consumer culture change the lives of Europeans?    What obstacles to lasting peace did European leaders face?    What were the causes and consequences of the Great Depression?

**819**

# INDIVIDUALS IN SOCIETY

## Gustav Stresemann

Foreign Minister Gustav Stresemann of Germany (right) leaves a meeting with Aristide Briand, his French counterpart. (Corbis)

**THE GERMAN FOREIGN MINISTER GUSTAV** Stresemann (1878–1929) is a controversial historical figure. Hailed by many as a hero of peace, he was denounced as a traitor by radical German nationalists and then by Hitler's Nazis. After World War II, revisionist historians stressed Stresemann's persistent nationalism and cast doubt on his peaceful intentions. Weimar Germany's most renowned leader is a fascinating example of the restless quest for convincing historical interpretation.

Stresemann's origins were modest. His parents were Berlin innkeepers and retailers of bottled beer, and of their five children only Gustav was able to attend high school. Attracted first to literature and history, Stresemann later turned to economics, earned a doctoral degree, and quickly reached the top as a manager and director of German trade associations. A highly intelligent extrovert with a knack for negotiation, Stresemann became a deputy in the German Reichstag (parliament) in 1907 as a business-oriented liberal and nationalist. When World War I erupted, he believed, like most Germans, that Germany had acted defensively and was not at fault. He emerged as a strident nationalist and urged German annexation of conquered foreign territories. Germany's collapse in defeat and revolution devastated Stresemann. He seemed a prime candidate for the hateful extremism of the far right.

Yet although Stresemann opposed the Treaty of Versailles as an unjust and unrealistic imposition, he turned back toward the center. He accepted the new Weimar Republic and played a growing role in the Reichstag as the leader of his own small pro-business party. His hour came in the Ruhr crisis, when French and Belgian troops occupied the district. Named chancellor in August 1923, he called off passive resistance and began talks with the French. His government also quelled communist uprisings; put down rebellions in Bavaria, including an attempted coup by Hitler; and ended runaway inflation with the introduction of a new currency. Stresemann fought to preserve German unity, and he succeeded.

Voted out as chancellor in November 1923, Stresemann remained as foreign minister in every German government until his death in 1929. Proclaiming a policy of peace and agreeing to pay reparations, he achieved his greatest triumph in the Locarno agreements of 1925 (see page 819). But the interlocking guarantees of existing French and German borders (and the related agreements to resolve peacefully all disputes with Poland and Czechoslovakia) did not lead the French to make any further concessions that might have disarmed Stresemann's extremist foes. He made little additional progress in achieving international reconciliation and sovereign equality for Germany. His premature death in office was a serious blow to German pragmatism that encouraged the turn to a more aggressive and nationalist foreign policy.

Stresemann was no fuzzy pacifist. Historians debunking his legend are right in seeing an enduring patriotism in his defense of German interests. But Stresemann, like his French counterpart Aristide Briand, was a statesman of goodwill who wanted peace through mutually advantageous compromise. A realist trained by business and politics in the art of the possible, Stresemann also reasoned that Germany had to be a satisfied and equal partner if peace was to be secure. His unwillingness to guarantee Germany's eastern borders (see Map 26.4 on page 791), which is often criticized as contributing to the coming of the Second World War, reflected his conviction that keeping some Germans under Polish and Czechoslovakian rule created a ticking time bomb in Europe.

Stresemann was no less convinced that war on Poland would almost certainly re-create the Allied coalition that had crushed Germany in 1918.* His insistence on the necessity of peace in the east as well as the west was prophetic. Hitler's 1939 invasion of Poland resulted in an even mightier coalition that almost annihilated Germany in 1945.

### QUESTIONS FOR ANALYSIS

1. What did Gustav Stresemann do to promote reconciliation in Europe? How did his policy toward France differ from that toward Poland and Czechoslovakia?
2. What is your interpretation of Stresemann? Does he arouse your sympathy or your suspicion and hostility? Why?

*Robert Grathwol, "Stresemann: Reflections on His Foreign Policy," *Journal of Modern History* 45 (March 1973): 52–70.

an obscure politician named Adolf Hitler leaped onto a table in a beer hall in Munich and proclaimed a "national socialist revolution." But Hitler's plot to seize control of the government was easily crushed, and Hitler was sentenced to prison, where he outlined his theories and program in his book *Mein Kampf* (mine komf) (*My Struggle*). Throughout the 1920s, Hitler's National Socialist Party attracted support primarily from fanatical anti-Semites, ultranationalists, and disgruntled ex-servicemen. In 1928 his party had just twelve insignificant seats in the Reichstag. Indeed, after 1923 liberal democracy seemed to take root in Weimar Germany. A new currency was established, and the economy stabilized.

The moderate businessmen who tended to dominate the various German coalition governments were convinced that economic prosperity demanded good relations with the Western Powers, and they supported parliamentary government at home. Elections were held regularly, and republican democracy appeared to have growing support among a majority of Germans.

There were, however, sharp political divisions in the country. Many unrepentant nationalists and monarchists populated the right and the army. Members of Germany's recently formed Communist Party were active on the left. The Communists, directed from Moscow, reserved their greatest hatred for the Social Democrats, whom they accused of betraying the revolution. The working classes were divided politically, but a majority supported the nonrevolutionary but socialist Social Democrats.

The situation in France was similar to that in Germany. Communists and Socialists battled for the support of the workers. After 1924 the democratically elected government rested mainly in the hands of coalitions of moderates, and business interests were well represented. France's great accomplishment was the rapid rebuilding of its war-torn northern region. The expense of this undertaking led, however, to a large deficit and substantial inflation. In 1926 Poincaré was recalled to office, while Briand remained minister for foreign affairs. The Poincaré government proceeded to slash spending and raise taxes, restoring confidence in the economy. The franc was stabilized at about one-fifth of its prewar value, and the economy remained fairly stable until 1930.

Britain, too, faced challenges after 1920. The wartime trend toward greater social equality continued, however, helping maintain social harmony. The great problem was unemployment. In June 1921 almost 2.2 million people—23 percent of the labor force—were out of work, and throughout the 1920s unemployment hovered around 12 percent. Yet the state provided unemployment benefits to those without jobs and supplemented the payments with subsidized housing, medical aid, and increased old-age pensions. These and other measures kept living standards from seriously declining, defused class tensions, and pointed the way toward the welfare state Britain would establish after World War II.

Relative social harmony was accompanied by the rise of the British Labour Party. Committed to the kind of moderate revisionist socialism that had emerged before World War I (Chapter 24), the Labour Party replaced the Liberal Party as the main opposition to the Conservatives. The new prominence of the Labour Party reflected the decline of old liberal ideals of competitive capitalism, limited government control, and individual responsibility. In 1924 and 1929, the Labour Party under Ramsay MacDonald (1866–1937) governed the country with the support of the smaller Liberal Party. Yet Labour moved toward socialism gradually and democratically, so that the middle classes were not overly frightened as the working classes won new benefits.

The British Conservatives showed the same compromising spirit on social issues. In 1922 Britain granted southern, Catholic, Ireland full autonomy after a bitter guerrilla war, thereby removing a key source of prewar friction. Despite conflicts such as the 1926 strike by coal miners, social unrest in Britain was limited in the 1920s and 1930s. Thus developments in both international relations and the domestic politics of the leading democracies gave cause for optimism in the late 1920s.

How did modernism revolutionize European culture?

How did consumer culture change the lives of Europeans?

**What obstacles to lasting peace did European leaders face?**

What were the causes and consequences of the Great Depression?

821

# ▼ What were the causes and consequences of the Great Depression?

This fragile optimism was short-lived. Beginning in 1929, a massive economic downturn struck the entire world with ever-greater intensity, and recovery was slow and uneven. Contemporaries labeled the economic crisis the Great Depression. Only with the Second World War did the depression disappear in much of the world.

The social and political consequences of the Great Depression were enormous. Mass unemployment and failing farms made insecurity and unemployment a reality for millions of ordinary people (Map 27.1). In Europe and the United States, governments instituted a variety of social welfare programs intended to manage the crisis. Yet the prolonged economic collapse shattered the fragile political stability of the mid-1920s and encouraged the growth of extremists on both ends of the political spectrum. Democratic government faltered, and authoritarian fascist parties gained power across Europe.

## The Economic Crisis

Though economic activity was already declining moderately in many countries by early 1929, the crash of the stock market in the United States in October of that year initiated a worldwide crisis. The American economy had prospered in the late 1920s, but there were large inequalities in income and a serious imbalance between actual investment and stock market speculation. Thus net investment—in factories, farms, equipment, and the like—actually fell from $3.5 billion in 1925 to $3.2 billion in 1929. In the same years, as money flooded into stocks, the value of shares traded on the exchanges soared from $27 billion to $87 billion. Such inflated prices should have raised serious concerns about economic solvency, but even experts failed to predict the looming collapse.

The American stock market boom was built on borrowed money. Many wealthy investors, speculators, and people of modest means had bought stocks by paying only a small fraction of the total purchase price and borrowing the remainder from their stockbrokers. Such buying "on margin" was extremely dangerous. When prices started falling, the hard-pressed margin buyers either had to put up more money, which was often impossible, or sell their shares to pay off their brokers. Thousands of people started selling all at once. The result was a financial panic.

The consequences were swift and severe. Battered investors and their fellow citizens started buying fewer goods. Prices fell, production began to slow down, and unemployment began to rise. Soon the entire American economy was caught in a spiraling decline.

The financial panic in the United States triggered an international financial crisis. Throughout the 1920s, American bankers and investors had lent large amounts of capital to many countries. Once the panic broke, New York bankers began recalling these short-term loans. It became very hard for European business people to borrow money, and the panicky public began to withdraw its savings from the banks. These banking problems eventually led to the crash of the largest bank in Austria in 1931 and then to general financial chaos. The recall of private loans by American bankers also accelerated the collapse in world prices when businesses around the world dumped industrial goods and agricultural commodities in a frantic attempt to get cash to pay debts.

The financial crisis led to a general crisis of production: between 1929 and 1933, world output of goods fell by an estimated 38 percent. As this happened, each country turned inward and tried to manage the crisis alone. Country after country followed the example of the United States when in 1930 it raised protective tariffs to their highest levels ever and tried to seal off shrinking national markets for American producers only. Such actions

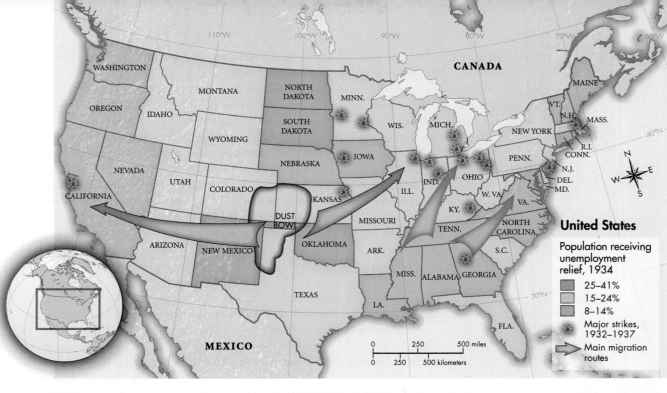

## Map 27.1 The Great Depression in the United States and Europe, 1929–1939

These maps show that unemployment was high almost everywhere, but that national and regional differences were also substantial.

**ANALYZING THE MAP** Which European countries had the highest rate of unemployment? How do the rates of people on unemployment relief in the United States compare to the percentage of unemployed workers in Europe? In the United States, what were the main channels of migration for workers?

**CONNECTIONS** What tactics of reform and recovery did European nations use to combat the deprivations of the Great Depression?

To complete this activity online, go to the Online Study Guide at bedfordstmartins.com/mckaywestunderstanding.

further limited international trade. Within this context of fragmented and destructive economic nationalism, a halting recovery only began in 1933.

Although opinions differ, two factors probably best explain the relentless slide to the bottom from 1929 to early 1933. First, the international economy lacked leadership able to maintain stability when the crisis came. Neither Britain nor the United States—the world's economic leaders at the time—successfully stabilized the international economic system in 1929. Second, almost every country pursued poor economic policies. Governments generally cut their budgets when they should have raised spending and run large deficits in order to stimulate their economies. After World War II, such a "counter-cyclical policy," advocated by the economist John Maynard Keynes, became a well-established weapon against downturn and depression. But in the 1930s, Keynes's prescription was generally regarded with horror by orthodox economists.

## Mass Unemployment

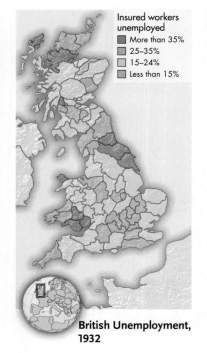

**Insured workers unemployed**
- ■ More than 35%
- ■ 25–35%
- ☐ 15–24%
- ☐ Less than 15%

**British Unemployment, 1932**

The lack of large-scale government spending contributed to the rise of mass unemployment. As the financial crisis led to cuts in production, workers lost their jobs and had little money to buy goods (see Map 27.1). Mass unemployment created great social problems. Poverty increased dramatically, although in most countries unemployed workers generally received some kind of meager unemployment benefits or public aid that prevented starvation. (See "Listening to the Past: George Orwell on Life on the Dole," page 826.) Millions of people lost their spirit, condemned to an apparently hopeless search for work. Homes and ways of life were disrupted in millions of personal tragedies. Young people postponed marriages, and birthrates fell sharply. There was an increase in suicide and mental illness. Poverty or the threat of poverty became a grinding reality. In 1932 the workers of Manchester, England, appealed to their city officials—a typical plea echoed throughout the Western world:

> We tell you that thousands of people . . . are in desperate straits. We tell you that men, women, and children are going hungry. . . . We tell you that great numbers are being rendered distraught through the stress and worry of trying to exist without work. . . . If you do not do this—if you do not provide useful work for the unemployed—what, we ask, is your alternative? Do not imagine that this colossal tragedy of unemployment is going on endlessly without some fateful catastrophe. Hungry men are angry men.[6]

Only strong government action could deal with mass unemployment, a social powder keg preparing to explode.

## The New Deal in the United States

The Great Depression and the response to it marked a major turning point in American history. President Herbert Hoover (1895–1972) and his administration initially reacted to the stock market crash and economic decline with dogged optimism but limited action. When the full force of the financial crisis struck Europe in the summer of 1931 and boomeranged back to the United States, banks failed and unemployment soared. Between 1929 and 1932 industrial production fell by about 50 percent.

In these tragic circumstances, Franklin Delano Roosevelt (1882–1945) won a landslide presidential victory in 1932 with promises of a "New Deal for the forgotten man." Roosevelt's basic goal was to reform capitalism in order to preserve it. Though Roosevelt rejected socialism and government ownership of industry in 1933, he nonetheless advocated forceful government intervention in the economy and instituted a broad range of government-supported social programs designed to stimulate the economy and provide jobs for ordinary people. Across Europe, governments engaged in similar actions in desperate attempts to relieve the economic crisis.

In the United States, innovative federal programs promoted agricultural recovery, a top priority. Almost half of the American population still lived in rural areas, and American farmers were hard hit by the depression. Roosevelt took the United States off the gold standard and devalued the dollar in an effort to raise American prices and rescue farmers. The Agricultural Adjustment Act of 1933 also aimed at raising prices and farm income by limiting agricultural production. These planning measures worked for a while, and in 1936 farmers repaid Roosevelt with overwhelming support.

The most ambitious attempt to control and plan the economy was the National Recovery Administration (NRA). Intended to reduce competition and fix prices and wages for everyone's benefit, the NRA broke with the American tradition of free competition and aroused conflicts among business people, consumers, and bureaucrats. It did not work well and was declared unconstitutional in 1935.

Roosevelt and his advisers then attacked the key problem of mass unemployment directly. The federal government accepted the responsibility of employing directly as many people as financially possible. New agencies were created to undertake a vast range of projects. The most famous of these was the Works Progress Administration (WPA), set up in 1935. One-fifth of the entire U.S. labor force worked for the WPA at some point in the 1930s, constructing public buildings, bridges, and highways.

In 1935 the U.S. government also established a national social security system with old-age pensions and unemployment benefits. The National Labor Relations Act of 1935 declared collective bargaining to be the policy of the United States. Union membership more than doubled from 4 million in 1935 to 9 million in 1940. In general, between 1935 and 1938 government rulings and social reforms chipped away at the privileges of the wealthy and tried to help ordinary people.

Relief programs like the WPA were part of the New Deal's fundamental commitment to use the federal government to provide for the welfare of all Americans. This commitment marked a profound shift from the traditional stress on family support and community responsibility. Embraced by a large majority in the 1930s, this shift in attitudes proved to be one of the New Deal's most enduring legacies.

Yet despite undeniable accomplishments in social reform, the New Deal was only partly successful as a response to the Great Depression. At the height of the recovery in May 1937, 7 million workers were still unemployed, in contrast to a high of 15 million in 1933. The economic situation then worsened seriously in the recession of 1937 and 1938, and unemployment had risen to 10 million when war broke out in Europe in September 1939. The New Deal never did pull the United States out of the depression; it took the Second World War to do that.

## The Scandinavian Response to the Depression

Of all the Western democracies, the Scandinavian countries under Social Democratic leadership responded most successfully to the challenge of the Great Depression. In the 1920s the Social Democrats passed important social reform legislation for both peasants and workers and developed a unique kind of socialism. Flexible and nonrevolutionary, Scandinavian socialism grew out of a strong tradition of cooperative community action. Even before 1900 Scandinavian agricultural cooperatives had shown how individual peasant families could join together for everyone's benefit. Labor leaders and capitalists were also inclined to work together.

When the economic crisis struck in 1929, socialist governments in Scandinavia built on this pattern of cooperative social action. Sweden in particular pioneered in the use of large-scale deficits to finance public works and thereby maintain production and

# LISTENING TO THE PAST

## George Orwell on Life on the Dole

*Periodic surges in unemployment were an old story in capitalist economies, but the long-term joblessness of millions in the Great Depression was something new and unexpected. In Britain especially, where the depression followed a weak postwar recovery, large numbers suffered involuntary idleness for years at a time. Whole families lived "on the dole," the weekly welfare benefits paid by the government.*

*One of the most insightful accounts of unemployed workers was written by the British journalist and novelist George Orwell (1903–1950), who studied the conditions in northern England and wrote* The Road to Wigan Pier *(1937), an excerpt of which follows. An independent socialist who distrusted rigid Marxism, Orwell believed that socialism could triumph in Britain if it came to mean commonsense "justice and liberty" for a broad sector of the working classes. Orwell's disillusionment with authoritarian socialism and Soviet-style communism pervades his other famous works,* Animal Farm *(1945) and* 1984 *(1949).*

❝ When you see the unemployment figures quoted at two millions, it is fatally easy to take this as meaning that two million people are out of work and the rest of the population is comparatively comfortable. . . . [Adding in the destitute,] you might take the number of underfed people in England (for *everyone* on the dole or thereabouts is underfed) as being, at the very most, five millions.

This is an enormous under-estimate, because, in the first place, the only people shown on unemployment figures are those actually drawing the dole — that is, in general, heads of families. An unemployed man's dependants do not figure on the list unless they too are drawing a separate allowance. . . . In addition there are great numbers of people who are in work but who, from a financial point of view, might equally be unemployed, because they are not drawing anything that can be described as a living wage.

Allow for these and their dependants, throw in as before the old-age pensioners, the destitute and other nondescripts, and you get an *underfed* population of well over ten millions. . . . Take the figures for Wigan, which is typical enough of the industrial and mining districts. . . . The total population of Wigan is a little under 87,000; so that at any moment more than one person in three out of the whole population — not merely the registered workers — is either drawing or living on the dole. . . .

Nevertheless, in spite of the frightful extent of unemployment, it is a fact that poverty — extreme poverty — is less in evidence in the industrial North than it is in London. Everything is poorer and shabbier, there are fewer motor-cars and fewer well-dressed people; but also there are fewer people who are obviously destitute. . . . In the industrial towns the old communal way of life has not yet broken up, tradition is still strong and almost everyone has a family — potentially, therefore, a home. In a town of 50,000 or 100,000 inhabitants there is no casual and as it were unaccounted-for population; nobody sleeping in the streets, for instance. Moreover, there is just this to be said for the unemployment regulations, that they do not discourage people from marrying. A man and wife on twenty-three shillings a week are not far from the starvation line, but they can make a home of sorts; they are vastly better off than a single man on fifteen shillings. . . .

But there is no doubt about the deadening, debilitating effect of unemployment upon everybody, married or single, and upon men more than upon women. . . . Everyone who saw Greenwood's play *Love on the Dole* must remember that dreadful moment when the poor, good, stupid working man beats on the table and cries out, "O God, send me some work!" This was not dramatic exaggeration, it was a touch from life. That cry must have been uttered, in almost those words, in tens of thousands, perhaps hundreds of thousands of English homes, during the past fifteen years.

But, I think not again — or at least, not so often. . . . When people live on the dole for years at a time they grow used to it, and drawing the dole, though it remains unpleasant, ceases to be shameful. Thus the old, independent, workhouse-fearing tradition is undermined. . . .

So you have whole populations settling down, as it were, to a lifetime of the P.A.C. . . . Take, for instance, the fact that the working class think nothing of getting married on the dole. . . . Life is still fairly normal, more normal than one really has the right to expect. Families are impoverished, but the family-system has not broken up. The people are in effect living a reduced version of their former lives.

employment. Scandinavian governments also increased such social welfare benefits as old-age pensions, unemployment insurance, subsidized housing, and maternity allowances. All this spending required a large bureaucracy and high taxes. Yet both private and cooperative enterprise thrived, as did democracy. Some observers saw Scandinavia's welfare socialism as an appealing middle way between sick capitalism and cruel communism or fascism.

Poster used in the British election campaign of 1931, when unemployment rose to a new record high. (Conservative Research Department/The Bridgeman Art Library)

suit which, for a little while and at a little distance, looks as though it had been tailored in Savile Row. The girl can look like a fashion plate at an even lower price. . . . You can stand on the street corner, indulging in a private daydream of yourself as Clark Gable or Greta Garbo, which compensates you for a great deal. . . .

Trade since the war has had to adjust itself to meet the demands of underpaid, underfed people, with the result that a luxury is nowadays almost always cheaper than a necessity. One pair of plain solid shoes costs as much as two ultra-smart pairs. . . . And above all there is gambling, the cheapest of all luxuries. Even people on the verge of starvation can buy a few days' hope ("Something to live for," as they call it) by having a penny on a sweepstake. . . . Twenty million people are underfed but literally everyone in England has access to a radio. What we have lost in food we have gained in electricity. Whole sections of the working class who have been plundered of all they really need are being compensated, in part, by cheap luxuries which mitigate the surface of life.

Do you consider all this desirable? No, I don't. But it may be that the psychological adjustment which the working class are visibly making is the best they could make in the circumstances. They have neither turned revolutionary nor lost their self-respect; merely they have kept their tempers and settled down to make the best of things on a fish-and-chip standard. The alternative would be God knows what continued agonies of despair; or it might be attempted insurrections which, in a strongly governed country like England, could only lead to futile massacres and a régime of savage repression. 》

**Source:** Excerpts from Chapter V in *The Road to Wigan Pier* by George Orwell. Copyright © 1958 and renewed 1986 by the Estate of Sonia B. Orwell. Reprinted by permission of Houghton Mifflin Harcourt Publishing Company, from *The Complete Works of George Orwell* by George Orwell. Copyright © George Orwell, 1986. Reproduced by permission of Bill Hamilton as the Literary Executor of the Estate of the Late Sonia Brownell Orwell and Secker & Warburg Ltd.

Instead of raging against their destiny they have made things tolerable by lowering their standards. But they don't necessarily lower their standards by cutting out luxuries and concentrating on necessities; more often it is the other way about — the more natural way, if you come to think of it. Hence the fact that in a decade of unparalleled depression, the consumption of all cheap luxuries has increased. The two things that have probably made the greatest difference of all are the movies and the mass-production of cheap smart clothes since the war. The youth who leaves school at fourteen and gets a blind-alley job is out of work at twenty, probably for life; but for two pounds ten on the hire-purchase system he can buy himself a

## QUESTIONS FOR ANALYSIS

1. According to Orwell, "extreme poverty" was less visible in the northern industrial towns than in London. How did family relations contribute to social stability in the face of growing poverty?
2. What were the consequences of long-term unemployment for English workers? How did joblessness change attitudes and behaviors?
3. Judging from Orwell's description, did radical revolution seem likely in England in the Great Depression? Why?

## Recovery and Reform in Britain and France

In Britain MacDonald's Labour government and then, after 1931, the Conservative-dominated coalition government followed orthodox economic theory. The budget was balanced, but spending was tightly controlled and unemployed workers received barely enough welfare to live. Nonetheless, the economy recovered considerably after 1932. By

How did modernism revolutionize European culture?

How did consumer culture change the lives of Europeans?

What obstacles to lasting peace did European leaders face?

What were the causes and consequences of the Great Depression?

**OSLOFROKOSTEN**

*HVA DEN ER OG GIR*

**Oslo Breakfast** Scandinavian socialism championed cooperation and practical welfare measures, playing down strident rhetoric and theories of class conflict. The Oslo breakfast exemplified the Scandinavian approach. It provided every schoolchild in the Norwegian capital with a good breakfast free of charge. (Courtesy, Directorate for Health and Social Affairs, Oslo)

1937 total production was about 20 percent higher than in 1929. In fact, for Britain the years after 1932 were actually somewhat better than the 1920s had been, the opposite of the situation in the United States and France.

This good but by no means brilliant performance reflected the gradual reorientation of the British economy. After going off the gold standard in 1931 and establishing protective tariffs in 1932, Britain concentrated increasingly on the national, rather than the international, market. The old export industries of the Industrial Revolution, such as textiles and coal, continued to decline, but new industries, such as automobiles and electrical appliances, grew in response to domestic demand. Moreover, low interest rates encouraged a housing boom. By the end of the decade, there were highly visible differences between the old, depressed industrial areas of the north and the new, growing areas of the south. These developments encouraged Britain to look inward and avoid unpleasant foreign entanglements.

Because France was relatively less industrialized and more isolated from the world economy, the Great Depression came late. But once the depression hit France, it stayed. Decline was steady until 1935, and a short-lived recovery never brought production or employment back up to predepression levels. Economic stagnation both reflected and heightened an ongoing political crisis. There was no stability in government. As before 1914, the French parliament was made up of many political parties that could never cooperate for long.

The French lost the underlying unity that had made government instability bearable before 1914. Fascist-type organizations agitated against parliamentary democracy and looked to Mussolini's Italy and Hitler's Germany for inspiration. In February 1934 French fascists rioted and threatened to take over the republic. At the same time, the Communist Party and many workers opposed to the existing system were looking to Stalin's Russia for guidance. The vital center of moderate republicanism was weakened by attacks from both sides.

**Popular Front** A short-lived New Deal–inspired alliance in France led by Léon Blum that encouraged the union movement and launched a far-reaching program of social reform.

Frightened by the growing strength of the fascists at home and abroad, the Communists, the Socialists, and the Radicals formed an alliance — the Popular Front — for the national elections of May 1936. Their clear victory reflected the trend toward polarization. The number of Communists in the parliament jumped from 10 to 72, while the Socialists, led by Léon Blum, became the strongest party in France, with 146 seats. The really quite moderate Radicals slipped badly, and the conservatives lost ground to the far right.

In the next few months, Blum's Popular Front government made the first and only real attempt to deal with the social and economic problems of the 1930s in France. Inspired by Roosevelt's New Deal, the Popular Front encouraged the union movement and launched a far-reaching program of social reform. Popular with workers and the lower middle class, these measures were quickly sabotaged by rapid inflation and cries of revolution from fascists and frightened conservatives. Wealthy people sneaked their money out of the country, labor unrest grew, and France entered a severe financial crisis. Blum was forced to announce a "breathing spell" in social reform.

Political dissension in France was encouraged by the Spanish Civil War (1936–1939), during which authoritarian fascist rebels overthrew the democratically elected republican government. Communists demanded that France support the Spanish republicans, while many French conservatives would gladly have joined Hitler and Mussolini in aiding the Spanish fascists. Extremism grew, and France itself was within sight of civil war. Blum was forced to resign in June 1937, and the Popular Front quickly collapsed. An anxious and divided France drifted aimlessly once again, preoccupied by Hitler and German rearmament.

# ←LOOKING BACK LOOKING AHEAD→

THE DECADES BEFORE AND ESPECIALLY AFTER World War I brought intense intellectual and cultural innovation. The results were both richly productive and deeply troubling. From T. S. Eliot's poem *The Waste Land* to Einstein's theory of relativity and the sleek glass and steel buildings of the Bauhaus, the intellectual products of the time stand among the highest achievement of Western arts and sciences. At the same time, mass culture, embodied in cinema, radio, and an emerging consumer culture, had transformative effects on everyday life. Yet the modern vision was often bleak and cold. The arrival of consumer society undermined traditional values, contributing to feelings of disorientation and pessimism. The situation was worsened by ongoing political and economic turmoil. The Treaty of Versailles had failed to create a lasting peace or resolve the question of Germany's role in postwar Europe. The Great Depression revealed the fragility of the world economic system and cast millions out of work. In the end, perhaps, the era's intellectual achievements and the overall sense of crisis and anxiety were closely related.

Writing in 1930, Sigmund Freud captured the general mood of gloom and foreboding. "Men have gained control over the forces of nature to such an extent that . . . they would have no difficulty in exterminating one another to the last man," wrote the famous psychologist. "They know this, and hence comes a large part of their current unrest, their unhappiness and their mood of anxiety."[7] Freud's dark words reflected the extraordinary human costs of World War I and the horrific power of modern weaponry. They also expressed his despair over the growing popularity of repressive dictatorial regimes. During the interwar years, many great European nations—including Italy, Germany, Spain, Poland, Portugal, Austria, and Hungary—would fall one by one to authoritarian or fascist dictatorships, and so succumb to the temptations of totalitarianism. Liberal democracy was severely weakened. European stability was threatened by the radical programs of Soviet Communists on the left and fascists on the right, and Freud uncannily predicted the great conflict to come. ∎

- **For a list of suggested readings for this chapter, visit** *bedfordstmartins.com/mckaywestunderstanding*.

- **For primary sources from this period, see** *Sources of Western Society*, Second Edition.

- **For Web sites, images, and documents related to topics in this chapter, see Make History at** *bedfordstmartins.com/mckaywestunderstanding*.

How did modernism revolutionize European culture?

How did consumer culture change the lives of Europeans?

What obstacles to lasting peace did European leaders face?

What were the causes and consequences of the Great Depression?

# Chapter 27 Study Guide

Online Study Guide
bedfordstmartins.com/mckaywestunderstanding

## Step 1

**GETTING STARTED** Below are basic terms about this period in the history of Western civilization. Can you identify each term below and explain why it matters? To do this exercise online, go to bedfordstmartins.com/mckaywestunderstanding.

| TERMS | WHO (OR WHAT) AND WHEN | WHY IT MATTERS |
|---|---|---|
| logical positivism, p. 805 | | |
| existentialism, p. 806 | | |
| theory of special relativity, p. 807 | | |
| id, ego, and superego, p. 808 | | |
| stream-of-consciousness technique, p. 809 | | |
| modernism, p. 810 | | |
| functionalism, p. 810 | | |
| Bauhaus, p. 810 | | |
| Dadaism, p. 811 | | |
| "new woman," p. 815 | | |
| Dawes Plan, p. 819 | | |
| Great Depression, p. 822 | | |
| Popular Front, p. 828 | | |

## Step 2

**MOVING BEYOND THE BASICS** The exercise below requires a more advanced understanding of the chapter material. Examine the contributions of artists and intellectuals to the culture of the Age of Anxiety by filling in the chart below with descriptions of the work and ideas of key artistic and intellectual figures of the period. When you are finished, consider the following questions: What connections can you make among the works of individuals in disparate fields? For example, what connections might there be between the psychological theories of Freud, the writing of Woolf, and the music of Stravinsky? To do this exercise online, go to bedfordstmartins.com/mckaywestunderstanding.

| ARTIST/INTELLECTUAL | KEY IDEAS | CHALLENGE TO STATUS QUO |
|---|---|---|
| Friedrich Nietzsche | | |
| Ludwig Wittgenstein | | |
| Jean-Paul Sartre | | |
| Albert Einstein | | |
| Sigmund Freud | | |
| Virginia Woolf | | |
| Pablo Picasso | | |
| Igor Stravinsky | | |

**PUTTING IT ALL TOGETHER** Now that you've reviewed key elements of the chapter, take a step back and try to see the big picture. Remember to use specific examples from the chapter in your answers. To do this exercise online, go to bedfordstmartins.com/mckaywestunderstanding.

## POSTWAR INTELLECTUAL AND ARTISTIC TRENDS

- Compare and contrast the intellectual climate in the decade before and after World War I. How would you explain the differences you note? What postwar trends were already becoming evident before the war?

- What is "modern" about modernism? How was modernism embodied in architecture, painting, and music in the early twentieth century?

## CONSUMER SOCIETY

- How did consumerism contribute to the development of an international mass culture? How did cultural connections between Western nations reflect economic connections between Western nations?

- What shared experiences were made possible by cinema and radio? How did political leaders use these new forms of communication to promote their policies?

## THE SEARCH FOR PEACE AND STABILITY

- What were the key sources of instability in the years following World War I? How successful were Western leaders at responding to postwar challenges? What problems did they leave unresolved?

- How much cooperation was there between Western governments in the 1920s? What examples of cooperative action can you present? What light does the breakdown of cooperation in the 1930s shed on the limits of 1920s policies and initiatives?

## THE GREAT DEPRESSION

- How did the policies and problems of the 1920s contribute to both the onset of the Great Depression and the failure of Western nations to develop a coordinated response?

- Compare and contrast the response to the Great Depression in the United States, France, Britain, Germany, and the Scandinavian countries. How would you explain the similarities and differences you note?

■ **In Your Own Words** Imagine that you must explain Chapter 27 to someone who hasn't read it. What would be the most important points to include and why?

# 28

# Dictatorships and the Second World War

## 1919–1945

The radical experiments in arts and culture that followed World War I shook the intellectual foundations of Western society. Radical experimentation also transformed notions of the relationship between the state and its citizens. In the age of anxiety, democratic government and liberal ideals of individual rights were in retreat, threatened and in many places overcome by new visions of social equality and national community. In Europe on the eve of the Second World War, popularly elected governments survived only in Great Britain, France, Czechoslovakia, the Low Countries, Scandinavia, and Switzerland.

Across the 1920s and 1930s, totalitarian regimes in the communist Soviet Union, fascist Italy, and Nazi Germany practiced a ruthless and dynamic tyranny. Their attempts to revolutionize state and society went far beyond familiar forms of conservative authoritarianism. Communist and fascist states ruled with unprecedented severity. They promised to greatly improve the lives of ordinary citizens and intervened radically in those lives in pursuit of utopian schemes of social engineering. Their drive for territorial expansion threatened neighboring nations and put the democracies on the defensive. The human costs were appalling. Millions died as Stalin forced communism on the Soviet Union in the 1930s. Attempts to build a "racially pure" New Order in Europe by Hitler's Nazi Germany led to the deaths of millions more in World War II and the Holocaust. ∎

**Life at Auschwitz.** This rough painting by an anonymous inmate of the Auschwitz-Birkenau Nazi concentration camp is preserved on the ceiling of a camp barracks. Guarded by an SS officer brandishing a whip, prisoners labor on a drainage canal under the worst conditions, while others carry a dead worker off the field. (DEA Library/Getty Images)

# Chapter Preview

▶ **What characteristics did totalitarian dictatorships share?**

▶ **How did Stalin and his followers build a totalitarian state?**

▶ **What kind of government did Mussolini establish in Italy?**

▶ **How and why did Nazi policies lead to World War II?**

▶ **What explains the Allied victory in World War II?**

# What characteristics did totalitarian dictatorships share?

Both conservative and radical dictatorships swept through Europe in the 1920s and 1930s. Although these two types of dictatorship shared some characteristics and sometimes overlapped in practice, in essence they were quite different.

## Conservative Authoritarianism and Radical Totalitarian Dictatorships

The traditional form of antidemocratic government in European history was conservative authoritarianism. Like Catherine the Great in Russia and Metternich in Austria, the leaders of such governments relied on obedient bureaucracies in their efforts to control society. Political opponents were often jailed or exiled, but old-fashioned authoritarian governments were limited in their power and objectives. They had neither the ability nor the desire to control many aspects of their subjects' lives. As long as the people did not try to change the system, they often had considerable personal independence.

After the First World War, authoritarianism revived, especially in the less-developed eastern part of Europe. But new kinds of radical dictatorship that went much further than conservative authoritarianism emerged in the Soviet Union, Germany, and to some extent Italy and other countries. And both Communist and fascist political parties were well established in all major European nations.

> **totalitarianism** A radical dictatorship that exercises "total claims" over the beliefs and behavior of its citizens by taking control of the economic, social, intellectual, and cultural aspects of society.

Some scholars use the term totalitarianism to describe these radical dictatorships, which made unprecedented "total claims" on the beliefs and behavior of their citizens. The totalitarian model emphasizes the characteristics that fascist and communist dictatorships had in common. The one-party totalitarian state used violent political repression and intense propaganda to gain complete power. Increasingly, the state tried to dominate the economic, social, intellectual, and cultural aspects of people's lives.

Most historians agree that totalitarianism owed much to the experience of total war in 1914–1918 (see Chapter 26). World War I required state governments to limit individual liberties and intervene in the economy in order to achieve one supreme objective: victory. Totalitarian politicians were inspired by the example of the modern state at war. They showed a callous disregard for human life and greatly expanded the power of the state in pursuit of social control.

Communist and fascist dictatorships shared other characteristics. Both rejected parliamentary government and liberal values. Classical liberalism (see Chapter 22) sought to limit the power of the state and protect the rights of the individual. Totalitarians, on the other hand, believed that liberal individualism undermined equality and unity. They rejected democracy in favor of one-party political systems ruled from above.

A charismatic leader typically dominated the totalitarian state—Stalin in the Soviet Union, Mussolini in Italy, Hitler in Germany. All three created political parties of a new kind, dedicated to promoting idealized visions of collective harmony. They used force and terror to intimidate and destroy political opponents, and they pursued policies of imperial expansion to exploit other lands. They censored the mass media and instituted propaganda campaigns meant to advance their goals. Finally, and perhaps most important, totalitarian governments engaged in massive projects of state-controlled social engineering dedicated to replacing individualism with a unified "people" capable of exercising the collective will.

## Communism and Fascism

Communism and fascism clearly shared a desire to revolutionize state and society. Yet some scholars argue that the differences between the two systems are more important than the similarities, and so move beyond the totalitarian model. What were the main differences between these two systems? To answer this question, it is important to consider the way ideology, or a guiding political philosophy, was linked to the use of state-sponsored repression and violence.

Following Marx, Soviet Communists strove to create an international brotherhood of workers. In the communist utopia ruled by the revolutionary working class, economic exploitation would supposedly disappear and society would be based on radical social equality (see Chapter 22). Under Stalinism—the name given to the Communist system during Stalin's rule—the state aggressively intervened in all walks of life to pursue this vision of social leveling. Using brute force to destroy the upper and middle classes, the Stalinist state nationalized private property, pushed rapid industrialization, and collectivized agriculture (see pages 837–842).

The fascist vision of a new society was quite different. Leaders who embraced fascism, such as Mussolini and Hitler, claimed that they were striving to build a new community on a national—not an international—level. Extreme nationalists, and often racists, fascists glorified war and the military. For them, the nation was the highest embodiment of the people, and the powerful leader was the materialization of the people's collective will.

Like communists, fascists promised to improve the lives of ordinary workers. Fascist governments intervened in the economy, but unlike communist regimes they did not try to level class differences and nationalize private property. Instead, they presented a vision of a community bound together by nationalism. In the ideal fascist state, all social strata and classes would work together to build a harmonious national community.

Communists and fascists differed in another crucial respect: the question of race. Where communists sought to build a new world around the destruction of class differences, fascists typically sought to build a new national community grounded in racial homogeneity. Fascists embraced the doctrine of eugenics, a pseudoscience that maintained that the selective breeding of human beings could improve the general characteristics of a national population. Eugenics was popular throughout the United States and Europe in the 1920s and 1930s and was viewed by many as a legitimate social policy. But fascists, especially the German National Socialists or Nazis, pushed these ideas to the extreme.

Adopting a radicalized view of eugenics, the Nazis maintained that the German nation had to be "purified" of groups of people deemed "unfit" by the regime. Such ideas ultimately led to the Holocaust, the attempt to purge Germany and Europe of all Jews

## Chapter Chronology

| | |
|---|---|
| 1921 | New Economic Policy (NEP) in U.S.S.R. |
| 1922 | Mussolini seizes power in Italy |
| 1924–1929 | Buildup of Nazi Party in Germany |
| 1927 | Stalin comes to power in U.S.S.R. |
| 1928 | Stalin's first five-year plan |
| 1929 | Lateran Agreement; start of collectivization in Soviet Union |
| 1929–1939 | Great Depression |
| 1931 | Japan invades Manchuria |
| 1932–1933 | Famine in Ukraine |
| 1933 | Hitler appointed chancellor in Germany; Nazis begin control of state and society |
| 1935 | Mussolini invades Ethiopia |
| 1936 | Start of great purges under Stalin; Spanish Civil War begins |
| 1937 | Japanese army attacks China |
| 1939 | Germany occupies Czech lands and invades western Poland; Britain and France declare war on Germany, starting World War II; Soviet Union occupies eastern Poland |
| 1940 | Germany defeats and occupies France |
| 1940 | Battle of Britain |
| 1941 | Germany invades U.S.S.R.; Japan attacks Pearl Harbor; United States enters war |
| 1941–1945 | The Holocaust |
| 1942–1943 | Battle of Stalingrad |
| 1944 | Allied invasion at Normandy |
| 1945 | Soviet and U.S. forces enter Germany; United States drops atomic bombs on Japan; World War II ends |

**fascism** A movement characterized by extreme, often expansionist nationalism, antisocialism, a dynamic and violent leader, and glorification of war and the military.

**eugenics** A pseudoscientific doctrine that maintains that the selective breeding of human beings can improve the general characteristics of a national population, which helped inspire Nazi ideas about "race and space" and ultimately contributed to the Holocaust.

How did Stalin and his followers build a totalitarian state?

What kind of government did Mussolini establish in Italy?

How and why did Nazi policies lead to World War II?

What explains the Allied victory in World War II?

835

## ▪ PICTURING THE PAST

### The Appeal of Propaganda

Totalitarian leaders used extensive propaganda campaigns to enlist the support of the masses. Italian dictator Benito Mussolini repeatedly linked his regime to the glory of ancient Rome. Here he has donned the costume of a legionnaire to lead a parade in front of the Roman Coliseum (top). The Soviet dictator Stalin presented himself as the friend of all humankind. In this propaganda poster (bottom), titled "The Great Stalin, the Banner of Friendship of the Peoples of the U.S.S.R.," he receives flowers from a diverse group of Soviet citizens, including ethnic Russians and East and Central Asians. This idealized testament to peaceful coexistence within the Soviet empire masked the tensions aroused by Russian domination. (Mussolini: Stefano Bianchetti/Corbis; Stalin: Bedford/St. Martin's)

**ANALYZING THE IMAGE** How do these images present the role of the dictatorial leader? How do they represent the relationship between the leader and the led?

**CONNECTIONS** How might these idealized portrayals have helped build support for their respective regimes? Was there any truth behind the propaganda?

To complete this activity online, go to the Online Study Guide at bedfordstmartins.com/mckaywestunderstanding.

and other groups by mass killing during World War II (see page 857). Though the Soviets sometimes persecuted specific ethnic groups, in general they justified their attacks using ideologies of class rather than race.

Perhaps because both championed the overthrow of existing society, communists and fascists were sworn enemies. The result was a clash of ideologies, which was in large part responsible for the horrific destruction and loss of life in the middle of the twentieth century. Explaining the nature of totalitarian dictatorships thus remains a crucial project for historians, even as they look more closely at the ideological differences between communism and fascism.

One important set of questions explores the way dictatorial regimes generate popular consensus. Neither Hitler nor Stalin ever achieved the total control each sought. Nor did they rule alone; modern dictators need the help of large state bureaucracies and large numbers of ordinary people. Which was more important for generating popular support: terror and coercion, or practical material rewards? Under what circumstances did people resist totalitarian tyranny? These questions lead us toward what Holocaust survivor Primo Levi called the "gray zone" of moral compromise, which defined everyday life in totalitarian societies. (See "Individuals in Society: Primo Levi," page 860.)

# ▼ How did Stalin and his followers build a totalitarian state?

A master of political infighting, Joseph Stalin (1879–1953) consolidated his power and eliminated his enemies in the mid-1920s. Then in 1928, as undisputed leader of the Soviet Union and the ruling Communist Party, Stalin launched the first five-year plan, a determined attempt to transform Soviet society into a radical communist state. The ultimate goal was to generate new attitudes, new loyalties, and a new socialist humanity.

## From Lenin to Stalin

By spring 1921 Lenin and the Bolsheviks had won the civil war, but they ruled a shattered and devastated land. In the face of economic disintegration, riots by peasants and workers, and an open rebellion by previously pro-Bolshevik sailors at Kronstadt, the tough but ever-flexible Lenin changed course. He repressed the Kronstadt rebels, and in March 1921 he replaced war communism (see Chapter 26) with the New Economic Policy (NEP), which re-established limited economic freedom in an attempt to rebuild agriculture and industry. Peasant producers were permitted to sell their surpluses in free markets, and private traders and small handicraft manufacturers were allowed to reappear. Heavy industry, railroads, and banks, however, remained wholly nationalized.

The NEP was a political and economic success. Politically, it was a necessary but temporary compromise with the Soviet Union's overwhelming peasant majority, the only force capable of overturning Lenin's government. The NEP brought rapid economic recovery, and by 1926 industrial output surpassed, and agricultural production was almost equal to, prewar levels. As the economy recovered and the government partially relaxed its censorship and repression, an intense struggle for power began in the inner circles of the Communist Party, for Lenin had left no chosen successor when he died in 1924. The principal contenders were Stalin and Trotsky.

Stalin was a good organizer but a poor speaker and writer, and he had no experience outside of Russia. Trotsky, who had planned the 1917 takeover and then created the Red Army, appeared to have all the advantages in the struggle to take power. Yet Stalin won

**five-year plan** A plan launched by Stalin in 1928, and termed the "revolution from above," aimed at modernizing the Soviet Union and creating a new communist society with new attitudes, new loyalties, and a new socialist humanity.

**New Economic Policy (NEP)** Lenin's 1921 policy to re-establish limited economic freedom in an attempt to rebuild agriculture and industry in the face of economic disintegration.

How did Stalin and his followers build a totalitarian state?

What kind of government did Mussolini establish in Italy?

How and why did Nazi policies lead to World War II?

What explains the Allied victory in World War II?

837

because he was more effective at gaining the all-important support of the party, the only genuine source of power in the one-party state. As general secretary of the party's Central Committee, he used his office to win friends and allies with jobs and promises.

Stalin also won because he was better able to relate Marxian teaching to Soviet realities in the 1920s. Stalin argued that the Russian-dominated Soviet Union had the ability to build socialism on its own. Trotsky maintained that socialism in the Soviet Union could succeed only if a socialist revolution swept throughout Europe. To many Russian communists, Trotsky's views sold their country short and promised risky conflicts with capitalist countries. Stalin's willingness to break with the NEP and "build socialism" at home appealed to young militants in the party.

With cunning skill, Stalin gradually achieved supreme power between 1922 and 1927. First he allied with Trotsky's personal enemies to crush Trotsky, and then he moved against all who might challenge him, including his former allies. Stalin's final triumph came at the party congress of December 1927, which condemned all "deviation from the general party line" formulated by Stalin.

## The Five-Year Plans

The party congress of 1927, which ratified Stalin's consolidation of power, marked the end of the NEP and the beginning of the era of socialist five-year plans, economic policies aimed at transforming the Soviet economy and, with it, Soviet society. By 1930 economic and social change was sweeping the country.

Stalin unleashed his "second revolution" for a variety of interrelated reasons. There were, first of all, ideological considerations. Stalin and his supporters were deeply committed to socialism as they understood it. They feared a gradual restoration of capitalism, wished to promote the working classes, and were eager to abolish the NEP's private traders, independent artisans, and property-owning peasants. Economic motivations were also important. A fragile economic recovery stalled in 1927 and 1928, and a new socialist offensive seemed necessary to ensure industrial and agricultural growth. Moreover, rapid economic development would allow the U.S.S.R. to catch up with the West. (See "Listening to the Past: Stalin Justifies the Five-Year Plan," page 840.)

The independent peasantry remained a major problem. For centuries the peasants had wanted to own the land, and finally they had it. Sooner or later, the communists reasoned, the peasants would embrace conservative capitalism. At the same time, the mainly urban communists believed that the villages could be squeezed to provide the enormous sums needed for all-out industrialization.

To resolve these issues, in 1929 Stalin ordered the collectivization of agriculture—the forced consolidation of individual peasant farms into large, state-controlled enterprises. Peasants all over the Soviet Union were compelled to move off their small plots onto large state-run farms, where central planners could control their work.

The increasingly repressive measures instituted by the state focused on the kulaks (KOO-lahx), the class of well-off peasants who had benefited the most from the market policies of the NEP. The kulaks were actually a very small group, but they were targeted as a great enemy of progress, and Stalin called for their "liquidation." Stripped of land and livestock, many starved or were deported to forced-labor camps for "re-education."

The forced collectivization of agriculture led to disaster. Peasant resistance caused chaos in the countryside, and large numbers of farmers slaughtered their animals and burned their crops rather than turn them over to state commissars. Nor were the state-controlled collective farms more productive. The output of grain barely increased, and collectivized agriculture was unable to make any substantial financial contribution to Soviet industrial development in the first five-year plan.

In Ukraine the drive against peasants became an assault on Ukrainians in general, who had sought independence after the First World War. In 1932 Stalin and his associates

**collectivization of agriculture** The forcible consolidation of individual peasant farms into large state-controlled enterprises in the Soviet Union under Stalin.

**kulaks** The better-off peasants who were stripped of land and livestock under Stalin and were generally not permitted to join collective farms; many of them starved or were deported to forced-labor camps for "re-education."

set levels of grain deliveries for the Ukrainian collective at excessively high levels, and they refused to relax those quotas or even allow food relief when Ukrainian communist leaders reported that starvation was occurring. The result was a terrible man-made famine in Ukraine in 1932 and 1933, which probably claimed 6 million lives.

Collectivization was a cruel but real victory for Stalinist ideologues. Millions of people died as a direct result, yet by the end of 1938, fully 93 percent of peasant families had been herded onto collective farms, effectively neutralizing them as a political threat. Nonetheless, the opposition of the peasantry had forced the state to make modest concessions. Peasants secured the right to limit a family's labor on the state-run farms and to cultivate tiny family plots, which provided them with much of their food.

The industrial side of the five-year plans was much more successful. A huge State Planning Commission oversaw the program by setting production goals and controlling deliveries of raw and finished materials. Despite numerous problems, Soviet industry produced about four times as much in 1937 as it had in 1928. No other major country had ever achieved such rapid industrial growth. Urban development went hand in hand with forced industrial growth: more than 25 million people migrated to cities during the 1930s, mostly peasants who left their villages to become laborers in Russia's growing industrial centers.

An industrial labor force was created almost overnight as peasant men and women began working in factories built across the country. Between 1930 and 1932, independent trade unions lost most of their power. The government could assign workers to any job anywhere in the country, and an internal passport system ensured that individuals could not move without the permission of the police. When factory managers needed more hands, they called on their counterparts on the collective farms, who sent them "unneeded" peasants.

Workers typically lived in deplorable conditions in hastily built industrial cities such as Magnitogorsk (Magnetic Mountain City) in the Ural mountains. Yet they also experienced some benefits of upward mobility. In a letter published in the Magnitogorsk newspaper, an electrician described the opportunities created by rapid industrialization:

> In old tsarist Russia, we weren't even considered people. We couldn't dream about education, or getting a job in a state enterprise. And now I'm a citizen of the USSR. Like all citizens I have the right to a job, to education, to leisure. . . . I live in a country where one feels like living and learning.[1]

We should read such words with care, since they appeared in a state-censored publication. Yet the enthusiasm was at least partly authentic. The great industrialization drive, concentrated between 1928 and 1937, was an awe-inspiring achievement purchased with enormous sacrifice on the part of ordinary Soviet citizens.

| ■ The Goals of the First Five-Year Plan |
| --- |
| Total industrial output to increase by 250 percent |
| Heavy industry to grow even faster than industry as a whole |
| Agricultural production to increase by 150 percent |
| 20 percent of Soviet peasants to join socialist collective farms |

**Day Shift at Magnitogorsk** Beginning in 1928, Stalin's government issued a series of ambitious five-year plans designed to rapidly industrialize the Soviet Union. The plans focused primarily on boosting heavy industry and included the building of a gigantic steel complex at Magnitogorsk in the Ural Mountains. Here steelworkers review production goals at the Magnitogorsk foundry. (Sovfoto)

How did Stalin and his followers build a totalitarian state?

What kind of government did Mussolini establish in Italy?

How and why did Nazi policies lead to World War II?

What explains the Allied victory in World War II?

**839**

*On February 4, 1931, Joseph Stalin delivered the following address, entitled "No Slowdown in Tempo!" to the First Conference of Soviet Industrial Managers. Published the following day in* Pravda, *the newspaper of the Communist Party, and widely publicized at home and abroad, Stalin's speech reaffirmed the leader's commitment to the breakneck pace of industrialization and collectivization set forth in the first five-year plan. Arguing that more sacrifices were necessary, Stalin sought to rally the people and generate support for the party's program. His address captures the spirit of Soviet public discourse in the early 1930s.*

*Stalin's concluding idea, that Bolsheviks needed to master technology and industrial management, reflected another major development. The Soviet Union was training a new class of communist engineers and technicians, who were beginning to replace foreign engineers and "bourgeois specialists," Russian engineers trained in tsarist times who were grudgingly tolerated after the revolution.*

❝ It is sometimes asked whether it is not possible to slow down the tempo somewhat, to put a check on the movement. No, comrades, it is not possible! The tempo must not be reduced! On the contrary, we must increase it as much as is within our powers and possibilities. This is dictated to us by our obligations to the workers and peasants of the U.S.S.R. This is dictated to us by our obligations to the working class of the whole world.

To slacken the tempo would mean falling behind. And those who fall behind get beaten. But we do not want to be beaten. No, we refuse to be beaten! One feature of the history of old Russia was the continual beatings she suffered because of her backwardness. She was beaten by the Mongol khans, . . . the Turkish beys, . . . and the Japanese barons. All beat her — because of her backwardness, cultural backwardness, political backwardness, industrial backwardness, agricultural backwardness. They beat her because to do so was profitable and could be done with impunity. . . . Such is the law of the exploiters — to beat the backward and the weak. It is the jungle law of capitalism. You are backward, you are weak — therefore you are wrong; hence you can be beaten and enslaved. You are mighty — therefore you are right; hence we must be wary of you. That is why we must no longer lag behind.

In the past we had no fatherland, nor could we have had one. But now that we have overthrown capitalism and power is in our hands, in the hands of the people, we have a fatherland, and we will uphold its independence. Do you want our socialist fatherland to be beaten and to lose its independence?

If you do not want this, you must put an end to its backwardness in the shortest possible time and develop a genuine Bolshevik tempo in building up its socialist economy. There is no other way. That is why Lenin said on the eve of the October Revolution: "Either perish, or overtake and outstrip the advanced capitalist countries."

We are fifty or a hundred years behind the advanced countries. We must make good this distance in ten years. Either we do it, or we shall go under. That is what our obligations to the workers and peasants of the U.S.S.R. dictate to us.

But we have yet other, more serious and more important, obligations. They are our obligations to the world proletariat. . . . We achieved victory not solely through the efforts of the working class of the U.S.S.R., but also thanks to the support of the working class of the world. Without this support we would have been torn to pieces long ago. . . .

Why does the international proletariat support us? How did we merit this support? By the fact that we were the first to hurl ourselves into the battle against capitalism, we were the first to establish working-class state power, we were the first to begin building socialism. By the fact that we are engaged on a cause which, if successful, will transform the whole world and free the entire working class. But what is needed for success? The elimination of our backwardness, the development of a high Bolshevik tempo of construction. We must march forward in such a way that the working class of the whole world, looking at us, may say:

## Life and Culture in Soviet Society

Daily life was difficult in Stalin's Soviet Union in the years before World War II. There were constant shortages, and housing was a particularly serious problem. Millions were moving into the cities, but the government built few new apartments. A relatively lucky family received one room for all its members and shared both a kitchen and a toilet with others on the floor.

Because consumption was reduced to pay for investment, there was little improvement in the average standard of living. Studies show that the average nonfarm wage purchased only about half as many goods in 1932 as it had in 1928. After 1932 real wages

There you have my advanced detachment, my shock brigade, my working-class state power, my fatherland; they are engaged on their cause, *our* cause, and they are working well; let us support them against the capitalists and promote the cause of the world revolution. Must we not justify the hopes of the world's working class, must we not fulfill our obligations to them? Yes, we must if we do not want to utterly disgrace ourselves.

Such are our obligations, internal and international.

As you see, they dictate to us a Bolshevik tempo of development.

I will not say that we have accomplished nothing in regard to management of production during these years. In fact, we have accomplished a good deal. . . . But we could have accomplished still more if we had tried during this period really to master production, the technique of production, the financial and economic side of it. In ten years at most we must make good the distance that separates us from the advanced capitalist countries. We have all the "objective" possibilities for this. The only thing lacking is the ability to make proper use of these possibilities.

And that depends on us. *Only* on us! . . . If you are a factory manager — interfere in all the affairs of the factory, look into everything, let nothing escape you, learn and learn again. Bolsheviks must master technique. It is time Bolsheviks themselves became experts. . . .

It is said that it is hard to master technique. That is not true! There are no fortresses that Bolsheviks cannot capture. We have solved a number of most difficult problems. We have overthrown capitalism. We have assumed power.

We have built up a huge socialist industry. We have transferred the middle peasants on the path of socialism. We have already accomplished what is most important from the point of view of construction. What remains to be done is not so much: to study technique, to master science. And when we have done that we shall develop a tempo of which we dare not even dream at present. And we shall do it if we really want to. 🗩

**Source:** Joseph Stalin, "No Slowdown in Tempo!" *Pravda*, February 5, 1931, excerpted from "Reading No. 14" in *Soviet Economic Development: Operation Outstrip, 1921–1965*, by Anatole G. Mazour.

### QUESTIONS FOR ANALYSIS

1. What reasons does Stalin give to justify an unrelenting "Bolshevik" tempo of industrial and social change? In the light of history, which reason seems most convincing? Why?

2. Imagine that the year is 1931 and you are a Soviet student reading Stalin's speech. Would Stalin's determination inspire you, frighten you, or leave you cold? Why?

3. Some historians argue that Soviet socialism was a kind of utopianism, where the economy, the society, and even human beings could be completely remade and perfected. What utopian elements do you see in Stalin's declaration?

rose slowly, but by 1937 workers could still buy only about 60 percent of what they had bought in 1928. Collectivized peasants experienced greater hardships.

Life was hard but by no means hopeless. Idealism and ideology had real appeal for many communists and ordinary citizens, who saw themselves building the world's first socialist society while capitalism crumbled and degenerated into fascism in the West. This optimistic belief in the future of the Soviet Union also attracted many disillusioned Westerners to communism in the 1930s.

On a more practical level, Soviet workers did receive important social benefits, such as old-age pensions, free medical services, free education, and day-care centers for children. Unemployment was almost unknown. Finally, there was the possibility of personal

How did Stalin and his followers build a totalitarian state?

What kind of government did Mussolini establish in Italy?

How and why did Nazi policies lead to World War II?

What explains the Allied victory in World War II?

841

advancement. Rapid industrialization required massive numbers of trained experts, such as skilled workers, engineers, and plant managers. Individuals who acquired specialized skills and technical education were in a position to join political and artistic elites in a new upper class, whose members were rich and powerful.

The radical transformation of Soviet society had a profound impact on women's lives. The Russian Revolution of 1917 immediately proclaimed complete equality of rights for women. In the 1920s divorce and abortion were made easily available, and women were urged to work outside the home. After Stalin came to power, he reversed this trend. The government now revoked many laws supporting women's emancipation in order to strengthen the traditional family and build up the state's population.

The most lasting changes for women involved work and education. Peasant women continued to work on farms, and millions of women toiled in factories and in heavy construction. The Soviets also opened higher education to women, who could now enter the ranks of the better-paid specialists in industry and science. By 1950, 75 percent of all doctors in the Soviet Union were women.

Alongside such advances, Soviet society demanded great sacrifices from women. The vast majority of women had to work outside the home to support their families. Men continued to dominate the very best jobs. Finally, rapid change and economic hardship led to many broken families, creating further physical and emotional strains for women.

Culture was thoroughly politicized for propaganda and indoctrination purposes. Party activists lectured workers in factories and peasants on collective farms while newspapers, films, and radio broadcasts recounted socialist achievements and capitalist plots. Whereas the 1920s had seen considerable experimentation in modern art and theater, in the 1930s the government clamped down. Stalin ordered intellectuals to become "engineers of human minds." They were instructed to exalt the lives of ordinary workers and glorify Russian nationalism.

Stalin seldom appeared in public, but his presence was everywhere — in portraits, statues, books, and quotations from his "sacred" writings. Although the government persecuted religion and turned churches into "museums of atheism," the state had both an earthly religion and a high priest — Marxism-Leninism and Joseph Stalin.

## Stalinist Terror and the Great Purges

In the mid-1930s, the push to build socialism and a new society culminated in ruthless police terror and a massive purging of the Communist Party. First used by the Bolsheviks in the civil war to maintain their power, terror as state policy was revived in the collectivization drive against the peasants. The top members of the party and government publicly supported Stalin's initiatives, but there was some grumbling. In late 1934 Stalin's number-two man, Sergei Kirov, was mysteriously murdered. Although Stalin himself probably ordered Kirov's murder, he blamed the assassination on what he called "fascist agents" within the Communist Party. Stalin used the incident to launch a reign of terror that purged the party of supposed traitors and solidified his own control.

State-sponsored repression picked up steam over the next two years. It culminated in the "great purge" of 1936–1938, a series of spectacular public show trials. In August 1936 sixteen "Old Bolsheviks" — prominent leaders who had been in the party since the Russian Revolution (Chapter 26) — confessed to all manner of contrived plots against Stalin in Moscow; all were executed. Then in 1937 the secret police arrested a mass of lesser party officials and newer members, torturing them and extracting confessions for more show trials. In addition to the party faithful, union officials, managers, intellectuals, army officers, and countless ordinary citizens were accused of counter-revolutionary activities and struck down. At least 8 million people were arrested, and millions of these were executed or never returned from prisons and forced-labor camps.

**Life in a Forced-Labor Camp**
Deported peasants and other political prisoners work under the most dehumanizing conditions to build the Stalin–White Sea Canal in far northern Russia, around 1933. In books and plays, Stalin's followers praised the project as a model for the regeneration of "reactionaries" and "kulak exploiters" through the joys of socialist work. (David King Collection)

Stalin and the remaining party leadership recruited 1.5 million new members to take the place of those purged. Thus more than half of all Communist Party members in 1941 had joined since the purges, and they experienced rapid social advance. Often the children of workers, they had usually studied in the new technical schools, and they soon proved capable of managing the government and large-scale production. Despite its human costs, the great purges brought substantial practical rewards to this new generation of committed communists. They would serve Stalin effectively until his death in 1953, and they would govern the Soviet Union until the early 1980s.

Stalin's mass purges remain baffling, for most historians believe that those purged posed no threat and were innocent of their supposed crimes. Certainly the highly publicized purges sent a warning to the people: no one was secure; everyone had to serve the party and its leader with redoubled devotion. Some scholars have argued that the terror was part of a fully developed totalitarian state, which must always fight real or imaginary enemies.

The long-standing interpretation that puts the blame for the great purges on Stalin has nevertheless been challenged. Some historians argue that many Soviet citizens shared Stalin's fear of subversive elements. Bombarded with ideology and political slogans, the population responded energetically to Stalin's directives. Investigations and trials snowballed into mass hysteria, resulting in a witch-hunt that claimed millions of victims. In this view of the 1930s, a deluded Stalin found large numbers of willing collaborators for crime as well as for achievement.[2]

## ▼ What kind of government did Mussolini establish in Italy?

Mussolini's fascist movement and his seizure of power in 1922 were important steps in the rise of dictatorships in Europe between the two world wars. Mussolini and his supporters were the first to call themselves "fascists" — revolutionaries determined to create a new totalitarian state based on extreme nationalism and militarism.

How did Stalin and his followers build a totalitarian state?

What kind of government did Mussolini establish in Italy?

How and why did Nazi policies lead to World War II?

What explains the Allied victory in World War II?

843

## The Seizure of Power

In the early twentieth century, Italy was a liberal state with civil rights and a constitutional monarchy. On the eve of World War I, the parliamentary regime granted universal male suffrage, and Italy appeared to be moving toward democracy. But there were serious problems. Much of the Italian population was still poor, and many peasants were more attached to their villages and local interests than to the national state. Moreover, the papacy, many devout Catholics, conservatives, and landowners remained strongly opposed to liberal institutions and relations between church and state were often tense. Class differences were also extreme, leading to the development of a powerful revolutionary socialist movement.

World War I worsened the political situation. To win the support of the Italian people for the war effort, the government had promised territorial expansion as well as social and land reform, which it could not deliver. Instead, unemployment and inflation soared after the war ended, creating mass hardship. In response, the Italian Socialist Party followed the Bolshevik example, and radical workers and peasants began occupying factories and seizing land in 1920. These actions scared and mobilized the property-owning classes. Moreover, after the war the pope lifted his ban on participation by Catholics in Italian politics, and a strong Catholic party quickly emerged. Thus by 1921 revolutionary socialists, antiliberal conservatives, and property owners were all opposed — though for different reasons — to the liberal parliamentary government.

Into these crosscurrents of unrest and fear stepped Benito Mussolini (1883–1945). Mussolini began his political career as a Socialist Party leader and radical newspaper editor before World War I. In 1914 he urged that Italy join the Allies, a stand for which he was expelled from the Italian Socialist Party. Later Mussolini fought at the front and was wounded in 1917. Returning home, he began organizing bitter war veterans like himself into a band of fascists — from the Italian word for "a union of forces."

At first Mussolini's program was a radical combination of nationalist and socialist demands. As such, it competed directly with the well-organized Socialist Party and failed to get off the ground. When Mussolini saw that his violent verbal assaults on rival Socialists won him growing support from conservatives and the frightened middle classes, he shifted gears in 1920 and became a sworn enemy of socialism. Mussolini and his private militia of Black Shirts grew increasingly violent. Few people were killed, but socialist newspapers, union halls, and local Socialist Party headquarters were destroyed, and the Black Shirts managed to push Socialists out of city governments in northern Italy.

Fascism soon became a mass movement, one which Mussolini claimed would help the little people against the established interests. As the government collapsed in 1922, largely because of the chaos created by his Black Shirt militias, Mussolini stepped forward as the savior of order and property. Striking a conservative, anti-communist note in his speeches and gaining the support of army leaders, Mussolini demanded the resignation of the existing government. In October 1922 a band of armed fascists marched on Rome to threaten the king and force him to appoint Mussolini prime minister of Italy. The threat worked. Victor Emmanuel III (r. 1900–1946) asked Mussolini to take over the government and form a new cabinet. Thus, after widespread violence and a threat of armed uprising, Mussolini seized power using the legal framework of the Italian constitution.

## The Regime in Action

Mussolini became prime minister in 1922, yet his long-term political intentions were by no means clear until 1924. At first, Mussolini moved cautiously to establish control. He promised a "return to order" and consolidated his support among Italian elites. Fooled by Mussolini's apparent moderation, the Italian parliament passed a new electoral law

**Black Shirts** Mussolini's private militia that destroyed socialist newspapers, union halls, and Socialist Party headquarters, eventually pushing Socialists out of the city governments of northern Italy.

that gave two-thirds of the representatives in the parliament to the party that won the most votes. This change allowed the Fascist Party and its allies to win an overwhelming majority in April 1924. Shortly thereafter, a group of fascist extremists kidnapped and murdered the Socialist politician Giacomo Matteotti (JAHK-oh-moh mat-tee-OH-tee). Alarmed by this outrage, a group of prominent parliamentary leaders demanded that Mussolini's armed squads be dissolved and all violence be banned.

Mussolini may not have ordered Matteotti's murder, but he took advantage of the resulting political crisis. Declaring his desire to "make the nation Fascist," he imposed a series of repressive measures. The government ruled by decree, abolished freedom of the press, and organized fixed elections. Mussolini arrested his political opponents, disbanded all independent labor unions, and put dedicated Fascists in control of Italy's schools. Mussolini trumpeted his goal in a famous slogan of 1926: "Everything in the state, nothing outside the state, nothing against the state." By the end of that year, Italy was a one-party dictatorship under Mussolini's unquestioned leadership.

Mussolini's Fascist Party drew support from broad sectors of the population, in large part because he was willing to compromise with the traditional elites that controlled the army, the economy, and the state. He left big business to regulate itself, and there was no land reform. Mussolini also drew increasing support from the Catholic Church. In the Lateran Agreement of 1929, he recognized the Vatican as an independent state, and he agreed to give the church significant financial support in return for the pope's support. Because he was forced to compromise with these conservative elites, Mussolini never established complete totalitarian control.

Mussolini's government nonetheless proceeded with attempts to bring fascism to Italy. The state engineered popular consent by staging massive rallies and sporting events, creating fascist youth and women's movements, and providing new welfare benefits.

**Lateran Agreement** A 1929 agreement that recognized the Vatican as an independent state, with Mussolini agreeing to give the church heavy financial support in return for public support from the pope.

**Fascist Youth on Parade** Totalitarian governments in Italy and Nazi Germany established mass youth organizations to instill the values of national unity and train young soldiers for the state. These members of the Balila, Italy's fascist youth organization, raise their rifles in salute at a mass rally in 1939. (Hulton-Deutsch Collection/Corbis)

How did Stalin and his followers build a totalitarian state?

**What kind of government did Mussolini establish in Italy?**

How and why did Nazi policies lead to World War II?

What explains the Allied victory in World War II?

845

Newspapers, radio, and film promoted a "cult of the Duce" (leader), portraying Mussolini as a powerful strongman who embodied the highest qualities of the Italian people.

Like other fascist regimes, Mussolini's government was vehemently opposed to liberal feminism and promoted instead traditional gender roles. The "new fascist man" was supposed to be a virile, patriotic warrior; his wife was the guardian of the home who raised children to support the values of the fascist state. Some women found great satisfaction in their devotion to family, national service, and the Italian "race."

Mussolini also gained popularity by manipulating popular pride in the grand history of the ancient Roman Empire. Propagandists criticized liberalism and parliamentary government as foreign imports that violated "Roman" traditions.[3]

Mussolini matched his aggressive rhetoric with military action: Italian armies invaded the African nation of Ethiopia in October 1935. After surprising setbacks at the hands of the poorly armed Ethiopian army, the Italians won in 1936, and Mussolini could proudly declare that Italy again had its empire. The war shocked international opinion and cemented ties between Italy and Nazi Germany. After a visit to Berlin in the fall of 1937, the Italian dictator pledged support for Hitler and promised that Italy and Germany would "march together right to the end."[4]

Italy's Ethiopian Campaign, 1935–1936

→ Italian campaigns, 1935–1936

Deeply influenced by Hitler's example (see below), Mussolini's government passed a series of anti-Jewish racial laws in 1938. Though the laws were unpopular, Jews were forced out of public schools and dismissed from professional careers. The fascist government stepped up anti-Semitic persecution late in World War II, when Italy was under Nazi control. Though Mussolini's repressive tactics were never as ruthless as those in Nazi Germany, his government did much to turn Italy into a totalitarian police state.

## ▼ How and why did Nazi policies lead to World War II?

The most frightening dictatorship developed in Nazi Germany. National Socialism (or Nazism) shared some of the characteristics of Italian fascism. But Nazism was far more interventionist than its Italian counterpart. Truly totalitarian in its aspirations, the dynamism of Nazi Germany, based on racial aggression and territorial expansion, led to history's most destructive war.

### The Roots of National Socialism

**National Socialism** A movement born of extreme nationalism and racism, led by Adolf Hitler, that ruled Germany from 1933 to 1945 and forced Europe into the Second World War.

National Socialism grew out of many complex developments, of which the most influential were extreme nationalism and racism. These two ideas captured the mind of the young Adolf Hitler (1889–1945), and he dominated Nazism until the end of World War II.

The son of an Austrian customs official, Hitler spent his childhood in small towns in Austria. A mediocre student, he dropped out of high school at age fourteen. Hitler then moved to Vienna, where he was exposed to extreme Austro-German nationalists who believed Germans to be a superior people and the natural rulers of central Europe. They advocated union with Germany and violent expulsion of "inferior" peoples from the Austro-Hungarian Empire.

In Vienna Hitler developed an unshakable belief in the crudest distortions of Social Darwinism (see Chapter 25), the superiority of Germanic races, and the inevitability of racial conflict. The Jews, he claimed, directed an international conspiracy of finance capitalism and Marxist socialism against German culture, German unity, and the German people. These ideas came to define Hitler's worldview and would play an immense role in the ideology and actions of National Socialism.

Hitler greeted the outbreak of the First World War as a salvation. The struggle and discipline of war gave life meaning, and Hitler served bravely on the western front. When Germany was defeated in 1918, Hitler's world was shattered. Convinced that Jews and Marxists had "stabbed Germany in the back," he vowed to fight on.

In late 1919 Hitler joined a tiny extremist group in Munich called the German Workers' Party. By 1921 Hitler had gained absolute control of this small but growing party, which had been renamed the National Socialist German Workers' Party, or Nazis, in 1920. Hitler became a master of mass propaganda and political showmanship. In wild, histrionic speeches, he worked his audience into a frenzy with demagogic attacks on the Versailles treaty, Jews, war profiteers, and Germany's Weimar Republic.

Party membership multiplied tenfold after early 1922. In late 1923 the Weimar Republic seemed on the verge of collapse, and Hitler, inspired by Mussolini's recent victory, organized an armed uprising in Munich—the so-called Beer Hall Putsch. Despite the failure of the poorly planned coup and Hitler's arrest, National Socialism had been born.

## Hitler's Road to Power

At his trial, Hitler violently denounced the Weimar Republic, and he gained enormous publicity. From the failed revolt, Hitler concluded that he had to come to power through electoral competition rather than armed rebellion. He used his brief prison term to dictate his book *Mein Kampf* (*My Struggle*). Here Hitler laid out his basic ideas on "racial purification" and territorial expansion that would increasingly define National Socialism.

In *Mein Kampf* Hitler claimed that Germans were a "master race" that needed to defend its "pure blood" from groups he labeled "racial degenerates," including Jews, Slavs, and others. The German race was destined to triumph and grow, and, according to Hitler, it needed *Lebensraum* (living space). This space could be found to Germany's east, in central Europe, which Hitler claimed was inhabited by the "subhuman" Slavs and Jews. The future dictator portrayed a vision of war and conquest in which the German master race would colonize and ultimately replace these "subhumans" across east-central Europe. He championed the idea of the leader-dictator or *Führer* (FEW-ruhr), who would embody the people's will and lead the German nation to victory. These ideas—a deadly combination of race and space—would ultimately propel Hitler's Germany into the Second World War.

In the years of relative prosperity and stability between 1924 and 1929, Hitler built up the Nazi Party. To appeal to middle-class voters, Hitler de-emphasized the anticapitalist elements of National Socialism and vowed to fight communism. The Nazis still remained a small splinter group in 1928, when they received only 2.6 percent of the vote in the general elections and twelve seats in the Reichstag, the German parliament. There the Nazi deputies pursued the legal strategy of using democracy to destroy democracy.

The Great Depression of 1929 brought the ascent of National Socialism. Now Hitler promised German voters economic as well as political salvation. His appeals for "national rebirth" appealed to a broad spectrum of voters, including middle- and lower-middle-class groups, as well as skilled workers striving for middle-class status. Seized by panic as bankruptcies increased, unemployment soared, and the communists made election gains, voters deserted the conservative and moderate parties for the Nazis. In the election of 1930 the Nazis won 6.5 million votes and 107 seats, and in July 1932 they gained 14.5 million votes—38 percent of the total. They were now the largest party in the Reichstag.

How did Stalin and his followers build a totalitarian state?

What kind of government did Mussolini establish in Italy?

How and why did Nazi policies lead to World War II?

What explains the Allied victory in World War II?

847

## ▪ Events Leading to World War II

| | |
|---|---|
| **1919** | Treaty of Versailles is signed |
| **1920** | Founding of National Socialist German Workers' Party (Nazis) |
| **1922** | Mussolini seizes power in Italy |
| **1927** | Stalin takes full control in the Soviet Union |
| **1929–1939** | Great Depression |
| **1931** | Japan invades Manchuria |
| **January 1933** | Hitler is appointed chancellor of Germany |
| **March 1933** | Reichstag passes the Enabling Act, granting Hitler absolute dictatorial power |
| **1935** | Nuremberg Laws deprive Jews of all rights of citizenship |
| **March 1935** | Hitler announces German rearmament |
| **October 1935** | Mussolini invades Ethiopia and receives Hitler's support |
| **March 1936** | German armies move unopposed into the demilitarized Rhineland |
| **1936–1939** | Civil war in Spain, culminating in taking of power by fascist regime under Franco |
| **October 1936** | Rome-Berlin Axis created |
| **1937** | Japan invades China |
| **March 1938** | Germany annexes Austria |
| **September 1938** | Munich Conference: Britain and France agree to German seizure of the Sudetenland from Czechoslovakia |
| **March 1939** | Germany occupies the rest of Czechoslovakia; appeasement ends in Britain |
| **August 1939** | Nazi-Soviet pact is signed |
| **September 1, 1939** | Germany invades Poland |
| **September 3, 1939** | Britain and France declare war on Germany |

The breakdown of democratic government helped the Nazis seize power. Unable to gain the support of a majority in the Reichstag, in summer 1930 Chancellor Heinrich Brüning (BROO-nihng) convinced the president, General Hindenburg, to authorize rule by decree under Article 48 of the constitution, which allowed the central government to govern without the consent of the parliament. Brüning tried to overcome the economic crisis by cutting back government spending and ruthlessly forcing down prices and wages. His conservative policies intensified Germany's economic collapse and convinced many voters that the country's republican leaders were stupid and corrupt, adding to Hitler's appeal. Division on the left also contributed to Nazi success. Even though the two left-wing parties together outnumbered the Nazis in the Reichstag, the Communists refused to cooperate with the Social Democrats.

Finally, Hitler excelled in the backroom politics of the Weimar Republic. In 1932 he cleverly gained the support of conservative politicians and key leaders in the army and big business. These people thought they could use Hitler for their own advantage and accepted his demand to be appointed chancellor in a coalition government, reasoning that he could be manipulated and controlled. On January 30, 1933, Adolf Hitler, leader of the largest political party in Germany, was legally appointed chancellor by President Hindenburg.

# State and Society in Nazi Germany

Hitler moved quickly to establish a dictatorship that would pursue the Nazi program of race and space. First, Hitler and the Nazi Party worked to consolidate their power. To maintain legal appearances, Hitler called for new elections. In February 1933, the Reichstag building was partly destroyed by fire. Hitler blamed the Communist Party, and he convinced President Hindenburg to sign dictatorial emergency acts that abolished freedom of speech and assembly as well as most personal liberties.

The façade of democratic government was soon torn asunder. When the Nazis won only 44 percent of the vote in the elections, Hitler outlawed the Communist Party and arrested its parliamentary representatives. Then on March 23, 1933, the Nazis pushed through the Reichstag the so-called Enabling Act, which gave Hitler absolute dictatorial power for four years. The Nazis deceitful stress on legality, coupled with divide-and-conquer techniques, had disarmed the opposition until it was too late for effective resistance.

**Enabling Act** An act pushed through the Reichstag by the Nazis that gave Hitler absolute dictatorial power for four years.

Germany became a one-party Nazi state. Elections were farces. The new regime took over the government bureaucracy intact, installing Nazis in top positions. Once the Nazis were firmly in command of the government, Hitler and the party turned their attention to constructing a National Socialist society defined by national unity and racial exclusion. First the Nazis attacked their political enemies. Communists, Social Democrats, and trade union leaders were forced out of their jobs or arrested and taken to hastily built concentration camps. Strikes and independent unions were outlawed.

Hitler then purged the Nazi Party of its more extremist elements. The Nazi storm troopers (the SA), the quasi-military band of 3 million toughs in brown shirts who had fought communists and beaten up Jews before the Nazis took power, expected top positions in the army. Now that the Nazis were in power, however, Hitler was eager to win support of the traditional military and maintain social order. He decided that the leadership of the SA had to be eliminated. On the night of June 30, 1934, Hitler's elite personal guard—the SS—arrested and shot without trial between 85 and 200 SA leaders and other political enemies. Afterward the SS grew rapidly. Under Heinrich Himmler (1900–1945), the SS took over the political police and the concentration-camp system.

The Nazi Party instituted a policy it called "coordination" that was meant to force society to conform to National Socialist ideology. Independent professional organizations were swallowed up by Nazi associations. Publishing houses were put under Nazi control, and universities and writers were quickly brought into line. Democratic, socialist, and Jewish literature was put on ever-growing blacklists. Students and professors burned forbidden books in public squares. Modern art and architecture—which the Nazis considered "degenerate"—were prohibited. Life became violently anti-intellectual. By 1934 a brutal dictatorship characterized by frightening dynamism and obedience to Hitler was largely in place.

Acting on its vision of racial purity, the party began a many-faceted campaign against those they deemed incapable of making a positive contribution to the "master race." The Nazis persecuted a number of supposedly undesirable groups based on their reputed racial characteristics. Jews headed the list, but Slavic peoples, Gypsies (Sinti and Roma), homosexuals, Jehovah's Witnesses, and people considered handicapped were also targets of state-sponsored repression.

Barbarism and race hatred were institutionalized with the force of science and law.[5] New university academies, such as the German Society for Racial Research, wrote studies that measured and defined racial differences; prejudice was thus presented in the guise of enlightened science. The ethical breakdown was exemplified in a series of sterilization laws, which led to the forced sterilization of some four hundred thousand supposedly "undesirable" citizens.

How did Stalin and his followers build a totalitarian state?

What kind of government did Mussolini establish in Italy?

**How and why did Nazi policies lead to World War II?**

What explains the Allied victory in World War II?

**849**

From the beginning, German Jews were a special object of Nazi persecution. By the end of 1934, most Jewish lawyers, doctors, professors, civil servants, and musicians had been banned from their professions. In 1935 the infamous Nuremberg Laws classified as Jewish anyone having three or more Jewish grandparents. The Nuremberg Laws deprived Jews of all rights of citizenship and outlawed marriage and sexual relations between Jews and those defined as German. For the vast majority of German citizens not targeted by such laws, the creation of a demonized outsider group may well have contributed to feelings of national unity and support for the Hitler regime.

In late 1938 the assault on the Jews accelerated. During a well-organized wave of violence known as Kristallnacht (the night of broken glass), Nazi gangs smashed windows, looted Jewish-owned shops, and destroyed homes and synagogues. German Jews were then rounded up and made to pay for the damage. Confronted with ever-increasing prejudice, by 1939 some 300,000 of Germany's 500,000 Jews had emigrated. Some Germans privately opposed these outrages, but most went along or looked the other way. This lack of opposition reflected the strong popular support enjoyed by Hitler's government.

## Popular Support for National Socialism

Why did millions of ordinary Germans back a brutally repressive regime? A combination of coercion and reward generated popular support for the racial state. Using the secret police and the growing concentration camp system, the regime persecuted its political and "racial" enemies. Yet for the large majority of ordinary German citizens who were not Jews, communists, or members of other outsider groups, Hitler's government brought new opportunities. The German "master race" clearly benefited from Nazi policies.

Hitler had promised the masses economic recovery and he delivered. The Nazi state launched a large public works program to help pull Germany out of the depression. Work began on highways, offices, sports stadiums, and public housing, which created jobs and instilled pride in national recovery. By 1938 unemployment had fallen to 2 percent, and there was a shortage of workers. Thus between 1932 and 1938, the standard of living for the average employed worker increased moderately. Business profits rose sharply.

The persecution of Jews brought substantial benefits to ordinary Germans. As Jews were forced out of their jobs and then their homes, Germans stepped in to take their place. In a process known as Aryanization (named after the "Aryan master race" prized by the Nazis for its supposedly pure German blood), many Jews were forced to sell their businesses to "racially pure" Germans at rock-bottom prices.

Economic recovery was accompanied by a great wave of social and cultural innovation intended to construct what Nazi propagandists called the *Volksgemeinschaft*—a "people's community" for all racially pure Germans. The party organized mass organizations to spread Nazi ideology and enlist volunteers for the Nazi cause. Millions of Germans joined the Hitler Youth, the League of German Women, and the German Labor Front. Mass rallies, such as annual May Day celebrations and Nazi Party conventions in Nuremberg, brought together thousands of participants. Reports on such events in the Nazi-controlled press brought the message home to millions more.

The Nazis made great attempts to control the private lives and leisure time of ordinary Germans. State-sponsored "Strength Through Joy" programs set up exercise classes, beautified workplaces, and took working-class Germans on free vacations. A series of newly invented holidays encouraged Germans to celebrate the values of the racial state at home. The government promised prosperity and proudly touted an array of inexpensive and people's products. Items such as the Volkswagen (the people's car) were intended to link individual desires for consumer goods to the collective ideology of the people's community. Such programs suggested that the regime sincerely wished to improve German living standards.

**Mothers in the Fatherland** Nazi ideologues promoted strictly defined gender roles for men and women. The Nazi state implemented a variety of social programs to encourage "racially correct" women to stay home and raise "Aryan" children. This colorful poster portrays the joy of motherhood and calls for donations to the Mother and Child division of the National Socialist People's Welfare office. A woman who had four children was awarded the bronze Cross of Honor for the German Mother (above). The medal came with a letter of appreciation signed by Hitler. (poster: akg-images; medal: Private Collection/Peter Newark Military Pictures/The Bridgeman Art Library)

Women played a special role in the Nazi state. Promising to "liberate women from women's liberation," Nazi ideologues championed a return to traditional family values. They outlawed abortion, discouraged women from holding jobs or obtaining higher education, and glorified domesticity and motherhood. In the later 1930s, facing labor shortages, the Nazis reluctantly reversed course and encouraged women to enter the labor force. At the same time, the millions of women enrolled in Nazi mass organizations experienced a new sense of community in public activities.

Few historians today believe that Hitler and the Nazis brought about a real social revolution. Yet Hitler's rule corresponded to a time of economic growth, and Nazi propagandists continually triumphed the supposed accomplishments of the regime. The vision of the people's community, the national pride of German recovery, and the feelings of belonging created by acts of racial exclusion led many Germans to support the regime.

Not all Germans supported Hitler, however. Indeed a number of groups actively resisted him after 1933. But opponents of the Nazis were never unified, which helps account for their lack of success. And the regime clamped down: tens of thousands of political enemies were imprisoned, and thousands were executed. In the first years of Hitler's rule, the principal resisters were communists and socialists in the trade unions, groups smashed by the expansion of the SS system. A second group of opponents arose in the Catholic and Protestant churches. However, their efforts were directed primarily at preserving religious life, not at overthrowing Hitler. In 1938 and again during the war, a few high-ranking army officers, who feared the consequences of Hitler's reckless aggression, plotted against him, but all were unsuccessful.

How did Stalin and his followers build a totalitarian state?

What kind of government did Mussolini establish in Italy?

How and why did Nazi policies lead to World War II?

What explains the Allied victory in World War II?

851

# Aggression and Appeasement

The nazification of German society fulfilled only part of the larger Nazi agenda. Even as it built up the people's community, the regime aggressively pursued policies meant to achieve German territorial expansion. At first, Hitler carefully camouflaged his expansionist foreign policy. Germany was still militarily weak, and the Nazi leader proclaimed his peaceful intentions. Then in March 1935 Hitler openly declared that Germany would no longer abide by the disarmament clauses of the Treaty of Versailles. He established a military draft and began to build up the German army. France, Italy, and Great Britain protested strongly and warned against future aggressive actions.

Yet the emerging united front against Hitler quickly collapsed. Britain adopted a policy of appeasement, granting Hitler everything he could reasonably want (and more) in order to avoid war. British appeasement, which practically dictated French policy, was motivated in large part by the pacifism of a population still horrified by the memory of the First World War. As in Germany, many powerful conservatives in Britain underestimated Hitler. They believed that Soviet communism was the real danger and that Hitler could be used to stop it.

When Hitler suddenly marched his armies into the demilitarized Rhineland in March 1936, brazenly violating the Treaties of Versailles and Locarno (Map 28.1), Britain refused to act. France could do little to halt the Germans without British support. Emboldened, Hitler moved ever more aggressively in international affairs. Italy and German established the so-called Rome-Berlin Axis in 1936. Japan, also under the rule of a fascist dictatorship, joined the Axis alliance.

At the same time, Germany and Italy intervened in the Spanish civil war (1936–1939), where their military aid helped General Francisco Franco's revolutionary fascist movement defeat the elected republican government. Republican Spain's only official aid in the fight against Franco came from the Soviet Union.

In late 1937 Hitler moved forward with plans to crush Austria and Czechoslovakia as the first step in his long-contemplated drive for living space in the east. By threatening Austria with invasion, Hitler forced the Austrian chancellor to put local Nazis in control of the government in March 1938. The next day, in the Austrian Anschluss (annexation), German armies moved in unopposed, and Austria became two more provinces of Greater Germany (see Map 28.1).

Simultaneously, Hitler demanded that territories inhabited mostly by ethnic Germans in western Czechoslovakia — the Sudetenland — be ceded to Nazi Germany. Though democratic Czechoslovakia was prepared to defend itself, appeasement triumphed again. In September 1938 British prime minster Arthur Neville Chamberlain flew to Germany three times in fourteen days. In these negotiations, Chamberlain and the French agreed with Hitler that Germany should immediately take over the Sudetenland. Returning to London from the Munich Conference, Chamberlain told cheering crowds that he had secured "peace with honor . . . peace for our time." Sold out by the Western Powers, Czechoslovakia gave in.

Chamberlain's peace was short-lived. In March 1939 Hitler's armies invaded and occupied the rest of Czechoslovakia. This time, there was no possible rationale of self-determination for Nazi aggression, since Hitler was seizing ethnic Czechs and Slovaks as captive peoples. When Hitler next used the question of German minorities in Danzig as a pretext to confront Poland, Chamberlain declared that Britain and France would fight if Hitler attacked his eastern neighbor. Hitler did not take these warnings seriously and pressed on.

In August 1939, in a dramatic about-face, sworn enemies Hitler and Stalin signed a so-called nonaggression pact that in fact paved the road to war. Each dictator promised to remain neutral if the other became involved in open hostilities. An attached secret protocol divided Poland and east-central Europe into German and Soviet zones. Stalin

**appeasement** The British policy toward Germany prior to World War II that aimed at granting Hitler whatever he wanted, including western Czechoslovakia, in order to avoid war.

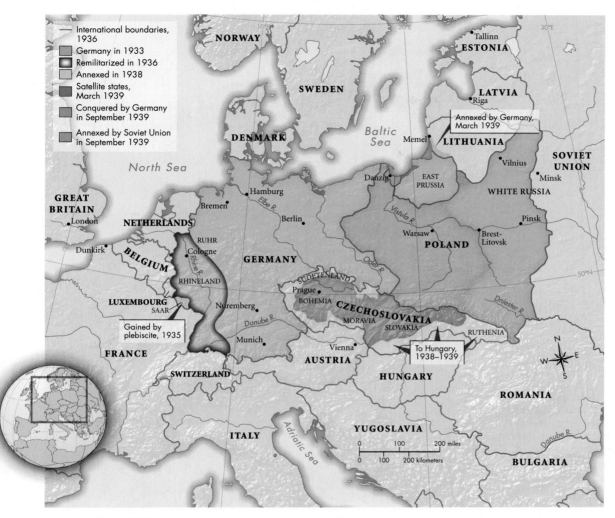

**Map 28.1 The Growth of Nazi Germany, 1933–1939** Until March 1939 Hitler's conquests brought ethnic Germans into the Nazi state; then he turned on the Slavic and Jewish peoples he had always hated. He stripped Czechoslovakia of its independence and prepared to attack Poland in September 1939.

agreed to the pact because he remained distrustful of Western intentions and Hitler offered immediate territorial gain.

For Hitler, everything was now set. On September 1, 1939, the Germans attacked Poland from three sides. Two days later, Britain and France, finally true to their word, declared war on Germany. The Second World War had begun.

## ▼ What explains the Allied victory in World War II?

Nazi Germany's unlimited ambition unleashed world war. Hitler's armies quickly conquered much of western and eastern Europe, establishing an empire based on Nazi ideas of race and space. At the same time, Japanese armies overran much of Southeast Asia and created their own racial empire. This aggression brought together a coalition of unlikely

How did Stalin and his followers build a totalitarian state?

What kind of government did Mussolini establish in Italy?

How and why did Nazi policies lead to World War II?

**What explains the Allied victory in World War II?**

853

German Bombers over Warsaw Germany opened its September 1939 attack on Poland by subjecting the Polish capital to repeated bombardment. By the end of the war, both sides had engaged in massive air campaigns against civilian targets, taking the lives of millions of civilians and leading finally to the use of the atomic bomb against Japan in 1945. (INTERFOTO/Alamy)

but powerful allies determined to halt the advance of fascism: Britain, the United States, and the Soviet Union.

## German Victories in Europe

Using mechanized forces in the first example of a blitzkrieg or "lightning war," Hitler's armies crushed Poland in four weeks. While the Soviet Union quickly took its part of the booty — the eastern half of Poland and the independent Baltic states of Lithuania, Estonia, and Latvia — French and British armies prepared their defenses in the west.

In spring 1940 the Nazi lightning war struck again. After occupying Denmark, Norway, and Holland, German motorized columns broke into France through southern Belgium, split the Franco-British forces, and trapped the entire British army on the French beaches of Dunkirk. By heroic efforts, the British withdrew their troops, but France was taken by the Nazis. By July 1940 Hitler ruled practically all of western continental Europe. Only Britain, led by Winston Churchill (1874–1965), remained unconquered.

To prepare for an invasion of Britain, Germany sought to gain control of the air. In the Battle of Britain, which began in July 1940, German planes attacked British airfields and key factories, dueling with British defenders high in the skies. Losses were heavy on both sides. In September 1940 Hitler turned from military objectives to indiscriminate bombing of British cities in an attempt to break British morale. British aircraft factories increased production, and the people of London defiantly dug in. By October Britain was beating Germany three to one in the air war, and the Battle of Britain was over. Unsuccessful in Britain, the Nazis turned south and invaded and occupied Greece and the Balkans.

Hitler now allowed his lifetime obsession of creating a vast eastern European empire to dictate policy. In June 1941 German armies attacked the Soviet Union, breaking the Nazi-Soviet pact (Map 28.2). By October, the Germans had reached the outskirts of Moscow. But the Soviets did not collapse, and when a severe winter struck, the invaders were stopped. Stalled in Russia, Hitler and his allies still ruled over a vast European empire. Hitler, the Nazi leadership, and the German army were positioned to accelerate construction of their New Order in Europe.

## Europe Under Nazi Occupation

Hitler's New Order was based on the guiding principle of National Socialism: racial imperialism. Occupied peoples were treated according to their place on the Nazi racial hierarchy. All were subject to harsh policies dedicated to ethnic cleansing and the plunder of resources for the Nazi war effort.

**Vichy France, 1940**

Within the New Order, the so-called Nordic peoples— the Dutch, Norwegians, and Danes—received preferential treatment, for the Germans believed they were racially related to the Aryan master race. France was divided into two parts. The German army occupied the north, including Paris. The southeast remained nominally independent. There Marshal Henri-Philippe Pétain formed a new French government—the so-called Vichy (VIH-shee) regime— that adopted many aspects of National Socialist ideology and willingly placed French Jews in the hands of the Nazis.

In all conquered territories, the Nazis used a variety of techniques to enrich Germans and support the war effort. Occupied nations were forced to pay for the costs of the war and for the occupation itself. Nazi administrators stole goods and money from local Jews, set currency exchanges at favorable rates, and forced occupied peoples to accept worthless wartime script. A flood of plunder reached Germany, which helped maintain high living standards and preserved morale well into the war. Nazi victory furthermore placed national Jewish populations across Europe under German control, and so eased the planning and implementation of the mass murder of Europe's Jews.

From the start, the Nazi leadership had cast the war in the east as a war of annihilation. They now set out to build an eastern colonial empire where Jews would be exterminated and Poles, Ukrainians, and Russians would be enslaved and forced to die out. German peasants would resettle the resulting abandoned lands.

With the support of military commanders, German policemen, and bureaucrats in the occupied territories, Nazi administrators and Himmler's elite SS corps now implemented a program of destruction and annihilation to create a "mass settlement space" for racially pure Germans. Across the east, the Nazi armies destroyed cities and factories, stole crops and farm animals, and subjected conquered peoples to forced starvation and mass murder. The murderous sweep of Nazi occupation destroyed the lives of millions.

In response to such atrocities, small but determined underground resistance groups fought back. They were hardly unified. Communists and socialists often disagreed with more centrist or nationalist groups on long-term goals and short-term tactics. The resistance nonetheless presented a real challenge to the Nazi New Order. Poland, under

**New Order** Hitler's program based on racial imperialism, which gave preferential treatment to the Nordic peoples; the French, an "inferior" Latin people, occupied a middle position, and Slavs and Jews were treated harshly as "subhumans."

How did Stalin and his followers build a totalitarian state?

What kind of government did Mussolini establish in Italy?

How and why did Nazi policies lead to World War II?

What explains the Allied victory in World War II?

855

Legend:
- Axis powers and their allies
- Occupied by Germany and its allies
- Allied powers and their allies
- Neutral nations
- Boundary of Greater Germany
- Major battle

Siege of Leningrad, Sept. 1941–Jan. 1944

Germans repulsed, Dec. 1941

Siege of Stalingrad, Aug. 21, 1942–Jan. 31, 1943

Germany surrenders, May 8, 1945

Siege, Sept. 1939
Uprising, Aug.–Sept. 1944

Battle of Britain, fall 1940

Invasion of Normandy, June 6, 1944

Battle of the Bulge, Dec. 1944

Axis troops occupy Vichy France, Nov. 10 and 11, 1942

Axis troops evacuated, May 1943

Joined Allies, Nov. 1942

Allies invade Sicily and Italy, July–Sept. 1943

Rome (Liberated June 1944)

Monte Cassino, May 1944

Salerno, Sept. 1943

Sicily, July 1943

Italian front Feb. 1945

Battle for Crete May 20–June 1, 1941

El Alamein, summer 1942

Russian front, spring 1944
Russian front, Nov. 1942
Russian front, Dec. 1941
Russian front, Feb. 1945
Western front, Feb. 1945

Moscow, Oct. 1941–Jan. 1942

Kursk, July–Aug. 1943

Dnieper, Aug.–Dec. 1943

Casablanca Nov. 1942

**■ MAPPING THE PAST**

## Map 28.2  World War II in Europe and Africa, 1939–1945

This map shows the extent of Hitler's empire before the Battle of Stalingrad in late 1942 and the subsequent advances of the Allies until Germany surrendered on May 7, 1945. Compare this map with Map 28.1 on page 853 to trace the rise and fall of the Nazi empire over time.

**ANALYZING THE MAP**  What was the first country conquered by Hitler (see Map 28.1)? Locate Germany's advance and retreat on the Russian front in December 1941, November 1942, spring 1944, and February 1945. How does this compare to the position of British and American forces on the battlefield at similar points in time?

**CONNECTIONS**  What implications might the battle lines on February 1945 have had for the postwar settlement in Europe?

To complete this activity online, go to the Online Study Guide at bedfordstmartins.com/mckaywestunderstanding.

**Key:**
— Boundary of Poland, 1938
▢ Germany, 1938
▢ Annexed by Germany, 1939
▢ German civil administration, 1942
▢ German military occupation, 1942
— Boundary of Greater Germany, 1942

**Nazi Occupation of Poland and East-Central Europe, 1939–1942**

German occupation longer than any other nation, had the most determined and well-organized resistance. The Nazis had closed all Polish universities and outlawed national newspapers, but the Poles organized secret classes and maintained an underground press. Underground members of the Polish Home Army, led by the government in exile in London, passed intelligence about German operations to the Allies and committed sabotage; communist groups in Poland likewise attacked the Nazis. The French resistance undertook similar actions, as did groups in Italy, Greece, Russia, and the Netherlands.

The German response was swift and deadly. The Nazi army and the SS tortured captured resistance members and executed hostages in reprisal for attacks. Responding to actions undertaken by resistance groups, the German army murdered the male populations of Lidice (Czechoslovakia) and Oradour (France) and leveled these entire towns.

## The Holocaust

The ultimate abomination of Nazi racism was the condemnation of all European Jews and other peoples considered racially inferior to persecution and then annihilation in the Holocaust, a great spasm of mass murder that took place during the Second World War.

Immediately after taking power, the Nazis began to use social, legal, and economic means to persecute Jews and other "undesirable" groups. Between 1938 and 1940, persecution turned deadly in the Nazi euthanasia (mercy killing) campaign, an important step toward genocide. Just as Germany began the war, some 70,000 people with physical and mental disabilities were forced into special hospitals, barracks, and camps where they were murdered. The victims were mostly ethnic Germans, and the euthanasia campaign was stopped after church leaders and ordinary families spoke out. The staff involved took what they learned in this program with them to the extermination camps the Nazis would build in the east (Map 28.3).

The German victory over Poland in 1939 brought some 3 million Jews under Nazi control, and Jews living in German-occupied territories were soon forced to move into centralized urban areas known as ghettos. In walled-off districts in cities large and small, hundreds of thousands of Polish Jews were forced to live in highly crowded and unsanitary conditions, without real work or adequate sustenance. Over 500,000 people died in the Nazi ghettos.

The racial violence reached new extremes when the German war of annihilation against the Soviet Union opened in 1941. Three military death squads known as Special Action Units (*Einsatzgruppen*) and other military groups followed the advancing German armies into central Europe. They moved from town to town shooting Jews and other target populations. In this way the German armed forces murdered some 2 million innocent civilians.

In late 1941 Hitler and the Nazi leadership, in some still-debated combination, ordered the SS to implement the mass murder of all Jews in Europe. What the Nazi leadership called the "final solution of the Jewish question" had begun. The Germans set up an industrialized killing machine. The SS established an extensive network of concentration camps, industrial complexes, and railroad transport lines to imprison and murder Jews as well as other so-called undesirables, and to exploit their labor before they died. In the occupied eastern territories, the surviving residents of the ghettos were loaded

**Holocaust** The systematic effort of the Nazi state to exterminate all European Jews and other groups deemed racially inferior during the Second World War.

How did Stalin and his followers build a totalitarian state?

What kind of government did Mussolini establish in Italy?

How and why did Nazi policies lead to World War II?

What explains the Allied victory in World War II?

857

**Map 28.3** **The Holocaust, 1941–1945** The leadership of Nazi Germany established an extensive network of ghettos and concentration and extermination camps to persecute their political opponents and those people deemed "racially undesirable" by the regime. The death camps, where the Nazi SS systematically murdered millions of European Jews, Soviet prisoners of war, and others, were located primarily in Nazi-occupied territories in eastern Europe, but the conditions in the concentration camps within Germany's borders were almost as brutal.

onto trains and taken to camps such as Auschwitz, where over one million people—the vast majority of them Jews—were murdered in gas chambers. Some few were put to work as expendable laborers. The Jews of Germany and then of occupied western and central Europe were likewise rounded up, put on trains, and sent to the camps. Even after it was quite clear that Germany would lose the war, the killing continued.

By 1945 the Nazis had killed about 6 million Jews. (See "Individuals in Society: Primo Levi," page 860.) Who was responsible for this terrible crime? Historians continue to debate this critical question. Some lay the guilt on Hitler and the Nazi leadership, arguing that ordinary Germans had little knowledge of the extermination camps or were forced to participate by Nazi terror and totalitarian control. Other scholars conclude that far more Germans knew about and were at best indifferent to the fate of "racial inferiors."

Yet the question remains: what inspired those who actually worked in the killing machine—the "desk murderers" in Berlin who sent trains to the east, the soldiers in the military units who shot Jews in the Polish forests, the guards at Auschwitz? Some historians

**The Holocaust** The Nazi drive to establish a racial empire in east-central Europe led to the Holocaust, the mass murder of approximately 6 million Jews during World War II. The Nazis also persecuted and killed millions of Slavic peoples, Gypsies (Sinta and Roma), Soviet prisoners of war, communists, and other groups deemed undesirable by the Nazi state. In this horrifying photograph, German soldiers and members of the Reich Labor Service look on as a member of a Special Action Unit (*Einsatzgruppe*) executes a Ukrainian Jew who kneels at the edge of a mass grave. (Library of Congress, LC-USZ61-671)

believe that extremist and widely shared anti-Semitism led "ordinary Germans" to become Hitler's "willing executioners." Others argue that heightened peer pressure, the desire to advance in the ranks, and the need to prove one's strength under the most brutalizing wartime violence turned average Germans into reluctant killers. The conditioning of racist Nazi propaganda clearly played a role. Whatever the motivation, numerous Germans were prepared to perpetrate ever-greater crimes, from mistreatment to arrest to mass murder.[6]

## Japanese Empire and the War in the Pacific

The racist war of annihilation in Europe was matched by racially inspired warfare in East Asia. In response to political divisions and economic crisis, a fascist government had taken control of Japan in the 1930s. As in Nazi Germany and fascist Italy, the Japanese system was highly nationalistic and militaristic, and it was deeply committed to imperial expansion. According to Japanese racial theorists, the Asian races were far superior to Westerners. Ultranationalists glorified the warrior virtues of honor and sacrifice, and they proclaimed that racially superior Japan would liberate East Asia from Western colonialists.

Japan soon acted on its racial-imperial ambitions. In 1931 Japanese armies invaded and occupied Manchuria, a vast territory bordering northeastern China. In 1937 Japan

How did Stalin and his followers build a totalitarian state? | What kind of government did Mussolini establish in Italy? | How and why did Nazi policies lead to World War II? | **What explains the Allied victory in World War II?**

**859**

# INDIVIDUALS IN SOCIETY

## Primo Levi

**MOST JEWS DEPORTED TO AUSCHWITZ WERE** murdered as soon as they arrived, but the Nazis made some prisoners into slave laborers, and a few of them survived. Primo Levi (1919–1987), an Italian Jew who was one of these laborers, lived to became one of the most influential witnesses to the Holocaust and its death camps.

Like much of Italy's small Jewish community, Levi's family belonged to the urban professional classes. Primo graduated from the University of Turin with highest honors in chemistry in 1941. But starting in 1938, when Italy introduced racial laws, he had faced growing discrimination, and in 1943 he joined the antifascist resistance movement. Quickly captured, he was deported to Auschwitz with 650 Italian Jews in February 1944. Stone-faced SS men picked only ninety-six men, Levi among them, and twenty-nine women from this transport to work in their respective labor camps; the rest were gassed upon arrival.

Levi and his fellow Jewish prisoners were kicked, punched, stripped, branded with tattoos, crammed into huts, and worked unmercifully. Hoping for some sign of prisoner solidarity in this terrible environment, Levi found only a desperate struggle of each against all and enormous status differences among prisoners. Many stunned and bewildered newcomers, beaten and demoralized by their bosses — the most privileged prisoners — simply collapsed and died. Others struggled to secure their own privileges, however small, because food rations and working conditions were so abominable that ordinary Jewish prisoners perished in two to three months.

Sensitive and noncombative, Levi found himself sinking into oblivion. But instead of joining the mass of the "drowned," he became one of the "saved" — a complicated surprise with moral implications that he would ponder all his life. As Levi explained in *Survival in Auschwitz* (1947), the usual road to salvation in the camps was some kind of collaboration with German power. Savage German criminals were released from prison to become brutal camp guards; non-Jewish political prisoners competed for jobs entitling them to better conditions, and, especially troubling for Levi, a small number of Jewish men plotted and struggled for the power of life and death over other Jewish prisoners.

Though not one of these Jewish bosses, Levi believed that he himself, like almost all survivors, had entered the "gray zone" of moral compromise. "Nobody can know for how long and under what trials his soul can resist before yielding or breaking," Levi wrote. "The harsher the oppression, the more widespread among the oppressed is the willingness, with all its infinite nuances and motivations, to collaborate."* According to Levi, there were no saints in the concentration camps: the Nazi system degraded its victims, forcing them to commit sometimes bestial acts against their fellow prisoners in order to survive.

For Levi, compromise and salvation came from his profession. Interviewed by a German technocrat for work in the camp's synthetic rubber program, Levi spoke fluent German, including scientific terminology, and so was chosen for this relatively easy labor. Work in the warm camp laboratory offered Levi opportunities to pilfer equipment that could then be traded to other prisoners for food and necessities. Levi also gained critical support from three prisoners who refused to do wicked and hateful acts. And he counted "luck" as essential for his survival: in the camp infirmary with scarlet fever in February 1945 as advancing Russian armies prepared to liberate the camp, Levi was not evacuated by the Nazis and shot to death like most Jewish prisoners.

After the war Primo Levi was haunted by the nightmare that the Holocaust would be ignored or forgotten. Ashamed that so many people whom he considered better than himself had perished, and wanting the world to understand the genocide in all its complexity so that never again would people tolerate such atrocities, he turned to writing about his experiences. He grappled tirelessly with his vision of individual choice and moral ambiguity in a hell designed to make the victims collaborate and persecute each other. Bearing witness to the Holocaust, Levi wrote and lectured tirelessly to preserve the memory of Jewish victims and guilty Nazis.

## QUESTIONS FOR ANALYSIS

1. Describe Levi's experience at Auschwitz. How did camp prisoners treat each other? Why?
2. What does Levi mean by the "gray zone"?
3. Will a vivid historical memory of the Holocaust help to prevent future genocide?

*Primo Levi, *The Drowned and the Saved* (New York: Vintage, 1989), pp. 43, 60. See also Levi, *Survival in Auschwitz: The Nazi Assault on Humanity*, rev. ed. 1958 (London: Collier Books, 1961). These powerful testimonies are highly recommended.

invaded China itself. In 1940 the Japanese entered into a formal alliance with Italy and Germany, and in summer 1941 Japanese armies occupied southern portions of the French colony of Indochina (now Vietnam and Cambodia).

The goal was to establish what the Japanese called the Greater East Asia Co-Prosperity Sphere. Under the slogan "Asia for Asians," propagandists maintained that Japanese expansion was intended to liberate East Asian people from the hated Western colonialists. By promising to create a mutually advantageous union for long-term development, the Japanese tapped local currents of nationalist sentiment. But the Co-Prosperity Sphere was a sham. Real power remained in the hands of Japanese military commanders and their superiors in Tokyo, and the occupiers exploited local peoples for Japan's wartime needs. In addition, the Japanese often exhibited great cruelty toward civilian populations and prisoners of war, which aroused local populations against the invaders.

Japanese expansion in the Pacific evoked a sharp response from the U.S. administration under President Roosevelt, and Japan's leaders came to believe that war with the United States was inevitable. They decided to launch a surprise attack on the U.S. fleet in Pearl Harbor in the Hawaiian Islands. On December 7, 1941, the Japanese sank or crippled every American battleship, but by chance all the American aircraft carriers were at sea and escaped unharmed. Pearl Harbor brought the Americans into the war in Europe and Asia.

As the Americans mobilized for war, Japanese armies overran more European and American colonies in Southeast Asia. By May 1942 Japan controlled a vast empire (Map 28.4) and was threatening Australia. The Americans pushed back and engaged the Japanese in a series of hard-fought naval battles. In July 1943 the Americans and their Australian allies opened a successful island-hopping campaign that slowly forced Japan out of its conquered territories.

## The "Hinge of Fate"

While the Nazis and the Japanese built their empires, Great Britain, the United States, and the Soviet Union joined together in a military pact Churchill termed the Grand Alliance. This was a matter of chance more than choice. Only the Japanese surprise attack had brought the United States into the war. Moreover, the British and Americans were determined opponents of Soviet communism, and disagreements between the Soviets and the capitalist powers sowed mutual distrust. Stalin repeatedly urged Britain and the United States to open a second front to relieve pressure on Soviet forces by attacking the Germans in western Europe, but Churchill and Roosevelt refused until the summer of 1944. Despite such tensions, the overriding goal of defeating the Axis powers brought together these reluctant allies.

To ease tensions, the Grand Alliance agreed on a policy of "Europe first." Only after Hitler was defeated would the Allies mount an all-out attack on Japan. The Allies also agreed to concentrate on immediate military needs, postponing political questions about the eventual peace settlement that might have divided them. To further encourage mutual trust, the Allies adopted the principle of the unconditional surrender of Germany and Japan. This policy cemented the Grand Alliance because it denied Hitler any hope of dividing his foes.

The military resources of the Grand Alliance were awesome. The United States harnessed its vast industrial base to wage global war and in 1943 outproduced the rest of the world combined. After a determined push, the Soviet Union's military strength was so great that it might well have defeated Germany without Western help.

The combined might of the Allies forced back the Nazi New Order on all fronts (see Map 28.2). In North Africa, fighting between British and Axis forces had resulted in significant German advances. At the Battle of El Alamein (el al-uh-MAYN) in May 1942, British forces decisively defeated combined German and Italian armies and halted the

How did Stalin and his followers build a totalitarian state?

What kind of government did Mussolini establish in Italy?

How and why did Nazi policies lead to World War II?

What explains the Allied victory in World War II?

861

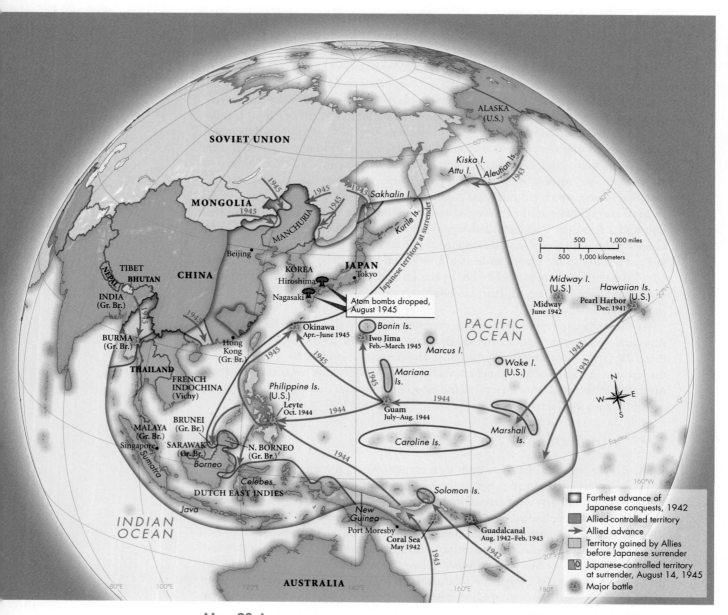

**Map 28.4 World War II in the Pacific** In 1942 Japanese forces overran an enormous amount of territory, which the Allies slowly recaptured in a long, bitter struggle. As this map shows, Japan still held a large Asian empire in August 1945 when the unprecedented devastation of atomic warfare suddenly forced it to surrender.

Axis penetration of North Africa. Winston Churchill later called the battle the "hinge of fate" that cemented Allied victory. Shortly thereafter, an Anglo-American force took control of Morocco and Algeria.

After driving the Axis power out of North Africa, in spring 1943 U.S. and British forces invaded Sicily and then mainland Italy. Mussolini was overthrown by a coup d'état, and the new Italian government accepted unconditional surrender. In response, Nazi armies invaded and seized control of northern and central Italy, and German paratroopers rescued Mussolini in a daring raid and put him at the head of a puppet government. Facing stiff German resistance, the Allies battled their way up the Italian peninsula.

Chapter 28
**Dictatorships and the Second**
**862** World War • 1919–1945

CHAPTER LOCATOR

What characteristics
did totalitarian
dictatorships share?

The spring of 1943 brought crucial Allied victories at sea and in the air. In the first years of the war, German submarines had successfully attacked North Atlantic shipping, severely hampering the British war effort. New antisubmarine technologies favored the Allies. Soon massive convoys of hundreds of ships were crossing the Atlantic, bringing much-needed troops and supplies from the United States to Britain.

The German air force had never really recovered from its defeat in the Battle of Britain. With almost unchallenged air superiority, the United States and Britain now mounted massive bombing raids on German cities. By the war's end, hardly a German city of any size remained untouched, and many lay in ruins.

The German forces suffered even worse defeats at the hands of the Red Army on the eastern front. Although the Germans had almost captured Moscow and Leningrad in early winter 1941, they were forced back by determined Soviet counterattacks. The Germans mounted a second and initially successful invasion of the Soviet Union in the summer of 1942, but the campaign turned into a disaster. The downfall came at the Battle of Stalingrad, when in November 1942 the Soviets surrounded and systematically destroyed the entire German Sixth Army. In summer 1943 the larger, better-equipped Soviet armies took the offensive and began to push the Germans back along the entire eastern front (see Map 28.2).

## Allied Victory

The balance of power was now clearly in Allied hands, yet bitter fighting continued in Europe for almost two years. Germany stepped up its efforts. The German war industry, under the Nazi minister of armaments Albert Speer, put to work millions of prisoners of war and slave laborers from across occupied Europe. Between early 1942 and July 1944, German war production tripled despite heavy Anglo-American bombing.

German resistance against Hitler also failed to halt the fighting. An unsuccessful attempt by conservative army leaders to assassinate Hitler in July 1944 only brought increased repression. Closely disciplined by the regime, frightened by the prospect of unconditional surrender, and terrorized by Nazi propaganda that portrayed the advancing Russian armies as Slavic beasts, the Germans fought on.

On June 6, 1944, American and British forces under General Dwight Eisenhower landed on the beaches of Normandy, France, in history's greatest naval invasion. More than 2 million men and almost half a million vehicles pushed inland and broke through the German lines. In March 1945 American troops crossed the Rhine and entered Germany. By spring of 1945 the Allies had also pushed the Germans out of the Italian peninsula. That April, Mussolini was captured in northern Italy by antifascist communist partisans and executed.

The Soviets, who had been advancing steadily since July 1943, reached the outskirts of Warsaw by August 1944. Over the next six months, the Soviets moved southward into Romania, Hungary, and Yugoslavia. In January 1945 the Red Army crossed Poland into Germany, and on April 26 met American forces on the Elbe River. As Soviet forces fought their way into Berlin, Hitler committed suicide in his bunker, and on May 8 the remaining German commanders capitulated.

The war in the Pacific also drew to a close. In spite of repeated U.S. victories, Japanese troops had continued to fight with enormous courage and determination. American commanders believed the conquest of Japan might cost a million American casualties and claim 10 to 20 million Japanese lives. In fact, Japan was almost helpless, its industry and cities largely destroyed by intense American bombing. Yet the Japanese seemed determined to fight on, ready to die for a hopeless cause.

On August 6 and 9, 1945, after much discussion at the upper levels of the U.S. government, American planes dropped atomic bombs on Hiroshima and Nagasaki in Japan.

How did Stalin and his followers build a totalitarian state?

What kind of government did Mussolini establish in Italy?

How and why did Nazi policies lead to World War II?

What explains the Allied victory in World War II?

863

**Nuclear Wasteland at Hiroshima** Only a handful of buildings remain standing in the ruins of Hiroshima in September 1945. Fearing the costs of a prolonged ground and naval campaign against the Japanese mainland, the U.S. high command dropped atomic bombs on Hiroshima and Nagasaki in August 1945. The bombings ended the war and opened the nuclear age. (AP Images)

The mass bombing of cities and civilians, one of the terrible new practices of World War II, now ended in the final nightmare—unprecedented human destruction in a single blinding flash. On August 14, 1945, the Japanese announced their surrender. The Second World War, which had claimed the lives of more than 50 million soldiers and civilians, was over.

Chapter 28
**Dictatorships and the Second**
**864**    **World War • 1919–1945**

CHAPTER LOCATOR    What characteristics
did totalitarian
dictatorships share?

THE FIRST HALF OF THE TWENTIETH CENTURY brought almost unimaginable violence and destruction. Shaken by the rapid cultural change and economic collapse that followed the tragedy of World War I, many Europeans embraced the radical politics of communism and fascism. For some, visions of a classless society or a racially pure national community offered a way out of the age of anxiety. Totalitarian dictators like Stalin and Hitler capitalized on the desire for social order, building dictatorial regimes that demanded total allegiance to an ideological vision. Even as these regimes rewarded supporters and promised ordinary people a new age, they ruthlessly repressed their enemies, real and imagined. The vision proved fatal: the great clash of ideologies that emerged in the 1920s and 1930s led to history's most deadly war, killing millions and devastating large swathes of Europe and East Asia.

Only the reluctant Grand Alliance of the liberal United States and Great Britain with the communist Soviet Union was able to defeat the Axis powers. After 1945, fascism was finished, discredited by total defeat and the postwar revelation of the Holocaust. To make sure, the Allies would occupy the lands of their former enemies. Rebuilding a devastated Europe proved a challenging but in the end manageable task: once recovery took off, the postwar decades brought an economic boom that led to levels of prosperity unimaginable in the interwar years. Maintaining an alliance between the capitalist West and the communist East was something else. Trust quickly broke down. Europe was divided into two hostile camps, and Cold War tensions between East and West would dominate European and world politics for the next fifty years. ■

- **For a list of suggested readings for this chapter, visit** *bedfordstmartins.com/mckaywestunderstanding*.

- **For primary sources from this period, see** *Sources of Western Society*, Second Edition.

- **For Web sites, images, and documents related to topics in this chapter, see Make History at** *bedfordstmartins.com/mckaywestunderstanding*.

How did Stalin and his followers build a totalitarian state?

What kind of government did Mussolini establish in Italy?

How and why did Nazi policies lead to World War II?

What explains the Allied victory in World War II?

## Step 1

**GETTING STARTED** Below are basic terms about this period in the history of Western civilization. Can you identify each term below and explain why it matters? To do this exercise online, go to bedfordstmartins.com/mckaywestunderstanding.

| TERMS | WHO (OR WHAT) AND WHEN | WHY IT MATTERS |
|---|---|---|
| totalitarianism, p. 834 | | |
| fascism, p. 835 | | |
| eugenics, p. 835 | | |
| five-year plan, p. 837 | | |
| New Economic Policy (NEP), p. 837 | | |
| collectivization of agriculture, p. 838 | | |
| kulaks, p. 838 | | |
| Black Shirts, p. 844 | | |
| Lateran Agreement, p. 845 | | |
| National Socialism, p. 846 | | |
| Enabling Act, p. 849 | | |
| appeasement, p. 852 | | |
| New Order, p. 855 | | |
| Holocaust, p. 857 | | |

## Step 2

**MOVING BEYOND THE BASICS** The exercise below requires a more advanced understanding of the chapter material. Examine the totalitarian regimes of the 1920s and 1930s by describing the ideologies and policies of the Soviet Union, Italy, and Germany. When you are finished, consider the following questions: How did ideology shape the policies of each government? What were the most important similarities and differences among these governments? To do this exercise online, go to bedfordstmartins.com/mckaywestunderstanding.

| | IDEOLOGY | SOCIAL POLICY | ECONOMIC POLICY | FOREIGN POLICY |
|---|---|---|---|---|
| The Soviet Union | | | | |
| Italy | | | | |
| Germany | | | | |

## AUTHORITARIAN STATES

- Compare and contrast totalitarian states with traditional conservative authoritarian regimes. How did totalitarian governments differ from their authoritarian predecessors?

- Compare and contrast Stalinism and Nazism. What were the most important differences between the two ideologies? How did both systems use the persecution of "outsiders" to promote loyalty and obedience to the regime?

## STALIN'S SOVIET UNION

- What hardships did Soviet citizens experience under Stalinism? Given these hardships, why were so many ordinary citizens enthusiastic about Stalinism?

- What role did violence, and the threat of violence, play in Stalin's rule? Could Stalin's economic and social policies have been implemented without a high degree of coercion? Why or why not?

## HITLER AND MUSSOLINI

- Compare and contrast the role of nationalism in Hitler's and Mussolini's ideologies. How did each use nationalism to gain support? How did their beliefs about the basis of national unity differ?

- Compare and contrast the efforts of Hitler and Stalin to gain the support of their respective populations. In this context, what did the two regimes have in common?

## THE SECOND WORLD WAR

- What role did race play in the German and Japanese drive for territorial expansion? Is it fair to describe World War II, in Europe and in the Pacific, as a racial war?

- In your opinion, why did the Allies win the war? What role did industrial production play in the Allied victory? What other factors were important?

■ **In Your Own Words** Imagine that you must explain Chapter 28 to someone who hasn't read it. What would be the most important points to include and why?

# 29

# Cold War Conflict and Consensus

## 1945–1965

In the immediate postwar years, Europeans struggled to overcome the effects of rampant death and destruction, and the victorious Allies worked to shape an effective peace treaty. Disagreements between the Soviet Union and the Western allies emerged during the peace process and quickly led to an apparently endless Cold War between the two new superpowers—the United States and the Soviet Union. Europe was divided into a Soviet-aligned Eastern bloc and a U.S.-aligned Western bloc, and Cold War rivalry spurred military, economic, and technological competition. Amid these overarching tensions, battered western Europe fashioned a great renaissance, building strong democratic institutions and vibrant economies. After a period of political repression, the Soviet Union and the East Bloc also saw some reforms, leading to stability there as well.

But the postwar period was by no means peaceful. Anti-Soviet uprisings across eastern Europe led to military intervention and tragedy for thousands. Colonial independence movements in the developing world sometimes erupted in violence, even after liberation was achieved. Cold War hostilities had an immense impact on the decolonization process, often to the detriment of formerly colonized peoples.

Global Cold War conflicts notwithstanding, the postwar decades witnessed the construction of a surprisingly durable consensus in both communist eastern Europe and liberal western Europe. At the same time, changing class structures, new roles for women and youths, and new migration patterns had a profound impact on European society, laying the groundwork for major transformations in the decades to come. ■

**Life in Eastern Europe.** This relief sculpture, a revealing example of socialist realism from 1952 that portrays a mail carrier, industrial workers, and peasants, adorns the wall of the central post office in Banská Bystrica, a regional capital in present-day Slovakia (the former Czechoslovakia). Citizens in the Soviet satellite nations of the East Bloc frequently saw similar works of public art, which idealized the dignity of ordinary laborers and the advantages of communism. (Georgios Makkas/Alamy)

# Chapter Preview

▶ Why was World War II followed so quickly by the Cold War?

▶ What explains postwar economic growth in western Europe?

▶ How did the Soviet Union dominate eastern Europe?

▶ What led to decolonization in the years after World War II?

▶ What kinds of societies emerged in Europe after 1945?

# ▼ Why was World War II followed so quickly by the Cold War?

In 1945 the Allies faced the momentous challenges of rebuilding the shattered European nations, dealing with Nazi criminals, and creating a lasting peace. Reconstruction began, and war crimes were punished, but the Allies failed to truly cooperate in peacemaking. By the end of 1947 Europe was rigidly divided into East and West Blocs allied with the Soviet Union and the United States, respectively. The resulting Cold War was waged around the world for the next forty years.

## The Legacies of the Second World War

In the summer of 1945 Europe lay in ruins. Across the continent, the fighting had destroyed cities and landscapes. Buildings, factories, farms, rail tracks, roads, and bridges had been obliterated. The human costs of the Second World War are almost incalculable (Map 29.1). The best estimates are that about 50 million human beings perished in the conflict.

The destruction of war furthermore left tens of millions homeless—25 million in the Soviet Union and 20 million in Germany alone, joined by countless French, Czechs, Poles, Italians, and others. The wartime policies of Hitler and Stalin had forced some 30 million people from their homes in the hardest hit nations of east-central Europe. The end of the war and the start of peace increased their numbers. Some 13 million

**Displaced Persons in the Ruins of Berlin** The end of the war in 1945 stopped the fighting, but not the suffering. For the next two years, millions of displaced persons wandered the streets of Europe searching for sustenance, lost family members, and a place to call home. (Fred Rampage/Getty Images)

Chapter 29
**Cold War Conflict and Consensus**
870    1945–1965

CHAPTER LOCATOR    Why was World War II
followed so quickly by
the Cold War?

ethnic Germans fled west before the advancing Soviet troops or were forced to leave the states of eastern Europe under the terms of the peace accords. Forced laborers from Poland, France, the Balkans, and other nations, brought to Germany by the Nazis, now sought to go home.

These **displaced persons** or DPs—their numbers increased by concentration camp survivors, released prisoners of war, and hundreds of thousands of orphaned children—searched for food and shelter. From 1945 to 1947 the newly established United Nations Relief and Rehabilitation Administration (UNRRA) opened over 760 DP camps and spent $10 billion to house, feed, clothe, and repatriate the refugees.

For DPs, going home was not always the best option. Soviet and eastern European nationals who had spent time in the West were seen as politically unreliable and were persecuted by the new Stalinist regimes of the Soviet bloc. Jewish DPs faced unique problems. Their communities had been destroyed, there was persistent anti-Semitism, and for the most part they were not welcome in their former homelands. After the creation of Israel in 1948 (see page 890), over 330,000 European Jews left the continent where they had experienced so much suffering and destruction for the new Jewish state. By 1957, when the last DP camp closed, the UNRRA had cared for and resettled many millions of refugees under the most difficult conditions.

Postwar authorities were also left to deal with the crimes committed by the Nazis. Across Europe and particularly in the east, almost 100,000 Germans and Austrians were convicted of wartime crimes. In Germany, Allied occupation governments set up denazification procedures meant to identify former Nazi Party members and punish those responsible for the worst crimes of the National Socialist state. At the Nuremberg trials (1945–1946), an international military tribunal organized by the four Allied powers—the Soviet Union, the United States, Britain, and France—tried and sentenced the highest-ranking Nazi military and civilian leaders who had survived the war. The twenty-two defendants were charged with war crimes and crimes against humanity. After testimony from victims of the regime, which revealed the full systematic horror of Nazi atrocities, twelve were sentenced to death.

The Nuremberg trials marked the last time the four Allies worked together to punish former Nazis. As the Cold War developed and as the Soviets and the Western allies drew increasingly apart, each carried out separate denazification programs in its own zone of occupation. In the west, U.S. military courts at first actively prosecuted leading Nazis. But the huge numbers implicated in Nazi crimes, West German opposition to the proceedings, and the need for stability in the looming Cold War made thorough denazification impractical. Except for the worst offenders, the West had quietly shelved denazification by 1948. The process was similar in the Soviet zone. At first, punishment was swift and harsh. As in the west, however, former Nazis who cooperated with the new regime could avoid prosecution, and many soon found leading positions in government and industry in both the Soviet and U.S. zones.

In the years immediately after the war, ordinary people across Europe came to terms with the war and slowly regained normal lives. Still, the revelation of Nazi barbarism, the destruction of so many lives, and the great disruptions of the postwar years had deeply

## Chapter Chronology

| | |
|---|---|
| **1945** | Yalta Conference; end of World War II; Potsdam Conference; Nuremberg trials |
| **1945–1960s** | Decolonization of Asia and Africa |
| **1945–1965** | United States takes lead in Big Science |
| **1947** | Truman Doctrine; Marshall Plan |
| **1948** | Founding of Israel |
| **1948–1949** | Berlin airlift |
| **1949** | Creation of East and West Germany; formation of NATO; establishment of COMECON |
| **1950–1953** | Korean War |
| **1953** | Death of Stalin |
| **1955–1964** | Khrushchev rises to power; de-Stalinization of Soviet Union |
| **1955** | Warsaw Pact founded |
| **1956** | Suez crisis |
| **1957** | Formation of Common Market |
| **1961** | Building of Berlin Wall |
| **1962** | Cuban missile crisis |
| **1964** | Brezhnev replaces Khrushchev as Soviet leader |

**displaced persons** Postwar refugees, including 13 million Germans, former Nazi prisoners and forced laborers, and orphaned children.

## Map 29.1 The Aftermath of World War II in Europe, ca. 1945–1950

By 1945 millions of people displaced by war and territorial changes were on the move. The Soviet Union and Poland took land from Germany, which the Allies partitioned into occupation zones. Those zones subsequently formed the basis of the East and West German states. Austria was detached from Germany, but the Soviets subsequently permitted Austria to reunify as a neutral state.

**ANALYZING THE MAP** Which groups fled west? Who went east? How would you characterize the general direction of most of these movements?

**CONNECTIONS** What does the widespread movement of people at the end of the war suggest about the war? What does it suggest about the ensuing political climate?

To complete this activity online, go to the Online Study Guide at bedfordstmartins.com/mckaywestunderstanding.

shaken European confidence. As German philosopher Theodor Adorno wrote in 1951, "There can be no poetry after Auschwitz." Against this background of postwar ruin, despair, and slow recovery, the victorious Allies struggled to shape a reasonable and lasting peace.

Chapter 29
**Cold War Conflict and Consensus**
872    1945–1965

CHAPTER LOCATOR

Why was World War II
followed so quickly by
the Cold War?

**The Big Three** In 1945 a triumphant Winston Churchill, an ailing Franklin Roosevelt, and a determined Stalin met at Yalta in southern Russia to plan for peace. Cooperation soon gave way to bitter hostility, and the decisions made by these leaders transformed the map of Europe. (Franklin D. Roosevelt Presidential Library)

## The Peace Accords and Cold War Origins

The most powerful allies in the wartime coalition — the Soviet Union and the United States — began to quarrel almost as soon as the unifying threat of Nazi Germany disappeared. The hostility between the Eastern and Western superpowers was the logical outgrowth of military developments, wartime agreements, and long-standing political and ideological differences that stretched back to the Russian Revolution (see Chapter 26).

In the early phases of the Second World War, the Americans and the British made military victory their highest priority. They avoided discussion of Stalin's war aims and the shape of the eventual peace settlement, fearing that hard bargaining on these points would encourage Stalin to consider making a separate peace with Hitler. By late 1943 discussion about the shape of the postwar world could no longer be postponed. The conference that the "Big Three" — Stalin, Roosevelt, and Churchill — held in the Iranian capital of Teheran in November 1943 thus proved of crucial importance in determining subsequent events.

At the Tehran Conference, the Big Three reaffirmed their determination to crush Germany, discussed Poland's postwar borders, and crafted a strategy to win the war. Over Churchill's objections, Roosevelt agreed to Stalin's request that American and British forces open a second front in France. This agreement was part of Roosevelt's general effort to meet Stalin's wartime demands whenever possible, and it had momentous political implications. It meant that the Soviet and the American-British armies would come together in defeated Germany along a north-south line and that only Soviet troops would liberate eastern Europe. Thus the basic shape of postwar Europe was emerging even as the fighting continued.

When the Big Three met again in February 1945 at Yalta on the Black Sea in southern Russia, advancing Soviet armies were within a hundred miles of Berlin. The Red Army had occupied Poland as well as Bulgaria, Romania, Hungary, part of Yugoslavia, and much of Czechoslovakia. The temporarily stalled American-British forces had yet to cross the Rhine into Germany. Moreover, the United States was far from defeating Japan. In short, the Soviet Union's position was strong and America's was weak.

There was little Roosevelt could do but double his bet on Stalin's peaceful intentions. The Allies agreed at the Yalta Conference that each of the victorious powers would occupy a separate zone of Germany, and that the Germans would pay heavy reparations to the Soviet Union. Stalin agreed to declare war on Japan after Germany was defeated. As for Poland, the Big Three agreed that the Soviet Union would permanently incorporate the eastern Polish territories its army had occupied at the start of the war, and that Poland would be compensated with German lands to the west. They also agreed in an ambiguous compromise that eastern European governments were to be freely elected but pro-Russian.

The Yalta compromise over elections in eastern Europe broke down almost immediately. Even before the conference, Bulgaria and Poland were under the control of communists. Elsewhere in eastern Europe, the advancing Soviets formed coalition governments that included Social Democrats and other leftist parties, but reserved key government posts for Moscow-trained communists. At the postwar Potsdam Conference of July 1945, the long-avoided differences over eastern Europe finally surged to the fore. The compromising Roosevelt had died and had been succeeded by the more determined President Harry Truman, who demanded immediate free elections throughout eastern Europe. Stalin refused point-blank. "A freely elected government in any of these East European countries would be anti-Soviet," he admitted simply, "and that we cannot allow."[1]

Stalin was determined to establish a defensive buffer zone of sympathetic states around the Soviet Union and at the same time expand the reach of communism and the Soviet state. Stalin believed that only communists could be truly dependable allies, and that free elections would result in independent and possibly hostile governments on his western border. With Soviet armies in central Europe, there was no way short of war for the United States to control the region's political future. The United States, for its part, wished to maintain liberal democracy and free-market capitalism in western Europe. The Americans quickly showed that they were willing to use their vast political, economic, and military power to maintain predominance in their own sphere of influence.

## West Versus East

The Cold War escalated over the next five years as both sides hardened their positions. In May 1945, as the fighting ended, Truman abruptly cut off all aid to the Soviet Union. In October he declared that the United States would never recognize any government established by force against the free will of its people. In March 1946 former British prime minister Churchill ominously informed an American audience that an "iron curtain" had fallen across the continent, dividing Germany and all of Europe into two antagonistic camps (Map 29.2).

Stalin had indeed consolidated his hold on eastern Europe. Recognizing that communists could not take power in free elections, he purged the last remaining noncommunist elements from the coalition governments set up after the war and established Soviet-style one-party communist dictatorships.

In the west, the large, well-organized Communist Parties of France and Italy returned to what they called the "struggle against capitalist imperialism." They criticized the growing role of the United States in western Europe and challenged their own governments with violent rhetoric and large strikes. At the same time, communist revolutionaries were

CHAPTER LOCATOR | Why was World War II followed so quickly by the Cold War?

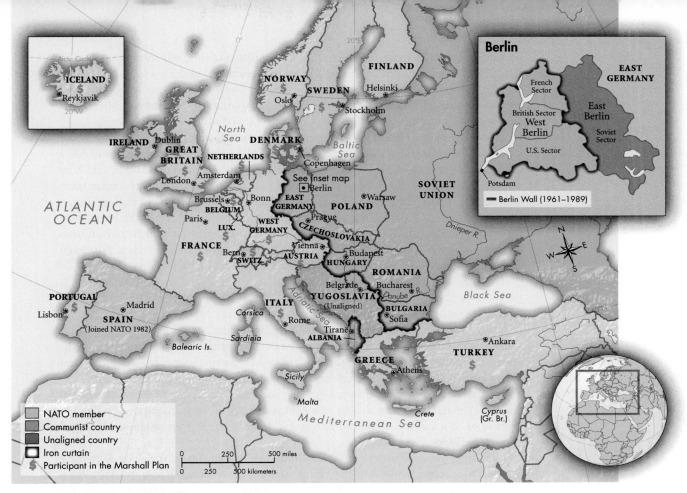

**Map 29.2 Cold War Europe in the 1950s** The Cold War divided Europe into two hostile military alliances that formed to the east and west of an "iron curtain."

waging bitter civil wars in Greece and China (see below and page 890). By the spring of 1947 it appeared to many Americans that Stalin and the Soviet Union were determined to export communism by subversion throughout Europe and around the world.

The United States responded with the Truman Doctrine, aimed at "containing" communism to areas already occupied by the Red Army. The United States, President Truman promised, would resist the expansion of communism anywhere on the globe. At first, Truman asked Congress for military aid to Greece and Turkey. With American support, both remained in the Western bloc. The U.S. government restructured its military to meet the Soviet threat, pouring money into defense spending and testing nuclear weapons. American determination hardened when the Soviets exploded their own atomic bomb in 1949. Emotional, moralistic denunciations of Stalin and communist Russia emerged as part of American public life. At home and abroad, the United States engaged in an anticommunist crusade.

The expansion of the U.S. military was only one aspect of Truman's policy of containment. In 1947 western Europe was still on the verge of economic collapse. Food was scarce across the continent, inflation was high, and black markets flourished. Recognizing that an economically and politically stable western Europe could be an effective block against the popular appeal of communism, U.S. Secretary of State George C. Marshall offered Europe economic aid—the Marshall Plan—to help it rebuild.

The Marshall Plan was one of the most successful foreign aid programs in history. When it ended in 1951, the United States had given about $13 billion in aid (equivalent to over $200 billion in today's dollars) to fifteen western European nations, and Europe's

**Truman Doctrine** America's policy geared to containing communism to those countries already under Soviet control.

**Marshall Plan** American plan for providing economic aid to western Europe to help it rebuild.

What explains postwar economic growth in western Europe?

How did the Soviet Union dominate eastern Europe?

What led to decolonization in the years after World War II?

What kinds of societies emerged in Europe after 1945?

economy was on the way to recovery. Marshall Plan funding was initially offered to East Bloc countries as well, but fearing Western interference in the Soviet sphere, Stalin rejected the offer. In 1949 the Soviets established the Council for Mutual Economic Assistance (COMECON), an economic organization of communist states intended to rebuild the East Bloc independently of the West.

In the late 1940s Berlin, the capital city of Germany, was on the front line of the Cold War. Like the rest of Germany, Berlin had been divided among the victorious Allies into east and west zones. In June 1948 the Western allies replaced the currency in West Germany and West Berlin, a first move in plans to establish a separate West German state. This action violated the peace accords, and in response Stalin blocked all traffic through the Soviet zone of Germany to Berlin in an attempt to reunify the city under Soviet control. Acting firmly, the Western allies coordinated around-the-clock flights of hundreds of planes over the Soviet roadblocks, supplying provisions to West Berliners. After 324 days, the Berlin airlift had proven successful, and the Soviets backed down.

The U.S. success in breaking the Berlin blockade had several lasting results. First, it paved the way for the creation of two separate German states in 1949: the Federal Republic of West Germany, aligned with the United States, and the German Democratic Republic (or East Germany), aligned with the Soviet Union.

The Berlin crisis also seemed to show that containment worked, and thus strengthened U.S. resolve to maintain a military presence in western Europe. In 1949 the United States formed NATO (the North Atlantic Treaty Organization), an anti-Soviet military alliance of Western governments that by 1955 included West Germany. The Soviets countered in 1955 by organizing the Warsaw Pact, a military alliance among the satellite nations of eastern Europe. In both political and military terms, Europe was divided into two hostile blocs.

The superpower confrontation in Europe quickly spread around the globe. When the Soviet-backed communist army of North Korea invaded South Korea in 1950, President Truman swiftly sent U.S. troops. In 1953 a fragile truce was negotiated, and the fighting stopped. In the end the Korean War was indecisive: Korea remained divided between the communist north and the liberal south. The war nonetheless showed that while the superpowers might maintain a fragile peace in Europe, they were willing to engage in open conflict in nonwestern territories (see also page 887).

In the decade after World War II, the Soviet-American confrontation became institutionalized. For the next forty-five years, the superpowers would struggle to win political influence and territorial control, and also to achieve technological superiority. Cold War hostilities directly fostered a nuclear arms race, the U.S. and Soviet space programs, and the computer revolution, all made possible by stunning achievements in science and technology.

## Big Science and New Technologies

With the advent of the Second World War, theoretical science was joined with practical technology (applied science) on a massive scale. Many leading university scientists went to work on top-secret projects to help their governments fight the war. The development by British scientists of radar to detect enemy aircraft was a particularly important outcome of this new kind of research. The air war also greatly stimulated the development of rocketry and jet aircraft, and it spurred further work on electronic computers. The most spectacular result of directed scientific research during the war was the atomic bomb.

The impressive results of directed research during World War II inspired a new research model—Big Science. By combining theoretical work with sophisticated engineering in a large organization, Big Science could tackle extremely difficult problems, from new weapons for the military to better products for consumers. Big Science was extremely expensive, requiring large-scale financing from governments and large corporations.

876

Chapter 29
**Cold War Conflict and Consensus**
1945–1965

CHAPTER LOCATOR | Why was World War II followed so quickly by the Cold War?

Highly specialized modern scientists and technologists typically worked as members of a team in a large bureaucratic organization.

Throughout the Cold War, both the capitalist United States and the socialist Soviet Union provided generous funding for scientific activity. Between 1945 and 1965 government spending on scientific research and development in the United States grew five times as fast as the national income, and by 1965 such spending took 3 percent of all U.S. income. As the Soviet Union recovered, it too devoted heavy subsidies to scientific research.

One reason for the parallel between the two countries was that science was not demobilized in either country after the war. Scientists remained a critical part of every major military establishment, and a large portion of all postwar scientific research supported the growing Cold War arms race. After 1945 roughly one-quarter of all men and women trained in science and engineering in the West—and perhaps more in the Soviet Union—were employed full-time in the production of weapons.

МЫ—МИРНЫЕ ЛЮДИ,

НО НАШ БРОНЕПОЕЗД СТОИТ НА ЗАПАСНОМ ПУТИ!

### ▪ PICTURING THE PAST

### A Soviet View of the Arms Race

This propaganda poster from the 1950s reads, "We are a peaceful people, but our armored train stands in ready reserve." The reference to the armored train recalls the Bolshevik use of trains in combat against the White armies during the Russian civil war of the early 1920s. (Sovfoto)

**ANALYZING THE IMAGE** What does the "armored train" of the 1950s look like? How does the artist portray the Soviet people, and how does this supposedly peaceful image express Cold War hostility?

**CONNECTIONS** Why might the Soviet citizens again need protection, and why would the artist reference the Russian civil war? How did the emergence of Big Science contribute to the global confrontation between the superpowers?

To complete this activity online, go to the Online Study Guide at bedfordstmartins.com/mckaywestunderstanding.

Sophisticated science, government spending, and military needs all came together in the space race of the 1960s. In 1957 the Soviets used long-range rockets developed in their nuclear weapons program to put a satellite in orbit. In 1961 they sent the world's first cosmonaut circling the globe. Embarrassed by Soviet triumphs, the United States made an all-out commitment to catch up with the Soviets and landed a crewed spacecraft on the moon in 1969. Four more moon landings followed by 1972.

Advanced nuclear weapons and the space race would have been impossible without the concurrent revolution in computer technology. The search for better weaponry in World War II had boosted the development of sophisticated data-processing machines. The invention of the transistor in 1947 further hastened the spread of computers. From the mid-1950s on, bulky vacuum tubes were increasingly replaced by this small, efficient electronic switching device. By the 1960s sophisticated computers were indispensable tools for a variety of military, commercial, and scientific uses.

Big Science also had more humane and tangible results for ordinary people. During the postwar green revolution, directed research into agriculture greatly increased the world's food supplies. The application of scientific techniques to industrial processes also made consumer goods less expensive and more readily available to larger numbers of people. The transistor, for example, was used in computers but also in portable radios, kitchen appliances, and any number of other electronic consumer products. In sum, epoch-making inventions and new technologies in the East and West Blocs alike created new sources of material well-being and entertainment as well as destruction.

# ▼ What explains postwar economic growth in western Europe?

As the Cold War divided Europe into two blocs, the future appeared bleak. Economic conditions were the worst in generations, and Europe was weak and divided, a battleground for Cold War ambitions. Yet Europe recovered, with the nations of western Europe in the vanguard. In less than a generation, western Europeans constructed democratic political institutions that paved the way for unprecedented economic growth. A true consumer revolution brought improved living standards and a sense of prosperity to ever-larger numbers of people. Western European countries also established the European Economic Community, the first steps toward broad European unity.

## The Search for Political and Social Consensus

After the war, economic conditions in western Europe were terrible. Infrastructure of all kinds barely functioned. Runaway inflation and a thriving black market testified to severe shortages and hardships. In 1948, as Marshall Plan dollars poured in, however, the economies of western Europe began to improve. The outbreak of the Korean War in 1950 further stimulated economic activity, and Europe entered a period of rapid economic progress that lasted into the late 1960s.

There were many reasons for this stunning economic performance. American aid got the process off to a fast start. Moreover, economic growth became a basic objective of all western European governments, who were determined to avoid a return to the dangerous and demoralizing stagnation of the 1930s.

The postwar governments in western Europe thus embraced new political and economic policies that led to a remarkably lasting social consensus. They turned to liberal democracy and generally adopted Keynesian economics (see Chapter 27) in successful attempts to stimulate their economies. In addition, whether they leaned to the left or to

Chapter 29
**Cold War Conflict and Consensus**
878    1945–1965

CHAPTER LOCATOR    | Why was World War II
followed so quickly by
the Cold War?

the right, national leaders applied an imaginative mixture of government planning and free-market capitalism to promote economic growth. They relied on limited regulation of the economy and established generous welfare provisions for both workers and the middle classes.

In politics, a new generation of European politicians emerged to guide national recovery. Across the west, newly formed Christian Democratic parties became important power brokers. Rooted in the Catholic parties of the prewar decades (see Chapters 24 and 28), the Christian Democrats offered voters tired of radical politics a center-right vision of reconciliation and recovery. The socialists and the communists, active in the resistance against Hitler, also increased their power and prestige, especially in France and Italy. They, too, provided fresh leadership and pushed for social change and economic reform.

**Christian Democrats**
Center-right political parties that rose to power in western Europe after the Second World War.

Across much of continental Europe, the Christian Democrats defeated their left-wing competition. In Italy the Christian Democrats won an absolute majority in the parliament in early 1948. In France the Popular Republican Movement, a Christian Democratic party, provided some of the best postwar leaders after General Charles de Gaulle (dih-GOHL) resigned from the office of prime minister in January 1946. West Germans, too, chose a Christian Democratic government that governed West Germany from 1949 until 1966.

As they provided effective leadership for their respective countries, the Christian Democrats drew inspiration from a common Christian and European heritage. They rejected authoritarianism and narrow nationalism; instead they placed their faith in democracy and liberalism. They championed a return to traditional family values and were steadfast cold warriors. Their anticommunist rhetoric was harsh and unrelenting.

Following their U.S. allies, the Christian Democrats advocated free-market economics. They promised voters prosperity and ample consumer goods. At the same time, they instituted welfare measures such as education subsidies, family and housing allowances, public transportation, and public health insurance throughout continental Europe. When necessary, Christian Democratic leaders accepted the need for limited government planning. In France the government established modernization commissions for key industries, and state-controlled banks funneled money into industrial development. In West Germany, the Christian Democrats promoted a "social-market economy" based on a combination of free-market liberalism, some state intervention, and an extensive social welfare network.

By contrast, in Great Britain the social-democratic Labour Party took power after the war and tried to establish a "cradle-to-grave" welfare state. Although the Labour Party suffered defeats throughout much of the 1950s and early 1960s, its Conservative opponents maintained much of the welfare state when they came to power. Many British industries were nationalized, or placed under state control. The British government gave its citizens free medical services and hospital care, retirement pensions, and unemployment benefits, all subsidized by progressive taxation. In eastern and western Europe alike, state-sponsored welfare measures meant that, by the early 1960s, Europeans had more food, better homes, and longer lives than ever before.

Western Europe's political recovery was spectacular in the generation after 1945. By the late 1950s, contemporaries were talking about a widespread "economic miracle." The booming economy complemented political transformation and social reform, creating solid foundations for a new European stability.

## Toward European Unity

The political and social consensus that emerged in the postwar decade was accompanied by the first tentative steps toward a more unified Europe. Christian Democrats were particularly committed to cultural and economic cooperation, and other groups shared their dedication. Many Europeans believed that only a new "European nation" could effectively rebuild the continent and reassert its influence in world affairs.

A number of new financial arrangements and institutions encouraged slow but steady moves toward European unity, as did cooperation with the United States. The Bretton Woods agreement of 1944 had already linked Western currencies to the U.S. dollar and established the International Monetary Fund and the World Bank to facilitate free markets and world trade. Founded in 1948, the Organization for European Economic Cooperation (OEEC) and the Council of Europe both promoted commerce and international cooperation among European nations.

European federalists hoped that the Council of Europe would quickly evolve into a European parliament with sovereign rights, but this did not happen. Britain consistently opposed conceding real political power—sovereignty—to the council. Many continental nationalists and communists agreed with the British. Frustrated in the direct political approach, European federalists turned to economics as a way of working toward genuine unity. In 1950 two French statesmen, the planner Jean Monnet and Foreign Minister Robert Schuman, called for an international organization to control and integrate all European steel and coal production. Christian Democratic governments in West Germany, Italy, Belgium, the Netherlands, and Luxembourg accepted the French idea and founded the European Coal and Steel Community in 1951 (the British refused to join). The immediate economic goal—a single continental steel and coal market without national tariffs or quotas—was rapidly realized. The more far-reaching political goal was to bind the six member nations so closely together economically that war among them would eventually become unthinkable.

In 1957 the six nations of the Coal and Steel Community signed the Treaty of Rome, which created the European Economic Community, generally known as the Common Market. The first goal of the treaty was a gradual reduction of all tariffs among the six in order to create a single market. Other goals included the free movement of capital and labor as well as common economic policies and institutions.

**Common Market** The European Economic Community, created by six western European nations in 1957 as part of a larger search for European unity.

The development of the Common Market fired imaginations and encouraged hopes of rapid progress toward political as well as economic union. In the 1960s, however, these hopes were frustrated by a resurgence of more traditional nationalism. French president Charles de Gaulle, elected to office in 1959, was at heart a romantic nationalist. De Gaulle viewed the United States as the main threat to genuine French (and European) independence. He withdrew all French military forces from NATO, developed France's own nuclear weapons, and vetoed the scheduled advent of majority rule within the Common Market. Thus the 1950s and 1960s established a lasting pattern: Europeans would establish ever-closer economic ties, but the Common Market remained a union of independent sovereign states.

## The Consumer Revolution

In the late 1950s western Europe's rapidly expanding economy led to a rising standard of living and remarkable growth in the number and availability of standardized consumer goods. As the percentage of income spent on necessities such as housing and food declined, near full employment and high wages meant that more Europeans could buy more things than ever before. Eager to rebuild their homes and families, western Europeans embraced the new products of consumer society.

The purchase of consumer goods was greatly facilitated by the increased use of installment purchasing, which allowed people to buy on credit. With the expansion of social security safeguards reducing the need to accumulate savings, ordinary people were increasingly willing to take on debt, and new banks and credit unions offered loans for consumer purchases. Free-market economics and government promotion of the consumer sector were thus quite successful. For example, the European automobile industry

Chapter 29
**Cold War Conflict and Consensus**
**880** 1945–1965

CHAPTER LOCATOR | Why was World War II followed so quickly by the Cold War?

**Life and Leisure in the Consumer Revolution** By the late 1950s a rapidly expanding economy was making more consumer goods available to more people on both sides of the iron curtain, transforming the way people spent their leisure time. British teens listened to the latest rock 'n' roll hits on long-playing record albums. The *Six-Five Special* album pictured here featured recordings from the successful BBC television series of the same name. Consumer goods were not as readily available in the East, and the state controlled what goods were produced. Citizens in Czechoslovakia, for example, tuned into state-controlled television broadcasts on this Czech-made ten-inch tabletop receiver. (television: Martin Hajek/Visual Connection Archive; album: Science Museum/Science & Society Picture Library)

expanded phenomenally. In 1948 there were only 5 million cars in western Europe; by 1965 there were 44 million. Car ownership was democratized and became possible for better-paid workers.

The consumer revolution had powerful ramifications in an era of Cold War competition. Politicians in both the East and the West claimed that their respective systems could best provide citizens with ample consumer goods. (See "Listening to the Past: The Nixon-Khrushchev 'Kitchen Debate,'" page 884.) In the competition over consumption, Western free markets clearly surpassed Eastern planned economies in the production and distribution of inexpensive products. Western leaders championed the arrival of prosperity and promised new forms of social equality based on equal access to consumer goods rather than forced class leveling—as in the East Bloc. The race to provide ordinary people with higher living standards would be a central if often overlooked aspect of the Cold War, as Soviet eastern Europe struggled to catch up to Western standards of prosperity.

## ▼ How did the Soviet Union dominate eastern Europe?

While western Europe surged ahead economically after the Second World War and increased its independent political power as American influence gradually waned, eastern Europe followed a different path. The Soviet Union first tightened its grip on the "liberated" nations of eastern Europe under Stalin and then refused to let go. Postwar recovery in eastern Europe proceeded along Soviet lines, and political and social developments there were strongly influenced by changes in the Soviet Union.

## Postwar Life Under Stalin

The "Great Patriotic War of the Fatherland" had fostered Russian nationalism and a relaxation of dictatorial terror. It also had produced a rare but real unity between Soviet rulers and most Russian people. Even before the war ended, however, Stalin was moving the Soviet Union back toward rigid dictatorship. As early as 1944 the leading members of the Communist Party were given a new slogan: "The war on Fascism ends, the war on capitalism begins."[2] By early 1946 Stalin was arguing that war was inevitable as long as capitalism existed. Stalin's new foreign foe in the West served as an excuse for reestablishing a harsh dictatorship. Rigid ideological indoctrination, attacks on religion, and the absence of civil liberties were soon facts of life for citizens of the Soviet empire. Millions of supposed political enemies were sent to prison, exile, or forced labor camps.

The new satellite states in Soviet-controlled east-central Europe, including Poland, Hungary, Czechoslovakia, Romania, Albania, Bulgaria, and East Germany, were remade on the Soviet model. Though there were significant differences in what was soon known as the East Bloc, developments followed a similar pattern. Popular Communist leaders who had led the resistance against Germany were ousted as Stalin sought to create obedient instruments of domination in eastern Europe. With Soviet backing, national Communist Parties established one-party dictatorships subservient to the Communist Party in Moscow. Dissenters were arrested, imprisoned, and sometimes executed.

Only Josip Broz Tito (1892–1980), the resistance leader and Communist chief of Yugoslavia, was able to proclaim independence and successfully resist Soviet domination. Tito stood up to Stalin in 1948, and because there was no Russian army in Yugoslavia, he got away with it. Yugoslavia became communist but remained outside of the Soviet-dominated East Bloc.

Within the East Bloc, the newly installed communist governments moved quickly to restructure national economies along Soviet lines. First, East Germany, Hungary, and Romania—countries that had fought against Russia in World War II—were forced to pay substantial war reparations to the Soviet Union. At the same time, Communist authorities introduced Soviet-style five-year plans (see Chapter 28) to cope with the enormous task of economic reconstruction. Most industries and businesses across the East Bloc were nationalized (turned over to state ownership). Such efforts created great disruptions in everyday life, even as they laid the groundwork for industrial development later in the decade.

Communist planners gave top priority to heavy industry and the military, and they neglected consumer goods and housing. In addition, East Bloc leaders were suspicious of Western-style consumer culture. Thus, for practical and ideological reasons, the provision of consumer goods clearly lagged in the East Bloc, leading to popular complaints and disillusionment with the constantly deferred promise of socialism.

For ordinary eastern Europeans, everyday life was hard throughout the 1950s. Socialist planned economies often led to production problems and persistent shortages of basic household items. Party leaders encouraged workers to perform almost superhuman labor to "build socialism," often for low pay and under poor conditions. In East Germany, popular discontent with this situation led to open revolt in June 1953. A strike by Berlin construction workers led to nationwide demonstrations that were put down by Soviet troops. Over 350 protesters were killed and thousands jailed; though when the revolt was over, the East German government instituted reforms designed to meet the most pressing demands of the demonstrators.

Chapter 29
**Cold War Conflict and Consensus**
882    1945–1965

CHAPTER LOCATOR | Why was World War II followed so quickly by the Cold War?

May Day in Nowa Huta In 1951 marchers in a Soviet-planned steel town outside of Kraków, Poland, carry posters of (from left to right) Marx, a Polish communist leader, Lenin, and Engels. (Wiktor Pental/visavis.pl)

Communist censors purged culture and art in aggressive campaigns that reimposed rigid anti-Western ideological conformity. The regime required artists and writers to conform to the dictates of socialist realism, which idealized the working classes and the Soviet Union. Artists who strayed from the party line were denounced. In short, the postwar East Bloc resembled the U.S.S.R. in the 1930s, although police terror was less intense (see Chapter 28).

## Reform and De-Stalinization

In 1953 the aging Stalin finally died, and the dictatorship that he had built began to change. Even as Stalin's heirs struggled for power, they realized that reforms were necessary because of the widespread fear and hatred of Stalin's political terrorism. The power of the secret police was curbed, and many forced-labor camps were gradually closed. Change was also necessary to spur economic growth, which had sputtered under Stalin's five-year plans. Moreover, Stalin's belligerent foreign policy had led directly to a strong Western alliance, which isolated the Soviet Union.

The Soviet Communist leadership was badly split on the question of just how much change should be permitted in order to preserve the system. Conservatives wanted to make as few changes as possible. Reformers, who were led by Nikita Khrushchev (1894–1971), argued for major innovations. To strengthen his position and that of his fellow reformers within the party, Khrushchev spoke out against Stalin and his crimes at a closed session of the Twentieth Party Congress in 1956.

The liberalization—or de-Stalinization, as it was called in the West—of the Soviet Union was genuine. Khrushchev's speech was read at Communist Party meetings held throughout the country, and it strengthened the reform movement. The Communist Party maintained its monopoly on political power, but Khrushchev shook up the party,

de-Stalinization The liberalization of the post-Stalin Soviet Union led by reformer Nikita Khrushchev.

# LISTENING TO THE PAST

## The Nixon-Khrushchev "Kitchen Debate"

*During the Cold War, the United States and the Soviet Union waged political battles in Europe and wars of influence in the former colonies. But the two superpowers also sparred over which system — communism or capitalism — provided the best lifestyle for its citizens.*

*In a late 1950s effort to relieve Cold War tensions, the Americans and Soviets allowed one another to set up public displays in each other's territory. The American National Exhibition in Moscow in 1959 included a model U.S. suburban home, complete with modern kitchen appliances, a television and stereo console, and a Cadillac sedan, all meant to demonstrate the superiority of capitalism to local visitors.*

*Against this backdrop, U.S. vice president Richard Nixon and Soviet premier Nikita Khrushchev met and engaged in an impromptu and sometimes ham-fisted argument over the merits of their respective political systems. As this exchange from the famous "kitchen debate" suggests, dishwashers were also on the front lines of the Cold War.*

❝ KHRUSHCHEV: We want to live in peace and friendship with Americans because we are the two most powerful countries and if we live in friendship then other countries will also live in friendship. But if there is a country that is too war-minded we could pull its ears a little and say: Don't you dare; fighting is not allowed now; this is a period of atomic armament; some foolish one could start a war and then even a wise one couldn't finish the war. Therefore, we are governed by this idea in our policy — internal and foreign. How long has America existed? Three hundred years?

NIXON: One hundred and fifty years.

KHRUSHCHEV: One hundred and fifty years? Well then we will say America has been in existence for 150 years and this is the level she has reached. We have existed not quite 42 years and in another seven years we will be on the same level as America. When we catch you up, in passing you by, we will wave to you. Then if you wish we can stop and say: Please follow up. Plainly speaking, if you want capitalism you can live that way. That is your own affair and doesn't concern us. We can still feel sorry for you but since you don't understand us — live as you do understand. . . . [*Wrapping his arms about a Soviet workman.*] Does this man look like a slave laborer? [*Waving at others.*] With men with such spirit how can we lose?

NIXON: [*Pointing to American workmen.*] With men like that we are strong. But these men, Soviet and American, work together well for peace, even as they have worked together in building this exhibition. This is the way it should be. Your remarks are in the tradition of what we have come to expect — sweeping and extemporaneous. Later on we will both have an opportunity to speak and consequently I will not comment on the various points that you raised, except to say this — this color television is one of the most advanced developments in communication that we have. I can only say that if this competi-

tion in which you plan to outstrip us is to do the best for both of our peoples and for peoples everywhere, there must be a free exchange of ideas. After all, you don't know everything.

KHRUSHCHEV: If I don't know everything you don't know anything about communism except fear of it.

NIXON: There are some instances where you may be ahead of us, for example in the development of the thrust of your rockets for the investigation of outer space; there may be some instances in which we are ahead of you — in color television, for instance.

KHRUSHCHEV: No, we are up with you on this, too. We have bested you in one technique and also in the other.

NIXON: You see, you never concede anything.

KHRUSHCHEV: I do not give up.

NIXON: Wait till you see the picture. Let's have far more communication and exchange in this very area that we speak of. We should hear you more on our televisions. You should hear us more on yours.

KHRUSHCHEV: That's a good idea. Let's do it like this. You appear before our people. We will appear before your people. People will see and appreciate this. . . .

NIXON: [*Halting Khrushchev at model kitchen in model house.*] You had a very nice house in your exhibition in New York. My wife and I saw and enjoyed it very much. I want to show you this kitchen. It is like those of our houses in California.

KHRUSHCHEV: [*After Nixon called attention to a built-in panel-controlled washing machine.*] We have such things.

NIXON: This is the newest model. This is the kind which is built in thousands of units for direct installation in the houses. [*He added that Americans were interested in making life easier for their women.*]

[*Mr. Khrushchev remarked that in the Soviet Union, they did not have "the capitalist attitude toward women."*]

NIXON: I think that this attitude toward women is universal. What we want to do is make easier the life of our housewives.

[*Nixon explained that the house could be built for $14,000 and that most veterans had bought houses for between $10,000 and $15,000.*]

NIXON: Let me give you an example you can appreciate. Our steelworkers, as you know, are on strike. But any steelworker could buy this house. They earn $3 an hour. This house costs about $100 a month to buy on a contract running 25 to 30 years.

Chapter 29
**Cold War Conflict and Consensus**
1945–1965

884

CHAPTER LOCATOR | Why was World War II followed so quickly by the Cold War?

**Nixon and Khrushchev discuss the merits of the American way during the famous kitchen debate.** (AP Images)

KHRUSHCHEV: We have steelworkers and we have peasants who also can afford to spend $14,000 for a house. . . .

KHRUSHCHEV: Don't you have a machine that puts food into the mouth and pushes it down? Many things you've shown us are interesting but they are not needed in life. They have no useful purpose. They are merely gadgets. We have a saying, if you have bedbugs you have to catch one and pour boiling water into the ear.

NIXON: We have another saying. This is that the way to kill a fly is to make it drink whisky. But we have a better use for whisky. [*Aside*] I like to have this battle of wits with the Chairman. He knows his business. . . .

KHRUSHCHEV: The Americans have created their own image of the Soviet man and think he is as you want him to be. But he is not as you think. You think the Russian people will be dumbfounded to see these things, but the fact is that newly built Russian houses have all this equipment right now. Moreover, all you have to do to get a house is to be born in the Soviet Union. You are entitled to housing. I was born in the Soviet Union. So I have a right to a house. In America, if you don't have a dollar — you have the right to choose between sleeping in a house or on the pavement. Yet you say that we are slaves of communism. . . .

NIXON: We do not claim to astonish the Russian people. We hope to show our diversity and our right to choose. We do not wish to have decisions made at the top by government officials who say that all homes should be built in the same way. Would it not be better to compete in the relative merits of washing machines than in the strength of rockets. Is this the kind of competition you want?

KHRUSHCHEV: Yes that's the kind of competition we want. But your generals say: "Let's compete in rockets. We are strong and we can beat you." But in this respect we can also show you something.

NIXON: To me you are strong and we are strong. In some ways, you are stronger. In others, we are stronger. We are both strong not only from the standpoint of weapons but from the standpoint of will and spirit. »

**Source:** Transcript of the "Kitchen Debate" at the opening of the American National Exhibition at Sokolniki Park in Moscow, July 24, 1959.

## QUESTIONS FOR ANALYSIS

1. Why do Nixon and Khrushchev spend so much time talking about the lives of workers in the United States and the Soviet Union?
2. Why were consumer goods, such as washing machines and television sets, such important symbols of modernity and progress for both Nixon and Khrushchev?
3. What does the kitchen debate reveal about the different ways in which communist and capitalist leaders viewed women's role in society?

brought in new members, and became Soviet premier in 1957. Under his reformist leadership, resources were shifted from heavy industry and the military toward consumer goods and agriculture. Stalinist controls over workers were relaxed. The Soviet Union's low standard of living finally began to improve and continued to rise substantially throughout the 1960s.

Khrushchev was proud of Soviet achievements and liked to boast that East Bloc living standards and access to consumer goods would soon surpass the West. (See "Listening to the Past: The Nixon-Khrushchev 'Kitchen Debate,'" page 884.) Socialist citizens in fact experienced a limited consumer revolution. Their options were more modest than those in the West, but eastern Europeans purchased automobiles, televisions, and other consumer goods in ever-increasing numbers in the 1960s.

## Foreign Policy and Domestic Rebellion

Khrushchev also de-Stalinized Soviet foreign policy. "Peaceful coexistence" with capitalism was possible, he argued, and great wars were not inevitable. Khrushchev even made concessions, agreeing in 1955 to real independence for a neutral Austria after ten long years of Allied occupation. Thus there was considerable relaxation of Cold War tensions between 1955 and 1957. At the same time, Khrushchev began wooing the new nations of Asia and Africa with promises and aid.

In the eastern European satellites, de-Stalinization stimulated rebelliousness. Poland took the lead in 1956, when extensive rioting brought a new government to power. The new first secretary of the Polish Communist Party argued that there were "many roads to socialism" and managed to win greater autonomy from Soviet control. The new leadership maintained Communist control even as it tolerated a free peasantry and an independent Catholic Church.

Hungary experienced a real and tragic revolution the same year. Led by students and workers, the people of Budapest installed Imre Nagy, a liberal communist reformer, as their new prime minister in October 1956. Nagy forced Soviet troops to leave the country, but the victory was short-lived. After the new government promised free elections and renounced Hungary's military alliance with Moscow, the Russian leaders ordered an invasion and crushed the revolution. Around 2,700 Hungarians died in the revolt. Fighting was bitter until the end, for the Hungarians hoped that the United States would come to their aid. When this did not occur, most people in eastern Europe concluded that their only hope was to strive for small domestic gains while following Russia obediently in foreign affairs.

The outcome of the Hungarian uprising weakened support for Soviet-style communism in western Europe. Across western Europe, tens of thousands of Communist Party members resigned in disgust. At the same time, Western leaders saw that the Soviets would use military force to defend their control over the Communist bloc, and that only open war between East and West had the potential to overturn authoritarian Communist rule. It seemed that Communist domination of east-central Europe was here to stay.

## The Limits of Reform

By late 1962 opposition to Khrushchev's reformist policies had gained momentum in party circles. Khrushchev's Communist colleagues began to see de-Stalinization as a threat to the dictatorial authority of the party. Moreover, Khrushchev's policy toward the West was erratic and ultimately unsuccessful. In 1958, in a failed attempt to close the open border between East and West Berlin, he ordered the Western allies to evacuate the city within six months. In response, the allies reaffirmed their unity in West Berlin, and Khrushchev backed down. Then in 1961 Khrushchev ordered the East Germans to build a wall between East and West Berlin, thereby sealing off West Berlin. The recently elected

Chapter 29
**Cold War Conflict and Consensus**
1945–1965

886

CHAPTER LOCATOR

Why was World War II
followed so quickly by
the Cold War?

U.S. president, John F. Kennedy, insisted publicly that the United States would never abandon Berlin. Hoping that the Berlin Wall would lessen Cold War tensions, Kennedy nonetheless allowed its construction.

Emboldened and seeing a chance to change the balance of military power decisively, Premier Khrushchev next ordered missiles with nuclear warheads installed in Fidel Castro's communist Cuba in 1962. President Kennedy countered with a naval blockade of Cuba. After a tense diplomatic crisis, Khrushchev agreed to remove the Soviet missiles in return for American pledges not to disturb Castro's regime. In a secret agreement, Kennedy also promised to remove U.S. nuclear missiles from Turkey.

Khrushchev's influence, already slipping, declined rapidly after the Cuban missile crisis. In 1964 the reformist premier was displaced in a bloodless coup. Under his successor, Leonid Brezhnev (BREHZH-nehf) (1906–1982), the Soviet Union began a period of stagnation and limited re-Stalinization. Soviet leaders, determined never to suffer Khrushchev's humiliation in the face of American nuclear superiority, also launched a massive arms buildup. Yet Brezhnev and company proceeded cautiously in the mid-1960s and avoided direct confrontation with the United States.

Despite popular protests and changes in leadership, the Soviet Union and its satellite countries had achieved some stability by the late 1950s. Communist regimes addressed dissent and uprisings with an effective combination of military force, political repression, and limited economic reform. Both sides in the Cold War basically accepted the division of Europe into spheres of influence. More violent conflicts now took place in the developing world, where decolonization was opening new paths for Cold War confrontation.

# ▼ What led to decolonization in the years after World War II?

In the postwar era, in one of world history's great turning points, Europe's long-standing overseas expansion was dramatically reversed. The retreat from imperial control—what Europeans called decolonization—remade the world map. Some one hundred new nations in Africa, Asia, and the Middle East joined the global community (Map 29.3).

## Decolonization and the Cold War

The most basic cause of imperial collapse was the rising demand of non-Western peoples for national self-determination, racial equality, and personal dignity. This demand spread from intellectuals to the masses in nearly every colonial territory after the First World War. By 1939 colonial empires had already been shaken, and the Second World War prepared the way for the eventual triumph of independence movements.

European empires had been based on an enormous power differential between the rulers and the ruled, a difference that had greatly declined by 1945. Western Europe was economically devastated and militarily weak immediately after the war. Moreover, the Japanese had driven imperial rulers from large parts of East Asia during the war in the Pacific. In East Asia, European imperialists confronted strong anticolonial nationalist movements that had developed under the Japanese occupation.

To some degree, the Great Powers also regarded their empires very differently after 1945 than before 1914, or even before 1939. Empire had rested on self-confidence and self-righteousness. The horrors of the Second World War destroyed such complacent arrogance and gave opponents of imperialism much greater influence in Europe. Increasing pressure from the United States, which had long presented itself as an enemy of empire, further encouraged Europeans to let go of their former colonies. Economically weakened,

**decolonization** The postwar reversal of Europe's overseas expansion caused by the rising demand of the colonized peoples themselves, the declining power of European nations, and the freedoms promised by U.S. and Soviet ideals.

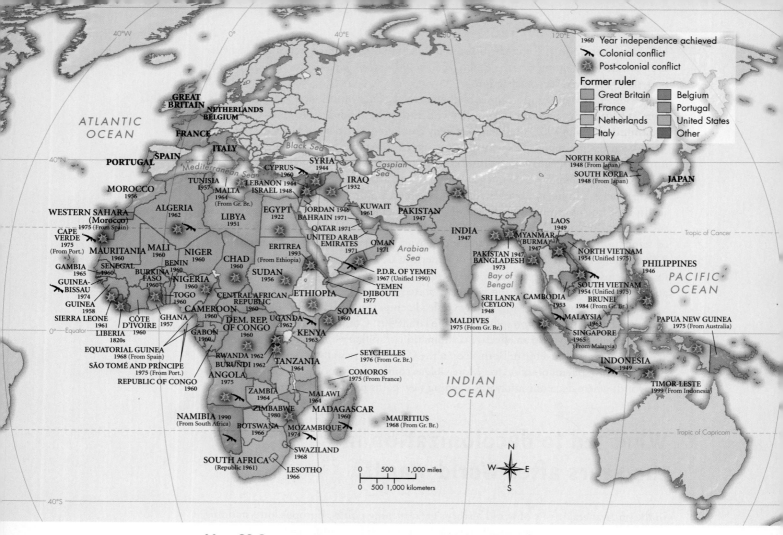

**Map 29.3 Decolonization in Africa and Asia, 1947 to the Present** Divided primarily along religious lines into two states, British India led the way to political independence in 1947. Most African territories achieved statehood by the mid-1960s as European empires passed away, unlamented.

and with their political power and moral authority in tatters, the imperial powers could hardly afford to engage in bloody colonial wars and wanted instead to concentrate on rebuilding at home.

Around the globe, the Cold War had an inescapable impact on decolonization. Liberation from colonial rule had long been a communist goal. The Soviets and Red Chinese advocated rebellion in the developing world and promised native peoples an end to colonial exploitation followed by freedom and equality in a socialist state. They supported communist independence movements with economic and military aid.

Western Europe and particularly the United States offered a competing vision of independence based on free-market economics and liberal democracy. Like the Soviet Union, the United Sates extended aid and arms to decolonizing nations. The Americans promoted cautious moves toward self-determination in the context of containment, attempting to limit the influence of communism in newly liberated states.

After they had won independence, the leaders of the new nations often found themselves trapped between the superpowers, compelled to voice support for one bloc or the other. Many new leaders followed a policy of nonalignment, remaining neutral in the Cold War and playing both sides for what they could get.

**nonalignment** Policy of postcolonial governments to remain neutral in the Cold War and play both the United States and the Soviet Union for what they could get.

Chapter 29
Cold War Conflict and Consensus
1945–1965

888

CHAPTER LOCATOR

Why was World War II
followed so quickly by
the Cold War?

# The Struggle for Power in Asia

The first major fight for independence that followed World War II, between the Dutch and anticolonial insurgents in the Dutch East Indies (today's Indonesia), in many ways exemplified decolonization in the Cold War world. The Dutch had been involved in Indonesia since the early seventeenth century (see Chapter 15), and in the crisis that followed the Second World War they hoped to use Indonesia's raw materials to support economic recovery. During the war, however, the Japanese had overrun the archipelago and encouraged hopes for independence from Western control. When the Dutch returned in 1945, they faced a determined group of rebels inspired by a powerful combination of nationalism, Marxism, and Islam. Four years of guerrilla war followed, and in 1949 the Netherlands reluctantly accepted Indonesian independence. The new Indonesian president became an effective advocate of nonalignment, receiving foreign aid from both the United States and the Soviet Union.

A similar combination of communism and anticolonialism inspired the independence movement in French Indochina (now Vietnam, Cambodia, and Laos). France was determined to re-establish colonial rule after the Japanese occupation collapsed at the end of World War II. Despite substantial American aid, the French army was defeated in 1954 by forces under the guerrilla leader Ho Chi Minh (hoh chee mihn) (1890–1969), who was supported by the Soviet Union and China. Indochina was divided: a shaky truce established the states of North and South Vietnam, which led to civil war and subsequent intervention by the United States.

India played a key role in decolonization. Nationalist opposition to British rule coalesced after the First World War under the leadership of British-educated lawyer Mohandas (Mahatma) Gandhi (1869–1948). In the 1920s and 1930s Gandhi (GAHN-dee) built a

**Gandhi Arrives in Delhi, October 1939** From the 1920s until his death in 1948, the Indian anticolonial leader Mahatma Gandhi led a determined and ultimately successful campaign against British imperialism. His advocacy of nonviolent resistance inspired the Indian masses, nurtured Indian national identity, and left a lasting model for later protest movements. Here Gandhi arrives for negotiations with the British viceroy after the outbreak of World War II. (Corbis)

mass movement preaching nonviolent "noncooperation" with the British. In 1935 Gandhi wrested from the frustrated and unnerved British a new, liberal constitution that was practically a blueprint for independence. The Second World War interrupted progress toward Indian self-rule, but when the Labour Party came to power in Great Britain in 1945, it was ready to relinquish sovereignty. British socialists had always been critical of imperialism, and the heavy cost of governing India had become a large financial burden.

Britain withdrew peacefully, but conflict between India's Hindu and Muslim populations posed a lasting dilemma for the South Asian subcontinent. As independence neared, the Muslim minority grew increasingly anxious about their status in an India dominated by the Hindu majority. Muslim leaders called for partition—the division of India into separate Hindu and Muslim states—and the British agreed. When independence was made official on August 15, 1947, predominantly Muslim territories on India's eastern and western borders became East Pakistan (today Bangladesh) and West Pakistan. A wave of massive migration and violence accompanied the partition of India. Seeking relief from ethnic conflict, some 10 million Muslim and Hindu refugees fled across the new borders, and an estimated five hundred thousand lost their lives in the riots that ensued. Gandhi was assassinated in January 1948 by a radical Hindu nationalist who opposed partition, and Jawaharlal Nehru became India's prime minister.

As the Cold War heated up in the following decade, Pakistan, an Islamic republic, developed close ties with the United States. Under the leadership of Nehru, India successfully established a liberal democratic state and maintained a policy of nonalignment, dealing with both the United States and the Soviet Union. Pakistan and India both joined the British Commonwealth, a voluntary and cooperative association of former British colonies.

If Indian nationalism drew on Western parliamentary liberalism, Chinese nationalism developed and triumphed in the framework of Marxist-Leninist ideology. After the withdrawal of the occupying Japanese army in 1945, China erupted in open civil war between the conservative Guomindang (Kuomintang, National People's Party), led by Jiang Jieshi (traditionally called Chiang Kai-shek; 1887–1975), and the Chinese communists, headed by Mao Zedong (MAOU dzuh-DUNG). Winning the support of the peasantry by promising to expropriate the holdings of the big landowners, the tougher, better-organized communists forced the Guomindang to withdraw to the island of Taiwan in 1949. The Chinese communists expelled foreigners and began building a new society that adapted Marxism to Chinese conditions and brought Stalinist-style repression to the Chinese people. The new government promoted land reform. It also extended education and health care programs to the peasantry, and it introduced five-year plans that successfully boosted industrial production.

## Independence and Conflict in the Middle East

In some areas of the Middle East, the movement toward political independence went relatively smoothly. The French League of Nations mandates in Syria and Lebanon had collapsed during the Second World War, and Saudi Arabia and Transjordan had already achieved independence from Britain. But events in the British mandate of Palestine and in Egypt showed that decolonization in the Middle East could be a dangerous and difficult process.

As part of the peace accords that followed the First World War, the British government had advocated a Jewish home-

**Israel, 1948**

Chapter 29
**Cold War Conflict and Consensus**
1945–1965

890

CHAPTER LOCATOR

Why was World War II
followed so quickly by
the Cold War?

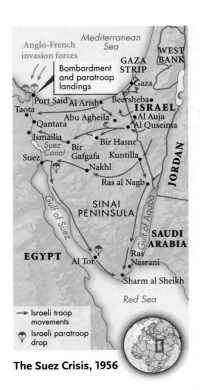

**The Suez Crisis, 1956**

land alongside the Arab population (see Chapter 26). This tenuous compromise unraveled after World War II. Neither Jews nor Arabs were happy with British rule, and violence and terrorism mounted on both sides. In 1947 the British decided to leave Palestine, and the United Nations voted in a nonbinding resolution to divide the territory into two states—one Arab and one Jewish. The Jews accepted the plan and founded the state of Israel in 1948. The Palestinians and the surrounding Arab nations did not, and they attacked the Jewish state as soon as it was proclaimed. The Israelis drove off the invaders and conquered more territory. Roughly nine hundred thousand Arab Palestinians fled or were expelled from their homes, creating a persistent refugee problem. The next fifty years would see four more wars between the Israelis and the Arab states and innumerable clashes between Israelis and Palestinians.

The Arab defeat in 1948 triggered a powerful nationalist revolution in Egypt in 1952, led by Gamal Abdel Nasser (1918–1970). The revolutionaries drove out the pro-Western king, and in 1954 Nasser became president of an independent Egyptian republic. A crafty politician, Nasser advocated nonalignment and expertly played the superpowers against each other.

In July 1956 Nasser abruptly nationalized the foreign-owned Suez Canal Company. Infuriated, the British and the French, along with the Israelis, secretly planned a military invasion. The resulting Suez crisis marked a watershed in the history of European imperialism. The Israeli army invaded the Sinai Peninsula bordering the canal, and British and French bombers attacked Egyptian airfields. World opinion, however, was outraged, and the United States feared that the invasion would propel the Arab states into the Soviet bloc. The Americans joined with the Soviets to force the British, French, and Israelis to back down. The Suez crisis showed that the European powers could no longer maintain their global empires, and it demonstrated the power and appeal of nonalignment.

## The African Awakening

In less than a decade, most African states won independence from European imperialism. In much of the continent south of the Sahara, decolonization proceeded relatively smoothly. Yet the new African states were quickly caught up in the struggles between the Cold War superpowers, and decolonization all too often left a lasting legacy of economic decline and political instability (see Map 29.3).

Starting in 1957 most of Britain's African colonies achieved independence with little or no bloodshed and became members of the British Commonwealth. Ghana, Nigeria, Tanzania, and other nations gained independence in this way, but there were exceptions to this smooth transfer of power. In Kenya in the early 1950s, British forces brutally crushed the Mau Mau rebellion, but nonetheless had to grant Kenyan independence in 1963. In the former British colony of South Africa, white settlers left the Commonwealth in 1961 and declared an independent republic in order to preserve the unequal advantages of apartheid—an exploitative system of racial segregation enforced by law.

The decolonization of the Belgian Congo was one of the great tragedies of the Cold War. Belgian leaders maintained a system of apartheid and dragged their feet in granting independence. These conditions sparked an anticolonial movement that grew increasingly aggressive in the late 1950s under the leadership of Patrice Lumumba. In January 1960 the Belgians gave in, announcing that the Congo would be independent six months later, a schedule that was irresponsibly fast. Lumumba was chosen prime minister in democratic elections, but when the Belgians pulled out on schedule, the new government was entirely unprepared. Chaos broke out when the Congolese army rioted against the Belgian military officers who remained in the country.

With substantial financial investments in the Congo, the United States and western Europe worried that the new nation might fall into Soviet hands. U.S. leaders cast Lumumba as a Soviet proxy, an oversimplification of his nonalignment policies, and American anxiety increased when Lumumba turned to the Soviet Union for aid and protection.

In a troubling example of containment in action, the CIA helped implement a military coup against Lumumba, who was assassinated in captivity in January 1961. The Congolese military set up a U.S.-backed dictatorship under the corrupt general Joseph Mobutu. Mobutu ruled until 1997 and became one of the world's wealthiest men, while the Congo remains one of the poorest and most politically troubled nations in the world.

French colonies in Africa followed several roads to independence. Like the British, the French offered most of their African colonies the choice of a total break with France or independence within a kind of French commonwealth. All but one of the new states chose association with France, largely because they identified with French culture and wanted aid from their former colonizer.

**French Checkpoint in Algeria, 1962** French soldiers search a civilian in Algiers, the capital of Algeria. Inspired by a potent mix of communism and Islamic radicalism, the Algerian National Liberation Front fought a lengthy and bloody struggle against the French colonial government that finally led to Algerian independence in 1962. (Agence France Presse/Hulton Archive/Getty Images)

Things were more difficult in the French colony of Algeria, a large Muslim state on the Mediterranean Sea, where some 500,000 French and Europeans had taken up permanent residency by the 1950s. Nicknamed *pieds noirs* ("black feet" in French), many of these Europeans had raised families in Algeria for three or four generations, and they enforced a two-tiered system of citizenship, maintaining complete control of politics and the economy. When Muslim rebels, inspired by Islamic fundamentalism and communist ideals, established the National Liberation Front (FLN) and revolted against French colonialism in the early 1950s, the presence of the pied noirs complicated matters. Worried about their positions in the colonies, the pied noirs pressured the French government to help them. In response, the French army sent some 400,000 troops to crush the FLN and put down the revolt.

The resulting Algerian war—long, bloody, and dirty, with numerous atrocities on both sides—lasted from 1954 to 1962. The excesses of the French army included systematic torture, the so-called resettlement or forced relocation of the Muslim population, and attacks on civilians who supported the insurgents. News reports turned French public opinion and indeed the government against the war, but efforts to open peace talks instigated a revolt by the Algerian French and threats of a coup d'état by the French army. In 1958 the immensely popular General Charles de Gaulle was reinstated as French prime minister as part of the movement to keep Algeria French, and his appointment calmed the army, the pied noirs, and the French public. Yet de Gaulle pragmatically accepted the principle of Algerian self-determination, and in 1962 he ended

Chapter 29
**Cold War Conflict and Consensus**
**892** 1945–1965

CHAPTER LOCATOR    Why was World War II followed so quickly by the Cold War?

the conflict. After more than a century of French rule, Algeria became independent, and its European population quickly fled to France.

By the mid-1960s most African states had won independence. The colonial legacy, however, had long-term negative effects. African leaders may have expressed support for socialist or democratic principles in order to win aid from the superpowers. In practice, however, corrupt and authoritarian African leaders like Mobutu in the Congo often established lasting authoritarian dictatorships and enriched themselves at the expense of their populations.

Even after decolonization, western European countries managed to increase their economic and cultural ties with their former African colonies in the 1960s and 1970s. Above all, they used the lure of special trading privileges and provided heavy investment in French- and English-language education to enhance a powerful Western presence in the new African states. This situation led a variety of critics to charge that western Europe (and the United States) had imposed a system of neocolonialism on the former colonies. According to this view, neocolonialism was a system designed to perpetuate Western economic domination and undermine the promise of political independence. The system was clearly better than open political domination, but, according to critics, it still worked to the former colony's disadvantage.

## ▼ What kinds of societies emerged in Europe after 1945?

While Europe staged its astonishing political and economic recovery, the basic structures of Western society were changing no less rapidly and remarkably. New forms of European migration, a changing class structure, and new roles for women and youths had dramatic impacts on everyday life in postwar Europe.

### Changing Class Structures

Rapid economic growth went a long way toward creating a new society in Europe after the Second World War. European society became more mobile. Old class barriers relaxed, and class distinctions became fuzzier.

Changes in the structure of the middle class were particularly influential in the general drift toward a less rigid class structure. In the nineteenth and early twentieth centuries, the model for the middle class had been the independent, self-employed individual who owned a business or practiced a liberal profession such as law or medicine. Ownership of property—very often inherited property—and strong family ties had often been the keys to wealth and standing within the middle class. After 1945 this pattern declined drastically in western Europe. A new breed of managers and experts—so-called white-collar workers—replaced traditional property owners as the leaders of the middle class. Ability to serve the needs of a big organization largely replaced inherited property and family connections in determining an individual's social position in the middle and upper-middle classes. At the same time, the middle class grew massively and became harder to define.

There were several reasons for these developments. Rapid industrial and technological expansion created a powerful demand for technologists and managers in large corporations and government agencies. Moreover, the old propertied middle class lost control of many family-owned businesses, and many small businesses simply passed out of existence as their former owners joined the ranks of salaried employees.

# INDIVIDUALS IN SOCIETY

## Armando Rodrigues, West Germany's "One-Millionth Guest Worker"

**POPPING FLASHBULBS GREETED PORTUGUESE** worker Armando Rodrigues when he stepped off a train in Cologne in September 1964. Celebrated in the national media as West Germany's one-millionth guest worker, Rodrigues was met by government and business leaders — including the minister of labor — who presented him with a motorcycle and a bouquet of carnations. A famous photograph of the event shows a modestly dressed Rodrigues mounted on his bike and surrounded by clapping dignitaries.

In most respects, Rodrigues was hardly different from the many foreign workers recruited to work in West Germany and other northern European countries. Yet given his moment of fame, he is an apt symbol of a troubled labor program that helped turn Germany into a multiethnic society.

By the late 1950s the new Federal Republic desperately needed able-bodied men to fill the low-paying jobs created by rapid economic expansion. West Germany had signed its first bilateral labor agreement with Italy in 1955, and treaties with other Mediterranean countries and Turkey soon followed.

Rodrigues and hundreds of thousands of other young men signed up for the employment program and then submitted to an arduous application process. Rodrigues traveled from his village to the regional Federal Labor Office, where he filled out forms and took written and medical exams. Months later, after he had received an initial one-year contract from a German employer, Rodrigues and twelve hundred other Portuguese and Spanish men boarded a special train reserved for foreign workers and embarked for the Federal Republic.

For labor migrants, life was hard in West Germany. In the first years of the guest worker program, most recruits were young men between the ages of twenty and forty who were either single or willing to leave their families at home. They typically filled low-level jobs in construction, mines, and factories, and lived in segregated barracks close to their workplaces, with six to eight workers in a room.

According to official plans, the so-called guest workers were supposed to return home after a specified period of time. Rodrigues went back to Portugal in the late 1970s, but despite government pressure, millions of temporary "guests" raised families and became permanent West German residents, building substantial ethnic minorities in the Federal Republic. Because of strict naturalization laws, however, they could not become West German citizens.

West Germans gave Rodrigues and his fellow migrants a mixed reception. Though they were a welcome source of inexpensive labor, the men who emigrated from what West Germans called "the southern lands" faced discrimination and prejudice. "Order, cleanliness, and punctuality seem like the natural qualities of a respectable person to us," wrote one official in 1966. "In the south, one does not learn or know this, so it is difficult [for a person from the south] to adjust here."*

Despite such hostility, foreign workers established a lasting and powerful presence in West Germany, and they were a significant factor in the country's swift economic recovery. Over time, West Germans came to terms with the tensions surrounding cultural integration and ethnic pluralism. Some forty-five years after Rodrigues arrived in Cologne, his motorcycle is on permanent display in the House of History Museum in Bonn. The exhibit is a remarkable testament both to the contribution of migrant labor to West German economic growth and to the benefits of multiculturalism in a democratic German society.

### QUESTIONS FOR ANALYSIS

1. How did Rodrigues's welcome at his 1964 reception differ from the general attitude toward guest workers in Germany at the time?
2. What were the long-term costs and benefits of West Germany's labor recruitment policies?

*Quoted in Rita Chin, *The Guest Worker Question in Postwar Germany* (New York: Cambridge University Press, 2007), p. 43.

**Armando Rodrigues received a standing ovation and a motorcycle when he got off the train in Cologne in 1964.** (DPA/Landov)

Chapter 29
Cold War Conflict and Consensus
1945–1965

894

CHAPTER LOCATOR | Why was World War II followed so quickly by the Cold War?

Similar processes were at work in the communist states of the East Bloc, where class leveling was an avowed goal of the authoritarian socialist state. The forced nationalization of industry, the expropriation of property, and aggressive attempts to open employment opportunities to workers and equalize wage structures effectively reduced class differences.

In both East and West, managers and civil servants represented the model for a new middle class of salaried specialists. Well-paid and highly trained, often with backgrounds in engineering or accounting, these pragmatic experts were primarily concerned with efficiency and with practical solutions to concrete problems.

The structure of the lower classes also became more flexible and open. There was a mass exodus from farms and the countryside. Meanwhile, the number of industrial workers in western Europe also began to decline, as new jobs for white-collar and service employees grew rapidly. This change marked a significant transition in the world of labor. In general, European workers were better educated and more specialized than before, and the new workforce bore a greater resemblance to the growing middle class of salaried specialists than to traditional industrial workers. The welfare benefits extended by postwar governments also worked to promote greater social equality by raising lower-class living standards and by being paid for in part by higher taxes on the wealthy.

## Patterns of Postwar Migration

Changing patterns of migration also had a significant impact on European society. From the 1850s to the 1930s, countless European immigrants had left the continent for colonies or foreign states (see Chapter 25). In the 1950s and 1960s the trend reversed. Europeans now saw an influx of migrants into their lands.

Some migration took place within national borders. Declining job prospects in Europe's rural areas encouraged many peasants and small farmers to seek better prospects in the cities. In the poorer nations in southern Europe such as Spain, Portugal, and Italy, millions moved to more developed regions of their own countries. The process was similar in the Soviet bloc, where the forced collectivization of agriculture and state subsidies for heavy industry opened opportunities in urban areas.

Many other Europeans moved across national borders seeking work. The general pattern was from south to north. Workers from less developed countries like Italy, Spain, and socialist Yugoslavia moved to the industrialized nations of the north, and particularly to Germany, which had lost 5 million people during the Second World War and was in desperate need of workers. In the 1950s and 1960s West Germany and other prosperous countries implemented a series of guest worker programs that were designed to recruit much-needed labor for the booming economy. By the early 1970s there were 2.8 million foreign workers in Germany and 2.3 million in France, where they made up 11 percent of the French workforce.

**guest worker programs** Government-run programs in western Europe designed to recruit labor for the booming postwar economy.

Most guest workers were young, unskilled single men who labored for low wages in entry-level jobs and sent much of their pay to their families at home. (See "Individuals in Society: Armando Rodrigues, West Germany's 'One-Millionth Guest Worker,'" opposite.) According to government plans, guest workers were supposed to return to their home countries after a specified period. In time, however, they built new lives and many chose to live permanently in their adoptive countries.

Europe was also changed by postcolonial migration, the movement of people from the former colonies (see pages 887–893) and the developing world into the prosperous states of Europe. In contrast to guest workers, who migrated as a result of formal recruitment programs, postcolonial migrants, who could often claim citizenship rights from their former colonizers, moved spontaneously to the former imperial powers. Immigrants from the Caribbean, India, Africa, and Asia moved to Britain; North Africans and especially Algerians moved to France; and Indonesians from the former Dutch East Indies migrated

**postcolonial migration** The postwar movement of people from former colonies and the developing world into Europe.

The *Empire Windrush* Docks in London  On June 22, 1948, almost five hundred Jamaicans seeking to immigrate to Great Britain arrived in London on the former troopship *Empire Windrush*. The event symbolized the changing patterns of postwar migration that would bring cultural and ethnic diversity to western Europe. (Keystone/Getty Images)

to the Netherlands. Postcolonial migrants also moved to eastern Europe, though in fewer numbers.

These new migration patterns had dramatic results. Immigrant labor fueled economic recovery. Growing ethnic diversity changed the face of Europe and enriched the cultural life of the continent. The new residents were not always welcome, however. Adaptation to European lifestyles could be difficult, and migrants often held on to their own languages and lived in separate communities. They often faced employment as well as housing discrimination, and they were targeted by the anti-immigration policies of xenophobic politicians. Some Europeans worried that Muslim migrants from North Africa and Turkey would fail to adapt to European values and customs. In the twenty-first century Europeans continue to deal with the challenges of a multicultural society.

## New Roles for Women

The postwar culmination of a one-hundred-year-long trend toward early marriage, early childbearing, and small family size in wealthy urban societies (see Chapter 23) had revolutionary implications for women. Above all, pregnancy and child care occupied a much smaller portion of a woman's life than in earlier times. The postwar baby boom did make for larger families and fairly rapid population growth, but the long-term decline in birth-

Chapter 29
**Cold War Conflict and Consensus**
896     1945–1965

CHAPTER LOCATOR

Why was World War II
followed so quickly by
the Cold War?

rates resumed by the 1960s. By the early 1970s about half of Western women were having their last baby by the age of twenty-six or twenty-seven.

This was a momentous transition. Throughout history male-dominated society insisted on defining most women as mothers or potential mothers, and motherhood was very demanding. In the postwar years, however, motherhood no longer absorbed the energies of a lifetime, and more and more married women looked for new roles in the world of work outside the family.

Women's roles in the workforce also changed after World War II. The ever-greater complexity of the modern economy meant that many women had to go outside the home to find cash income. Three major forces helped women searching for jobs. First, the economy boomed from about 1950 to 1973 and created strong demand for labor. Second, the economy continued its gradual shift away from the old male-dominated heavy industries, to the more dynamic white-collar service industries in which some women had always worked, such as government, education, trade, and health care. Third, young Western women shared fully in the postwar education revolution (see page 898) and could take advantage of the growing need for office workers and well-trained professionals. Thus more and more married women became full-time and part-time wage earners.

In eastern Europe, women accounted for almost half of all employed persons, and many women made their way into previously male professions, such as medicine and engineering. In western Europe and North America, there was a good deal of variation, with the percentage of married women in the workforce rising from a range of roughly 20 to 25 percent in 1950 to a range of 30 to 60 percent in the 1970s.

All was not easy for women entering paid employment. Married women entering (or re-entering) the labor force faced widespread and long-established discrimination in pay, advancement, and occupational choice in comparison to men. Moreover, many women could find only part-time work with low pay and scanty benefits. Finally, married working women still carried most of the child-rearing and housekeeping responsibilities. Trying to live up to society's seemingly contradictory ideals was one reason for many women to accept part-time employment; women working full-time typically faced an exhausting "double day"—on the job and at home.

The injustices that married women encountered as wage earners contributed greatly to the subsequent movement for women's equality and emancipation. When in the 1960s a powerful feminist movement arose in the United States and western Europe to challenge the system, it found widespread support among working women.

## Youth Culture and the Generation Gap

Postwar Europe also witnessed remarkable changes in youth roles and lifestyles, as the bulging cohort of so-called baby boomers born after World War II created a distinctive and very international youth culture. In the 1950s young people across western Europe and the United States created unique subcultures rooted in fashion and musical taste that set them off from their elders and fueled anxiety about a growing "generation gap."

Youth styles in the United States often provided inspiration for movements in Europe. Groups like the British Teddy Boys, the West German *Halbstarken* (half-strongs), and the French *blousons noirs* (black jackets) modeled their rebellious clothing and cynical attitudes on the bad-boy characters played by U.S. film stars such as James Dean and Marlon Brando. American jazz and rock 'n' roll spread rapidly in western Europe, aided by the invention of the long-playing record album (or LP) and the 45 rpm "single" in the late 1940s, and the growth of the corporate music industry.

Youths played a key role in the consumer revolution. Postwar prosperity gave young people more purchasing power than ever before. Marketing experts and manufacturers quickly recognized that the young people they now called "teenagers" had money to spend.

**British Teddy Boys, 1953** These young men are dressed in the "Teddy boy" style with velvet collars, narrow ties, and peg trousers that combine British Edwardian and American fashion. Like other subcultures in the 1950s, the Teds used their appearance to express their youthful rebelliousness. Teddy Boys quickly earned a reputation for street fighting, low-level criminal activity, and attacks on Britain's growing West Indian community. (© Henry Grant Collection/Museum of London)

An array of advertisements and products now consciously targeted the youth market. As the baby boomers entered their late teens, they eagerly purchased trendy clothing and the latest pop music hits, as well as record players, transistor radios, magazines, hairstyles, and makeup, all marketed for the "young generation."

The new youth culture became an inescapable part of European society. One clear sign of this new presence was the rapid growth in the number of universities—and college students. In contrast to the United States, university education in Europe had been limited for centuries to a small elite. In 1950 only 3 to 4 percent of western European youths went on to higher education. Then, as government subsidies made education more affordable to the masses, enrollments skyrocketed. By 1960 at least three times more students attended some kind of university than had before World War II, and the number continued to rise sharply until the 1970s.

The rapid expansion of higher education opened new opportunities for the middle and lower classes, but it also meant that classrooms were badly overcrowded. Many students felt that they were not getting the kind of education they needed for jobs in the modern world. At the same time, some students feared that universities would soon do nothing but turn out docile technocrats both to stock and to serve "the establishment." Thus it was no coincidence that students became leaders in a counterculture that attacked the ideals of the affluent society and shocked the West in the late 1960s.

CHAPTER LOCATOR    Why was World War II followed so quickly by the Cold War?

THE UNPRECEDENTED HUMAN AND PHYSICAL destruction of the Second World War left Europeans shaken, searching in the ruins for new livelihoods and a workable political order. A tension-filled peace settlement left the continent divided into two hostile political-military blocs, and the resulting Cold War, complete with the possibility of atomic annihilation, threatened to explode into open confrontation. Albert Einstein voiced a common anxiety when he said, "I do not know with what weapons World War III will be fought, but World War IV will be fought with sticks and stones."

Despite such fears, the division of Europe led to the emergence of a remarkably enduring world system. In the West, liberal democracy and the Western alliance brought social and political consensus. In the East, a combination of political repression and partial reform likewise limited dissent and encouraged stability. During the height of the Cold War, Europe's former colonies won liberation in a process that was often flawed, but that nonetheless resulted in political independence for millions of people. And large-scale transformations, including the rise of Big Science and rapid economic growth, opened new opportunities for women and immigrants and contributed to stability on both sides of the iron curtain.

By the early 1960s Europeans had entered a remarkable age of affluence that almost eliminated real poverty on most of the continent. Superpower confrontations had led not to European war but to peaceful coexistence. The following decades, however, would see substantial challenges to this postwar consensus. Youth revolts and a determined feminist movement, an oil crisis and a deep economic recession, and political dissent and revolution in the socialist bloc would shake and remake the foundations of Western society. ■

- **For a list of suggested readings for this chapter, visit** *bedfordstmartins.com/mckaywestunderstanding*.

- **For primary sources from this period, see** *Sources of Western Society*, Second Edition.

- **For Web sites, images, and documents related to topics in this chapter, see Make History at** *bedfordstmartins.com/mckaywestunderstanding*.

What explains postwar economic growth in western Europe?

How did the Soviet Union dominate eastern Europe?

What led to decolonization in the years after World War II?

What kinds of societies emerged in Europe after 1945?

# ▪ Chapter 29 Study Guide

## Step 1

**GETTING STARTED** Below are basic terms about this period in the history of Western civilization. Can you identify each term below and explain why it matters? To do this exercise online, go to bedfordstmartins.com/mckaywestunderstanding.

| TERMS | WHO (OR WHAT) AND WHEN | WHY IT MATTERS |
|---|---|---|
| displaced persons, p. 871 | | |
| Truman Doctrine, p. 875 | | |
| Marshall Plan, p. 875 | | |
| Council for Mutual Economic Assistance (COMECON), p. 876 | | |
| NATO, p. 876 | | |
| Warsaw Pact, p. 876 | | |
| Christian Democrats, p. 879 | | |
| Common Market, p. 880 | | |
| de-Stalinization, p. 883 | | |
| decolonization, p. 887 | | |
| nonalignment, p. 888 | | |
| guest worker programs, p. 895 | | |
| postcolonial migration, p. 895 | | |

## Step 2

**MOVING BEYOND THE BASICS** The exercise below requires a more advanced understanding of the chapter material. Compare and contrast eastern and western Europe in the postwar period by describing the key social, economic, and political developments in the decades following World War II. When you are finished, consider the following questions: In what ways did eastern and western Europe diverge in the decades following World War II? In what ways did the two regions remain connected? To do this exercise online, go to bedfordstmartins.com/mckaywestunderstanding.

| | SOCIETY | ECONOMY | POLITICS |
|---|---|---|---|
| Eastern Europe | | | |
| Western Europe | | | |

**Step 3**

**PUTTING IT ALL TOGETHER** Now that you've reviewed key elements of the chapter, take a step back and try to see the big picture. Remember to use specific examples from the chapter in your answers. To do this exercise online, go to bedfordstmartins.com/mckaywestunderstanding.

### POSTWAR EUROPE AND THE ORIGINS OF THE COLD WAR

- Why did cooperation between the Western Allies and the Soviet Union break down so quickly once World War II was over? Was the Cold War inevitable? Why or why not?

- How did developments in science and technology reflect the priorities of the Cold War? In what ways does the legacy of the Cold War continue to shape science and technology today?

### ECONOMIC AND POLITICAL DEVELOPMENTS

- Compare and contrast pre– and post–World War II Western Europe. How did the experience of the 1930s and World War II contribute to the drive toward European unity?

- What steps did the Soviet Union take to consolidate its hold on eastern Europe in the decades following World War II? How did eastern Europeans respond to their new circumstances?

### THE END OF EMPIRES

- What forces contributed to postwar decolonization? How did decolonization reflect Europe's altered position in the world?

- How did the Cold War shape decolonization? How did newly independent peoples try to use the Cold War to their advantage?

### POSTWAR SOCIAL TRANSFORMATIONS

- How did the class structure of western and eastern Europe change after World War II? What role did government play in social change on both sides of the iron curtain?

- Compare and contrast the place of women and youths in European society before and after World War II. What changes do you note? How would you explain them?

■ **In Your Own Words** Imagine that you must explain Chapter 29 to someone who hasn't read it. What would be the most important points to include and why?

# 30

# Challenging the Postwar Order

## 1960–1991

As Europe entered the 1960s, the consensus established in the postwar era appeared stable and secure. Centrist politicians in western Europe agreed that abundant jobs and extensive state spending on welfare benefits would continue to improve living standards at all levels of society. In the Soviet Union and the East Bloc, although conditions varied country by country, modest economic growth and limited reforms amid continued political repression likewise contributed to a sense of stability. Cold War tensions relaxed, and it seemed that a remarkable age of affluence would ease political differences and lead to social harmony.

In the late 1960s, however, this hard won consensus began to unravel. In 1968 counterculture protesters across the globe challenged dominant certainties. In the early 1970s the astonishing postwar economic advance ground to a halt, with serious social consequences. In western Europe, a new generation of more conservative political leaders drastically cut welfare benefits to deal with economic decline and growing global competition. New political groups—including feminists and environmentalists, national separatists and new-right populists—criticized centrist politics from across the political spectrum.

In the East Bloc, postwar leaders continued to vacillate between reform and repression, leading to frustrating stagnation. In the 1980s a broad movement to transform the communist system took root in Poland, and efforts to reform and revitalize the communist system in the Soviet Union snowballed out of control. In 1989 revolutions swept away communist rule throughout the entire Soviet bloc as the Cold War reached a dramatic conclusion.  ■

**Life in a Divided Europe.** Watchtowers, armed guards, and min̶e̶.̶.̶.̶ ̶.̶.̶.̶ed the communist eastern side of the Berlin Wall, the primary symbol of Cold War division in Europe. In the liberal West, to the contrary, ordinary folk turned the easily accessible wall into an ad hoc art gallery — this whimsical graffiti art appeared in the late 1980s. (Saba Laudanna, photographer)

## Chapter Preview

▶ Why did the postwar consensus of the 1950s break down?

▶ What were the consequences of economic decline in the 1970s?

▶ What led to the decline of Soviet power in eastern Europe?

▶ Why did revolution sweep through eastern Europe in 1989?

# ▼ Why did the postwar consensus of the 1950s break down?

Looking at the wealth and prosperity of the early 1960s, commentators asserted that western Europe had entered an age of affluence. Newly elected Social Democratic governments moved to normalize relations with the East Bloc and increased their countries' spending on welfare provisions. In the East, tensions lessened, eased by modest economic growth and forced underground by political repression. On both sides of the iron curtain, it seemed that the stability was here to stay.

Challenges to the postwar consensus emerged in the mid-1960s, first in the form of a student counterculture that confronted the values of mainstream society with radical politics and lifestyle rebellions. Discontent spread to the East Bloc as well, particularly in Czechoslovakia, where in 1968 a rapid push toward liberalization was crushed by Soviet military force.

## Cold War Tensions Thaw

The first decades of postwar reconstruction had been overseen by the center-right Christian Democrats (see Chapter 29). Now, buoyed by the rapidly expanding economy, politics shifted to the left. In Britain, the Labour Party took power in 1964. In the Scandinavian countries of Denmark, Norway, and Sweden, Social Democratic parties maintained a leading role throughout the period. In West Germany, Willy Brandt (1913–1992) became the first Social Democratic West German chancellor in 1969.

**détente** The progressive relaxation of Cold War tensions.

One result of the victory of Social Democrats was the policy of détente (day-TAHNT), the progressive relaxation of Cold War tensions. While the Cold War between the Soviet Union and the United States continued, western Europe took major steps toward genuine peace along the iron curtain. West German chancellor Willy Brandt took the lead. In December 1970 he flew to Poland for the signing of a historic treaty of reconciliation. In a dramatic moment, Brandt laid a wreath at the tomb of the Polish unknown soldier and another at the monument commemorating the armed uprising of Warsaw's Jewish ghetto against occupying Nazi armies. "I wanted," Brandt said later, "to ask pardon in the name of our people for a million-fold crime which was committed in the misused name of the Germans."[1]

**A West German Leader Apologizes for the Holocaust** In 1970 West German chancellor Willy Brandt knelt before the Jewish Heroes' Monument in Warsaw, Poland, to ask forgiveness for the German mass murder of European Jews and other groups during the Second World War. Brandt's action, captured in photo and film by the onlooking press, symbolized the chancellor's policy of Ostpolitik, the normalization of relations between the East and West Blocs. (AP Images)

Brandt's trip to Poland was part of his policy of reconciliation with eastern Europe, termed *Ostpolitik* (German for eastern policy). Brandt aimed at nothing less than a comprehensive peace settlement for central Europe and the two German states established after 1945. In this context, Brandt negotiated treaties with the Soviet Union, Poland, and Czechoslovakia that formally accepted existing state boundaries in return for a mutual renunciation of force or the threat of force. Using the imaginative formula of "two German states within one German nation," Brandt's government also broke decisively with the past and entered into direct relations with East Germany. Brandt aimed for modest practical improvements rather than reunification, which at that point was completely impractical.

The policy of détente reached its high point when the United States, Canada, the Soviet Union, and all European nations (except isolationist Albania and tiny Andorra) signed the Final Act of the Helsinki Conference in 1975. The thirty-five participating nations agreed that Europe's existing political frontiers could not be changed by force. They also accepted numerous provisions guaranteeing the human rights and political freedoms of their citizens. Although the East continued to curtail certain domestic freedoms and violate human rights guarantees (see pages 921–922), the agreement was generally effective in maintaining international peace.

(see pages 921–922)

## Chapter Chronology

| | |
|---|---|
| 1961 | Building of Berlin Wall suggests permanence of the East Bloc |
| 1962–1965 | Second Vatican Council |
| 1963 | Friedan, *The Feminine Mystique* |
| 1964–1973 | U.S. involvement in Vietnam War |
| 1966 | Formation of National Organization for Women (NOW) |
| 1968 | Soviet invasion of Czechoslovakia; "May events" protests in France |
| 1973 | OPEC oil embargo |
| 1975 | Final Act of the Helsinki Conference |
| 1979 | Margaret Thatcher becomes British prime minister; founding of West German Green Party; Soviet invasion of Afghanistan |
| 1985 | Mikhail Gorbachev named Soviet premier |
| 1987 | United States and Soviet Union sign arms reduction treaty |
| 1989 | Soviet withdrawal from Afghanistan |
| 1989–1991 | Fall of communism in eastern Europe |
| December 1991 | Dissolution of the Soviet Union |

Newly empowered Social Democrats also engaged in reform at home. Building on the welfare systems established in the 1950s, politicians increased state spending on public services even further. Social Democrats were committed to capitalist free markets. At the same time, however, they viewed welfare provisions as a way to ameliorate the inequalities of a competitive market economy. Despite doctrinal differences, the center-right Christian Democrats also supported spending on public benefits and entitlements—as long as the economy prospered. With the economic slowdown of the mid-1970s, growing inflation and unemployment strained state budgets and undermined support for the welfare state consensus (see pages 913–916).

(see pages 913–916)

## The Affluent Society

The political shift to the left in the 1960s was accompanied by rapid social change across western Europe. High wages meant that more people could afford the products provided by the consumer revolution that began in the 1950s (see Chapter 29), and the arrival of a full-blown consumer society had a profound impact on daily life. Labor-saving devices in family homes—vacuum cleaners, refrigerators, washing machines, and many others—transformed housework.

Europeans at all levels of society had more money to spend on leisure time and recreational pursuits. With month-long paid vacations required by law in most western European countries and with widespread automobile ownership, travel came within the reach of the middle class and much of the working class. At home, more and more Europeans oriented their leisure time around television.

Intellectuals and cultural critics disparaged the new consumer society. Some worried that consumerism created a conformity that wiped out regional and national traditions

CHAPTER LOCATOR | Why did the postwar consensus of the 1950s break down? | What were the consequences of economic decline in the 1970s? | What led to the decline of Soviet power in eastern Europe? | Why did revolution sweep through eastern Europe in 1989?

905

Braniff Airways Hostesses, ca. 1968 Sporting the latest "mod" styles, hostesses for Braniff International Airways wear uniforms made by world-renowned Italian fashion designer Emilio Pucci. The 1960s counterculture helped popularize the use of kaleidoscopic fluorescent colors and wild shapes in fashion, the fine arts, and advertising. (Braniff Archives)

and undermined intellectual activity. The great majority of people, they concluded, now ate the same foods, wore the same clothes, and watched the same programs on television, sapping creativity and individualism. Other critics complained that these changes threatened to Americanize European culture.

Worries about the Americanization of Europe were overstated—European nations preserved distinctive national cultures even during the consumer revolution—but social change was nonetheless unavoidable. The moral authority of religious doctrine lost ground before the growing individualism of consumer society. Even in traditionally Catholic countries, such as Italy, Ireland, and France, outward signs of popular belief seemed to falter. At the Second Vatican Council, convened from 1962 to 1965, Catholic leaders agreed on a number of reforms meant to democratize and renew the church while broadening its appeal. Their resolutions did little to halt the slide toward secularization. In Protestant lands—Great Britain, Scandinavia, the Netherlands, and most of West Germany—the decline in church membership was even greater.

Family ties also weakened, and the number of adults living alone grew remarkably. Men and women married later, the nuclear family became smaller and more mobile, and divorce rates rose rapidly. By the 1970s the baby boom of the postwar decades was over, and population growth leveled out. It even began to decline in northwest Europe.

## The Growing Counterculture Movement

One of the dramatic results of economic prosperity and a more tolerant society was the emergence of a youthful counterculture that came of age in the mid-1960s to challenge the assumptions of the affluent society. What accounts for the emergence of the counterculture in the mid-1960s? Simple demographics played an important role. Young soldiers returning home after World War II in 1945 eagerly established families, and the next two decades brought a dramatic increase in the number of births per year in Europe and the United States. The children born during this baby boom grew up in an era of political liberalism and unprecedented material affluence. Impressed by the U.S. civil rights movement and dismayed by ongoing Western imperialism and war, the baby boomers had the education—and perhaps most importantly the freedom from material want—to act on their concerns about inequality and social justice.

Counterculture movements in both Europe and the United States drew inspiration from the American civil rights movement of the late 1950s and early 1960s. If dedicated African Americans and their white supporters could successfully reform entrenched power structures, student leaders reasoned, so could they. At the University of California–Berkeley in 1964 and 1965, students consciously adapted the tactics of the civil rights movement, including demonstrations and sit-ins, to challenge limits on free speech and academic freedom at the university. Soon students across the United States and in western Europe were engaged in active protests.

Many student activists in western Europe and the United States embraced an updated, romanticized version of Marxism, creating a movement that came to be known as the New Left. Adherents of the New Left argued that Marxism in the Soviet Union had been perverted to serve the needs of a repressive totalitarian state. Western capitalism, with its cold disregard for social equality, was little better. What was needed was a more humanitarian style of socialism that could avoid the worst excesses of both capitalism and Soviet-style communism. New Left critics also attacked what they saw as the conformity of consumer society. The so-called culture industry, they argued, fulfilled only false needs and so contributed to the alienation of Western society.

New Left A movement of students in the West who advocated simpler, purer societies based on an updated, romanticized version of Marxism.

Such ideas fascinated student intellectuals, but much counterculture activity revolved around a lifestyle rebellion that apparently had broader appeal. Politics and lifestyles merged, a process captured in the 1960s slogan "the personal is the political." Nowhere was this more obvious than in the so-called sexual revolution. The 1960s brought frank discussion about sexuality in general, a new willingness to engage in premarital sex, and a growing acceptance of homosexuality. Much of the new openness about sex crossed generational lines, but for the young the idea of sexual emancipation was closely linked to radical politics. Sexual openness and "free love," the sixties generation argued, not only moved people beyond traditional norms, but might also form the foundation of a more humane society.

Along with sexual openness, drug use and rock music were at the center of the lifestyle revolt. For many in the counterculture, drugs were a way to break free from conventional morals. The popular music of the 1960s championed countercultural lifestyles. Rock bands like the Beatles, the Rolling Stones, and many others sang songs about drugs and casual sex. Counterculture "scenes" developed in cities such as San Francisco, Paris, and West Berlin. Carnaby Street, the center of "swinging London" in the 1960s, was famous for its clothing boutiques and record stores, underscoring the close connections between generational revolt and consumer culture.

## The United States and Vietnam

The growth of the counterculture movement was closely linked to the course of the Vietnam War. American involvement in Vietnam was in large measure a product of the Cold War and the policy of containment (see Chapter 29). From the late 1940s on, most Americans and their leaders viewed the world in terms of a struggle to stop the spread of communism. As western Europe began to revive and China established a communist government in 1949, efforts to contain communism shifted to Asia.

After Vietnam won independence from France in 1954, U.S. president Dwight D. Eisenhower (r. 1953–1961) refused to sign the Geneva Accords that temporarily divided the country into two zones—a socialist north and an anticommunist south. When the South Vietnamese government declined to hold elections that would unify the north and south zones, Eisenhower provided the south with military aid. President John F. Kennedy (r. 1961–1963) later increased the number of American "military advisers," and in 1964 President Lyndon B. Johnson (r. 1963–1969) greatly expanded America's role in the Vietnam conflict, providing South Vietnam with massive military aid and a half million American troops.

The undeclared war in Vietnam, fought nightly on American television, eventually divided the nation. Initial support was strong. Most Americans saw the war as part of a legitimate defense against communism. But an antiwar movement quickly emerged on college campuses. In October 1965 student protesters joined forces with old-line socialists, New Left intellectuals, and pacifists in antiwar demonstrations in fifty American cities. The protests spread to western Europe. By 1967 a growing number of critics in the United States and Europe denounced the American presence in Vietnam as a criminal intrusion into a complex and distant civil war.

CHAPTER LOCATOR | Why did the postwar consensus of the 1950s break down? | What were the consequences of economic decline in the 1970s? | What led to the decline of Soviet power in eastern Europe? | Why did revolution sweep through eastern Europe in 1989?

907

Criticism reached a crescendo after the Vietcong Tet Offensive in January 1968. This comprehensive attack on major South Vietnamese cities failed militarily. The Vietcong suffered heavy losses, but the Tet Offensive signaled that the war was not close to ending, as Washington had claimed. America's leaders lost heart, and within months President Johnson announced that he would not stand for reelection and called for negotiations with North Vietnam.

President Richard M. Nixon (r. 1969–1974) sought to gradually disengage America from Vietnam beginning in 1968. Intensifying the continuous bombardment of the enemy while simultaneously pursuing peace talks with the North Vietnamese, Nixon suspended the draft and cut American forces in Vietnam from 550,000 to 24,000 in four years. In 1973 Nixon reached a peace agreement with North Vietnam that allowed remaining American forces to complete their withdrawal, and that gave the United States the right to resume bombing if the accords were broken.

America's disillusionment with the war had far-reaching repercussions. In early 1974, when North Vietnam launched a general invasion against South Vietnamese armies, the U.S. Congress refused to permit any American military response. After more than thirty-five years of battle, the South Vietnamese were forced in 1975 to accept a unified country under a communist dictatorship.

## Student Revolts and 1968

The intensification of the Vietnam War in the late 1960s was accompanied by world-wide opposition. In European and American cities, students and sympathetic followers organized massive demonstrations against the war, and then extended their protests to support colonial independence movements, to demand an end to the nuclear arms race, and to call for world peace and liberation from social conventions of all kinds.

Youth activism erupted in 1968 in a series of protests and riots that circled the globe. One of the most famous and perhaps far-reaching of these revolts occurred in France in May 1968, when angry students and striking workers brought the French economy to a standstill. A group of students inspired by New Left ideals initially occupied buildings and took over the University of Paris. Violent clashes with police followed. When police tried to clear the area around the university on the night of May 10, a pitched street battle took place.

The so-called May events might have been a typically short-lived student protest against American involvement in Vietnam and the abuses of capitalism, but the demonstrations triggered a national revolt. By May 18 some 10 million workers were out on strike, and protesters occupied factories across France. For a brief moment, it seemed as if counterculture dreams of a revolution from below would come to pass. The French

| ■ 1968: Protests Around the World |
| --- |
| **The United States:** African Americans riot after the assassination of civil rights leader Martin Luther King, Jr.; antiwar demonstrators battle police at the Democratic National Convention in Chicago. |
| **Mexico:** Police in Mexico City shoot and kill several hundred protesters calling for political reform. |
| **Japan:** Demonstrations against the war in Vietnam erupt in Tokyo. |
| **Poland:** Students in Warsaw march to protest government censorship. |
| **Czechoslovakia:** Young people in Prague are in the forefront of the attempt to reform communism from within. |
| **Western Europe:** Large-scale youth protests in Paris, Berlin, London, and other cities. |

**Student Rebellion in Paris** These rock-throwing students in the Latin Quarter of Paris are trying to force education reforms and even topple de Gaulle's government. In May 1968, in a famous example of the protest movements that swept the world in the late 1960s, Parisian rioters clashed repeatedly with France's tough riot police in bloody street fighting. De Gaulle remained in power, but a major reform of French education did follow. (Bruno Barbey/Magnum Photos)

Fifth Republic was on the verge of collapse, and a shaken President de Gaulle surrounded Paris with troops.

In the end, however, the idealistic goals of the students did not really correspond to the practical demands of the striking workers. When the government promised workplace reforms, including immediate pay raises, the strikers returned to work. President de Gaulle dissolved the French parliament and called for new elections. His conservative party won almost 75 percent of the seats, showing that the majority of the French people supported neither general strikes nor student-led revolutions. The May events nonetheless marked the high point of counterculture protest in Europe; in the early 1970s the movement declined.

As the political enthusiasm of the counterculture waned, committed activists were divided among themselves about the best way to continue to fight for social change. Some began to work for change from within the system. They entered national politics and joined emerging feminist, antinuclear, and environmental groups that would play an important role in the coming decades (see pages 916–919).

Other groups, however, followed a more radical path. Across Europe, but particularly in Italy and West Germany, fringe New Left groups tried to bring radical change by turning to violence and terrorism. The Italian Red Brigades and the West German Red Army Faction robbed banks, bombed public buildings, and kidnapped and killed politicians and business leaders. After spasms of violence in the late 1970s, security forces succeeded in incarcerating most of the terrorist leaders, and the movement fizzled out.

Counterculture protests generated a great deal of excitement and trained a generation of activists, but New Left ideologies focused on alienation and dehumanization captured in slogans like "Power to the imagination" resulted in little practical political change. Lifestyle rebellions involving sex, drugs, and rock music transformed individual behavior, but they did not lead to revolution.

## The 1960s in the East Bloc

The building of the Berlin Wall in 1961 and the failure of NATO to intervene suggested that communism was here to stay. It also encouraged socialist regimes to experiment with some economic and cultural liberalization. East Bloc economies clearly lagged behind those of the West. To address this problem, socialist leaders now implemented cautious forms of decentralization and limited market policies. The results were mixed. Initiatives in Hungary and East Germany brought some improvement. In other East Bloc countries, however, economic growth flagged.

Recognizing that the emphasis on heavy industry could lead to popular discontent, Communist planning commissions redirected resources to the consumer sector. Again, the results varied across the East Bloc. By 1970, for example, ownership of televisions in East Germany, Czechoslovakia, and Hungary approached that of the West, and other consumer goods were also more available. In Poland, however, the economy stagnated in the 1960s. In Albania and Romania, where leaders held fast to Stalinist practices, provision of consumer goods faltered. In general, ordinary people in the East Bloc grew increasingly tired of the shortage of consumer goods that seemed an endemic part of socialist society.

In the 1960s Communist regimes also granted cautious cultural freedoms. In the Soviet Union, the cultural thaw allowed dissidents to publish critical works of fiction, and this relative tolerance spread to eastern European countries as well. In East Germany, for example, during the Bitterfeld Movement — named after a conference of writers, officials, and workers in Bitterfeld, an industrial city south of Berlin — the regime encouraged intellectuals to take a more critical view of life in the East Bloc, so long as they did not directly oppose communism itself.

Despite some cultural openness, the most outspoken dissidents were harassed and often forced to immigrate to the West, and an underground literature critical of communism emerged in the Soviet Union and the East Bloc. Written and published secretly to avoid regime censors, and then passed hand to hand by dissident readers, such literature emerged in Russia, Poland, and other countries in the mid-1950s and blossomed in the 1960s. These unofficial networks of communication kept critical thought alive and built contacts among dissidents, building the foundation for the protest movements of the 1970s and 1980s.

Modest prosperity and limited cultural tolerance only went so far. The citizens of East Bloc countries sought political liberty as well, and the limits on reform were sharply revealed in Czechoslovakia during the 1968 "Prague spring." In January 1968 reform elements in the Czechoslovak Communist Party gained a majority and voted out the long-time Stalinist leader in favor of Alexander Dubček (1921–1992), whose new government launched dramatic reforms. Dubček (DOOB-chehk) and his allies called for "socialism with

**The East German Trabi** This small East German passenger car, produced between 1963 and 1990, was one of the best-known symbols of everyday life in East Germany. Though the cars were notorious for their poor engineering, the growing number of Trabis on East German streets nonetheless testified to the increased availability of consumer goods in the East Bloc in the 1960s and 1970s. (Visual Connection Archive)

a human face." They relaxed state censorship and replaced rigid bureaucratic planning with local decision making by trade unions, managers, and consumers. The reform program proved enormously popular.

Although Dubček constantly proclaimed his loyalty to the Soviet Union and the Warsaw Pact, the determination of the Czechoslovak reformers to build a more liberal and democratic socialism frightened hard-line Communists. These fears were particularly strong in Poland and East Germany, where leaders knew they lacked popular support. Moreover, the Soviet Union feared that a liberalized Czechoslovakia would eventually be drawn to neutrality or even to the democratic West. Thus the Eastern bloc leadership launched a concerted campaign of intimidation against the Czechoslovak reformers, and five hundred thousand Russian and allied eastern European troops occupied Czechoslovakia in August 1968. The Czechoslovaks made no attempt to resist militarily, and the arrested leaders surrendered to Soviet demands. The reform program was abandoned, and the Czechoslovak experiment in humanizing communism came to an end.

Shortly after the invasion of Czechoslovakia, Soviet premier Leonid Brezhnev (1906–1982) declared the so-called **Brezhnev Doctrine**, according to which the Soviet Union and its allies had the right to intervene in any socialist country whenever they saw the need. The 1968 invasion of Czechoslovakia was the crucial event of the Brezhnev era: it showed that only the threat of the Soviet military was holding the East Bloc together. At the same time, it demonstrated the determination of the ruling elite to maintain the status quo throughout the Soviet bloc.

**Brezhnev Doctrine** Doctrine created by Leonid Brezhnev that held that the Soviet Union had the right to intervene in any socialist country whenever it saw the need.

**The Invasion of Czechoslovakia** Armed with Czechoslovakian flags, courageous Czechs in downtown Prague try to stop a Soviet tank and repel the invasion and occupation of their country by the Soviet Union and its eastern European allies. This dramatic confrontation was ultimately unsuccessful. Realizing that military resistance would be suicidal, the Czechs capitulated to Soviet control. (AP Images)

CHAPTER LOCATOR | Why did the postwar consensus of the 1950s break down?　　What were the consequences of economic decline in the 1970s?　　What led to the decline of Soviet power in eastern Europe?　　Why did revolution sweep through eastern Europe in 1989?

911

# ▼ What were the consequences of economic decline in the 1970s?

The great postwar economic boom came to a close in the early 1970s, opening a long period of economic stagnation, widespread unemployment, and social dislocation. Politics in western Europe shifted to the right. By the end of the 1980s the postwar stability based on economic prosperity, generous welfare provisions, and consensus politics had been deeply shaken, and the West had restructured its economy and entered the information age.

## Economic Crisis and Hardship

Starting in the early 1970s the West entered into a long period of economic decline. One of the early causes of the downturn was the collapse of the international monetary system, which since 1945 had been based on the American dollar. In the postwar decades, the United States spent billions of dollars on foreign aid and foreign wars, weakening the value of American currency. In 1971 President Nixon attempted to reverse this trend by abruptly stopping the exchange of U.S. currency for gold. The value of the dollar fell sharply, and inflation accelerated worldwide. Fixed rates of exchange were abandoned, and uncertainty replaced predictability in international trade and finance.

Even more damaging to the global economy was the dramatic reversal in the price and availability of energy. The great postwar boom had been fueled in part by cheap oil from the Middle East. The fate of the developed world was thus increasingly linked to this turbulent region, and strains began to show in the late 1960s. In 1967, in the Six-Day War between Israel and its Arab neighbors, Israel quickly defeated its adversaries and expanded its territory in the former territories of Palestine, angering Arab leaders. The conflict exacerbated anti-Western feeling in the Arab states. By 1971 OPEC, the Arab-led Organization of Petroleum Exporting Countries, had watched the price of crude oil decline consistently compared with the rising price of Western manufactured goods. OPEC decided to reverse that trend by presenting a united front against Western oil companies.

**OPEC** The Arab-led Organization of Petroleum Exporting Countries.

The stage was set for a revolution in energy prices when Egypt and Syria launched an attack on Israel in October 1973, setting off the fourth Arab-Israeli war. With the help of U.S. military arms, Israel again achieved a quick victory. OPEC then declared an embargo on oil shipments to the United States, Israel's ally, and within a year crude oil prices quadrupled.

Coming on the heels of upheaval in the international monetary system, the revolution in energy prices plunged the world into its worst economic decline since the 1930s. The energy-intensive industries that had driven the economy up in the 1950s and 1960s now dragged it down. Unemployment rose; productivity and living standards declined; inflation soared. By 1976 a modest recovery was in progress, but when a fundamentalist Islamic revolution struck Iran and oil production collapsed in that country in 1979, the price of crude oil doubled, and the world economy was rocked again. Unemployment and inflation rose dramatically before another uneven recovery began in 1982. Economists coined a new term — stagflation — to describe the combination of stagnant growth and high inflation that led to a worldwide recession.

**stagflation** Term coined in the early 1980s to describe the combination of stagnant growth and high inflation that led to a worldwide recession.

Anxious observers worried that the Common Market would disintegrate in the face of severe economic dislocation and that economic nationalism would halt steps toward European unity. Yet the Common Market — now officially known as the European Economic Community — continued to attract new members. In 1973 Denmark and Iceland, in addition to Britain, finally joined. Greece joined in 1981, and Portugal and Spain entered in 1986. The nations of the European Economic Community cooperated more closely in international undertakings, and the movement toward unity for western Europe stayed alive.

The developing world was hit hard by slowed growth, and the global economic downturn widened the gap between rich and poor countries. Governments in the developing world borrowed heavily from the United States and western European bankers in attempts to restructure their economies, setting the stage for a serious international debt crisis. At the same time, the East Asian countries of Japan and then Singapore, South Korea, and Taiwan started exporting high-tech consumer goods to the West. Competition from these East Asian "tiger economies" shifted manufacturing jobs away from the highly industrialized countries of northern Europe.

Even as the world economy slowly began recovering in the 1980s, it could no longer create enough jobs to replace those that were lost. By the end of the 1970s, the foundations of economic growth had begun shifting to high-tech information industries, such as computing and biotechnology, and to services, including medicine, banking, and finance. Scholars spoke of the shift as the arrival of "the information age" or postindustrial society. Technological advances streamlined the production of many goods, making many industrial jobs superfluous. In western Europe, heavy industry, such as steel, mining, automobile manufacture, and shipbuilding, lost ground.

**postindustrial society** Society that relies on high-tech and service-oriented jobs for economic growth rather than on heavy industry and manufacturing jobs.

One telling measure of the troubled economy was the misery index, which combined rates of inflation and unemployment in a single, powerfully emotional number. Misery increased on both sides of the Atlantic, but the increase was substantially greater in western Europe. By 1985 the unemployment rate there had risen to its highest level since the Great Depression. Nineteen million people were without work.

Yet on the whole, the welfare system fashioned in the postwar era prevented mass suffering and degradation. The responsive, socially concerned national state undoubtedly contributed to the preservation of political stability and democracy in the face of economic difficulties that might have brought revolution and dictatorship in earlier times.

The energetic response of governments to support social needs helps explain why total government spending in most European countries continued to rise sharply during the 1970s and early 1980s. In 1982 western European governments spent an average of more than 50 percent of all national income on social programs, as compared to 37 percent fifteen years earlier. In all countries, people were willing to see their governments increase spending, but they resisted higher taxes. This imbalance contributed to the rapid growth of budget deficits, national debts, and inflation. By the late 1970s a powerful reaction against government's ever-increasing role had set in.

## The Conservative Backlash

The transition to a postindustrial society was led by a new generation of conservative political leaders who were willing to make the difficult reforms necessary to restructure the economy, even though this typically led to social dislocation and growing inequality. The new conservatives of the 1980s followed a philosophy that came to be known as neoliberalism because of its distant roots in the laissez-faire policies favored by nineteenth-century liberals such as Adam Smith (see Chapter 18). Neoliberal theorists argued that government should cut support of social services such as housing, education, and health insurance; limit business subsidies; and retreat from regulation of all kinds. Neoliberals also called for privatization — the sale of state-managed industries to private owners. Placing government-owned industries such as transportation and communication networks in private hands, they argued, would both tighten government spending and lead to greater workplace efficiency. The main goal was to increase private profits, which neoliberals believed were the real engine of economic growth.

**neoliberalism** Philosophy of 1980s conservatives who argued for decreased government spending on social services and privatization of state-run industries.

CHAPTER LOCATOR | Why did the postwar consensus of the 1950s break down? | **What were the consequences of economic decline in the 1970s?** | What led to the decline of Soviet power in eastern Europe? | Why did revolution sweep through eastern Europe in 1989?

913

The effects of neoliberal policies are best illustrated by events in Great Britain. The broad shift toward greater conservatism, coupled with growing voter dissatisfaction with high taxes and runaway state budgets, helped elect Margaret Thatcher (b. 1925) prime minister in 1979. A convinced neoliberal, Thatcher was determined to scale back the role of government, and in the 1980s she pushed through a series of controversial free-market policies that transformed postwar Britain. Thatcher's Conservative Party government cut spending on health care, education, and public housing. The Conservatives reduced taxes and privatized or sold off government-run enterprises. In one of the most popular actions, Thatcher encouraged low- and moderate-income renters in state-owned housing projects to buy their apartments at rock-bottom prices. This initiative, part of Thatcher's broader privatization campaign, created a whole new class of property owners, thereby eroding the electoral base of Britain's socialist Labour Party. (See "Individuals in Society: Margaret Thatcher," page 915.)

Though she never eliminated all social programs, Thatcher's policies helped replace the interventionist ethos of the welfare state with a greater reliance on private enterprise and the free market. There were significant human costs involved in this transition. In the first three years of her first term, heavy industries such as steel, coal mining, and textiles shut down, and unemployment rates in Britain doubled to over 12 percent. The gap between rich and poor widened, and increasing poverty led to discontent and crime. Working-class strikes and protests sometimes led to violent riots. By 1990 Thatcher's popularity had fallen to record lows, and she was replaced by Conservative Party leader John Major.

In the United States, two-term president Ronald Reagan (r. 1981–1989) followed a similar path, though his success in cutting government was more limited. With widespread popular support and the agreement of most congressional Democrats as well as Republicans, Reagan in 1981 pushed through major cuts in income taxes. But Reagan and Congress failed to limit government spending, which increased as a percentage of national income in the course of his presidency. A massive military buildup was partly responsible, but spending on social programs also grew rapidly. The harsh recession of the early 1980s required the government to spend more on unemployment benefits, welfare benefits, and medical treatment for the poor. Moreover, Reagan's antiwelfare rhetoric mobilized the liberal opposition and eventually turned many moderates against him. The budget deficit soared, and U.S. government debt tripled in a decade.

West Germany also turned to the right. In 1982 Christian Democrat Helmut Kohl (r. 1982–1998) became chancellor. Like Thatcher, Kohl cut taxes and government spending. His policies led to increasing unemployment in heavy industry but also to solid economic growth. In foreign policy, Kohl drew close to President Reagan. The chancellor agreed to deploy U.S. Pershing II and cruise missiles on West German territory, and so contributed to renewed

**The Social Consequences of Thatcherism** As police watch in the background, picketers outside the largest coal mine in Britain hold up a poster reading "Save the Pits" during the miner's strike of 1984–1985. Prime Minister Margaret Thatcher broke the strike, weakening the power of Britain's trade unions and easing the turn to free-market economic reforms. Thatcher's neoliberal policies revived economic growth but cut state subsidies for welfare benefits and heavy industries, leading to lower living standards for many working-class Britons and, as this image attests, to popular protest. (Bride Lane Library/Pepperfoto/Getty Images)

**MARGARET THATCHER, THE FIRST WOMAN**
elected to lead a major European state, was one of the late twentieth century's most significant leaders. The controversial "iron lady" attacked socialism, promoted capitalism, and changed the face of modern Britain.

Raised in a lower-middle-class family in a small city in southeastern England, Thatcher entered Oxford in 1943 to study chemistry. She soon discovered a passion for politics. Elected president of student Conservatives, she ran for Parliament in 1950 in a solidly Labour district to gain experience. Articulate and attractive, she gained the attention of Denis Thatcher, a wealthy businessman who drove her to campaign appearances in his Jaguar. Married a year later, the new Mrs. Thatcher abandoned chemistry, went to law school, gave birth to twins, and became a tax attorney. In 1959 she returned to politics and won a seat in the Conservative triumph.

For the next fifteen years Thatcher served in Parliament and held various ministerial posts when the Conservatives governed. In 1974, as the economy soured and the Conservatives lost two close elections, a rebellious Margaret Thatcher adroitly ran for the leadership position of the Conservative Party and won. In the 1979 election, as the Labour government faced rampant inflation and crippling strikes, Thatcher promised to reduce union power, lower taxes, and promote free markets. Attracting swing votes from skilled workers, she was elected prime minister.

A self-described "conviction politician," Thatcher rejected postwar Keynesian efforts to manage the economy, arguing that governments had created inflation by printing too much money. Thus her government reduced the supply of money and credit, and it refused to retreat as interest rates and unemployment soared. Her popularity plummeted. But Thatcher maintained her position, in part through an aggressive pursuit of foreign policy. In 1982 the generals ruling Argentina suddenly seized the Falkland Islands off the Argentine coast, the home of 1,800 British citizens. Ever a staunch nationalist, Thatcher detached a naval armada that recaptured the Falklands without a hitch. Britain admired Thatcher's determination and patriotism, and she was reelected in 1983.

Thatcher's second term was the high point of her influence. Her wholehearted commitment to privatization transformed British industry. More than fifty state-owned companies, ranging from the state telephone monopoly to the nationalized steel trust, were sold to private investors. Small investors were offered shares at bargain prices to promote "people's capitalism." Thatcher also curbed the power of British labor unions with various laws and actions. Most spectacularly, when in 1984 the once-mighty coal miners rejected more mine closings and doggedly struck for a year, Thatcher stood firm and beat them. This outcome had a profound psychological

**Margaret Thatcher as prime minister.** (AP Images/Staff-Caulkin)

impact on the public, who blamed her for growing unemployment. Thatcher was also accused of mishandling a series of protest hunger strikes undertaken by the Irish Republican Army — in 1981 ten IRA members starved themselves to death in British prisons — but she held her ground, refusing to compromise with those she labeled criminals. As a result, the revolt in Northern Ireland entered one of its bloodiest phases.

Elected to a third term in 1987, Thatcher became increasingly stubborn, overconfident, and uncaring. Working with her neoliberal ideological soul mate, U.S. president Ronald Reagan, she opposed greater political and economic unity within the European Community. This, coupled with rising inflation, stubborn unemployment, and an unpopular effort to assert financial control over city governments, proved her undoing. In 1990, as in 1974, party stalwarts suddenly revolted and elected a new Conservative leader. The transformational changes of the Thatcher years nonetheless endured, consolidated by her Conservative successor and largely accepted by the New Labour prime minister, the moderate Tony Blair.

## QUESTIONS FOR ANALYSIS

1. Why did Margaret Thatcher want to change Britain, and how did she do it?
2. How do Thatcher's policies reflect the conservative backlash of the 1970s and 1980s?

CHAPTER LOCATOR  | Why did the postwar consensus of the 1950s break down? | What were the consequences of economic decline in the 1970s? | What led to the decline of Soviet power in eastern Europe? | Why did revolution sweep through eastern Europe in 1989?

915

superpower tensions. In power for sixteen years, Kohl and the Christian Democrats presided over the dismantling of the Berlin Wall in 1989, the reunification of East and West Germany in 1990, and the end of the Cold War (see pages 930–932).

The most striking temporary exception to the general drift to the right in European politics was François Mitterrand (r. 1981–1995) of France. After his election as president in 1981, Mitterrand and his Socialist Party led France on a lurch to the left. Working at first in a coalition that included the French Communist Party, Mitterrand launched a vast program of nationalization and public investment designed to spend the country out of economic stagnation. By 1983 this attempt had clearly failed, and Mitterrand's Socialist government made a dramatic about-face. They reprivatized industries and imposed a wide variety of austerity measures.

Despite persistent economic crises and high social costs, by 1990 the developed nations of western Europe and North America were far more productive than they had been in the early 1970s. Western Europe was at the center of the emerging global economy, and its citizens were far richer than those in Soviet bloc countries (see pages 905–906). Yet the collapse of the postwar consensus and the remaking of Europe in the transitional decades of the 1970s and 1980s generated new forms of protest and dissent across the political spectrum.

## Challenges and Victories for Women

The 1970s marked the arrival of a broad-based feminist movement devoted to securing genuine gender equality and promoting the general interests of women. Three basic reasons accounted for this major development. First, ongoing changes in underlying patterns of motherhood and paid work created novel conditions and new demands (see Chapter 29). Second, a vanguard of feminist intellectuals articulated a powerful critique of gender relations, which stimulated many women to rethink their assumptions and challenge the status quo. Third, dissatisfied women recognized that they had to band together if they were to influence politics and secure fundamental reforms.

**Italian Feminists** These women demonstrate in Rome in 1977 for the passage of legislation legalizing abortion, which the pope and the Catholic Church have steadfastly opposed. The demonstrators raise their hands in a feminist salute during the peaceful march. (Bettmann/Corbis)

Feminists could draw on a long heritage of protest, stretching back to the French Revolution and the women's movements of the late nineteenth century (see Chapters 20 and 23). They were also inspired by more recent works, such as the foundational book *The Second Sex* (1949) by the French writer and philosopher Simone de Beauvoir (1908–1986). Drawing on history, philosophy, psychology, biology, and literature, Beauvoir argued that women had almost always been trapped by particularly inflexible and limiting conditions. Only through courageous action and self-assertive creativity could a woman become a completely free person and escape the role of the inferior "other" that men had constructed for her gender. (See "Listening to the Past: Simone de Beauvoir, a Feminist Critique of Marriage," page 918.)

*The Second Sex* inspired a generation of women intellectuals, and by the late 1960s and the 1970s a broad-based feminist movement had spread through the United States and Europe. In the United States, Betty Friedan's (1921–2006) pathbreaking study *The Feminine Mystique* (1963) pointed the way. Friedan called attention to the stifling aspects of women's domestic life, devoted to the service of husbands and children. In 1966 Friedan helped found the

National Organization for Women (NOW) to press for women's rights. NOW flourished, growing from seven hundred members in 1967 to forty thousand in 1974.

Many other women's organizations rose to follow NOW in Europe and the United States. The new feminists challenged patriarchy, the domination of society by men, and attacked sexism, the inequalities faced by women simply because they were female. Advocates of women's rights pushed for new statutes in the workplace: laws against discrimination, equal pay for equal work, and measures such as maternal leave and affordable day care designed to help women combine careers and family responsibilities.

The movement further concentrated on gender and family questions, including the right to divorce (in some Catholic countries), legalized abortion, the needs of single mothers, and protection from rape and physical violence. In almost every country, the effort to decriminalize abortion served as a catalyst in mobilizing an effective, self-conscious women's movement.

In countries that had long placed women in a subordinate position, the legal changes were little less than revolutionary. In Italy, for example, new laws abolished restrictions on divorce and abortion, which had been strengthened by Mussolini and defended by the Catholic Church in the postwar era. By 1988 divorce and abortion were common in Italy, which had the lowest birthrate in Europe. More generally, the sharply focused women's movement of the 1970s won new rights for women. Subsequently, the movement became more diffuse, a victim of both its successes and the resurgence of an antifeminist opposition.

In addition to the feminist movement, many newly empowered women were active in the antinuclear peace movement, which had its roots in the anti-Vietnam protests of the 1960s and took on new life as the Cold War heated up in the late 1970s. Appalled by the Soviet invasion of Afghanistan in 1979, the United States and NATO took a number of countermeasures, including an agreement to station limited-range nuclear missiles in Europe (see page 925). Concerned citizens quickly realized that if a low-level tactical nuclear war broke out between the superpowers, western Europe and particularly West Germany would suffer the consequences. In 1981 hundreds of thousands of demonstrators marched in protest in major cities across western Europe. West European leaders went ahead with the missile deployment, but determined citizens' groups continued to call attention to the costs of modern war.

## The Rise of the Environmental Movement

Like feminist activists and peace advocates, newly formed environmental groups had roots in the 1960s counterculture. Early environmentalists drew inspiration from writers like biologist Rachel Carson, whose book *Silent Spring*, published in the United States in 1962, was quickly translated into twelve European languages. Carson's book warned of the dangers

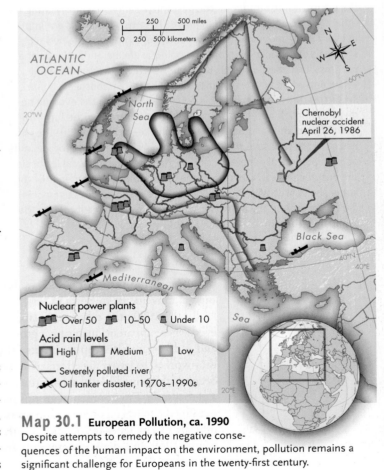

**Map 30.1 European Pollution, ca. 1990**
Despite attempts to remedy the negative consequences of the human impact on the environment, pollution remains a significant challenge for Europeans in the twenty-first century.

CHAPTER LOCATOR    Why did the postwar consensus of the 1950s break down?    **What were the consequences of economic decline in the 1970s?**    What led to the decline of Soviet power in eastern Europe?    Why did revolution sweep through eastern Europe in 1989?

917

# Simone de Beauvoir, a Feminist Critique of Marriage

*Having grown up in Paris in a middle-class family and become a teacher, novelist, and intellectual, Simone de Beauvoir (1908–1986) turned increasingly to feminist concerns after World War II. Her most influential work was* The Second Sex *(1949), a massive declaration of independence for contemporary women.*

*As an existentialist, Beauvoir believed that all individuals must accept responsibility for their lives and strive to overcome the tragic dilemmas they face. Studying the experience of women since antiquity, Beauvoir argued that men had generally used education and social conditioning to create a dependent "other," a negative nonman who was not permitted to grow and strive for freedom. Marriage — on men's terms — was part of this unjust and undesirable process. Beauvoir's conclusion that some couples could establish free and equal unions was based in part on her experience with philosopher Jean-Paul Sartre, Beauvoir's encouraging companion and sometime lover.*

❝ All human existence is transcendence and immanence at the same time; to go beyond itself, it must maintain itself; to thrust itself toward the future, it must integrate the past into itself; and while relating to others, it must confirm itself in itself. These two moments are implied in every living movement: for *man*, marriage provides the perfect synthesis of them; in his work and political life, he finds change and progress, he experiences his dispersion through time and the universe; and when he tires of this wandering, he establishes a home, he settles down, he anchors himself in the world; in the evening he restores himself in the house, where his wife cares for the furniture and children and safeguards the past she keeps in store. But the wife has no other task save the one of maintaining and caring for life in its pure and identical generality; she perpetuates the immutable species, she ensures the even rhythm of the days and the permanence of the home she guards with locked doors; she is given no direct grasp on the future, nor on the universe; she goes beyond herself toward the group only through her husband as mouthpiece.

Marriage today still retains this traditional form. . . . The male's vocation is action; he needs to produce, fight, create, progress, go beyond himself toward the totality of the universe and the infinity of the future; but traditional marriage does not invite woman to transcend herself with him; it confines her in immanence. She has no choice but to build a stable life where the present, prolonging the past, escapes the threats of tomorrow, that is, precisely to create a happiness. . . .

It is through housework that the wife comes to make her "nest" her own; this is why, even if she has "help," she insists on doing things herself; at least by watching over, controlling, and criticizing, she endeavors to make her servants' results her own. By administrating her home, she achieves her social justification; her job is also to oversee the food, clothing, and care of the familial society in general. Thus she too realizes herself as an activity. But, as we will see, it is an activity that brings her no escape from her immanence and allows her no individual affirmation of herself. . . .

Few tasks are more similar to the torment of Sisyphus than those of the housewife; day after day, one must wash dishes, dust furniture, mend clothes that will be dirty, dusty, and torn again. The housewife wears herself out running on the spot; she does nothing; she only perpetuates the present; she never gains the sense that she is conquering a positive Good, but struggles indefinitely against Evil. . . .

Washing, ironing, sweeping, routing out tufts of dust in the dark places behind the wardrobe, this is holding away death but also refusing life: for in one movement time is created and destroyed; the housewife only grasps the negative aspect of it. . . .

So the wife's work within the home does not grant her autonomy; it is not directly useful to the group, it does not open onto the future, it does not produce anything. It becomes meaningful and dignified only if it is integrated into existences that go beyond them-

of the rampant overuse of pesticides. It had a striking impact on the growth of environmental movements in Europe.

By the 1970s the destructive environmental costs of industrial development were everywhere apparent, inspiring a growing ecology movement to challenge government and industry to clean up their acts. The new ecologists had two main agendas. First, they worked to lessen the effects of industrial development on the natural environment. Second, they linked local environmental issues to poverty, inequality, and violence on a global scale. Environmental groups pursued these goals in many ways. Some used the mass media to reach potential supporters; some worked closely with politicians and public officials to change state policies. Others took a more activist stance. In Denmark in March 1969, in a dramatic example, student protesters at the University of Copenha-

**Simone de Beauvoir as a teacher in 1947, when she was writing *The Second Sex*.** (Hulton-Deutsch Collection/Corbis)

Marriage must combine two autonomous existences, not be a withdrawal, an annexation, an escape, a remedy. . . . The couple should not consider itself a community, a closed cell: instead, the individual as individual has to be integrated into a society in which he can thrive without assistance; he will then be able to create links in pure generosity with another individual equally adapted to the group, links founded on the recognition of two freedoms.

This balanced couple is not a utopia; such couples exist sometimes even within marriage, more often outside of it; some are united by a great sexual love that leaves them free in their friendships and occupations; others are linked by a friendship that does not hamper their sexual freedom; more rarely there are still others who are both lovers and friends but without seeking in each other their exclusive reason for living. Many nuances are possible in the relations of a man and a woman: in companionship, pleasure, confidence, tenderness, complicity, and love, they can be for each other the most fruitful source of joy, richness, and strength offered to a human being. **"**

**Source:** Simone de Beauvoir, *The Second Sex*, trans. Constance Borde and Sheila Malovany-Chevallier. Originally published in French as *Le deuxiéme sexe* copyright © 1949 by Editions Gallimard, Paris. English translation copyright © 2009 by Constance Borde and Sheila Malovany-Chevallier. Used by permission of Alfred A. Knopf, a division of Random House, Inc. and Geroges Borchardt, Inc. for Editions Gallimard.

selves, toward the society in production or action: far from enfranchising the matron, it makes her dependent on her husband and children; she justifies her existence through them: she is no more than an inessential mediation in their lives. . . .

The drama of marriage is not that it does not guarantee the wife the promised happiness — there is no guarantee of happiness — it is that it mutilates her; it dooms her to repetition and routine. The first twenty years of a woman's life are extraordinarily rich; she experiences menstruation, sexuality, marriage, and motherhood; she discovers the world and her destiny. She is mistress of a home at twenty, linked from then on to one man, a child in her arms, now her life is finished forever. Real activity, real work, are the privilege of man: her only occupations are sometimes exhausting but never fulfill her. . . .

## QUESTIONS FOR ANALYSIS

1. How did Beauvoir analyze marriage and marriage partners in terms of existential philosophy?
2. To what extent does a married woman benefit from a "traditional" marriage, according to Beauvoir? Why?
3. What was Beauvoir's solution to the situation she described? Was her solution desirable? Realistic?
4. What have you learned about the history of women that supports or challenges Beauvoir's analysis? Include developments since World War II and your own reflections.

gen took over a scientific conference on natural history. They locked the conference hall doors, sprayed the professors in attendance with polluted lake water, and held up an oil-doused duck, shouting, "Come and save it . . . you talk about pollution, why don't you do anything about it!"[2]

Environmental protest also took on institutional forms. In West Germany in 1979 environmentalists founded the Green Party, a political party intended to fight for environmental causes. The West German Greens met with astounding success when they elected members to parliament in the 1983 elections, the first time in sixty years that a new political party had been seated in Germany. Their success was a model for like-minded activists across Europe and the United States. Green Party members have been elected to parliaments in Belgium, Italy, and Sweden.

**Green Party Representatives Enter Parliament**

In 1983 members of the environmentally conscious West German Green Party won enough votes to send several representatives to the parliament for the first time, an important victory for the protest movements that emerged in the 1970s and 1980s. (Bildarchiv Preussischer Kulturbesitz/Art Resource, NY)

**ANALYZING THE IMAGE** How do the Green Party representatives (center) use visual presentation and symbolism to portray their political beliefs? How would you describe the reaction of the more traditionally dressed members of parliament?

**CONNECTIONS** What does the Green Party victory in 1983 tell us about political debate in a postindustrial society? Are there continuities with the social activism of the 1960s counterculture, or is this something new?

To complete this activity online, go to the Online Study Guide at bedfordstmartins.com/mckaywestunderstanding.

## Separatism and Right-Wing Extremism

The 1970s also saw the rise of determined separatist movements across Europe. In Ireland, Spain, Belgium, and Switzerland—and in Yugoslavia and Czechoslovakia in the East Bloc—regional ethnic groups struggled for special rights, political autonomy, and even national independence from ruling governments. This new separatist nationalism was most violent in Spain and Northern Ireland. In the ethnic Basque region of northern Spain, the ETA (short for Basque Homeland and Freedom) tried to use bombings and assassinations to force the government to grant territorial independence. After the death in 1975 of the Spanish fascist dictator Francisco Franco, who had ruled Spain for almost forty years, a new constitution granted the Basque region special autonomy, but it was not enough. The ETA stepped up its terrorist campaigns, killing over four hundred people in the 1980s.

The Provisional Irish Republican Army (IRA), a paramilitary organization in Northern Ireland, used similar tactics. Though Ireland had won autonomy in 1922, Great Britain retained control of six primarily Protestant counties in the north of the country (see Chapter 27). In the late 1960s violence reemerged as the IRA attacked British security forces its members saw as occupying the district. On Bloody Sunday in January 1972, British soldiers shot and killed thirteen demonstrators, who had been protesting anti-Catholic discrimination, in the town of Derry, and the violence escalated. For the next thirty years the IRA attacked soldiers and civilians in Northern Ireland and in Britain itself. Over two thousand British soldiers, civilians, and IRA members were killed during "the Troubles" before negotiations between the IRA and the British government opened in the late 1990s.

Mainstream European politicians also faced challenges from new political forces on the far right in the 1970s and 1980s. New right politicians promoted themselves as the champions of ordinary (white) workers, complaining that immigrants swelled welfare rolls and stole jobs from native-born Europeans. Though their programs at times veered close to open racism, they began to win seats in national parliaments in the 1980s.

# ▼ What led to the decline of Soviet power in eastern Europe?

In the postwar decades, the Communist states of the East Bloc had achieved a shaky social consensus based on a rising standard of living, an extensive welfare system, and the inevitable political repression. When the Marxist utopia still had not arrived in the 1970s, propagandists told citizens that their totally egalitarian society would be realized sometime in the future. In the long run, leaders claimed, socialism would prove that it was better than capitalism. Such claims were an attempt to paper over serious tensions in socialist society.

When Mikhail Gorbachev burst on the scene in 1985, the new Soviet leader opened an era of reform that was as sweeping as it was unexpected. Although many believed that Gorbachev would soon fall from power, his reforms rapidly transformed Soviet culture and politics, and drastically reduced Cold War tensions. But communism, which Gorbachev wanted to revitalize, continued to decline.

## State and Society in the East Bloc

In the 1970s Communist leaders in eastern Europe and the Soviet Union adopted the term really existing socialism to describe the accomplishments of their societies. Agriculture had been successfully collectivized, with 80 to 90 percent of Soviet and East Bloc farmers working on huge collective farms. Industry and business had been nationalized, and only a small percentage of the economy remained in private hands in most East Bloc countries. The state had also gone some way to level class differences. Though party members clearly had greater access to better opportunities and resources, the gap between rich and poor was far smaller than in the West. An extensive system of government-supported welfare benefits were available to all.

**really existing socialism**
A term used by Communist leaders to describe the socialist accomplishments of their societies, such as nationalized industry and collective agriculture.

Everyday life under really existing socialism was defined by an uneasy mixture of outward conformity and private disengagement—or apathy. The Communist Party dominated public life. Mass organizations instituted huge rallies, colorful festivals, and new holidays that exposed citizens to the values of the socialist state. East Bloc citizens might participate in party-sponsored public events, but at home, and in private, they grumbled about and often sidestepped Communist authority.

CHAPTER LOCATOR | Why did the postwar consensus of the 1950s break down? | What were the consequences of economic decline in the 1970s? | **What led to the decline of Soviet power in eastern Europe?** | Why did revolution sweep through eastern Europe in 1989?

921

East Bloc living standards were well above those in the developing world, but well below living standards in the West. Centralized economic planning continued to lead to shortages of the most basic goods. Though the secret police persecuted those who openly challenged the system and generated mountains of files on ordinary people, those who put up and shut up had little to fear.

Women in particular experienced the contradictions of the socialist system. On the one hand, the state advocated equal rights for women and encouraged them to join the workforce in positions formerly reserved for men, such as medicine, in numbers greater than those in the West. In addition, an extensive system of state-supported child care freed women to take outside employment. On the other hand, women rarely made it into the upper ranks of business or politics. And East Bloc women faced the same double burden as those in the West—on top of their full-time jobs, they were expected to do the shopping, the cooking, and the cleaning at home.

The countries of eastern Europe—like those in the West—were hit hard by the energy crisis and stagflation of the 1970s. For a time, access to inexpensive oil provided by the Soviet Union provided a buffer, but this cushion began to fall apart in the 1980s. For a number of reasons, East Bloc leaders refused to make the economic reforms that might have made the socialist system more effective.

First, the transformation to Western-style postindustrial societies would have required fundamental changes in the Communist system. As in the West, it would have hurt the already tenuous living standard of industrial workers. But East Bloc governments were dedicated to the working class: coal miners, shipbuilders, factory and construction workers. To pursue the sorts of reforms required to develop a postindustrial economy would have undermined the livelihoods and support of these basic constituencies, which were already showing signs of wear.

East Bloc regimes also refused to cut spending on the welfare state, which was, after all, one of the proudest achievements of socialism. In addition, socialist governments continued to provide subsidies to heavy industries such as steel and mining. High-tech industries failed to take off in eastern Europe, in part because the West maintained embargos on technology exports. The industrial goods produced in the East Bloc became increasingly uncompetitive in the new global system. To stave off total collapse, Communist governments borrowed massive amounts of hard currency from Western banks, helping to convince ordinary people that communism was bankrupt, and setting up a cycle of indebtedness that helped bring down the East Bloc in 1989.

Economic decline was not the only reason people increasingly questioned the socialist system. The best career and educational opportunities were reserved for party members or handed out as political favors, leaving many talented people underemployed and resentful. Tight controls on travel continually called attention to the burdens of daily life in a repressive society. The one-party state had repeatedly quashed popular reform movements and retreated from economic liberalization, even when presented in a nonthreatening way. The liberal freedoms and consumer prosperity of the West were evident for all to see in the television broadcasts that streamed across the iron curtain every evening. Many East Bloc citizens came to doubt the legitimacy of communism altogether.

## Reform Movements in Czechoslovakia and Poland

Economic and social stagnation in the East Bloc encouraged small numbers of dedicated people to try to change society from within. Developments in Czechoslovakia and Poland were the most significant, and determined reform movements emerged in both countries in the mid-1970s. Remembering a history of violent repression and Soviet invasion, reformists carefully avoided direct challenges to government leaders. Nor did they try to reform the Communist Party itself. Instead, they worked to build a civil society from

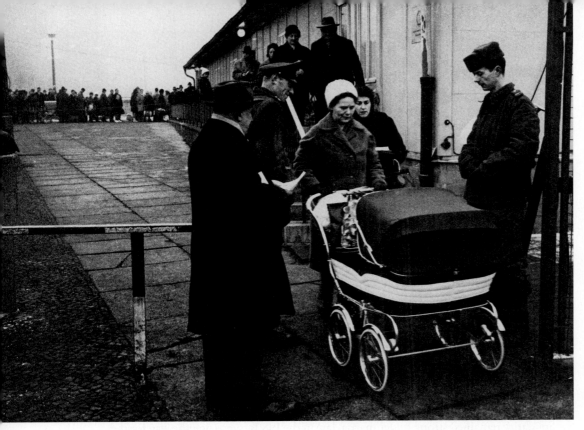

**Crossing the Border Between East and West Berlin** During the Christmas season of 1965, West Berliners were given special permission to visit relatives in the walled-off eastern part of the city. The limits on travel in the East Bloc were one of the most hated aspects of life under Communist rule. (Bildarchiv Preussischer Kulturbesitz/Art Resource, NY)

below—to create a realm of freedom beyond formal politics where civil liberties and human rights could be exercised within the Communist system.

In Czechoslovakia in 1977 a small group of citizens, including future Czechoslovak president Václav Havel (see pages 929–930), signed a manifesto that came to be known as Charter 77. The group called on Communist leaders to respect civil and human rights. They also criticized censorship and argued for improved environmental policies. Despite government retaliation, Czech leaders challenged passive acceptance of Communist authority and contributed to growing public dissatisfaction.

In Poland the Communists had never been able to monopolize society. Most agricultural land remained in private hands, and the Catholic Church thrived. The Communists also failed to manage the economy effectively. The 1960s saw little economic improvement, and in 1970 Poland's working class rose in protest. A new Communist leader came to power, and he wagered that massive inflows of Western capital and technology, especially from rich and now-friendly West Germany, could produce a Polish economic miracle. Instead, bureaucratic incompetence and the first oil shock in 1973 put the economy into a nosedive. Workers, intellectuals, and the church became increasingly restive. Then Cardinal Karol Wojtyla (voy-TIH-lah), archbishop of Kraków, was elected pope in 1978. In June 1979 he returned to Poland from Rome, preaching love of Christ and country and the "inalienable rights of man." Pope John Paul II drew enormous crowds and electrified the Polish nation.

In August 1980 the sixteen thousand workers at the Lenin Shipyards in Gdansk (formerly known as Danzig) laid down their tools and occupied the plant. As other workers joined "in solidarity," the strikers advanced the ideals of civil society, including the right to form free-trade unions, freedom of speech, release of political prisoners, and economic

**CHAPTER LOCATOR** | Why did the postwar consensus of the 1950s break down? | What were the consequences of economic decline in the 1970s? | What led to the decline of Soviet power in eastern Europe? | Why did revolution sweep through eastern Europe in 1989?

923

reforms. After eighteen days the government gave in and accepted the workers' demands in the Gdansk Agreement.

Led by Lenin Shipyards electrician Lech Walesa (lehk vah-LEHN-suh) (b. 1943), the workers proceeded to organize a free and democratic trade union called **Solidarity**. Joined by intellectuals and supported by the Catholic Church, it became a national union with 9.5 million members. Cultural and intellectual freedom blossomed in Poland, and Solidarity enjoyed tremendous public support. Nonetheless, Solidarity worked cautiously to shape an active civil society, refusing to challenge directly the Communist monopoly on political power. Yet the ever-present threat of calling a nationwide strike gave them real power in ongoing negotiations with the Communist bosses.

Solidarity's combination of strength and moderation postponed a showdown, as the Soviet Union played a waiting game of threats and pressure. After a confrontation in March 1981 Walesa settled for minor government concessions, and Solidarity dropped plans for a massive general strike. Criticism of Walesa's moderate leadership gradually grew, and Solidarity lost its cohesiveness. The worsening economic crisis also encouraged radical actions among disgruntled Solidarity members, and the Polish Communist leadership shrewdly denounced Solidarity for promoting economic collapse and provoking a possible Soviet invasion. In December 1981 Communist leader General Wojciech Jaruzelski (VOY-chek yahr-oo-ZEL-skee) suddenly proclaimed martial law, outlawed Solidarity, and arrested its leaders.

Solidarity survived in part because of the government's unwillingness (and probably its inability) to impose full-scale terror. Moreover, cultural and intellectual life remained vigorous as the faltering Polish economy continued to deteriorate. Thus popular support for Solidarity remained strong under martial law in the 1980s, preparing the way for the union's political rebirth toward the end of the decade.

**Solidarity** Outlawed Polish trade union that worked for workers' rights and political reform throughout the 1980s.

**Lech Walesa and Solidarity** An inspiration for fellow workers at the Lenin Shipyards in the dramatic and successful strike against the Communist bosses in August 1980, Walesa played a key role in Solidarity before and after it was outlawed. Speaking here to old comrades at the Lenin Shipyards after Solidarity was again legalized in 1988, Walesa personified an enduring opposition to Communist rule in eastern Europe. (Georges Merrillon/Gamma)

The rise and survival of Solidarity showed the desire of millions of eastern Europeans for greater political liberty and the enduring appeal of cultural freedom, trade-union rights, patriotic nationalism, and religious feeling. Not least, Solidarity's challenge encouraged fresh thinking in the Soviet Union.

## From Détente Back to Cold War

The Soviets and the leaders of the Soviet satellite states also faced challenges from abroad as optimistic hopes for détente in international relations gradually faded in the late 1970s. Brezhnev's Soviet Union ignored the human rights provisions of the Helsinki agreement, and East-West political competition remained very much alive outside Europe. The Soviet invasion of Afghanistan in December 1979, which was designed to save an increasingly unpopular Marxist regime, was especially alarming to the West. Many Americans feared that the oil-rich states of the Persian Gulf would be next, and once again they looked to the NATO alliance to thwart communist expansion.

**The Soviet War in Afghanistan, 1979–1989**

- Afghanistan
- Soviet Union
- → Soviet invasion
- Controlled by Soviet forces

President Jimmy Carter (r. 1977–1981) tried to lead NATO beyond verbal condemnation and urged economic sanctions against the Soviet Union, but only Great Britain among the European allies supported the American initiative. The alliance showed the same lack of concerted action when the Solidarity movement rose in Poland. Some observers concluded that NATO had lost the will to act decisively in dealing with the Soviet bloc.

The Atlantic alliance endured, however, and the U.S. military buildup launched by Carter in his last years in office was greatly accelerated by President Reagan. Increasing defense spending enormously, the Reagan administration deployed short-range nuclear missiles in western Europe and built up the navy to preserve American power in the post-Vietnam age. The broad shift toward greater conservatism in the 1980s gave Reagan allies in western Europe. Margaret Thatcher was a forceful advocate for a revitalized Atlantic alliance, and under Helmut Kohl West Germany and the United States once again coordinated military and political policy toward the Soviet bloc.

## Gorbachev's Reforms in the Soviet Union

Cold War tensions aside, the Soviet Union's Communist Party elite seemed secure in the early 1980s. The long-established system of administrative controls continued to stretch downward from the central ministries and state committees to provincial cities, and from there to factories, neighborhoods, and villages. Organized opposition was impossible, and average people left politics to the bosses.

Although the extensive state and party bureaucracy safeguarded the elite, it promoted apathy in the masses. When the ailing Brezhnev finally died in 1982, his successor, Yuri Andropov (r. 1982–1984), tried to invigorate the system. Relatively little came of his efforts, but they combined with a sharply worsening economic situation to set the stage for the emergence in 1985 of Mikhail Gorbachev (r. 1985–1991).

Gorbachev believed in communism, but he realized it was failing to keep up with Western capitalism and technological developments, and that the Soviet Union's status as a superpower was eroding. Thus Gorbachev wanted to save the Soviet system by revitalizing it with fundamental reforms. Gorbachev was also an idealist who wanted to improve conditions for ordinary citizens. Understanding that the endless waste and expense of the

CHAPTER LOCATOR | Why did the postwar consensus of the 1950s break down? | What were the consequences of economic decline in the 1970s? | **What led to the decline of Soviet power in eastern Europe?** | Why did revolution sweep through eastern Europe in 1989?

925

**Mikhail Gorbachev** In his acceptance speech before the Supreme Soviet (the U.S.S.R.'s parliament), newly elected president Mikhail Gorbachev vowed to assume "all responsibility" for the success or failure of perestroika. Previous Soviet parliaments were little more than tools of the Communist Party, but this one actively debated and even opposed government programs. (Boris Yurchenko/AP Images)

**perestroika** Economic restructuring and reform implemented by Soviet premier Gorbachev in 1985.

**glasnost** Soviet premier Gorbachev's popular campaign for openness in government and the media.

Cold War arms race had had a disastrous impact on living conditions in the Soviet Union, he realized that improvement at home required better relations with the West.

Gorbachev's first set of reform policies was designed to transform and restructure the economy in order to provide for the real needs of the Soviet population. To accomplish this economic restructuring, or **perestroika** (pehr-uh-STROY-kuh), Gorbachev and his supporters permitted an easing of government price controls on some goods, more independence for state enterprises, and the setting up of profit-seeking private cooperatives to provide personal services for consumers. These timid economic reforms initially produced a few improvements, but shortages grew as the economy stalled at an intermediate point between central planning and free-market mechanisms. By late 1988 widespread consumer dissatisfaction posed a serious threat to Gorbachev's leadership and the entire reform program.

Gorbachev's campaign "to tell it like it is" was much more successful. Very popular in a country where censorship, dull uniformity, and outright lies had long characterized public discourse, the newfound openness, or **glasnost** (GLAZ-nohst), of the government and the media marked an astonishing break with the past. Long-banned émigré writers sold millions of copies of their works in new editions, while denunciations of Stalin and his terror became standard fare in plays and movies. Thus initial openness in government pronouncements quickly went much further than Gorbachev intended and led to something approaching free speech and free expression.

Democratization was the third element of reform. Beginning as an attack on corruption in the Communist Party, it led to the first free elections in the Soviet Union since 1917. Gorbachev and the party remained in control, but a minority of critical independents was elected in April 1989 to a revitalized Congress of People's Deputies. An active civil society began to emerge—a new political culture at odds with the Communist Party's monopoly of power and control. Democratization ignited demands for greater autonomy and even for national independence by non-Russian minorities, especially in the Baltic region and in the Caucasus.

Finally, Gorbachev brought new thinking to the field of foreign affairs. He withdrew Soviet troops from Afghanistan in February 1989 and sought to reduce East-West tensions. Of enormous importance, the Soviet leader sought to halt the arms race with the United States and convinced President Reagan of his sincerity. In a Washington summit in December 1987, the two leaders agreed to eliminate all land-based intermediate-range missiles in Europe, setting the stage for more arms reductions. Gorbachev also encouraged reform movements in Poland and Hungary and pledged to respect the political choices of the peoples of eastern Europe, repudiating the Brezhnev Doctrine.

## ▼ Why did revolution sweep through eastern Europe in 1989?

In 1989 Gorbachev's plan to reform communism in order to save it snowballed out of control. A series of largely peaceful revolutions swept across eastern Europe (Map 30.2), overturning existing communist regimes. The revolutions of 1989 had momentous consequences. First, the peoples of eastern Europe joyfully reentered the mainstream of con-

**▪ MAPPING THE PAST**

**Map 30.2  Democratic Movements in Eastern Europe, 1989**
Countries that had been satellites in the orbit of the Soviet Union began to set themselves free in 1989.

**ANALYZING THE MAP**  Which countries experienced the largest number of demonstrations? Which countries and/or states within the Soviet Union experienced the fewest?

**CONNECTIONS**  How did Gorbachev's reforms in the Soviet Union contribute to the spread of democratic movements in eastern Europe, and which specific action of his hastened the end of the Cold War?

To complete this activity online, go to the Online Study Guide at bedfordstmartins.com/mckaywestunderstanding.

temporary European life and culture. Second, West Germany quickly absorbed its East German rival and emerged as the most influential country in Europe. Third, a complicated anticommunist revolution swept through the Soviet Union as the multinational empire broke into a large Russia and fourteen other independent states.

## The Collapse of Communism in Eastern Europe

Solidarity and the Polish people led the way to revolution in eastern Europe. In 1988 widespread labor unrest and strikes, raging inflation, and the outlawed Solidarity's refusal to cooperate with the military government had brought Poland to the brink of economic

CHAPTER LOCATOR | Why did the postwar consensus of the 1950s break down? | What were the consequences of economic decline in the 1970s? | What led to the decline of Soviet power in eastern Europe? | **Why did revolution sweep through eastern Europe in 1989?**

927

collapse. Thus Solidarity pressured Poland's Communist leaders into another round of negotiations that might work out a sharing of power to resolve the political stalemate and the economic crisis. The subsequent agreement in early 1989 legalized Solidarity and declared that a large minority of representatives to the Polish parliament would be chosen by free elections that June. Still guaranteed a parliamentary majority and expecting to win many of the contested seats, the Communists believed that their rule would hold for at least four more years.

Lacking access to the state-run media, Solidarity succeeded nonetheless in mobilizing the country and winning most of the contested seats in an overwhelming victory. Moreover, many voters crossed off the names of unopposed party candidates, so that the Communist Party failed to win the majority its leaders had anticipated. Solidarity members entered the Polish parliament, and a dangerous stalemate quickly developed. But Solidarity leader Lech Walesa adroitly obtained a majority by securing the allegiance of two minor pro-communist parties that had been part of the coalition government after World War II. In August 1989 Tadeusz Mazowiecki (b. 1927), the editor of Solidarity's weekly newspaper, was sworn in as Poland's new noncommunist prime minister, and in 1990 Lech Walesa was elected president.

In its first year and a half, the new Solidarity government cautiously introduced political changes. It eliminated the secret police, the Communist ministers in the government, and finally Communist Party leader Jaruzelski himself, but it did so step-by-step in order to avoid confrontation with the army or the Soviet Union. However, in economic affairs, the Solidarity-led government was radical from the beginning. It applied economic **shock therapy**, an intense dose of neoliberal policy designed to make a clean break with state planning and move quickly to market mechanisms and private property.

**shock therapy** The Solidarity-led government's radical take on economic affairs that abruptly ended state planning and moved to market mechanisms and private property.

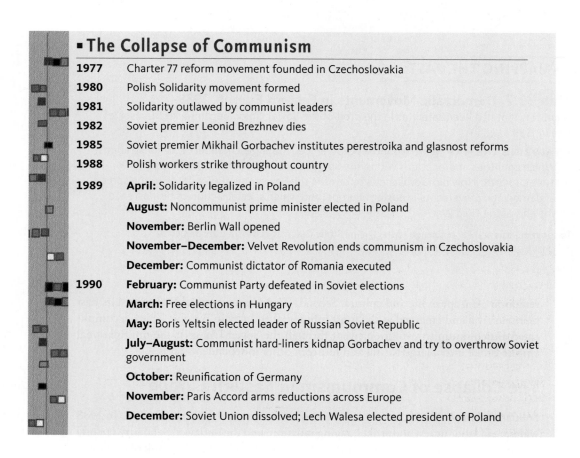

## ▪ The Collapse of Communism

| | |
|---|---|
| **1977** | Charter 77 reform movement founded in Czechoslovakia |
| **1980** | Polish Solidarity movement formed |
| **1981** | Solidarity outlawed by communist leaders |
| **1982** | Soviet premier Leonid Brezhnev dies |
| **1985** | Soviet premier Mikhail Gorbachev institutes perestroika and glasnost reforms |
| **1988** | Polish workers strike throughout country |
| **1989** | **April:** Solidarity legalized in Poland |
| | **August:** Noncommunist prime minister elected in Poland |
| | **November:** Berlin Wall opened |
| | **November–December:** Velvet Revolution ends communism in Czechoslovakia |
| | **December:** Communist dictator of Romania executed |
| **1990** | **February:** Communist Party defeated in Soviet elections |
| | **March:** Free elections in Hungary |
| | **May:** Boris Yeltsin elected leader of Russian Soviet Republic |
| | **July–August:** Communist hard-liners kidnap Gorbachev and try to overthrow Soviet government |
| | **October:** Reunification of Germany |
| | **November:** Paris Accord arms reductions across Europe |
| | **December:** Soviet Union dissolved; Lech Walesa elected president of Poland |

Hungary followed Poland. In May 1988, in an effort to retain power by granting modest political concessions, the Communist Party replaced party boss János Kádár (KAH-dahr) with a reform communist. But opposition groups rejected piecemeal progress, and in the summer of 1989 the Hungarian Communist Party agreed to hold free elections in March 1990. Welcoming Western investment and moving rapidly toward multiparty democracy, Hungary's Communists now enjoyed considerable popular support, and they believed, mistakenly, that they could defeat the opposition in the upcoming elections.

In an effort to strengthen their support at home and also put pressure on East Germany's hard-line Communist regime, the Hungarians opened their border to East Germans and tore down the barbed wire barrier with Austria. Then tens of thousands of dissatisfied East German "vacationers" poured into Hungary, crossed into Austria as refugees, and continued on to immediate resettlement in West Germany. In a desperate but ad hoc attempt to stabilize the situation, the East German government opened the Berlin Wall in November 1989, and people danced for joy atop that grim symbol of the prison state. East Germany's Communist leaders were swept aside, and a reform government took power and scheduled free elections.

In Czechoslovakia, communism died quickly in November–December 1989. This so-called Velvet Revolution grew out of popular demonstrations led by students, intellectuals, and a dissident playwright turned moral revolutionary named Václav Havel

**Demonstrators During the Velvet Revolution** Hundreds of thousands of Czechoslovakian citizens flooded the streets of Prague daily in peaceful protests after the police savagely beat student demonstrators in mid-November 1989. On the night of November 24 three hundred thousand people roared "Dubček-Havel" when Alexander Dubček, the aging reformer ousted in 1968 by the Soviets, stood on a balcony with Václav Havel, the leading opponent of communism. That night the Communists agreed to share power, and a few days later they resigned from the government. (Corbis)

CHAPTER LOCATOR | Why did the postwar consensus of the 1950s break down? | What were the consequences of economic decline in the 1970s? | What led to the decline of Soviet power in eastern Europe? | **Why did revolution sweep through eastern Europe in 1989?**

**929**

(VAH-slahf HAH-vuhl) (b. 1936). The protesters practically took control of the streets and forced the Communists into a power-sharing arrangement, which quickly resulted in the resignation of the Communist government. As 1989 ended, the Czechoslovakian assembly elected Havel president.

Only in Romania was revolution violent and bloody. Faced with mass protests in December 1989, Nicolae Ceaușescu (chow-SHES-kou) (1918–1989), alone among eastern European bosses, ordered his ruthless security forces to slaughter thousands, thereby sparking a classic armed uprising. After Ceaușescu's forces were defeated, the tyrant and his wife were captured and executed by a military court. A coalition government emerged from the fighting.

## German Unification and the End of the Cold War

The sudden death of communism in East Germany in 1989 reopened the "German question" and raised the threat of renewed Cold War conflict over Germany. Taking power in October 1989, East German reform communists, supported by leading East German intellectuals and former dissidents, wanted to preserve socialism by making it genuinely democratic and responsive to the needs of the people. These reformers supported closer ties with West Germany, but they feared unification and wanted to preserve a distinct East German identity.

Their efforts failed, and over the next year East Germany was absorbed into an enlarged West Germany. Three factors were particularly important in this sudden absorption. First, in the first week after the Berlin Wall was opened, almost 9 million East Germans—roughly half of the total population—poured across the border into West Germany. Almost all returned to their homes in the East, but their experience in the West aroused long-dormant hopes of unity among ordinary citizens.

Second, West German chancellor Helmut Kohl and his closest advisers skillfully exploited the historic opportunity. In November 1989 Kohl presented a ten-point plan for a step-by-step unification in cooperation with both East Germany and the international community. Kohl then promised the citizens of East Germany an immediate economic bonanza—a one-for-one exchange of all East German marks in savings accounts and pensions into much more valuable West German marks. This offer helped a well-financed conservative-liberal Alliance for Germany, which was set up in East Germany and was closely tied to Kohl's West German Christian Democrats, to overwhelm those who argued for the preservation of some kind of independent socialist society in East Germany. In March 1990 the Alliance outdistanced the Socialist Party and won almost 50 percent of the votes in an East German parliamentary election. The Alliance for Germany quickly negotiated an economic union on favorable terms with Chancellor Kohl.

Finally, in the summer of 1990 the crucial international aspect of German unification was successfully resolved. Unification would once again make Germany the strongest state in central Europe and would directly affect the security of the Soviet Union. But Gorbachev swallowed hard and negotiated the best deal he could. In October 1990 East Germany merged into West Germany, forming henceforth a single nation under the West German laws and constitution.

The reunification of Germany accelerated the pace of agreements to liquidate the Cold War. In November 1990

**The Reunification of Germany, 1990**

delegates from twenty-two European countries joined those from the United States and the Soviet Union in Paris and agreed to scale down their armed forces. The delegates also affirmed that all existing borders in Europe were legal and valid. The Paris Accord was for all practical purposes a general peace treaty, bringing an end to World War II and the Cold War that followed.

Peace in Europe encouraged the United States and the Soviet Union to scrap a significant portion of their nuclear weapons in a series of agreements. In September 1991 President George H. W. Bush also canceled the around-the-clock alert status for American bombers outfitted with atomic bombs, and Gorbachev quickly followed suit. For the first time in four decades, Soviet and American nuclear weapons were not standing ready to destroy capitalism, communism, and life itself.

## The Disintegration of the Soviet Union

As 1990 began, revolutionary changes had triumphed in all but two eastern European states — tiny Albania and the vast Soviet Union. The great question now became whether the Soviet Union would follow its former satellites and whether reform communism would give way to a popular anticommunist revolution.

In February 1990, as competing Russian politicians presented their programs and nationalists in the non-Russian republics demanded autonomy or independence from the Soviet Union, the Communist Party suffered a stunning defeat in local elections throughout the country. Democrats and anticommunists won clear majorities in the leading cities of the Russian Soviet Republic (SFSR), the largest republic in the Soviet Union. Moreover, in Lithuania the people elected a nationalist as president, and the newly chosen parliament declared Lithuania an independent state.

Gorbachev responded by placing an economic embargo on Lithuania, but he refused to use the army to crush the separatist government. The result was a tense political stalemate that undermined popular support for Gorbachev. Separating himself further from Communist hard-liners, Gorbachev asked Soviet citizens to ratify a new constitution that formally abolished the Communist Party's monopoly of political power and expanded the power of the Congress of People's Deputies. Retaining his post as party secretary, Gorbachev convinced a majority of deputies to elect him president of the Soviet Union.

Gorbachev's eroding power and his unwillingness to risk a universal suffrage election for the presidency strengthened his great rival, Boris Yeltsin (1931–2007). A radical reform communist, Yeltsin embraced the democratic movement, and in May 1990 he was elected parliamentary leader of the Russian Soviet Republic. He announced that Russia itself would put its interests first and declare its independence from the Soviet Union. Gorbachev tried to save the Soviet Union with a new treaty that would link the member republics in a looser, freely accepted confederation, but six of the fifteen Soviet republics rejected Gorbachev's pleas.

Opposed by democrats and nationalists, Gorbachev was also challenged again by the Communist old guard. After Gorbachev was defeated at the Communist Party congress in July 1990, a gang of hard-liners kidnapped him and his family in the Caucasus and tried to seize the Soviet government in August 1991. The attempted coup collapsed in the face of massive popular resistance that rallied around Yeltsin. As the spellbound world watched on television, Yeltsin defiantly denounced the rebels from atop a stalled tank in central Moscow and declared the "rebirth of Russia." The army supported Yeltsin, and Gorbachev was rescued and returned to power as head of the Soviet Union.

The leaders of the coup wanted to preserve Communist power, state ownership, and the multinational Soviet Union, but they succeeded only in destroying all three. An anticommunist revolution swept the Russian Soviet Republic as Yeltsin and his supporters

CHAPTER LOCATOR | Why did the postwar consensus of the 1950s break down? | What were the consequences of economic decline in the 1970s? | What led to the decline of Soviet power in eastern Europe? | **Why did revolution sweep through eastern Europe in 1989?**

931

**Yeltsin Resists a Coup by Russian Communist Hard-Liners** Standing atop a tank in Moscow in August 1991, the president of the Russian Soviet Republic, Boris Yeltsin, reads a statement denouncing the conspirators who were attempting to halt Gorbachev's reforms and hold the Soviet empire together. Yeltsin's brave public demonstration helped foil the coup and paved the way for the dissolution of the Soviet Union. (AP Images)

outlawed the Communist Party and confiscated its property. Under Yeltsin's leadership, Russia declared its independence, withdrew from the Soviet Union, and renamed the Russian Soviet Republic the Russian Federation. All the other Soviet republics also left. The Soviet Union ceased to exist on December 25, 1991. The independent republics of the old Soviet Union then established a loose confederation, the Commonwealth of Independent States, which played only a minor role in the 1990s.

# ⬅ LOOKING BACK **LOOKING AHEAD** ➡

THE UNEXPECTED AND RAPID COLLAPSE of communism in Europe capped three decades of turbulent historical change. In the 1960s powerful challenges to the status quo steered western Europe to the left and attempted (but failed) to wrest power from the communists in the East. In the 1970s a global recession had devastating effects for everyday people in the West and East Blocs alike. And in the 1980s conservative Western leaders made the hard choices necessary to face economic decline and new global competition.

With the world economy on the road to recovery and new free-market systems in place across the former East Bloc, all of Europe would now have the opportunity to enter the information age. After forty years of Cold War division, the continent regained an underlying unity as faith in democratic government and market economics became the common European creed. In 1991 hopes for peaceful democratic progress were almost universal. According to philosopher Francis Fukuyama, the world had reached "the end of history," because the collapse of the Cold War would lead to peaceful development based on growing tolerance, free-market economics, and liberal democracy.

The post–Cold War years saw the realization of some of these hopes, but the new era brought its own problems and tragedies. New ethnic and nationalist tensions flared, leading to a disastrous civil war in the former Yugoslavia. The struggle to rebuild the shattered societies of the former East Bloc countries was far more difficult than observers had hoped. Poor economic growth continued to complicate attempts to deal with the wide-open global economy. New conflicts with Islamic nations in the Middle East involved some European nations in open war. The European Union expanded, but political disagreements, environmental issues, increased anxiety about non-Western immigrants, and a host of other problems undermined moves toward true European unity. History was far from over: the realities of a post–Cold War world continued to produce difficult challenges as Europe entered the twenty-first century. ■

- **For a list of suggested readings for this chapter, visit** *bedfordstmartins.com/mckaywestunderstanding*.

- **For primary sources from this period, see** *Sources of Western Society, Second Edition*.

- **For Web sites, images, and documents related to topics in this chapter, see Make History at** *bedfordstmartins.com/mckaywestunderstanding*.

CHAPTER LOCATOR | Why did the postwar consensus of the 1950s break down? | What were the consequences of economic decline in the 1970s? | What led to the decline of Soviet power in eastern Europe? | Why did revolution sweep through eastern Europe in 1989?

933

# Chapter 30 Study Guide

Online Study Guide
bedfordstmartins.com/mckaywestunderstanding

## Step 1

**GETTING STARTED** Below are basic terms about this period in the history of Western civilization. Can you identify each term below and explain why it matters? To do this exercise online, go to bedfordstmartins.com/mckaywestunderstanding.

| TERMS | WHO (OR WHAT) AND WHEN | WHY IT MATTERS |
|---|---|---|
| détente, p. 904 | | |
| New Left, p. 907 | | |
| Brezhnev Doctrine, p. 911 | | |
| OPEC, p. 912 | | |
| stagflation, p. 912 | | |
| postindustrial society, p. 913 | | |
| neoliberalism, p. 913 | | |
| really existing socialism, p. 921 | | |
| Solidarity, p. 924 | | |
| perestroika, p. 926 | | |
| glasnost, p. 926 | | |
| shock therapy, p. 928 | | |

## Step 2

**MOVING BEYOND THE BASICS** The exercise below requires a more advanced understanding of the chapter material. Compare and contrast western Europe in 1960 and 1980 by filling in the chart below with descriptions of the social, economic, and political characteristics of western Europe in 1960 and 1980. (You may want to review Chapter 29 before proceeding with this exercise.) When you are finished, consider the following questions: How would you explain the differences you note between western Europe in 1960 and 1980? What continuities can you identify between the two periods? To do this exercise online, go to bedfordstmartins.com/mckaywestunderstanding.

| | SOCIETY | ECONOMY | POLITICS |
|---|---|---|---|
| Western Europe: 1960 | | | |
| Western Europe: 1980 | | | |

## PUTTING IT ALL TOGETHER
Now that you've reviewed key elements of the chapter, take a step back and try to see the big picture. Remember to use specific examples from the chapter in your answers. To do this exercise online, go to bedfordstmartins.com/mckaywestunderstanding.

### REFORM AND PROTEST IN THE 1960S

- To what extent was the counterculture of the 1960s a product of postwar affluence? What other factors contributed to its emergence?

- Compare and contrast eastern Europe in the 1960s and the 1980s. Why did discontent with Communist rule produce revolution at the end of the 1980s, but not in the 1960s?

### CHANGING CONSENSUS IN WESTERN EUROPE

- How did global developments and trends shape European life in the 1970s and 1980s?

- What forms did protest and dissent take in western Europe in the 1970s and 1980s? In your opinion, which protest movements were most significant? Why?

### THE DECLINE OF "REALLY EXISTING SOCIALISM"

- What were the sources of economic and social stagnation in eastern Europe in the 1970s and 1980s? How did Communist authorities respond to the challenges they faced?

- In your opinion, could communism have been successfully "reformed from within"? Why or why not? What light does Gorbachev's experience in the Soviet Union shed on this question?

### THE REVOLUTIONS OF 1989

- How would you explain the relatively peaceful nature of the revolutions of 1989? Given that authorities had used force to suppress dissent many times in the past, why, with the exception of Nicolae Ceauşescu in Romania, did they choose not to do so in 1989?

- What do the revolutions of 1989 tell us about the nature of Soviet power and authority prior to 1989? What were the essential ingredients of Soviet control? When and how were they lost?

■ **In Your Own Words** Imagine that you must explain Chapter 30 to someone who hasn't read it. What would be the most important points to include and why?

# 31

# Europe in an Age of Globalization

## 1990 to the Present

On November 9, 2009, the twentieth anniversary of the fall of the Berlin Wall, jubilant crowds filled the streets around the Brandenburg Gate at the former border between East and West Berlin. International leaders and tens of thousands of onlookers applauded as former Polish president Lech Walesa pushed over a line of one thousand eight-foot-tall foam dominos, symbolizing communism's collapse.

The crowd had reason to celebrate. The end of the Cold War had opened a new chapter in European and world history. Capitalism spread across the former East Bloc and the Soviet Union (now the Russian Federation), bringing potential for democratic reform. Some of these hopes were realized, but the new era also brought its own problems and tragedies. In eastern Europe, the process of rebuilding shattered societies was more difficult than optimists had envisioned in 1991. Across the West and around the world, individuals experienced the benefits and disadvantages of globalization and the digital revolution. The ongoing influx of immigrants into western Europe brought ethnic diversity to formerly homogeneous societies, which sometimes led to fear and conflict.

As Europe faced serious tensions and complex changes at the turn of the century, it also came together to form a strong new European Union that would prove a formidable economic competitor to the United States. Though old ties between Europe and the United States began to loosen, the nations of the West—and the world—could not ignore the common challenges they now faced. Finding solutions to ever-present problems regarding security, energy, the environment, and human rights would require not only innovation, but also cooperation. ■

**Life in an Age of Globalization.** Established in 1895, the Venice Biennale is a major international contemporary art exhibition held every other year in Venice, Italy. Housed at a park where art is displayed in thirty permanent national pavilions, the show draws visitors from around the world and suggests the effect of globalization on the arts. Here a woman takes in a work by the Italian artist Gian Marco Montesano commissioned for the Italian pavilion at the 53rd Biennale in 2009. (AFP/Getty Images)

# Chapter Preview

▶ How did life change in Russia and eastern Europe after 1989?

▶ How did globalization affect European life?

▶ What explains Europe's increasing ethnic diversity?

▶ What challenges will Europe face in the coming decades?

# ▼ How did life change in Russia and eastern Europe after 1989?

Establishing liberal democratic governments and free markets in the former East Bloc countries and the Soviet Union, now renamed Russia, would not prove an easy task. While Russia initially moved toward economic reform and political openness, the nation returned to its authoritarian traditions in the early 2000s. The transition to democracy and capitalism in the former communist countries of east-central Europe was also difficult and the results were mixed. Some countries, such as Poland, the Czech Republic, Hungary, and the Baltic states, established relatively prosperous democracies. Others, such as Romania and Bulgaria, lagged behind. In multiethnic Yugoslavia, the collapse of communism led to a disastrous civil war and the violent dissolution of the country.

## Economic Shock Therapy in Russia

Politics and economics were closely intertwined in Russia after the attempted communist coup in 1991 and the dissolution of the Soviet Union (see Chapter 30). President Boris Yeltsin, his democratic supporters, and his economic ministers wanted to create conditions that would prevent a return to communism and would also right the faltering economy. In January 1992, applying the type of economic shock therapy used by Poland (see Chapter 30), the Russians moved quickly to privatize the market, freeing prices on

**Rich and Poor in Today's Russia** A woman sells knitted scarves in front of a department store window in Moscow in September 2005. The collapse of the Soviet Union and the use of shock therapy to reform the Russian economy created new wealth but also new poverty. (TASS/Sovfoto)

Chapter 31
**Europe in an Age of Globalization**
938    **1990 to the Present**

90 percent of all Russian goods, with the exception of bread, vodka, oil, and public transportation. The government also launched a rapid privatization of industry and turned thousands of factories and mines over to new private companies.

President Yeltsin and his economic reformers believed that shock therapy would revive production and bring widespread prosperity after a brief period of hardship. The results of the reforms were in fact quite different. Prices increased 250 percent on the very first day, increasing twenty-six times in the course of 1992. At the same time, Russian production fell 20 percent. Nor did the situation stabilize quickly. After 1995, rapid but gradually slowing inflation raged, and output continued to fall. According to most estimates, in 1996 the Russian economy produced at least one-third and possibly as much as one-half less than in 1991. The Russian economy crashed again in 1998 in the wake of Asia's financial crisis.

Rapid economic liberalization worked poorly in Russia for several reasons. Soviet industry had been highly monopolized and strongly tilted toward military goods. Production of many items had been concentrated in one or two gigantic factories or in interconnected combines that supplied the entire economy. With privatization these state monopolies became private monopolies that cut production and raised prices in order to maximize their financial returns. Moreover, corporate managers and bureaucrats forced Yeltsin's government to hand out enormous subsidies to reinforce the positions of big firms and to avoid bankruptcies. Finally, new corporate leaders included criminals who intimidated would-be rivals in attempts to prevent the formation of new businesses.

Runaway inflation and poorly executed privatization brought a profound social revolution to Russia. The new capitalist elite acquired great wealth and power, while large numbers of people fell into poverty, and the majority struggled to make ends meet. Managers, former Communist officials, and financiers who came out of the privatization process with large shares of the old state monopolies stood at the top of the reorganized society.

Perhaps the most telling statistic, which reflected the hardship caused by the collapse of the Soviet welfare state and growing poverty, was the catastrophic decline in the life expectancy of the average Russian male from sixty-nine years in 1991 to only fifty-eight years in 1996. Under these conditions, effective representative government failed to develop, and many Russians came to equate democracy with the corruption, poverty, and national decline they experienced throughout the 1990s.

## Russian Revival Under Vladimir Putin

The widespread disillusionment in the first decade of postcommunist Russia set the stage for the "managed democracy" of Vladimir Putin (VLAH-duh-mihr POO-tihn) (b. 1952). First elected president as Yeltsin's chosen successor in 2000, Putin won in a landslide in March 2004. An officer in the secret police in the Communist era, Putin

## Chapter Chronology

| | |
|---|---|
| 1980s–1990s | Emergence of globalization |
| 1990s–2000s | New waves of legal and illegal immigration to Europe |
| 1990–1991 | Persian Gulf War |
| 1991 | Maastricht Treaty |
| 1991–2001 | Civil war in Yugoslavia |
| 1992–1997 | Decline of Russian economy |
| 1993 | Creation of the European Union |
| 1997–1998 | Global economic downturn |
| 1999 | Protests against World Trade Organization in Seattle |
| 2000–2008 | Resurgence of Russian economy under Putin |
| 2001 | September 11 terrorist attack on the United States; war in Afghanistan begins |
| 2002 | Euro introduced in European Union |
| 2003 | Iraq war begins |
| 2004 | Train bombings in Madrid by Islamic extremists |
| 2005 | Young Muslims riot in France; subway bombing in London by Islamic extremists |
| 2006 | Sectarian conflict in Iraq increases |
| 2008 | Worldwide financial crisis |
| 2009 | Ratification of Treaty of Lisbon; young Muslims riot in France; Copenhagen summit on climate change |

CHAPTER LOCATOR | How did life change in Russia and eastern Europe after 1989? | How did globalization affect European life? | What explains Europe's increasing ethnic diversity? | What challenges will Europe face in the coming decades?

939

and his United Russia Party maintained relatively free markets in the economic sphere but re-established semi-authoritarian political rule.

The combination of Putin's autocratic politics and the turn to market economics—aided greatly by high prices for oil and natural gas, Russia's most important exports—led to a decade of strong economic growth. In 2008 the Russian economy had been expanding for over nine years, encouraging the growth of a new middle class. That same year, the global financial crisis and a rapid drop in the price of oil reversed these trends. Economic growth ground to a halt, and the economy continued to falter in 2009 and 2010.

During his term as president, Putin championed a return to an assertive anti-Western Russian nationalism. He opposed the expansion of NATO in the former East Bloc and increasingly challenged the United States in world affairs. Putin expressed pride in the accomplishments of the Soviet Union and downplayed the abuses of the Stalinist system. Putin's carefully crafted manly image and his forceful interaction in international diplomacy soothed the country's injured pride and symbolized its national revival.

Putin's government moved to limit political opposition. The arrest and imprisonment for tax evasion of the corrupt billionaire oil tycoon Mikhail Khodorkovsky, who had openly supported opposition parties, showed that Putin and the United Russian Party would use state powers to stifle dissent. The Russian government also cracked down on the independent media. The suspicious murder in 2006 of journalist Anna Politkovskaya, a prominent critic of Russian human rights abuses and Russia's war in Chechnya, reinforced Western worries that the country was returning to Soviet-style press censorship.

Putin also took an aggressive and at times interventionist stance toward the Commonwealth of Independent States, a loose confederation of the newly independent regions on the borders of the former Soviet Union (Map 31.1). Conflict has been particularly intense in the oil-rich Caucasus region to the south, where an unstable combination of nationalist separatism and ethnic and religious tensions challenge Russian dominance. Since the breakup of the Soviet Union, Russian troops have repeatedly invaded Chechnya (CHECH-nyuh), a tiny republic of 1 million Muslims on Russia's southern border that in 1991 had declared its independence from the Russian Federation. The cost of the conflict in Chechnya has been high. Thousands on both sides have lost their lives, and both sides have committed serious human rights abuses.

Moscow declared an end to military operations in Chechnya in April 2009, but Chechen insurgents, inspired by separatist nationalism and Islamic radicalism, continued their violent struggle for independence. The ongoing civil war in Chechnya also contributed to an ongoing crisis in the independent state of Georgia, which won independence from Russia in 1991. Russian troops invaded Georgia in 2008 to support a separatist movement in South Ossetia (ah-SEE-shuh), which eventually established a breakaway independent republic.

Putin stepped down when his term limits expired in 2008. His handpicked successor, Dimitri Medvedev (mehd-VEHD-yehf) (b. 1965), won the Russian presidential elections that year and then appointed Putin prime minister, leading observers to conclude that the former president was still the dominant leader. Medvedev cast himself as a relative liberal compared to the former president, and Russian citizens enjoy a relatively open cultural life. Yet by 2010 it seemed clear that Russia had slowed attempts to establish a Western-style democracy and instead reinstituted a system of authoritarian presidential control.

## Coping with Change in Eastern Europe

Developments in eastern Europe were similar to those in Russia in important ways. The postcommunist former satellites worked to replace state planning and socialism with market mechanisms and private property. Western-style electoral politics also took hold;

Chapter 31
**Europe in an Age of Globalization**
**1990 to the Present**

940

**Map 31.1** **Russia and the Successor States, 1991–2010** After the failure of an attempt in August 1991 to depose Gorbachev, an anticommunist revolution swept the Soviet Union. Led by Russia and Boris Yeltsin, the republics that formed the Soviet Union declared their sovereignty and independence. Eleven of the fifteen republics then formed a loose confederation called the Commonwealth of Independent States, but the integrated economy of the Soviet Union dissolved into separate national economies, each with its own goals and policies. Conflict continues to simmer over these goals and policies, as evidenced by the ongoing civil war in Chechnya and the recent conflict between Russia and Georgia over South Ossetia.

as in Russia, the transition has been marked by ineffective political parties and intense battles between presidents and parliaments.

Economic growth in the former communist countries was varied, but most observers agreed that Poland, the Czech Republic, and Hungary were the most successful. The reasons for these successes included considerable experience with limited market reforms before 1989, flexibility and lack of dogmatism in government policy, and an enthusiastic embrace of capitalism by a new entrepreneurial class.

Poland, the Czech Republic, and Hungary also did far better than Russia in creating new civic institutions, legal systems, and independent media outlets that reinforced political freedom and national revival. Lech Walesa in Poland and Václav Havel in Czechoslovakia were elected presidents of their countries. After Czechoslovakia's Velvet Revolution in 1989, Havel and the Czech parliament accepted a "velvet divorce" in 1993 when Slovakian nationalists wanted to break off and form their own state. Above all, the

CHAPTER LOCATOR

How did life change in Russia and eastern Europe after 1989?

How did globalization affect European life?

What explains Europe's increasing ethnic diversity?

What challenges will Europe face in the coming decades?

941

popular goal of adopting the liberal democratic values of western Europe reinforced political moderation and compromise. In 1997 Poland, Hungary, and the Czech Republic were accepted into the NATO alliance, and in 2004 these countries plus Slovakia gained admission to the European Union (EU) (see pages 947–948).

Romania and Bulgaria lagged behind in the postcommunist transition. Western traditions were much weaker there, and both countries were much poorer than their neighbors to the north. Romania and Bulgaria did make progress after 2000, however, and joined NATO in 2004 and the EU in 2007.

The social consequences of reconstruction in the former East Bloc were similar to those in Russia. Ordinary citizens and the elderly were the big losers, while the young and former Communists were the big winners. Inequalities between richer and poorer regions also increased. Capital cities such as Warsaw, Prague, and Budapest concentrated wealth, power, and opportunity as never before, while provincial centers stagnated and old industrial areas declined. Crime and gangsterism increased in both the streets and the executive suites.

Though few former East Bloc residents wanted to return to communism, they nonetheless expressed some longings for the stability of the old system. They missed the guaranteed jobs and generous social benefits provided by the Communist state, and they found the individualism and competitiveness of capitalist democracy cold and difficult. Germans coined the term Ostalgie—a combination of the German words for "East" and "nostalgia"—to label this fondness for the lifestyles and culture of the vanished East Bloc.

At the same time, many East Bloc citizens had never fully accepted communism, primarily because they equated it with Russian imperialism and the loss of national independence. The crowds that toppled communist regimes in 1989 believed that they were liberating the nation as well as the individual. Thus, when communism died, nationalism was reborn. Reflecting this new sense of popular nationalism, conservative politicians found success in Poland, the Czech Republic, and other former East Bloc countries.

**Ostalgie** German term referring to nostalgia for the lifestyles and culture of the vanished East Bloc.

## Tragedy in Yugoslavia

The great postcommunist tragedy was Yugoslavia, which under Josip Tito had been a federation of republics and regions under centralized Communist rule (see Chapter 29). After Tito's death in 1980, power passed increasingly to the sister republics, which encouraged a revival of regional and ethnic conflicts that were exacerbated by charges of ethnically inspired massacres during World War II and a dramatic economic decline in the mid-1980s.

The revolutions of 1989 accelerated the breakup of Yugoslavia. Serbian president Slobodan Milosevic (SLOH-buh-dayn muh-LOH-suh-vihch) (1941–2006) intended to grab land from other republics and unite all Serbs, regardless of where they lived, in a "greater Serbia." In 1989 Milosevic abolished self-rule in the Serbian province of Kosovo, where Albanian-speaking, primarily Islamic peoples constituted the overwhelming majority. Milosevic's moves strengthened the cause of national separatism in the Serbian-controlled federation, and in June 1991 Slovenia and Croatia declared their independence from Yugoslavia. Milosevic's armies invaded to reassert Serbian control.

In 1992 the civil war spread to Bosnia-Herzegovina, which had also declared its independence. Serbs—about 30 percent of that region's population—refused to live under the more numerous Bosnian Muslims (Map 31.2). Yugoslavia had once been a tolerant and largely successful multiethnic state. The new goal of both sides in the Bosnian civil war was ethnic cleansing: the attempt to establish ethnically homogeneous territories by intimidation, forced deportation, and killing. Serbian armies and irregular militias attempted to "cleanse" the territory of its non-Serb residents through murder, rape, de-

**ethnic cleansing** The attempt to establish ethnically homogeneous territories by intimidation, forced deportation, and killing.

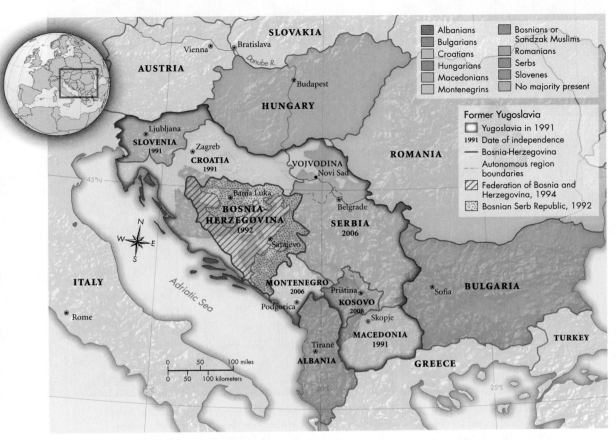

**Map 31.2 The Breakup of Yugoslavia, 1991–2006** Yugoslavia had the most ethnically diverse population in eastern Europe. The republic of Croatia had substantial Serbian and Muslim minorities. Bosnia-Herzegovina had large Muslim, Serbian, and Croatian populations, none of which had a majority. In June 1991 Serbia's brutal effort to seize territory and unite all Serbs in a single state brought a tragic civil war.

struction, and the herding of refugees into concentration camps. Before the fighting in Bosnia ended, some three hundred thousand people were dead, and millions had been forced to flee their homes.

While appalling scenes of horror shocked the world, the Western nations had difficulty formulating an effective and unified response. The turning point came in July 1995 when Bosnian Serbs overran Srebrenica—a Muslim city previously declared a United Nations safe area. Pursuing their ethnic cleansing campaign, Serb forces killed 7,400 of the city's Muslim civilians, primarily men and boys. Public outrage prompted NATO to bomb Bosnian Serb military targets intensively, and the Croatian army drove all the Serbs from Croatia. In November 1995 President Bill Clinton helped the sides hammer out an accord that gave the Bosnian Serbs about 49 percent of Bosnia and the Muslim-Croatian peoples the rest.

The Albanian Muslims of Kosovo had been hoping for a restoration of self-rule, but they gained nothing from the Bosnian agreement. In early 1998 Kosovar militants formed the Kosovo Liberation Army (KLA) and began to fight for independence. Serbian repression of the Kosovars increased, and in 1998 Serbian forces attacked both KLA guerrillas and unarmed villagers, displacing 250,000 people within Kosovo.

By January 1999 the Western Powers, led by the United States, were threatening Milosevic with air raids if he did not withdraw Serbian armies from Kosovo and accept

**Kosovo Liberation Army (KLA)** Military organization formed in 1998 by Kosovar militants who sought independence from Serbia.

CHAPTER LOCATOR | How did life change in Russia and eastern Europe after 1989? | How did globalization affect European life? | What explains Europe's increasing ethnic diversity? | What challenges will Europe face in the coming decades?

943

**Escape from Srebrenica** A Bosnian Muslim refugee arrives at the United Nations base in Tuzla and with anguished screams tells the world of the Serbian atrocities. Several thousand civilians were murdered at Srebrenica, and Western public opinion finally demanded decisive action. Efforts continue to arrest the Serbs believed responsible and to try them for crimes against humanity. (J. Jones/ Corbis)

self-government for Kosovo. Milosevic refused, and in March 1999 NATO began bombing targets in Serbia. Serbian forces responded by driving about 865,000 Albanian Kosovars into exile. NATO redoubled its bombing campaign, which eventually forced Milosevic to withdraw and allowed the Kosovars to regain their homeland. A UN–NATO peacekeeping force occupied the territory, bringing the ten-year cycle of Yugoslavian civil wars to a close.

## ▼ How did globalization affect European life?

**globalization** The emergence of a freer, more technologically connected global economy, accompanied by a worldwide exchange of cultural, political, and religious ideas.

Contemporary observers often assert that the world has entered a new era of globalization. Such assertions do not mean that there were never international connections before. Europe has long had close ties to other parts of the world. Yet new global relationships did emerge in the last decades of the twentieth century.

First, the expansion and ready availability of highly efficient computer and media technologies led to ever-faster exchanges of information and entertainment around the world. Second, the growth of multinational corporations restructured national economies on a global scale. Third, an array of international governing bodies, such as the European Union, the United Nations, the World Bank, and the World Trade Organization, increasingly set policies that challenged the authority of traditional nation-states. Taken together, these global transformations had a remarkable impact—both positive and negative—on many aspects of Western society.

Chapter 31
**Europe in an Age of Globalization**
**944** **1990 to the Present**

## The Digital Age and the Changing Economy

The development of sophisticated personal computer technologies and the Internet at the end of the twentieth century, coupled with the deregulation of national and international financial systems, had a revolutionary impact on international trade. The ability to rapidly exchange information and capital meant that economic activity was no longer centered on national banks or stock exchanges, but rather flowed quickly across international borders. Large cities like London, Moscow, New York, and Hong Kong became global centers of banking, trade, and financial services. The influence of the powerful companies and organizations headquartered in these new global cities extended far beyond the borders of the traditional nation-state.

Multinational corporations flourished in the new global climate. Conglomerates such as Siemens and Vivendi exemplified the new business model. Siemens, with international headquarters in Germany and offices around the globe, is one of the world's largest engineering companies, with holdings in energy, construction, health care, financial services, and industrial production. Vivendi, a media and telecommunications company headquartered in France, controls an international network of products, including music and film, publishing, television broadcasting, pay-TV, Internet services, and video games.

The growing global reach of multinational corporations and the development of sophisticated information technologies have had astonishing effects on everyday life. Compact discs and downloadable audio files replaced vinyl records and cassettes, and digital cameras eliminated the need for film. E-mail and text messaging changed the way friends and families exchanged news, and letter writing with pen and paper became a quaint relic of the past. Many people now relied on the Internet to access consumer goods, entertainment, and information from around the globe. The smart phone, with its multimedia telecommunications features, combined all these activities and more in one small handheld device.

Though globalization in some ways fueled the booming economy, the close connections between national economies also made the entire world vulnerable to economic panics and downturns. In 1997 a banking crisis in Thailand spread to Indonesia, South Korea, and Japan, and then echoed around the world. The resulting decline in prices for raw materials such as petroleum and natural gas hit Russia especially hard. The crisis then spread to Latin America, where most countries entered a severe economic downturn in 1998.

A decade later, in 2008, the global recession triggered by a crisis in the U.S. housing market and financial system created the worst worldwide economic crisis since the Great Depression of the 1930s. The United States government spent massive sums in attempts to recharge the economy, but unemployment, a weak housing market, and stagnant production continued.

The recession quickly swept through Europe. One of the worst hit was Iceland, where in October 2008 the currency and banking system collapsed outright. Other countries across Europe were also rocked by the crisis. Ireland and Latvia were forced to make painful cuts in government spending to balance national budgets. By 2010 Britain was deeply in debt, and Spain, Portugal, and Greece were close to bankruptcy. National governments used a variety of initiatives to revive their economies, even as experts worried about the long-term effects of the recession on European stability and demonstrators protested against cuts in social programs.

## The Human Side of Globalization

In addition to the financial vulnerabilities inherent in a global economy, the varied forces of globalization encouraged far-reaching social change tied closely to the technological advances of the postindustrial society (see Chapter 30). Low labor costs in the industrializing world — including the former East Bloc, South America, and East Asia —

CHAPTER LOCATOR | How did life change in Russia and eastern Europe after 1989? | How did globalization affect European life? | What explains Europe's increasing ethnic diversity? | What challenges will Europe face in the coming decades?

945

**Financial Meltdown in Iceland** These protesters are on their way to the parliament in Reykjavik, the capital of Iceland, in March 2010 to protest the government's proposed debt repayment policies after the collapse of the Icelandic banking system. One protester carries a sign reading "Stop the Financial Casino." Iceland's financial meltdown, sparked by a major recession in the United States, underscored the close links between national economies in the new era of globalization. (S. Olads/EPA/Corbis)

encouraged corporations to outsource labor-intensive manufacturing jobs to these regions. Free trade policies and lowered tariffs made it less expensive to manufacture goods such as steel, automotive parts, computer components, and all manner of consumer goods in developing countries, and then import them for sale in the West.

Globalization dramatically changed the nature of work in western Europe. In France in 1973, for example, some 40 percent of the employed population worked in industry—in mining, construction, manufacturing, and utilities. About 49 percent worked in services, including retail, the hotel and restaurant trades, transportation, communications, financial and business services, and social and personal services. In 2004 only 24 percent of the French worked in industry, and 72 percent worked in services. The numbers varied country by country, yet across Europe the trend was clear: by 2005 only about one in three workers was still employed in the manufacturing sector.[1]

The deindustrialization of Europe established a multitiered society. In the top tier was a small, affluent group of highly paid experts, executives, and professionals—about one-quarter of the total population—who managed the new information industries. In the second, larger tier, a struggling middle class experienced stagnating incomes and a declining standard of living. Workers from the formerly well-paid industrial sector faced unemployment and cuts in both welfare and workplace benefits.

In the bottom tier—in some areas as much as a quarter of the population—a poorly paid underclass performed the unskilled jobs of a postindustrial economy. In Europe and the United States inclusion in this lowest segment of society was often predicated on race and ethnicity. In London, unemployment rates among young black men soared above those of their white compatriots, and the connections between race and poverty were similar in other urban areas.

Geographic contrasts further revealed the unequal aspects of globalization. Regions in Europe that had successfully made the move to a postindustrial economy, such as north-

Chapter 31
**Europe in an Age of Globalization**
**946**    **1990 to the Present**

ern Italy and southern Germany and Austria, were centers of affluence and prosperity. Regions that had depended on heavy industry or were historically underdeveloped, including the former East Bloc countries, the factory districts north of London, and the largely rural areas of southern Italy and Spain, lagged behind. In addition, a global north-south divide increasingly separated the relatively affluent countries of Europe and North America from the industrializing nations of Africa and South America. Though India, China, and other East Asian nations experienced solid growth, other industrializing nations struggled to overcome decades of underdevelopment.

## The New European Union

Global economic pressures encouraged the expansion and consolidation of the European Community (EC), which in 1993 rechristened itself the European Union (EU) (Map 31.3). With its roots in Europe's Common Market (see Chapter 29), the EU worked to add the free movement of European labor, capital, and services to the existing free trade in goods. In addition, member states sought to create a monetary union in which all EU countries would share a single currency. Membership in the monetary union required states to meet the financial criteria defined in the 1991 Maastricht Treaty, which also set legal standards and anticipated the development of common policies on defense and foreign affairs.

Western European elites generally supported the step toward economic integration embodied in the Maastricht Treaty. They felt that membership requirements, which imposed financial discipline on national governments, would combat Europe's ongoing economic problems, and they viewed the establishment of a single European currency as an irreversible historic step toward basic political unity. This unity would allow western Europe as a whole to regain its place in world politics and to deal with the United States as an equal.

Support for the Maastricht Treaty was not universal. Ordinary people, leftist political parties, and populist nationalists expressed skepticism and considerable opposition to the new rules. Many people resented the EU's bureaucracy, which sought to impose common standards on everything from cheese to day care. Critics argued that EU standards undermined national practices and local traditions. Moreover, increased unity meant yielding power to distant "Eurocrats" and political insiders, supposedly limiting popular sovereignty and democratic control.

Above all, many ordinary citizens feared that the new Europe was being created at their expense. Joining the monetary union required national governments to meet stringent fiscal standards, impose budget cuts, and contribute to the EU operating budget. The resulting reductions in health care and social benefits hit ordinary citizens and did little to reduce western Europe's high unemployment rate. When put to the public for a vote, ratification of the Maastricht Treaty was usually very close. In France, for example, the treaty passed with just 50.1 percent of the vote.

Even after the Maastricht Treaty was ratified, battles over budgets and high unemployment throughout the EU in the 1990s raised questions about the meaning of European unity and identity. Would the EU expand to include the postcommunist nations of eastern Europe, and if it did, how could Muslim Turkey's long-standing application be ignored? How could a European Union of twenty-five to thirty countries have any real cohesion and common identity? Conversely, would a large, cohesive Europe remain closely linked with the United States in the NATO alliance? Would—or could—the EU develop an independent military defense policy? In the face of these questions, western Europeans proceeded cautiously in considering new requests for EU membership.

Then on January 1, 2002, the euro finally replaced the national currencies of all eurozone residents. The establishment of the European monetary union built confidence and increased willingness to accept new members. On May 1, 2004, the European Union began admitting its former East Bloc neighbors, and by 2007 the EU was home

**European Union (EU)** The economic, cultural, and political alliance of twenty-seven European nations.

**Maastricht Treaty** The basis for the formation of the European Union, which set financial and cultural standards for potential member states and defined criteria for membership in the monetary union.

CHAPTER LOCATOR | How did life change in Russia and eastern Europe after 1989? | How did globalization affect European life? | What explains Europe's increasing ethnic diversity? | What challenges will Europe face in the coming decades?

947

The European Union
- Original members, 1951
- New members, 1973
- New members, 1981
- New members, 1986
- German reunification, 1990
- New members, 1995
- New members, 2004
- New members, 2007
- Candidate countries, 2010
- € Euro Zone countries, 2010

## ▪ MAPPING THE PAST

### Map 31.3  The European Union, 2010

No longer divided by ideological competition and the Cold War, much of today's Europe has banded together in a European Union that facilitates the open movement of people, jobs, and currency across borders.

**ANALYZING THE MAP**  Trace the expansion of membership from its initial founding as the European Economic Union to today. How would you characterize the members who joined during 2004–2007? Whose membership is still pending?

**CONNECTIONS**  Which countries are and are not part of the Euro Zone, and what does this suggest about how successful the European Union has been in adopting the euro?

To complete this activity online, go to the Online Study Guide at bedfordstmartins.com/mckaywestunderstanding.

to 493 million citizens in twenty-seven different countries. It included most of the former East Bloc and, with the Baltic republics, several territories that had once been inside the Soviet Union.

This rapid expansion underscored the need to reform the EU's unwieldy governing structure. In June 2004 a special commission presented a new EU constitution that created a president, a foreign minister, and a voting system weighted to reflect the populations of the different states. The proposed constitution moved toward a more centralized federal system, but each state retained veto power over taxation, social policy, foreign affairs, and other sensitive areas. After many contentious referendum campaigns across the continent, the constitution failed to win the unanimous support that it needed to take effect. Ultimately, nationalist fears about losing sovereignty and cultural identity outweighed the perceived benefits of a more unified Europe.

In 2007 the rejected constitution was replaced by the Treaty of Lisbon. The new treaty kept many sections of the constitution, but further streamlined the EU bureaucracy and reformed its political structure. By November 2009 it had been ratified by all the EU states. When the Treaty of Lisbon went into effect on December 1, 2009, it capped a fifty-year effort to unify what had been a deeply divided and war-torn continent.

**Turkey's Struggle for EU Membership** Turkey's leaders and the general population seek to join the European Union, but the road to membership is proving difficult. The EU has required Turkey to make many constitutional reforms and to give greater autonomy to Turkish Kurds. Yet even as the other nations standing in line gain admission, the Turks face ever more demands, leading to accusations that the real roadblock is Europe's anti-Muslim feeling. (CartoonStock Limited)

## Supranational Organizations

Beyond the European Union, the trend toward globalization empowered a variety of other supranational organizations whose interests and activities crossed the borders of the world's nation-states. The United Nations (UN), established in 1945 after World War II, remains one of the most important players on the world stage. Representatives from all independent countries meet in the UN General Assembly in New York City to manage international agreements and crises. The governing Security Council — which includes the United States, Russia, France, Great Britain, and China — has the power to veto resolutions passed by the General Assembly. The many offices of the UN deal with issues such as world hunger and poverty, and the International Court of Justice in The Hague, Netherlands, hears cases that violate international law. The UN also sends troops to police crisis situations in attempts to preserve peace between warring parties.

A number of nonprofit international financial institutions — including the World Bank, the International Monetary Fund (IMF), and the World Trade Organization (WTO) — have also gained power in a globalizing world. Initially founded in the years following World War II to help rebuild war-torn Europe, the IMF and the World Bank now provide loans to the developing world. Their funding comes primarily from donations from the United States and western Europe, and they often extend loans on the condition that recipient countries adopt free trade, deregulation, and other neoliberal economic policies. After the 1990s the World Bank and the IMF played active roles in shaping economic and social policy in the former East Bloc.

With headquarters in Geneva, Switzerland, the WTO is one of the most powerful supranational financial institutions. It sets trade and tariff agreements for over 150 member countries and so helps manage a large percentage of the world's import-export policies. Like the IMF and the World Bank, the WTO promotes neoliberal policies around the world.

The rise of these institutions was paralleled by the emergence of a variety of so-called **nongovernmental organizations (NGOs)**. Some NGOs act as lobbyists for specific issues; others conduct international programs and activities. Exemplary NGOs include Doctors

**World Trade Organization (WTO)** A powerful supranational financial institution that sets trade and tariff agreements for over 150 member countries and so helps manage a large percentage of the world's import-export policies. Like the IMF and the World Bank, the WTO promotes neoliberal policies around the world.

**nongovernmental organizations (NGOs)** Independent organizations with specific agendas, such as humanitarian aid or environmental protection, that conduct international programs and activities.

CHAPTER LOCATOR | How did life change in Russia and eastern Europe after 1989? | How did globalization affect European life? | What explains Europe's increasing ethnic diversity? | What challenges will Europe face in the coming decades?

949

**Antiglobalization Activism** French protesters carry the figure of Ronald McDonald through the streets to protest the trial of José Bové, a prominent leader in campaigns against the human and environmental costs associated with globalization. Bové was accused of demolishing a McDonald's franchise in a small town in southern France. With its worldwide fast-food restaurants that pay little attention to local traditions, McDonald's has often been the target of antiglobalization protests. (Witt/Haley/Sipa)

Without Borders, a charitable organization of physicians headquartered in France; Greenpeace, an international environmental group; and Oxfam, a British-based group dedicated to alleviating famine, disease, and poverty in the developing world.

The rise of globalization has also encouraged the growth of new forms of global protest, often aimed at the leaders and economic structures of globalization itself. Such protest is typically aimed at global corporations and financial groups, which have done little to resolve the world's serious inequalities and problems, such as environmental pollution, unfair labor practices, and poor health and human rights policies.

The general tone of antiglobalization protest was captured in 1999 at the meeting of the World Trade Organization in Seattle, Washington. Tens of thousands of grassroots protesters from around the world, including environmentalists, consumer and antipoverty activists, and labor-rights groups, marched in the streets and disrupted the meeting. Similar protests took place at later meetings of the WTO, the World Bank, and other supranational groups, as activists struggled with powerful public officials to influence the course of world development.

## ▼ What explains Europe's increasing ethnic diversity?

As the twenty-first century opened and globalization began to affect European society and politics, Europeans also saw changes in the ethnic makeup of their nations. On the one hand, Europe experienced a remarkable decline in birthrates that seemed to predict a shrinking and aging population in the future. On the other hand, the European Union attracted rapidly growing numbers of refugees as well as legal and illegal immigrants from the former Soviet Union, the Middle East, Africa, and Asia. The unexpected arrival of so many newcomers raised difficult questions about ethnic diversity and the costs and benefits of multiculturalism.

### The Prospect of Population Decline

Population is still growing rapidly in many poor countries, but not in the world's industrialized nations, where in many countries birthrates have fallen below the 2.1 children per family necessary to maintain a stable population. If the current baby bust continues, the long-term consequences could be dramatic, though hardly predictable. At the least, Europe's population would decline and age. The number of people of working age would drop, and the percentage of the population over sixty would rise. Social security taxes paid by the shrinking labor force would need to soar to meet the skyrocketing costs of pensions and health care for seniors—a recipe for generational tension and conflict.

Chapter 31
**Europe in an Age of Globalization**
**1990 to the Present**
950

Why, in times of peace, were Europeans failing to reproduce? The economic conditions of the 1980s and much of the 1990s played a role. High unemployment fell heavily on young people and often frustrated their plans to settle down and have children. Some observers have also argued that a partial rejection of motherhood and parenting was critical, noting that many Europeans chose to have no children or only one child.

The ongoing impact of careers for married women and the related drive for gender equality were decisive factors in the long-term decline of postwar birthrates. After World War II, Western women married early, had their children early, and then turned increasingly to full-time employment, where they suffered from the discrimination that drove the women's movement. As the twenty-first century opened, women had attained many (but not all) of their objectives. They did as well as or better than men in school, and educated young women earned almost as much as their male counterparts.

Research has shown that European women and men in their twenties, thirties, and early forties still wanted two or even three children—about the same number as their parents had wanted. Many women, however, postponed the birth of their first child into their thirties in order to finish their education and establish themselves in their careers. Then, finding that balancing a child and a career was more difficult than anticipated, new mothers tended to postpone and eventually forgo the second child. The better educated and the more economically successful a woman was, the more likely she was to stop with a single child or to have no children at all.

By 2005 some population experts believed that European women were no longer postponing having children. At the least, birthrates appeared to have stabilized. Moreover, the frightening implications of dramatic population decline had emerged as a major public issue. Opinion leaders, politicians, and the media started to press for more babies and more support for families with children. Europeans may yet respond with enough vigor to limit the extent of their population decline and avoid societal disaster.

## Changing Immigration Flows

As European demographic vitality waned in the 1990s, a surge of migrants from Africa, Asia, and eastern Europe headed for western Europe. Some migrants entered the European Union legally, but increasing numbers did not. Large-scale immigration, both legal and illegal, emerged as a critical and controversial issue.

Western Europe drew heavily on North Africa and Turkey for manual laborers from about 1960 until about 1973, when unemployment started to rise and governments abruptly stopped the inflow. Many foreign workers stayed on, however, eventually bringing their families and establishing permanent immigrant communities. The postcolonial immigration that began in the 1950s also continued (see Chapter 29).

A new and different surge of migration into western Europe began in the 1990s. The collapse of communism and civil wars in Yugoslavia sent hundreds of thousands of refugees fleeing westward. Conflicts in Afghanistan, Iraq, Somalia, and Rwanda—to name only four countries—brought thousands more from Central Asia and Africa. Illegal immigration into the European Union also exploded, rising from an estimated 50,000 people in 1993 to perhaps 500,000 a decade later.

Though many migrants in the early twenty-first century applied for political asylum and refugee status, most were eventually rejected and classified as illegal job seekers. Economic opportunity undoubtedly was a major attraction for illegal immigrants. Germans, for example, earned on average five times more than neighboring Poles, who in turn earned much more than people farther east and in North Africa.

Illegal immigration was aided by powerful criminal gangs that profited from people smuggling. Gangs also contributed to the large number of young female illegal immigrants from eastern Europe, especially Russia and Ukraine. Often lured by criminals promising

CHAPTER LOCATOR | How did life change in Russia and eastern Europe after 1989? | How did globalization affect European life? | What explains Europe's increasing ethnic diversity? | What challenges will Europe face in the coming decades?

951

legitimate jobs, and sometimes simply kidnapped and sold for a few thousand dollars, these women were smuggled into the most prosperous parts of Europe and forced into prostitution.

## Ethnic Diversity in Contemporary Europe

By 2010 immigration to Europe had changed the ethnic makeup of the continent, though the effects were unevenly distributed. In 2005 immigrants composed about 10 percent of most western European nations, while the former East Bloc nations had far fewer foreign residents. One way to measure the effect of these new immigrants is to consider the rapid rise of their numbers. Since the 1960s the foreign population of western European nations has grown by five to ten times. In the Netherlands in 1960, for example, only 1 percent of the population was foreign born. In 2006 the foreign-born made up 10 percent. For centuries the number of foreign residents living in Europe had been relatively small. Now, permanently displaced ethnic groups or **diasporas** brought ethnic diversity to the continent.

**diasporas** Enclaves of ethnic groups settled outside of their homelands.

The new immigrants were divided into two main groups. A small percentage of the recent arrivals were highly trained specialists who could find work in education, business, and the high-tech industry. Many immigrants, however, did not have access to high-quality education or language training, which limited their employment opportunities and made integration more difficult. They often lived in separate city districts marked by poor housing and crowded conditions, which set them apart from more established residents.

A variety of new cultural forms, ranging from sports and cuisine to music, the fine arts, and film, brought together native and foreign traditions and transformed European lifestyles. The makeup of the teams who play European football (soccer) clearly reflected the new diversity. In the 1950s and 1960s regional football teams were made almost en-

**The Changing Face of London's Arsenal Football Club** Growing ethnic diversity is transforming many aspects of everyday life in contemporary Europe, including the ethnic makeup of European football (soccer) teams. In 1950 the Arsenal Football Club of northern London was composed entirely of white ethnic Britons. Today, its roster includes diverse players from around the globe. (1950 team: J. A. Hampton/Hulton Archive/Getty Images; 2010 team: Stuart MacFarlane/Arsenal Football Club)

Chapter 31
**Europe in an Age of Globalization**
952    **1990 to the Present**

tirely of local players. By 2005 a single football club in North London included players from across Europe as well as from the Ivory Coast, Brazil, and the United States.[2]

Food is another important case in point. Recipes and cooks from former colonies in North Africa enlivened French cooking, while the döner kebab — the Turkish version of a gyros sandwich — became Germany's "native" fast food. Controversy raged when the British foreign minister announced in 2001 that chicken tikka masala — a spicy Indian stew — was Great Britain's new national dish. In fact, tikka masala is a hybrid, a remarkable example of the way that peoples, recipes, and ingredients from Central Asia, Persia, and Europe had interacted for over four centuries.

The new ethnic diversity associated with globalization has inspired numerous works in literature and the fine arts. Short stories and novels by Jhumpa Lahiri, an ethnic Bengali born in London, explore the clash between immigrant and host cultures as well as the conflict between first- and second-generation immigrants. The bestselling novel *White Teeth* (2000), by British author Zadie Smith, likewise uses family settings to describe the at times painful contact between Bangladeshi Muslims and British Jews and Christians. Museums and annual art exhibitions regularly feature the works of non-Western artists who further explore the conflicts and new forms generated by cultural interaction.

This multiculturalism has also had a profound effect on popular music and film. Rai, a folk music that originated in the Bedouin culture of North Africa, exemplifies the new forms that emerge from cultural mixing. In the 1920s rai traveled with Algerian immigrants to France. In its current form, it blends Arab and North African folk music, U.S. rap, and French and Spanish pop styles. Lyrics range from sentimental love stories to blunt and sometimes bawdy descriptions of daily life.

Feature films have also been an important venue for dramatizing the experience of cross-cultural contact, and they reach large audiences. In *Bend It Like Beckham* (2002), by Indian-Anglo director Gurinder Chada, a teenage girl from Pakistan becomes an accomplished high school soccer player. She falls in love with her Irish coach, challenging the traditional values of her family, first-generation Punjabi-Sikhs from northern India. The French film *The Class* (2008), set in a high school in a working-class neighborhood in Paris, portrays a teacher's attempts to understand and inspire his students, who come from France, North and sub-Saharan Africa, and East Asia.

The growth of immigration and ethnic diversity has generated intense controversy and conflict in western Europe, raising questions about who, exactly, could or should be European, and about the way these new citizens might change European society. Some commentators have accused the newcomers of taking jobs from the unemployed and undermining national unity. The idea that cultural and ethnic diversity could be a force for vitality and creativity has run counter to deep-seated beliefs about national homogeneity. Government welfare programs intended to support struggling immigrants have been seen as a misuse of money, especially in times of economic downturn.

Immigration is a highly charged political issue. By the 1990s in France, some 70 percent of the population believed that there were "too many Arabs," and 30 percent supported right-wing politician Jean Marie Le Pen's calls to rid France of its immigrants altogether. Le Pen's National Front and other far-right political parties, such as the Danish People's Party and Austria's Freedom Party, successfully exploited popular prejudice about what they called "foreign rabble" to make impressive gains in national elections.

## Europe and Its Muslim Citizens

General concerns with migration have often fused with fears of Muslim migrants and Muslim residents who have grown up in Europe. Islam is now the largest minority religion in Europe. Muslim residents make up about 25 percent of the population in Marseilles and Rotterdam, 15 percent in Brussels, and about 10 percent in Paris, Copenhagen, and London.[3]

multiculturalism The mixing of ethnic styles in daily life and in cultural works such as film, music, art, and literature.

CHAPTER LOCATOR | How did life change in Russia and eastern Europe after 1989? | How did globalization affect European life? | **What explains Europe's increasing ethnic diversity?** | What challenges will Europe face in the coming decades?

953

### National Front Campaign Poster

This 2009 campaign poster calls on viewers to vote for the far-right French National Front in elections to the European Parliament. It portrays the familiar French image of Lady Liberty with European Union stars circling her head. (Handout/Reuters)

**ANALYZING THE IMAGE** How is Lady Liberty depicted? What type of mood is the creator trying to elicit in voters via this image?

**CONNECTIONS** According to the National Front, which issue facing Europe today is a key contributor to Lady Liberty's distress? How effective do you think emotional appeals like this one are in garnering support for far-right parties across Europe?

To complete this activity online, go to the Online Study Guide at bedfordstmartins.com/mckaywestunderstanding.

The worries increased after the September 11, 2001, al-Qaeda attack on New York's World Trade Center (see page 959) and the subsequent war in Iraq. Terrorist attacks in Europe organized by Islamic extremists heightened anxieties. In March 2004 radical Moroccan Muslims living in Spain exploded bombs planted on trains bound for Madrid, killing 191 commuters and wounding 1,800 more. A year later an attack on the London transit system carried out by British citizens of Pakistani descent killed over 50 innocent people.

The vast majority of Europe's Muslims clearly support democracy and reject radical extremism, but these attacks and lesser actions by Islamic militants nonetheless sharpened the European debate on immigration. A shrill chorus warned that, in addition to the security danger, Europe's Muslim population posed a threat to the West's entire Enlightenment tradition, which embraced freedom of thought, representative government, toleration, separation of church and state, and, more recently, equal rights for women and gays. Conservative critics proclaimed that Islamic extremists and radical clerics rejected these fundamental Western values and preached the supremacy of Islamic laws for Muslims living in Europe.

Nationalist-minded politicians tried to exploit widespread doubts that immigrant populations from Muslim countries would ever assimilate to the different national cultures. Moreover, conservative critics claimed, many so-called moderate Islamic teachers were really anti-Western radicals playing for time. (See "Individuals in Society: Tariq Ramadan," opposite.) Time was on the side of Euro-Islam, the critics warned. Europe's Muslim population, estimated at some 20 million in 2010, appeared likely to grow to 30 million by 2025 and to increase rapidly thereafter.

Admitting that Islamic extremism could pose a serious challenge, more mainstream observers have focused instead on the problem of integration. Whereas the first generation

**Tariq Ramadan.** (Salvatore Di Nolfi/Keystone)

## RELIGIOUS TEACHER, ACTIVIST PROFESSOR, AND

media star, Tariq Ramadan (b. 1962) is Europe's most famous Muslim intellectual. He is also a controversial figure, praised by many as a moderate bridge-builder and denounced by others as an Islamic militant in clever disguise.

Born in Switzerland of Egyptian ancestry, Ramadan is the grandson of Hassan al-Banna, the charismatic founder of the powerful Muslim Brotherhood. Al-Banna, who was assassinated in 1949, fought to reshape Arab nationalism within a framework of Islamic religious orthodoxy and anti-British terrorism. Tariq grew up in Geneva, where his father had sought refuge in 1954 after Nasser's anti-Islamic crackdown in Egypt. He attended mainstream public schools, played soccer, and absorbed a wide-ranging Islamic heritage. For example, growing up fluent in French and Arabic, he learned English mainly from listening to Pakistani Muslims discuss issues with his father, who represented the Muslim Brotherhood and its ideology in Europe.

Ramadan studied philosophy and French literature as an undergraduate at the University of Geneva, and then earned a doctorate in Arabic and Islamic studies. Marrying a Swiss woman who converted to Islam, Ramadan moved his family to Cairo in 1991 to study Islamic law and philosophy. It proved to be a pivotal experience. Eagerly anticipating the return to his Muslim roots, Ramadan gradually realized that only in Europe did he feel truly at home. In this personal experience he found the message that Western Muslims should participate fully as active citizens and feel "at home" in their adopted countries. In developing this message, Ramadan left the classroom and became a publicly prominent intellectual, writing nonscholarly books and making audio cassettes that sell in the tens of thousands.

Slim and elegant in well-tailored suits and open collars, Ramadan is a brilliant speaker. His public lectures in French and English draw hundreds of Muslims and curious non-Muslims. Ramadan argues that Western Muslims basically live in security, have fundamental legal rights, and can freely practice their religion. He notes that Muslims in the West are often more secure than are believers in the Muslim world, where governments are frequently repressive and arbitrary. According to Ramadan, Islamic teaching requires Western Muslims to obey Western laws, although in rare cases they may need to plead conscientious objection and disobey on religious grounds. Becoming full citizens and refusing to live in parallel as the foreign Other, Muslims should work with non-Muslims on matters of common concern, such as mutual respect, better schools, and economic justice.*

Ramadan is most effective with second- and third-generation college graduates. He urges them to think for themselves and to distinguish the sacred revelation of Islam from the nonessential cultural aspects that their parents brought from African and Asian villages.

With growing fame has come growing controversy. In 2004, preparing to take up a professorship in the United States, he was denied an entry visa on the grounds that he had contributed to a Palestinian charity with ties to terrorists. Defenders disputed the facts and charged that his criticism of Israeli policies and the invasion of Iraq were the real reasons for the denial. Ramadan's critics also claim that he says different things to different groups: hard-edged criticism of the West found on tapes for Muslims belies the reasoned moderation of his books. Some critics also argue that his recent condemnation of Western capitalism and globalization is an opportunistic attempt to win favor with European leftists and does not reflect his self-proclaimed Islamic passion for justice. Yet, in 2010 the U.S. State Department lifted the ban that prevented Ramadan from entering the United States, and the scholar's reputation remains intact.† An innovative bridge-builder, he symbolizes the growing importance of Europe's Muslim citizens.

## QUESTIONS FOR ANALYSIS

1. What is Ramadan's message to Western Muslims? How did he reach his conclusions?
2. Do you think Ramadan's ideas are realistic? Why?

*See, especially, Tariq Ramadan, *Western Muslims and the Future of Islam* (Oxford: Oxford University Press, 2004).
†See Ian Buruma, "Tariq Ramadan Has an Identity Issue," *The New York Times Magazine*, February 4, 2007.

**CHAPTER LOCATOR** | How did life change in Russia and eastern Europe after 1989? | How did globalization affect European life? | **What explains Europe's increasing ethnic diversity?** | What challenges will Europe face in the coming decades?

955

# William Pfaff, "Will the French Riots Change Anything?"

*In late November 2005 young Muslim males rioted for several nights in the suburbs of Paris and other French cities. Receiving saturation coverage from the media, their explosion of car-burning and arson ignited controversy and debate throughout France and across Europe. Similar outbreaks occurred in 2007 and 2009. What caused the riots, and why did they persist? Anti-immigrant conservatives interpret the events as an example of the inevitable conflict between Christians and Muslims. More liberal observers have argued that dismal living conditions and failures of assimilation were to blame.*

*One penetrating commentary, written after the unrest in 2005 and aimed at an American audience, came from William Pfaff, a noted author and political columnist with many years of European experience. As you read Pfaff's analysis, note in particular the portrait he draws of daily life in France's immigrant ghettos and the role of religion in French Muslim society.*

❝ The rioting in France's ghetto suburbs is a phenomenon of futility — but a revelation nonetheless. It has no ideology and no purpose other than to make a statement of distress and anger. It is beyond politics. It broke out spontaneously and spread in the same way, communicated by televised example, ratified by the huge attention it won from the press and television and the politicians, none of whom had any idea what to do.

It has been an immensely pathetic spectacle, whose primary meaning has been that it happened. It has been the most important popular social phenomenon in France since the student uprisings of 1968. But those uprisings . . . had consequences for power. The new riots have nothing to do with power.

They started with the accidental electrocutions of two boys hiding from the police, who they thought were after them. The police say there was no pursuit and they had no interest in the boys. However, under the policies of the minister of interior — the presidential candidate Nicolas Sarkozy — there had been a general police crackdown in these ugly suburban clusters of deteriorating high-rise apartments built years ago to house immigrant workers. They were meant to be machines for living. The police attention meant random identity checks, police suspicion, and harassment of young men hanging about — maybe

dealing in drugs, maybe simply doing nothing because there is nothing for them to do. (In the past, they at least had to do national military service, which was a strong integrative force, but now France has a professional army.)

Their grandfathers came to France, mostly from North Africa, to do the hard labor in France's industrial reconstruction after the Second World War. Their fathers saw the work gradually dry up as Europe's economies slowed, following the first oil shock in the early 1970s. After that came unemployment. The unemployment rate in the zones where there has been the most violence is nearly 40 percent and among young people it is higher. Many of the young men in these places have never been offered a job. When they applied, their names often excluded them.

Their grandfathers were hard-working men. Their fathers saw their manhood undermined by unemployment. These young men are doomed to be boys. They often take their frustration out on their sisters and girlfriends, who are more likely to have done well in school and found jobs — and frequently a new life — outside the ghetto. . . .

The Muslim mothers and wives of the French ghetto are often confined in the home. Drugs are big business in the American ghetto; they are not that big in France. The crimes of the French ghetto are robbery and shoplifting, stealing mobile phones, stealing cars for joyrides, burning them afterward to eliminate fingerprints, or burning cars just for the hell of it, as well as robbing middle-class students in the city and making trouble on suburban trains, looking for excitement.

Religion is important . . . in the French ghetto, it provides the carapace that protects against the France that excludes Muslims. To the European Muslim, it seems that all of the powerful in the world are in collusion to exclude Muslims — or are at war with them. The war in Iraq, on television, is the constant backdrop to Muslim life in Europe. There are itinerant imams who can put the young ghetto Muslim on the road to danger and adventure in Afghanistan, Pakistan, Iraq — or elsewhere. There are plenty more who preach a still deeper ghettoization: a retreat inside Islamic funda-

of Muslim migrants had found jobs as unskilled workers in Europe's great postwar boom, they and their children had been hard hit after 1973 by the general economic downturn. Immigrants also suffered from the ongoing decline of European manufacturing due to globalization. Provided for modestly by the welfare state and living in dilapidated housing projects, many Muslims of the second and third generations were finding themselves outcasts in their adopted countries. In short, observers suggested, economic prospects and discrimination had more influence on immigrant attitudes about their host communities than did religion.

Chapter 31
**Europe in an Age of Globalization**
956    **1990 to the Present**

Angry youths set vehicles on fire in October 2005 as riots erupt on the streets around Clichy-Sous-Bois, a Paris suburb in which foreign-born residents make up over 35 percent of the population. The riots began after two teenage boys were electrocuted and died while hiding from police in a local power substation. (Jean-Michel Turpin/Corbis)

a citizen just like everyone else, with all the rights and privileges of citizenship — including the right to be unemployed.

Nicolas Sarkozy's zero tolerance of crime and of the petty mafias in the ghetto contributed to touching off these riots, but until recently he was the only French politician to say there has to be affirmative action to get an immigrant elite out of the ghettos and into important roles in French life, where they can pull their communities after them. Some affirmative action has been attempted in recruiting candidates for the elite *grandes écoles* [state schools] that train the French administrative and political class, where the cultural hurdles are immense for candidates. Virtually no children of the Muslim immigration are prominent in mainstream electoral politics; the political parties have yet to make a serious effort to include them. The present government has one junior minister of Algerian origin. I am not aware of any Muslims of immigrant origin in French diplomacy or the top ranks of police and military.

President Jacques Chirac has announced a civilian national service agency to give training and employment to 50,000 young people from the troubled zones by 2007. The age of apprenticeship has been lowered to fourteen, with a corresponding drop in the age of compulsory academic schooling and new measures to support apprenticeships. There will be more money for schools, local associations, and housing construction and renovation. This is change. Whether it is enough, and in time, is another matter. 〞

**Source:** William Pfaff, "The French Riots: Will They Change Anything?" *The New York Review of Books*, vol. 52, no. 20, December 15, 2005, pp. 88–89. Copyright © 2005 NYREV, Inc. Reprinted with permission from The New York Review of Books.

### QUESTIONS FOR ANALYSIS

1. Describe the situation of young Muslims in France. What elements of their situation strike you most forcefully? How might these contribute to ongoing outbreaks of civic unrest?
2. France has maintained that, since all citizens are equal, they should all be treated the same way. Why has this policy failed for French Muslims? What alternatives would you suggest? Why?

mentalism, totally shutting out a diabolized secular world.

One would think there would be a revolutionary potential in these ghettos, vulnerability to a mobilizing ideology. This seems not to be so. We may be living in a religious age, but it is not one of political ideology. In any case, it is difficult to imagine how the marginalized, thirteen- to twenty-three-year-old children of the Muslim immigration could change France other than by what they are doing, which is to demonstrate that the French model of assimilating immigrants as citizens, and not as members of religious or ethnic groups, has failed for them. It has failed because it has not seriously been tried.

The ghettoization of immigrant youth in France is the consequence of negligence. It has been as bad as the ghettoization through political correctness of Muslims in Britain and the Netherlands, where many people who thought of themselves as enlightened said that assimilation efforts were acts of cultural aggression. The immigrant in France is told that he or she is

This argument was strengthened by widespread rioting in France in 2005 and again in 2009 by hundreds of young second- and third-generation Muslim immigrants. Almost always French by birth, language, and education, marauding groups labeled "Arabs" in press reports torched hundreds of automobiles in Paris suburbs and large cities. (See "Listening to the Past: William Pfaff, 'Will the French Riots Change Anything?'" above.) The rioters complained bitterly of high unemployment, systematic discrimination, and exclusion.

An articulate minority used such arguments to challenge anti-migrant, anti-Muslim discrimination and its racist overtones. They argued that Europe needed newcomers—

CHAPTER LOCATOR | How did life change in Russia and eastern Europe after 1989? | How did globalization affect European life? | **What explains Europe's increasing ethnic diversity?** | What challenges will Europe face in the coming decades?

957

preferably talented newcomers—to limit the impending population decline and provide valuable technical skills. Some scholars conclude that Europe must recognize that Islam is now a European religion and a vital part of European life. This recognition might open the way to eventual political and cultural acceptance of European Muslims and head off the resentment that can drive Europe's Muslim believers to separatism and acts of terror.

# ▼ What challenges will Europe face in the coming decades?

As the first decade of the twenty-first century drew to a close, European societies were faced with a number of critical challenges. Growing distance between the United States and Europe revealed differences in international policies and values. Washington's traditional western European allies criticized the U.S.-led war on terror. Environmental problems revealed the dangers of heavy dependence on fossil fuels for energy consumption. At the same time, the relative wealth of European societies prompted reflection on European identity, Europe's humanitarian mission, and Europe's place in the larger community of nations.

## Growing Strains in U.S.-European Relations

In the fifty years after World War II, the United States and western Europe generally maintained close ties, usually working together to promote international consensus under U.S. guidance, as represented by the NATO alliance. For example, a U.S.-led coalition attacked Iraqi forces in Kuwait in the 1990–1991 Persian Gulf War, freeing Kuwait from attempted annexation by Iraqi dictator Saddam Hussein. Over time, however, the growing power of the European Union and the new unilateral thrust of Washington's foreign policy created strains in familiar transatlantic relations.

There were many reasons for the growing gap between the United States and Europe. For one, the European Union was now the world's largest trading block, challenging the predominance of the United States. European businesses invested heavily in the United States, reversing a decades-long economic relationship in which investment dollars had flowed the other way. For another, under President George W. Bush (r. 2001–2009), the United States often ignored international opinion in pursuit of its own interests. Washington refused to ratify the Kyoto Treaty of 1997, which was intended to limit global warming. Nor did the United States join the International Criminal Court. These unilateral positions troubled EU leaders, as did unflagging U.S. support for Israel in the ongoing Arab-Israeli crisis.

Geopolitical issues relating to NATO widened the gap further. Despite the absence of a Cold War enemy, NATO continued to expand. In 1999 Poland, Hungary, and the Czech Republic joined the alliance. By 2010 France had returned to full membership, and the addition of new countries from eastern Europe and the Balkans had swelled the total number of member states to twenty-eight.

With so many members, it could prove difficult for NATO to win unanimous support for its actions. France, for example, did not support NATO's engagement in Bosnia in 1999 (see pages 943–944) because the alliance failed to get UN approval for the action. NATO allies only reluctantly supported U.S. president Barack Obama's 2010 push for increased troop levels in Afghanistan (see page 961). Differences also emerged over the response to the popular revolts that shook a number of Arab nations, particularly Libya, in 2011. As the EU expanded, some argued that Europe should establish its own independent military and defense policy. Meanwhile, Russian leaders were angered

Chapter 31
**Europe in an Age of Globalization**
**1990 to the Present**

**958**

by NATO's expansion into former East Bloc countries adjacent to Russia, particularly when President Bush moved to deploy missile defense systems in Poland and the Czech Republic in 2008.

The Iraq war, which began in 2003 (see page 960), likewise placed heavy strains on U.S.-European relations. Some of America's traditional allies, including France and Germany, opposed the war. The only substantial support for the war came from Great Britain, under Prime Minister Tony Blair (r. 1997–2007). Even there, the majority of the population was opposed, and Blair's popular approval eroded rapidly. Hostility increased when U.S. secretary of defense Donald Rumsfeld suggested that France and Germany now represented "old Europe," in contrast to the "new" European countries, including Poland, Spain, and Italy, which supported U.S. actions. By 2006 even these supporters had withdrawn their small troop contingents from Iraq.

There was also a values gap. Ever more secular Europeans had a hard time understanding the religiosity of many Americans and of the openly Christian President Bush. Relatively lax gun control laws and the use of the death penalty in the United States were viewed with dismay. U.S. reluctance to reform its health care system shocked Europeans, who took their extensive state-financed medical benefits for granted. Public opinion polls showed that the depth of anti-American sentiment among ordinary European citizens was worse in 2008 than it had been during the war in Vietnam.

The election of Barack Obama, America's first African American president, in 2008 brought some improvement to U.S.-European relations. Though Obama's policies proved divisive at home, the new president was wildly popular among ordinary Europeans. When Obama visited Germany during his 2008 presidential campaign, over two hundred thousand Berliners cheered as he called for a new approach to diplomatic relations and international justice as well as a renewal of the U.S.-European alliance.

After his election, Obama made a number of changes in foreign policy that set his administration apart from that of George W. Bush. His attempts to open diplomatic negotiations with countries hostile to U.S. interests, such as North Korea and Iran, and his willingness to advocate climate change control measures won support in Europe. Obama announced that he would not deploy missiles in central Europe and agreed to reductions in nuclear arms, easing tensions with Russia. When Obama traveled to Oslo, Norway, in December 2009 to accept the Nobel Peace Prize, Europeans hoped that this symbolic recognition would encourage the president to bring a more cooperative face to U.S. foreign policy. Despite these changes, President Obama and the United States continued to fight two unpopular wars in the Middle East, making it difficult to resolve divisions in U.S.-European interests.

## The War on Terror and European Security

On the morning of September 11, 2001, two hijacked passenger planes from Boston crashed into and destroyed the World Trade Center towers in New York City. Shortly thereafter a third plane smashed into the Pentagon, and a fourth, believed to be headed for the White House or the U.S. Capitol, crashed into a field in rural Pennsylvania. These terrorist attacks, perpetrated by the radical Islamic group al-Qaeda, took the lives of more than three thousand people and put the safety of ordinary citizens at the top of the West's agenda.

At first, the terrorist attacks seemed to bridge the growing gap between the United States and its European allies. Stunned and horrified, the peoples and governments of Europe and the world joined Americans in heartfelt solidarity. Over time, however, tensions between Europe and the United States reemerged and deepened, particularly after President Bush declared a unilateral U.S. **war on terror** — a determined effort to fight terrorism in all its forms, around the world.

Shortly after the September 11 attacks, the United States announced it would invade Afghanistan to destroy the perpetrators of the crime — Saudi-born millionaire Osama

**war on terror** American policy under President Bush to fight global terrorism in all its forms.

CHAPTER LOCATOR | How did life change in Russia and eastern Europe after 1989? | How did globalization affect European life? | What explains Europe's increasing ethnic diversity? | What challenges will Europe face in the coming decades?

959

**Dutch Troops in Afghanistan** The commander of a Dutch army platoon serving with NATO forces in the war in Afghanistan speaks with an Afghan village elder during a routine patrol in January 2010. Sending European troops to support U.S. and NATO efforts to end the Taliban insurgency in this central Asian country was unpopular with ordinary Europeans and contributed to growing strains in U.S.-European foreign relations. (Deshakalyan Chowdhury/AFP/Getty Images)

bin Laden's al-Qaeda network and Afghanistan's reactionary Muslim government, the Taliban. Building a broad international coalition that included western Europe, Russia, and Pakistan, the United States joined with local anti-Taliban resistance fighters to quickly topple the Taliban government. The war in Afghanistan, however, was not over. U.S. and European NATO troops failed to find bin Laden, and the Taliban insurgents retreated into the mountainous southern regions of the country, where they continued to engage in guerrilla warfare. By 2010, as President Obama deployed thirty thousand additional U.S. troops to quell the insurgency, Germany, Italy, the Netherlands, and other NATO contributors were facing growing popular discontent with the war. Although bin Laden was eventually found and killed by U.S. commandos at his hideout in Pakistan in May 2011, the Afghan war continued to strain NATO alliances.

Even as fighting continued in Afghanistan, in late 2001 the Bush administration turned its attention to Saddam Hussein's Iraq. Many in the administration argued that a U.S.-led intervention could turn Iraq into a pro-American democracy. A remade Iraq, they believed, would transform the Middle East in ways that were favorable to the United States. The most effective prowar argument, however, played on American fears of renewed terrorism and charged that Saddam Hussein was still developing weapons of mass destruction in disregard of his 1991 promise to end all such programs.

Many Americans shared the widespread doubts held by Europeans about the wisdom of an American attack on Iraq. Protesters and some politicians in the United States and Europe argued for a peaceful settlement of the Iraqi crisis, especially after UN inspectors found no weapons of mass destruction in the country. Though the UN failed to approve an invasion, in March 2003 the United States and Britain, with token support from a handful of other European states, invaded Iraq. They quickly overwhelmed the Iraqi army, and Saddam's dictatorship collapsed.

Chapter 31
**Europe in an Age of Globalization**
**960**   **1990 to the Present**

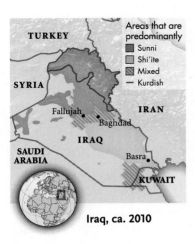

**Iraq, ca. 2010**

Areas that are predominantly
- Sunni
- Shi'ite
- Mixed
- Kurdish

America's subsequent efforts to establish a stable pro-American Iraq proved difficult, if not impossible. Poor postwar planning and management by President Bush and his top aides was one factor, but there were others. Modern Iraq, a creation of Western imperialism after World War I (see Chapter 26), is a fragile state with three distinct groups: non-Arab Kurds, Arab Sunni Muslims, and Arab Shi'ite Muslims. Ethnic and religious tensions among these groups directly contributed to instability in occupied Iraq, and by 2006 a sectarian conflict had taken hold in Baghdad. American soldiers were increasingly caught in the crossfire between Sunni and Shi'ite militias.

The fighting had reached a high point in 2006–2007, when President Bush announced that he would initiate new counterinsurgency policies and send additional troops to bolster U.S. forces. By the time President Obama took office in 2009, this troop surge had successfully reduced violence across the country. Though insurgents continued to mount attacks, the number of casualties had declined dramatically, and the Obama administration moved forward with agreements negotiated by President Bush to withdraw all U.S. troops by the end of 2011. The Iraqi government, however, continued to struggle with ethnic divisiveness and security concerns.

The U.S. invasion of Iraq caused some European leaders to question Washington's general rationale for the war on terror. Europeans shared U.S. worries about stability in the Middle East, and they faced their own problems with Islamic terrorism. But European leaders worried that the tactics used in the war, exemplified by Washington's readiness to use its military without international agreements or UN backing, violated international law. Moreover, the U.S.-led war raised serious human rights concerns. The revelation of the use of harsh interrogation by American forces in the Iraqi prison Abu Ghraib shocked European public opinion. U.S. willingness to engage in "extraordinary rendition"—secretly moving terrorism suspects to countries that allow coercive interrogation techniques—further disturbed European observers.

Indeed, leaders in Europe questioned the very idea of a war on terror. Because terrorism is a stateless phenomenon, military victory in a single state, they argued, would hardly end terrorism. Instead, they maintained, terrorism was better fought through police and intelligence measures than through military action. Thus, European security services focused on tighter EU borders, stepped-up airport security, increased public surveillance, and additional support for antiterrorist police investigations. Acknowledging their common goal of preventing future attacks, security forces in Europe also coordinated counterterrorism efforts with experts in the United States to investigate and stop international terrorist groups.

## The Dependence on Fossil Fuels

One of the most significant challenges facing Europe and indeed the world in the twenty-first century is the search for adequate energy resources. Maintaining standards of living in industrialized countries requires extremely high levels of energy use, and current supplies are heavily dependent on fossil fuels, including oil, coal, and natural gas.

Global conflicts over access to limited energy resources have become an increasingly familiar aspect of life in the twenty-first century. In 2008 Europe and Russia combined had 12 percent of the world's population but consumed about 40 percent of the world's annual natural gas production, 25 percent of the world's oil, and 16 percent of the world's coal. Scholars argue that such high levels of usage are unsustainable over the long run.

CHAPTER LOCATOR | How did life change in Russia and eastern Europe after 1989? | How did globalization affect European life? | What explains Europe's increasing ethnic diversity? | **What challenges will Europe face in the coming decades?**

**961**

Struggles to control and profit from these shrinking resources often cut across ethnic, religious, and national lines, leading to intractable conflicts and tense new geopolitical arrangements. The need to preserve access to oil has led to a transformation in military power in the post–Cold War world. During the Cold War, the largest areas of military buildup were in central Europe and in East Asia. Today military power is increasingly concentrated in oil-producing areas such as the Middle East, which holds about 65 percent of the world's oil reserves.

Russian territory has massive quantities of oil and natural gas, and the global struggle for energy has placed Russia in a powerful but strained position. The Russian invasions of Chechnya and Georgia were attempts to maintain political influence in these formerly Soviet borderlands, and also to preserve control of the region's rich energy resources.

Beyond military invasions, Russian leaders use their control over energy to assert political influence. The Russian energy corporation Gazprom sells Europe 28 percent of its natural gas, and the EU treads softly in order to maintain this supply. There have been over fifty politically motivated disruptions of natural gas supply in the former Soviet republics, including one in January 2009 when Russia shut off supplies to Ukraine for three weeks, closing factories and leaving hundreds of thousands without heat.

— Oil pipeline
— Gas pipeline
■ Supplied by Russia

**Primary Oil and Gas Pipelines to Europe, ca. 2005**

## Environmental Problems and Progress

Even if the supply of fossil fuels were not of concern, the use of these energy sources has led to serious environmental problems. Burning oil and coal releases massive amounts of carbon dioxide ($CO_2$), the leading cause of global warming, into the atmosphere. Thus, fossil fuel usage directly contributes to climate change and the degradation of the world's oceans. Climatologists meeting in March 2009 in Copenhagen concluded that climate change was proceeding dramatically faster than previously predicted and that some climatic disruption is now unavoidable. Rising average temperatures were melting glaciers and leading to the retreat of glacial ice packs, resulting in the drying up of freshwater sources across the world. Moreover, in the next fifty years rising sea levels will threaten low-lying coastal areas with flooding and inundation. Since the 1990s the EU has spearheaded efforts to control energy consumption and contain climate change. EU leaders have imposed tight restrictions on emissions, and Germany, the Netherlands, and Denmark have become world leaders in harnessing alternate energy sources.

In addition to the problems presented by global warming, the world's oceans and freshwater lakes have been threatened by overuse and pollution. Usable water resources have been jeopardized by a number of toxins and waste products. The environmental disaster that resulted when an offshore oil-drilling rig exploded in the Gulf of Mexico in April 2010, spewing millions of gallons of oil into the gulf waters, underscored the close connections between energy needs and water pollution.

In a revealing example of the international reach of the new global institutions, the EU has issued stringent policies in an effort to limit the human impact on water resources. In 2003 the EU implemented a new Common Fisheries Policy. The new regulations were designed to halt the dumping of hazardous pollutants into rivers and oceans and to preserve noncommercial species from harm during fishing. They also addressed public health issues by requiring the strict labeling of seafood for poisonous contaminants. To maintain stocks of commercially valuable fish, the EU placed caps on total allowable

**global warming** The increase of average temperatures around the world, caused primarily by carbon dioxide emissions from the burning of fossil fuels.

Chapter 31
**Europe in an Age of Globalization**
962    **1990 to the Present**

catch, limited the number of fishing boats in specific regions, and regulated fishing technology.

Though EU efforts to regulate energy use and control pollution showed some success, the overall effort to control energy consumption has been an uphill battle, underscoring the interconnectedness of the contemporary world. Developing nations have had a difficult time balancing environmental concerns and economic growth. In December 2009 the representatives of 192 nations met in Copenhagen, Denmark, and agreed to reduce $CO_2$ emissions responsibly and extend financial support to developing countries to help them deal with the effects of global warming. Whether leaders have the political will to carry out this and other plans to limit the human impact on the environment, however, remains uncertain.

## Promoting Human Rights

European residents entering the twenty-first century enjoyed some of the highest living standards in the world, the result of fifty years of peace, security, and overall economic growth. The agonies of war in the former Yugoslavia vividly recalled the horrors of World War II and cast in bold relief the ever-present reality of collective violence in today's world. For some Europeans, the realization of this contrast—that they had so much and so many others had so little—kindled a desire to help. As a result, European intellectuals and opinion makers began to envision a new historic mission for Europe: the promotion of domestic peace and human rights around the world.

**Demonstrating for Peace** Holding torches, some 3,500 people form the peace sign in Heroes Square in central Budapest, the capital of Hungary in 2006. The rally marked the third anniversary of the U.S.-led invasion of Iraq. Millions long for peace, but history and current events suggest that bloody conflicts will continue. Yet Europeans have cause for cautious optimism: despite episodes of intense violence and suffering, since 1945 wars have been localized, cataclysmic catastrophes like World Wars I and II have been averted, and Europe has become a world leader in the push for global human rights. (Peter Kollanyi/epa/Corbis)

CHAPTER LOCATOR | How did life change in Russia and eastern Europe after 1989? | How did globalization affect European life? | What explains Europe's increasing ethnic diversity? | **What challenges will Europe face in the coming decades?**

963

European leaders and humanitarians believed that more global agreements and new international institutions were needed to set moral standards and to regulate countries, political leaders, armies, corporations, and individuals. In practice, this meant more curbs on the sovereign rights of the world's states, just as the states of the European Union had imposed increasingly strict standards of behavior on themselves in order to secure the rights and welfare of EU citizens.

In practical terms, western Europe's evolving human rights mission would require, first of all, military intervention to stop civil wars and to prevent tyrannical governments from slaughtering their own people. Thus the European Union joined with the United States to intervene militarily in Bosnia, Croatia, and Kosovo. The states of the EU also vigorously supported UN initiatives to verify the compliance of anti–germ warfare conventions, outlaw the use of land mines, and establish a new international court to prosecute war criminals.

Europeans also pushed for broader definitions of individual rights. Abolishing the death penalty in the European Union, for example, they condemned its continued use in China, the United States, and Saudi Arabia. Rights for Europeans in their personal relations also continued to expand. In the Netherlands, for example, a growing network of laws gave pensions and full worker's rights to prostitutes. They also legalized gay and lesbian marriages, the smoking of marijuana in licensed coffee shops, and assisted suicide (euthanasia) for the terminally ill.

As the first decade of the twenty-first century drew to a close, western Europeans also pushed to extend their broad-based concept of social and economic rights to the world's poor countries. These efforts were often related to sharp criticism of globalization and unrestrained neoliberal capitalism. Europe's moderate Social Democrats joined human rights campaigners in 2001 to secure drastic price cuts from international pharmaceutical corporations selling drugs to combat Africa's AIDS crisis. Strong advocates of greater social equality and state-funded health care, European socialists embraced morality as a basis for action and the global expansion of human rights as a primary goal.

---

# ← LOOKING BACK LOOKING AHEAD →

THE TWENTY-FIRST CENTURY opened with changes and new challenges for the Western world. The collapse of the East Bloc brought democracy to central and eastern Europe, but left millions struggling to adapt to a radically different way of life. High-tech information systems that quickened the pace of communications and the global reach of new supranational institutions made the world a smaller place, but globalization left some struggling to maintain their livelihoods. New contacts between peoples, made possible by increased migration, revitalized European society, but raised concerns about cultural difference and sometimes led to violent confrontations.

One thing is sure: despite the success of European democracy and liberalism, and despite the high living standards enjoyed by most of those on the European subcontinent, the challenges won't go away. The search for solutions to environmental degradation and conflicts between ethnic and religious groups, and the promotion of human rights across the globe, will clearly occupy European and world leaders for some time to come.

However these issues play out, the study of the past puts the present and the future in perspective. Others before us have trodden the paths of uncertainty and crisis, and the historian's ability to analyze and explain the choices they made helps us understand our current situation and helps save us from exaggerated self-pity in the face of

Chapter 31
**Europe in an Age of Globalization**
**964**    **1990 to the Present**

our own predicaments. Perhaps our Western heritage may rightly inspire us with measured pride and self-confidence. We stand, momentarily, at the head of the long procession of Western civilization. Sometimes the procession has wandered, or backtracked, or done terrible things. But it has also carried the efforts and sacrifices of generations of toiling, struggling ancestors. Through no effort of our own, we are the beneficiaries of those sacrifices and achievements. Now that it is our turn to carry the torch onward, we may remember these ties with our forebears.

To change the metaphor, we in the West are like card players who have been dealt many good cards. Some of them are obvious, such as our technical and scientific heritage, our environmental resources, and our commitment to human rights and individual freedoms. Others are not so obvious, sometimes half-forgotten or even hidden up the sleeve. Think, for example, of the almost miraculous victory of peaceful revolution in eastern Europe in 1989 — in what Czech playwright-turned-president Václav Havel called "the power of the powerless." Here we again see the regenerative strength of the Western ideals of individual rights and representative government in the European homeland. We hold a good hand.

Our study of history, of mighty struggles and fearsome challenges, of shining achievements and tragic failures, gives a sense of the essence of life itself: the process of change over time. Again and again we have seen how peoples and societies evolve, influenced by ideas, human passions, and material conditions. This process of change will continue as the future becomes the present and then the past. Students of history are better prepared to make sense of this unfolding process because they have already observed it. They understand that change is rooted in existing historical forces, and they have tools to explore the intricate web of change that propels life forward. Students of history are prepared for the new and unexpected in human development, for they have already seen great breakthroughs and revolutions. They have an understanding of how things really happen. ∎

- **For a list of suggested readings for this chapter, visit** *bedfordstmartins.com/mckaywestunderstanding.*

- **For primary sources from this period, see** *Sources of Western Society,* Second Edition.

- **For Web sites, images, and documents related to topics in this chapter, see Make History at** *bedfordstmartins.com/mckaywestunderstanding.*

CHAPTER LOCATOR | How did life change in Russia and eastern Europe after 1989? | How did globalization affect European life? | What explains Europe's increasing ethnic diversity? | What challenges will Europe face in the coming decades?

965

# ▪ Chapter 31 Study Guide

Online Study Guide
bedfordstmartins.com/mckaywestunderstanding

## Step 1

**GETTING STARTED** Below are basic terms about this period in the history of Western civilization. Can you identify each term below and explain why it matters? To do this exercise online, go to bedfordstmartins.com/mckaywestunderstanding.

| TERMS | WHO (OR WHAT) AND WHEN | WHY IT MATTERS |
|---|---|---|
| Ostalgie, p. 942 | | |
| ethnic cleansing, p. 942 | | |
| Kosovo Liberation Army (KLA), p. 943 | | |
| globalization, p. 944 | | |
| European Union (EU), p. 947 | | |
| Maastricht Treaty, p. 947 | | |
| World Trade Organization (WTO), p. 949 | | |
| nongovernmental organizations (NGOs), p. 949 | | |
| diasporas, p. 952 | | |
| multiculturalism, p. 953 | | |
| war on terror, p. 959 | | |
| global warming, p. 962 | | |

## Step 2

**MOVING BEYOND THE BASICS** The exercise below requires a more advanced understanding of the chapter material. Fill in the chart below with descriptions of European society, economics, politics, and culture in 1900, 1950, and 2000. When you are finished, consider the following questions: What were the most important trends in European life over the course of the twentieth century? How would you explain the general shift from competition to cooperation among European nations? What obstacles to European unity still remain? To do this exercise online, go to bedfordstmartins.com/mckaywestunderstanding.

| | SOCIETY | ECONOMICS | POLITICS | CULTURE |
|---|---|---|---|---|
| Europe in 1900 | | | | |
| Europe in 1950 | | | | |
| Europe in 2000 | | | | |

## PUTTING IT ALL TOGETHER Now that you've reviewed key elements of the chapter, take a step back and try to see the big picture. Remember to use specific examples from the chapter in your answers. To do this exercise online, go to bedfordstmartins.com/mckaywestunderstanding.

### RUSSIA AND EASTERN EUROPE AFTER THE COLD WAR

- Compare and contrast the Russian/Soviet state in 1914, 1945, and 2010. What continuities do you see in the Russian/Soviet state over the course of the twentieth century? What are the most important differences?

- How would you explain the pattern of post–Cold War development in eastern Europe? Why were some states more successful than others? Why did the end of the Cold War lead to tragedy in Yugoslavia?

### GLOBALIZATION

- How did new global connections change the economic relationship between Europe and the rest world? What were the advantages and disadvantages of this altered relationship?

- In your opinion, what groups within Europe have gained the most from globalization? Which have the lost the most?

### MULTICULTURALISM

- Compare and contrast the issues and debates surrounding legal and illegal immigration in Europe and the United States. How would you explain the differences you note?

- How do you imagine Europe's population will have changed fifty years from now? What current social and cultural conflicts and challenges will remain? What new challenges will have emerged?

■ **In Your Own Words** Imagine that you must explain Chapter 31 to someone who hasn't read it. What would be the most important points to include and why?

## Chapter 15

1. Quoted in C. M. Cipolla, *Guns, Sails, and Empires: Technological Innovation and the Early Phases of European Expansion, 1400–1700* (New York: Minerva Press, 1965), p. 132.
2. Quoted in F. H. Littell, *The Macmillan Atlas: History of Christianity* (New York: Macmillan, 1976), p. 75.
3. J. M. Cohen, ed. and trans., *The Four Voyages of Christopher Columbus* (New York: Penguin Books, 1969), p. 37.
4. Thomas Benjamin, *The Atlantic World: Europeans, Africans, Indians, and Their Shared History, 1400–1900* (Cambridge, U.K.: Cambridge University Press, 2009), pp. 35–59.
5. Quoted in C. Gibson, ed., *The Black Legend: Anti-Spanish Attitudes in the Old World and the New* (New York: Knopf, 1971), pp. 74–75.
6. Cited in Geoffrey Vaughn Scammell, *The First Imperial Age: European Overseas Expansion, c. 1400–1715* (London and New York: Routledge, 2002), p. 432.
7. Herbert S. Klein, "Profits and the Causes of Mortality," in David Northrup, ed., *The Atlantic Slave Trade* (Lexington, Mass.: D. C. Heath and Co., 1994), p. 116.
8. Voyages: The Trans-Atlantic Slave Trade Database, http://www.slavevoyages.org/tast/assessment/estimates.faces (accessed May 9, 2009).
9. C. Cotton, trans., *The Essays of Michel de Montaigne* (New York: A. L. Burt, 1893), pp. 207, 210.

## Chapter 16

1. H. Kamen, "The Economic and Social Consequences of the Thirty Years' War," *Past and Present* 39 (April 1968): 44–61.
2. John A. Lynn, "Reconstructing French Army Growth," in *The Military Transformation of Early Modern Europe*, ed. Clifford J. Rogers (Boulder, Colo.: Westview Press, 1995), p. 125.
3. J. H. Elliott, *Imperial Spain, 1469–1716* (New York: Mentor Books, 1963), pp. 306–308.
4. H. Rosenberg, *Bureaucracy, Aristocracy, and Autocracy: The Prussian Experience, 1660–1815* (Boston: Beacon Press, 1966), p. 43.
5. Ibid., *Bureaucracy, Aristocracy, and Autocracy*, p. 40.
6. For a revisionist interpretation, see J. Wormald, "James VI and I: Two Kings or One?" *History* 62 (June 1983): 187–209.

## Chapter 17

1. Quoted in A. G. R. Smith, *Science and Society in the Sixteenth and Seventeenth Centuries* (New York: Harcourt Brace Jovanovich, 1972), p. 97.
2. Quoted in Butterfield, *The Origins of Modern Science* (New York: Macmillan, 1951), p. 47.
3. Ibid., p. 120.
4. Quoted in John Freely, *Aladdin's Lamp: How Greek Science Came to Europe Through the Islamic World* (New York: Knopf, 2009), p. 217.
5. Quoted in L. M. Marsak, ed., *The Enlightenment* (New York: John Wiley & Sons, 1972), p. 56.
6. Quoted in G. L. Mosse et al., eds., *Europe in Review* (Chicago: Rand McNally, 1964), p. 156.
7. Quoted in G. P. Gooch, *Catherine the Great and Other Studies* (Hamden, Conn.: Archon Books, 1966), p. 149.

8. See E. Fox-Genovese, "Women in the Enlightenment," in *Becoming Visible: Women in European History*, 2d ed., ed. R. Bridenthal, C. Koonz, and S. Stuard (Boston: Houghton Mifflin, 1987), esp. pp. 252–259, 263–265.
9. Quoted in Emmanuel Chukwudi Ezc, ed., *Race and the Enlightenment: A Reader* (Oxford: Blackwell, 1997), p. 33.

## Chapter 18

1. Jan de Vries, *The Industrious Revolution: Consumer Behavior and the Household Economy, 1650 to the Present* (Cambridge, U.K.: Cambridge University Press, 2008).
2. Jan de Vries, "The Industrial Revolution and the Industrious Revolution," *The Journal of Economic History* 54, 2 (June 1994): 249–270, discusses the industrious revolution of the second half of the twentieth century.
3. R. Heilbroner, *The Essential Adam Smith* (New York: W. W. Norton, 1986), p. 196.
4. Figures obtained from Voyages: The Trans-Atlantic Slave Trade Database, http://www.slavevoyages.org/tast/assessment/estimates.faces (accessed June 11, 2009).
5. Pierre Marie François Paget, *Travels Round the World in the Years 1767, 1768, 1769, 1770, 1771* (London, 1793), vol. 1, p. 262.
6. Orlando Patterson, *Slavery and Social Death* (Cambridge, Mass.: Harvard University Press, 1982), p. 255.

## Chapter 19

1. Quoted in R. Cobb, *The Police and the People: French Popular Protest, 1789–1820* (Oxford, U.K.: Clarendon Press, 1970), p. 238.
2. Peter Laslett, *Family Life and Illicit Love: Essays in Historical Sociology* (Cambridge, U.K.: Cambridge University Press, 1977) and G. Gullickson, *Spinners and Weavers of Auffay: Rural Industry and the Sexual Division of Labor in a French Village, 1750–1850* (Cambridge, U.K.: Cambridge University Press, 1986), p. 186.
3. Louis Crompton, *Homosexuality and Civilization* (Cambridge, Mass.: Belknap Press, 2003), p. 321.
4. George E. Haggerty, ed., *Encyclopedia of Gay Histories and Cultures* (New York: Garland Publishing, 2000), pp. 1311–1312.
5. Pier Paolo Viazzo, "Mortality, Fertility, and Family," in *Family Life in Early Modern Times, 1500–1789*, ed. David I. Kertzer and Marzio Barbagli (New Haven, Conn.: Yale University Press, 2001), p. 180.
6. P. P. Viazzo, "Mortality, Fertility, and Family," in *The History of the European Family*, vol. 1, ed. D. Kertzer and M. Barbagli (New Haven, Conn.: Yale University Press, 2001), pp. 176–178.
7. Alysa Levene, "The Estimation of Mortality at the London Foundling Hospital, 1741–99," *Population Studies* 59, 1 (2005): 87–97.
8. Cited in Robert Woods, "Did Montaigne Love His Children? Demography and the Hypothesis of Parental Indifference," *Journal of Interdisciplinary History* 33, 3 (2003): 421.
9. James Van Horn Melton, *Absolutism and the Eighteenth-Century Origins of Compulsory Schooling in Prussia and Austria* (Cambridge, U.K.: Cambridge University Press, 2003), p. 46.
10. J. V. H. Melton, "The Theresian School Reform of 1774," in *Early Modern Europe*, ed. James B. Collins and Karen L. Taylor (Oxford, U.K.: Blackwell, 2006).

11. I. Woloch, *Eighteenth-Century Europe: Tradition and Progress, 1715–1789* (New York: W. W. Norton, 1982), pp. 220–221.
12. Neil McKendrik, John Brewer, and J. H. Plumb, *The Birth of a Consumer Society: The Commercialization of Eighteenth-Century England* (Bloomington: Indiana University Press, 1982).
13. Quoted in K. Pinson, *Pietism as a Factor in the Rise of German Nationalism* (New York: Columbia University Press, 1934), pp. 43–44.

## Chapter 20

1. Quoted in G. Wright, *France in Modern Times*, 4th ed. (New York: W. W. Norton, 1987), p. 34.
2. G. Pernoud and S. Flaisser eds., *The French Revolution* (Greenwich, Conn.: Fawcett, 1960), p. 61.
3. Quoted in L. Gershoy, *The Era of the French Revolution, 1789–1799* (New York: Van Nostrand, 1957), p. 150.
4. Cited in Kim Klooster, *Revolutions in the Atlantic World: A Comprehensive History* (New York and London: New York University Press, 2009), p. 74.

## Chapter 21

1. N. F. R. Crafts, *British Economic Growth During the Industrial Revolution* (Oxford: Oxford University Press, 1985), p. 32.
2. P. Bairoch, "International Industrialization Levels from 1750 to 1980," *Journal of European Economic History* 11 (Spring 1982): 269–333.
3. Quoted in W. A. Hayek, ed., *Capitalism and the Historians* (Chicago: University of Chicago Press, 1954), p. 126.
4. Crafts, *British Economic Growth*, p. 95.
5. H-J. Voth, *Time and Work in England, 1750–1830* (Oxford: Oxford University Press, 2000), pp. 268–270; also pp. 118–133.
6. Quoted in E. R. Pike, *"Hard Times": Human Documents of the Industrial Revolution* (New York: Praeger, 1966), p. 109.
7. See especially J. Brenner and M. Rama, "Rethinking Women's Oppression," *New Left Review* 144 (March–April 1984): 33–71, and sources cited there.
8. Pike, *"Hard Times,"* p. 208.
9. Quoted in D. Geary, ed., *Labour and Socialist Movements in Europe Before 1914* (Oxford: Berg, 1989), p. 29.

## Chapter 22

1. Quoted in F. B. Artz, *From the Renaissance to Romanticism: Trends in Style in Art, Literature, and Music, 1300–1830* (Chicago: University of Chicago Press, 1962), pp. 276, 278.
2. Quoted in G. O'Brien, *The Economic History of Ireland from the Union to the Famine* (London: Longmans, Green, 1921), pp. 23–24.
3. A. de Tocqueville, *Recollections* (New York: Columbia University Press, 1949), p. 94.
4. W. L. Langer, *Political and Social Upheaval, 1832–1852* (New York: Harper & Row, 1969), p. 361.

## Chapter 23

1. S. Marcus, "Reading the Illegible," in *The Victorian City: Images and Realities*, ed. H. J. Dyos and Michael Wolff, vol. 1 (London: Routledge & Kegan Paul, 1973), p. 266.
2. Quoted in E. Chadwick, *Report on the Sanitary Condition of the Labouring Population of Great Britain*, ed. M. W. Flinn (Edinburgh: University of Edinburgh Press, 1965; original publication, 1842), pp. 315–316.
3. J. McKay, *Tramways and Trolleys: The Rise of Urban Mass Transport in Europe* (Princeton, N.J.: Princeton University Press, 1976), p. 81.
4. Quoted in R. Roberts, *The Classic Slum: Salford Life in the First Quarter of the Century* (Manchester, U.K.: University of Manchester Press, 1971), p. 95.

5. For a thorough discussion, see S. Marcus, *The Other Victorians: A Study of Sexuality and Pornography in Mid-Nineteenth-Century England* (New York: Basic Books, 1966).
6. See the pioneering work of J. de Vries, *The Industrious Revolution: Consumer Behavior and the Household Economy* (Cambridge, U.K.: Cambridge University Press, 2008), especially pp. 186–237.
7. Roberts, *The Classic Slum*, p. 35.
8. Quoted in R. P. Neuman, "The Sexual Question and Social Democracy in Imperial Germany," *Journal of Social History* 7 (Winter 1974): 281.
9. A. Comte, *The Positive Philosophy of Auguste Comte*, trans. H. Martineau, vol. 1 (London: J. Chapman, 1853), pp. 1–2.

## Chapter 25

1. Quoted in Earl of Cromer, *Modern Egypt* (London, 1911), p. 48.
2. Quoted in I. Howe, *World of Our Fathers* (New York: Harcourt Brace Jovanovich, 1975), p. 290.
3. Quoted in W. L. Langer, *European Alliances and Alignments, 1871–1890* (New York: Vintage Books, 1931), p. 290.
4. Quoted in G. H. Nadel and P. Curtis, eds., *Imperialism and Colonialism* (New York: Macmillan, 1964), p. 94.
5. Rudyard Kipling, *The Five Nations* (London, 1903).
6. Quoted in W. L. Langer, *The Diplomacy of Imperialism*, 2d ed. (New York: Alfred A. Knopf, 1951), p. 88.
7. Quoted in K. M. Panikkar, *Asia and Western Dominance: A Survey of the Vasco da Gama Epoch of Asian History* (London: George Allen & Unwin, 1959), p. 116.
8. A. Burton, "The White Women's Burden: British Feminists and 'The Indian Women,' 1865–1915," in *Western Women and Imperialism: Complicity and Resistance*, ed. N. Chauduri and M. Strobel (Bloomington: Indiana University Press, 1992), pp. 137–157.

## Chapter 26

1. On the mood of 1914, see J. Joll, *The Origins of the First World War* (New York: Longman, 1992), pp. 199–233.
2. Quoted in George L. Mosse, *Fallen Soldiers: Reshaping the Memory of the World Wars* (New York: Oxford University Press, 1990), p. 64.
3. V. G. Liulevicius, *War Land on the Eastern Front: Culture, National Identity, and German Occupation in World War I* (New York: Cambridge University Press, 2000), pp. 54–89; quotation on p. 71.
4. Quoted in F. P. Chambers, *The War Behind the War, 1914–1918* (London: Faber & Faber, 1939), p. 168.
5. Quoted in H. Nicolson, *Peacemaking 1919* (New York: Grosset & Dunlap Universal Library, 1965), pp. 8, 31–32.
6. Quoted in C. Barnett, *The Swordbearers: Supreme Command in the First World War* (New York: Morrow, 1964), p. 40.

## Chapter 27

1. P. Valéry, *Variety*, trans. M. Cowley (New York: Harcourt Brace, 1927), pp. 27–28.
2. T. S. Eliot, *The Waste Land*, in *The Norton Anthology of Poetry Revised*, ed. A. W. Allison et al. (New York: Norton, 1975), p. 1034.
3. C. E. Jeanneret-Gris (Le Corbusier), *Towards a New Architecture* (London: J. Rodker, 1931), p. 15.
4. Quoted in A. H. Barr, Jr., *What Is Modern Painting?* 9th ed. (New York: Museum of Modern Art, 1966), p. 25.
5. R. Huelsenbeck, "Collective Dada Manifesto (1920)," in *The Dada Painters and Poets*, ed. Robert Motherwell and Jack D. Flam (Boston: G. K. Hall, 1981), pp. 242–246.
6. Quoted in S. B. Clough et al., eds., *Economic History of Europe: Twentieth Century* (New York: Harper & Row, 1968), pp. 243–245.
7. S. Freud, *Civilization and Its Discontents* (New York: W. W. Norton, 1961), p. 112.

## Chapter 28

1. Quoted in S. Kotkin, *Magnetic Mountain: Stalinism as a Civilization* (Berkeley: University of California Press, 1997), pp. 221–222.

2. R. Thurston, *Life and Terror in Stalin's Russia, 1934–1941* (New Haven, Conn.: Yale University Press, 1996), esp. pp. 16–106; also M. Malia, *The Soviet Tragedy: A History of Socialism in Russia, 1917–1991* (New York: Free Press, 1995), pp. 227–270.

3. Quoted in C. Duggan, *A Concise History of Italy* (New York: Cambridge University Press, 1994), p. 227.

4. Quoted in ibid., p. 234.

5. M. Burleigh and W. Wippermann, *The Racial State: Germany 1933–1945* (New York: Cambridge University Press, 1991).

6. D. Goldhagen, *Hitler's Willing Executioners: Ordinary Germans and the Holocaust* (New York: Vintage Books, 1997); for an alternate explanation, see C. Browing, *Ordinary Men: Reserve Police Battalion 101 and the Final Solution in Poland* (New York: Harper, 1992).

## Chapter 29

1. Quoted in N. Graebner, *Cold War Diplomacy, 1945–1960* (Princeton, N.J.: Van Nostrand, 1962), p. 17.

2. Quoted in D. Treadgold, *Twentieth Century Russia*, 5th ed. (Boston: Houghton Mifflin, 1981), p. 442.

## Chapter 30

1. Quoted in Kessing's Research Report, *Germany and East Europe Since 1945: From the Potsdam Agreement to Chancellor Brandt's "Ostpolitik"* (New York: Charles Scribner's Sons, 1973), pp. 284–285.

2. See R. Guha, *Environmentalism: A Global History* (New York: Longman, 2000), p. 79.

## Chapter 31

1. *Quarterly Labor Force Statistics, Volume 2004/4* (Paris: OECD Publications, 2004), p. 64.

2. Judt, quoted in *Postwar: A History of Europe Since 1945* (New York: Penguin, 2005*)*, p. 783.

3. J. Klausen, *The Islamic Challenge: Politics and Religion in Western Europe* (New York: Oxford University Press, 2006), p. 16; Malise Ruthven, "The Big Muslim Problem!" *New York Review*, December 17, 2009, p. 62.

# Index

Consumer revolution, 567, 572(i), 878, 880–881
  in East Bloc, 886
  in 18th century, 563, 571(b)
  youths and, 897–898
Consumer society, 567–573
  critics of, 815, 905–906, 907
  emergence of, 813–817, 905–906
Contagious disease. See Disease
Containment policy (U.S.), 875, 876
  in Congo, 892
  Vietnam War and, 907
Continental Europe
  colonial trade and, 538
  industrialization in, 623–628, 626(m)
Continental System, of Napoleon, 607–608, 609–610
Contraception. See Birth control
Conversations on the Plurality of Worlds (Fontenelle), 499(i)
Conversion. See also Missions and missionaries
  to Christianity, 545
Conway, Anne, 497
Cook, James, 547
Cookbooks, 691(i)
Coordination policy, 849
Copenhagen
  climate change meeting in (May, 2009), 962
  CO$_2$ emissions meeting in (December, 2009), 962
Copernican hypothesis, 491–492, 494, 498
Copernicus, Nicolaus, 491–492, 496, 498
Corinne (Staël), 656(b)
Corner of the Table, A (Chabas), 683(i)
Corn Laws (England, 1815), 659, 660, 737
Corporations. See also Guilds
  industrialization and, 628
  multinational, 944, 945
  outsourcing by, 946
Corsica, 605
Cort, Henry, 620
Cortés, Hernando, 422, 431–433, 432(i)
Cortés, Martín, 432(i)
Cosmography, 423
Cosmology, of Aristotle, 490–491, 490(i)
Cosmonaut, 878
Cossacks (Russia), 469
Cottage industry, 528, 529–531, 530(m)
  in England, 616, 616(m)
  factories and, 632
  putting-out system in, 528–529
  workers in, 529–531, 632–633
Cottages. See Housing
Cotton and cotton industry. See also Textile industry
  factories in, 617
  in India, 420
  romanticization of slavery and, 507(i)
  in United States, 712–713
  workers in, 632(i)
Council for Mutual Economic Assistance (COMECON), 876

Council of Europe, 880
Counterculture, 904, 906–907, 917
  clothing and, 906(i)
  growth of, 898
  student revolts and, 908–909
Counterinsurgency policies, in Iraq, 961
Counter-Reformation, 498
Countryside. See Rural areas
Counts. See Nobility
Coup d'état
  in China, 762
  by Napoleon III, 705
  in Soviet Union, 931, 932(i)
Court (households and palaces), of Louis XIV (France), 460–461, 460(i)
Courtesans, 558
Courtiers. See Nobility
Cowry shells, as currency, 548
Crash. See Financial crash
Credit
  purchase of consumer goods and, 880
  in Spain, 464
Creoles, 543, 545
Crime and criminals. See also Law(s); Punishment
  in eastern Europe, 942
  illegal immigration and, 951–952
  people smuggling and, 951–952
Crimean War, 714, 714(m)
Crises. See Age of crisis
Croatia, 942, 943, 943(m), 964
Croats, 647, 667, 943
Cromwell, Oliver, 479–480, 480(i), 537
Crops. See also Agriculture; Farms and farming
  in Columbian Exchange, 437
  farming and, 522
  nitrogen-storing, 523
  rotation of, 523
Cross-dressing, by women, 558
Crystal Palace exhibition, 621(i)
Cuba, 427
Cuban missile crisis, 887
Cubells y Ruiz, Enrique Martinez, 695(i)
Cubism, 811
Cults, of Duce, 846
Cultural nationalism, 649
Cultural relativism, 444
Culture(s). See also Popular culture; Western world
  consumer, 562–563, 813–817
  counterculture, 898, 904, 906–907
  European expansion and, 443–446
  French, 461
  immigrants and, 952, 953
  mass, 813–815
  middle-class, 682–683
  modernism and, 810–813
  postcolonial migrations and, 896
  in Russia, 470(i), 940
  Soviet, 842, 926
  youth, 897–898
Curie, Marie, 807

Curie, Pierre, 807
Currency
  Bretton Woods agreement and, 880
  euro as, 947
  in France, 594
  single European, 947
Customs union. See Zollverein
Cuzco, 433
Czechoslovakia, 793, 819, 905, 910, 920
  communism in, 882
  Little Entente and, 817
  Nazis in, 852
  "Prague spring" in, 910–911
  reform movement in, 908(f), 922–923
  Soviets in, 874, 904
  "velvet divorce" in, 941
  Velvet Revolution in, 929–930, 929(i)
Czech people
  in Austrian Empire, 647, 666, 723
  independence and, 783
Czech Republic. See also Bohemia
  economy of, 941
  in postcommunist era, 938, 941–942

Dadaism, 803(i), 811, 811(i), 812
Da Gama, Vasco, 422, 425, 426(m)
Daily life. See Lifestyle
D'Alembert, Jean le Rond, 501(i), 502, 503, 507(i)
Dali, Salvador, 811
Damascus, 794
Dance, modernism in, 812, 812(i)
Danish phase, of Thirty Years' War, 454
Danton, Georges Jacques, 598, 604
Danzig, 852
Darwin, Charles, 696–697, 696(i)
Daughters. See Girls; Women
David, Jacques-Louis, 589(i)
David d'Angers, Pierre, 591(i)
Dawes, Charles G., 819
Dawes Plan, 819
Dean, James, 897
Death
  in 18th century, 527
  in 17th century, 526
Death penalty
  abolishing, 964
  European-U.S. gap in, 959
Death rate. See Mortality
Debt
  in East Bloc, 922
  in France, 588
  in Iceland, 946(i)
  in U.S., 914
Debt crisis, 913
Debt peonage, 541
Decentralization, political and economic, 910
Dechristianization, in France, 601
Declaration of Independence (U.S.), 587
Declaration of Pillnitz, 597
Declaration of the Rights of Man and of the Citizen (France), 592, 593

rebellion in (1641), 479
recession in, 945
Irish Republican Army (IRA), 915(b), 921
Iron and iron industry
in England, 616, 620
German, 628(i)
industrialization and, 618
workers in, 636
"Iron curtain" speech (Churchill), 874
Iron law of wages, 622
Irrigation, in India, 756
**Isabella** (Castile). *See* Ferdinand and Isabella
(Spain)
Islam. *See also* Arabs and Arab world;
Muslims
colonial independence and, 889
as European religion, 953, 958
intellectual thought from, 955(b)
Islamic fundamentalism
in Algeria, 892
revolution in Iran and, 912
terrorism and, 954, 959
Islamic radicalism, September 11, 2001,
attacks and, 954, 959
Island-hopping campaign (Second World
War), 861
**Ismail** (Egypt), 741, 754
Israel. *See also* Arab-Israeli wars; Jews and
Judaism; Palestine
establishment of, 871, 891
in 1948, 890(m)
Suez crisis and, 891
U.S. support for, 958
Istanbul. *See also* Constantinople (Istanbul)
Constantinople as, 420–421
Young Turks in, 718
Italian people, 744(i)
Italy, 959, 960. *See also* Rome
Austria and, 645, 707–708
after Congress of Vienna, 706
Enlightenment in, 503
Ethiopia and, 846, 846(m)
European unity and, 880
exploration and, 422
fascism in, 798, 844–846
after First World War, 794
First World War and, 775–776, 844
guest workers from, 894(b)
industrialization in, 624, 624(f)
Jews in, 860(b)
kingdom of the Two Sicilies and,
645–646, 707(m), 708
Marxian socialism in, 731
migration from, 743, 895
papal rule in, 706
revolt in (1820), 647(m)
Rome-Berlin Axis and, 852
Second World War and, 857, 862,
863, 879
totalitarianism in, 834
Treaty of Versailles and, 792
in Triple Alliance, 768

in Triple Entente, 776
unification of, 706–708, 707(m)
women in, 916(i), 917
**Ivan III the Great** (Russia), 468
**Ivan IV the Terrible** (Russia), 468–469, 474

Jacobin club (France), 597, 598
*Jacob's Room* (Woolf), 809
Jakarta, 545
Jamaica, migration from, 896(i)
**James I** (England), 445, 477, 478
**James II** (England), 481
Jamestown, 434
Janissary corps, Ottoman, 475
**Jansen, Cornelius,** 576
Jansenism, 576
Japan, 945
atomic bombing of, 854(i), 863, 864(i)
in Axis alliance, 852
China and, 760, 861
empire of, 859–861
after First World War, 792
imperialism and, 740, 750, 757–760,
758–759(b)
industrialization in, 624
Korea and, 760
Meiji Restoration in, 757
military in, 757, 759(i), 859
protests in, 908(f)
Russo-Japanese War and, 715, 760
in Second World War, 859–861, 862(m),
863–864, 874
society in, 757–760
trade with, 442
West and, 740, 757–760, 913
**Jaruzelski, Wojciech,** 924, 928
Jasperware, 622(i), 623(i)
**Jaurès, Jean,** 730
Java, 419(i), 545, 750
Jazz, 897
**Jefferson, Thomas,** 587, 607
Jehovah's Witnesses, Nazis and, 849
Jena, battle at, 606
**Jenner, Edward,** 578–579
Jesuits, 545, 573–574
education by, 562
**Jesus of Nazareth.** *See* Christianity
*Jewish Bride, The* (Rembrandt), 482(i)
Jewish Heroes' Monument (Warsaw), 904(i)
*Jewish State, The . . .* (Herzl), 724
Jews and Judaism. *See also* Anti-Semitism;
Israel; Zionism
in Americas, 545
in Austria, 515, 574
in Dutch Republic, 483
emancipation of, 725
emigration of, 850
in England, 480
in fascist Italy, 846
in France, 594, 855
Glückel of Hameln on, 482(b)
Holocaust and, 832, 833(i), 835–837,
857–859, 858(m), 859(i), 860(b)

homeland for, 890–891
migration from Europe and, 744
Nazis and, 835–837, 847, 849, 850
Nuremberg Laws against, 850
Palestine and, 724(b), 725, 793, 797(i)
racial ideas about, 444
in Russia, 726(b)
scientific thought and, 499–500
after Second World War, 871
as slaves, 421
Zionism and, 724
**Jiang Jieshi (Chiang Kai-shek),** 890
**Joad, Cyril,** 807
Jobs. *See* Careers; Labor
**John Paul II** (Pope), 923
**Johnson, Lyndon B.,** 907
**Joliet, Louis,** 462
**Jonson, Ben,** on death of son, 560–561
**Joseph II** (Austria), 513, 514–515,
514(i), 574
*Journal* (Columbus), 426–427
Journeymen's associations, 537
**Joyce, James,** 809
*Juan de Pareja* (Velázquez), 438(i)
Judaism. *See* Jews and Judaism
Judiciary and judicial system, in
England, 481
"June Days" (Paris), 666
Junkers, 467, 720
Just price, 566

**Kádár, János,** 929
**Kafka, Franz,** 809
Kampuchea. *See* Cambodia
**Kandinsky, Wassily,** 811
**Kant, Immanuel,** 503, 506, 510
Kapp Putsch, 790
"Karawane" (Ball), 811(i)
**Kellogg, Frank B.,** 819
Kellogg-Briand Pact (1928), 819
**Kemal, Mustafa** (Atatürk), 795
**Kennedy, John F.**
Berlin Wall and, 886–887
Cuban missile crisis and, 887
Vietnam War and, 907
Kenya, independence for, 891
**Kepler, Johannes,** 492–493, 494, 496
**Kerensky, Alexander,** 785, 786
**Keynes, John Maynard,** 824
Keynesian economics, 878
Khartoum, massacre at, 749
Khedive (Egypt), 741
**Khodorkovsky, Mikhail,** 940
**Khrushchev, Nikita**
Cuban missile crisis and, 887
de-Stalinization and reform by, 883–886
"kitchen debate" and, 884–885(b), 885(i)
Kiel, mutiny at, 790
**Kierkegaard, Søren,** 806
**King, Martin Luther, Jr.,** 908(f)
"King Cholera," 675(i)
Kingdom of the Two Sicilies, 645–646,
707(m), 708

# CONTEMPORARY EUROPE

**NORWAY**
Bergen
Oslo

**SWEDEN**
Stockholm
Göteborg

*North Sea*

**SCOTLAND**
Edinburgh
Glasgow

**NORTHERN IRELAND**
Belfast

Aarhus
**DENMARK**
Copenhagen

*Baltic Sea*

**RUSSIA**
Kaliningrad
Gdańsk

**IRELAND**
Dublin

**UNITED KINGDOM**
Liverpool
**WALES**
Birmingham
**ENGLAND**
*Thames R.*
London

Cork

Berlin

**POLAND**
Warsaw

*Elbe R.*

*Vistula R.*

**ATLANTIC OCEAN**

*English Channel*

**NETHERLANDS**
Amsterdam
Rotterdam

Antwerp
Brussels
**BELGIUM**

*Rhine R.*

**GERMANY**

Frankfurt

Prague
**CZECH REP.**
Kraków

Brno

**SLOVAKIA**
Miske

Seine R.
Paris

Luxembourg
**LUXEMBOURG**

*Oder R.*

*Danube R.*
Vienna
Bratislava

**FRANCE**

Loire R.

*Bay of Biscay*

Munich
**AUSTRIA**
Innsbruck
Graz
Budapest
**HUNGARY**

**LIECHTENSTEIN**
Zürich
Bern
Vaduz
**SWITZERLAND**
Lyons
*Rhône R.*
A L P S
Milan
*Po R.*

**SLOVENIA**
Ljubljana
Zagreb
**CROATIA**

San Marino
**SAN MARINO**
*Adriatic Sea*

**BOSNIA AND HERZEGOVINA**
Sarajevo
**SERBIA**
Belgrade

**ANDORRA**
Andorra la Vella

*Ebro R.*

**PYRENEES**

Marseilles
**MONACO**

**APENNINES**

Split

Oporto

**PORTUGAL**

Madrid

**SPAIN**

Barcelona

*Corsica*

Rome
**ITALY**

Podgorica
**MONTENEGRO**

Tiranë
**ALBANIA**

Lisbon

Seville

Gibraltar
(Gr. Br.)

*Balearic Is.*

Naples

*Sardinia*

*Tyrrhenian Sea*

*Ionian Sea*

Algiers

Palermo
*Sicily*

Rabat

Tunis

Valletta
**MALTA**

**MOROCCO**

**TUNISIA**

*Mediterranean*

**ALGERIA**

Tripoli

**LIBYA**

## Elevation

| Feet | Meters |
|---|---|
| Over 13,120 | Over 4,001 |
| 6,561–13,120 | 2,001–4,000 |
| 1,641–6,560 | 501–2,000 |
| 661–1,640 | 201–500 |
| 0–660 | 0–200 |
| Below sea level | Below sea level |

⊛ National capital
• Major city

0    150    300 miles
0    150    300 kilometers

THE CONTEMPORARY WORLD

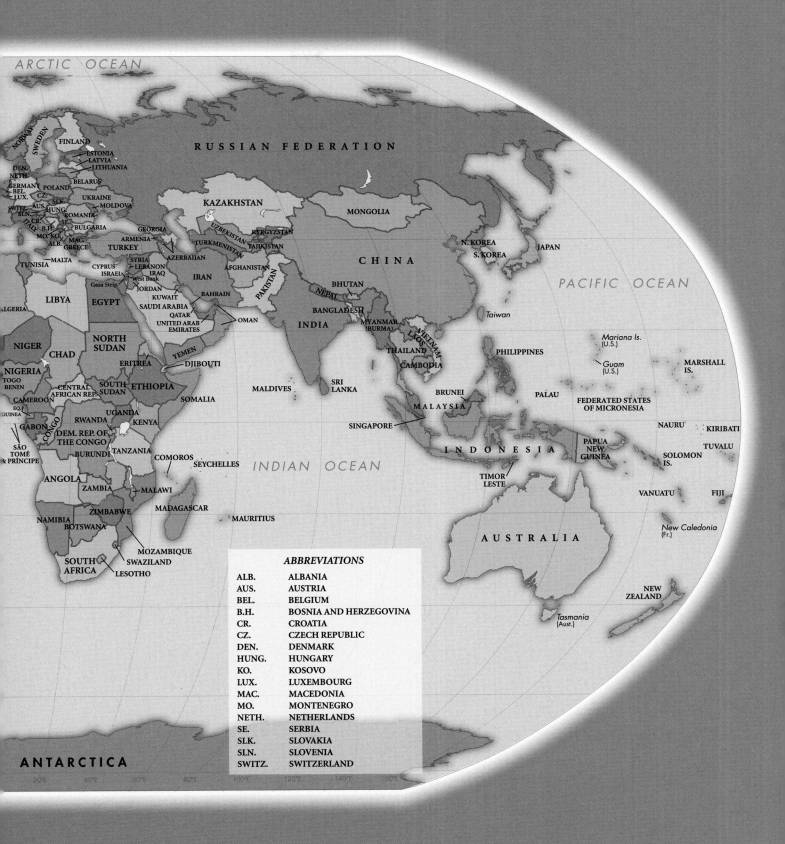

ARCTIC OCEAN

RUSSIAN FEDERATION

NORWAY
SWEDEN
FINLAND
ESTONIA
LATVIA
LITHUANIA
DEN.
NETH.
GERMANY
BEL.
LUX.
POLAND
BELARUS
CZ.
SLK.
UKRAINE
SWITZ.
AUS.
HUNG.
MOLDOVA
SLN.
ROMANIA
CR.
B.H.
SE.
BULGARIA
MO. KO.
MAC.
ALB. GREECE
TUNISIA
MALTA

KAZAKHSTAN
MONGOLIA
N. KOREA
S. KOREA
JAPAN

PACIFIC OCEAN

GEORGIA
ARMENIA
TURKEY
AZERBAIJAN
CYPRUS
SYRIA
LEBANON
ISRAEL
IRAQ
West Bank
Gaza Strip
JORDAN
KUWAIT

UZBEKISTAN
TURKMENISTAN
KYRGYZSTAN
TAJIKISTAN
AFGHANISTAN
IRAN
PAKISTAN

CHINA

BHUTAN
NEPAL

Taiwan

Mariana Is.
(U.S.)

LIBYA
EGYPT
ALGERIA
NIGER
CHAD
NORTH
SUDAN
SAUDI ARABIA
QATAR
UNITED ARAB
EMIRATES
BAHRAIN
OMAN
YEMEN
INDIA
BANGLADESH
MYANMAR
(BURMA)
LAOS
VIETNAM
THAILAND
CAMBODIA

PHILIPPINES

Guam
(U.S.)

MARSHALL
IS.

NIGERIA
TOGO
BENIN
CAMEROON
EQ.
GUINEA
GABON
CONGO
CENTRAL
AFRICAN REP.
SOUTH
SUDAN
ERITREA
DJIBOUTI
ETHIOPIA
SOMALIA
MALDIVES
SRI
LANKA
BRUNEI
PALAU
FEDERATED STATES
OF MICRONESIA

SÃO
TOMÉ
& PRÍNCIPE
DEM. REP. OF
THE CONGO
RWANDA
UGANDA
KENYA
BURUNDI
TANZANIA
COMOROS
SEYCHELLES
MALAYSIA
SINGAPORE
INDONESIA
PAPUA
NEW
GUINEA
NAURU
KIRIBATI
TUVALU
SOLOMON
IS.

INDIAN OCEAN

ANGOLA
ZAMBIA
MALAWI
ZIMBABWE
NAMIBIA
BOTSWANA
MADAGASCAR
MAURITIUS

TIMOR
LESTE

AUSTRALIA

VANUATU
FIJI

New Caledonia
(Fr.)

SOUTH
AFRICA
MOZAMBIQUE
SWAZILAND
LESOTHO

NEW
ZEALAND

Tasmania
(Aust.)

ANTARCTICA

20°E    40°E    60°E    80°E    100°E    120°E    140°E    160°E

| ABBREVIATIONS | |
|---|---|
| ALB. | ALBANIA |
| AUS. | AUSTRIA |
| BEL. | BELGIUM |
| B.H. | BOSNIA AND HERZEGOVINA |
| CR. | CROATIA |
| CZ. | CZECH REPUBLIC |
| DEN. | DENMARK |
| HUNG. | HUNGARY |
| KO. | KOSOVO |
| LUX. | LUXEMBOURG |
| MAC. | MACEDONIA |
| MO. | MONTENEGRO |
| NETH. | NETHERLANDS |
| SE. | SERBIA |
| SLK. | SLOVAKIA |
| SLN. | SLOVENIA |
| SWITZ. | SWITZERLAND |

# About the Authors

**John P. McKay** (Ph.D., University of California, Berkeley) is professor emeritus at the University of Illinois. He has written or edited numerous works, including the Herbert Baxter Adams Prize–winning book *Pioneers for Profit: Foreign Entrepreneurship and Russian Industrialization, 1885–1913*.

**Bennett D. Hill** (Ph.D., Princeton University), late of the University of Illinois, published *English Cistercian Monasteries and Their Patrons in the Twelfth Century*, *Church and State in the Middle Ages*, and numerous articles and reviews. A Benedictine monk of St. Anselm's Abbey in Washington, D.C., he was also a visiting professor at Georgetown University.

**John Buckler** (Ph.D., Harvard University), late of the University of Illinois, published numerous books, including *Theban Hegemony, 371–362 B.C.*; *Philip II and the Sacred War*; and *Aegean Greece in the Fourth Century B.C.* With Hans Beck, he most recently published *Central Greece and the Politics of Power in the Fourth Century*.

**Clare Haru Crowston** (Ph.D., Cornell University) teaches at the University of Illinois, where she is currently associate professor of history. She is the author of *Fabricating Women: The Seamstresses of Old Regime France, 1675–1791*, which won the Berkshire and Hagley Prizes. She edited two special issues of the *Journal of Women's History*, has published numerous journal articles and reviews, and is a past president of the Society for French Historical Studies.

**Merry E. Wiesner-Hanks** (Ph.D., University of Wisconsin–Madison) taught first at Augustana College in Illinois, and since 1985 at the University of Wisconsin–Milwaukee, where she is currently UWM Distinguished Professor in the department of history. She is the coeditor of the *Sixteenth Century Journal* and the author or editor of more than twenty books, most recently *The Marvelous Hairy Girls: The Gonzales Sisters and Their Worlds* and *Gender in History*.

**Joe Perry** (Ph.D., University of Illinois at Urbana-Champaign) is associate professor of modern German and European history at Georgia State University. He has published numerous articles and is author of the recently published book, *Christmas in Germany: A Cultural History*. His current research interests include issues of consumption, gender, and television in East and West Germany after World War II.

# About the Cover Art

### *At the Café*, Jean Béraud, ca. 1900

Born in St. Petersburg, Russia, to French parents, Jean Béraud (1849–1935) specialized in painting scenes of daily life that give the viewer a sense of the personalities of his subjects. In this portrait, a young man, smoking a cigarette, and a young woman, wearing a fashionable turban-style hat and drinking a glass of wine, stare at something or someone in the distance. In the bustling cities of early-twentieth-century Europe, young men and women found new places for meeting and socializing in cafés, coffeehouses, restaurants, dance halls, and streetcars. Diaries and letters from the early twentieth century evoke the excitement and romance encountered in the city but also reveal the alienation and loneliness that accompanied its anonymity.

(The Bridgeman Art Library)